Counseling Boys and Young Men

Suzanne Degges-White, PhD, LMHC, LCAC, LPC, NCC, is an associate professor of counselor education in the Department of Leadership and Counselor Education at the University of Mississippi in University, MS. She received her master's degree in community counseling and her PhD in counseling and counselor education at the University of North Carolina at Greensboro, where she also earned a graduate certificate in women's studies. She is a licensed counselor in private practice serving children, adolescents, adults, and couples. Suzanne's research interests include development over the life span, gender issues in counseling, and the use of creative and innovative techniques in counseling. She has been the recipient of multiple grants and research awards for her work. Suzanne is the coeditor of the book, *Integrating the Expressive Arts Into Counseling Practice* and the coauthor of *Friends Forever: How Girls and Women Forge Lasting Relationships.*

Bonnie Colon, MS, LMHC, NCC, NCSC, is an assistant clinical professor in the counseling and development program in the Department of Graduate Studies in Education at Purdue University Calumet in Hammond, IN. She received her master's degree in counseling at Purdue University Calumet. She is a licensed and certified professional school counselor in both Indiana and Illinois and has 15 years of experience working as a high school counselor. She is a board member for public relations of the Indiana School Counselor Association and is an active advocate for the profession of school counseling in the state of Indiana.

Counseling Boys and Young Men

Suzanne Degges-White, PhD, LMHC, LCAC, LPC, NCC

Bonnie Colon, MS, LMHC, NCC, NCSC

Editors

SPRINGER PUBLISHING COMPANY
NEW YORK

Springer Publishing Company, LLC
11 West 42nd Street
New York, NY 10036
www.springerpub.com

Acquisitions Editor: Nancy Hale
Production Editor: Joseph Stubenrauch
Composition: Newgen Imaging

ISBN: 978–0-8261-0918-7
E-book ISBN: 978–0-8261-0919-4

12 13 14 15/ 5 4 3 2 1

The author and the publisher of this Work have made every effort to use sources believed to be reliable to provide information that is accurate and compatible with the standards generally accepted at the time of publication. The author and publisher shall not be liable for any special, consequential, or exemplary damages resulting, in whole or in part, from the readers' use of, or reliance on, the information contained in this book. The publisher has no responsibility for the persistence or accuracy of URLs for external or third-party Internet Web sites referred to in this publication and does not guarantee that any content on such Web sites is, or will remain, accurate or appropriate.

Library of Congress Cataloging-in-Publication Data

Counseling boys and young men / [edited by] Suzanne Degges-White, Bonnie R. Colon.
    p. cm.
   Includes index.
   ISBN 978-0-8261-0918-7
   1. Young men—Counseling of. 2. Boys—Counseling of. 3. Adolescent psychology.
   4. Counseling psychology. I. Degges-White, Suzanne. II. Colon, Bonnie R.
   BF724.C637 2012
   158.30835'1—dc23   2012013784

Special discounts on bulk quantities of our books are available to corporations, professional associations, pharmaceutical companies, health care organizations, and other qualifying groups.

If you are interested in a custom book, including chapters from more than one of our titles, we can provide that service as well.

For details, please contact:
Special Sales Department, Springer Publishing Company, LLC
11 West 42nd Street, 15th Floor, New York, NY 10036–8002s
Phone: 877–687-7476 or 212–431-4370; Fax: 212–941-7842
Email: sales@springerpub.com

Printed in the United States of America by Gasch Printing.

We dedicate this book to boys and young men, the parents and families who love them, and the counselors committed to helping them live happy, productive lives.

Contents

Contributors   *xiii*
Preface   *xix*
Acknowledgments   *xxv*

Part I: Understanding and Promoting Healthy Development

1. The Developmental Path: From Boyhood to Older Adolescence   *1*
   Thomas A. Grzesik, Samantha M. Grzesik, and Katie J. Vena
   Physiological Development   *1*
   Emotional and Social Development Through Play   *3*
   Cognitive Development and Gender   *5*
   Learning to Follow Society's Code of Conduct   *12*
   Case Study: Growing Up as a Boy From an Attachment and Morality
   Perspective: Stefan's Story   *15*
      Ages 0 to 5   *15*
   Through the Lens of Attachment Theory   *17*
   Through the Lens of Moral Development Theory   *17*
      Ages 5 to 9   *18*
   Through the Lens of Attachment Theory   *19*
   Through the Lens of Moral Development Theory   *19*
      Ages 10 to 11   *20*
      Ages 12 to 14   *20*
   Through the Lens of Attachment Theory   *21*
   Through the Lens of Moral Development Theory   *22*
      Ages 15 to 18 (Catholic High School)   *22*
   Through the Lens of Attachment Theory   *24*
   Through the Lens of Moral Development Theory   *24*
   Conclusion   *25*

2. Talking to the Beat of a Different Drum: Speaking So He Can Listen and Listening So He Can Speak   *29*
Keith M. Davis
   Working With Young Males in Counseling   *29*
   Case Study: Elementary School Boys Aged 9 to 11; Travis Aged 13   *36*
   Conclusions and Additional Resources   *38*

3. Understanding Male Adolescent Diversity   *41*
Shawn L. Spurgeon and Daniel M. Paredes
   The Adolescent Male Client   *41*
   Approach to Counseling the Adolescent Male or Young Man   *46*
   Tips for Counselors   *51*
   Conclusion   *53*

4. When Learning Is "Different": Readin', Writin', 'Rithmetic, and Giftedness?   *59*
Tony Michael, Ian S. Turnage-Butterbaugh, Rebekah H. Reysen, Edward Hudspeth, and Suzanne Degges-White
   Reading Disorder   *60*
   Disorder of Written Expression   *63*
   Mathematics Learning Disorder   *65*
   Giftedness   *66*
   Summary   *67*
   Case Study: Trey, Age 13   *67*
   Suggested Resources   *69*

5. Untold Stories of Potential: Career Counseling With Male Children and Adolescents   *73*
Kevin B. Stoltz and Susan R. Barclay
   Career Adaptability   *75*
   Career Development in Childhood   *76*
   How Career Identity Develops   *78*
   Career Identity Development: Super's Causal Model   *81*
   Play: A Career Counseling Intervention With Males in Early and Middle Childhood   *82*
   Career Counseling With Adolescent Males   *85*
   Conclusion   *91*
   Appendix A   *94*

Part II: Relationship Development and Relationship Concerns

6. Relationship Development With Family and Friends   *97*
Caroline S. Booth, Miriam L. Wagner, and Robin G. Liles
   Family Networks   *98*
   Peer Networks   *102*
   Counseling Implications   *107*
   Case Study: Finding His Place: Nathaniel, 5 Years Old   *109*

7. Working With Boys From Single-Parent Homes   *119*
  S. Kent Butler and M. Ann Shillingford
    Single-Parent Families Today   *119*
    Effects of Being Raised in a Single-Parent Household   *119*
    Living in the Middle of a High-Conflict Divorce   *120*
    Evidence-Based Interventions and Innovative Approaches   *126*
    Case Study: Abrahim, Age 12   *128*
    Case Study: Jessie, Age 13   *130*
    Summary   *132*
    Additional Resources   *132*

8. Romantic Relationships: From Wrestling to Romance   *135*
  Christine Borzumato-Gainey, Suzanne Degges-White,
  and Carrie V. Smith
    Romantic Relationships as Normal Development   *135*
    Communication   *136*
    Sexual Development   *137*
    Sexual Relationship Development   *138*
    Teen Fatherhood   *141*
    Dating Violence   *145*
    Case Study: Teen Heartthrob   *145*
    Case Study: Teen Father   *147*
    Resources   *150*

9. Counseling Gay and Questioning Boys and Young Men   *155*
  Edward P. Cannon and John F. Marszalek
    Sexual Orientation, Sexual Behavior, and Sexual Identity   *156*
    Recommendations for Counselors and Other Helping
    Professionals   *159*
    Case Study: Martin, Age 16   *162*
    Helpful Internet Resources   *166*
    Recommended Books for Youth   *167*
    Recommended Books for Counselors and Helping
    Professionals   *167*

Part III: Emotional and Mental Health Concerns

10. Attention Deficit/Hyperactivity Disorder in Young Males   *171*
  Imelda Bratton
    Prevalence and Diagnosis of Attention Deficit/Hyperactivity
    Disorder   *171*
    Suggested Interventions for Treating ADHD   *172*
    Counseling, Activity-Based, and Expressive Interventions   *173*
    Case Study: A Journey Through Tyler's World   *175*
    Suggested Resources   *182*

11. Navigating the Challenges of Connecting With Male Youth:
Empowering Real-Time Interventions Through Adventure-Based
Counseling   *185*
*Torey L. Portrie-Bethke, David Christian, William Brown, and
Nicole R. Hill*
Adventure-Based Counseling With Young Males   *185*
A History of ABC   *187*
Current Applications of ABC   *191*
Male Developmental Considerations   *196*
The Future of ABC   *216*

12. Autism Spectrum Disorders: Helping Young Males Connect   *221*
Rita Brusca-Vega and Suzanne Beike
Understanding Autism Spectrum Disorders   *222*
Treating Autism Spectrum Disorders   *225*
Case Study: Brian—A Third Grader With ASD   *237*
Case Study: Eugene—A Young Adult With ASD   *239*
Concluding Remarks   *242*

13. Understanding and Treating Victimization and Abuse   *247*
Nancy E. Sherman and Bill M. Blundell
Prevalence of the Problem   *247*
Signs and Symptoms of Maltreatment   *248*
Sibling Abuse   *251*
Abuse of Parents   *251*
Impact of Maltreatment   *252*
Treatment   *254*
Case Study: Bart, Age 14   *256*
Resources for Professionals   *260*
Resources for Sexual Abuse   *260*

14. Understanding the Child's World of Grief   *263*
Corie Schoeneberg and George R. Sesser
The Impact of Loss   *263*
Importance of Facilitating the Grief Process   *264*
Child-Centered Play Therapy   *265*
Case Study: CCPT With Tom, a 7-Year-Old Boy   *267*
Implications for Counselors and Play Therapists   *276*

15. Emotional Concerns: When Life Doesn't Feel "Right"   *279*
Rachel M. Hoffman
Emotional Concerns in Adolescents and Young Adults   *279*
Anxiety Disorders   *279*
Mood Disorders   *280*
Body Image and Eating Disorders   *281*
Self-Injurious Behaviors   *283*
Suicide: Risk Assessment and Prevention   *284*
Interventions   *285*

Case Study: Helping Jake Move Out of the Dark   *286*
Further Reading   *290*

Part IV: Behavior Disorders and Concerns

16. Identifying the Cycle: Assessing Addictions in Young Men   *295*
W. Bryce Hagedorn, Jesse Fox, and Tabitha L. Young
Addictions in Adolescent Males   *295*
Definitions and Criteria of Addiction   *296*
Assessment Strategies   *298*
Chemical Addictions   *301*
Process Addictions   *311*
Conclusion   *317*

17. Stopping the Cycle: Treating Addictions in Young Men   *327*
W. Bryce Hagedorn, Jesse Fox, and Tabitha L. Young
Strategies for Treating Young Men With Addictive Disorders   *327*
The Family's Involvement   *329*
Case Study: Don't Bet on It   *338*
Conclusion   *341*

18. Out of Bounds: Oppositional Defiant Disorder and Conduct
Disorder   *343*
Margery J. Shupe
Overview   *343*
Suggested Interventions/Treatment Strategies   *347*
Case Study: Alex, Age 7   *349*
Conclusion   *354*
Additional Resources   *355*

19. Bullying and Its Opposite: Harnessing the Power of the Heroes in
the School Room, Therapy Room, and on the Playground   *359*
James R. Porter and Brian J. Mistler
Overview   *359*
Interventions and Best Practices for Individual and Group
Therapy   *360*
Clinical Work With a Victim of Bullying   *365*
Case Study: Richard, Age 12   *365*
School Interventions and Strategies   *367*
Case Study: Systematic Prevention Program   *371*
Conclusions and Summary   *374*

20. Anger Management for Adolescents   *379*
Kevin A. Fall and Stephanie Eberts
The Dynamics of Anger   *379*
A Theoretical Framework for Understanding and Treating
Anger   *381*
Case Study: The Case of Jason   *384*
Summary   *395*
Suggested Resources   *396*

21. Gang Membership and Interventions   *399*
   Lori A. Wolff and Edward Hudspeth
      Background of Gangs in the United States   *399*
      Gang Prevention and Intervention Program Strategies   *402*
      Specific Gang Prevention and Intervention Program Components
      and Evaluation   *404*
      Case Study: Reggie, Age 11   *409*

Conclusion   *417*
Index   *419*

Contributors

Susan R. Barclay, PhD, LPC, NCC
Graduate
Higher Education and Student Personnel Program
University of Mississippi
University, Mississippi

Suzanne Beike, PhD
Assistant Professor
Special Education Program
Purdue University Calumet
Hammond, Indiana

Bill M. Blundell, MA, LCPC
Counselor
The Antioch Group
Peoria, Illinois

Caroline S. Booth, PhD, LPC, NCC
Assistant Professor
Department of Human Development and Services
North Carolina A & T State University
Greensboro, North Carolina

Christine Borzumato-Gainey, PhD, LPC
Mental Health Counselor
Elon University
Elon, North Carolina

Imelda Bratton, PhD
Assistant Professor
Department of Counseling and Student Affairs
Western Kentucky University
Bowling Green, Kentucky

William Brown
Master's Degree Student
Clinical Mental Health Counseling Program
Department of Applied Psychology
Antioch University New England
Keene, New Hampshire

Rita Brusca-Vega, EdD
Associate Professor
Special Education Program
Purdue University Calumet
Hammond, Indiana

S. Kent Butler, PhD
Associate Professor
Department of Educational and Human Sciences
University of Central Florida
Orlando, Florida

Edward P. Cannon, PhD, LPC, LMFT
Assistant Professor and Coordinator
Clinical Mental Health Counseling Program
University of Colorado
Denver, Colorado

David Christian, MS, LPC-Intern
Doctoral Student and School Counselor Intern
Department of Counseling and Higher Education
University of North Texas
Denton, Texas

Keith M. Davis, PhD, NCC, NCLSC
Professor and Director
Clinical Mental Health Counseling Program
Appalachian State University
Boone, North Carolina

Suzanne Degges-White, PhD, LMHC, LCAC, LPC, NCC
Associate Professor
Department of Leadership and Counselor Education
University of Mississippi
University, Mississippi

Stephanie Eberts, PhD
Assistant Professor
Professional Counseling Program
Texas State University
San Marcos, Texas

Kevin A. Fall, PhD
Associate Professor and Program Coordinator
Professional Counseling Program
Texas State University
San Marcos, Texas

Jesse Fox, MA
Doctoral Student
Counselor Education Program
University of Central Florida
Orlando, Florida

Samantha M. Grzesik, MSEd
Early Intervention Coordinator
EB Pediatric Resources
Chicago, Illinois

Thomas A. Grzesik, MS, CRC, LCPC
Counselor in Private Practice
Schererville, Indiana

W. Bryce Hagedorn, PhD, LMHC, NCC, MAC, QCS
Associate Professor and Program Director
Counselor Education Program
University of Central Florida
Orlando, Florida

Nicole R. Hill, PhD, LPC
Interim Dean
Graduate School
Professor
Department of Counseling and Counselor Education
Division of Health Sciences
Idaho State University
Pocatello, Idaho

Rachel M. Hoffman, PhD, PCC-S (OH)
Clinical Director
Meridian Community Care
Adjunct Faculty Member
Youngstown State University
Youngstown, Ohio

Edward Hudspeth, PhD, NCC, LPC, RPh, RPT-S, ACS
Clinical Assistant Professor
Department of Leadership and Counselor Education
University of Mississippi
University, Mississippi

Robin G. Liles, PhD, LPC, NCC
Associate Professor
Department of Human Development and Services
North Carolina A & T State University
Greensboro, North Carolina

John F. Marszalek, PhD, LPC, NCC
Core Faculty and Program Coordinator
Mental Health Counseling Program
School of Counseling and Social Service
Walden University
Minneapolis, Minnesota

Tony Michael, MA, LPC
Doctoral Student
Counselor Education and Supervision Program
University of Mississippi
University, Mississippi

Brian J. Mistler, PhD
Licensed Psychologist and Director of Student Health Services
Ringling College of Art and Design
Sarasota, Florida

Daniel M. Paredes, PhD, NCC, LPC, ACS
Clinical Counselor and Diversity Counseling Coordinator
North Carolina A & T State University
Greensboro, North Carolina

James R. Porter, PhD, LMHC
Private Psychotherapist
Gainesville, Florida

Torey L. Portrie-Bethke, PhD, NCC
Assistant Professor
Clinical Mental Health Counseling Program
Department of Applied Psychology
Antioch University New England
Keene, New Hampshire

Rebekah H. Reysen, MEd
Learning Specialist
Center for Excellence in Teaching & Learning
University of Mississippi
University, Mississippi

Corie Schoeneberg, EdS, LPC, RPT, NCC
Private Practitioner and Adjunct Instructor
Counselor Education Program
University of Central Missouri
Warrensburg, Missouri

George R. Sesser, PsyD, LP, LPC
Professor
Counselor Education Program
Department of Educational Leadership and Human Development
University of Central Missouri
Warrensburg, Missouri

Nancy E. Sherman, PhD, NCC, LCPC, ACS
Professor and Clinical Coordinator
Clinical Mental Health Counseling Program
Bradley University
Peoria, Illinois

M. Ann Shillingford, PhD
Assistant Professor
School Psychology and Counselor Education Program (SPACE)
School of Education
College of William & Mary
Williamsburg, Virginia

Margery J. Shupe, LPCC–S
Associate Professor
Department of School and Community Counseling
Xavier University
Cincinnati, Ohio

Carrie V. Smith, BBA
Graduate Student
Department of Leadership and Counselor Education
University of Mississippi
University, Mississippi

Shawn L. Spurgeon, PhD, LPC-MHSP, ACS
Assistant Professor
Mental Health Counseling
Department of Educational Psychology and Counseling
University of Tennessee
Knoxville, Tennessee

Kevin B. Stoltz, PhD, NCC, ACS, LPC
Associate Professor
Department of Leadership and Counselor Education
University of Mississippi
University, Mississippi

Ian S. Turnage-Butterbaugh, MS
Doctoral Student and Instructor
University of Mississippi
University, Mississippi

Katie J. Vena, MS
Program Director
South Shore Academy
Valparaiso, Indiana

Miriam L. Wagner, EdD
Associate Professor and Chair
Human Development and Services Department
North Carolina A & T State University
Greensboro, North Carolina

Lori A. Wolff, PhD, JD
Professor
Department of Leadership and Counselor Education
University of Mississippi
University, Mississippi

Tabitha L. Young, PhD, LMHC, NCC
Assistant Professor
Department of Leadership and Counselor Education
University of Mississippi
University, Mississippi

Preface

This book is designed to provide readers with a better understanding of the unique challenges faced by today's young males and to share the most effective strategies for counseling boys and young men. The cultural expectations of young girls and women have long been the topic of books, articles, and media attention, but there has been a lack of attention to the specific needs of young boys and young men. Therefore, the content of this book represents a multidimensional exploration of issues and concerns that this group brings into the counseling office. By presenting a holistic view of the development of young males within their social, emotional, and behavioral realms, this book highlights many of the potential pitfalls they may face and relevant interventions to be used by clinicians.

When selecting topics for the chapters in this book, current statistics and our rapidly changing culture shaped our choices. The content provides readers with information related to areas beyond those typically found in books addressing the counseling concerns of children and adolescents. The media is an overwhelming and greatly uncontrollable influence on our youth, and the current culture heavily emphasizes the importance of "having it your way" and "getting it while it is hot." Coupled with the increasing pressure to grow up fast and the ability of the Internet to provide information on taboo or titillating topics at the speed of a keyboard click, young people are confronted with knowledge and images beyond their maturity at record rates. Counselors must be willing to help young males make sense of the overabundance of data they are being fed, as they try to create their evolving identities. Thus, we have invited experts in the field to share their knowledge, experience, and strategies for best meeting the needs of these modern men-in-the-making.

As the capabilities of technology escalate, new doors to new vices (online gaming, easily accessible graphic pornography, "instant" friendships, etc.) are being opened. Counseling professionals are being asked to treat young men for behaviors that the practitioner may feel unprepared to address. By covering timely and critical topics, this book serves as a primer for both experienced and newly trained clinicians. The authors not only provide descriptions of contemporary presenting issues, innovative strategies, and novel case studies but also help readers visualize how to recognize and treat clients wrestling with specific behavioral issues or emotional concerns. Where relevant, chapters offer lists of additional resources (e.g., websites, books, organizations) to assist the reader in learning more about areas of particular interest.

We have organized this book around four aspects of clinical interest. The first section is titled *Understanding and Promoting Healthy Development* and its purpose is to help readers understand the developmental processes of males from cradle to early adulthood. The normal developmental path for young males is presented in terms of physical, emotional, and moral development in the first chapter and a detailed case example is presented. Also in this section are chapters that emphasize the ways in which therapy with young males is different than with young females, as well as a comprehensive discussion of how to adequately assess the issues and concerns of your adolescent male clients within a contextually focused perspective. This section also includes a look at the developmental problems that arise when young males suffer from learning disorders. Males are diagnosed with this type of disorder more frequently than females and, most unfortunately, research shows that individuals with learning disorders are twice as likely as others to report emotional distress and to attempt suicide (see Knopf, Park, & Paul Mulye, 2008). It is clear that we must recognize that learning disorders impact more than just academic performance. We also take a look at giftedness in young males and the ways in which this can negatively influence a young boy's life as academic excellence can lead to bullying and ostracism by a boy's peers. We close this section with a look at career counseling for young men. The traditional world of work has changed dramatically, as factories and industries have moved offshore or replaced manpower with machine power and technology. It is essential that we help our young men prepare for career paths that no longer reflect the typical trajectory outlined by early career theorists.

Just as "no man is an island" and "it takes a village to raise a child," young boys grow up within a web of multiple relationships. Our second section, *Relationship Development and Relationship Concerns*, provides perspectives on a young male's relationships within the family and with peers and romantic interests. The first chapter outlines normal relationship development with parents, siblings, and same-sex peers, and our second chapter explores some of the struggles faced by young boys growing up in single-parent homes, which currently comprise over a quarter of the homes in which children are residing. Kreider and Ellis (2011) reported findings from the U.S. Census Bureau that while 75% of White children live with both parents in their home, only 67% of Hispanic and 37% of African American children live in two-parent households, suggesting that there are huge inequalities in the lives of youth that counselors must be willing to acknowledge and address through advocacy and special programming. In the chapter on single-parent homes, the authors outline the special needs of young boys in families of divorce, as well as homes in which a parent has been incarcerated and those in which military deployment has removed a parent from a young boy's daily life.

Romantic relationships are explored in the following chapter and the authors take a look at concerns including adolescent sexual activity, "sexting," dating violence, and teen fathers. The final chapter in this section addresses gay and questioning young males. Studies show gay men usually recognized that they were somehow "different" from their heterosexual peers around age 5 or 6 and society is increasingly supportive of young men "coming out" in their early teen years; however, the individual decision may be fraught with tension and anxiety, and depending on the environment or geographical location, a young man's peers may respond with diverse reactions ranging from nonchalant acceptance to physical violence perpetrated against him. This chapter will provide readers with useful strategies to assist these young males as they seek to determine and develop their sexual identities.

Our third section, *Emotional and Mental Health Concerns*, focuses on a variety of mental health issues that may impede a young male's healthy functioning. Knopf et al. (2008) reported that adolescent males are more likely to have mental health difficulties than their female peers, yet they are less likely to seek treatment, according to studies. Males have consistently been more frequently diagnosed with attention deficit hyperactivity disorder (ADHD) than females, and we include a look at ADHD and its treatment via innovative methods—one case study illustrates the use of sand-play therapy for ADHD, and a separate chapter provides a rich base of knowledge on the use of adventure-based counseling as a treatment for young men with ADHD. It is a unique platform for connecting with young males that goes beyond the office and into the realm of metaphorical and actual adventure. In another chapter, authors explore working with young males who have suffered victimization and abuse. They also provide information addressing clinical work with boys who have abused their siblings or their parents.

A chapter on grief and loss is next in this section. Grief is a complicated emotion, and many young males are unprepared to work through this emotion, as our culture still seems to frown on the expression of sadness and vulnerability in males. Information on helping the boys cope with loss is shared, as well as a case study outlining grief counseling with a young boy. This is followed by a chapter looking at mood disorders in young males. It has been reported that around 20% of male high school students have acknowledged at least some mild depressive symptoms, and research also shows that the suicide death rate for adolescent males is 2.5 times that of adolescent females (see Knopf et al., 2008). Clearly, we need to understand more about the emotional life of young men, and this chapter provides welcome knowledge about emotional concerns and suicide assessment for this population.

Oftentimes, a young man's inability to seek help for his emotional distress may lead him to attempt to soothe himself through behaviors that are nonproductive or even lethal. These choices are discussed in the final section, *Behavior Disorders and Concerns.* Substance use and abuse disorders are found more often in young males than females. Addictions to substances have been joined in their negative influence on the lives of young men by addictions to processes, such as gaming, sexual activities, and gambling. To best meet counselors' needs, we have included two chapters on addictive behaviors—one on identifying and assessing these behaviors and another providing strategies for treatment. The authors of these two chapters address the variety of addictive behaviors that are keeping young men from healthy interactions and normal development. Males who suffer with oppositional defiant disorder or conduct disorder create heartache for families and distress for many others in their environments. In a chapter addressing these disorders, the author describes symptoms and strategies for helping young men and their families combat the damage of these problems. A chapter on bullying provides information on the dynamics of bullying, as well as how to involve the bully, the bullied person, and by-standers in an effort to mitigate this harmful interaction among youth. A chapter on helping boys and young men deal with their anger is provided so that clinicians can help young males find more productive ways of handling the anger that may arise from unmet needs or desires, or from sadness or loss, emotions they are typically uneducated in handling. The final chapter in the book is focused on street gangs and their members. Unfortunately, the prevalence of gangs has continued to rise over the past decade, and research presented in this chapter suggests that society-level interventions are necessary to fully combat the ability of gangs to function and grow their membership. Programming initiatives are described and a unique case study is presented showing the efficacy of a novel treatment, play therapy, with an 11-year-old boy who was on the cusp of falling into gang membership.

Throughout this book, our authors provide a textured exploration of the challenges faced by young men today, as well as the challenges faced by clinicians who work with these young men. Communication and emotional expression practices of young males are described and suggestions for building a productive therapeutic alliance are shared explicitly and through the case studies presented. In summary, the aim of this book is to raise the awareness of practitioners to the many ways in which young men need assistance navigating from boyhood to manhood.

REFERENCES

Knopf, D., Park, M. J., & Paul Mulye, T. (2008). *The mental health of adolescents: A national profile, 2008.* San Francisco, CA: National Adolescent Health Information Center, University of California, San Francisco.

Kreider, R. M., & Ellis, R. (2011). Living arrangements of children: 2009. *Current Population Reports,* P70–P126. Washington, DC: U.S. Census Bureau.

Acknowledgments

This project grew out of the realization that while our boys and young men need counseling techniques and approaches that are targeted to their unique developmental and temperamental needs, there was an absence of literature on this topic. So, we turned to the experts in the field and asked if they would share their wisdom and experience with readers, which they did with skill and clarity. Therefore, we acknowledge that it is their commitment to the well-being of boys and young men that allowed this book to take shape. We also greatly appreciate the support shown by our editorial team, Jennifer Perillo, who helped shape the project from its origin, and Nancy Hale, who has seen it through to its completion. We also offer sincere gratitude to Katie Corasaniti, who keeps the ball rolling and keeps us on track!

Part I: Understanding and Promoting Healthy Development

1

The Developmental Path: From Boyhood to Older Adolescence

THOMAS A. GRZESIK, SAMANTHA M. GRZESIK, AND KATIE J. VENA

PHYSIOLOGICAL DEVELOPMENT

The developmental path of males and females from childhood throughout adulthood varies by gender. Although the physical disparities are apparent, the divergent physiological pathways are not. A host of neurobiological differences between genders affects differences in learning, behavior, and emotional regulation and expression. Although these differences may be quite striking, neither the male nor the female brain is superior in functioning to that of the other, even though the male brain tends to be about 10% to 15% larger than the female brain (Bonomo, 2010).

On average, the brain stops growing between the ages of 12 and 14, but structures of the brain may develop into early adulthood (Scholastic, 2008). Gender differences in the size and function of various components are evident early on. The prefrontal cortex is responsible for carrying out future decisions, making right and wrong choices, and weighing risks and rewards. The limbic system is the center of emotional responses. Since the prefrontal cortex develops late and the limbic system matures early, this often has an effect on the decision and choice making of teenagers (Scholastic). Teenagers are more apt to make decisions without thinking through an issue logically or rationally. During mental tasks (e.g., speaking), males do not engage both cerebral hemispheres to accomplish the task, whereas females rely on both (National Center for Infants, Toddlers, and Families, 2011).

Males also have a greater volume of gray matter, and females possess more white matter. White matter allows neural activity to be sent and spread throughout different parts of the brain, while gray matter retains neural activity in a localized position (Gurian, 2010). This may be a reason females tend to be more empathic and openly emotional. Moreover, throughout the day, a male brain needs time to recharge and will periodically enter a state of rest, but a female brain rarely does so. As a result, males and females tend to approach tasks and learning differently. Females are more easily able to handle multitasking because their corpus callosum is significantly larger, and this structure transmits signals between both hemispheres (Bonomo, 2010). Another brain structure that is distinctive in size is the inferior parietal lobule (IPL) that is responsible for processing spatial attention, perception, and sensory integration. The IPL is larger in males, and research shows that the left side is particularly larger than the right (Sabbatini, 1997). Information processing is also different between female and male brains. Information even travels to different parts of the brain for males and females. In addition, the hippocampus (short- and long-term memory), the occipital lobe (visual processing), the frontal lobes (emotion center), and the temporal lobe (organization of sensory input) are not as active in males as in females. Thus, females tend to associate more sensation and emotions to their experiences and keep records of each moment in their memory (Gurian, 2010). Throughout development, on average, males carry out spatial tasks such as mentally visualizing the shape and rotation of an object better than females. However, females, on average, can execute tasks such as emotion recognition and particular verbal functions better than males due to more cortical areas (National Center for Infants, Toddlers, and Families, 2011). In regards to learning, females are more proficient in reading and writing, while males perform better in advanced mathematics and physics (Bonomo, 2010).

Besides differences in specific brain structures, the neurophysiological make-up is gender unique. Female neural activity is consistently busier than in males. Females also have more nerve fibers in their skin and are more sensitive to pain (Gurian, 2010). Males process pain slower than females and are less sensitive to pain. Nerve connections that assist in listening are more developed in females, giving them better auditory skills (Bonomo, 2010). The neurochemical and hormone differences between the genders affect physiology and behavior. Males have a significantly higher level of the aggression/desire-seeking chemical known as testosterone (Ginger, 2003). However, females have higher levels of oxytocin and serotonin. Oxytocin is a chemical neurotransmitter in the brain that is associated with bonding, sometimes referred to as the hormone of love. Females tend to bond easier and more often with others. Serotonin helps stabilize mood and is referred to as the "happy feeling" chemical (Gurian,

2010). Because of possessing less serotonin, males are more at risk to display impulsive behaviors. According to Zimmer (2011), there is a specific region in the brain that evaluates conflict, the cognitive control network. The network functions more poorly in childhood but develops with age. During the adolescent years, teenagers are more likely to be impulsive without thinking about the consequences or the risks associated with the consequences or behavior. As young males develop, more risks occur such as venturing off without parents, increasing autonomy, experimenting with new drugs, alcohol, and risk-taking behaviors. Due to experience, environment, and genetics, adolescents may have decreasing levels of cognitive control. These levels may lead to the developing of anxiety, depression, addictions, and other affective and cognitive disorders.

Both boys and girls follow similar developmental paths, and multilevel development is occurring from conception through death. This chapter will present development from conception through late adolescence and will focus on the uniqueness of boys. In exploring this uniqueness, a number of developmental theories and postulates were explored, including the role of play in children's development.

EMOTIONAL AND SOCIAL DEVELOPMENT THROUGH PLAY

Developmental theorists Jean Piaget and Lev Vygotsky emphasized the importance of play in the development of a child. Early in life, young boys are already identifying and choosing gender-appropriate toys (Dunn & Hughes, 2001; Martin, Wood, & Little, 1990). Within the Piaget Sensorimotor Stage (birth to about age 2), it was noted that even at age 1, there is a difference in the preference of toys between boys and girls (Snow, Jacklin, & Maccoby, 1983). From a very early age, boys show an interest toward vehicles, weapons, building blocks, and progress to toys involving construction and mechanical systems. They show a propensity for building things. They favor objects that are animated and devices with functions that can be manually activated (Baron-Cohen, 2005). Girls focused on playing with dolls and related objects, and boys found interest in playing with tools, toy cars, and airplanes. Servin, Bohlin, and Berlin (1999) found that boys continue to show a preference for action/manipulative type toys from the age of 1 to 5. More recently, Golonblack et al. (2008) conducted a longitudinal study involving the sex type behavior of boys and girls from 2½ to 8 years old. They focused on the types of toys each sex played with, and they found that sex type behavior increased through the preschool years to at least 8 years of age.

Vygotsky (1978) believed that play is a significant tool for learning and development. According to Vygotsky, "play traits are the result of proximal development of the child. In play, a child always behaves beyond his average age, above his daily behavior; in play, it is as though he were a head taller than himself. As in the focus of a magnifying glass, play contains all development tendencies in a condensed form and is itself a major source of development" (p. 102).

According to Newman and Newman (2009), play is an important experience that enhances physical skills, motor coordination, and perceptive skills, as well as social and personality development. As children grow into middle childhood and participate in team sports, they learn the value of cooperation through the division of labor. Team play also fosters interpersonal relationships and further develops social skills. Play can also influence the building of familial relationships. According to Kazura (2000), play can be a significant vehicle in the development of father–child relationships. Children who were socially attached to their fathers demonstrated much higher levels of play activity than those who demonstrated an insecure attachment to their fathers.

In general, play is critical to a child's physical, intellectual, social, emotional, and personality development. It also enables a child to develop environmental awareness (Hendrick & Weissman, 2005). According to Maccoby (1998), children between the ages of 3 and 9 spend most of their time that is not managed and controlled by adults in some form of play activity. As compared to girls, boys more often participate in aggressive, competitive, risk taking, physically rough and tumble, and conquering types of play activity.

According to Connell (2002), the left hemisphere of the brain is essentially responsible for auditory and verbal language skills that include listening, speaking, and writing. The left hemisphere functions as a means of processing information in a sequential and analytical manner and, in turn, allows us to focus on details. The right hemisphere provides the functional means for visual–spatial and visual–motor activity that include sports, architecture, sculpturing, painting, and carpentry. The right hemisphere allows for a holistic style of processing information. This is evident in the different styles and preferences of play between boys and girls.

Due to the advanced biological development of the left hemisphere in girls as compared to boys, girls are better able to read and write than boys at an early school age. It was found that boys are better able to learn using nontraditional methods, such as movement and visual–spatial skills consistent with their more developed right hemisphere (Gurian, 2001).

These differences in brain function between boys and girls can explain the sex differences in the type and style of play. These differences continue along the cognitive developmental path. The associated behavioral differences also appear in social schemas such as play. The consequences of play permeate all aspects of development, that is, psychosocial, cognitive, behavioral, emotional, spiritual, moral, and so on.

COGNITIVE DEVELOPMENT AND GENDER

Boys' cognitive development is significantly influenced by the strength of their right hemisphere functioning and the weakness of their left hemisphere functioning. Spatial abilities refer to *space relations,* and this involves the ability to think in three dimensions and to picture mentally the shape, size, and position of objects when shown only a picture or pattern. It is important for carpenters, architects, machinists, engineers, dentists, dress designers, and others whose work requires them to visualize solid forms or spaces. Spatial abilities also include *mechanical reasoning*; this is the understanding of mechanical principles and devices and the laws of everyday physics. This ability is important for mechanics, engineers, and a variety of factory positions (Bennett, Seashore, & Wesman, 1991). Within a broader definition of visual–spatial abilities is *form perception*, which is the ability to perceive pertinent detail in objects or in pictorial or graphic material and to make visual comparisons and discriminations and see slight differences in shapes and shadings of figures and widths (Field & Field, 2004).

Learning Styles and Gender

Boys and girls learn differently, as these brain differences suggest, and they should be afforded a teaching style specific to their needs (Gurian, 2001). According to Geist and King (2008), girls' learning styles encompass their read/write or auditory approach; boys learn best through visual and kinesthetic means (as cited in Bevan, 2001; Fleming, 2005; Molumby, 2004; Singham, 2003). Females are typically visual learners, and they learn best through presentation and demonstration. For example, they may absorb and understand the lesson by drawing things out or visualizing a problem on a chalkboard. Males, though, are typically kinesthetic learners who learn best through hands-on methods. Problem solving by the kinesthetic learner is facilitated by allowing them to use related objects during the course of the solution or to physically act out a scenario. It is important that motion/movement interaction be incorporated for this learning style. These learners also benefit from the use of everyday problems being included in the course of learning and understanding mathematics (Geist & King, 2008). This style of learning is an extension of a biological learning trait of boys that has been further developed and socialized through play.

As cited in Bonomo (2010), Sax (2006) addressed gender-based differences between boys and girls in the following table:

Girls	Boys
Girls can multitask better than boys because the corpus callosum in females is 26% larger than in males. The corpus callosum is the nervous tissue that sends signals between the two halves of the brain.	In the male brain, a larger area is devoted to spatial mechanical functioning and half as much to verbal emotive functioning.
Girls have the ability to transition between lessons more quickly and are less apt to have attention span issues.	Boys utilize the cerebral cortex less often than girls, and they access the primitive areas of the brain more often while performing the same types of activities or tasks.
The neural connectors that create listening skills are more developed in the female brain and therefore enhance listening skills, memory storage, and tone of voice discrimination in girls.	For the male brain to renew or recharge, it will go into rest states, while the female brain does so without rest states or sleep.
Girls make fewer impulsive decisions than boys due to a higher serotonin level.	Boys have less serotonin and less oxytocin, which makes them more impulsive and less likely to sit still to talk to someone.
The female brain has 15% more blood flow than the male brain, allowing for enhanced integrated learning.	Boys structure or compartmentalize learning because they have less blood flow to the brain.
Because girls have more cortical areas devoted to verbal functioning, they are better at sensory memory, sitting still, listening, tonality, and the complexities of reading and writing (the skills and behaviors that tend to be rewarded in school).	Boys' brains are better suited to symbols, abstractions, and pictures. Boys in general learn higher math and physics better than girls. Boys prefer video games for the physical movement and destruction. Boys get into more trouble for not listening, moving around, sleeping in class, and incomplete assignments.

Gender Implications for Education

In addition to the neurological and biological differences mentioned earlier in this chapter, research has shown that there are sex differences in hearing, vision, and smell. Girls acquire binocular vision much sooner than boys do. The sense of smell for females is estimated to be 100,000 times more sensitive than that of a male. The sense of hearing is also much more sensitive in girls than in boys, especially at higher frequencies, which are critical for speech discrimination. Some boys who have been classified as delayed learners perhaps may have been able to grasp learning much sooner if the teacher had spoken louder (Sax, 2006).

According to Sax (2006), there are differences in the autonomic nervous system between males and females. He explains that the female autonomic system is more influenced by the parasympathetic nervous system, and the male autonomic nervous system is more influenced by the sympathetic nervous system. An interesting point made by Sax is the influence of the parasympathetic nervous system on digestion, heart rate, vasodilatation, and increased continuous blood flow with a subsequent response to higher ambient temperatures. He pointed out that studies have shown that boys learn better in colder temperatures and girls learn better in warmer temperatures. The ideal classroom temperature for a boy is 69°F and 75°F for girls. He also explained that boys' learning is facilitated by instruction that is presented in a loud, concise, and precise manner. In contrast, he explained that girls learn better when instruction is presented in a softer, less demanding manner. As a proponent of single-sex schools, Sax's research shows that there has been significant success in higher achievement in single-sex schools. He has found that single-sex schools have allowed both boys and girls to flourish in subjects that have been traditionally dominated by the opposite sex. An interesting side note is that research shows that the teachers' gender does not have a significant bearing on the motivation of boys and girls. Research has shown that academic outcome is influenced by the nature and quality of the didactic delivery and the motivation generated by the individual student (Martin & Marsh, 2005).

According to King, Gurian, and Stevens (2010), traditional education has resulted in a gender gap, with boys falling behind girls in academic achievement. This is especially true in reading. They have found that boys tend to be graphic thinkers and respond better to an academic environment that provides kinesthetic techniques and a competitive structure. They attributed gendered learning differences to physical differences in the brain, as well as psychosocial influences. They also suggested that boys would benefit in a learning environment that is kinesthetic and visually oriented with material that is consistent with boys' interests. These researchers found that tailoring teaching methods to boys' learning style increases motivation and academic achievement.

Another researcher, Zaman (2008), suggested that teacher bias against boys' classroom behavior might lead to the disproportionate number of boys versus girls who are expelled from school. Furthermore, she opined that a lack of gender sensitivity could become an insidious negative attitude by a teacher, which, in turn, has a direct negative impact on a boy's motivation to learn and subsequent academic achievement. She proposed that teachers undergo gender sensitivity screening and training in order to promote a learning environment more supportive and beneficial for boys.

In another study addressing the learning behaviors of girls and boys, Hancock and Stock (1996) found that girls develop strategies through planned behavior (e.g., focusing on the preparation for tests within a much earlier timeframe than boys do). They also found that a learning style dominant in boys involves aural comprehension. It was suggested that this may be the reason why boys read at a lower level than girls do, but boys are better listeners. It was found that the sixth-grade boys were not as concerned with tests, texts, and surface processing of information but more concerned with independent study behaviors and the processing of aural classroom interaction at a deep level. The authors suggested that these study strategy differences between boys and girls might be the source of ongoing gender differences in academic achievements.

Other researchers (Tyre, Murr, Juarez, Underwood, Springen, & Wingert, 2006) have found not only that boys start off elementary school with lower literacy skills than girls do, but that they are less frequently encouraged to read, which only widens the literacy gap. They also reported that girls exhibit consistently higher scores in reading and writing throughout elementary, middle, and high school. From a greater likelihood to suffer from disabilities such as emotional disturbances, learning problems, and speech impediments in elementary school, young males are more likely to engage in physical fights, use illegal substances, and drop out of high school than girls are. However, Pollack (1998) noted that in mathematics and science, boys surpass girls at a significant rate. These differences in learning and processing have led Pollack to develop the following suggestions for parents when enhancing the educational experiences and achievements of young males:

1. Provide praise for your son's school achievements.
2. Become involved and remain involved.
3. Actively keep track of your son's emotional life.
4. Prevent and dissuade schools from misjudging your son.
5. Help to influence the school's mission.

Pollack recommended the following for schools to help improve the achievement levels of boys:

1. Provide subject matter that is boy-friendly.
2. Implement teaching methodology that is specific to the learning styles of boys.
3. Allow every boy the opportunity to learn at his pace.
4. Establish same-sex classes in order to experiment with this approach to teaching.
5. Increase the number of male teachers.

6. Find mentoring programs that allow for compatibility between the student and the mentor.
7. Establish safe places for boys (guy spaces) to help develop appropriate emotional and social growth.

The Importance of Attachment in Development

John Bowlby and Mary Ainsworth are responsible for the initial development of the evolving theory of attachment. Bowlby (as cited in Bretherton, 1992) set forth the supposition that the genesis of the attachment relationship between caregiver and infant begins with proximity. Frequent close proximity to the caregiver fulfills a basic security need of the infant. Based on empirical evidence, Bowlby postulated that in order to develop in a mentally healthy manner, the infant and young child should experience an environment that is warm and intimate through continuous relationship with his caretaker that provides mutual satisfaction and enjoyment.

The experience of attachment is both internal and external. The attachment experiences that are stored in memory control the reactions of an individual following loss (death) or separation from an attachment figure (Bretherton, 1992). Reynolds (2002), as cited in Gurian and Stevens (2005), proposed that an attachment system that emphasizes learning optimizes a young child's ability to learn. A profound emotional connection encouraged between the parent and the child at the inception of bonding occurs during the first moment of introrecognition and physical contact. Attachment is a developmental process of parent/caregiver and child mutuality that allows the ongoing process of affectionate caregiving that enhances the innate bond throughout life (Gurian & Stevens, 2005). Attachment can extend beyond the death of one of the shareholders. Attachment is a developed emotional bond. For the vast majority of people, the need for close physical proximity to the caregiver diminishes significantly during early childhood with eventual virtual extinction.

Bowlby determined that attachment disruption or poor attachment could lead to separation anxiety (as cited in Bretherton, 1992). This anxiety manifests as a pervasive fear of abandonment that can be experienced at the mere thought of a caregiver's unavailability. Excessive levels of separation anxiety are related to negative family experiences that include repeated threats of abandonment or rejection by parents or exposure to a parent's illness or death for which the child feels a sense of responsibility. Bowlby suggested that poor attachment during the early developmental stages could affect personality development and possibly lead to personality disorders.

Mary Ainsworth (as cited in Bretherton, 1992) performed field studies of infant–mother relationships in Uganda. In essence, Ainsworth determined that infants with secure attachment to their mother seemed content and did not cry as often as insecurely attached infants. She also noted that infants who have not yet formed attachments showed no differential behavior toward the mother (Ainsworth, 1963, 1967). Waters (2004) recounted that Ainsworth and her collaborators developed a standard laboratory procedure called the Strange Situation, an observational means of determining a child's style or type of attachment. According to Newman & Newman (2009), the attachment types are classified in four pattern categories: (a) A child who has a *secure attachment* is spontaneous in the exploration of the environment and will interact with strangers in the presence of their caregiver. After a period of separation, the child may openly greet the caregiver. If there was distress during the separation, the return of the caregiver will reduce the distress of the child. (b) Children who fit an *anxious-avoidant attachment* pattern avoid contact with their caregiver after separation and/or will ignore efforts toward interaction. These children do not show the same level of distress at being separated as do other children. (c) Children who reveal an *anxious-resistant* attachment are cautious in the presence of a stranger, and there is a disruption in their spontaneous exploratory behavior due to separation from the caregiver. Upon the return of the caregiver, the child shows signs of wanting to be close to the caregiver, but there is also a show of negative or angry behavior with a poor response to soothing or comfort. (d) Children that fall within a *disorganized attachment* pattern have no consistent strategy for managing separation or stress. Their behavior is contradictory and unpredictable with expressions of extreme fear and confusion.

Bowlby determined that attachment is a lasting psychological relationship or connectedness between human beings (Waters & Cummings, 2000). It seems logical that the effects of an experience as strong as attachment would have a continuing effect on relationships, and research is showing this to be true (Crowell, Treboux, & Waters, 2002; Waters, 2004). Based on these studies, it is apparent that attachment has a profound and continuing effect on individuals and their subsequent encounters from birth through adulthood. However, Bowlby suggested that a change in attachment patterns could occur in both childhood and adult relational interactions (as cited in Crowell & Treboux, 1995). He put forth that this change could be the result of new emotional relationships in combination, with the development of formal operational thought resulting in the individual being able to reflect on and reinterpret the efficacy of past and present experiences.

According to Crowell and Treboux (1995), children develop expectations of a parent's potential behavior in various situations setting forth postulates regarding close relationships and how they fit into daily life and stressful situations. Bowlby proposed that those internal working models of the world include others and oneself, and once these models are formed, they tend to remain stable and usually operate at the unconscious level. These models are believed to be based on attachment relationships, and they provide the basis for the organization of memory that includes the roles that shape one's access to knowledge about the self, the attachment object, and resulting qualities of the relationship.

Based on Bowlby's postulates regarding mental representations (as cited in Crowell & Treboux, 1995), attachment research has shifted away from behavioral observations of infants toward methodologies geared toward determining the cognitive and effective foundations of the attachment behavior system throughout the life span. Waters noted (as cited in Crowell & Treboux) that even though it is not specific to the attachment behavior system, mental representations allow the means through which the subjective view and experience of a person, as opposed to merely the objective features of experience, can have a bearing on behavior and development. According to Crowell and Treboux, mental representations conceptualize attachment as a binding process among people across time and space. Waters sets forth (as cited by Crowell & Treboux) that the understanding of the binding nature of attachment among people across time and space is provided through mental representations. Bretherton (as cited by Crowell & Treboux) opined that Bowlby's induction of mental representations into attachment theory provides a life span insight of the attachment behavior system and allows for an understanding of the developmental change in the expression of attachment and its continuing importance of development of behavior in relationships.

Mental representations are the residual effects of attachment behavior experienced between the child and the caregiver. Unlike the infant–caregiver attachment experience, the dyadic attachment relationship between older adolescents or between adults is reciprocal. According to Ainsworth and Weiss (as cited by Crowell & Treboux, 1995), attachment relationships manifest in a variety of ways such as camaraderie, sexual bonds, sense of competence, and mutual experience.

In the same vein as mental representation, Peter Fonagy discussed attunement and contingent communication. Fonagy (as cited by Sonkin, 2005) explained that the key legacy of secure attachment is the ability of individuals to reflect rationally on thier internal emotional experience while reflecting on the mind of another. The individual gains this ability through the verbal and nonverbal cues exchanged between child and caregiver, allowing a child to see himself or herself through the eyes of the caregiver. This is what Fonagy terms attunement and contingent communication. He suggested that individuals lacking secure attachment are void of this reflective function due to repressed emotional responses as they exist in dismissing attachments or are extremely heightened in emotional responses as indicated in preoccupied attachment. In each case, the individuals lack the ability to identify their own internal experience or reflect on the experience of another. These insecure approaches to regulating contemporaneous attachments indicate a compromise in the individual's capacity for reflection on self or on others.

Gurian and Sevens (2005) noted multiple research efforts that suggested that children with positive attachment experiences through nurturing within a secured attachment system develop positive self-esteem and good relational skills, become confident and inquisitive, form a conscience, and learn more successfully. They attributed a biological reason for the relationship of secure attachment to increased learning. Specifically, they set forth "the organic mechanisms in the brain by which the brain learns requires secured attachment in order to grow fully" (p. 71). Furthermore, bonding and attachment have an insidious influence on a child that affects the nervous system, as well as their emotional, social, and intellectual development. Poor or insecure bonding in attachment can have a devastating effect on all aspects of a child's life, including experiences while in school. The environments in which children and adolescents live are critical in promoting mental health and mitigating the possibilities of depression, anxiety disorders, and other affective, behavioral, and cognitive disorders. An individual's environment may significantly influence the course of his or her thought-processing behaviors (Erk, 2008). Family issues are a primary trigger of depression and anxiety in children and adolescents who are already predisposed to these disorders. Child abuse (including physical, verbal, sexual, and emotional) significantly increases risks to physical, cognitive, and emotional development, as well as the well-being of the youth.

Poor attachment for boys can lead to violence and learning disorders, whereas, for girls, it can lead to anorexia, bulimia, and depression. Due to a boy's kinesthetic nature that can involve fidgeting and pulling away, it is much more difficult for the caregivers to provide meaningful touch at an early age in the attachment experience. As cited by Gurian and Stevens (2005), Nancy Bayley's research at UCLA (as cited in Blum, 1998), boys, more than girls, during early childhood experience learning difficulties resulting from poor attachment. Bayley concluded that insecure attachment resulted in test scores that revealed lower adolescent intellectual skills for male infants than for female infants who did not experience secure attachment. This is another example of the differences in the structure and function of male versus female brains.

LEARNING TO FOLLOW SOCIETY'S CODE OF CONDUCT

Human development does not occur in a vacuum. We are social beings that adhere to a societal code of conduct. This code of conduct is known as morality. In developing a sense of morals, a child navigates through this code of conduct with the help of caregivers, siblings, peers, educators, mass communications, and so on, as well as through trial and error. Lawrence Kohlberg established six stages of moral development (Bailey, 2011). His stages are as follows:

Level I: Preconventional Morality

(Children up to Ages 10 to 13)

Stage 1: Orientation to Obedience and Punishment
Kohlberg explained that during Stage 1, children are not yet speaking members of society. and they view morality as an external influence dictated by older people. Children learn that there is goodness or rewards in obedience and punishment or badness in disobedience.

Stage 2: Individualism and Instrumental Exchange
In Stage 2, the child has continuing awareness that disobedience is wrong with a consequence of punishment, but now understands that punishment is a risk that needs to be avoided. Also during this stage, a child develops an egoist persona in which decisions are made to suit one's own needs and desires. Other people are valued in terms of utility. Furthermore, vengeance is considered a moral obligation.

Level II: Conventional Morality

(Children in Their Early Teens up to Middle Age)

Kohlberg set forth that most people do not go beyond this level. This is the level in which the acceptance of the rules and regulations of an individual's subgroup and group unfolds.

Stage 3: Interpersonal Conformity
At this stage, children learn the importance of morality within their lives and within the general population. They develop the belief that it is important to live up to the expectations of family and society. They understand the value of the attributes of good behavior, such as the reciprocity of feelings, trust, and protection, as well as mutual emotions involving love and empathy. A child learns the complexities of peer pressure. Moral focus is placed on group standards and following group mores and dictates. Furthermore, a child learns that individual vengeance is no longer accepted, and retribution is now a function of the collective. As an individual, the child learns that forgiveness is preferred over revenge.

Stage 4: Law and Order (Maintaining the Social Order)

During Stage 4, the developing individual expands the importance of relationships and conformity outside of smaller groups, such as family and friends, to society as a whole. The individual participates at a higher level within the moral code and is now focused on obeying laws, respecting authority, and contributing in a manner directed toward helping sustain social order. The conformity to the moral code goes unquestioned for most people. It is now accepted that it is not just for one to forego rewarding positive contributing efforts to maintaining society or to not punish recalcitrant members.

Stage 4½: The Cynic

Kohlberg found that some people transition through or remain in an area of development that is between the conventional stages and the post-conventional levels of 5 and 6. These individuals question the rigidity of conventional morality, but have not yet found a higher level of moral function. They still find themselves controlled by conventional morality, but develop a disdain for a lack of debate and compromise within the conventional stages and find themselves becoming cynical toward leadership and the utility of society in general.

Level III: Postconventional Morality

This level focuses on ethical obligations including nonmalfeasance, justice, autonomy, and justice. Very few people reach this level and seldom prior to middle age.

Stage 5: Social Contract and Individual Rights

During this stage, individuals begin to question the overall value of society. They question the status quo and explore ways in which society can improve the rights and values of its members. In doing so, these individuals take a developmental approach and determine if emerging rights and values have met the initial goals in the formation of the society. The assumption made by these individuals is that societal members would all want to enjoy liberty, the right to thrive, and protection, as well as democratic processes that can address and change harmful laws while improving society. These individuals are opposed to retributive punishment because it does not comport with human rights and welfare. Emphasis is placed on individual rights and freedoms established by the whole society.

Stage 6: Universal Ethical Principles

At this stage, the individual promotes abstract principles in place of concrete rules or moral decision making. The ultimate attainment within this stage is justice for all through the development of individual human rights.

Although not every young male will follow this linear path to optimal morality, it is useful as a guide in understanding the behavior—and misbehavior—of youth. In a semistructured interview with 29 young males, aged 6 to 19, living in a residential care facility, the younger boys staunchly avowed that abusive behaviors were wrong. However, the older young men expressed their belief that physical and verbal abuse of others was acceptable if they "deserved it." These young men seemed to see abuse as a way to punish or get revenge against someone who had wronged them. Some of these same youths showed a sense of isolation in that they denigrated friendships as being superficial and lacking value. Others, who described their families as supportive, both spoke out against abuse as unacceptable and expressed their belief that while they did not need to be liked and accepted by everyone, they did value their close friends to whom they could turn to for validation and acceptance. The ways in which even one young man's attachment behaviors and sense of morality can vary over time are broad. Following is a case study of a young male's development from birth to late adolescence using attachment and morality development as the measure of his progress.

CASE STUDY: GROWING UP AS A BOY FROM AN ATTACHMENT AND MORALITY PERSPECTIVE: STEFAN'S STORY

Ages 0 to 5

Family Constellation and Relationship Development
My name is Stefan and I am currently middle aged. I grew up in the inner city of a large Midwestern community. Both my paternal and maternal grandparents were Polish immigrants. I was a middle child and, during this stage, I had a brother two years older and another three years younger. My mother did not graduate from high school. My father graduated from high school in three years.

My caregivers were my mother, father, and paternal grandmother. My crib was in my parents' bedroom. During my waking hours while lying in my crib, I remember being upset if my mother did not have her foot within reach of my hands. I recall regular interaction with my mother. She was not an overtly affectionate person, but, in retrospect, her affection was always genuine and present. My father worked two jobs and was not available to me during most of my waking hours. He was fair with punishment and not abusive. I recall having a good feeling when he was present. My paternal grandmother, who was a widow, lived with us. She was bilingual in Polish and English. I had a very close relationship with her. She was nurturing and protective.

I recall that my mother was somewhat jealous of the relationship I had with my grandmother. I was clearly clingy during this stage. I was very reluctant to leave my grandmother or mother. In fact, I remember my grandmother attempting to hand me over to her friend. I became very resistant and bit her friend.

I do not recall a lot of interaction with my brothers during this stage. I remember having a feeling of rejection by my mother after my younger brother was born. I was 3½ years old. I developed a closer relationship with my grandmother following the birth of my brother. I was enthralled with my father's career as a firefighter. Some of my earliest fond memories were going with my mother and brothers to visit my father at the fire station.

My earliest memory of quality interaction with my mother relates to the evenings I would sit on her lap while she read a book to me. My grandmother provided me with basic childcare while my parents were at work. I accompanied her to many of her social activities. In retrospect, it seemed that I was her favorite grandchild.

Physical Challenges

When I was between two and three years old, I underwent eye surgery. I recall waking up and repeatedly kicking at something. I was alone and frightened. My mother and father appeared shortly after I awoke. I recall that I wanted my little red teddy bear named Timmy with me during my surgery. One of my parents handed the bear to me shortly after I awoke. The limited vision that I experienced after the surgery resulted in my inability to judge the proximity of my caregivers. I was very frightened by the experience. I panicked when a caregiver did not respond to my calls. I recall running through the house and bumping into doors and walls while searching for a caregiver. The teddy bear seemed to provide me with a sense of comfort, if I knew my caregivers were nearby.

My speech was delayed during my first three years due to tongue-tie (ankyloglossia). This was surgically corrected, and my speech followed a normal course. The development of my eye, hand, and foot coordination was delayed due to uncorrected hyperopia (farsightedness). Following eye surgery and with the use of eyeglasses, I eventually succeeded in attaining normal motor coordination, although this took until I was nine or ten. I did not learn how to skip until the end of kindergarten. Cognitively, I developed at a stage-appropriate pace.

Entering School

I was terrified my first day of kindergarten. I did not want to leave my mother. I cried and clung to her. I do not recall the immediate aftermath of that incident; however, I slowly adjusted to a normal daily kindergarten routine.

> At age 6, I was completing kindergarten. I attended kindergarten during the morning session. My mother was a room mother for my older brother's third grade class at a Catholic grade school. During special event days at his school, my mother always helped serve treats to the students. I recall accompanying her to many of these events. Sister Angeline, the first grade teacher, always made a special effort to talk with me whenever I was at the school. She would remark that she could not wait until I was in her first grade class.

THROUGH THE LENS OF ATTACHMENT THEORY

According to Bowlby (1956), the nature of dependence and independence in the form of child and caregiver relationships is manifested through attachment. In essence, John Bowlby set forth in his attachment theory that it is a basic human need to be securely attached to another person(s) (Holmes, 1993). This theory is partly based on Freudian theory, field studies involving mother and infant relationships, as well as various ethological studies (MacDonald, 2001). The synthesis of his research led him to the formulation that a child's internal self and pursuit of external needs are the result of a collective attachment history.

During my Infancy and Early Childhood Stage, I experienced external attachment with my parents. My internal attachment was somewhat insecure during this developmental stage. I sensed some emotional distance between my mother and me, but I was satisfied with the internal attachment I had with my father. Initially, my strongest attachment was with my grandmother. The consistent relationship with my grandmother acted as a bridge to the ongoing development of my parental attachments. My sense of security was tenuous during this stage of my life.

In order to experience separation anxiety, there must be a history of attachment (Bretherton, 1992). Based on my display of separation anxiety as demonstrated by the biting incident, my behavior following eye surgery, and my initial difficulty adjusting to kindergarten, it was apparent that my internal and external attachments were not in harmony. I was not able to grasp the idea of proximity.

THROUGH THE LENS OF MORAL DEVELOPMENT THEORY

I do not recall any specific personal instances of punishment during this stage; however, I have a recollection that my father did administer punishment. Although I do not recall specific instances, Kohlberg's premise regarding obedience and punishment was most likely realized during this stage.

Ages 5 to 9

My first day in first grade was disastrous. I was disruptive and recalcitrant. Sister Angeline made me stand in a corner of the room during lunch hour. I felt fear and shame. I remember she eventually allowed my older brother to take me home for lunch after what seemed like a very long stay in the corner. Questions arose such as, "What will my parents think and will they punish me?" Also, my first thought regarding Sister Angeline was that she no longer liked me. I did not understand how she could be so mean to me. On the way home for lunch, my fourth grade brother explained why I was wrong and why I was punished. I do not recall if I fully understood his explanation, but I do recall that my behavior was not a major problem for the remainder of first grade. Also, this seems to be the period of time that I began to pursue a close relationship with my brother.

My caregiver relationships did not significantly change from the prior developmental stage. I recall having what seemed like a lot of autonomy during my outdoor playtime. I developed friendships with the two girls who lived next door. With the boys, I played games that were action oriented such as Cops and Robbers. The games I played with the girls were domestically oriented. Combined boy and girl games were "Captain, May I?" "Tag," and "Hide-and-Go-Seek." I do not recall playing athletic games such as "Catch" during this developmental stage. At seven, I learned how to ride a two-wheel bicycle. This was a very proud moment for me. I received praise from my entire family.

My language and cognitive skills were age appropriate. I maintained average grades. In retrospect, I was an underachiever. I did not like school. I was still having difficulty with motor activity. Occasionally, I would trip and fall while running. During this period, I was undergoing some type of vision therapy.

I continued to develop a close relationship with my older brother. We spent a lot of time playing various board and card games. Also, he would allow me to participate in outdoor activities with him and his friends, such as sledding and exploring. Although the relationship with my older brother was positive, it was just the opposite with my younger brother. I resented the close relationship he had with my mother.

I recall my father almost losing his life in his role as a firefighter during a major multilevel structure fire. He attempted to save two children from a burning building. He would have died in that fire if he had not stumbled down a staircase. His near death caused me to experience a prolonged period of anxiety.

Before third grade, we moved to a new neighborhood. I was very upset by the move away from my friends. Also, I was apprehensive about going to a new school and developing new acquaintances. My initial experience in the new neighborhood was poor. Peers ridiculed me for having thick glasses and wearing cowboy boots. I eventually developed new friendships. My grades were deficient during the first half of the third grade. Following participation in a schoolwide standardized test, my parents had a conference with the teacher. It was agreed that I would be allowed to complete homework and take tests at my own pace. This was an embarrassing experience for me. I knew the cause of my poor performance was my attitude toward school and not my academic ability. I put forth an earnest effort toward my schoolwork and received outstanding grades for the next few months. After proving that I had the ability to excel, I edged back toward mediocrity.

THROUGH THE LENS OF ATTACHMENT THEORY

Attachment theory extends to other nonprimary caregivers within the family system (Bretherton, 1992). During my primary grade years, I developed a close attachment with my older brother. At this stage, our attachment was more external than internal. Internal attachment was maintained through a sense of proximity with my caregivers. However, I did begin developing an internal attachment with my brother concomitant with the incident when he rescued me from my punishment in the corner of the first grade room. This was the beginning of a close bond that we would share until his death at age 46. According to Waters and Cummings (2000), the secure base phenomenon of attachment sets forth that individuals develop representations of their own secure base experience through the formation of representational skills. My father's near death represented a basic concept, although concrete in nature, that my external attachments to him could have been lost. This evoked an internal response in the form of separation anxiety.

THROUGH THE LENS OF MORAL DEVELOPMENT THEORY

The incident involving my misbehavior during my first day of first grade represents an example of classic Stage 1 moral development. Punishment is tied to wrongness. Although my brother was not quite 9 years old, it appears that he was functioning at a preliminary level of conventional morality. He essentially explained to me that he would always try to live up to the expectations of the family and was a course I should follow. He also stressed a Stage 2 premise that punishment is a risk that one naturally wants to avoid (Newman & Newman, 2009).

Ages 10 to 11

During these years, I just assumed that everyone my age followed the same rules. During the fifth grade, however, I first experienced bullying. Three boys from the neighborhood taunted and threatened me on a regular basis. I finally made a decision that I had to take a stand. I discussed my options with my older brother, and he encouraged me to take action. I made a decision to confront each of these boys individually. I got in a fight with one of the boys and, fortunately, I got the better of him. The remaining two boys decided that they did not want to have a physical confrontation with me. We all eventually became friends. I felt a sense of respect. However, I also felt guilty having to resort to physical means in order to establish myself as a respected member of my peer group. It was from this point forward that I began to develop leadership skills. I did not always use these skills properly. However, as I progressed through the developmental stages, I eventually put these leadership skills to good use.

Ages 12 to 14

In sixth grade (Catholic grade school), my world revolved around athletics and friends. All my friends were boys. Most of my free time was spent playing football or baseball.

During the initial years of this stage, my caregiver relationships did not significantly change. Toward the later years of this stage, I became openly defiant to my mother and covertly defiant to my father. I continued to maintain a positive relationship with my grandmother. I continued to have an active relationship with my older brother. I would play sports with him and occasionally accompany him to social events. I began developing a good relationship with my younger brother. Although he was still favored by my mother, it did not significantly affect me. I recall that I became protective of my younger brother. In fact, I became his role model.

My motor skills significantly improved during pubescence. I excelled in football and baseball. I enjoyed playing athletic games and socializing with my teammates. I also recall a strong desire to impress my father with my athletic accomplishments.

Language and cognitive skills remained age appropriate. During the sixth grade and part of the seventh grade, I was an avid reader. Most of the books that I read were adventure stories. My grades were average to below average. I was performing significantly below my potential. This poor academic performance led to parental reprisals that included a decrease in my social activities. The reprisals were enforced by my father. I increased my academic efforts for a few months and then fell back into mediocrity. My motivation for increasing my grades was external. I knew that I could achieve at a higher level, therefore the grades I received did not personally (internally) matter. I wanted to increase my grades to regain my social privileges.

In the midst of my seventh grade year, I developed a defiant behavior pattern. In retrospect, my behavior was reinforced through acceptance by my peer group. I felt a very strong bond with my friends during this time. I frequently questioned the fairness of rules, and it was not unusual for me to break various rules. I recall having ambivalent feelings about my behavior.

I was a leader, but my leadership was not always directed toward positive behavior. In eighth grade, my friends and I caused some minor damage to the school. We were apprehended by school officials. Our parents were notified and eventually met with the school officials. The penalty issued by the school required us to perform cleaning and yard maintenance chores over the course of several weekends. I was surprised that my father did not impose his own punishment. He had a very sincere conversation with me regarding moral character, reputation, and values. My worst punishment was my father's disappointment in me. For maybe the first time, I fully understood the intrinsic qualities of consequences.

I was in seventh grade when I first became romantically involved with a girl. This relationship lasted for a few months. It ended when I kissed another girl at a party. In eighth grade, I developed my second girlfriend relationship. During this relationship, I attended a few of her family's activities. I never attempted to take sexual advantage of her. I do not recall what led to the end of this relationship.

THROUGH THE LENS OF ATTACHMENT THEORY

Crowell et al. (2002) suggest that a child's expectations of self in the attachment figure(s) progresses into the operational reality of close relationships and this perceived and/or real attachment further directs the child's belief formation and expectations of the attachment relationship. During my middle school stage, I miscalculated the potential attachment relationship with my parents. I measured independent thought by defiance and detachment. This maladaptive attachment behavior was further supported by the attachment I developed with my social group.

Attachment Theory literature reveals that there is a difference between emotion regulation within an attachment concept and emotion regulation from the nonattachment relationships. This explains the often temporary relationships individuals have with perceived friends. In my case, interaction with the social groups did not become extinct before the end of this developmental stage. The emotional ties with my caregivers still remained despite my external behavior.

THROUGH THE LENS OF MORAL DEVELOPMENT THEORY

Kohlberg's theory holds that children develop morally through social experiences and conflict. He explains that a child's moral reasoning is developed through these experiences and through internal–external debate pertaining to a dilemma. He further theorized that the stages of moral development are consecutive and invariant in sequence, with no skipping or returning to a stage. It is important to note that even in Kohlberg's moral decision-making model in which he utilizes dilemmas as a platform, the attained moral level can be obfuscated by the basic need to survive. It is not uncommon for an individual to make a moral choice at a base or preconventional level in order to avoid punishment, even though there has already been a realization of moral thought at a conventional level (Crain, 1985). I perceived my social group as an authority figure. My thoughts at that time were not going against the wishes of the group for fear of shunning or punishment. At the same time, I had reached a stage where my behavior outside the group conformed to laws. My morals were otherwise good, and interaction with most authority figures was with respect. This was a matter of ambivalence as opposed to a dichotomy. In essence, this was an ongoing dilemma during this stage of my life.

Ages 15 to 18 (Catholic High School)

I continued to play sports my freshman year in high school. I injured my right knee during football season, and upon my return to the team, I broke my left wrist. I was finished playing sports for the year. Prior to the injuries, I was on the first team. My motor skills were above average. Despite my social and school agenda, I still had time to read adventure novels. My verbal skills were above average. I had some deficits in spatial/mathematic relationships. It appears my eyesight affected my visual–spatial perception abilities.

After the property damage incident in eighth grade, the relationship with my father became stronger. He began to discuss mature topics such as careers and politics. Even though he worked two jobs, he attended the few football games I played during my freshman year. The summer before my sophomore year, he took my brothers and me on a fishing trip. Unfortunately, my father died of a heart attack one week before the start of my sophomore year. He had never experienced a serious illness.

The death of my father changed my emotional status. This change continued beyond the initial bereavement. I no longer felt as if our family still existed. My father had been the operational figure in our family dynamics. The family still functioned, but it was different. Approximately six months after the death of my father, my older brother joined the Air Force. My mother continued to work. She did not drive; therefore, all of the activities that required driving became my responsibility. This responsibility included grocery shopping and driving my mother, grandmother, and younger brother to various events. Along with these responsibilities, I also gained a lot of freedom. I was able to use the car at my discretion. My mother did not strictly enforce the curfew on weekends. I felt a sense of responsibility for the upbringing of my younger brother. He was three grades behind me. Most of my involvement with my younger brother pertained to academics and behavior. Unfortunately, I was not a consistently good role model.

During my sophomore year, I reinjured my knee and I was advised by my physician to refrain from further athletic activity. The exclusion from sports put another void in my life. The voids were filled with negative behavior. I lost interest in the academic aspect of school. I associated with delinquents during my sophomore year; however, I still associated with my usual friends, and I continued to perform my responsibilities at home.

My grades were poor my sophomore year. I was required to attend summer school. It seemed like I significantly matured during that summer. I attended summer school at the local public school. I had a few long conversations with one of the teachers. His assessment of me resulted in a positive and confident self-assessment. My grades improved significantly during my junior year. I no longer associated with delinquents, but my behavior remained somewhat defiant. Although I was arrested on a few occasions for fighting and curfew during this stage, I was never charged with an infraction. Fortunately, the local juvenile detectives became familiar with the active teenagers in their district. A conversation with one of these detectives several years later revealed that they arrested people from my group of friends in order to remind us that there were limits to bad behavior. I sensed their motivation. They were confident that most, if not all of us, would get through the teenage years without becoming societal problems.

I developed a few strong romantic relationships during the latter part of high school. At the time of graduation, I maintained the relationship with my current girlfriend, and we were eventually married.

Just before my senior year, my grandmother died. I was very close to her. Initially, her death caused me to become depressed and angry. I spent a lot of time reflecting about her involvement in my life. She was a very spiritual (religious) person. Her actions and words helped to shape my spiritual (religious) and moral self. Developmentally, both of my parents provided me with a spiritual and moral framework. Even though I was not the most civilly obedient adolescent, I was very aware of the moral implications of all of my actions.

THROUGH THE LENS OF ATTACHMENT THEORY

The experience of attachment is both internal and external. The attachment experiences that are stored in memory control the reactions of an individual following loss (death) or separation from an attachment figure (Bretherton, 1992). Initially, the death of my father had a significantly negative impact on me during my high school years. During this developmental stage, I dwelled on the external detachment and, as a result, placed myself back in a moral dilemma similar to the one I experienced in the previous stage. Later during this stage, I began having success academically, interpersonally, and socially. I became a member of the Student Council during my senior year. My attachment with my mother became stronger.

My grandmother's attitude toward the death of my father was inspirational. Emotionally and spiritually, she still maintained an attachment with her son. I finally realized that the internal attachment with my father was still available to me. The realization of internal attachment continued following the death of my grandmother. I no longer experienced anxiety or despair at the end of this stage. I felt secure in my attachments.

THROUGH THE LENS OF MORAL DEVELOPMENT THEORY

Kohlberg's use of dilemmas as a means of demonstrating moral development and reasoning assumes that an individual will utilize a purely moral/ethical reason for making a decision. It appears that he discounts the emotional components of survival, although he attributed emotions as part of the moral development. Survival can pertain to concrete aspects of life such as food and shelter, or survival within a social context.

During this stage, I reached the conventional level of morality. Attachment issues I experienced during this developmental stage influenced this level of morality. I was capable of understanding and even debating dilemmas at a postconventional level; however, I was uncomfortable pursuing that level of morality while experiencing significant attachment ambivalence.

It is likely that only a small percentage of people have ever reached Stage 6 of Kohlberg's moral development model. Nevertheless, today's Stage 6 might be tomorrow's Stage 1. During my early childhood and primary grade stages, family therapy would have provided me with behavioral interventions that would have properly shaped my reaction to separation. My parents would have received education in healthy mutual attachment development. A successful outcome would obviate therapeutic intervention at later stages.

Intervention during my middle school and high school stages would have involved eclectic talk therapy of an empathetic and nonconfrontational nature. Education pertaining to the possible reasons for my behavior would have been an initial approach. After I developed a trusting relationship with the therapist, behavior modification would be employed to remediate immediate problems and concerns. This could include the implementation of a cognitive-based program in order to develop a long-term strategy to preempt misunderstanding or irrational thoughts. Choice Therapy and Gestalt techniques, for example, empty chair, would also be appropriate.

CONCLUSION

In summation, this chapter has focused on the research related to differential development between the sexes. Developmental differences of note include those in the physical, emotional, and social realms. From early in life, young boys are already experiencing specific physiological changes as they enter a world in which they are socialized early toward the appropriate gender role. Boys and girls both share a need for attachment, belonging, and social support, yet they often work toward these outcomes quite differently. Throughout the remaining chapters, this book will address the risks and consequences of less-than-optimal development, and the authors will share suggestions for useful and creative interventions.

REFERENCES

Ainsworth, M. D. S. (1963). The development of infant–mother interaction among the Uganda. In B. M. Foss (Ed.), *Determinants of infant behavior* (pp. 67–104). New York: Wiley.

Ainsworth, M. D. S. (1967). *Infancy in Uganda: Infant care and growth of love.* Baltimore: Johns Hopkins University Press.

Bailey, B. C. *Kohlberg's stages of moral development.* Retrieved May 16, 2011 from http://Pegasus.cc.ucf.edu/~ncoverst/Kohlberg's%20Stages%20of%20 Moral%20Development.htm

Baron-Cohen, S. (2005). Paper appeared in Phi Kappa Phi Forum 2005 (Special issue on the Human Brain). Cambridge, UK: Cambridge University.

Bennett, G. K., Seashore, H. G., & Wesman, A. G. (1991). *Differential Aptitude, tests for personnel and career assessment: Technical manual.* San Antonio, TX: The Psychological Corporation, Harcourt Brace Jovanovich.

Bevan, R. (2001). Boys, girls and mathematics: Beginning to learn from the gender debate. *Mathematics in School, 30(4),* 2.

Blum, D. (1998). *Sex on the brain: The biological differences between men and women.* New York, NY: Penguin Books.

Bonomo, V. (2010). Gender matters in elementary education: Research-based strategies to meet the distinctive learning needs of boys and girls. *Educational Horizons, 88(4),* 257–264.

Bowlby, J. (1956). The growth of independence in the young child. *Royal Society of Health Journal,* 76, 587–591.

Bretherton, I. (1992). The origins of attachment theory: John Bowlby and Mary Ainsworth. *Developmental Psychology, 28,* 759–775.

Connell, D. (2002). Left brain/right brain. *Instructor,* September, 28–32, 89.

Crain, W. C. (1985). *Theories of development* (pp.118–136). Upper Saddle River, NJ: Prentice Hall.

Crowell, J. A., & Treboux, D. (1995). A review of adult attachment measures: Implication for theory and research. *Social Development, 4,* 294–327.

Crowell, J. A., Treboux, D., & Waters, E. (2002). Stability of attachment representations: The transition to marriage. *Developmental Psychology, 38,* 467–479.

Dunn, J., & Hughes, C. (2001). "I got some swords and you're dead!" Violent fantasy, antisocial behavior, friendship, and moral sensibility in young children. *Child Development, 72,* 491–505.

Erk, R. (2008). *Counseling treatment for children and adolescents with DSM-IV-TR Disorders.* Upper Saddle River, NJ: Pearson Education,.

Field, J. E., & Field, T. F. (2004). *The transitional classification of jobs.* Athens, GA: Eliot & Fitzpatrick.

Fleming, N. D. (2005). *Teaching and learning styles: VARK strategies* (Rev. ed.). Christchurch, NA: Neil Fleming.

Geist, E., & King, M. (2008). Different, not better: Gender differences in mathematics learning achievement. *Journal of Instructional Psychology, 35,* 43–52.

Ginger, S. (2003). Female brains vs. male brains. *International Journal of Psychotherapy, 8(2),* 139–145.

Golonblack, S., Rust, J., Zervoulis, K., Croudace, T., Golding, J., & Hines, M. (2008). Developmental trajectories of sex-typed behavior in boys and girls: A longitudinal general population study of children aged 2.5–8 years. *Child Development, 79,* 1583–1593.

Gurian, M. (2001). *Boys and Girls Learn Differently.* San Francisco, CA: Wiley.

Gurian, M. (2010). *The purpose of boys: Helping our sons find meaning, significance, and direction in their lives. San Francisco, CA: Jossey-Bass.*

Gurian, M., & Stevens, K. (2005). *The minds of boys.* San Francisco: Jossey-Bass/ John Wiley.

Hancock, T. E., & Stock, W. A. (1996). Gender and developmental differences in the academic study of behaviors of elementary school children. *Journal of Experimental Education, 65(1),* 18–39.

Hendricks, J., & Weissman, P. (2005). *The whole child: Development education for the early years:* Upper Saddle River, NJ: Prentice Hall.

Holmes, J. (1993). *John Bowlby and Attachment Theory.* London, UK: Routledge.

Kazura, K. (2000). Father's qualitative and quantitative involvement: An investigation of attachment, play, and social interactions. *Journal of Men's Studies, 9,* 41–57.

King, K., Gurian, M., & Stevens, K. (2010). Gender-friendly. *Educational Leadership, November.*

Maccoby, E. E. (1998). *The two sexes: Growing up apart, coming together.* Cambridge, MA: Harvard University Press.

MacDonald, S. G. (2001). The real and the researchable: A brief review of the contribution of John Bowlby. *Perspectives in Psychiatric Care,* 37(2), 60–64 (1907–1990).

Martin, A., & Marsh, H. (2005). Motivating boys and motivating girls: Does teacher gender really matter? *Australian Journal of Education,* 49(3), 320–334.

Martin, C. L., Wood, C. H., & Little, J. K. (1990). The development of stereotype components. *Child Development, 61,* 1891–1904.

Molumby, N. L. (2004). *The application of different teaching strategies reflective of individual students' learning modalities in the university flute studio class.* Retrieved from http://rave.ohiolink.edu/etdc/view?acc%5Fnum=osu1086122579

National Center for Infants, Toddlers, and Families. (2011). Zero to three. Washington, DC: Author.

Newman, B. M., & Newman, P. R. (2009). *Development through life: A psychological approach.* Belmont, CA: Wadsworth/Thomson Learning.

Pollack, W. (1998). *Real boys.* New York: Random House.

Sabbatini, R. (1997). Are there differences between brains of males and females? Retrieved from www.cerebromente.org.br/n11/mente/eisntein/cerebro-homens.html

Sax, L. (2006). Six degrees of separation: What teachers need to know about the merging science of sex differences. *Educational Horizons, 84(3),* 190–212.

Scholastic. (2008). Teens and decision making: What brain science reveals. Retrieved from http://headsup.scholastic.com/articles/teens-and-decision-making-what-brain-science-reveals/?vm=r

Servin, A., Bohlin, G., & Berlin, L. (1999). Sex differences in 1-, 3-, and 5-year-olds toy-choice in a structured play session. *Scandinavian Journal of Psychology, 40,* 43–48.

Singham, M. (2003). The achievement gap: Myths and reality. *Phi Delta Kappa 84*(8), 586.

Snow, M. E., Jacklin, C. N., & Maccoby, E. E. (1983). Sex-of-child differences in father-child interactions at one year of age. *Child Development, 49,* 227–232.

Sonkin, D. J. (2005, January/February). *Attachment theory and psychotherapy. The therapist.* Retrieved March 30, 2007 from http://Daniel-onkin.com//attachment_psychotherapy.htm

Tyre, P., Murr, A., Juarez, V., Underwood, A., Sprigen, K., & Wingert, P. (2006). The trouble with boys. *Newsweek, 147(5),* 44–52.

Vygotsky, L. S. (1978). *Mind in society.* Cambridge, MA: Harvard University Press.

Waters, T. (2004). Learning to love: From your mother's arms to your lover's arms. *The Medium (Voice of the University of Toronto), 30(19),* 1–4.

Waters, T., & Cummings, E. M. (2000). A secure base from which to explore close relationships. *Child Development, 71(1),* 164–172.

Zaman, A. (2008). Gender sensitive teaching: a reflective approach for early child-hood Education teacher training programs. *Education, 129(1)*, 110–118.

Zimmer, C. (2011). The train: Fast driving, drugs, and unsafe sex: The risk-loving behavior of teenagers may result from a neurological gap in the developing brain. *Discover, 32*, 28–29.

2

Talking to the Beat of a Different Drum: Speaking So He Can Listen and Listening So He Can Speak

KEITH M. DAVIS

WORKING WITH YOUNG MALES IN COUNSELING

Anyone who has worked with younger boys and male adolescents in counseling has most likely experienced the frustration in the development of rapport and connection in a therapeutic environment. Research has clearly demonstrated that males, in general, are less inclined to seek helping services, including counseling, than are females (Addis & Mahalik, 2003; Kiselica & Englar-Carlson, 2008). Often, when younger males are engaging in counseling services, it is because parents or other adults have referred them and not because they have sought it on their own. This often feels to younger males that counseling is a mandated and forced, perhaps even a punitive, process. Indeed, Kiselica and Englar-Carlson (2008) pointed out that many boys and male adolescents do not willingly choose to be in counseling, but rather have significant adults in their lives (e.g., parents, guardians, school personnel, and legal authorities) that have made the choice for them. As a result, it is no surprise that boys and adolescent males often show up to counseling resistant and not willing to listen or express themselves.

This book chapter will examine: (a) reasons why young boys and male adolescents are typically referred for counseling and psychotherapy, (b) how traditional psychotherapy is not well-suited for boys and male adolescents, (c) the relational styles of boys and male adolescents, (d) suggested interventions and best practices for creating male-friendly environments, and (e) both group and individual approaches in a case study format.

Reasons Why Boys and Male Adolescents Are Referred for Counseling

While some boys may not completely understand why they have been referred to counseling, a significant amount do understand that counseling has been advised as the result of having "been in trouble," often through perceived disruptive behavior (e.g., anger, aggression, fighting, or defiance). Research and prevalence rates statistics from the *Diagnostic and Statistical Manual of Mental Disorders 4th Edition Text Revision* (*DSM-IV-TR*; American Psychiatric Association, 2000) clearly demonstrate that boys and adolescent males are disproportionately represented with such diagnoses as attention-deficit hyperactivity disorder (ADHD), oppositional defiant disorder, and conduct disorder—diagnoses that often manifest in perceived disruptive and/or aggressive behaviors toward others or property. Many of these boys and male adolescents often show up to counseling angry, defiant, and resistant to the counseling process and counselor. The counselor, encountering a boy or male adolescent who is resistant and not cooperative to the counseling process, may assume the popular notion that they are not open, expressive, and forthcoming about their feelings, nor capable of understanding their own feelings or the feelings of others. Thus, the counselor is tasked with an attempt to develop rapport and connection with a boy who simply does not see the utility of counseling.

Traditional Psychotherapy and Relational Styles of Boys and Male Adolescents

Increasingly, the counseling and psychotherapy fields have seen an increase in research regarding the relational style of boys and male adolescents and how such relational styles influence the counseling relationship. An understanding of the relational style of boys and male adolescents is critical for those counselors who are attempting to build rapport and connect with their younger male clientele. First and foremost, it is important to debunk the "myth" and "assumption" that boys and male adolescents have difficulty accessing their emotions.

Emerging research has demonstrated that the traditional psychotherapy environment is not well suited for many boys and male adolescents (Haen, 2011; Kiselica & Englar-Carlson, 2008; Kiselica, Englar-Carlson, & Horne, 2008; Kiselica, Englar-Carlson, Horne, & Fisher, 2008). Kiselica and Englar-Carlson (2008) state:

> There is a fundamental mismatch between the way counseling and psychotherapy tend to be conducted and the relational styles of most boys and this mismatch plays a major role in the failure of many professionals to establish rapport with boys. (p. 50)

The authors continue to explain that this fundamental mismatch is grounded in the traditional counseling environment being more suited for those individuals with more social personalities who "...thrive in situations that provide them with the opportunity to engage others in an emotionally intimate and engaging manner" (p. 50). It is not that boys and male adolescents are not capable of being social personality types, but rather for many boys with more "realistic" and "conventional" personality types (Bruch, 1978; Holland, 1973), they prefer activity-oriented and exploratory approaches that "...involve the manipulation and organization of data and objects..." (p. 50). In short, boys and adolescent males tend to be more about "doing" rather than deep and highly expressive "feeling" when it comes to relating to their worlds and each other.

Comparisons of the biological and social development between girls and boys demonstrate that boys enter the world hardwired to be more active and exploratory, traits that counter the expectation that boys should remain still and compliant throughout a school day (Gurian & Stevens, 2007; Kiselica, Englar-Carlson, & Horne, 2008). It is through shared activity and exploration that many boys and male adolescents form deep bonds of friendship, connection, and intimacy. Such shared activity and exploration among boys and adolescent males often result in a socialization process known as "action empathy" (Levant, 1995, pp. 229–251)—the ability to "...take action based on how a person sees things from another's point of view" (Kiselica, Englar-Carlson, Horne, & Fisher, 2008, p. 32). The idea of action empathy is equally founded in the research by McNelles and Connolly (1999), who used the term "activity-centered intimacy" (p. 156) to denote a pathway to achieving connectedness that does not necessarily rely on the verbal sharing of feelings (Haen, 2011). These more "covert" styles of achieving intimacy and connectedness between boys and male adolescents challenge the assumption that boys and adolescent males are "emotional mummies" (Kiselica et al., 2008, p. 34). Citing research by Cancian (1987), Kiselica et al. (2008) state:

> One of the problems with the treatment of boys and men in counseling and psychotherapy is that, as conceptions of intimacy have become more feminized, there has been a tendency for mental health professionals to pathologize boys and men for having an action-oriented approach to the world. (p. 34)

Similarly, Haen (2011), citing the above work by Kiselica et al. (2008) states, "There has been a propensity to evaluate boys' relational styles by female standards, a pattern that can distort the conclusions and patholo-gize boys' styles of connecting to others" (p. 22).

For those counselors who are, and will be, working with boys and male adolescents, an understanding of their relational style is a giant step in developing rapport and connectedness, resulting in more effective engagement in the therapeutic process. Equally important, boys and men across cultures tend to be more socialized to work in groups, spending more time in coordinated and structured group activities than females (Benenson, Apostoleris, & Parness, 1997). Thus, working within a group context, rather than individually, may be less intimidating for them.

Based on research, and my own experience in working with boys and adolescent males for the last 17 years, the following section will describe some specific interventions and practices that have been helpful in the development of rapport and connection with them. Kiselica et al. (2008) describe perfectly the importance of counselors working with boys and male adolescents to create a *male-friendly* environment. They define a *male-friendly* environment as:

> ...tapping into the natural ways boys relate to the world and employing a wide range of strategies and activities that appeal to male youth and have shown through research to facilitate the establishment and maintenance of rapport with young boys and adolescent males. (p. 51)

Suggested Interventions and Best Practices for Working With Boys and Male Adolescents

Even before becoming familiar with research on counseling boys and adolescent males, and by virtue of being male myself, it had always made intuitive sense to me to use a more activity- and action-oriented approach in working with them when I became a professional school counselor (both at the high school and elementary level). I often recalled my own childhood and adolescence, remembering group activities with other boys that often left me feeling connected and safe in a form of "brotherhood" that was often lacking in other aspects of my life. Whether it was through playing sports, outdoor games, building forts, hunting lizards and snakes, or playing music (I was a drummer and played in several bands, including the school band), the sense of connection and intimacy was undeniable. My own personal love of music, both playing and listening, led me to the idea of working with boys and adolescent males using drumming in a therapeutic manner.

The use of drums, drumming, and percussion for therapeutic purposes has been documented through research as an effective way to build and maintain rapport with boys and adolescent males, and is a more effective way to express and manage aggression and anger. As an example, Michael Currie (2004, 2006, 2008, 2011) developed a program called Doing Anger Differently (DAD), a school-based program for young boys and male adolescents who display high levels of anger and aggression. Allowing percussion and drumming to act as a metaphor for expressing anger, Currie (2006) employs a series of Latin American percussion exercises that helps boys use percussion as a nonverbal metaphor to express their anger and rage. Currie states:

> These emotions often manifest in overwhelming bodily arousal, but elude speech. As music is isomorphic with emotion, the percussion exercises can provide a bridge between the body (i.e. the physical affect) and speaking about the emotion. This bridge allows boys to speak where previously they have acted violently.
>
> Adolescent boys love to play the drums, preferring a drumming group to routine school classes where they are often in conflict with teachers. The percussion exercises provide a context or participants to enter into intense and meaningful group relationships. After a short time the group provides a locus of enjoyment and membership—often the first time a boy may have experienced this, given the troubled backgrounds of many participants. (para. 2,3)

As another example of therapeutic drumming with boys and adolescent males, Harris and Wilbur (1998) reported how the use of drums and drumming with adolescent males helped in creating a sense of community, promoting healing, and expressing emotions. Tom Harris, of the previous cited work, coordinates and conducts the *Inner Harbour Therapeutic Drumming Program* (Georgia), which uses traditional West African drumming instruction and performance for adolescent males diagnosed with severe behavioral and emotional issues. The program aims to help reduce feelings of anger and depression, and according to the website (n.d.):

> Drumming participants report that 30 minutes of drumming reduces feelings of anger and depression and replaces them with feelings of rejuvenation and feeling alive, stronger, and hopeful. Groups who are dysfunctional, or having difficulties, quickly find ways to work together and be supportive of each other when they begin to drum. These immediate benefits are enhanced by increasing skills in cooperation, awareness, frustration tolerance, and mental focus, among others. (para. 6)

Adding to these examples of how drumming with boys and male adolescents helps develop rapport and expression of inner thoughts and feelings, I offer my own rationale and experience from 17 years of working with them.

While working as a professional school counselor, both in high school and elementary school, it was not uncommon for me to develop groups of boys and adolescent males who were referred for counseling for a variety of behavioral issues. For reasons mentioned previously, the majority of the boys often approached counseling with resistance, seeing it as a punitive process from school administration. I knew that if rapport was not immediately established, the chances for successful outcomes would be difficult. Most of the boys referred to me simply knew they were "in trouble," so there was no real need on my part to lecture about the tenets of more productive behavior.

Drumming Groups

Much like the work of Currie (2004, 2006, 2008, 2011) and Harris and Wilbur (1998), my approach to working with boys and adolescent males has consisted primarily of the use of drumming groups, or what I referred to as drumming circles. As a drummer for many years myself, I have always been fortunate to have access to a variety of drums (e.g., Native American [pow wow, frame drums], African [djembes, ashikos], and Latin [congas, bongos]). In my practice, I have never encountered a boy that has not been intrigued with drums, regardless of perceived skill level.

Beginning and Building Rapport

When the boys arrive for group, typically four to eight boys per group, I generally have all the drums placed in the center of the room. It is not uncommon for them to be curious and excited to see such a display of drums. Capitalizing on their instant curiosity, I invite them to experiment with each drum until they find the one they perceive suits them. Once each boy is settled with a drum, I talk about the drum, the importance of respect for the drum, and how each drum needs to be cared for. Typically, each drum needs a little tuning, so I first teach each boy how to carefully show respect for the drum by "fine-tuning" it, much like we as boys and men need to be "fine-tuned" every now and then. Once the drums are tuned, we begin with a simple beat; I model a simple one-handed beat on the drum. I ask the boys to repeat what they hear from me, each boy becoming familiar with the feel and sound of their individual drum. This modeling is important, as it teaches respect for the drum, following instruction, and creating a unified "rhythm" among the group. I will then ask each boy in the group to take a turn leading the rest of the group in a simple beat, asking questions such as "How does the drum feel?" or "How do you feel beating the drum?" Questions then begin connecting action with feelings. We then conclude our first meeting with thanking the drum and processing how the drums and overall group felt to them.

Building Empathy

I generally like to spend the first couple of sessions just having the boys become accustomed to the drums, the group process, and connecting activity to feelings. Once the boys have grown accustomed to the drums and being in a group, we begin to move deeper into how drums can be a reflection of making inner feelings more external. I ask questions that explore how they are currently feeling, and how those feelings would sound on the drum. For example, if a boy is particularly angry, sad, or happy on a given day, I have the boy make a sound on the drum to represent to the group how that may sound. Once the boy demonstrates the "feeling" sound, I then have the other boys in the group repeat it, emphasizing that feelings and emotions are real and legitimate, and that the drum is a helpful way to express such feelings, rather than directing such feelings toward another (e.g., anger or aggression). Having the boys repeat such drumming "feelings" helps to begin a process of empathy, the ability to actually feel how another might be feeling on a particular day. When a boy takes a turn drumming his feelings, then having the other boys repeat his beat, I then ask the group of boys how they felt repeating the beat, or can they identify a time when they have felt similarly. This further emphasizes and demonstrates empathy and begins a process of what I call "activity with dialogue," the combination of an activity with the process of verbally expressing how one feels in the present or in particular situations (e.g., conflict in classroom, on the playground, or with parents and friends).

Feelings Ensemble

Once the group of boys has met with me in a drumming circle several times, I begin a process of further connecting emotions and feelings to drumming. Building on the original work of Bowman (1987) and further modified by Davis (2007), the *Feelings Ensemble* facilitates the connection of specific emotions to everyday situations the boys may encounter (see Davis [2007] for further explanation of how this activity is conducted). As facilitator, I will ask the boys for specific feelings (e.g., anger, sadness, depression), and we will compose a group composition that represents the particular feeling. Again, this is a tactile and kinesthetic way for boys to outwardly express their inner feelings and more importantly facilitates a safer way for them to verbally express how they are feeling (i.e., activity with dialogue). During group process, when a boy is "talking" about a particular feeling, I will then have him drum how that feeling sounds, then have the other boys in the group drum a response to the feeling, connecting through dialogue specific situations when they feel that particular way.

CASE STUDY: ELEMENTARY SCHOOL BOYS AGED 9 TO 11; TRAVIS AGED 13

Group Context

While working as a professional school counselor at both the high school and elementary levels it was not uncommon for me to receive multiple referrals for boys and adolescent males with a variety of behavioral concerns (e.g., anger, aggression, conflict with adult authority figures). Given the time constraints of professional school counselors, group work is often a more equitable way for a professional school counselor to maximize contact with boys and adolescent males (Davis & Adams, 1998). Boys and adolescent males are accustomed to being in groups, so drumming circles are an ideal setting to help them.

The majority of boys and adolescent males I have worked with represent a variety of behavioral concerns, socioeconomic levels, and racial/ethnic make-ups. The use of drums and drumming is compatible with most boys and male adolescents. Drums and drumming are common across the cultural spectrum, each culture having some connection with drum history and music-making, as represented in the variety of drums used in my group experiences (e.g., Native American, African, and Latin).

Given the disproportionate amount of boys who are referred to counseling for behavioral concerns, it is not surprising the majority of my groups have been with boys and adolescent males. As one example of a group of boys I worked with, while working as an elementary school counselor, I formed a group of fourth and fifth grade boys who had been identified through classroom guidance activities as living in a home where some form of domestic violence took place. Living in such an unpredictable and unstable environment, it was not surprising that many of these boys demonstrated aggressive behaviors at school (e.g., fights, defiance to adults, vandalism). These boys were primarily from lower socioeconomic families living in a rural environment, were of Caucasian and African American descent, and ranged in age from 9 to 11 years. Our drumming group met twice weekly for approximately 6 weeks, for a total of 12 meetings. Each drumming group session lasted approximately 30 minutes. Group sessions were a combination of drumming, relating the drumming to feelings through activity-oriented dialogue, and forming strategies for how to channel feelings in more productive ways, rather than toward others and property.

Often, our groups would conclude with the making of drums for the boys, often from coffee cans, old pots, pans, or boxes. In follow-up meetings with parents/guardians, I also encouraged the purchase, if possible, of some form of drum, or helped in making additional drums available, as explained earlier. This would ensure that each boy might have an opportunity to continue to have an outlet to express his feelings in a more productive way.

Individual Context

Clearly, there are times when forming and conducting a group may not be feasible. Drumming is also an effective way to build and maintain rapport when working with boys and adolescent males individually. This was often the case when I began working in private practice, where forming groups was much more of a challenge given schedule conflicts and confidentiality issues. However, the format for using drums in an individual setting is similar.

As an example of working individually with boys and adolescent males, I recall a 13-year-old Caucasian boy who was brought to my office by his parents. "Travis" was an angry boy who had "conquered" several therapists before coming to me. His parents, nearly at their wits' end, were required by the local school district to have Travis in counseling to work through his chronic aggressive behavior at school, where he was a seventh grader. Travis had been in several fights at school, defied all adult authority figures, and was basically just one mad kid. When Travis arrived in my office for our first session, his body language was guarded, he commented that he had been to several therapists already, and was basically tired of the whole process. My initial impression was that Travis simply had not connected with previous therapists and was resistant to any further therapy. Realizing that I probably had one shot to connect with Travis in this initial session, I decided that we would drum together.

I always keep a couple of drums and a set of bongos in my office. Pointing to the drums, I asked Travis if he had ever played a drum before. Attempting to remain "cool," I noticed intrigue with Travis as he replied that he had never played. I invited him to experiment with the drums and bongos to see how they felt to him. After a few minutes of experimentation, Travis chose a drum, and I chose another. Much like working in a group, I began with a simple single beat and had Travis repeat it with me. I asked Travis how he felt beating the drum, for which he replied "it's kinda' cool." I replied, "Yeah drums are a pretty cool way for me to express how I feel." I modeled for Travis on the drum my own feelings of being happy, sad, or mad. I then asked him to do the same, and we each repeated our drumbeats together.

As our first session came to end, it appeared to me that Travis was excited about drumming, and that he and I had formed a nice connection built on trust and respect. I thanked Travis for his hard work and that I would look forward to seeing him again if he liked. Travis actually asked me if he could come back the following day! Our weekly follow-up sessions were spent drumming, relating drumming to his feelings, and learning better and more effective ways to deal and cope with his angry feelings, which I learned in subsequent sessions were largely the result of his parents' constant bickering and arguing with one another. As our time began to come to a close together, I was able to talk with Travis' parents about getting him a drum so that he could maintain a way to express his feelings. I learned that Travis' aggressive behavior had decreased at school, and my recommendation for him to join the middle school band as a percussionist was followed up by his parents, thus providing another useful way for Travis to manage his behavior at school.

CONCLUSIONS AND ADDITIONAL RESOURCES

Counselors and other mental health professionals who will be working with boys and adolescent males will face unique challenges in developing rapport and connection in a therapeutic environment. It is highly likely that the majority of boys and male adolescents who show up in counseling offices are not doing so by choice, but rather have been mandated for counseling by significant adults and authority figures in their lives (Kiselica & Englar-Carlson, 2008), with such mandates predicated on their perceived problem behaviors (e.g., being in trouble). As a result, it is highly unlikely and unrealistic in such conditions for a counselor to expect that boys and adolescent males will simply show up and be forthcoming and highly expressive in their thoughts and feelings. However, boys and adolescent males are capable of expressing feelings and emotions if a *male-friendly* environment is created.

There is increasing evidence in the counseling and psychotherapy research that in order for counselors and other mental health professionals to work effectively with boys and adolescent males, an understanding of their relational styles are critical. The traditional psychotherapy environment has been demonstrated through research to be poorly suited for boys and male adolescents. Boys and men are socialized to work in groups, and it is through these shared activity-oriented groups that they are very capable of forming deep bonds of friendship, connection, and intimacy, providing a trusting environment to express themselves through activity-oriented dialogue.

My own success and experience in working with boys and adolescent males has primarily been through the use of drumming and drumming groups. However, I have also had similar success with other activity-oriented groups such as playing basketball, football, board games, cleaning up playgrounds and parks, and creative and expressive arts activities. Basically, any approach or activity that does not require coerced participation of males solely in the acts of sitting and talking can be implemented. For those counselors who may not have access to a variety of drums, the use of old coffee cans, pots, pans, boxes, or any form of noisemakers can be used (see Davis, 2007) to help boys and adolescent males access and express their emotions. For further ideas and suggestions on how to develop rapport with boys and adolescent males, help them to access and express their emotions more productively, and create *male-friendly* environments for counseling, a reading of the references is recommended.

REFERENCES

Addis, M. E., & Mahalik, J. R. (2003). Men, masculinity, and the contexts of help seeking. *American Psychologist, 58*, 5–14.

American Psychiatric Association. (2000). *Diagnostic and Statistical Manual of Mental Disorders* (4th ed.): Text Revision. Washington DC: Author.

Benenson, J. F., Apostoleris, N. H., & Parnass, J. (1997). Age and sex differences in dyadic and group interaction. *Developmental Psychology, 33*, 538–543.

Bowman, R. P. (1987). Approaches for counseling children through music. *Elementary School Guidance & Counseling, 21*, 284–291.

Bruch, M. A. (1978). Holland's typology applied to client-counselor interaction: Implications for counseling men. *The Counseling Psychologist, 7*, 26–32.

Cancian, F. M. (1987). *Love in America: Gender and self-development.* Cambridge: Cambridge University Press.

Currie, M. (2004). Doing anger differently: A group percussion therapy for angry adolescent boys. *International Journal of Group Psychotherapy, 54*, 275–294.

Currie, M. (2006). *Doing Anger Differently: From discharge to discourse.* Retrieved from http://www.psychology.org.au/publications/inpsych/dad/

Currie, M. (2008). *The Doing Anger Differently manual: A school group work program for talking about aggression.* Melbourne, Australia: Melbourne University Press.

Currie, M. (2011). Doing anger differently: Working creatively with angry and aggressive boys. In C. Haen (Ed.), *Engaging boys in treatment: Creative approaches to the therapy process* (pp. 197–217). New York: Routledge/Taylor & Francis Group, LLC.

Davis, K. M. (2007). Feelings ensemble and symphony. In S. S. Atkins & L. D. Williams (Eds.), *Sourcebook in expressive arts therapy* (pp. 123–125). Boone, NC: Parkway.

Davis, K. M., & Adams, J. R. (1998). Group counseling in middle schools: How middle level school counselors contribute to the overall development of middle school children. *Current Issues in Middle Level Education, 7*, 6–16.

Gurian, M., & Stevens, K. (2007). *The minds of boys: Saving our sons from falling behind in school and life.* San Francisco: Jossey-Bass.

Haen, C. (2011). Boys and therapy: The need for creative reformulation. In C. Haen (Ed.), *Engaging boys in treatment: Creative approaches to the therapy process* (pp. 3–39). New York: Routledge/Taylor & Francis Group, LLC.

Harris, T., & Wilbur, J. (1998, Fall). Percussion discussion: Using drums to reconnect youth. *Reaching Today's Youth*, 42–44.

Holland, J. L. (1973). *Making vocational choices: A theory of careers.* Englewood Cliffs, NJ: Prentice Hall.

Inner Harbour Therapeutic Drumming Program. (n.d.). Retrieved from http://www.youthvillages.org/what-we-do/residential-programs/inner-harbour-campus/recreation-and-actvities/therapeutic-drumming-program.aspx

Kiselica, M. S., & Englar-Carlson, M. (2008). Establishing rapport with boys in individual counseling and psychotherapy: A male-friendly perspective. In M. S. Kiselica, M. Englar-Carlson, & A. Horne (Eds.), *Counseling troubled boys: A guidebook for professionals* (pp. 49–65). New York: Routledge/Taylor & Francis Group, LLC.

Kiselica, M. S., Englar-Carlson, M., & Horne, A. M. (Eds.). (2008). *Counseling troubled boys: A guidebook for professionals.* New York: Routledge/Taylor & Francis Group, LLC.

Kiselica, M. S., Englar-Carlson, M., Horne, A. M., & Fisher, M. (2008). A positive psychology perspective on helping boys. In M. S. Kiselica, M. Englar-Carlson, & A. Horne (Eds.), *Counseling troubled boys: A guidebook for professionals* (pp. 31–48). New York: Routledge/Taylor & Francis Group, LLC.

Levant, R. F. (1995). Toward a reconstruction of masculinity. In R. F. Levant & W. S. Pollack (Eds.), *A new psychology of men* (pp. 229–251). New York: Basic Books.

McNelles, L. R., & Connolly, J. A. (1999). Intimacy between adolescent friends: Age and gender differences in intimate affect and intimate behaviors. *Journal of Research on Adolescence, 9*(2), 143–159.

3

Understanding Male Adolescent Diversity

SHAWN L. SPURGEON AND DANIEL M. PAREDES

Adolescent males face a number of issues and challenges as they expand their development and increase their awareness of their own identity. Adolescents can take on many tasks and roles as they move forward into adulthood. It is important for clinicians to understand these roles as well as the clinical issues they will face when working with this population. The chapter will highlight some of the challenges the adolescent male client will face. It will provide some useful tips for counselors to consider when working with adolescents as well as a framework for understanding relevant approaches for engaging adolescent males in the therapeutic milieu.

THE ADOLESCENT MALE CLIENT

Not only are men less likely to seek professional mental health help than adult women (Mahalik, Good, & Englar-Carlson, 2003), adolescent males are less likely to engage in a counseling relationship than adolescent females due to the different developmental issues they face and the socialization experiences they internalize (Sen, 2004). Given this situation, it is important for clinicians to be aware of the core issues adolescent males bring with them to the counseling session. Even within the academic realm, males face different challenges. Boys are also more likely than girls to struggle with learning disorders in their youth, as well as much more likely to drop out of school before graduation (Taylor & Lorimer, 2002; U.S. Department of Commerce, 2010). When counselors understand these issues, it helps to promote a more therapeutic situation for the adolescent as well as provide a framework for building a strong counseling relationship with the client.

Gender Roles

Gender roles are those cognitively construed connections that help to establish an individual as a human being and that help to categorize an individual within a group of acceptable societal behaviors (Tobin, Menon, Menon, Spatta, Hodges, & Perry, 2010). Gender-type behaviors are often connected to the socialization experiences and racial identities of adolescent males (Ueno & McWilliams, 2010). Differences in gender expectations and attainment can be seen in educational and occupational pursuits, social interactions, peer relationships, and community involvement (Mello, 2008).

Researchers believe that gender roles are maintained throughout the adolescent male's development by a continued focus on engaging in those activities that reinforce those roles (Godley, Hedges, & Hunter, 2011; Steinfeldt, Rutkowski, Vaughan, & Steinfeldt, 2011). Most boys are aware of gender differences by age 4; this awareness is greatly increased during adolescence due to socialization and developmental challenges faced during that time (Tobin et. al., 2010). For example, antisocial behavior among adolescent boys is deplored by society but completely acceptable in sporting events such as football and basketball (Steinfeldt et al., 2011). Often times, the expected gender roles for adolescent males can create stressful situations for them, and these can lead to more pervasive and detrimental behaviors such as illicit drug use (Godley et al., 2011). In addition, Wimer and Levant (2011) found that there is a direct relationship between how strongly a young man embraces masculine ideology and his willingness to seek academic assistance, if needed, in college. Our society has created a stereotype that conflates help-seeking with weakness, resulting in many young men who are left behind academically and socially. Counselors need to further their understanding of the role gender plays in adolescent male development.

Sexual Orientation

Although there have been studies aimed at clearly identifying and understanding the roots of sexual orientation, researchers have discredited them as false and unfounded due to the complexity of sexual identity (Kail & Cavanaugh, 2010). The interplay of genes, hormones, and social learning makes it difficult to pinpoint accurately the forces that shape sexual attraction. Rotheram-Borus and Langabeer (2001) postulated that sexual experimentation is part of a learning process designed to help adolescents better understand the relevance of sexual attraction to their lives. Although most adolescent dating involves members of the opposite sex, Carver, Egan, and Perry (2004) report that approximately 15% of adolescents experience a period of time when they question their sexual attraction to members of their own sex.

Gay adolescent males are at risk for victimization and often experience elevated levels of depression and mental health challenges (Kail & Cavanaugh, 2010). Gay adolescent males report greater incidences of verbal and physical victimization, higher levels of distress, and poorer academic performances than their heterosexual counterparts (Poteat, Mereish, DiGiovanni, & Koenig, 2011). Meyer (2003) reports that increased rates of suicide among gay adolescent youth can be attributed partly to discrimination, public scrutiny, conflict related to disclosure of sexual orientation to family members, and mistreatment in communities and schools. One of the major challenges for mental health counselors is to identify and assist adolescent males who are struggling with issues related to sexual orientation. Please see Chapter 9 for a more detailed description of this topic.

Ethnicity

Phinney (2005) defined ethnic identity as feeling a connection to an ethnic group and learning the rituals and customs of that group's unique culture and heritage. The process in which ethnic identity occurs has been extensively researched, and although there is some disagreement about the stages through which it occurs, there is consensus that it is developmental in nature. Typically, individuals move from a lack of awareness of their ethnic roots to a greater understanding and self-appreciation for the rituals and customs from which their own identities have developed (Kail & Cavanaugh, 2010). One of the major challenges related to ethnic identity is the within-family variations, especially when children are raised in a dominant culture, while their parents have been taught to value the important traditions developed by their forefathers (Costigan & Dokis, 2006).

Adolescent males who achieve a strong ethnic identity are more likely to find life satisfying and tend to have better relationships with family and adolescents from other ethnic backgrounds (Wakefield & Hudley, 2007). A challenge adolescent males face is trying to develop an ethnic identity while maintaining an understanding of the culture in which they reside (Kail & Cavanaugh, 2010). The developmental tasks associated with ethnic identity for adolescent males can be particularly challenging, given the complexity of increased cultural awareness and an inherent desire to increase their sense of belonging. Benish, Quintana, and Wampold (2011) advocated for a culturally adapted approach to working with adolescent males as the most effective way to help them fully engage in the therapeutic milieu.

Cultural Identity in Adolescence

Although there are always within-group differences, researchers have revealed significant differences in the lived experience of adolescents based on ethnic identity and family origin. Fuligni, Tseng, and Lam (1999) found that Asian American and Latin American adolescents were significantly more committed to their family expectations of providing assistance, respect, and support to the family than adolescents of European descent. They found, however, that these values were not always directly related to academic performance and that the students with the highest commitment to their families often had lower grades than other students. This suggested that these adolescents may have to spend more time taking care of family responsibilities than academic obligations. Counselors should be aware of the conflicting priorities that these students may be facing and perhaps take on an advocacy role for these young men who are trying to manage school and family tasks successfully. Unfortunately, regarding the dropout rates for male adolescents, it is apparent that a significant difference exists based on ethnicity; almost 11% of Black males and 19% of Hispanic males leave high school without completion compared to only 6.3% of White males. Counselors working with diverse populations must recognize the pull of the streets for these students and work to develop school/community programming that would encourage these students to remain in school.

Other researchers have found that ethnic identity can be a cause for significant discrimination within the high school setting, beyond the typical Black/White racial line. Rosenbloom and Way (2004) explored the experiences of African American, Asian American, and Latino adolescents in public school, and each group identified a form of discrimination they faced. African Americans and Latino students noted that they bore the expressed discrimination from the adults in their world, including teachers and law enforcement officers. The Asian American students were verbally and physically harassed by their peers; this was attributed to the perceived favoritism granted to this group by the teachers. In a study of the social expectations of high school students who identified as African American, Hispanic, or European American, clear divisions in their perceptions of videotaped social interactions were uncovered (Yager & Rotheram-Borus, 2000). When viewing a brief video clip, students were asked to describe what they believed would happen next between the characters in the film. Hispanic and European American students were more likely to offer group-oriented responses; African

American and Hispanic students were more likely to offer expressive and aggressive responses. Overall, the young men in the study were typically more expressive and aggressive than group-oriented and assertive. It was suggested that these differences in interpretation of events might also contribute to cross-ethnic conflicts for diverse student groups. It is also interesting to note that in research addressing race and friendship, Rude and Herda (2010) discovered that interracial friendships were the least stable for adolescents and that race issues are still worthy of further exploration.

Ethnicity also creates a divide for mental health diagnoses and treatment as well as involvement in the juvenile justice system. In summarizing results from the Youth Risk Behavior Surveillance System, Knopf, Park, and Paul Mulye (2008) noted that while males in both the 10 to 14 and the 15 to 19 age groups had higher suicide death rates than same-aged females, Hispanic students had higher suicide rates than their non-Hispanic African American peers and their White peers, who were the least likely to complete a suicide attempt. Hispanic adolescents also reported the highest depression rates, but non-Hispanic African American youth, aged 6 to 18, were the least likely to receive any type of outpatient treatment for depressive symptoms.

Although self-reports of involvement in risky or illegal behaviors show males as more prone to negative activities than females, demographic factors predict who is adjudicated or incarcerated for their involvement in these behaviors. Within the justice system, males represent over twice the number of females who find themselves involved (Puzzanchera & Kang, 2011). And, although there are almost twice as many White youth involved than minority youth, the representation is far from proportional! For youth who are incarcerated, discrepancies abound (Saavedra, 2010). Statistics show that Whites make up 59% of the youth population, but represent only 30% of incarcerated youth. However, Hispanic youth are 19% of the overall youth population, but account for 25% of the incarcerated youth. The most shocking statistic, perhaps, is that African Americans comprise only 15% of the youth population, but represent 45% of incarcerated youth. Awareness of the cultural expectations, biases, and prejudices working against diverse youth is imperative for any counselor who will be working with these young men.

It is important that counselors working within diversely populated schools or communities be aware of any cultural bias perceived by your clients. We should not assume that institutionalized or individual biases are nonexistent even if they are not readily apparent to the adults within a system. Inviting clients to talk about their perspective and their own view of how their identity may be perceived within their current context is essential to fully understanding the world through the eyes of your clients.

APPROACH TO COUNSELING THE ADOLESCENT MALE OR YOUNG MAN

Heretofore, we have focused on a selection of demographic status to consider in counseling young men. At this point, we will transition into discussing how to work with such clients. This section has been divided into the process of counseling commonly described in skills texts (e.g., Egan, 2002; Hackney & Cormier, 2009)—assessment, conceptualization and diagnosis, and intervention. We also will focus on counselor self-evaluation of countertransference.

Assessment

Assessment with adolescent and young male clients is a process similar to, but different than, the process for assessing adults. Challenges to the assessment process are in many ways going to be informed by our conceptualization of the client. This is a function of the fact that clients of this age group present with such a broad spectrum of profiles. Clients of this age may lack the emotional vocabulary to articulate how they feel, may be reluctant to participate in counseling [i.e., they have presented because a guardian, teacher, or other stakeholder thinks that they need counseling (Karver & Caporino, 2010; Vernon, 1999)], may lack the cognitive development necessary for advanced problem-solving skills, and may lack the communication skills to resolve interpersonal problems. Finally, we would challenge counselors to think of work with every adolescent as an opportunity to apply a multicultural counseling competence framework (Arredondo et al., 1996; Liu & Clay; 2002; Sue, 2001) to guide the information collection process.

Conceptualization and Diagnosis

The process of collecting information about the client and his concerns (i.e., assessment) is circularly nourished by the process of conceptualizing and diagnosing the adolescent male or young male client (Erford, 2007; Mears, 2010; Whiston, 2009). As information is collected about the client, subsequent questions will emerge so that a full biopsychosocial–spiritual understanding of the client can be attained. Many agencies will have a default set of demographic questions included on intake forms, but in order to complete an accurate and multiculturally sensitive assessment, a series of checklists is not sufficient. In order to gain a contextual understanding of the client's challenges and strengths, follow-up questions must be asked. Multicultural counseling frameworks such as the multicultural counseling competencies and related frameworks provide a useful tool for the conceptualization process (Arredondo et al., 1996; Sue, Arredondo, & McDavis, 1992; Sue, 2001). However, the challenge is to balance out the emic and etic points of view so that the assessment process is not distracted by an attempt to identify a discrete description for every possible cultural variable. Some categories of information to gather and example questions are presented in Table 3.1. The exact wording of questions, however, should be adapted to be congruent with the counselor's personal style and with the language that the client understands.

Information gathered during the assessment process should be integrated into models the counselor has developed for their work through an understanding of empirically supported treatments, multicultural counseling frameworks, and their own preferred theoretical orientation. Follow-up questions that both confirm and challenge preliminary conceptualization hypotheses should be introduced into the assessment process throughout the counseling relationship. The conceptualization of the client, his strengths, his limitations, and presenting issues should be used to coconstruct counseling goals and objectives.

TABLE 3.1

Assessment Questions for Culturally Diverse Young Men

Ethnicity	Gender role
• How do you identify ethnically? • What does being [ethnicity] mean to you?	• What are some things that men/women should do? • What are some of the things you do that make you "manly?" • Who taught you what it means to be a man?
Sexual orientation	Socioeconomic status
• How do you identify sexual orientation-wise? Straight? Gay? Bisexual? (Closed-ended examples of identifying labels might help.)	• How are things at home money-wise?
Career aspiration(s)	Immigration history (if applicable)
• What would you like to do when you graduate? • What interests you about [post-graduation plans]? • What role, if any, did family/mentors play in your making this choice?	• What can you tell me about the process of coming to [city where client lives]? • Are there any opportunities that are complicated by your immigration status? (Be mindful of not conveying the assumption that the client is undocumented.)

(Continued)

TABLE 3.1

Assessment Questions for Culturally Diverse Young Men (*Continued*)

Religious and/or spiritual affiliation	Hobbies/subculture
• What is the difference between religion and spirituality to you? • What role does your higher power (God) play in the presenting concern? What about its resolution? • What are some of the benefits/drawbacks of being part of your church community?	• What do you and your friends do for fun? • What extracurriculars/organizations are you involved in? • What are the good and bad things about being part of these groups? • Is membership in these groups a self-imposed or other-imposed part of your identity?
Family affiliation	Use of social media
• What role do you play in your family? • What is the role of extended family or other key people in your life?	• How much time do you spend on social media? • What's the difference between your acquaintances/associates and your real friends?
Self-care activities	Music preferences
• What's the difference between self-care and distraction to you? • What activities are part of your self-care?	• What kind of music do you listen to? • What does your music preferences say about you?
Relationship status	Drug and alcohol use
• What serious dating relationships have you had? • Was this relationship mostly face-to-face or mostly online? • What did you learn about yourself through your relationships?	• What kinds of alcohol have you tried? • What kinds of drugs have you tried? [Closed ended questions/examples of drugs may be necessary]
Disability status	Academic history
• Do you have any documented disabilities? • If so, what accommodations have you been provided?	• What are your grades like? • How accurately do/did your grades reflect how smart you really are? • What do you like/dislike about school?
Employment history	
• What jobs have you had?	

Choosing Interventions

Intervention selection with the diverse adolescent male or young man depends entirely on an individual client's profile (Lewis, 2002; Vernon, 1999). The interventions selected by the counselor should take into account the cognitive and affective strengths identified in the assessment process, the relevant cultural factors, external factors (i.e., community risk factors, parental involvement), and the client's motivation to change (Gross

& Capuzzi, 2000; Lewis, 2002; Maag & Forness, 2002). Skilled counselors also might take into consideration that the outward appearance presented by the adolescent client is sometimes a façade hiding distress (Garbarino, 2001; Gross & Capuzzi, 2000).

Insight-oriented talk-focused techniques consistent with person-centered therapy are appropriate choices for work with adolescents (Kaslow & Thompson, 1998; Kazdin & Weisz, 1998; Liddle, Jackson-Gilfort, & Marvel, 2006). It might be helpful to keep in mind, however, that adolescents sometimes perceive vulnerability as a limitation and therefore may present as reluctant, or perhaps, oppositional (Doucette, 2004; Garbarino, 1999). Techniques to break through defenses not readily breached with talk therapy include the use of creativity-based interventions (music, writing, visual media) and physical activities (sports, outdoor challenges).

Talk-Based Interventions
The first choice for most counselors is likely some sort of talk-based intervention. Significant parts of most training programs, certainly those modeled after the Council for the Accreditation of Counseling and Related Educational Program (CACREP) *Standards* (CACREP, 2009), will include training in basic helping skills and in the use of various talk-based counseling theories. The literature does support the use of techniques consistent with the most common theories (i.e., those addressed in frequently used theories textbooks such as Gerald Corey's *Theory and Practice of Counseling and Psychotherapy*, Sam Gladding's *Counseling Theories: Essential Concepts and Applications*, or Linda Seligman's and Lourie Reichenberg's *Theories of Counseling and Psychotherapy: Systems, Strategies, and Skills*). Examples of theories informing the techniques appropriate for adolescents include person-centered counseling (Lemoire & Chen, 2005), cognitive behavioral therapy (Kaslow & Thompson, 1998; Kazdin & Weisz, 1998; Kendall & Barmish, 2007; Villalba & Lewis, 2007), reality therapy/choice theory (Glasser, 1998; Walter, Lambie, & Ngazimbi, 2008), and family therapy (Bitter, 2009; Liddle, Jackson-Gilfort, & Marvel, 2006).

Creativity-Based Interventions
An indirect means of inviting clients to share their underlying psychological processes is the use of creativity-based interventions (Bradley & Gould, 1999; Tyson & Baffour, 2004; Utley & Garza, 2011). Creativity-based techniques could include the use of music, writing, or performance. With music, clients might be afforded an opportunity to express themselves through another's words. This is especially helpful because adolescent males sometimes lack the skills or trust in their counselor to articulate how they feel or what their experience of a presenting issue is. Clients could be asked to identify a song or several songs that are relevant to

their circumstances. Affective and cognitive connections to the presenting issues can then be processed in session (Gold, Wigram, & Voracek, 2007; Keen, 2004).

It would be wise for counselors to be prepared to listen to music that might be out of their own preferred genre(s). If financial circumstances limit the client's ability to search for songs in between sessions, searching for appropriate music could be done jointly in session on the Internet. Popular music sellers (iTunes, Amazon, Rhapsody), lyric databases, performer websites, and YouTube could provide access to the needed songs. Alternatively, if the client has stated that part of his preferred activities is to create music, it might be helpful to ask him to develop a song that explains his experience with the presenting issue. Although it is possible to have a studio in house (Palomo & Jencius, 2007) or to otherwise use computer-based recording software in counseling, asking for a recording or live performance of the client's music are probably more common. As part of the process of getting "buy-in" from the client for the exercise, examples of how other musicians/lyricists/rappers use music to address topics that are difficult to discuss could be presented.

Writing, whether it be artistic in the classical sense (poems, short stories, screenplays) or perhaps less artistic (letter writing, journaling), could provide a means to help the adolescent male address difficult emotions or thoughts creatively (Bradley & Gould, 1999; Hoffman, Gimenez Hinkle, & White Kress, 2010). White and Murray (2002) note that letter writing affords adolescent clients an opportunity to externalize their problems, consider resolution to their problems that might not be readily apparent in a verbal context, and provide an opportunity for the client and counselor to revisit a particular subject multiple times. They also note that letters could be part of contingency planning in counseling allowing a client to revisit an encouraging letter during difficult or otherwise special times. Journaling, similarly, might provide an opportunity for the client to reevaluate their presenting concern, a barrier to resolution, or possible assets available to resolve their concern (Kendall & Barmish, 2007).

Drawing, painting, photography, or other visual media could also provide a means to access information that is difficult to articulate. Asking a client who has shared an interest in visual media to apply their interest to create a representation of their experience of the presenting issue and a representation of the issue after it has been resolved could facilitate the assessment and goal-setting process. Visual media also could provide a means for approaching topics that might not otherwise be addressed. Todd Drake, an artist in North Carolina, for example, has developed an exhibition called *Esse Quam Videri Project*, which features self-portraits of Muslims in the United States. The exhibition has travelled to museums and college campuses and has been used to facilitate discussion about identity and discrimination in the United States. Although only a few of the participants in this exhibition were young men, this technique could similarly be used with diverse clients in individual or group counseling settings.

Physical Activity–Based Interventions

Physical activity–based interventions provide yet another innovative avenue to assist young male clients. Examples include sophisticated, organized group activities such as ropes courses (Gillen & Balkin, 2006; Glass & Myers, 2001; Portrie-Bethke, Hill, & Bethke, 2009) or activities requiring significantly less equipment and training than outdoor adventure-based interventions (Bradley & Gould, 1999; Paone, Malott, & Maldonado, 2008; Roaten & Schmidt, 2009). Others have noted that activities can be as simple as walking around a school yard (Doucette, 2004).

Adventure-based counseling is characterized by presenting participants with a series of physical challenges. Gillen and Balkin (2006) noted, however, that even without formal ropes courses or large outdoor facilities, the principles underlying adventure-based counseling could be used. The example they provide is tasking a group with using a tennis ball as a means to facilitate ordered group discussion while simultaneously asking participants to decrease the time between ball passes. In this case, the group becomes oriented to passing the ball and may not realize that the related behavior is self-disclosing. This example highlights the essence of all activity-based interventions—changing the context for counseling so that the client's defenses are more readily compromised. Please see Chapter 11 for detailed information on adventure-based counseling.

Considerations for the use of activity-based counseling include being careful to select interventions that are congruent with the client's developmental level; are challenging, but not too difficult; and that, if asked, the counselor would be willing to engage in as well. Additionally, if the young man is underage, it might be helpful to keep in mind that even innocuous seeming tasks could have cultural significance for the client's family and should be accounted for in selecting an intervention.

TIPS FOR COUNSELORS

Adolescence represents a challenging time when youth try to move toward a stronger self-understanding and self-knowledge while respecting and understanding the environment in which they reside. Counselors can serve as conduits of change when they understand the clinical issues this population faces as well as the interventions and techniques designed for developing a strong and therapeutic relationship in the counseling milieu. Also, there are important aspects for working with adolescent males the counselors need to understand and consider as they move forward in the counseling process.

Monitoring Countertransference

Working with adolescents can be challenging because it is inherently a time of significant change on multiple dimensions. We would argue that all work with adolescents is an example of multicultural counseling. In that spirit, we recommend that counselors approach this work as a process requiring constant self-reflection for biases and needs for development. Collins, Arthur, and Wylie-Wong (2010) provide an especially detailed 13-step cultural auditing process to help counselors identify what cultural variables are at play in a specific counseling relationship. Along with the self-reflection process for cultural critical incidents Collins and Pieterse (2007)present, counselors who periodically review sources of bias and countertransference in their work with adolescents will be better equipped for the challenges.

Although counselors would be wise to monitor issues of countertransference in service provision to young men, we would encourage counselors to also be mindful of how transference could be used. One example would be minding how clients perceive the counselor (e.g., grandmother, uncle, brother, cousin, peer) and using that influence intentionally to help the client attain their goals. Counselors need to be willing to challenge their adolescent male clients as well as analyze their thoughts and feelings when these situations present themselves. Oftentimes, a stronger understanding of self can be developed as a result of clinical supervision and can thus provide a better support system for the adolescent male client.

Cognitive Development

It is important for counselors to remember that adolescence is a time of changing developmental tasks and that these tasks need to be fully understood by the adolescents in order for them to achieve optimal growth (Kail & Cavanaugh, 2010). As such, counselors need to understand that adolescence is not a time for "little adults" to grow but is part of a complex human developmental matrix. The cognitive skills of an adolescent are not the same as an adult, and this fact needs to be taken into account when working with them, especially adolescent males. Multiple theories of cognitive development have been postulated, and the common trait among them is that they see cognitive development of adolescents as a distinct and unique entity along the developmental continuum.

Counselors need to be aware of the developmental processes related to adolescent males in order to provide the most therapeutic situation for them. It is important to note that adolescent males tend to engage in risk-taking behaviors and often do not consider the consequences of their actions due to heightened levels of impulsivity (Steinfeldt et al., 2011). As a result, they are less likely to process and understand the "why" question. An effective technique for understanding the cognitive processing of adolescent males is to engage them in conversations that allow them to talk about the details as concretely as possible. Once they are able to process what they have done, they are more likely to understand the "why" question.

Testing Boundaries

Counselors tend to struggle with clients who test boundaries, mainly because they believe it reflects on their abilities and clinical skills (Cochran & Cochran, 2006). Counselors need to understand that testing boundaries is a natural part of the developmental experiences of adolescent males. The way a counselor responds to the adolescent male's boundary testing may influence the strength of the therapeutic relationship. Adolescent males need to see that the people they are confiding in are "real," and testing boundaries is one method they employ to do it. When they believe the counselor is willing to challenge them and to hold them accountable for their behavior while remaining objective and not personalizing the testing of boundaries, a stronger therapeutic relationship can be developed.

CONCLUSION

Adolescent males remain an important and critical part of society. It is important that professional counselors gain the knowledge necessary for effectively engaging this population in the counseling relationship. When counselors are able to understand this population better, they can develop more effective interventions for working with them as they struggle with their core issues. This knowledge includes a better understanding of the developmental challenges they face as well as an understanding of the environment in which they live. When counselors are able to navigate these variables and strengthen their understanding of adolescent males, they can serve as stronger advocates and support persons.

REFERENCES

Arredondo, P., Toporek, R., Brown, S., Jones, J., Locke, D., Sanchez, J., & Stadler, H. (1996). Operationalization of the multicultural counseling competencies. *Journal of Multicultural Counseling and Development, 24,* 42–78.

Benish, S. G., Quitana, S., & Wampold, B. E. (2011). Culturally adapted psychotherapy and the legitimacy of myth: A direct-comparison meta-analysis. *Journal of Counseling Psychology, 58*(3), 279–289. doi: 10.1037/a0023626.

Bitter, J. R. (2009). The mistaken notion of adults with children. *The Journal of Individual Psychology, 65(2)*, 135–155.

Bradley, L. J., & Gould, L. J. (1999). Individual counseling: Creative interventions. In A. Vernon (Ed.), *Counseling children and adolescents* (2nd ed., pp. 65–96). Denver, CO: Love.

Carver, P. R., Egan, S. K., & Perry, D. G. (2004). Children who question their heterosexuality. *Developmental Psychology, 40*, 43–53.

Cochran, J. L., & Cochran, N. H. (2006). *The heart of counseling: A guide to developing therapeutic relationships.* Belmont, CA: Thomson/Brooks Cole.

Collins, S., Arthur, N., & Wong-Wylie, G. (2010). Enhancing reflective practice in multicultural counseling through cultural auditing. *Journal of Counseling and Development, 88*, 340–347.

Collins, N. M., & Pieterse, A. L. (2007). Critical incident analysis based training: An approach for developing active racial/cultural awareness. *Journal of Counseling and Development, 85*, 14–23.

Costigan, C. L., & Dokis, D. P. (2006). Relations between parent-child acculturation differences and adjustment within immigrant Chinese families. *Child Development, 77*, 1252–1267.

Council for the Accreditation of Counseling and Related Educational Program. (2009). *2009 CACREP Standards.* Alexandria, VA: Author.

Doucette, P. A. (2004). Walk and talk: An intervention for behaviorally challenged youths. *Adolescence, 39*, 373–388.

Egan, G. (2002). *The skilled helper: A problem-management and opportunity-development approach to training* (7th ed.). Pacific Grove, CA: Brooks/Cole.

Erford, B. T. (2007). *Assessment for counselors.* Boston: Lahaska Press.

Fuligni, A. J., Tseng, V., & Lam, M. (1999). Attitudes toward family obligations among American adolescents with Asian, Latin American, and European backgrounds. *Child Development, 70*, 1030–1044.

Garbarino, J. (1999). Lost boys. Why our sons turn violent and how we can save them. *Our Children, 24*, 32–33.

Garbarino, J. (2001). *Lost boys: Why our sons turn violent and how we can save them.* New York: The Free Press.

Gillen, M. C., & Balkin, R. S. (2006). Adventure counseling as an adjunct to group counseling in hospital and clinical settings. *Journal for Specialists in Group Work, 31*, 153–164.

Glass, J. S., & Myers, J. E. (2001). Combining the old and the new to help adolescents: Individual psychology and adventure-based counseling. *Journal of Mental Health Counseling, 23*, 104–114.

Glasser, W. (1998). *Choice Theory: A new psychology of personal freedom.* New York: Harper Perennial.

Godley, S. H., Hedges, K., & Hunter, B. (2011). Gender and racial differences in treatment process and outcome among participants in the adolescent community reinforcement approach. *Psychology of Addictive Behaviors, 25(1)*, 143–154.

Gold, C., Wigram, T., & Voracek, M. (2007). Predictors of change in music therapy with children and adolescents: The role of therapeutic techniques. *Psychology and Psychotherapy: Theory, Research and Practice, 80*, 577–589.

Gross, D. R., & Capuzzi, D. (2000). Defining youth at risk. In D. Capuzzi & D. R. Gross (Eds.), *Youth at risk: A prevention resource for counselors, teachers, and parents* (3rd ed., pp. 3–22). Alexandria, VA: American Counseling Association.

Hackney, H. L., & Cormier, S. (2009). *The professional counselor: A process guide to helping* (6th ed.). Upper Saddle River, NJ: Pearson.

Hoffman, R., Gimenez Hinkle, M., & White Kress, V. (2010). Letter writing as an intervention in family therapy with adolescents who engage in nonsuicidal self-injury. *The Family Journal: Counseling and Therapy for Couples and Families, 18*, 24–30.

Kail, R. V., & Cavanaugh, J. C. (2010). *Human development: A life-span view* (5th ed.). Belmont, CA: Wadsworth.

Karver, M. S., & Caporino, N. (2010). The use of empirically-supported strategies for building a therapeutic relationship with an adolescent with oppositional defiant disorder. *Cognitive and Behavioral Practice, 17*, 222–232.

Kaslow, N., & Thompson, M. P. (1998). Applying the criteria for empirically supported treatments to studies of psychosocial interventions for child and adolescent depression. *Journal of Clinical Psychology, 27*, 146–155.

Kazdin, A. E., & Weisz, J. R. (1998). Identifying and developing empirically supported child and adolescent treatments. *Journal of Consulting and Clinical Psychology, 66*, 19–36.

Keen, A.W. (2004). Using music as a therapy tool to motivate troubled adolescents. *Social Work in Health Care, 39*, 361–373.

Kendall, P. C., & Barmish, A. J. (2007). Show-that-i-can (Homework) in cognitive-behavioral therapy for anxious youth: Individualizing homework for Robert. *Cognitive and Behavioral Practice, 14*, 289–296.

Knopf, D., Park, M. J., & Paul Mulye, T. (2008). *The mental health of adolescents: A national profile, 2008*. San Francisco, CA: National Adolescent Health Information Center, University of California, San Francisco.

Lemoire, S. J., & Chen, C. P. (2005). Applying person-centered counseling to sexual minority adolescents. *Journal of Counseling and Development, 83*, 146–154.

Lewis, J. A. (2002). Working with adolescents: The cultural context. In J. Carlson & J. A. Lewis (Eds.), *Counseling the adolescent* (4th ed., pp. 3–16). Denver, CO: Love.

Liddle, H. A., Jackson-Gilfort, A., & Mavel, F. A. (2006). An empirically supported and culturally specific engagement and intervention strategy for African American adolescent males. *American Journal of Orthopsychiatry, 75*, 215–225.

Liu, W. M., & Clay, D. L. (2002). Multicultural counseling competencies: Guidelines in Working with children and adolescents. *Journal of Mental Health Counseling, 24*, 177–187.

Maag, J. W., & Forness, S. R. (2002). Depression in children and adolescents. In J. Carlson & J. A. Lewis (Eds.), *Counseling the adolescent* (4th ed., pp. 135–165). Denver, CO: Love.

Mahalik, J. R., Good, G. E., & Englar-Carlson, M. (2003). Masculinity scripts, presenting concerns, and help seeking: Implications for practice and training. *Professional Psychology: Research & Practice, 34*, 123–131.

Mears, G. (2010). Assessment, case conceptualization, diagnosis, and treatment planning. In B. T. Erford (Ed.). *Orientation to the counseling profession* (pp. 269–297). Boston: Pearson.

Mello, Z. R. (2008). Gender variation in developmental trajectories of educational and occupational expectations and attainment from adolescence to adulthood. *Developmental Psychology, 44*(4), 1069–1080.

Meyer, I. H. (2003). Prejudice, social stress, and mental health in lesbian, gay, and bisexual populations: Conceptual issues and research evidence. *Psychological Bulletin, 129,* 674–697.

Palomo, D., & Jencius, M. (2007). *Digital music in mental health services.* Retrieved from http://www.counseloraudiosource.net/Archive/Courses/

Paone, T. R., Malott, K. M., & Maldonado, J. M. (2008). Exploring group activity therapy with ethnically diverse adolescents. *Journal of Creativity in Mental Health, 3*, 285–302.

Puzzanchera, C., & Kang, W. (2011). *Easy access to juvenile court statistics: 1985–2008.* Retrieved from http://www.ojjdp.gov/ojstatbb/ezajcs/

Phinney, J. S. (2005). Ethnic identity development in minority adolescents. In C. B. Fisher & R. M. Lerner (Eds.), *Encyclopedia of applied developmental science* (Vol. I, pp. 420–423). Thousand Oaks, CA: Sage.

Portrie-Bethke, T. L., Hill, N. R., & Bethke, J. G. (2009). Strength-based mental health counseling for children with ADHD: An integrative model of adventure-based counseling and Adlerian play therapy. *Journal of Mental Health Counseling, 31*, 323–339.

Poteat, V. P., Mereish, E. H., DiGiovanni, C. D., & Koenig, B. W. (2011). The effects of general and homophobic victimization on adolescents' psychosocial and educational concerns: The importance of intersecting identities and parent support. *Journal of Counseling Psychology, 58(4),* 597–609.

Roaten, G. K., & Schmidt, E. A. (2009). Using experiential activities with adolescents to promote respect for diversity. *Professional School Counseling, 12*, 309–314.

Rosenbloom, S. R., & Way, N. (2004). Experiences of discrimination among African American, Asian American, and Latino adolescents in an urban high school. *Youth and Society, 35,* 420–451.

Rotheram-Borus, M. J., & Langabeer, K. A. (2001). Developmental trajectories of gay, lesbian, and bisexual youths. In A. R. D'Augelli & C. Patterson (Eds.), *Lesbian, gay, and bisexual identities among youth: Psychological perspectives* (pp. 97–128). New York: Oxford University Press.

Rude, J., & Herda, D. (2010). Best friends forever? Race and the stability of adolescent friendships. *Social Forces, 89*, 585–608.

Saavedra, J. D. (2010). *Just the facts: A snapshot of incarcerated youth.* Washington, DC: National Council of La Raza.

Sen, B. (2004). Adolescent propensity for depressed mood and help seeking: Race and gender differences. *Journal of Mental Health Policy and Economics, 7,* 133–145.

Steinfeldt, J. A., Rutkowski, L. A., Vaughan, E. L., & Steinfeldt, M. C. (2011). Masculinity, moral atmosphere, and moral functioning of high school football players. *Journal of Sport and Exercise Psychology, 33,* 215–234.

Sue, D. W. (2001). Multidimensional facets of cultural competence. *The Counseling Psychologist, 29,* 790–821.

Sue, D. W., Arredondo, P., & McDavis, R. (1992). Multicultural counseling competencies and standards: A call to the profession. *Journal of Counseling and Development, 70,* 477–485.

Taylor, D., & Lorimer, M. (2002). Helping boys succeed. *Educational Leadership, 60,* 68–70.

Tobin, D. D., Menon, M., Menon, M., Spatta, B. C., Hodges, E. V. E., & Perry, D. G. (2010). The intrapsychics of gender: A model of self-socialization. *Psychological Review, 117(2),* 601–622.

Tyson, E. H., & Baffour, T. D. (2004). Arts-based strengths: a solution-focused intervention with adolescents in an acute-care psychiatric setting. *The Arts in Psychotherapy, 31,* 213–227.

Ueno, K., & McWilliams, S. (2010). Gender-typed behaviors and school adjustment. *Sex Roles, 63,* 580–591. doi: 10.1007/s11199-010-9839-6.

U.S. Department of Commerce, Census Bureau. (2011). *Current Population Survey (CPS), October 1967 through October 2009.*

Utley, A., & Garza, Y. (2011). The therapeutic use of journaling with adolescents. *Journal of Creativity in Mental Health, 6,* 29–41.

Vernon, A. (1999). Counseling children and adolescents: Developmental considerations. In A. Vernon (Ed.), *Counseling children and adolescents* (2nd ed., pp. 1–30). Denver, CO: Love.

Villalba, J. A., & Lewis, L. (2007). Children, adolescents, and isolated traumatic events: Counseling considerations for couples and family counselors. *The Family Journal: Counseling and Therapy for Couples and Families, 15,* 30–35.

Wakefield, W. D., & Hudley, C. (2007). Ethnic and racial identity and adolescent well-being. *Theory Into Practice, 46,* 147–154.

Walter, S. M., Lambie, G. W., & Ngazimbi, E. E. (2008). A Choice Theory counseling group succeeds with middle school students who displayed disciplinary problems. *Middle School Journal, 2,* 4–12.

Whiston, S. C. (2009). *Principles and applications of assessment in counseling* (3rd ed.). Belmont, CA: Brooks/Cole, Cengage Learning.

White, V. E, & Murray, M. A. (2002). Passing note: The use of therapeutic letter writing in counseling adolescents. *Journal of Mental Health Counseling, 24,* 166–176.

Wimer, D. J., & Levant, R. F. (2011). The relation of masculinity and help-seeking style with the academic help-seeking behavior of college men. *Journal of Men's Studies, 19,* 256–274.

Yager, T. J., & Rotheram-Borus, M. J. (2000). Social expectations among African American, Hispanic, and European American adolescents. *Cross-Cultural Research, 34,* 283–305.

4

When Learning Is "Different": Readin', Writin', 'Rithmetic, and Giftedness?

TONY MICHAEL, IAN S. TURNAGE-BUTTERBAUGH,
REBEKAH H. REYSEN, EDWARD HUDSPETH, AND
SUZANNE DEGGES-WHITE

Boys are much more frequently diagnosed with learning disorders compared with girls, and this chapter addresses the basic learning disorders: reading disorder (RD), disorder of written expression, and mathematics learning disorder (MLD). Summaries of the typical presenting symptoms of learning disorders as well as information relating to the most effective treatments will be presented. Also addressed will be the ways in which learning disorders negatively influence the social development and acceptance of young males. We also touch on giftedness as a learning difference, as this can present barriers as well.

Learning disorders not only hamper academic development but also can delay or disrupt normal emotional, social, and psychological development. Students with learning disorders are at a greater risk of developing low self-esteem issues (Bruininks, 1978). They are also more likely to misbehave in the classroom (Rutter, Tizard, & Whitmore, 1970), which can create significant problems in the development of positive student–teacher relationships, relationships with peers, and academic achievement. Research also indicates that students with learning disabilities are at an increased risk of suicidal ideation (Bender, Rosenkrans, & Crane, 1999).

Learning disorders are also quick to complicate the commonplace events of daily life. These young men may have negative experiences or struggles, including difficulties with following directions, learning routines, counting their money, navigation, understanding words and ideas, and general vocabulary skills. If left untreated, learning disorders may lead to educational problems (including behavioral problems), low self-esteem, and reading struggles that persist into adulthood and can influence job performance. In a review of the literature addressing the emotional and psychological difficulties among youth with learning disorders, Johnson (2002) cited studies that suggested that these youth were more likely to be involved in juvenile delinquent behaviors, exhibit antisocial behaviors and conduct disorder, express higher levels of depression, and be the target of bullying. The need for assessment and effective interventions for learning disorders is apparent. Following are sections that are designed to help readers better understand the three specific subtypes of learning disorders: RD, disorder of written expression, and MLD.

READING DISORDER

A young boy with RD typically shows significant impairment in reading accuracy, speed, or comprehension to the level that the impairment hinders academic success and/or daily activities. Boys with RD execute reading assignments below the anticipated level based on their general intelligence, educational opportunities, and physical health. There are two basic forms of RD: reading problems and reading comprehension problems (APA, 2000).

Reading problems such as difficulty in understanding sounds, letters, and words are sometimes called dyslexia. Dyslexia can affect spelling and writing as well. Symptoms of dyslexia include problems with letter and word recognition, slow reading speed, reversal of words or letters when reading, and difficulty in pronouncing words aloud (phonics). Reading comprehension problems include difficulties in understanding the meaning of words, sentences, and paragraphs. Symptoms include absence of words when reading aloud, memory problems, remedial vocabulary skills, and poor comprehension of what was read. This form of RD can be more difficult to detect compared with dyslexia and is sometimes misdiagnosed. Many individuals show symptoms of some form of RD. According to the International Dyslexia Association (2008), possibly, as many as 15% to 20% of the population exhibits some symptoms of dyslexia. These symptoms include slow or inaccurate reading, poor spelling skills, poor writing, or mixing up similar words; the level of struggle ranges from mild to severe. Demographically speaking, research indicates that RD is more common in males and that the disorder is genetic in nature. Contrary to the popular opinion, an RD is not always identified in early childhood; many older adults are being diagnosed. The precise origin of RD is still not entirely apparent, though anatomical and brain imagery analyses demonstrated a difference in brain development and functioning in individuals with dyslexia. It is important that counselors, educators, and parents recognize that RD is neither due to lack of willingness to learn nor due to lack of intelligence. With appropriate teaching methods, those with any form of RD can learn successfully.

When evaluating reading ability, it is important to remember the importance of diagnosing on an *individual* basis. The first few variables a clinician needs to assess include client age, intelligence testing scores, previous educational experiences, and particular cultural attributes. The rationale for assessing specific cultural factors is that the language spoken at home may be different from the language used in academics. After gathering all of the relevant assessment data, an RD may be diagnosed when a child's reading achievement is considerably lower than what would be projected based on assessment data and when the reading difficulties impede the individual's ability to do schoolwork or manage daily life in noteworthy ways. If there are any existing physical conditions (i.e., mental retardation, poor eyesight, or hearing loss), the reading deficit must be in excess of what one would generally relate with the physical condition. If an RD or any other learning disorder is suspected, a comprehensive evaluation that screens hearing, eyesight, and intelligence levels should be performed. In addition, testing ought not to contain reading areas alone, but all areas of learning and learning processes. In school-age children, this evaluation may involve a team of educators, school counselors, educational psychologists, and child psychiatrists. Possible signs and symptoms of an RD based on grade level are shown in Table 4.1.

Treatment and Intervention Strategies

RD, like other learning disorders, falls under the Federal Individuals with Disabilities Education Act (IDEA), which calls for certain services to be available to those affected by the disorder. Specific definitions of learning disabilities vary across states, and, unfortunately, some school districts are less willing than others to recognize specific learning disabilities. Any

TABLE 4.1

Symptoms of Reading Disorders

Preschool	Difficulty rhyming, trouble finding the right word, problems pronouncing words
Grades K-4	Confuses basic words when reading, slow to learn new skills, cotently misspells words and makes frequent errors
Grades 5-8	Poor organization skills, spelling one word differently in a single document, difficulty with reading comprehension, dislikes reading and writing to the point that he or she avoids reading aloud

child with a diagnosed learning disability, including RD, should qualify for an Individual Education Program (IEP), which specifies the personalized instruction that will be provided to the student to address the disability at school.

There are many effective programs and techniques to address individual reading needs. Most beneficial programs typically include three characteristics: a phonics base, a multisensory component, and a highly structured foundation. A phonics base involves breaking words down into their smallest visual components—letters and the sounds associated with them. A multisensory component involves attempts to form and strengthen mental associations among visual, auditory, and kinesthetic means of inspiration. Thus, the student simultaneously sees, feels, and says the sound–symbol association. For example, a child may trace the letter or combination of letters with his or her finger while pronouncing a word aloud. Highly structured foundation, the third component for success, starts at the remedial level of the single letter–sound. Over time, the structure subsequently works up to a pair of letters representing a single speech sound (digraphs), then syllables, followed by words and sentences in a corresponding systematic manner as repetitive practice operates to shape key connections between sounds and written symbols (Kolligian & Sternberg, 1987; National Reading Panel, 2000; Spear-Swerling & Sternberg, 1994).

Generally, individuals with RD lack motivation in reading due to the difficulty of the task. Here is a summary of innovative techniques to help stimulate interest (Atkinson, Wilhite, Frey, & Williams, 2002; Jenkins & O'Connor, 2002; Fleming & Forester, 1997):

1. *Brainstorming* involves asking a student to consider the title of a selection that he or she is about to read, sharing the thoughts aloud. The facilitator writes down all the information that comes to mind as the student reads the title. This information is then used for further recall, and through this process, comprehension will be activated.
2. *Visual aids*, as they entail the usage of pictures, drawings, photographs, and other visual materials, are often helpful in activating a students' prior knowledge base. The facilitator may show a picture of the topic before reading about it in order to assist with the retrieval of appropriate knowledge. Incidentally, this also creates interest.
3. *The prequestion process* involves students being provided with questions to help them complete their reading assignments. These questions are purposeful as they are prepared before the reading time by the facilitator and tend to focus on the importance of paying attention.
4. *Sampling the vocabulary* includes a technique where unknown keywords are taught to a student before he or she has read the material so that new words, background information, and comprehension can improve

together. The facilitator lists all the words in the assignment that may be important for students to understand. The words are arranged to show their relationship to the learning task. It is important to add words that students likely already understand to connect relationships between the "known" and the "unknown."

5. *Metacognition* refers to the individual's instinctive awareness of his or her own knowledge and the person's capability to comprehend, manage, and influence his or her own cognitive processes. Metacognitive skills involve questioning on the terms of "what," "where," and "when." An example of this is by asking a student, "What were your first ideas after reading the chapter?" or "How is this character similar and different to another character?" In short, metacognition is simply referred to as the notion of "thinking about thinking" and the skill appears to have success with individuals who are diagnosed with RD.

DISORDER OF WRITTEN EXPRESSION

As a distinct diagnosis, disorder of written expression has evaded a thorough understanding and operational definition in both the existing literature and clinical practice. Therefore, unlike other learning disabilities that are well defined and easily understood, it is difficult to ascertain the complexities, subtleties, and components of how the disorders of written expression manifest themselves. However, the Diagnostic and Statistical Manual (DSM-IV-TR) outlines some diagnostic features and criteria for the disorder. The essential feature is described as "writing skills (as measured by an individually administered standardized test or functional assessment of writing skills) that fall substantially below those expected given the individuals' chronological age, measured intelligence, and age-appropriate education" (APA, 2000, pp. 54–55). Thus, a variety of developmental factors must be considered in determining the appropriateness of this diagnosis and severity of the disorder. In other words, what may seem like a problem for one individual may be developmentally appropriate or acceptable for another individual.

Similar to RD, a disturbance in written expression must cause a significant impediment to academic achievement or daily life in which writing skills are required (APA, 2000). These difficulties may manifest themselves in a myriad of ways, including difficulties with text composition, grammatical or punctuation errors, paragraph organization, spelling errors, and handwriting. However, a diagnosis is seldom given if the only symptom is spelling errors or poor handwriting in the absence of other difficulties with writing (APA, 2000). Additionally, Bernstein (2011) pointed out that writing is a complex process, which requires the mastery and integration of many *subskills*, including cognition, language, and motor skills. Since writing involves both cognition and motor skills, and a diagnosis of disorder of written expression is not given if motor skills alone are impaired, it is generally understood and documented that written expression disorders involve both impaired *transcription skills* and *neuropsychological processes* (Berninger & Amtmann, 2006).

Reliable information on prevalence rates for expressive-writing disorders is lacking due to very little accurate information about the expression disorders among the general population (Lindstrom, 2007). As a result, researchers and practitioners are left with cautionary estimates ranging from 8% to 15% of the population (Lindstrom, 2007), but these figures are based on the presence of other frequently comorbid learning disorders. Age of onset for written expression disorders is a little clearer; incidents of written expression problems sharply increase around the fourth grade and then begin to decline through the end of middle school and beginning of high school (Berninger & Amtmann, 2006). The DSM-IV-TR suggests that the disorder may become evident as early as first grade; however, it cautions early diagnoses due to the absence of formal writing instruction before the second grade in most school settings (APA, 2000).

Treatment and Intervention Strategies

Little is also known about the prognosis and treatment of expressive-writing disorders. However, untreated written-expression problems typically continue to manifest themselves throughout schooling. Berninger and Amtmann (2006) suggested that a critical period in writing development exists and that early assessment and treatment may be particularly important in the remediation of transcription skills. However, this is easier said than done. As Scott and Vitale (2000) pointed out, due to the complexity of writing and the various symptoms of written-expression disorder, teachers often have difficulty in accurately assessing the full range of writing skills. As a result, children with written-expression disorders that go undiagnosed or untreated are often mislabeled as lazy or unmotivated later in schooling (Berninger & Amtmann, 2006).

Even when appropriately assessed or identified by counselors and educators, little is known about the treatment of expressive-writing disorders. Treatment is usually approached in one of the following three ways:

1. *Basic writing techniques*, such as handwriting and/or spelling techniques, and skills
2. *Morphological* or *phonological awareness training*
3. *Bypass strategies*, which are typically computer-based and which compensate for deficits in cognitive processes utilized during writing

However, Berninger and Amtmann cautioned against the use of some computer-based strategies because little empirical evidence is available to support their efficacy and they may pose additional challenges to some students. In such cases, traditional paper-and-pencil strategies may still be the most appropriate for a large portion of those with written-expression disorders.

MATHEMATICS LEARNING DISORDER

Both foreign and domestic studies have been conducted on MLD, which indicate that approximately 5% to 8% of school-age children qualify as having MLD (Gross-Tsur, Manor, & Shalev, 1996). MLD has been referred to in a variety of ways over the years, including *specific arithmetic difficulties* (McLean & Hitch, 1999), *arithmetic learning disabilities* (Koontz & Berch, 1996), and *dyscalculia* (Wadlington & Wadlington, 2008), just to name a few.

Defining MLD has not been easy and remains a source of debate by researchers. One universally accepted set of standards that clinicians and educators can consult, however, is found in the Diagnostic and Statistical Manual (DSM-IV-TR) diagnostic criteria (APA, 2000). This set of criteria include testing at a mathematical achievement level that is far below one's peers considering factors such as age, educational level, and intelligence. As in other learning disorders, the child's level of ability must interfere with mathematics-based tasks on either a personal or academic level.

Mathematics, as a discipline, is comprised of many different components; these include arithmetic, algebra, statistics, measurement, and geometry. Doing well in arithmetic, an area to which young children are introduced early on, requires the ability to solve problems, understand mathematical facts, perform mathematical procedures, and understand various mathematical concepts. Research has shown that students with MLD are more likely to have difficulty with strategies for counting (Dowker, 2005b), recalling mathematical facts (Jordan & Hanich, 2000), identifying place values (e.g., the tens place), solving word problems (Russell & Ginsburg, 1984), and following through on multiple steps in arithmetic problems (Bryant, Bryant, & Hammill, 2000).

Existing Programs

The most effective strategies for assisting MLD students are still not fully determined and continue to be a topic of much debate among researchers (Butler, Beckingham, & Lauscher, 2005). There are a variety of interventions and programs in existence to help students with MLD, and it appears that individual instruction is favored. Two examples are the Mathematics Recovery and the Numeracy Recovery programs. The interventions used in these programs are geared towards specific areas in which the students are the most weak (Dowker, 2005a).

Developed in Australia by Wright, Martland, and Stafford (2000) and Wright, Martland, Stafford, and Stanger (2002), the Mathematics Recovery program is geared toward aiding students aged 6 and 7. This program involves a half-hour of one-on-one instruction between teacher and student every day for a period of 12 to 14 weeks. The Numeracy Recovery program, created by Dowker (2001, 2003), was initially tested with a similar age group of students in Oxford, England. It is a bit more intensive as it incorporates half-hour, one-on-one instruction for approximately 30 weeks. Both programs focus on individual instruction addressing the students' weakest areas. As with other remedial programs, students must be motivated and committed to enhancing their skill set for any program to be effective.

GIFTEDNESS

Giftedness may be defined in many ways, but it tends to address aptitude, or the natural abilities possessed by an individual, or talents, which refers to the mastery of an area or activity (Gagné, 1991, as cited in Lassig, 2003). Whereas the problems with hindered learning have been discussed, there is debate on whether those boys who excel in learning face any additional difficulties in their development. As with the general population, development of social and emotional problems is complex and dependent on much more than the individual. For the most part, gifted children are as well adjusted as other nongifted children (Bailey, 2011; Neihart, Reis, Robinson, & Moon, 2002). This statement is a generalization to the gifted population as a whole and does not negate areas of concern and potential risk for some subgroups. In giftedness-specific research, numerous potential concerns are noted and many are disputed. One report may describe gifted children as more resilient (Neihart, 2002), whereas another describes giftedness as a vulnerability (Silverman, 1997). However, asynchronous development (Silverman, 1997) is one commonly agreed upon potential source of problems.

Asynchronous development is best defined as uneven or out-of-sync development. The facets of development are staggered rather than congruent. An example would be a child with a chronological age of 6, a mental age of 11, and emotional age of 7. He or she might be able to reason and discuss complex topics, yet, emotionally, he or she may become overly sad when seeing a news report on war in the Middle East. Socially, the child may be bored with same-aged peers, yet be unable to accept the responsibilities of someone his or her mental age. It is thought that advanced mental ability, in the absence of emotional maturity, may produce intensity and sensitivity in gifted children (Lovecky, 1992).

Webb, Meckstroth, and Tolan (1982) noted that peer relationships with same-aged peers might suffer due to the intellectual differences because of developmental asynchrony. Similarly, in a study considering self-concept, self-esteem, and peer relationships, Janos, Fung, and Robinson (1985) found that gifted children see themselves as different, which in turn may affect peer relationships. Finally, Reis and Renzulli (2004) reported that gifted children exhibit advanced social competence, which often results in fewer friendships with same-aged peers. As a result, gifted children may hide their talents in order to increase peer acceptance. All in all, asynchrony is a potential source for difficulty both socially and emotionally. When asynchronous development is identified, supportive measures are necessary. For many, this can be accomplished by linking gifted children with similar gifted children or by encouraging them to seek involvement in multiple peer groups (Webb et al., 1982).

Although few studies report gender differences within the gifted populations, according to Kerr, Hallowell, and Schroeder-Davis (1991) research indicates that males (1) have more adjustment problems, (2) show more traits of anxiety and depression, and (3) are referred more often for behavioral disruptions. Colangelo, Kerr, Christensen, and Maxey (1993) also noted that underachievement is more pronounced in gifted males. With these gender-specific issues in mind, it is important to note that asynchronous development may be a potential cause.

SUMMARY

For a young boy to succeed in school and later in a career, he must be able to master the basics of reading, writing, and arithmetic, as well as the social skills necessary for his environment. However, a learning difference will effectively derail a young man's academic development and, in many ways, potentially his emotional and social development. Following is an illustrative case study showing the multiple ways in which a learning disorder may negatively affect a young man.

CASE STUDY: TREY, AGE 13

Trey is a 13-year-old, middle socioeconomic class, African American male student in a public junior high school. His teachers typically report that he persistently speaks out and disrupts classes with inappropriate comments. Other students in his classes frequently complain to the teacher about Trey disturbing them and trying to copy their answers on assignments. They also complain that he has a strong need for attention. Trey seldom remains on task when given class time to complete written assignments, and he seems to have significant difficulty focusing for any length of time. Due to his frequent behavioral issues, the school counselor recommended that Trey be evaluated for the presence of any learning disabilities. The results of the assessments revealed that Trey has a diagnosable RD. Based on the recommendation of a family friend, Trey's parents sought counseling for Trey, as they wanted him to feel more confident with his reading skills, and, ideally, be more well-behaved in school.

Counselor was familiar with learning disordered youth and was aware of the struggles they faced in the schools—both in learning and in fitting in with their peers. Academic interventions selected for Trey included a multisensory, phonics strategy that focused on using metacognitive skills each day after school with family members' assistance. One metacognitive exercise in particular called for Trey to be given the descriptive acronym *"RUN,"* which stood for "What did I *Read*? What do I *Understand*? What do I *Need* to still ask?" Every night, a family member would draw three columns on a sheet of paper with each column labeled with one of the questions. A conversation would follow as the family member asked Trey to answer each question and explain how it related to the assignment. In the school, Trey was placed into a small group with peers to discuss the daily assigned reading.

Within individual counseling sessions, the counselor also focused on positive reinforcement as Trey suffered from poor self-esteem and difficulty staying on task. Trey was encouraged to identify his negative feelings and destructive thoughts. Over time, Trey and his parents were taught to use different words rather than the derogatory labels such as "stupid" or "dumb," which even Trey had begun to apply to himself. The counselor explained how these negative terms had contributed to Trey's difficulties in his social world. In addition, Trey developed a list of affirming qualities and positive abilities he saw in himself. With the help of his counselor and parents, Trey was encouraged to continue to develop some of his unique abilities, one of which was playing the drums. As Trey developed his percussion skills, his confidence and his social skills also grew. With the highly structured support and teamwork from his counselor, family, and school, Trey made monumental strides in his self-esteem, emotional control, social development, reading ability, and comprehension scores over the next few school years.

SUGGESTED RESOURCES

- LD online: www.ldonline.org/indepth/reading
- National Center for Learning Disabilities: www.ncld.org
- The International Dyslexia Association: www.interdys.org
- Learning Disabilities Association of America: www.ldanatl.org
- *Assessing and Differentiating Reading and Writing Disorders: Multidimensional Model* by Linda. J. Lombardino (October 31, 2011)
- Parent Technical Assistance Center Network: www.parentcenternetwork.org

REFERENCES

American Psychiatric Association. (2000). *Diagnostic and statistical manual of mental disorders* (4th ed., text rev.). Washington, DC: Author.

Atkinson, T. S., Wilhite, K. L., Frey, L. M., & Williams, S. C. (2002). Reading instruction for the struggling reader: Implications for teachers of students with learning disabilities or emotional/behavioral disorders. *Preventing School Failure, 46*(4), 158.

Bailey, C. L. (2011). An examination of the relationships between ego development, Dabrowski's theory of positive disintegration, and the behavioral characteristics of gifted adolescents. *Gifted Child Quarterly, 55*(3), 208–222.

Bender, W. N., Rosenkrans, C. B., & Crane, M. (1999). Stress, depression, and suicide among students with learning disabilities: Assessing the risk. *Learning Disability Quarterly, 22*, 143–156. doi: 10.2307/1511272

Berninger, V. W., & Amtmann, D. (2006). Preventing written expression disabilities through early and continuing assessment and intervention for handwriting and/or spelling problems: Research into practice. In H. L. Swanson, K. R. Harris, & S. Graham (Eds.), *Handbook of learning disabilities* (pp. 345–363). New York, NY: The Guilford Press.

Bernstein, B. E. (2011). *Written expression learning disorder.* Retrieved from http://emedicine.medscape.com/article/1835883-overview

Bruininks, V. L. (1978). Peer status and personality characteristics of learning disabled and nondisabled students. *Journal of Learning Disabilities, 11*, 484–489. doi: 10.1177/002221947801100804

Bryant, D. P., Bryant, B. R., & Hammill, D. D. (2000). Characteristic behaviors of students with LD who have teacher-identified math weaknesses. *Journal of Learning Disabilities, 33*, 168–177.

Butler, D. L., Beckingham, B., & Lauscher, H. J. (2005). Promoting strategic learning by eighth-grade students struggling in mathematics: A report of three case studies. *Learning Disabilities Research & Practice, 20*, 156–174.

Colangelo, N., Kerr, B. A., Christensen, P., & Maxey, J. (1993). A comparison of gifted underachievers and gifted high achievers. *Gifted Child Quarterly, 37*(4), 155–160.

Dowker, A. D. (2001). Numeracy recovery: A pilot scheme for early intervention with young children with numeracy difficulties. *Support for Learning, 16,* 6–10.

Dowker, A. D. (2003). Interventions in numeracy: Individualized approaches. In I. Thompson (Ed.), *Enhancing primary mathematics teaching* (pp. 127–138). Maidenhead, UK: Open University Press.

Dowker, A. D. (2005a). Early identification and intervention for students with mathematics difficulties. *The Journal of Learning Disabilities, 38,* 324–332.

Dowker, A. D. (2005b). *Individual differences in arithmetic: Implications for psychology, neuroscience and education.* Hove, UK: Psychology Press.

Fleming, J., & Forester, B. (1997). Infusing language enhancement into the reading curriculum for disadvantaged adolescents. *Language, speech and hearing services in schools, 28*(2), 177.

Gross-Tsur, V., Manor, O., & Shalev, R. S. (1996). Developmental dyscalculia: Prevalence and demographic features. *Developmental Medicine and Child Neurology, 38,* 25–33.

Janos, P. M., Fung, H. C., & Robinson, N. M. (1985). Self-concept, self-esteem, and peer relations among gifted children who feel "different." *Gifted Child Quarterly, 29*(2), 78–82.

Jenkins, J. R., & O'Connor, R. (2002). Early identification and intervention for young children with reading/learning disabilities. In R. Bradley, L. Danielson, & D. Hallahan (Eds.), *Identification of learning disabilities* (pp. 99–149). Hillsdale, NJ: Erlbaum.

Johnson, B. (2002). Behaviour problems in children and adolescents with learning disabilities. *Internet Journal of Mental Health, 1*(2), 45–54.

Jordan, C. N., & Hanich, B. (2000). Mathematical thinking in second grade children with different forms of LD. *Journal of Learning Disabilities, 33,* 567–578.

Kerr, B., Hallowell, K., & Schroeder-Davis, S. (1991). *Handbook for counseling the gifted and talented.* Alexandria, VA: American Association for Counseling and Development.

Kolligian, J., & Sternberg, R. J. (1987). Intelligence, information processing, and specific learning disabilities: A triarchic synthesis. *Journal of Learning Disabilities, 20,* 8–17. doi: 10.1177/002221948702000103

Koontz, K. L., & Berch, D. B. (1996). Identifying simple numerical stimuli: Processing inefficiencies exhibited by arithmetic learning disabled children. *Mathematical Cognition, 2,* 1–23.

Lassig, C. J. (2003) Gifted and talented education reforms: Effects on teachers' attitudes. In B. Bartlett, F. Bryer, & D. Roebuck (Eds.), *Proceedings 1st annual international conference on cognition, language, and special education Research: Reimagining practice: Researching change* (Vol. 2, pp. 141–152), Surfers Paradise, Australia: Griffith University.

Lindstrom, J. H. (2007). Determining appropriate accommodations for postsecondary students with reading and written expression disorders. *Learning Disabilities Research and Practice, 22,* 229–236.

Lovecky, D. V. (1992). Exploring social and emotional aspects of giftedness in children. *Roeper Review, 15*(1), 18–24.

McLean, J. F., & Hitch, G. J. (1999). Working memory impairments in children with specific arithmetic learning difficulties. *Journal of Experimental Child Psychology, 74,* 240–260.

National Reading Panel. (2000). *Teaching children to read: An evidence-based assessment of the scientific research literature on reading and its implications for reading instruction.* Washington, DC: National Institute of Child Health and Human Development.

Neihart, M. (2002). Risk and resilience in gifted children: A conceptual framework. In M. Neihart, S. M. Reis, N. M. Robinson, & S. M. Moon (Eds.), *The social and emotional development of gifted children: What do we know?* (pp. 113–122), Waco, TX: Prufrock Press, Inc.

Neihart, M., Reis, S. M., Robinson, N. M., & Moon, S. M. (Eds.). (2002). *The social and emotional development of gifted children: What do we know?* Waco, TX: Prufrock Press, Inc.

Reis, S. M., & Renzulli, J. S. (2004). Current research on the social and emotional development of gifted and talented students: Good news and future possibilities. *Psychology in the Schools, 41*(1), 119–130.

Russell, R. L., & Ginsburg, H. P. (1984). Cognitive analysis of children's mathematical difficulties. *Cognition and Instruction, 1,* 217–244.

Rutter M., Tizard J., & Whitmore K. (1970). *Education, health and behaviour.* London, UK: Longmans.

Scott, B. J., & Vitale, M. R. (2000). Informal assessment of idea development in written expression: A tool for classroom use. *Preventing School Failure, 44,* 67–72.

Silverman, L. K. (1997). The construct of asynchronous development. *Peabody Journal of Education, 72*(3–4), 36–58.

Spear-Swerling, L., & Sternberg, R. J. (1994). The road not taken: An integrative theoretical model of reading disability. *Journal of Learning Disabilities, 27,* 91–103, 122. doi: 10.1177/002221949402700204

The International Dyslexia Association. (2008). *Just the facts....* Retrieved from http://www.interdys.org/ewebeditpro5/upload/BasicsFactSheet.pdf

Wadlington, E., & Wadlington, P. L. (2008). Helping students with mathematical disabilities to succeed. *Preventing School Failure, 53,* 2–7.

Webb, J. T., Meckstroth, E. A., & Tolan, S. S. (1982). *Guiding the gifted child: A practical source for parents and teachers.* Scottsdale, AZ: Great Potential Press.

Wright, R., Martland, J., & Stafford, A. (2000). *Early numeracy: Assessment for teaching and intervention,* London, UK: Chapman.

Wright, R., Martland, J., Stafford, A., & Stanger, G. (2002). *Teaching number: Advancing children's skills and strategies.* London, UK: Chapman.

5

Untold Stories of Potential: Career Counseling With Male Children and Adolescents

KEVIN B. STOLTZ AND SUSAN R. BARCLAY

In today's work environment, the responsibility of managing a career falls on the individual rather than on the organization (Hall, 1996; Savickas, 2011). Over a decade ago, Hall (1996) and Arthur and Rousseau (1996) proclaimed the end of the conventional career and recognized a new work paradigm that required employees to be untethered from traditional ways of viewing and understanding the career. The corporate structure of the 20th century dictated a contract of lifetime employment with progressive advancement within one organization. Employers presented workers with career paths and, later, developmental training to "groom" employees for growth within the organization. This was the standard of the 20th century. However, the work environment has changed drastically with the global economy. Gone are the promises of lifetime employment within a corporation. Changing jobs over the life span is common. The U.S. Department of Labor (2008) reported that individuals in the United States born between 1957 and 1964 held an average of 10.8 jobs over their working careers. Due to the rapid pace of technological advancements, entire careers come into and out of the marketplace in relatively short periods. This fast-paced evolutionary work environment requires workers to update knowledge and skills continually to meet the ever-changing demands.

In the face of the new work paradigm, Savickas (2011) calls for workers to consider time-limited work projects instead of lifetime employment.

A natural antecedent to this is that periods of educational pursuit are becoming the norm in this new work economy. Lifelong learning, an adaptable nature, and strong identity are required to stay competitive and adaptable for these new work projects (Savickas, 2011). Career counseling has begun to meet this new paradigm with career counseling theories (e.g., A Rich Context Approach, Blustein, 1997, 2006; Happenstance Theory, Krumboltz, 2009; Career Construction Theory, Savickas, 2002, 2005, 2011) and various techniques to assist all clients with both developing career adaptability and using their self-understanding to develop autonomy and adaptability in the 21st century work environment. However, adolescent males are in danger of being unprepared for this new work environment.

Adolescent male employment has declined steadily since 1989 and is currently at 21% below the high of that year [Bureau of Labor Statistics (BLS), 2011]. Without employment opportunities, these young males have little ability to begin to develop the skills, knowledge, and the adaptabilities to succeed in this competitive work environment. Research indicates that males are more likely than females to leave high school without completing (Chapman, Laird, & KewalRamani, 2010; Heckman & LaFontaine, 2007). Males without a high school diploma are at the greatest risk of chronic unemployment and earning less money over the life span (BLS, 2011; Chapman et al., 2010; ChildTrends Databank, 2011). In addition, male enrollment in colleges has declined continually over the past several decades. Current enrollment figures across the United States indicate females are more likely than males to enter postsecondary schools and complete their college degrees (Pollard, 2011; U.S. Census Bureau, 2009). Although the reasons for dropping out of high school or not pursuing a college degree may be many, one significant contributor may be a lack of career information (Brown, 2003; Gray, 2009; Vilhjalmsdottir, 2010). These statistics indicate that adolescent males may benefit from concentrated career counseling, which assists them in making productive career decisions to become more adaptable in the new work economy.

In this chapter, we present one new career theory, Career Construction Theory (CCT; Savickas, 2002, 2005, 2011), which can be applied when working with adolescent males for assisting this group to build career adaptability and meet the challenges of the new work paradigm. First, we present a definition of career adaptability and outline the development of the construct. Then, we review two developmental career theories that aid in understanding the developmental nature of career self-concept and identity. Next, we present the CCT as an integrated theory to address career adaptability. Finally, we discuss career interventions that support both early development and adolescent development. Each section includes case vignettes to clarify the approach and meaning of career construction counseling.

CAREER ADAPTABILITY

Broadly defined, career adaptability is the cognitive, behavioral, and emotional skills and self-identity awareness that an individual possesses and applies to career functioning (Savickas, 2002, 2005, 2011). Originally, Super and Kansel (1981) presented career adaptability as career maturity. In their discussion, Super and Kansel reasoned that tying career maturity to career transition and developmental levels in adulthood did not capture the essence of the learning and skills adults have acquired over their life span. In addition, the adult career client was not facing the working world for the first time usually, as is typical for early adulthood. This reasoning caused them to reflect and propose the term *career adaptability* as the representative phrase for an adult's accumulated skills, emotional regulation, and knowledge.

Super, Savickas, and Super (1996) revisited career adaptability and discussed the importance of the construct. Savickas (2002) presented dimensions of career adaptability as "developmental lines" (p. 167) and posited that, as individuals begin to experience the pressure of societally imposed tasks (e.g., becoming concerned about their careers, exploring the world of work), they begin to use their "attitudes, beliefs, and competencies" (Savickas, 2011, p. 139) to address the imposed tasks. This conceptualization led to the application of the concept of career adaptability to childhood, adolescence, and adulthood (Hartung, Porfeli, & Vondracek, 2008). The culmination of early childhood experiences, personal skills, attitudes, and abilities come together to create individual career adaptability. In addition, Savickas (2002) went on to focus a sizable discussion on assessing career adaptability, demonstrating the emerging importance of this concept in CCT. Currently, career adaptability continues to be a focus of research (Del Corso & Rehfuss, 2011; Ebberwein, Krieshok, Ulven, & Prosser, 2004; Koen, Klehe, Van Vianen, Zikic, & Nauta, 2010; Rehfuss, 2009; Rottinghaus, Day, & Borgen, 2005).

The importance of career adaptability in the new career paradigm signals that career counseling must begin to include an idiographic component as the centerpiece of career interventions. No longer can we rely solely on the matching paradigm of career guidance (Parsons, 1909) or the vocational education approach of career development (Super, 1990) to help people become more adaptive to the ever-evolving work environment (Savickas, 2011). Guidance and career education, although important in career counseling in the new paradigm, do not focus on understanding the individual in the context of a life story. Counselors use guidance to help people discover traits and explore work environments that resemble those traits. Career education seeks to teach about stages and readiness to engage in predictable work life tasks. Career construction counseling includes these two approaches, yet focuses on constructing the career as a life project steeped in the cultural context. This life project includes the lived experiences of each individual, and career counselors concentrate on assisting the person to construct a life story that is open to changes, shifts, interruptions, and revision in the work life. This theory is the subject of much research in adults (Del Corso & Rehfuss, 2011; Ebberwein et al., 2004; Koen et al., 2010; Rehfuss, 2009; Rottinghaus et al., 2005); however, there is little focus on developing research and interventions from a gender-specific perspective, especially in adolescence. In this chapter, we present applications of this new career theory to male children and adolescent career development. Career identity development and adaptability will be the main topics discussed from CCT.

CAREER DEVELOPMENT IN CHILDHOOD

Hartung, Porfeli, and Vondracek (2005) posited that childhood and adolescence are of primary importance in career development because these periods are the beginnings of engaging with the world of work. Early experiences either support or deter the child from developing curiosity, fantasy, skills, interests, and self-confidence (Ginzberg, Ginsburg, Axelrod, & Herma, 1951; Super, 1990). Activities in childhood and adolescence lay the foundation for adult career functioning (Hartung et al., 2008). During these years, the child forms attitudes, beliefs, and skills that are the foundational elements of career adaptability (Savickas, 2002).

Savickas (2002, 2011) outlined four dimensions of career adaptability: concern, control, curiosity, and confidence. *Career concern* is simply an understanding of time and the need to think and plan for the future (Savickas, in press). As young children grow, they gain more awareness that planning is an element of time progression. Children and adolescents with high career concern interact with adults and society with an attitude that time is limited and people must organize and plan for the future. Those with less career concern may lack energy for and anticipation of a future by showing little interest in planning. For example, an adolescent takes time to plan and prepare before executing an art project in class. He studies the assignment, ensures that he has the materials to complete the project, and schedules his time to work on the project. The planning activities are the beginnings of career concern. Another young man simply begins working on the project and finds that he does not have the materials needed. He takes time to get the materials and then realizes that he is running out of time to complete the project. He hurries through the project and does not work to his greatest potential. This is an example of poor planning and less career concern.

Career control is the dimension that indicates how self-assured and motivated children are about having an effect on their own future. Control indicates an individual's level of autonomy, internal decision making, self-determination, and how much the child attributes his or her own actions to success in endeavors (Blustein & Flum, 1999). An early example of control is the child's ability to both learn and govern appropriate intrapersonal responses and emotional control (Savickas, in press). In adolescence, control reflects an intrapersonal process of self-motivation in facing life tasks (e.g., self-motivation to perform well in school). Boys with higher levels of control are able to relate their actions to their success and can take responsibility when they do not act toward goals (e.g., "I studied hard for the test and made a good grade" or "I know I did not apply myself, and I will do better on the next test"). Those with lower control tend to attribute outcomes to external or environmental causes and have low levels of autonomy and self-determination (e.g., "That lousy teacher always makes the test too hard, and so I fail").

Career curiosity is the ability of the individual to possess interest in experiencing the world and especially different types of work (Savickas, in press). Taking initiative to learn about work and being open to having new experiences is an important skill in the new career paradigm (Krumboltz, 2009). Curiosity in young boys entails exploring the environment and constructing an understanding of the social systems in the world, including learning about work. In adolescence, career curiosity manifests as engagement with the wider social environment and exploring actual work roles. This is a time of much experimentation, and those with low curiosity demonstrate less involvement and experimentation. An example of high curiosity would be the young boy who approaches his father and asks to go to work with him so that he can see what his father does for a living. The boy reads about his father's work and learns what to expect when visiting the workplace. During the visit, the boy asks many questions and is able to explore the worksite with intention. A young man low in curiosity would not approach his father or seek additional information if asked to go. He would show little interest or motivation.

Career confidence is the last dimension of career adaptability. Confidence is the belief of individuals that they can succeed when facing a challenge (Savickas, in press). Confidence gives children the courage to face challenges and carry out plans successfully. In early childhood, boys with higher levels of confidence may wander further from their caretaker and need less encouragement when attempting new behaviors (e.g., swimming or riding a bike). In adolescence, confidence is more apparent. Boys with high levels of confidence are self-assured and face tense social situations with resolve and courage (e.g., standing up to a bully). Seeking a summer job with little assistance and little fear or trepidation is another example of confidence.

These dimensions of career adaptability represent aspects of an individual's ability to overcome challenges and meet the life tasks set before the person. Society dictates many life tasks, and meeting these sequential steps to adulthood are key factors in developing a positive self-concept. CCT explains the development of self-concept within a constructivist frame, which recognizes that context has influence on how people construct their lives and careers. Thus, context is an important consideration in early childhood career development.

The first context in which children begin forming opinions about life is within the family structure. Research consistently shows that family has significant impact on the career construction process for children. Super (1957) posited that parents are the first source for children's values and attitudes toward vocational preferences and that "the experiences to which the family has exposed the developing child and youth" (p. 244) provide the foundation for preferred occupational exploration and entry. Both Gottfredson (1981) and Roe (1954) discussed parental influence in their theories. Schultheiss (2003) maintained that melding relational theory and career theory provides the greatest understanding of how individuals approach careers.

In their study, Keller and Whiston (2008) found that parental support behaviors, such as collaborating with their children regarding career issues, believing in their children's abilities, and trusting their children to make good decisions, were paramount for children to gain the self-efficacy to construct and move into careers eventually. These findings are similar to the confidence dimension of career adaptability. According to Noack, Dracke, Gniewosz, and Dietrich (2010), parent-led exploration activities provide children and adolescents with the essential components to developing a vocational self-identity, which is an important component in Super's (1957) theoretical framework. As children hear their parents discuss work experiences, children assimilate that information and form clearer understandings about career (Noack et al., 2010). This is an example of building curiosity in children and adolescents. Thus, research supports that parental influence is an important variable in child and adolescent career development. In the following section, we discuss the acquisition of career identity from family and the broader environmental influences of school, friends, and society.

HOW CAREER IDENTITY DEVELOPS

Several theorists discussed early career development. Ginzberg et al. (1951) posited that early childhood was a time of fantasy regarding career interests. Eventually, this fantasy period gives way to the development of specific and serious interests. Super (1957) put forth a theory that combined all of early childhood into one stage called *growth*. Later, Super (1990) expanded on his theory and constructed a causal model demonstrating that early childhood experiences set the foundation for later career development. He posited that curiosity was the foundational element in developing career planning and decision making. With this model, Super began to represent the critical nature of early childhood development. Roe (1954) drew attention also to the importance of early childhood experiences as laying the foundation for career choices. Roe focused on the psychodynamic process of parenting in developing her theory. She hypothesized that parental demeanors toward children had an unconscious guiding effect on children's adult career choice. Specifically, she posited that warm, overprotective parents would yield a person with interest in the arts and entertainment. In contrast, a cold, avoiding, and negating parenting style would result in a child having interests in technology, outdoor activities, or science. The core of this model was that parent's style of approaching the child with either a warm or a cold demeanor dictated career choice. Although descriptive and informational, Roe's theory has not garnered convincing empirical support (Watson & McMahon, 2005).

A newer developmental theory that has received empirical support and continues to be tested in the career literature (Helwig, 2008) is Gottfredson's (1981, 2002) Theory of Circumscription and Compromise. Gottfredson outlined a developmental theory that describes four progressive stages of career self-concept development. Each stage has a central focal point that influences the child's self-concept and eventually leads back to career choices within a zone of tolerable alternatives. The stages and focal points are (a) orientation to size and power, (b) orientation to sex typing, (c) orientation to social valuation, and (d) orientation to unique self. The social context influences each stage, and children respond to these contexts individually. However, Gottfredson noted that masculine and feminine responses fall along gender lines generally.

Extrapolating from Gottfredson (1981, 2002), in the first stage, orientation to size and power, male children will be influenced by the parental hierarchy of power in the family. Males can often identify with an adult male's power and size; however, many times women are also vested with the primary caregiver role. Thus, male children may perceive the female caregiver as having more power over the child's daily routines. In this stage, young boys are learning how power is used, and they begin to identify with the source of that power. This early identity begins to form attitudes about how the male child interacts with family and authority figures. In addition, the boy begins to make unconscious resolutions concerning how he will navigate environmental barriers and opportunities. Young boys with traditional male parental role models are apt to identify with traditional roles for work. Boys with nontraditional parental role models are more inclined to pursue nontraditional roles and interests (Chusmir, 1990; Lease, 2003).

In Stage 2 of Gottfredson's (1981, 2002) theory, males are focused on sex typing and begin to notice and reject female activities and interests. Boys may get social messages that playing with specific toys (e.g., dolls, playhouses) are not male endeavors, and therefore, young boys may begin to develop separated work roles as an identity. In families where fathers are involved in the daily activities of childcare and have more contact with the children, these role divisions may be less pronounced. Traditional family roles are expected to impact boys in such ways that boys will form interests in traditional masculine ways (Hartung et al., 2005).

Stage 3 represents a time when boys are attending to the perceived social value in activities and interests. If male traits and activities (e.g., football, hunting, and fishing) are more valued in the social context, boys are inclined to strive to develop those interests and activities. If value were placed equally on activities or more weighted toward feminine activities (e.g., culinary arts, interior design), then the theory would hold that males might be more open to experimenting with a wider range of activities.

Finally, in the fourth stage, males have developed an internal identity on which the immediate environment has less influence. Thus, the final stage is dependent on all the earlier stages of development. This stage is when the male has developed a career self-concept through the circumscription of work fields based on his accumulated experiences. This circumscription and identity development occurred unconsciously and is not readily available in consciousness (Gottfredson, 1981). In Stage 4, males will begin to narrow selections of career based on three dimensions: least tolerable level of prestige and highest tolerable level of effort. Additionally, males will use sex typing to develop a zone of acceptable alternatives. In this stage, males spend much time exploring environments that will allow the expression of the internal self-concept. This is an especially important time for males to receive counseling that centers on the expression of the self-concept.

Males will respond to each developmental task with which they are confronted with a specific set of coping resources based on the early context and orientations referred to by Gottfredson (1981, 2002). Exploring the early family context and how males developed through these stages is helpful in understanding how males engage in problem solving and resolution. In addition, they come to career counseling with specific interests and abilities based on their early family experiences.

With Gottfredson's theory, there is an understanding of how the context and child meld together to develop a boy's career self-concept. Much of this development is unconscious, yet continues to play an important role in the career decision-making process. In career counseling, the counselor can elicit much of this unconscious material by listening to stories from the male's early childhood. These short stories of early experiences allow the counselor to get a glimpse of the developmental stages and important role models, both fictional and real, which helped the child to construct a *novella* of the past. Additionally, these early memories are consistent with personality themes that help clients begin to understand their own problem-solving strategies (Adler, 1937; Bruhn, 1990; Singer & Salovey, 1991). After co-constructing the stories with the male client, the counselor assists the client in understanding how this novella informs the present and future.

CAREER IDENTITY DEVELOPMENT: SUPER'S CAUSAL MODEL

Super (1990) developed a comprehensive theory of career self-concept development that begins in early childhood. He constructed a model of early childhood career development that centered on children's exploratory behavior motivated by curiosity. Super posited that children interact with the contextual environment through exploration. If these interactions are positive, either internally or externally, children will maintain their exploratory behavior. However, conflict arises if children meet negative experiences during their investigations of the world. When children reach conflict, they are apt to withdraw if the conflict is great, according to Super. This is a detrimental stance for the child to take, which can lead to eventual withdrawal and apathy toward exploratory behavior. This would cause a child significant developmental difficulties in forming a coherent and crystallized career self-concept.

When children receive internal or external reward for exploratory behavior, they begin to identify key figures in early life (Super, 1990). Children view these key figures (role models) as helpful, and these key figures provide a role modeling effect on children. As children watch their role models, they develop a sense of autonomy and gain further ability to explore and take appropriate developmental risks to continue learning. This continues and gives children a sense of accomplishment and self-esteem. In addition, children learn about the temporal aspects of planning and preparing for the future. This sense of planfulness fosters the ability to problem solve. According to Savickas (2002), the ability to problem solve is synonymous with the dimensions of career adaptability. Super (1990) stressed the importance of helping children to develop a strong penchant for curiosity and exploration. He saw these early exploratory behaviors as foundational to career adaptability and overall career development. Hartung et al. (2008) agreed with both Super (1990) and Savickas (2002) and stated that children's "attitudes, beliefs, and competencies represent the core dimensions of career adaptability" (p. 63). In summary, children are in a continual process of developing the attitudes, skills, beliefs, and behaviors that will be the foundation of their abilities to make and execute career plans toward fruition over the entire life course.

Children form these attitudes, skills, beliefs, and behaviors in the local context of family, school, media, and community. Hartung et al. (2008) went on to illuminate that children's play is essential to the development of career adaptability. Play activities teach important skills of planning, problem solving, imagining, physical dexterity and prowess, and interpersonal skills. Play activities and social components have specific influences that are often unconscious, yet counselors can witness and reflect these influences by engaging with children during play.

In this section, we presented theories of career identity development and how curiosity plays an important role in developing the foundation of career development in children. This section ended with the importance of childhood play and activities as the genesis of career identity. In the next section, we discuss how to use children's play as a career intervention with males.

PLAY: A CAREER COUNSELING INTERVENTION WITH MALES IN EARLY AND MIDDLE CHILDHOOD

Children's play becomes a focal point for understanding early career development, and play is a primary way of providing mental health intervention to children who are in danger of developing less than adequate social, cognitive, and emotional skills in life. These skills are related directly to career adaptability, and thus, counselors can conceptualize play therapy as a way of addressing the developmental lines of career adaptability, as well as other psychosocial lines of development.

Researchers (Hartung et al., 2008; Watson & McMahon, 2005) posited that the beginnings of career are founded in childhood. With this understanding comes a requirement to develop interventions for young children who are at risk of developmental issues. Exposure to traumatic events and crises can place children at risk of delayed formation of positive self-concepts and interests in the immediate environment (Tyndall-Lind, Landreth, & Giordano, 2001). Additionally, children who come from homes with parents who have substance abuse issues or high parental discord may also be at risk in forming a positive self-concept and attitudes of exploring interests (Trice, Hughes, Odom, Woods, & McClellan, 1995). Working with these children from a purely career guidance and education perspective would be very difficult because young children are still in the process of forming interests and skills and crystallizing their self-concept identity. However, CCT, especially the construct of career adaptability, applies to this young age. Focusing on concern, control, curiosity, and competence are appropriate interventions for this age group. As with many interventions for young children, the intention is to aid the child in getting back on the developmental track in all lines of development.

The inclusion of career development interventions is an often overlooked and under-researched aspect of treatment, yet these children are at risk of experiencing career developmental issues over the life span. Focusing on adaptability in early intervention approaches with children seems to be a necessary and judicious way of helping these children develop holistically. As evidenced by education and employment statistics, males may benefit from earlier career interventions centered on developing the lines of career adaptability.

One major emerging area of intervention with young boys for various counseling difficulties is play therapy (Cione, Coleburn, Fertuck, & Fraenkel, 2011; Cochran, Cochran, Nordling, McAdam, & Miller, 2010; Paone & Douma, 2009; Pastore, 2010). Play therapy allows children to play the stories of their experiences in the family and communal context. In session, the counselor witnesses these experiences and emotions (Kottman, 2003). According to Kottman, the crucial *C*s (Bettner & Lew, 1996) are important dimensions that indicate children's success in developing a foundation for future abilities. The *C*s are *connected*, *capable*, *counting*, and *courage*. We would add to these the dimensions of career adaptability. In essence, *capable* is similar to control, *courage* is similar to confidence, and *counting* includes aspects of control and confidence. Adding career concern and curiosity to the crucial *C*s is not a far reach, as these dimensions reflect aspects of connectedness. Concern about the future in the context of others is understood easily as individual behavior often affects relationships. Curiosity is often curtailed by connection to others, and focusing on allowing children to be curious and explore is an essential part of play therapy (Landreth, 1991, Kottman, 2003).

Counselors using play therapy with young male children can address the dimensions of career adaptability by encouraging curiosity in the playroom. This is a tenet of play therapy and is useful to male children who lack exploratory skills and behaviors. Supporting exploration in the playroom helps males develop curiosity. Counselors can also train parents to promote curiosity in their boys. For example, counselors can encourage overattending parents to lessen overattending behaviors to allow their sons to explore in safe environments. Having parents take their sons on nature walks, pointing out the various plants and insects, allowing their sons to touch and feel are all examples of promoting exploratory behavior, which increases curiosity.

Play therapy is important to other dimensions of career adaptability. Kottman (2003) discussed recognizing effort as a way of encouraging the child. This is a way of including the adaptability dimension of control. Males exert effort in the playroom to explore and play out experiences. By recognizing their efforts, the counselor supports a boy's self-agentic behavior. This recognition helps boys understand that they own their behaviors and ultimately their future—the essence of control. Counselors can train parents to support the adaptability dimension of control by teaching parents to recognize their sons' attempts to engage in tasks around the home. Training parents to recognize and support the efforts, and not the outcomes, of boy's activities is an important aspect of this approach. For example, parents can learn to encourage and support their sons' efforts at taking out the trash, even when the trash bag bursts and garbage spills all over the floor. Recognizing that their son remembered, and made efforts, to complete the task are the positive control aspects of career adaptability.

A focus on strengths and assets, also suggested by Kottman (2003), promotes the adaptability dimension of confidence. Kottman stated that a key element is to focus constantly on the child's "feeling of accomplishment and pride" (p. 145). Doing so relates the accomplishment to the child's activity and supports the adaptability dimension of confidence. During a play session, for example, the counselor will focus not so much on the male client's ability to carry out activities with intention, but the resulting satisfaction the male client displays in completing the activity. Statements like "You're really happy with the way you parked the fire truck" or "You're delighted by the way you threw the basketball" are ways of acknowledging the child's accomplishments without focusing on his ability. Helping parents to recognize their sons' sense of accomplishment and seizing opportunities to utilize similar statements will help build confidence in their sons.

Although Kottman (2003) does not address concern directly, planning and execution is a large part of play therapy. By recognizing the planning and effort that goes into the execution of behaviors, the counselor can support the child's planning ability as well as the other dimensions of career adaptability at work in the play therapy sessions. For example, a young boy who sets up an elaborate battle scene in the sand tray, taking much time and care to place all the characters, is displaying planfulness and concern. Recognizing the effort that went into planning the battlefield, a counselor might comment, "You really took time to plan that battle scene." Such a comment is a way of recognizing the time component and planfulness of the male client. In addition, helping parents see and comment on their sons' ability to plan is a way to build a future focus for career concern.

Play therapy offers many exploratory toys and experiences for males to express all aspects of their future work personalities. Toys, often characterized by play themes (e.g., aggressive toys for acting out, Landreth, 1991), can also be conceptualized as the six work environments theorized by Holland (1992). For example, guns and handcuffs can be an expression of exerting power like Holland's *enterprising* personality. Art material may be seen as an expression of the *artistic* personality. Using blocks for building can be seen as a *realistic* personality. By viewing these activities through Holland's theory, the counselor can reflect specific career interests to the male child and help him to learn about his individual interests and about jobs that may reflect those interests.

The first author will explain a particular example from a play session to illustrate this additive approach to play therapy with young males. In session, an 8-year-old male repeatedly built towers of blocks and then went to the easel to draw the towers in detail. I reflected his efforts of planning and constructing the tower (concern, control, and confidence). When he went to the easel, I reflected his decisions to draw the tower with accuracy and his efforts to get the drawing just right (control, confidence). Next, he would knock the tower down with blocks and begin again. I reflected his curiosity about how the tower would fall and in what direction (curiosity). Finally, I reflected his interest in these activities and related them to carpentry, building trades, engineering, and architecture. I did not suggest these as jobs to the boy, but presented these occupations as they related to his various interests. I viewed this as a way of giving the child career and job information for future career decision making.

In this section, we presented play therapy as one important intervention for working with young males. Play therapy is appropriate with males because they may have higher activity levels and are less willing to engage in talk therapy. We presented, also, how counselors can use play therapy to recognize emerging career interests in males and support development in the dimensions of career adaptability. In the next section, we elaborate on building career adaptability with adolescent males.

CAREER COUNSELING WITH ADOLESCENT MALES

Adolescent males are emerging from childhood and beginning to find a place in the social world. During this time, males are exploring their abilities, interests, skills, and talents and asking, "How do I take these elements to the social and working world?" (Gottfredson, 1981, 2002; Super, 1990). Males in this age group have developed the cognitive abilities to tell coherent stories that have all the elements of adult stories, including the ability to reason how these stories connect to the self.

With increased cognitive abilities in adolescents, counselors can engage male children in both activities and conversations. Activities should coincide with expressed client interests to engage the work self-concept. For example, with *realistic* (Holland, 1992) male clients, a walk in a park or tossing the football in the parking lot may be appropriate activities to illicit interests and conversations. With *enterprising* (Holland) clients, competitive games or prompting the client into persuasive debates may be helpful in prompting these interests. For strengthening career adaptability, the counselor should point out the young man's strengths and abilities and foster a sense of accomplishment in the activities. More focused conversations can take place once the young man gets comfortable and used to exploring his abilities, attitude, skills, and interests.

To guide these conversations, we recommend the *Career Story Interview* (Savickas, 2011). This interview consists of a series of questions (see Appendix A) that counselors can tailor to appropriate developmental levels. The intention of the first question is to evoke career concern and planning. Adolescents with lower career concern may be evasive or have little to offer in response to this question. The male client may attempt to offer fantasy careers in which the young man has expressed little interest or has displayed little or moderate ability. The counselor needs to stay engaged and can support motivation for concern by listening and reflecting that the young man has not really given this much thought. For example, "I really have not thought about what you could help me with concerning my career. That seems so far away, and I really do not have any idea. I suppose I will get a job around here somewhere when the time comes." In response to this statement, the counselor would not attempt to provide the client with career information or direction. That would serve to build resistance in the client. The counselor would reflect the tentative nature of the client's exploration by saying, "You are not sure how or what to plan for, and you believe you still have lots of time, but you know when the time comes you can make a decision to find work." This type of response both acknowledges the client's present state and supports the client's confidence, control, and autonomy. In addition, the counselor may restate the question as "So, if you were ready to begin constructing your career, how do you think I could be of help?" The answer to this question signifies the client's present state of readiness and the tasks the client is engaged in solving. In this example, the task is developing more concern. Concern is a necessary ingredient in readiness to consider co-constructing a narrative with the client.

The counselor utilizes the second question to ask the young man about his heroes or role models that he saw as special when he was younger. This is a key question to investigating the emerging self-concept in adolescent males. Many times, young men will offer family members as heroes or role models. Although useful, these role models are not chosen, because one's family is usually placed upon individuals rather than chosen. The role models for whom the counselor is looking are the ones the adolescent actually chooses or finds interesting. Fantasy heroes and role models are very common. An example with one client was Spiderman. This adolescent explained that he thought "Spidey" was cool because he had special powers and used those powers to fight evil. The counselor reflected that the client thought Spidey was powerful and wise in defeating evil. The client agreed and furthered that "I would like to do something like Spiderman. He is a very good person, but I do not have his powers." In this response, the counselor noticed the desire to be powerful and effective; however, the young man demonstrated a lack of confidence and control in not having the special powers of Spiderman. As a follow-up, the counselor questioned, "What powers do you possess that make you effective?" The young man paused and finally said, "I am not really sure." The counselor said, "Perhaps, that is something we can discuss to help you know what special attributes you have that can help you be successful; would you like to do that later?" The young man answered, "Yes." The counselor recycled to this discussion later in the interview.

Using the third question of the interview, the counselor asks clients to explore their manifest interests by revealing their favorite magazines, websites, and other media-associated activities. The answers to these questions reveal preferred environments and specific interests that the client investigates regularly. Responses help the counselor understand the client's Holland type and can be used as resources for further career exploration. A male adolescent client who states he enjoys *U.S. News & World Report* would not be providing enough information for the counselor to ascertain a preferred environment. Therefore, the counselor would ask the client to which section of the magazine the client was drawn. Perhaps the young man answers, "I enjoy the arts and entertainment section. I especially like to read about the upcoming movies, plays, and concerts." The counselor can conclude that the male adolescent prefers an *artistic* environment based on his manifest interest in the arts.

Moving on to the next question, the counselor solicits names of movies or books the client likes, and the counselor probes the client about those movies or books for deeper meaning in the material. Individuals are drawn to stories that have personal meaning, and the client constructs this meaning idiosyncratically. Thus, having the client tell the counselor about the story in the book or movie and the hero or heroine in the story are excellent ways to view what clients may fight or see as obstacles in their own career and life construction (Savickas, 2011). The importance of having clients relate the story is key in this question, as the personalized meaning comes from the client relating the story. One male adolescent related to the movie *Dirty Harry*. He liked the detective, Harry Callahan, because Callahan fought for what was right and did not let petty people or laws stop him from being moral and making the world safer. The client admired Callahan's independence and ability to make his own decisions. Earlier, in the intake interview, this young man complained that his father was always trying to influence his decisions about work and was overly protective of him. The movie is a good example of how the young man was trying to overcome his father's management so that he could exercise his own adaptability dimension of control.

Many times, adolescents have free time, and asking how they use that time can lead to areas of interest that clients have not explored as possible career applications. "What are your hobbies and what do you enjoy about them?" is an appropriate question during the counseling interview. With this question, the counselor is helping the client explore other aspects of the self-concept to broaden applicable interests and explore specific skills. For example, one adolescent male answered this question with, "I like to collect and polish rocks." At first answer, the counselor may be tempted to think about geology as a career for exploration. However, the client went on to say, "I like taking the rough surface and polishing it to make it round, smooth, and to expose the deep colors and contours of the rock." Notice the *artistic* (Holland, 1992) interests in this narrative. The counselor needs to illicit as much narrative about the activity so as not to close the discussion prematurely. These types of narrative broaden and deepen the interest categories from the third question and serve to refine the interests further for the client.

With the next question, the counselor inquires about a favorite motto or saying that the adolescent may hear or say regularly. The boy's chosen motto or saying indicates a problem-solving strategy that he may use regularly when facing life tasks or challenges (Savickas, 2011). One young man related the motto, "One Step at a Time." Earlier, the counselor had noted a comment from the boy's father when the father brought the young man to counseling. The father had stated that his son was very slow and seemed to focus for a long time on problems before he would act. The male adolescent did poorly in math class, even though he enjoyed math, and did not like the fast-paced world of sports. In session, the young man related that his father was always putting pressure on him to hurry up, and he did not feel comfortable rushing through activities. In math class, he felt time was always pushing him along before he could take the steps that he needed in solving the problems. This time pressure eroded his confidence, and he began thinking that he was incompetent in many areas. The counselor reflected the one-step process to the client and added that many careers include long periods for planning activities prior to execution. The counselor went on to accentuate the "steps" part of the motto. "Steps" indicated to the counselor that linear, progressive activities, like those of the *conventional* type, were a strong interest for this young man.

The next question, which focuses on school subjects, may also assess interpersonal relationships for males in school. The counselor inquires about both favored and disfavored subjects in school. The adolescent may answer with genuine interests that can expose specific skills or areas to refine the interests from earlier questions. However, the answer might relate to the teacher of the subject and not the subject matter. This is an important caveat in learning about the client. Asking what makes the teacher interesting and how the client learned from the teacher are good follow-up questions. Likewise, asking what makes the teacher dislikable or boring is another follow-up question. Responses to these questions can serve to deepen an understanding of interpersonal relationships or how the adolescent learns best. For example, one young man related that he enjoyed algebra. He said he was not very good at it and only earned a "C," but he really enjoyed the teacher. "She was able to encourage me even though I did not do so well," he said. He went on to say, "She would take time to show me examples and point out problems in the book that I could do to practice more. She was a very special person because she really seemed to care whether I learned or not. I would like to be a teacher like that." Here is an example of Holland's (1992) *social* type and not an attraction to the *investigative* (Holland) type that one may expect from an interest in algebra.

Finally, the interview ends with a request for three early recollections and a headline to represent each. The purpose of this question is to investigate on what the adolescent male focuses as a life theme or preoccupation (Savickas, in press). Early recollections help to define personality characteristics (Adler, 1937). According to Savickas, these early memories also expose life traumas, disappointments, and themes that the individual confronts regularly in life.

One young man remembered his fifth birthday party that his family gave for him. His mother had invited many of his friends, and the house was very crowded and full of friends and relatives. He did not like all the attention and noise, so he went to the basement to escape the commotion. He fell asleep and missed the party. His mother yelled at him for leaving the party, and he remembered being very angry because he did not want the party. His headline read *Mother Triumphant in Hosting a Party: Boy Sleeps Peacefully by Himself.* In the fifth grade, the young man remembered breaking his arm and going to school. When the kids gathered around him to look at his cast, he began to feel overwhelmed and frightened, thinking that the teacher would yell at him. The headline for this memory was *Boy Breaks Arm: School in Pandemonium.* The counselor co-constructed the theme with the client from these two early memories. The theme was that of avoiding attention and trying not to be noticed. The male adolescent expressed difficulty in making friends at school and complained that others did not interact with him or even notice him. In addition, he felt uncomfortable with too many people around him and did not like to be the center of jokes or attention. *Enterprising* occupations may not be ideal for this male client because of his discomfort with energized environments and being in the spotlight. He may prefer Holland types, such as *conventional, realistic,* or *investigative,* which do not involve working with or around people and which reflects his independent nature best.

Once the counselor has collected the narrative responses to all of the career story interview questions, the counselor is ready to reflect on the content and offer to co-construct the narrative with the adolescent. Weaving all the pieces together takes some reflection on the part of the counselor. The co-construction is usually done in a separate session to allow the counselor time to integrate the separate stories and build a more complete narrative. Because this is a co-constructing process, the counselor uses tentative language with the young man in order to elicit edits and revisions in the story. Once constructed, the counselor should point out the strengths and accomplishments of the adolescent to support the dimensions of career adaptability. In addition, the counselor helps the client to construct a success formula so the young man can take a statement of success forward in life to apply to new challenges.

Many times, an area of trauma or pain is uncovered in the early memories. This trauma or pain is referred to as a *preoccupation* by Savickas (2011). The counselor can reframe the preoccupation through cognitive techniques and help the male client re-story the preoccupation into a parable of strength or convert into an occupation. The young man who complained of not having friends also talked about a career in engineering. He shared with the counselor the trauma of moving continually from first grade through eighth grade. He had little opportunity to develop friendships and found it difficult to relate to peers. New environments challenged him constantly. The one constant this male client found was mathematics. He liked math and found it peaceful to run calculations by hand instead of using a computer. He would often sit in his bedroom and run calculations for hours. His counselor related the story of John Nash from the movie *A Beautiful Mind,* demonstrating that math calculations can model interpersonal relationships. This had an effect on the young man. He realized that he could share his interest in math with people and discuss complex interactions from a mathematical perspective, yet could still make time to remove himself from others when needed. This was a way to both share and practice his interest. He also began planning to study math and planned an academic career in higher math. The success formula, as developed by the client and the counselor, read, *I feel successful when I can work alone and then create and share ideas that help others to live better.*

In this section, we presented the use of narrative building from CCT with adolescent males. Although this may appear easy, frequently young males are not overly verbal or willing to engage in storytelling. Captivating the young male with activities and storytelling is an important aspect of this approach. The young man must be engaged in the process and be willing to share these life stories. Having a solid therapeutic relationship and being willing to engage in various activities will promote engagement by the male adolescent. In addition, encouraging thickening of the stories given is an important aspect of this approach. One of the biggest mistakes in using this approach is relying on nondirective techniques as the sole intervention in exploring the stories. The counselor must engage in the story and ask purposeful questions to thicken the story and to understand more of the context and self-identity development that has occurred.

CONCLUSION

In this chapter, we have presented a need for attending to career counseling with male children and adolescents. Changes in the world of work have placed greater demands on individuals to be self-constructing in their careers. With this focus on the individual managing the career, people must be adaptable to the ever-changing work world. CCT explains these dimensions of career adaptability, and we have offered a framework for applying this theory to career counseling with male children and adolescents. Helping these individuals develop career adaptability is of primary importance in the new economy, and CCT offers promise as a theory for supporting this goal.

REFERENCES

Adler, A. (1937). Significance of early recollections. *International Journal of Individual Psychology, 3,* 283–287.

Arthur, M. B., & Rousseau, D. M. (1996). A career lexicon for the 21st century. *Academy of Management Executive, 10*(4), 28–39. doi: 10.5465/AME.1996.3145317

Bettner, B. L., & Lew, A. (1996). *A parent's guide to understanding and motivating children.* Newton Centre, MA: Connexions Press.

Blustein, D. L. (1997). A context-rich perspective of career exploration across the life roles. *The Career Development Quarterly, 45,* 260–274.

Bluestein, D. L. (2006). *The psychology of working: A new perspective for career development, counseling, and public policy.* Hillsdale, NJ: Lawrence Erlbaum.

Blustein, D. L., & Flum H. (1999). A self-determination perspective of interests and exploration in career development. In M. L. Savickas & A. R. Spokane (Eds.), *Vocational interest: Meaning, measurement, and counseling use* (pp. 345–368). Palo Alto, CA: Davies-Black.

Brown, B. L. (2003). The benefits of career and technical education. *Trends and Issues Alert, 49.* Columbus, OH: ERIC Clearinghouse on Adult, Career, and Vocational Education.

Bruhn, (1990). Cognitive–perceptual theory and the projective use of autobiographical memory. *Journal of Personality Assessment, 55,* 95–114.

Bureau of Labor Statistics. (2011). *Working in the 21st century.* Retrieved from www.bls.gov

Cione, G. F., Coleburn, L. A., Fertuck, E. A., & Fraenkel, P. (2011). Psychodynamic play therapy with a six-year-old African American boy diagnosed with ADHD. *Journal of Infant, Child & Adolescent Psychotherapy, 10*(1), 130–143. doi: 10.1080/15289168.2011.576593.

Chapman, C., Laird, J., & KewalRamani, A. (2010). *Trends in high school dropout and completion rates in the United States: 1972–2008—Compendium report.* National Center for Education Statistics. Retrieved from http://nces.ed.gov/pubs2011/2011012.pdf

ChildTrends Databank (2011, February). *High school dropout rates: Indicators on children and youth.* Retrieved from www.childtrendsdatabank.org

Chusmir, L. H. (1990). Men who make nontraditional career choices. *Journal of Counseling and development, 69,* 11–16.

Cochran, J. L., Cochran, N. H., Nordling, W. J., McAdam, A., & Miller, D. T. (2010). Monitoring two boys' processes through the stages of child-centered play therapy. *International Journal of Play Therapy, 19*(2), 106–116. doi: 10.1037/a0019092.

Del Corso, J., & Rehfuss, M. C. (2011). The role of narrative in career construction theory. *Journal of Vocational Behavior, 79*(2), 334–339. doi: 10.1016/j.jvb.2011.04.003.

Ebberwein, C. A., Krieshok, T. S., Ulven, J. C., & Prosser, E. C. (2004). Voices in transition: Lessons on career adaptability. *The Career Development Quarterly, 52,* 292–308.

Ginzberg, E., Ginsburg, J. W., Axelrod, S., & Herma, J. L. (1951). *Occupational choice.* New York: Columbia University Press.

Gottfredson, L. S. (1981). Circumscription and compromise: A developmental theory of occupational aspirations. *Journal of Counseling Psychology Monograph, 28*(6), 545–579. doi: 10.1037/0022–0167.28.6.545.

Gottfredson, L. S. (2002). Gottfredson's theory of circumscription, compromise, and self-creation. In D. Brown & Associates (Eds.), *Career choice and development* (4th ed., pp. 85–148). San Francisco: Jossey-Bass.

Gray, K. (2009). *Getting real: Helping teens find their future* (2nd ed.). Thousand Oaks, CA: Corwin Press.

Hall, D. T. (1996). *The career is dead—Long live the career.* San Francisco, CA: Jossey Bass.

Hartung, P. J., Porfeli, E. J., & Vondracek, F. W. (2005). Child vocational development: A review and reconsideration. *Journal of Vocational Behavior, 66,* 385–419. doi: 10.1016/j.jvb.2004.05.006.

Hartung, P. J., Porfeli, E. J., & Vondracek, F. W. (2008). Career adaptability in childhood. *The Career Development Quarterly, 57,* 63–74.

Heckman, J. J., & LaFontaine, P. A. (2007). *The American high school graduation rate: Trends and levels.* The Institute for the Study of Labor. Retrieved from http://ftp.iza.org/dp3216.pdf

Helwig, A. A. (2008). From childhood to adulthood: A 15-year longitudinal career development study. *The Career Development Quarterly, 57,* 38–50.

Holland, J. L. (1992). *Making vocational choices: A theory of vocational personalities and work environment* (2nd ed.). Odessa, FL: Psychological Assessment Resources.

Keller, B. K., & Whiston, S. C. (2008). The role of parental influences on young adolescents' career development. *Journal of Career Assessment, 16,* 198–217. doi: 10.1177/1069072707313206.

Koen, J., Klehe, U.-C., Van Vianen, A. E. M., Zikic, J., & Nauta, A. (2010). Job-search strategies and reemployment quality: The impact of career adaptability. *Journal of Vocational Behavior, 77*(1), 126–139. doi: 10.1016/j.jvb.2010.02.004.

Kottman, T. (2003). *Partners in play: An Adlerian approach to play therapy* (2nd ed.). Alexandria, VA: American Counseling Association.

Krumboltz, J. D. (2009). The happenstance learning theory. *Journal of Career Assessment, 17,* 135–154. doi: 10.1177/1069072708328861.

Landreth, G. L. (1991). *Play therapy: The art of the relationship.* Bristol, PA: Accelerate Development.

Lease, S. H. (2003) Testing a model of men's nontraditional occupational choices. *Career Development Quarterly, 51,* 244–258.

Noack, P., Kracke, B, Gniewosz, & Dietrich, J. (2010). Parental and school effects on students' occupational exploration: A longitudinal and multilevel analysis. *Journal of Vocational Behavior, 77,* 50–57. doi: 10.1016/j.jvb.2010.02.006.

Paone, T. R., & Douma, K. B. (2009). Child-centered play therapy with a seven-year-old boy diagnosed with intermittent explosive disorder. *International Journal of Play Therapy, 18*(1), 31–44. doi: 10.1037/a0013938.

Parsons, F. (1909). *Choosing a vocation.* Boston: Houghton-Mifflin.

Pastore, V. L. (2010). A hero's journey: A boy who lost his parents and found himself. In E. Gil, E. Gil (Eds.), *Working with children to heal interpersonal trauma: The power of play* (pp. 117–148). New York: Guilford Press.

Pollard, K. (2011, April). *The gender gap in college enrollment and graduation.* Population Reference Bureau. Retrieved from http://www.prb.org/Articles/2011/gender-gap-in-education.aspx

Rehfuss, M. C. (2009). The future career autobiography: A narrative measure of career intervention effectiveness. *The Career Development Quarterly, 58,* 82–90.

Roe, A. (1954). A new classification of occupations. *Journal of Counseling Psychology, 1,* 215–220. doi: 10.1037/h0061426.

Rottinghaus, P. J., Day, S. X., & Borgen, F. H. (2005). The Career Futures Inventory: A measure of career-related adaptability and optimism. *Journal of Career Assessment, 13*(1), 3–24. doi: 10.1177/1069072704270271.

Savickas, M. L. (2002). The theory and practice of career construction. In. S. D. Brown & R. W. Lent (Eds.), *Career development and counseling* (4th ed., pp. 149–205). San Francisco: Jossey-Bass.

Savickas, M. L. (2005). The theory and practice of career construction. In S. D. Brown & R. W. Lent (Eds.), *Career development and counseling* (pp. 42–70). Hoboken, NJ: John Wiley.

Savickas, M. L. (2011). *Career counseling.* Washington, DC: American Psychological Association.

Savickas, M. L. (in press). Career construction. In S. D. Brown, & R. W. Lent (Eds.) *Career development and counseling: Putting theory and research to work* (2nd ed.). Hoboken, NJ: John Wiley & Sons.

Schultheiss, D. E. P. (2003). A relational approach to career counseling: Theoretical integration and practical application. *Journal of Counseling & Development, 81,* 301–310.

Singer, J. L., & Salovey, P. (1991). Organized knowledge structures and personality: Person schemas, self-schemas, prototypes, and scripts. In M. J. Horowitz

(Ed.), *Person schemas and maladaptive interpersonal patterns* (pp. 33–79). Chicago: University of Chicago Press.

Super, D. E. (1957). *The psychology of careers.* New York: Harper & Row.

Super, D. E. (1990). A life-span, life-space approach to careers. In D. Brown, L. Brooks, & Associates (Eds.), *Career choice and development* (2nd ed., pp. 197–261). San Francisco: Jossey-Bass.

Super, D. E., & Kansel, E. G. (1981). Career development in adulthood: Some theoretical problems and a possible solution. *British Journal of Guidance & Counseling, 9,* 194–201.

Super, D. E., Savickas, M. L., & Super, C. M. (1996). The life-span, life-space approach to careers. In S. D. Brown & R. W. Lent (Eds.), *Career development and counseling* (3rd ed., pp. 121–178). San Francisco: Jossey-Bass.

Trice, A. D., Hughes, M. A., Odom, C., Woods, K., & McClellan, N. C. (1995). The origins of children's career aspirations: IV. Testing hypotheses from four theories. *The career Development Quarterly, 43,* 307–322.

Tyndall-Lind, A., Landreth, G. L., & Giordano, M. A. (2001). Intensive group play therapy with child witnesses of domestic violence. *International Journal of Play Therapy, 10*(1), 53–83. doi: 10.1037/h0089443.

U.S. Census Bureau. (2009). The 2012 statistical abstract. Retrieved from http://www.census.gov/compendia/statab/2012/tables/12s0281.pdf

U.S. Department of Labor. (2008). *Number of jobs held, labor market activity, and earnings growth among the youngest baby boomers: Results from a longitudinal survey.* Retrieved from http://www.bls.gov/news.release/pdf/nlsoy.pdf

Vilhjalmsdottir, G. (2010). Occupational thinking and its relation to school dropout. *Journal of Career Development, 37*(4), 677–691. doi: 10.1177/0894845309357052.

Watson, M., & McMahon, M. (2005). Children's career development: A research review from a learning perspective. *Journal of Vocational Behavior, 67,* 119–132. doi: 10.1016/j.jvb.2004.08.011.

APPENDIX A

Career Story Interview

1. How can I help you in constructing your career?
2. Who do you admire/Whom did you admire when growing up (depending on the age of the boy)? Tell me about three heroes or role models.

    a. What do you admire about each of these heroes/role models?
    b. In what ways are you like these heroes/role models?
    c. In what ways are you different from each of these people?

3. What magazines do you read regularly? What do you like best about those magazines? What television shows do you watch? Why?
4. Tell me about your favorite book/movie. What's the story in the book/movie?

5. What type of activities do you enjoy doing in your spare time? What do you enjoy about these hobbies?

6. What are your favorite subjects? What do you like about these subjects? What are your least favorite subjects? What do you dislike about these subjects?

7. Tell me about your earliest memories. In particular, I'd like to hear about things you recall happening to you when you were approximately 6 years old or younger.

   a. If the (local paper) were going to publish this story, what would be the headline?

Part II: Relationship Development and Relationship Concerns

6

Relationship Development With Family and Friends

CAROLINE S. BOOTH, MIRIAM L. WAGNER, AND ROBIN G. LILES

Carol Gilligan (1993) was one of the first theorists to suggest a gendered approach to human development. Her inclusion of gender as a salient factor in development remains a valuable beginning point for any discussion of relationship development. While many consider relationships to be a feminine domain, researchers recognize that relationships exist across all individuals (Way, 2011). Males, from childhood to adolescence, have some of the most complex and developmentally important relationships, which have the power to affect their self-concept and interpersonal skills lifelong. These relationships might be especially significant in understanding young males as statistics show this population to be more at risk for academic, social, and emotional problems (Watts & Borders, 2005).

Culturally, boys are believed, and even expected, to be autonomous, independent, activity-oriented, and "emotionally illiterate" (Way, 2011). Some have suggested that this stems from an evolutionary perspective on gender that stipulates that males are inherently more aggressive and females are more nurturing as a result of their biological destinies (Lim & Ang, 2009). This belief combined with social expectations about toughness seemingly makes emotional expression and connection among boys of any age somewhat taboo. However, researchers have noted with increasing consistency how boys have complex relational existences that are unique and evolve over the life span.

This chapter will examine the social and relational development of boys from childhood to the teenage years. Familial relationships of boys will be discussed along with peer friendships and social networks. Both familial and peer relationships will be examined in the context of childhood and adolescence. Next, counseling implications will be shared for the practitioner working with these populations of males.

FAMILY NETWORKS

Scholars of human development have long understood the importance of family on the development of children and their self-concept (Hay & Ashman, 2003). In fact, it has been suggested that early family relationships become the model by which other relationships develop and evolve. Bowlby's (1977, 1988) attachment theory provides a useful framework for understanding the importance of these early relationships. Bowlby believed that children in infancy respond to their caretaker's behavioral patterns, and this forms the foundation for the first internal representation of self. Building on attachment theory, emotional security theory (Davies & Cummings, 1994) extends Bowlby's ideas about caretaker relationships to include all family relationships as influential to the interpersonal relationship development process. These early familial representations evolve into a working model for attachment that children generalize to relationships with others across the life span (Ma & Huebner, 2008). Positive relationships with caretakers and family members can translate into emotional security, psychological well-being, and good interpersonal skills (NICHD Early Child Care Research Network, 2009). Conversely, conflictual parent–child relationships can interfere with a child's social relationships, result in chronic stress, or contribute to maladaptive behaviors (Cummings, Schermerhorn, Keller, & Davies, 2006; Simon & Furman, 2010).

Childhood

Parental relationships are known to be integral to the development of self-concept in children (Hattie, 1992). Self-concept is considered an important factor because of the positive correlation between self-concept and achievement, motivation, and self-regulation and a myriad of other developmental processes such as racial identity (Hay, 2003). As such, those children whose parents have a more positive opinion and relationship with their child, will, in turn, have a higher self-concept. Conversely, those children with a weaker or more negative parental relationship features are theoretically more likely to experience less desired developmental outcomes. Children with high self-concept tend to meet with greater academic and social success, while those with lower self-concept often have lowered aspirations, negative attitudes, and external locus of control (Hay & Ashman, 2003). It is also believed that the influence of the parental relationship on self-concept is strongest during childhood (Hay, 2003).

These theoretical suppositions have been supported in multiple research findings studying the impact of parental attitudes and beliefs on the development of boys. Much of this research has focused on boys displaying deviant behavior. For instance, more negative parental relationships and harsh parental disciplinary styles have been found to be correlated with anxiety/depression symptoms (Alanko et al., 2009), attachment insecurity (Allen, Porter, McFarland, McElhaney, & Marsh, 2007), and a myriad of unwanted behavioral displays (Tremblay, Tremblay, & Saucier, 2004) in boys. These negative behaviors, in turn, can lead to further relationship difficulties with parents whose sons ultimately feel unaccepted and less loved (Tremblay et al., 2004).

Although most parents would like to believe that they treat their male and female children the same, some believe that parents exert different influences on sons than they do on daughters (Hay & Ashman, 2003). Butler-Por (1987) reported that parental expectations were higher for sons than for daughters. Hay and Ashman (2003) substantiated this finding in their research that studied 380 adolescent males and 275 adolescent females. They discovered that parental relationships were important for the emotional stability of males but not for that of females. The authors suggested this might be because males, more so than females, are expected to adhere to stereotypical gender roles. As a result, the authors hypothesized that parents may be showing more attention and responsiveness toward their sons' activities and achievements than their daughters', suggesting a parental preference based on gender.

This idea that parents show attention to male children as it relates to gender norm expression seems to be somewhat substantiated in an analysis of the gender role literature. Multiple researchers have documented that males expressing gender atypical traits often describe poor parental relationships in childhood when compared to those who express gender compliant traits (Alanko et al., 2009; Isay, 1999). These poor relationships are often characterized by coldness from fathers and overcontrolling attitudes from mothers who may each be reacting to their own personal fears about their son's behaviors (Alanko et al., 2009) and feelings of parental failure (Tremblay et al., 2004). Isay (1999) reported similar findings through case examples describing how homosexual men reported that nonsupportive parental relationships in childhood negatively affected their interpersonal development and emotional resilience. Specifically, many reported parental efforts to force display of more typical gendered behaviors.

Additional research has investigated the importance of the separate maternal and paternal relationship to boys, although this research has been more conflicting with some reporting the paternal relationship as more significant, while another research reports the opposite (Stolz, Olsen, Barber, & Clifford, 2010). A sampling of this research reveals findings suggesting that maternal relationships with boys are negatively correlated with dimensions such as aggression (MacKinnon-Lewis, Starnes, Volling, & Johnson 1997), while the father–son relationship has been described as more conditional with some sons reporting paternal relationships characterized by more judgment and one-sided communication (Tremblay et al., 2004). However, it is believed that the father–son relationship can be integral to the development of the boy and that this reciprocal relationship can help both father and son develop across the life span (Diamond, 2007). Stolz et al. (2010) believe that the relative significance of the father–son and mother–son relationship to a boy's development is largely moderated by child personality, which may explain the mixed research in this area. All of these findings recognize that both parental relationships are significant to boys' overall development and well-being in childhood.

A substantial body of literature has also examined the importance of other familial relationships to boys. Of particular significance are sibling relationships, which are known to have a substantial impact on the development of the individual. These sibling relationships are believed to be an extension of parent–child relationship patterns (Brody, 2004, Hoffman, 2010, MacKinnon-Lewis et al., 1997). These relationships shape the individual through both direct and indirect pathways. Although the context for siblings can be similar, parental treatment, birth order, and gender all create a clearly unique relational experience (Hoffman, 2010). Male siblings are believed to be more conflictual and antagonistic when compared to female siblings who are believed to be more supportive and affectionate (Hoffman, 2010). Personality variables can also moderate the quality of the sibling relationship.

Furman and Buhrmester (1985) identified four dimensions that affect the quality of the sibling relationship. These dimensions are present between each sibling dyad and are described as warmth/proximity, relative power/status, conflict, and rivalry. Other authors have identified the balance between emotional affection/empathy and conflict (Hoffman, 2010) as significant in sibling relationships because these dimensions provide a foundation for development of interpersonal conflict skills. Borrowing from Bandura's (1973) ideas on social learning, these early sibling relationships provide a model for relationships outside the family, and these relationship models have been found to be either positive or negative in nature. This "training ground" for relationships is actually so powerful that quality of sibling relationships has been shown to predict future adult well-being (Bank, Burreston, & Snyder, 2004). Boys, particularly if they are older, are more likely to be involved in bullying activities toward their sibling (Hoffman, 2010). These sibling conflicts seem to be particularly significant and predictive for boys for future peer conflict and other antisocial developmental outcomes (Bank et al., 2004; MacKinnon-Lewis et al., 1997).

Grandparents are another familial relationship that has been gaining increasing attention in recent years. However, much of this research is centered on grandparents raising grandsons and does not address the role a grandparent relationship has on a developing boy. There is a definite need for continued research in this area.

Adolescence

Erikson (1963) describes adolescence as a time of identity formation but also a time for connectedness, as relationships remain an integral part of the human experience (Maslow, 1968). For adolescents, this relational connectedness helps to define the self in context. As such, it is a culturally held belief that peers emerge as the most important relationships for adolescent males. However, there is conflicting research regarding whether parental or peer relationships are more influential for adolescents (Hay & Ashman, 2003). Emphasizing the importance of both relationships, Feiring and Taska (1996) liken the importance of both parent and peer relationships as a partnership in the adolescent male's socialization and development. This view validates the importance of each, although the nature of the boy's relationship to the parent and family can change during this period. Some research has even highlighted that parent–child conflict is greatest during the time of adolescence as young males seek to become more autonomous (Campione-Barr & Smetana, 2010). However, positive parental relationships and support of adolescent independence during this time correlates with the development of an adolescent self that is more synchronized with parental values and ideals (Zentner & Renauld, 2007). Conversely, adolescents whose parents are more controlling and restrictive are more likely to construct an ideal self in opposition to parents' beliefs and values.

These findings seem to be replicated when examining literature related to adolescent males and parenting. The parental relationship has been shown to be beneficial or detrimental to young males, depending on the quality and nature of the relationship. Harsh discipline, authoritarian parenting styles, and low parental involvement have been shown to correlate with more negative youth outcomes such as violence (Margolin, Youga, & Ballou, 2002), school misbehavior, and suicide (Fotti, Katz, Afifi, & Cox, 2006). Conversely, supportive parenting and more positive parent–son relationships have been shown to predict positive behaviors such as self-regulation (Moilanen, Shaw, Fitzpatrick, 2010). Parental relationship has also been found to be a significant factor in adolescents' peer relationships as parents frequently attempt to manage their sons' peer networks with varying degrees of success (Mounts, 2007; Soenens, Vansteenkiste, & Niemiec, 2009).

During adolescence, sibling relationships retain the significance they held in childhood, but research in this area is somewhat limited (Campione-Barr & Smetana, 2010). It has been reported that adolescents actually report the most conflict with siblings during this period than with any other relationship (Campione-Barr & Smetana, 2010). Positive sibling relationships have been shown to be positively related to dimensions such as prosocial behaviors and self-regulation (Padilla-Walker, Harper, & Jensen, 2010), positive value acquisition (Kretschmer & Pike, 2010), and academic achievement (Yuan, 2009), as well as less-valued dimensions such as the deviant behaviors of delinquency and bullying (Yuan, 2009) and other risky behaviors (East & Hanna, 2009). Continuing the trend from childhood, sibling adolescent relationships are still considered important to well-being although the strength of this effect in context with other dimensions is still being studied (Yuan, 2009).

While parents and sibling relationships are known to be significant to adolescents, grandparent relationships have also emerged as significant for adolescents. Multiple studies have documented the importance of the grandparent–adolescent relationship (Attar-Schwartz, Tan, & Buchanan, 2009; Flouri, Buchanan, Tan, Griggs, & Attar-Schwartz, 2010; Pratt, Norris, Lawford, & Arnold, 2010). These relationships have been found to have important moderating influences on stress and pathology as well serving other important functions in the developmental lives of adolescents. However, how these relationships may vary based on male versus female grandchildren has been largely unstudied.

PEER NETWORKS

In addition to the complexities inherent in family relationships, peer relationships are also known to be a complex endeavor, particularly for children (Rudolph, 2010). These relationships are known to be important factors in children's emotional and psychological development (NICHD Early Child Care Research Network, 2009). There has been extensive study of peer networks and how they influence the developing male. Interestingly, gender differences in peer affiliation are evident from as early as toddlerhood, and these differences tend to persist and magnify across the life span.

Childhood

Numerous researchers have studied the peer networks and relational patterns of children and noted significant gender differences (Poulin &

Pederson, 2007; Rose, 2007; Rose & Rudolph, 2006). Rose and Rudolph (2006) examined this body of research and found that both girls and boys interact with same-sex peers much more commonly than with opposite-sex peers, with these preferences emerging as early as age 3 (Serbin, Moller, Gulko, Powlishta, & Coltrane, 1994). These same-sex peer groupings do show functional differences based on gender, and this has been recorded as beginning in preschool as well. Multiple researchers have described how boys engaged in free play were more likely than girls to play in same-sex groups, whereas girls were more likely to play in same-sex dyads (Fabes, Martin, & Harnish, 2003; Gest, Davidson, Rulison, Moody, & Welsh, 2007). This has led to the conclusion that boys form more closely knit and distinctive peer groups than girls (Fabes et al., 2003). Rose and Rudolph (2006) also discovered that girls tend to spend more time in social conversation, while boys tend to engage in more organized (such as sports and games) and "rough and tumble" play. Finally, boy peer relationships are believed to involve less reciprocal relationships and more competitive-type play than the relationships of girls (Rose & Rudolph, 2006). Interestingly, they found that these sex differences in relating to peers emerged by age 6, and these differences became more pronounced with age.

Emotional intimacy does not readily come to mind when discussing male peer networks because it has often been assumed that boy's friendships were in a deficit position to girl's friendships because of a perceived lack of intimacy among boys (Underwood, 2007). However, Way (2011) argues that boys experience incredibly intimate peer friendships that peak during early and middle adolescence. These relationships are characterized by emotional connecting, discussions of hopes and dreams, and secret sharing. Other researchers have reported findings that reinforce this notion and suggest that many of these intimate relationships are formed and nurtured through shared activities (McNelles & Connolly, 1999). These activities can be very action-oriented such as participating in a joint task, sporting activity, or shared video gaming (Kiselica & Englar-Carlson, 2010).

Boys have also been documented to join and relate in more group activities than females, who forge supportive relationships through more longer-lasting, dyadic activities (Maccoby, 1990; Rose & Rudolph, 2006). This idea that boys are more likely to engage in larger group friendship activities has been repeatedly validated in the literature (Rose, 2007). However, this belief is moderated by the idea that boys may have larger peer groups, whereas girls may have more reciprocal friendships, as boy peer groups can frequently consist of not only friends, but acquaintances and playmates as well (Rose, 2007). It should be noted that these larger peer groups are believed to be more beneficial for boys than girls because of the potential for disclosure-based conflict in groups of females (Rose, 2007).

Maccoby (1998) surmises these gendered play experiences create a childhood where boys and girls essentially grow up in different worlds with different peer networks, play styles, and relational styles. It has been hypothesized that this pattern is nearly universal and continues throughout childhood to early adolescence (Gest et al., 2007). This segregation is also noted to perpetuate gender stereotypes and accentuate the development of gendered goals and values through the process of separate socialization experiences for boys and girls (Maccoby, 1998). It should be noted that a hypothesized by-product of this separated peer structure is increased difficulty with opposite-sex friendships in adolescence (Gest et al., 2007).

Very little is known about opposite-sex friendships in childhood because there is scant research on this type of peer network, which is considered rare (Rose, 2007). Most available research substantiates this idea, with mixed-gender friendship rates reported as low as 5% (Rose, 2007). However, McDougall and Hymel (2007) examined *children's perceptions* of friendships and reported that almost all thought mixed-gender friendships were possible and 90% believed that they had a cross-gender friend. However, it is believed that these cross-gender friends are rarely children's closest reciprocal friends, and it has been suggested that many times these friendships exist outside of the regular peer group and are often "underground" in nature (Rose, 2007). Interestingly, McDougall and Hymel (2007) discovered that cross-gendered friendships were described as more "boy-like" by both girls and boys in the study, seeming to suggest that girls moderated their play style, but boys did not. This could provide validation for Gest et al. (2007), who predict future difficulties for boys in opposite-sex friendships and dating relationships based on their lack of awareness and familiarity with feminine ways of being (Rose, 2007).

Although gender is salient in peer group structure, it seems less relevant in terms of social hierarchies of children. Multiple ethnographic studies have reported that both boys and girls have distinct social hierarchies in their peer groups (Gest et al., 2007). These hierarchies are first evident in preschool and persist throughout childhood. Adler and Adler (1996) studied third to sixth graders and identified four prominent status levels among both boys and girls. These levels were *popular, wannabes, middle group*, and *social isolates*. It is believed that girls' status hierarchies are more often connection oriented and based on language, social exclusion, or ridicule, whereas boys' hierarchies are more tightly knit and based on tangible dominance dimensions such as sports (Gest et al., 2007; Rose & Rudolph, 2006). However, research findings indicate that such gender differences in peer network hierarchies might be small in magnitude when compared to the overall similarities between these two populations (Gest et al., 2007).

Adolescence

As previously stated, the primary goal of adolescence is identity development (Erikson, 1963), which is operationalized as "the process of establishing oneself as unique from others, but in the context of close relationships" (McLean, Breen, & Fournier, 2010, p. 166). It has long been reported that adolescent peer networks are important to interpersonal development and well-being (Laursen, Furman, & Mooney, 2006). This has been described as a need to feel a sense of belonging and be a part of a group (Dixon, Scheidegger, & McWhirter, 2009), as well as a time when interpersonal connections can shift from parents to friends (Laursen et al., 2006). This process is known as individuation (Grotevant & Cooper, 1985), and it underscores the importance of relationships to identity development, self-concept, and well-being.

It has been suggested that adolescent males change and expand their peer networks in several ways from the social networks of childhood. Researchers believe that adolescent males gradually move away from more intimate same-sex friendships as they reach later adolescence in favor of more culturally appropriate male relationships based on dominance and competition (Way, 2011). This stereotypical male relationship experience is also characterized by toughness, emotional restriction, and denial of emotional needs (Feder, Levant, & Dean, 2010). Adolescent males have commented that they consciously avoid any displays of physical or emotional pain and tease others who do not conform to this standard in compliance with the masculine norm, even though they recognize this to be hurtful (Oransky & Marecek, 2009). This finding and other research reveals the pressures adolescent males feel to demonstrate and embody this masculine ideal (Tolman, Spencer, Harmon, Rosen-Reynoso, & Striepe, 2004). This social conformity speaks to the need for peer approval that becomes increasingly important for boys as they progress through adolescence (Yoo, 2009). This peer approval has been found to be so influential that adolescent males have reported engaging in behaviors such as exercising or tattooing to fit into the peer norm (Yoo, 2009). This effect has been labeled peer contagion whereby adolescents affiliate with peers who are similar, but these similar attitudes, behaviors, and preferences in turn heighten as a result of participation in the peer group (Cohen & Prinstein, 2006). It is believed that this emulation will result in an increase in status both socially and internally (Cohen & Prinstein, 2006). This belief was substantiated in an experimental design conducted by Cohen and Prinstein (2006), who found that adolescent males incorporated or internalized behaviors and attitudes when higher status peers (versus lower status peers) endorsed them.

Adolescent males also begin to create more opposite-sex friendships, also known as heterosocial interactions (Grover, Nangle, Serwik, & Zeff,

2007) although same-sex friendships still dominate (Poulin & Pederson, 2007). This peer group transition to more mixed-sex groups allows adolescents to practice adult roles and behaviors and increase social competence (Grover et al., 2007). This transition is also viewed as an important developmental step that correlates to overall well-being (Grover et al., 2007). Adolescent males who enjoy higher social status, display antisocial behavior (perceived as independent behavior), and physically mature sooner typically initiate mixed-sex friendship networks sooner than their peers (Poulin & Pederson, 2007). All of these qualities seem to substantiate the notion of a more masculine ideal.

This masculine relationship style even spills over into the heterosexual dating realm where competition and power aspects of interpersonal relationships can supersede the emotional aspects (Giordano, Longmore, & Manning, 2006). As a result, adolescent males are frequently uncomfortable with these emotional and intimate relational aspects and project a "false self" to others that can be very different from the subjective self (Sippola, Buchanan, & Kehoe, 2007). This can make the transition to heterosexual dating relationships very difficult and confusing and substantiates notions that heterosexual masculinity comes at the expense of denigrating the feminine (Cohan, 2009). Conversely, adolescent males who have the ability to express emotions, provide emotional support to peers, and the capability to self disclose are more likely to successfully engage in heterosexual, romantic relationships (Sippola et al., 2007).

This transition to heterosexual dating relationships is even more confusing for male adolescents as recent social customs dictate that sexual experience is a rite of passage and key identity component for the young male. Rather than waiting until marriage as their grandparents did, the new expectation is most males will have sexual experience, including intercourse, by the age of 18 (Hofferth & Hayer, 1987). As such, the heterosexual masculine ideal becomes heightened through sexual "conquests" that advance the status and dominance of a male within their like-minded peer groups (Cohan, 2009). Some researchers have even suggested that these fraternal peer groups powerfully socialize adolescent male's attitudes and beliefs about sexuality, women, and romantic relationships, and this shared value system can unwittingly serve to advance misogynistic and homophobic attitudes (Cohan, 2009). This dominant heterosexual masculine ideology also makes identity development for homosexual, bisexual, and questioning (HBQ) males all the more complicated as peer groups exert considerable influence for these individuals to conform to group expectations (Wilson, Harper, Hidalgo, Jamil, Torres, & Fernandez, 2010).

A final area of adolescent peer groups concerns the concept of deviant peers (Soenens et al., 2009). Many adolescents of both genders begin to affiliate with peers involved in problem/antisocial behaviors, and there is a known correlation between association and participation in these behaviors (Soenens et al., 2009). Those adolescents with poor parental relationships and those exposed to uncorrected coercive relationships from their siblings can be especially prone to these negative peer encounters (Hoffman, 2010).

COUNSELING IMPLICATIONS

Beginning in the 1990s, gender scholars became increasingly aware of the psychology of boys and men (Kiselica & Englar-Carlson, 2010). Following years of specialized study of females spurned by the feminist movement, researchers began taking a closer look at the "new psychology of men" with an emphasis on the restrictive socialization processes shaping development of males and masculinity (Levant & Pollack, 1995). Multiple constructs related to male development have subsequently been studied. Although traditional ideals of masculinity continue to persist in society, this research has created a new understanding whereby some of the components of the masculine ideal, such as emotional restriction, are now believed to be less psychological healthy (Kiselica, Englar-Carson, Horne, & Fisher, 2008). In fact, some have said that the strict male ideological view of relationships can actually handicap boys and adolescents from understanding and experiencing their emotional world and vulnerabilities (Kindlon & Thompson, 1999).

While multiple researchers have recognized the limitations of narrow male ideologies, some have cautioned against approaching the counseling relationship with this deficit approach. Kiselica and Englar-Carlson (2010) have created a positive psychology/positive masculinity model of psychotherapy for boys and men that recognizes the unique strengths of males throughout the life span. These authors report that the masculine ideology has positive value, and they have identified 10 unique strengths from this paradigm that can be useful starting points for relating and connecting to boys and males in counseling. One of these strengths is an understanding of how boys' unique relational lives are constructed. Some of their recommendations related to relationships are for practitioners to recognize male's ways of caring, relating, and empathizing. Specifically, they state how boys' relational and empathic styles are more action oriented, where activities and doing are central ways of expression. Other noteworthy strengths of male relationships are a preference for group paradigms and the use of humor to attain intimacy. Kiselica and Englar-Carlson also recognize that boys are daring, risk-taking, and like to be heroes. It is believed that focusing on these positive paradigm dimensions in counseling can provide boys and adolescent males with building blocks to define the self in such a way that promotes optimum well-being. They encourage practitioners to approach counseling with boys in such a way that not only troubles can be shared but strengths can be discussed as well. Boys can be affirmed for who they are within their own gender paradigm. Practitioners can do this by using the male relational style in the therapeutic relationship as such and implementing more activity-based counseling techniques.

Another researcher has noted similar recommendations for work with boys. In his book, *Boys of few words: Raising our sons to communicate and connect*, Cox (2006) noted that boys are more functional versus relational communicators. While this task-oriented style is effective in some circumstances, this can create emotional language deficits where boys struggle to articulate and understand their emotions. Cox believes that the by-product of this is that boys can become limited in initiating and sustaining relationships and can even become disinterested or disengaged by those expressive relationship components that they do not understand. As such, helping boys obtain the tools and language to effectively communicate relationally can be an important intervention for boys. Counselors and other helping professionals can also assist parents and other key figures (e.g., teachers) in understanding how their sons communicate and relate to others.

Although it is known that parental support is vital to the development of boys' self-concept, it is also believed that the early parental relationship provides a model and building block for subsequent relationships (sibling, peer, teacher, romantic, etc.), self-efficacy, and ultimately, life satisfaction (Danielson, Samdal, Hetland, & Wold, 2009). As such, it is important to recognize the springboard that these early relationships provide in terms of relationship competence and male behavior (MacKinnon-Lewis et al., 1997). Therefore, any of these relationship dyads could be powerful entry points for counselors. The cumulative nature of these relationships also underscores the importance of the family in providing a healthy foundational structure for boys to relate to the world. Parents, siblings, and grandparents need to recognize what is right with their boys to help them internalize these beliefs into their self-concept (Kiselica & Englar-Carlson, 2010). Counselors can work with these families to help them appreciate and understand boys' unique way of relating and provide tools to increase the qualitative experience of each member in these relationships.

From the research on the importance of sibling relationships to future well-being, it is known that empathy is an important component of conflict resolution and prosocial behavior (Hoffman, 2010). This prosocial behavior is negatively correlated with aggression, bullying, and other less-desired behavioral dimensions. As such, it would be important for the practitioner to be aware of the power that empathic understanding in relationships can have on the functioning of boys and adolescents. Being aware of other's feelings provides an important linkage between behavior and consequences that can be of great benefit to boys and their socioemotional understanding of relationships. Kiselica and Englar-Carlson (2010) describe males' empathic processes as being more action oriented, where they tend to take action based on another's point of view. Understanding this expression of empathy would be important for counselors to communicate with the relational partners of boys.

Any discussion of relational development of males needs to include recognition of the multicultural components that provide context and nuance to relationships. These cultural constructs are described as the beliefs, customs, practices, and social behaviors of a particular nation or people. These beliefs and customs permeate throughout people's interactions with one other. According to Robinson-Wood (2009), "the internalization of cultural values is influenced by acculturation, migration status, income, education, generational status, and racial/ethnic identity development" (p. 8). While a discussion of how each multicultural dimension influences a boy's relationship development is beyond the scope of this chapter, it should be noted that the interrelationship of these contextual dimensions influences how boys socially construct their relationship systems and masculine ideologies (Kiselica & Englar-Carlson, 2010).

In summary, boys and adolescent males use their early relationships to create their gendered selves. The relationships they formulate with family and friends serve as a foundation and context for identity development, as well as a starting point for behaviors and beliefs that can persist lifelong. This underscores the importance of each of these early relationships to the young male, although the relative importance of each will no doubt be studied for generations to come. The most important implication for practitioners will be to recognize the importance these relationships hold for young males as they navigate the complex realities of growing up in the 21st century.

Counselors are always in a key position to help educate those who interact with boys and adolescent males. Through educating parents, siblings, school personnel, and other key figures in boys' lives, perhaps the frequency of negative outcomes for boys can be reduced. Ultimately, everyone needs to pay attention and empower boys for their positive ways of being and relating to others. Through these small advocacy efforts, perhaps the connotation of "boys will be boys" can change to recognize the unique strengths and rich relational existences that each boy possesses.

CASE STUDY: FINDING HIS PLACE: NATHANIEL, 5 YEARS OLD

The following case study describes two family counseling sessions with a family presenting with "child misbehavior." The case is developed in three parts with corresponding teaching questions. This case would be useful in counselor education family counseling programs.

Part A

Sarah was completing the last of her required hours for counseling licensure when she met the Betts family. This Betts were a family of four. When they arrived in the counseling office, Sarah invited the parents to sit on the sofa. She also brought the children (sister and brother) over to a shelf with toys. Both children immediately engaged in play, with the older daughter quietly introducing one toy after another to her younger brother.

Returning to the office sitting area, Sarah began gathering initial assessment data. Sarah learned that the mother (Angela) and father (Dan) were married for 8 years. Both parents worked out of the home. They were Caucasian. Dan was an automotive technician, and Angela worked as a medical record-keeper at the local hospital. Angela reported that both she and Dan completed 2-year programs at the local community college to obtain their job skills. Neither parent had attended a 4-year college/university. Angela also stated that she and Dan were married shortly after graduating high school, and that they had known one another "since we were kids."

Angela and Dan also talked about their two children, Alison and Nathaniel. Alison was 10 years old. According to Angela and Dan, Alison was a "good little girl" who "never" gave them "problems." Angela went on to say that Alison was successful in networking with her friends and that she was an excellent student. Angela and Dan both readily agreed that she was a "blessing" to their family. Dan said, "Angela just loves her little brother, and she takes great care of him."

Nathaniel was 5 years old and had just entered kindergarten. As soon as Sarah initiated her line of questioning regarding Nathaniel, Angela and Dan became visibly less comfortable. Tears came to Angela's eyes, and with a quavering voice she said, "We are so worried about him! He gets in trouble all of the time, and look at this!" She handed Sarah a piece of paper on what was written: *Nathaniel had to sit in time-out twice today. Please work with him at home and let him know that school is serious and he has to pay attention.*

1. Although the information is sketchy, what are your initial and intuitive case conceptualizations regarding this family system?
2. Which family system theory or theories best supports your conceptualizations?
3. Thinking theoretically, and from your initial/intuitive case conceptualizations, develop a list of clarifying questions you would choose to address at this time in this case.

Part B

On observation, Sarah noted that Alison and Nathaniel were actively and positively engaged in quiet play. From her limited time, Sarah could not identify—nor sense—anything negatively outstanding in Nathaniel's behavior. In fact, on the contrary, Sarah was impressed with the children's obvious enjoyment of one another's company. Sarah described these thoughts to the parents, finishing with: "Well, Nathaniel certainly seems to be getting along well now."

"Yes," said Dan, "that's because he's with his sister. She can always calm him down."

"Alison is always like this," continued Angela. "I don't ever remember her getting into trouble. She's a straight-A student. She was a good baby, too, quiet and easy."

Sarah followed with questions about Nathaniel's earliest years. Angela and Dan described him as a "happy baby." They both were obviously pleased to report that he "walked early," and Dan went on to say that Nathaniel "loves sports." Dan admitted that he worried about his own athletic ability and whether he would be "up to helping" Nathaniel learn baseball, football, and basketball.

Sarah went on to ask if Nathaniel enjoyed friendships with other little boys his age. "Oh yes!" said Angela. "He plays with his cousin all the time. They're about the same age. His cousin is probably his best friend."

"What about before kindergarten, did Nathaniel attend day-care?" Sarah asked.

"No, he stayed with my mom," responded Dan. "He and his cousin both stayed with her. My sister and I paid my mom for her help with the kids. She didn't want any money, but we just felt like it was the right thing to do."

"What about your mother, then?" asked Sarah. "How would she describe Nathaniel?"

Dan responded, saying, "Oh man, she just loves him to death. Avery, too, that's his cousin."

"What about your sister," queried Sarah, "How do you think she views Nathaniel's behavior?"

Dan laughed. "Well, she's a little on the laid-back side. She's always saying 'boys will be boys!' No, I don't think she minds Nathaniel too much. I mean really, compared to Avery, Nathaniel is pretty easy-going."

At this point, Sarah was quiet. The only sound in the room was that of the children playing. When Dan was talking, Angela's eyes had been lowered, hands folded. After a short interval of silence, Angela's shoulders slumped, and she began to sob. Dan put his arm around her shoulders. The children stopped playing and stared at their mother.

Angela said through her tears, "It's hopeless. Nathaniel will never learn to be quiet and to behave in school."

Sarah softly asked, "And how long has Nathaniel been in school?"

"Six weeks," said Angela.

1. How would you describe Dan, Angela, Alison, and Nathaniel from a developmental point of view? What particular developmental challenges is each family member facing?
2. Thinking developmentally, how would you make sense of this family system?
3. Given these developmental perspectives, how would you proceed with this family?

Part C

Sarah was perplexed. Granted she had spent no direct time with Nathaniel, her conceptualizations largely stemmed from indirect observations as Nathaniel played with his sister. Furthermore, Angela and Dan had related nothing particularly concerning to Sarah. In fact, as a mother of three sons herself, Sarah was struck with Nathaniel's "normalcy." Angela and Dan, nor any professional observations, suggested to Sarah that Nathaniel had a behavioral problem.

On the other hand, Sarah found Angela's and Dan's apprehension and nervousness largely confusing, perhaps even misplaced. In particular, Sarah was concerned about Angela's tears, her clearly apparent worry and anxiety, and the effect it was having upon her family.

1. At this point, who do you believe is the "identified patient?"
2. How would you proceed with treatment planning for the "identified patient" and his or her family? Would you choose to involve the teacher in your plan?
3. What assessment plan would you put into place to ascertain treatment efficacy?

REFERENCES

Adler, P. A., & Adler, P. (1996). Dynamics of inclusion and exclusion in preadolescent cliques. *Social Psychology Quarterly, 58*(3), 145–162.

Alanko, K., Santtila, P., Witting, K., Varjonen, M., Jern, P., Johansson, A., von Der Pahlen, B., & Sandnabba, N. K. (2009). Psychiatric symptoms and same-sex sexual attraction and behavior in light of childhood gender atypical behavior and parental relationships. *Journal of Sex Research, 46*(5), 494–504. doi:10.1080/00224490902846487.

Allen, J. P., Porter, M., McFarland, C., McElhaney, K. B., & Marsh, P. (2007). The relation of attachment security to adolescents' paternal and peer relationships, depression, and externalizing behavior. *Child Development, 78*(4), 1222–1239. doi:10.1177/0143034304043688.

Attar-Schwartz, S., Tan-J, & Buchanan, A. (2009). Adolescents' perspectives on relationships with grandparents: The contribution of adolescent, grandparent, and parent-grandparent relationship variables. *Children and Youth Services Review, 31*(9), 1057–1066.

Bandura, A. (1973). *Aggression. A social teaming theory analysis.* Englewood Cliffs, NJ: Prentice Hall.

Bank, L., Burraston, B., & Snyder, J. (2004). Sibling conflict and ineffective parenting as predictors of adolescent boys' antisocial behavior and peer difficulties: Additive and interactional effects. *Formal of Research on Adolescence, 14*(1), 99–125. doi:10.1111/j.1532–7795.2004.01401005.x.

Bowlby, J. (1977). The making and breaking of affectional bonds. *British Journal of Psychiatry, 130*, 201–210.

Bowlby, J. (1988). *A secure base: Clinical applications of attachment theory.* London: Tavistock.

Brody, G. H. (2004). Siblings' direct and indirect contributions to child development. Current *Directions in Psychological Science, 13*(3), 124–126. doi:10.1111/j.0963–7214.2004.00289.x.

Butler-Por, N. (1987). *Underachievers in school: Issues and intervention.* Chichester, UK: John Wiley.

Campione-Barr, N., Smetana, J. G. (2010). Who said you could wear my sweater? Adolescent siblings conflicts and associations with relationships quality. *Child Development, 81*(2), 464–471. doi:10.1111/j.1467–8624.2009.01407.x.

Cohan, M. (2009). Adolescent heterosexual males talk about the role of male peer groups in their sexual decision-making. *Sexuality and Culture, 13*(3), 152–177. doi:10.1007/s12119–009-9052–3.

Cohen, G. L., & Prinstein, M. J. (2006). Peer contagion of aggression and health risk behavior among adolescent males: An experimental investigation of effect on public conduct and private attitudes. *Child Development, 77*, 967–983. doi:10.1111/j.1467–8624.2006.00913.x.

Cox, A. J. (2006). *Boys of few words.* New York: Guilford Press.

Cummings, E., Schermerhorn, A. C., Keller, P. S., & Davies, P. T. (2006). Parental depressive symptoms, children's representations of family relationships, and child adjustment. *Social Development, 17*(2), 278–305. doi:10.1111/j.1467–9507.2007.00425.x.

Danielson, A. G., Samdal, O., Hetland, J., & Wold, B. (2009). School-related social support and students' perceived life satisfaction. *Journal of Educational Research, 102*(4), 303–318.

Davies, P. T., & Cummings, E. M. (1994). Marital conflict and child adjustment: An emotional security hypothesis. *Psychological Bulletin, 116*, 387–411.

Diamond, M. J. (2007). *My father before me: How fathers and sons influence each other throughout their lives.* New York: Norton.

Dixon, A. L., Scheidegger, C., & McWhirter, J. J. (2009). The adolescent mattering experience: Gender variations in perceived mattering, anxiety, and depression. *Journal of Counseling & Development, 87*(3), 302–310.

East, P. L., & Hanna, M. D. (2009). Adolescents' relationships with siblings. In R. M. Lerner & L. Steinberg (Eds.), *Handbook of adolescent psychology* (pp. 43–73). Hoboken, NJ: John Wiley and Sons.

Erikson, E. H. (1963). *Childhood and society* (2nd ed.). New York: Norton.

Fabes, R. A., Martin, C. L., & Hanish, L. D. (2003). Qualities of young children's same-, other-, and mixed-sex play. *Child Development, 74*(3), 921–932.

Feder, J., Levant, R. F., & Dean, J. (2010). Boys and violence: A gender-informed analysis. *Psychology of Violence, 1*(8), 3–12. doi:10.1037/2152–0828.1.S.3.

Feiring, C., & Taska, L. S. (1996). Family self-concept: Ideas on its meaning. In B. A. Bracken (Ed.), *Handbook of self-concept: Development, social and clinical considerations* (pp. 317–373). New York: Wiley.

Flouri, E., Buchanan, A., Tan, J., Griggs, J., & Attar-Schwartz, S. (2010). Adverse life events, area socio-economic disadvantage, and adolescent psychopathology: The role of closeness to grandparents in moderating the effect of contextual stress. *The International Journal on the Biology of Stress, 13*(5), 402–412. doi:10.3109/10253891003671690.

Fotti, S. A., Katz, L. Y., Afifi, T. O., Cox, B. J. (2006). The associations between peer and parental relationships and suicidal behaviors in early adolescents. *The Canadian Journal of Psychiatry, 51*(11), 698–703.

Furman, W., & Buhrmester, D. (1985). Children's perception of the qualities of sibling relationships. *Child Development, 55,* 448–461.

Gest, S. D., Davidson, A. J., Rulison, K. L., Moody, J., & Welsh, J. A. (2007). Features of groups and status hierarchies in girls' and boys' early adolescent peer networks. *New Directions for Child and Adolescent Development, 118,* 43–60.

Gilligan, C. (1993). *In a different voice: Psychological theory and women's development.* Boston, MA: Harvard University Press.

Giordano, P. C., Longmore, M. A., & Manning, W. D. (2006). Gender and the meanings of adolescent romantic relationships: A focus on boys. *American Sociological Review, 71*(2), 260–287.

Grotevant, H. D., & Cooper, C. R. (1985). Patterns of interaction in family relationships and the development of identity exploration in adolescence. *Child Development, 56,* 415–428.

Grover, R. L., Nangle, D. W., Serwik, A., & Zeff, K. R. (2007). Girl friend, boy friend, Girl friend, boyfriend: Broadening our understanding of heterosocial competence. *Journal of Clinical Child and Adolescent Psychology, 36*(4), 491–502. doi:10.1080/15374410701651637.

Hattie, J. A. (1992). *Self-concept.* Hillsdale, NJ: Erlbaum.

Hay, I. (2003). Family strain, gender, and delinquency. *Sociological Perspectives, 46*(1), 107–135. doi:10.1525/sop.2003.46.1.107.

Hay, I., & Ashman, A. F. (2003). The development of adolescents' emotional stability and general self-concept: The interplay of parents, peers, and gender. *International Journal of Disability, Development, and Education, 50*(1), 77–91. doi:10.1080/1034912032000053359.

Hofferth, S. L. & Hayes, C. D. (1987). *Risking the future: Adolescent sexuality, pregnancy, and childbearing: Vol. 2. Working papers and statistical reports.* Washington, DC: National Academy Press.

Hoffman, L. (2010). The impact of opposite-sex younger siblings: A hypothesis concerning gender differences. *Journal of Infant, Child & Adolescent Psychotherapy, 9*(2–3), 68–85. doi:10.1080/15289168.2010.510983.

Isay, R. A. (1999). Gender in homosexual boys: Some developmental and clinical considerations. *Interpersonal and Biological Processes, 62*(2), 187–194.

Kindlon, D. & Thompson, M. (1999). *Raising Cain: Protecting the emotional life of boys.* New York: Random House.

Kiselica, M. S., & Englar-Carlson, M. (2010). Identifying strengths and building upon male strengths: The positive psychology/positive masculinity model of psychotherapy with boys and men. *Psychotherapy: Theory, Research, Practice, Training, 47*(3), 276–287. doi:10.1037/a0021159.

Kiselica, M. S., Englar-Carlson, M., Home, A. M., & Fisher, M. (2008). A positive psychology perspective on helping boys. In M. S. Kiselica & M. Englar-Carlson (Eds.), *Counseling troubled boys: A guidebook for professionals* (pp. 31–48). New York: Routledge Taylor & Francis Group.

Kretschmer, T., & Pike, A. (2010). Associations between adolescent siblings' relationship quality and similarity and differences in values. *Journal of Family Psychology, 24*(4), 411–418. doi:10.1037/a0020060.

Laursen, B., Furman, W., & Mooney, K. S. (2008). Predicting interpersonal competence and self-worth from adolescent relationships and relationship networks: Variable-Centered and person-centered perspectives. *Merrill-Palmer Quarterly, 52*(3), 572–600.

Levant, R. F., & Pollack, W. S. (1995). Introduction. In R. F. Levant & W. S. Pollack (Eds.). *A new psychology of men* (pp. 1–8). New York: Basic Books.

Lim, S. H., & Ang, R. P. (2009). Relationship between boys' normative beliefs about aggression and their physical, verbal, and indirect aggressive behaviors. Adolescence, 44(175), 635–650.

Ma, C. Q., & Huebner, E. S. (2008). Attachment relationships and adolescents' life satisfaction: Some relationships matter more to girls than boys. *Psychology in the Schools, 45*(2), 177–190.

Maccoby, E. (1990). Gender and relationships: A developmental account. *American Psychologist, 45,* 513–520.

Maccoby, E. E. (1998). *The two sexes: Growing up apart, coming together.* Cambridge, MA: Harvard University Press.

MacKinnon-Lewis, C., Starnes, R., Volling, B., & Johnson, S. (1997). Perceptions of parenting as predictors of boys' sibling and peer relations. *Developmental Psychology, 33*(6), 1024–1031. doi:10.1037/0012–1649.33.6.1024.

Margolin, A., Youga, J., & Ballou, M. (2002). Voices of violence: A study of male adolescent aggression. *Journal of Humanistic Counseling, Education, and Development, 41,* 215–231.

Maslow, A. H. (1968). *Toward a psychology of being.* New York: Van Nostrand.

McDougall, P. & Hymel, S. (2007). Same-gender versus cross-gender friendship conceptions: Similar or different? *Merrill-Palmer Quarterly, 53,* 347–380.

McLean, K. C., Breen, A., & Fournier, M. A. (2010). Adolescent identity development: Narrative meaning-making and memory telling. *Journal of Research on Adolescence, 20*(1), 166–187.doi:10.1111/j.1532–7795.2009.00633.x.

McNelles, L. R., & Connolly, J. A. (1999). Intimacy between adolescent friends: Age and gender differences in intimate affect and intimate behaviors. *Journal of Research on Adolescence, 9*(2), 143–159. doi:10.1207/s15327795jra0902_2.

Moilanen, K. L., Shaw, D. S., & Fitzpatrick, A. (2010). Self-regulation in early adolescence: Relations with mother-son relationship quality and maternal regulatory support and antagonism. *Journal of Youth and Adolescence, 39*(11), 1357–1367. doi:10.1007/s10964–009–9485-x.

Mounts, N. S. (2007). Adolescents' and their mothers' perceptions of parental management of peer relationships. *Journal of Research on Adolescence, 17*(1), 169–178. doi:10.1111/j.1532–7795.2007.00517.x.

NICHD Early Child Care Research Network. (2009). Family-Peer linkages: The meditational role of attentional processes. *Social Development, 18*(4), 875–895. doi:10.1111/j.1467–9507.2008.00510.x.

Oransky, M., Marecek, J. (2009). I'm not going to be a girl: Masculinity and emotions in boys' friendships and peer groups. *Journal of Adolescent Research, 24*(2), 218–241.doi:10.1177/0743558408329951.

Padilla-Walker, L. M., Harper, J. M., & Jensen, A. C. (2010). Self-regulation as a mediator between sibling relationship quality and early adolescents' positive and negative outcomes. *Journal of Family Psychology, 24*(4), 419–428.

Poulin, F. & Pederson, S. (2007). Developmental changes in gender composition of friendship networks in adolescent girls and boys. *Developmental Psychology, 43*(6), 1484–1496.

Pratt, M. W., Norris, J. E., Lawford, H., & Arnold, M. L. (2010). What he said to me stuck: Adolescents' narratives of grandparents and their identity development in emerging adulthood. In K. C. McLean & M. Pasupathi (Eds.) *Narrative development in adolescence: Creating the storied self* (pp. 93–112). New York: Springer.

Robinson-Wood, T. (2009). *The convergence of race, ethnicity, and gender: Multiple identities in counseling* (3rd ed.). Upper Saddle River, NJ: Pearson.

Rose, A. J. (2007). Structure, content, and socioemotional correlates of girls' and boys' friendships: Recent advances and future directions. *Journal of Developmental Psychology, 53*(3), 489–506. doi:10.1353/mpq.2007.0019.

Rose, A. J., & Rudolph, K. D. (2006). A review of sex differences in peer relationship processes: Potential trade-offs for the emotional and behavioral development of girls and boys. *Psychological Bulletin, 132*(1), 98–131. doi:10.1037/0033–2909.132.1.98.

Rudolph, K. D. (2010). Implicit theories of peer relationships. *Social development, 19*(1), 113–129. doi:10.1111/j.1467–9507.2008.00534.x.

Serbin, L. A., Moller, L. C., Gulko, J., Powlishta, K. K., & Colburne, K. A. (1994). The emergence of gender segregation in toddler playgroups. In C. Leaper (Ed.) *Childhood gender segregation: Causes and consequences* (pp.7–18). San Francisco: Jossey-Bass.

Simon, V. A., & Furman, W. (2010). Interparental conflict and adolescents' romantic relationship conflict. *Journal of Research on Adolescence, 20*(1), 188–209. doi:10.1111/j.1532–7795.2009.00635.x.

Sippola, L. K., Buchanan, C. M., Kehoe, S. (2007). Correlates of false self in adolescent romantic relationships. *Journal of Clinical Child and Adolescent Psychology, 36*(4), 515–521.

Soenens, B., Vansteenkiste, M., & Niemiec, C. P. (2009). Should parental prohibition of adolescents' peer relationships be prohibited? *Personal Relationships, 16*(4), 507–530. doi:10.1111/j.1475–6811.2009.01237.x.

Stolz, H. E., Olsen, J. A., Barber, B. K., & Clifford, L. M. (2010). Disentangling fathering and mothering: The role of youth personality. *Fathering, 8*(2), 163–180. doi:10.3149/fth.1802.163.

Tolman, D. L., Spencer, R., Harmon, T., Rosen-Reynoso, M., & Striepe, M. (2004). Getting close, staying cool: Early adolescent boys' experiences with romantic relationships. In N. Way & J. Y. Chu (Eds.) *Adolescent boys: Exploring diverse cultures of boyhood* (pp. 235–255). New York: New York University Press.

Tremblay, G., Tremblay, R. E., & Saucier, J-F. (2004). The development of parent-child relationship perceptions in boys from childhood to adolescence: A comparison between disruptive and non-disruptive boys. *Child and Adolescent Social Work, 21*(4), 407–426.

Underwood, M. K. (2007). Gender and children's friendships: Do girls' and boys' friendships constitute different peer cultures, and what are the trade-offs for development? *Journal of Developmental Psychology, 53*(3), 319–324. doi:10.1353/mpq.2007.0022.

Watts, R. & Borders, L. (2005). Boys perceptions of the male role: Understanding gender role conflict in adolescent males. *The Journal of Men's Studies, 13*(2), 267–280.

Way, N. (2011). *Deep secrets: Boys' friendships and the crisis of connection.* Boston, MA: Harvard University Press.

Wilson, B. D. M., Harper, G. W., Hidalgo, M. A., Jamil, O. B., Torres, R. S., & Fernandez, M. I. (2010). Negotiating dominant masculinity ideology: Strategies used by gay, bisexual and questioning male adolescents. *American Journal of Community Psychology, 45*(1–2), 169–185. doi:10.1007/s10464–009-9291–3.

Yoo, J. (2009). Peer influence on adolescent boys' appearance management behaviors. *Adolescence, 44*(176), 1017–1031.

Yuan, A. S. V. (2009). Sibling relationships and adolescents' mental health: The interrelationship of structure and quality. *Journal of Family Issues, 30*(9), 1221–1244. doi:1244.10.1177/0192513X09334906.

Zentner, M., & Renaud, O. (2007). Origins of adolescents' ideal self: An intergenerational perspective. *Journal of Personality and Social Psychology, 92*(3), 557–574.

7

Working With Boys From Single-Parent Homes

S. KENT BUTLER AND M. ANN SHILLINGFORD

SINGLE-PARENT FAMILIES TODAY

Growing up today, young males face a much wider array of challenges than any prior generation faced. Many of these challenges affect emotional development and may leave lasting impacts on young men's lives. One such challenge is growing up in a single-parent home. These family constellations include single mothers or fathers, divorced parents sharing custody, military families where one parent is deployed, or families plagued by incarceration.

In the United States, approximately 26% of homes are classified as single-parent (U.S. Census Bureau, 2011). Families and Living Arrangements reported in 2006 that there were 12.9 million one-parent families: 2.5 million single-father families and 10.4 million single-mother families. This figure is up from the 1970s when the two-parent household was virtually the norm. Today's cultural values and societal mores have evolved in many ways, and family constellations have taken on many new faces. Although we generally acknowledge the resilience of children to weather a variety of challenges, there are challenges and risk factors specific to children in single-parent families that may benefit from the involvement of professional clinicians.

EFFECTS OF BEING RAISED IN A SINGLE-PARENT HOUSEHOLD

Many children are born into single-parent homes, but situations such as parental divorce, death of a parent, military deployment of a parent,

119

or abandonment by a parent may place a child in this situation during their youth. Single-parented children are often at risk for a variety of psychological, emotional, and behavioral problems including juvenile delinquency, substance abuse, and interpersonal violence (Schroeder, Osgood, & Oghia, 2010). Researchers have also shown that boys raised in single-parent homes are significantly more likely to be victims of child sexual abuse (Holmes, 2007). Researchers believe this might occur as the boys are under less supervision than those in two-parent homes and perhaps because their need for emotional connection and affection may go unmet due to a single parent's physical or emotional unavailability to the boy. Further, as Cavanagh and Huston (2008) discovered, young boys are much more negatively affected by family instability in terms of peer relationships and social competency than young girls are. Of note, they found that significant family transitions experienced by young boys in their early years would have negative consequences years later in elementary school, including the display of aggressive behaviors. It is clear that boys are affected by shifts in their support systems and networks, perhaps even more so than young girls are.

Children usually recognize when parents are experiencing feelings of anxiety. This is especially true for boys and young men when the single-parent is their mother. These boys often attempt to take on the role of the male head of household and may become discouraged when they are unable to effectively help the struggling parent. This is only one example of the effects of single-parent households on boys and young men. Following are sections addressing more examples including the effects of high-conflict divorces, the loss of a father figure from the household, sons of deployed military forces, and sons of incarcerated parents.

LIVING IN THE MIDDLE OF A HIGH-CONFLICT DIVORCE

In the midst of a hostile separation, parents may not take into consideration the effect that their behaviors have on their children. Children get caught in a parental tug-of-war and can be unable to cope with the stress. Major issues that surface for children involved in high-conflict divorce include feeling pushed to take sides with one parent or the other, incidents in which they find themselves taking on the role of confidant or missing spouse for their custodial parent, and the development of negative behaviors such as skills related to parental manipulation.

During high-conflict divorce cases, parental behaviors may lead to alienation and damage the parent–child relationship. According to Mitcham and Henry (2007), the alienation may arise when one parent seeks control over the other by placing the child in the middle and attempting to sway the child's opinion of the targeted parent. Boyan and Termini (1999) further promulgated that children's behaviors may exhibit expressions of intense dislike or hatred of the targeted parent, open denigration versus exceptional praise of one parent over the other, or the utter refusal to communicate or spend quality time with the target parent, and offering very poorly supported rationalizations.

"Missing Dad": When Dad Is Not Around for His Son

"By Divine design, fathers were created to offer their children protection, correction, and connection. Mothers offer some of the same qualities; it is just that fathers do it in a different way. And when this fatherly presence is absent or lacking, it creates a cavernous void in the emotional life of the person." — Dr. Dan Collins

The old adage, *sons need their fathers*, is often verbalized in situations in which sons are not performing at their developmental best. Single mothers often bear the greatest part of the burden of the childrearing when there is limited access to dad or a father figure. Unfortunately, a mother may become a victim of her circumstances and be unjustly criticized and blamed for the father's absence. This may create problems for the children in the home as they learn to cope with whatever temperament develops in their mothers who are saddled with the responsibility of solo childrearing.

"Too many fathers missing from too many homes, from too many lives" — President Obama

For boys and young males caught in this dynamic, life is often confusing. They are caught between trying to be a kid and being the man of the house. Unknowingly—or, more tragically, intentionally—mothers may place their sons in this conflicted role paradox. Young males may try to live up to their mother's unrealistic expectations of maturity and responsibility, but this compromises normal developmental processes and takes the child out of step with his peers.

Maintaining discipline can be difficult for women who have sons who are growing bigger, taller, and stronger than they are. Clearly, men and women do not provide the same parenting skills or represent the same level of authority in many homes. According to Klinger (1998), even mothers with the best intentions cannot take on the role of a substitute father. While there are many competing factors that interfere with parents from all ethnic backgrounds, the most common for caregivers of African American males is the influence of the streets. Often the communities where these young men reside offer a plethora of opportunities to make poor life choices. Parenting can be complicated by a host of factors that involve both the family constellation and the external environment. Mothers often wonder how to parent a child who has been schooled by the streets and comes home unwilling to respect, to listen, or to abide by the house rules. Often the mother who is busy trying to keep a roof over the family's heads becomes disillusioned or increasingly tolerant of the once unacceptable behavior and begins to ignore much of their children's unsavory behavior.

"Missing in Action": Special Challenges for Military Families

The present U.S. military situation is another contributing factor in the advent of single-parent homes. According to recent statistics, almost three-quarters of a million children have had to see a parent head off to deployment and out of their day-to-day lives (Johnson et al., 2007). The resulting lack of communication from parents or about the situation in war-torn areas are just two aspects of the perplexing turmoil that can result when parents must leave the family and enter a war zone. Lincoln, Swift, and Shorteno-Fraser (2008) noted that one of the most difficult experiences a child could face is the deployment of a parent to an active war zone coupled with no predetermined date of return to the states. Unfortunately, research shows that boys are much likelier to suffer negative consequences of family disruption than their female counterparts are (Jensen et al., 1996). These consequences can include depression, anxiety, and behavioral problems (Campbell, Brown, & Okwara, 2011).

Depending on their ages, children have varying responses to extended deployments of their parents. The following chart highlights some of the symptoms we should be cognizant of in infants, toddlers, pre-schoolers, school age children, and teenagers. According to Pincus, House, Christenson, and Adler (2001), it is a plausible assumption that sudden maladaptive changes in a child's behavior or mood may stem from predictable stress of having a deployed parent. Not only is it stressful just to have the parent out of the home, the widespread and graphic media coverage of military activity can exacerbate the stress (Huebner & Mancini, 2005). The length of separation is also directly related to the severity of the negative consequences (Chandra et al., 2010) (see Table 7.1).

If a child is having a difficult time adapting to the stress of a deployed parent and seems unable to return to at least some semblance of a normal routine and behavior, or if he displays significant symptoms over an extended period, it may be wise to seek help from a mental health counselor.

According to Pincus et al. (2001), children of deployed parents who reside in single-parent or blended families are more vulnerable to psychiatric hospitalization. Lincoln et al. (2008) also noted that several sources have shown that deployment is related to higher rates of

TABLE 7.1

Negative Changes in Children

	Ages	Behaviors	Moods	Remedy
Infant	<1 year	Refuses to eat	Listless	Support for parent, pediatrician
Toddlers	1–3 years	Cries, tantrums	Irritable, sad	Increased attention, holding, hugs
Preschool	3–6 years	Potty accidents, clingy	Irritable, sad	Increased attention, holding, hugs
School age	6–12 years	Whines, body aches	Irritable, sad	Spend time, maintain routines
Teenagers	12–18 years	Isolates, uses drugs	Anger, apathy	Patience, limit-setting, counseling

Source: Pincus, S. H., House, R., Christenson, J., & Adler, L. E. (2001). The emotional cycle of deployment: A military family perspective. *U.S. Army Medical Department Journal.* Retrieved from: http://www.hooah4health.com/deployment/familymatters/emotionalcycle2.htm

child maltreatment. They also noted that research shows that the level of resiliency and connection to their stateside parent has a significant influence on how well the children handle the temporary loss of one parent. Yet, they also note that a parent's return to the family is not stress-free! The return of a deployed parent can create additional stressors on the family depending on how well the family handled the absence and how the combat duty has affected the returning family member. Some of the key areas for assessing and predicting how well a young male will handle the stress related to a deployed parent include whether his parent spent time in a combat zone, the length of the separation from his parent, and the level of psychological or physical injury suffered by his parent (Lincoln et al.). However, despite the obstacles present, a vast majority of spouses and family members successfully navigate the deployment period, keeping optimism high, as they look forward to the return of their loved ones and successfully reintegrating the family upon their return. Counselors working with children in homes in which a parent has been deployed should be aware that extra support for the family and children may be necessary as the military member returns, as this is a time of especial stress for everyone involved.

Boys Coping With an Incarcerated Parent

A parent in jail poses yet another set of challenges to children as they learn to navigate home life sans a parent. Glaze and Maruschak (2008) reported

that th... ion children in the United States dealing with an
inca... at African American children are 7.5 times more
likely... the imprisonment of a parent. In addition, as
ma... entences for criminals with prior histories, this
nu... aration time lengthens. Unfortunately, boys
s... difficult time handling this loss than girls do.
I... ng males with incarcerated parents, Murray
and... that these boys suffered a greater risk of
psyc... ternalizing problems in adolescence and over the
life s... (2009) found that aggressive behavior levels are
high... erated parents as early as 3 years of age! And the
mala... ontinue throughout their lives. Thus, it would be
of g... ide programming and assistance to the sons of
incarcerated parents ... early as possible.

©2012 LEGO

Separation or arrested attachment-formation from a primary caregiver at an early age is a risk for the development of later attachment problems as Bowlby (1969, 1973, 1980) has described. Having a parent wrested out of the house by law enforcement officers can be even more disturbing and traumatic than any other form of parental loss. A young boy may be awoken by sirens blaring and officers pounding on the family's door and then witness their father or mother being manhandled and led out to a waiting squad car. Under the tacit "boys' code of conduct" to be strong and manly, the young male may be unable to express his fear or sadness and bottle up these feelings, which can later lead to misplaced anger and rage. Phillips et al. (2004) noted that these young males most likely are already living in poverty, which is a huge risk factor for future problems, and that the loss of a parent only increases the emotional and social well-being risks. These additional risks can include frequent moves, changing caregivers, substance abuse, mental health problems in their custodial parent, exposure to violence, and an increased risk for abuse. Research has also shown that boys who have incarcerated fathers more frequently exhibited below-average self-concepts, as rated by their teachers, than those without incarcerated fathers (Friedman & Esselstyn, 1965).

"Children who have a parent in jail or prison often learn the many nuances of the phrase 'guilty by association' the hard way" (Rollins, 2010, p. 39). The incarceration factor may be seen as a triumph or a burden, depending on the family's circumstances. Depending on the boy's peer group, having a parent in prison may be seen as a "badge of honor" or it may color the community's perception of the boy and brand him "a chip off the old block." Both perceptions may encourage the youth to feel justified in heading in the same direction of their incarcerated parent. Societal assumptions and experiences bordering on self-blame, shattered attachments, and withdrawal may lead to frustration and school failure, drug or alcohol usage, school truancy, and aggressive/violent behavior by our younger generation when they have incarcerated parents. According to the Old Mill Center for Children & Families (2011), children of incarcerated parents are seven times more likely than their counterparts to be eventually incarcerated themselves. Sadly, their parents, even prior to incarceration were generally physically and/or emotionally unavailable to their children.

Maintaining healthy relationships while a parent is incarcerated can be a balancing act for a young man. Visits to the imprisoned parent may be stressful in many ways, as noted by Murray and Farrington (2008). Visits may involve physical discomforts such as searches, having to "visit" through a glass window, and long-distance travel. All of these factors may cause visits to be infrequent, and often a caregiver may promise a visit, but cancel or delay it if circumstances such as transportation and work schedules create conflicts. Oftentimes, the son of an inmate may be teased or bullied at school because of the parents' situation. In trying to protect the family name, some young males may act out in ways that only exacerbate the problem. By acting out and retaliating against their aggressors, adults may see them as exhibiting the same negative behaviors of their parents. When they are accused of following the same pathway as their parent, this may turn into a self-fulfilling prophecy. Other young males may respond in the opposite direction by turning inward, isolating themselves from peers, and wrestling with feelings of shame and embarrassment. This isolation may turn into depression and/or other psychological impairments. Research indicates that the group process moves children/youth through the sorrow, anger, confusion, guilt, and so on more quickly than individual counseling in many instances. However, depending on the child, behavior or mental health conditions may dictate that they initially receive individual rather than group counseling.

A recent qualitative study investigated the insights of imprisoned parents regarding the pieces of information they believed their children needed to know in order to stay out of jail, themselves (Thombre et al., 2009). Several main themes permeated their findings: prison was viewed as an adult day care in which prisoners had no control over how their time was spent; the imprisonment created an emotional drain for children and other family members; and that incarceration perpetuated itself throughout family generations. The participants believed that their children needed to be taught decision-making skills to avoid making the choices that would land them in prison. They also believed that their children needed to be educated to understand how the law worked and to value education, in and of itself. When asked what they believed their kids needed to understand about the prison system, they noted the following responses: the realities of prison life; appropriate ways of interacting with law enforcement officers; the value of discipline; and the impact of prison on an entire family. These topics can serve as excellent areas of exploration and education for counseling sessions with the children of incarcerated parents.

EVIDENCE-BASED INTERVENTIONS AND INNOVATIVE APPROACHES

In light of the significant challenges that boys and young men face due to the family structure, interventions and strategies have long been researched and implemented to provide needed supports. Counseling literature suggests that both theoretical as well as innovative approaches should be utilized by counselors working with this population. The following section presents research-supported best practices.

Schools

Outside the home environment, the school community is where children will receive a significant amount of support and services in the hopes of producing productive citizens. Several researchers have addressed ways in which schools may maintain best practices in support of children from disenfranchised households. For instance, Petsch & Rochlen (2009) recommended that school counselors recognize the needs of children residing in homes where a parent is incarcerated and thus advocate for counseling services for them. Advocacy should include education of the school community about the effects of parental incarceration on children and discussion of how parental incarceration may exacerbate displays of negative behaviors. According to Petsch and Rochlen, advocacy should also include attending professional development workshops and presentations addressing the topic as well as collaborating with teachers to develop a culturally sound social justice curriculum. Similarly, Shillingford and Edwards (2008) presented a theoretical approach that school counselors may take in supporting children when parents are imprisoned. The authors delineated how effective the use of choice theory was in supporting a young boy who resided with his mother during his father's incarceration. Through modeling, role-play, and other techniques from a choice theoretical approach, the Professional School Counselor (PSC) was able to assist the young boy in reducing negative behaviors while positively increasing his academic performance and communication skills.

Military deployments provide yet another opportunity for PSCs to provide supportive care for children who are experiencing parental separation. Rush and Akos (2007) reported on the necessity of PSCs in providing a group counseling approach to meet the needs of children of deployed parents. To this end, group therapeutic factors help to foster a safe environment whereby children may begin to develop coping skills and assist students in understanding their emotions surrounding their loved one's deployment. Another issue that may interfere in a child's growth and development surrounds divorce. Connolly and Green (2009) discussed the usefulness of school-based interventions for young children affected by their parent's separation and subsequent divorce and recommended group intervention programs to help decrease negative externalizing behaviors fostered by the family status.

Evidence-based research supports the utilization of specific counseling interventions to support children in single-parent households whether their living situation is due to divorce, military deployment, or incarceration. The interventions described as follows, although not specific to only boys and young men, seem to be beneficial to their emotional development. Other interventions and approaches that may be practical to counselors and therapists outside of the school community include art, play, and/or music therapies, among other practices.

Art Therapy

Art therapy involves creating and processing art in order to increase self-awareness and coping strategies for individuals experiencing stressful life situations. In light of the effects of single-parent household experiences on children, art therapy is extremely beneficial in exploring the emotional responses of boys and young men. Both boys and men frequently have difficulty verbally expressing their emotions; therefore, art or other expressive therapies can be effective approaches to help them process their thoughts and feelings. Art therapy takes a holistic approach and may help male clients connect their social, emotional, and developmental selves.

Although at first some adolescents may be reluctant to engage in creating art, counselors are typically successful in encouraging them to use art in place of words. Art therapy can involve the use of such objects as paper, crayons, pencils, and clay as well as unexpected items such as Legos, dominoes, and wood. Use of these items should be encouraged by therapists in order to support male clients in making meaning of their life situations through symbolic representations. Trauma and other concerns buried in the client's subconscious may be unearthed by the therapeutic relationship built between the child and therapist during the art sessions. In cases where children struggle to articulate their thoughts and feelings, this supportive mode of intervention is ideal in drawing out the child's innermost inhibitions and hence slowly helps begin the recovery process.

Art therapy may be useful in supporting young boys residing in single-parent households as it leads to the externalizing of their experiences and fosters the procurement of more enriching lives. The art therapist helps the male client to communicate any pain that he may be facing and gives him the opportunity to express himself in a nonverbal, nonthreatening way. Finally, the art therapist may use the construction of art to help the young man become aware of his behaviors, understand the impact of his behaviors on others, and learn alternative methods of relating or reacting to life situations.

CASE STUDY: ABRAHIM, AGE 12

Presenting Problem

Abrahim is a 12-year-old African American young man. He was referred to Tim, a mental health therapist, by his PSC. Abrahim has a learning disability and receives special education services from the school. In spite of the support that he receives at school, he appears unmotivated and angry. His teachers report that he does not always complete in-class assignments or homework. At home, his mother is concerned that he is often yelling at his siblings and refuses to do his chores. She is contemplating sending Abrahim to live with his grandparents. Abrahim's father, Rashid, has been in Afghanistan for the past year and prior to that was deployed elsewhere. He communicates with his family via Skype but is not always able to maintain lengthy conversations. When Rashid does reach his family, Abrahim appears reluctant to communicate with him and is brief with his responses.

Art Therapy Intervention

Tim, the therapist, discovers that Abrahim enjoys art and spends a significant amount of his time drawing. Tim determines that he will draw on Abrahim's strength and interest and utilize art therapy as an intervention. Tim is a registered art therapist and has a working knowledge of how to use this approach with his client. He encourages Abrahim to use the art material of his choice to formulate various aspects of his life (e.g., his family life, peers). Abrahim's art expressions shift quickly from the expected attempts of a child of his age and abilities to replicate lifelike images of objects in the office or standard subjects such as houses or animals into more abstract, "process-heavy," darker, and disorganized images.

Through the process of exploration, Tim and Abrahim are able to discover that Abrahim's anger is toward his father for being away for such a long time. Although he understands the military process of deployment, it appears to be difficult for him to personalize his father's commitment and accept it. He discovered that he missed his father and had been internalizing those feelings. Instead of expressing his fear and anxiety, Abrahim was externalizing anger and resentment. The relationship he built with Tim through the use of art allowed him to develop a more positive outlook about his life and his family. He was better able to communicate his feelings of fear to his mother as well as talk with his father more openly. Abrahim also felt more comfortable talking with his PSC, who, as time progressed, was given liberty to collaborate with teachers who, in turn, provided more social and emotional support at school.

Processing Questions

1. What do you think was the role of the therapist, Tim, during the art therapy sessions? How might you utilize this approach in your own practice?
2. Did Abrahim have to be good at drawing in order to receive the full benefits of the sessions?

Outcome Description

The intimate nature of art therapy will encourage children like Abrahim to begin the process of social and emotional growth. Art therapy may also promote behavioral change so that internalized feelings are addressed openly and negative externalized behaviors are replaced with conduct that is more functional.

Music Therapy

Music therapy is yet another innovative approach that can be used to support children. Brooke (2008) indicated that music therapy is a safe and supported approach through which individuals have the freedom and opportunity for authentic expression of their thoughts and emotions. Music therapy has been documented as a favorable mode of supporting children by:

• Stimulating the senses and involving the whole child
• Facilitating varied developmental skills
• Providing a calming and relaxing atmosphere
• Allowing them to feel good about themselves
• Helping them manage pain and stressful events
• Encouraging self-expression and communication

Due to the often emotionally and financially challenging atmosphere of the single-parent household, boys may not have the supports they require to develop the social and psychological skills that they will need as adults. Music therapy can help these children move forward beyond the pain and isolation to a more positive healing process. Music therapy can be structured or unstructured and can be delivered in a group or individual setting. The therapist can choose to utilize songs for self-exploration, encourage the young man to compose his own songs for self-expression, or use musical intonations for exploration of feelings.

CASE STUDY: JESSIE, AGE 13

Presenting Problem

Jessie has lived with his mother all his life. He has never met his father, and his mother refuses to share any information with him. At age 13, he has been experiencing developmental challenges, as do all adolescents. This has been compounded by the absence of and lack of information about his father. Jessie's mother shared that although his academic performance at school is acceptable, both at home and at school, he is defiant, disrespectful, and displays at-risk behaviors. For example, Jessie recently began smoking and staying out late with his friends and coming home at midnight or later. Jessie was suspended from school for three days because of a violent act toward another student. When asked by the school principal why he fought the student, he said that he did not know. Jessie has exhibited similar acts of misbehavior not only at school but also at home. His mother feels deeply distressed by her son's behaviors and has decided to seek help.

Music Therapy Intervention

Upon arrival at the therapist's office, Jessie immediately expresses to the therapist, Lola, that he does not have a problem and that everything is okay. "I really don't see why people keep making a big deal out of everything." Jessie is reluctant to talk about his school suspension or his behaviors that resulted in this consequence. Lola engages Jessie in general conversation to build rapport and discovers that he likes drawing and music. Over the next three sessions, Lola uses music therapy and begins to observe improvements in his willingness to talk during their sessions. She invites Jessie to create music using instruments she has in her office as well as to select prerecorded music she has available. Although he is initially hesitant to express himself, he does agree to bring in music selections that he feels communicate his feelings. Jessie is able to use different genres of music to explore and externalize how he feels about his father and express his feelings of rejection from his father. Jessie says that musicians use words and tunes that say what he doesn't have words to say. Lola asks that Jessie create an autobiographical playlist that includes music that he believes tells his life story and to bring it to their final termination session. Jessie is able to process his loss and the ambiguity surrounding his father as he also is able to acknowledge his own strengths and his own story through music.

Outcome Description

Lola, the therapist, was able to provide Jessie with a safe, nonjudgmental environment where he could express himself in a format that was comfortable for him. Through music therapy, Jessie is able to develop more effective communication skills. This development will also support him in being more open with his mother who, in turn, ideally, will be more willing to talk about his father with him. This approach will also assist Jessie in handling the pain that he is experiencing for his stressful life situations. For example, Jessie should now feel confident in understanding that his father's absence does not subtract from his self-worth or dictate his own future. A collaborative partnership between school, therapist, and home should provide Jessie with the support system necessary for overcoming any lingering negative emotional responses.

Other Innovative Approaches

Movement therapy, play therapy, bibliotherapy, and adventure therapy are other innovative approaches that have been used successfully with children. These approaches have been found to explore social and emotional functioning and to enhance self-definition. For example, movement or dance therapy bypasses the traditional "talk" therapy and allows the child the opportunity for unstructured, creative self-expression through body movement. Therapists focus on body attitude, posture, and breath flow, a system called Laban Analysis (Bernstein, 1986). Movement therapists determine that regardless of the social trauma that children may experience, their inert strengths remain intact and healthy, pending a safe, supportive atmosphere for expression.

Similarly, bibliotherapy has been found to be supportive of children's self-expression if it is done in an open, nonrestrictive way without time limitations. Using stories, children are able to explore the worlds of other characters instead of focusing solely on their own behaviors. This process not only normalizes feelings and experiences but also empowers children with the tools to cope with situations that they would otherwise not be able to handle.

Adventure therapy utilizes activity-based approaches such as problem-solving activities, wall climbing, and rope challenges, to help individuals bring meaning to their life situations (see Chapter 11 for a more complete description). Through the insights developed by these nonverbal and verbal activities, individuals are able to explore new ways of solving problems and thus procure behavioral change.

SUMMARY

This chapter focused on single-parent homes, and the authors have provided information addressing the many issues that are too commonly experienced for children living in these environments. It is our intent to provide counselors with best practices that will help mitigate the problems faced by clients living within these conditions. By presenting art and music therapy interventions and case studies, we have provided examples of ways in which counselors can creatively work with their male clients who are trying to cope with the absence of their fathers. The hope is that counselors will have working knowledge of the struggles that boys and young men face and be better able to support them through these innovative best practice strategies.

ADDITIONAL RESOURCES

Military Single-Parent Homes

American Association of Child & Adolescent Psychiatry: http://aacap.org/cs/root/facts_for_families/families_in_the_military
National Military Family Association: http://www.militaryfamily.org/
Our Military Kids: http://www.ourmilitarykids.org/

Divorce Single-Parent Homes

Children & Divorce: http://www.childrenanddivorce.com/
Help Guide: http://www.helpguide.org

For Single Parents

American Psychology Association. (2009). *Children in single-parent households and stepfamilies benefit most socially from time with grandparents.* http://www.apa.org/news/press/releases/2009/02/children-grandparents.aspx
FamilyDoctor.org: http://familydoctor.org/online/famdocen/home/articles/844.html

HealthLine: http://www.healthline.com/galecontent/single-parent-families#page2
The Single Parent Network: www.singleparentsnetwork.com

REFERENCES

Bernstein, P. L. (1986). *Theoretical approaches in dance-movement therapy* (Vol. 1). Dubuque, IA: Kendall/Hunt.

Boyan, B. B., & Termini, A. M. (1999). *Cooperative parenting and divorce: A parent guide to effective co-parenting.* Kennesaw, GA: Active Parenting.

Bowlby, J. (1969). *Attachment and loss: Vol. I. Attachment.* London: Hogarth Press and the Institute of Psycho-Analysis.

Bowlby, J. (1973). *Attachment and loss: Vol. II. Separation, anxiety and anger.* London: Hogarth Press/Institute of Psycho-Analysis.

Bowlby, J. (1980). *Attachment and loss: Vol. III. Loss, sadness and depression.* London: Hogarth Press/Institute of Psycho-Analysis.

Brooke, S. L. (2008). *The creative therapies and eating disorders.* Springfield, IL: Charles Thomas Publisher Ltd.

Campbell, C. L., Brown, E. J., & Okwara, L. (2011). Addressing sequelae of trauma and interpersonal violence in military children: A review of the literature and case illustration. *Cognitive and Behavioral Practice, 18,* 131–143.

Cavanagh, S. E., & Huston, A. C. (2008). The timing of family instability and children's social development. *Journal of Marriage and Family, 70,* 1258–1269.

Chandra, A., Lara-Cinisomo, S., Jaycox, L. H., Tanielian, T., Burns, R. M., Ruder, T., & Han, B. (2010). Children on the homefront: The experience of children from military families. *Pediatrics, 125,* 16–25.

Connolly, M. E., & Green, E. J. (2009). Evidence-based counseling interventions with children of divorce: Implications for elementary school counselors. *Journal of School Counseling, 7,* 1–37.

Friedman, S., & Esselstyn, T. C. (1965). The adjustment of children of jail inmates. *Federal Probation, 29,* 55–59.

Geller, A., Garfinkel, I., Cooper, C. E., & Mincy, R. B. (2009). Parental incarceration and child well-being: Implications for urban families. *Social Science Quarterly, 90,* 1186–1202.

Glaze, L. E., & Maruschak, L. M. (2008). *Parents in prison and their minor children.* Washington, DC: Bureau of Justice Statistics.

Holmes, W. C. (2007). Men's childhood sexual abuse histories by one-parent versus two-parent status of childhood home. *Journal of Epidemiology and Community Health, 61,* 319–325.

Huebner, A. J., & Mancini, J. A. (2005). *Adjustments among adolescents in military families when a parent is deployed.* Final report to the Military Family Research Institute and Department of Defense Quality of Life Office. Department of Human Development, Virginia Polytechnic Institute and State University. Retrieved from: http://www.unirel.vt.edu/news/Huebner_Mancini_teens_study.pdf

Jensen, P. S., Martin, D., & Watanabe, H. (1996). Children's response to separation during Operation Desert Storm. *Journal of the American Academy of Child and Adolescent Psychiatry, 35,* 433–441.

Johnson, S. J., Sherman, M. D., Hoffman, J. S., James, L. C., Johnson, P. L., Lochman, J. e., et al. (2007). *The psychological needs of U.S. military service members and their families: A preliminary report* (Presidential Task Force on Military Deployment Services for Youth, Families and Service Members). Washington, DC: American Psychological Association.

Klinger, R. (1998). What can be done about absentee fathers? *U.S.A. Today Magazine, 127*(2638), 136.

Lincoln, A., Swift, E., & Shorteno-Fraser, M. (2008). Psychological adjustment and treatment of children and families with parents deployed in military combat. *Journal of Clinical Psychology, 64,* 984–992.

Mitcham, M., & Henry, W. J. (2007). High-conflict divorce solutions: Parenting coordination as an innovative co-parenting intervention. *The Family Journal: Counseling & Therapy for Couples and Families, 15*(4), 368–373. doi:10.1177/106648070303751.

Murray, J., & Farrington, D. P. (2008). Parental imprisonment: Long-lasting effects on boys' internalizing problems through the life course. *Development and Psychopathology, 20,* 273–290.

Old Mill Center for Children & Families. (2011). *Kid connection for children of incarcerated parents.* Retrieved from: http://www.omill.org/articles/KidConnectionIncarceratedParents.html

Petsch, P., & Rochlen, A. B. (2009). Children of Incarcerated Parents: Implications for School Counselors. *Journal of School Counseling, 7,* 40–67.

Phillips, S. D., Burns, B. J., Wagner, H. R., & Barth, R. P. (2004). Parental arrest and children involved with child welfare services agencies. *American Journal of Orthopsychiatry, 74,* 174–186.

Pincus, S. H., House, R., Christenson, J., & Adler, L. E. (2001). The emotional cycle of deployment: A military family perspective. *U.S. Army Medical Department Journal.* Retrieved from: http://www.hooah4health.com/deployment/family-matters/emotionalcycle2.htm

Rollins, J. (2010). Endangered innocence. *Counseling Today.* Retrieved from: http://ct.counseling.org

Rush, C. M., & Akos, P. (2007). Supporting children and adolescents with deployed caregivers: A structured group approach for school counselors. *Journal for Specialists in Group Work, 32,* 113–125.

Schroeder, R. D., Osgood, A. K., & Oghia, M. J. (2010). Family transitions and juvenile delinquency. *Sociological Inquiry, 80,* 579–604.

Shillingford, M. A., & Edwards, O. W. (2008). Professional school counselors using choice theory to meet the needs of children of prisoners. *Professional School Counseling, 12,* 62–65.

Thombre, A., Montague, D. R., Maher, J., & Zohra, I. T. (2009). If I could only say it myself: How to communicate with children of incarcerated parents. *Journal of Correctional Education, 60,* 66–90.

U.S. Census Bureau. (2007). *Single-Parent households showed little variation since 1994, Census Bureau Reports.* Retrieved on October 29, 2011 from: http://www.census.gov/newsroom/releases/archives/families_households/cb07-46.html

8

Romantic Relationships: From Wrestling to Romance

CHRISTINE BORZUMATO-GAINEY, SUZANNE DEGGES-WHITE, AND CARRIE V. SMITH

ROMANTIC RELATIONSHIPS AS NORMAL DEVELOPMENT

Adolescence is marked by the shift from a family focus to a peer and culture focus. Unlike girls with hundreds of phone hours logged with their friends, the world of courtship requires adolescent boys to leave behind comfortable forms of camaraderie. Sports gear, video games, and the various other ways that boys connect with each other and form an identity are insufficient for romantic relationships. In fact, the often rough physical expression shared in same-sex friendships may leave boys confounded with the new relationship requirements. For most boys, the entrance into intimate relationships is filled with uncertainty.

According to Erikson's (1980) stages of development, adolescents are wrestling with identity development as they try to determine where they fit within their social environments. They rely heavily on their peer groups as mirrors of their own development and typically form tight bonds with their friends. The social world of male adolescents is often heavily ensconced in same-gender organizations and institutions such as gym class or sports teams, and it is through these settings that males are encouraged to hone their competitive skills and engage in male-to-male aggression in socially acceptable ways.

However, as boys move forward into late adolescence and young manhood, they feel drawn to seek intimacy and solidarity with others (Erikson, 1980). Tabares and Gottman (2003) noted that the romantic relationships in which teenagers engage are helping them to develop the competencies they will bring to each subsequent relationship they experience throughout their lives. Even 15 years ago, about three-quarters of eighth and ninth graders had already begun to date (Foshee, Linder, Bauman, et al., 1996). The social and emotional skills that adolescents are attempting to master include intimacy, communication, conflict management, and emotional regulation (Barber & Eccles, 2003).

As they begin to feel the newly arising urge to find an outlet for their romantic longings, adolescent males face the very real and very frightening risk of rejection by potential partners. Young men often wrestle with self-doubt and a lack of confidence in relation to their ability to win the attention of the girls of their choice, but society requires that they wear a mask of bravado to hide their vulnerability. In regards to romantic relationships, girls spend their teen years yearning for the fairy-tale prince, while boys spend their teen years trying to figure out how to appear as a prince but not lose face in the competitive masculine world in which he moves. The world of adolescent romance is awash in drama, melodrama, and the playing of roles!

COMMUNICATION

Both neuroscientists and social scientists tend to agree that adolescent boys are notably less experienced interpersonal communicators than their female counterparts are. Even *in utero*, female brain structures are more attuned to forming social connections than the male brain (Degges-White & Borzumato-Gainey, 2011). Communication in private, one-on-one situations demands the ability to convey thoughts and feelings (to a degree) in order to share personal hopes and needs, manage conflicts, and build a sense of solidarity. Much of the psychological literature suggests that boys are socialized to avoid or deny softer emotions; boys will ruthlessly tease other boys who break the machismo code. In turn, some boys may learn to suppress their emotions and objectify the females in their lives. Yet some theorists propose that adolescent romantic relations are an important socialization arena in which positive emotions toward partners bring new attitudes and feelings.

Decades ago, in a brief journal article titled, *Counseling Adolescent Males*, the author noted that as teens began contemplating the development of romantic relationships, they were often insecure and anxious (Coleman, 1981). They were seen to wrestle with questions about their self-concept and self-esteem, such as *Am I good looking enough? Am I man enough?* Thirty years later, things have not much changed! In a 2006 study comparing the meaning of romantic relationships, the authors found boys reported a significantly lower level of confidence in these navigational skills despite having similar levels of emotional engagement (Giordano, Longmore, & Manning, 2006). Yet growth in the character of a boy's communication style and the shift toward emotional expression dependent upon the quality of the romantic relationship may be too big an expectation for immature partners in youthful relations. Often, a boy's status among his peers will outweigh his communication skills, and his potential romantic partner will sacrifice her desire for emotional attachment with a skilled communicator for the status that comes with a popular boyfriend.

Dueling Messages

We live in an increasingly noncommittal culture. In the early part of the twentieth century, during the teen years, young people were expected to meet their life partner. Clearly the cultural scripts have changed. Although parents and other adults typically understand that teens will gain interest in the opposite sex, they want teens to enter romantic relationships within prohibitive guidelines such as not lasting "too long" and not becoming sexually involved. However, the majority of adolescents will be involved in a romantic relationship during their youth, and these relationships will play a significant role in the emotional, social, and psychological experiences and development of these young people (O'Sullivan, Cheng, Harris, & Brooks-Gunn, 2007).

Teens are also receiving compelling messages from the entertainment industry about the need to be noncommittal in highly sexual relationships. Movies, television shows, online material, and music offer constant reminders of the importance of sex with no strings attached. Rap music and hip-hop music remind teens of the pleasure of sex and the acceptability of male aggression against other males and women. In a content analysis study on gangsta rap music, a subgenre of hip-hop, Armstrong (2001) found that almost one out of four songs (22%) included lyrics that were overtly misogynistic in their depictions of assault, forcible rape, and murder. Within their own peer networks, boys will often reinforce the competition and conqueror approach to relationships. Boys tease each other for showing sincere interest in a girl. Males into adulthood comment upon the attractiveness of the vanquished female. While schools may often teach "abstinence only" education curricula, for many young people, nature's pull is stronger than parental and school caveats— almost one half of adolescents will have engaged in sexual intercourse by high school graduation (Abma, Martinez, Mosher, & Dawson, 2004).

SEXUAL DEVELOPMENT

At the onset of puberty, physical changes create a heightened sensitivity and serious need in boys to understand their bodies. Erections and ejaculation force them into regular, sexually focused thoughts. As the sexual world begins to open, boys are riddled with questions and uncertainty on issues as diverse as masturbation and bondage. Most troubling is the pressure to become sexually active with a partner before even their basic questions are answered. As Erikson (1980) aptly described the psychosocial stages connected to this period, the young adolescent goes from puberty to genitality in late adolescence. The boy's sexual identity and sexual self are driving his development as he moves into adulthood. Counselors must be comfortable discussing sexuality and anatomy with their adolescent male clients, and they must also be willing to be the one to first broach this topic, especially if they are female.

Many health classes do not fully address the variety and depth of teen concerns. The most common concern for teen boys is penis size, and this is rarely addressed by school health classes (Forrest, 2000). It is perhaps partly due to competitiveness among boys and partly due to the human need to feel "normal," but each boy wants reassurance that his penis is normal in size, shape, and capacity in relation to his peers. Boys' jokes are often filled with references to penis size and sexual prowess. Teen boys report much less interest in the topics that *are* covered in health classes such as menses, respectfulness, and safe sex. Books are available for boys to learn the answers to their questions, but the Internet is a more likely source of information today. At the end of this chapter, we have provided several contemporary written and online references for adolescent males that share relevant information more openly than books available to former generations.

SEXUAL RELATIONSHIP DEVELOPMENT

Young boys are "trained" at an early age to engage in the *male gaze*, which describes the sexual lens through which females are viewed. Even in a study of young adolescents (Royer, Keller, & Heidrich, 2009), boys valued a romantic partner's attractiveness significantly more than the females in the study did. Learning to appreciate physical appearance is taught early to young boys by their male caregivers in such diverse settings as admiring professional sports team cheerleaders on television and being waited on by the waitresses at Hooters. The history of erotic representation is centuries old, but more recently there has been an explosion in pornographic magazines and easily accessed websites that are often a source of arousal for boys. Even without proximity to attractive live females or virtual females on the Internet, the media continues to be a strong influence in the sexual lives of adolescents (Brown, L'Engle, Pardun, Guo, Kenneavy, & Jackson, 2005). Unfortunately, the advent and, now, ubiquity of cameras built into cell phones have led to astonishing rates of "sexting," which is the sending of explicit sexual messages and images to others via cell phones. In a report from The National Campaign to Prevent Teen and Unplanned Pregnancy (2008), some unsettling findings were presented. Teenage girls and boys both note that sexting is done to be "fun and flirtatious," and 20% of teens have sent nude or semi-nude photos of themselves to someone via their phone. The more time an adolescent spends in the company of print, video, or audio content with a high sexual focus, the earlier he will actually begin sexual experimentation and activity, and it is clear that technology makes it easier to find personal engagement with sexual materials.

Yet in stark contrast, traditional Judeo-Christian morality emphasizes heterosexuality and lifelong monogamy. And, in concordance, families with higher cohesiveness usually raise male adolescents who are less likely to be sexually active (Smith & Guthrie, 2005). The influence of family communications and family expectations play a significant role in the level of sexual activity engaged in during adolescence. And, as expected for this age group, peer approval of sexual activity has been linked as a motivating factor in the timing of initial sexual intercourse (Ott, Millstein, Ofner, & Halpern-Felsher, 2006). The more a boy's friends encourage and approve of sexual intercourse, the earlier he will initiate it. And research shows that around 8% of youth under age 14 have had sexual intercourse (Carver, Joyner, & Udry, 2003), and approximately 46% of high school students have had sexual intercourse (CDC, 2010). Regarding condom use, it may come as a surprise that a couple is *less likely* to engage in safe sex if intercourse is interpreted as an expression of intimacy or love (Ott et al., 2006). Moreover, perhaps not surprisingly, cultural context and ethnicity differences exist in the level of sexual activity and experience engaged in by adolescent males.

Cultural Differences in Sexual Behaviors

In studies comparing adolescents of diverse ethnicities, there are clear differences in the sexual initiation timeline between groups. The role of family honor and respect can be teased out of the data for some groups. For instance, Okazaki (2002) found that Asian Americans were less likely to engage in premarital sex, as it was seen to be a disgrace for the family. In fact, in a study exploring sexual behaviors, Rosenthal & Feldman (1999) found that Asian American adolescents were the latest to engage in any of the sexual behaviors assessed.

On the other end of the spectrum, African American adolescents are the most sexually active group. The CDC (2010) reported that 65% of Black high school students reported having had sexual intercourse compared to 49% of Hispanic students and 42% of White students. Many researchers have tried to determine the specific cultural factors that play into the high rates of sexual engagement for African American youth (Milbrath, Ohlson, & Eyre, 2009). Anderson (1990) proposed that young Black males regarded strong sexual prowess and frequent sexual activity as a method of enhancing self-esteem and status in response to having so many other avenues in the dominant culture being closed to him. It is also worth noting that there is significantly more discussion of sexuality and its consequences within African American families (O'Sullivan, Meyer-Bahlburg, & Watkins, 2001). Because young African American females are often taught that males cannot always be counted on for long-term emotional or financial support in a relationship, the males may even more highly value the ability to seduce their female partners, who tend to take a pragmatic, rather than romantic, view of their relationships (Milbrath et al., 2009). Cultural stereotypes of males as "players" were also found embedded in the groups of high school students they studied, suggesting that the females who acquiesced to sexual requests were aware that they may be being "played," but were also aware of the egalitarian role they played in relationships, themselves.

For Hispanic adolescent males, there is also a cultural model that awards prestige to males who exhibit hypermasculinity that is often coupled with sexual success with a girlfriend. However, in maintaining that masculinity, or *machismo*, a Hispanic teen may put down his girlfriend in front of his friends while professing his love to her when alone together. In fact, it is the profession of love and displays of romance that are typically the currency that earns sexual submission from adolescent girls (Milbrath et al., 2009). The role of religiosity may even play a surprising role in a couple's decision, or a female adolescent's agreement, to engage in sexual intercourse. One of Milbrath et al.'s Mexican American participants described her culture's antipathy for divorce due to the Catholic belief system and went on to say that it was important that she and her boyfriend determine sexual compatibility to help avoid an eventual divorce if they were to wed and found that they were incompatible. Young adolescent females develop a strong desire for a romantic relationship replete with roses and displays of chivalry, but for Hispanic females, they also develop in a culture in which women are typically expected to submit to the male partner's wishes. Further, within the Hispanic culture, shows of possessiveness and jealousy by an adolescent male translate into a declaration of love for his romantic partner (Dietrich, 1998). Thus, these adolescent males must be educated about their responsibility to respect females as well as the importance of using condoms, as Latina youth rank at the bottom of the list for frequency of condom use at sexual debut (Cavanagh, 2004). This is especially important long term, as studies show that the choice to use or not use a condom at one's sexual debut is a predictor of future usage (Shafii, 2007).

Although White adolescents are the least likely to have sexual intercourse by high school, they are the most "romantic" of adolescent couples. They are much more likely to tell others that they are a couple and much more likely to hold hands as a sign of affection. They are also more likely to engage in group activities as a couple and more likely to meet the parents of their romantic partner. The "fairy-tale" narrative is clearly more reflective of this group's dominant courtship pattern.

TEEN FATHERHOOD

The United States teenage birth rate fell to its lowest point in 2009 with 39.1 births per 1,000 females (Ventura & Hamilton, 2011). Yet the United States still has the highest teen pregnancy rate of any Western industrialized nation. While not all adolescent females are impregnated by teenage males, 2007 saw a birth rate of 18.7 births per 1,000 fathers ages 15–19 (National Vital Statistics, 2010). The national prevalence of children being born to teenage parents has prompted more research in the field of responsible fatherhood. Most of the research has focused on minority teens as the highest teen birth rates exist among minority youth in inner city areas (Weinman, Smith, & Buzi, 2002). These young dads typically battle greater stressors than their White counterparts, including the burdens of "paternity decisions, financial responsibilities, continuing both his and the mother's education, and residency" (Miller, 1997). The majority of teenage fathers do not marry the mothers of their first child, and, because of the high school dropout rate, they are seldom able to acquire lucrative jobs, thus resulting in a substantial loss in income each year (National Campaign to Prevent Teen and Unplanned Pregnancy, 2008). In addition, reports show that many young fathers faced with financial instability become disinterested in child rearing as a way to avoid failing "to provide" for their new family (Tuffin, Rouch, & Frewin, 2010).

In addition to financial concerns, numerous studies have shown a correlation between teen fatherhood and behavioral problems. Specifically, many young fathers have experience with drugs, sexually transmitted diseases, and violence (Smith, Buzi, & Weinman, 2002). In one study, more than 50% of a sample of 500 teenage fathers had at one time been involved in juvenile delinquency. The study described juvenile delinquency as car theft, burglary, bullying, attacking to inflict pain or death, or rape (Thornberry, Wei, Stouthamer-Loeber, &Van Dyke, 2000).

The combination of general adolescent stressors, an unplanned pregnancy, and the need to act as the provider is often too much for a young man to handle. Trying to successfully manage these conflicting dynamics may lead to even more complex psychological problems. These difficulties, and the lack of access to resources to battle these problems, may lead an adolescent father to abandon his responsibilities as a parent all together. While society continues to highlight the shortcomings of teenage fathers, it does little to offer adolescent dads the resources required to thrive, or much less, to function as responsible parents. Many teen fathers would like to be involved both during and after the pregnancy, but feel ill equipped to provide support physically, emotionally, and financially (Miller, 1997).

Research has also underscored the importance of having a father present in a child's life. Paternal involvement in a child's life can lead to a decrease in school dropouts, drug abuse problems, and future incarceration (National Fatherhood Initiative, 2006). Involvement with their children also has positive effects for adolescent fathers. Playing an active role in their child's life may help "promote the fathers' psychological development, contribute to the fathers' self-esteem, and strengthen the father–child relationship" (Lemay, Cashman, Elfenbein, & Felice, 2010). Many teen dads grew up without positive male role models themselves, and, therefore, lack effective examples to emulate. In a recent study, when adolescent fathers were asked to provide examples of "good fathers," less than a quarter of them identified their own fathers as positive examples (Lemay et al., 2010). Such a statistic is just one indicator of the cyclical nature of teen pregnancy in the United States from generation to generation.

Even school counselors, who may have the most direct access to teen fathers, often ignore the needs of this population. In a survey of school counselors, researchers found that counselors do not recommend pregnancy-related services to the fathers with the same frequency as they do to the mothers (Kiselica, Gorczynski, & Capps, 1998). If they did communicate any type of programming to the fathers, it was usually related to job training or financial responsibility. Less than 45% of the time, school counselors referred adolescent fathers to prenatal care services compared to 93% of the time for expectant teen mothers (Kiselica et al., 1998). They also hesitated to refer these young men to assertiveness training, which then puts the onus on a teenage father to ask an adult for help. While it is imperative that adolescent fathers gain knowledge in career services, they also need parent skill training as parenting begins when the mother becomes pregnant. Financial support is only one type of support that a young father can give the mother of his child. Fathers need education regarding healthy pregnancy as well as how to access resources including physical and mental health professionals. Even before an unplanned pregnancy occurs, schools need to improve sex education policies. Educators have shifted toward "abstinence only" curricula despite the fact that research shows no increase in sexual activity when students are informed about contraception (Kohler, Manhart, & Lafferty, 2008).

Existing Programming

There has been a recent increase in research and dialogue on the subject of adolescent fathers. In the past, almost all of the research regarding teen pregnancy centered on the well-being and training of the mother. Now, with the interest in responsible fatherhood and family at the forefront of media, experts are beginning to examine the needs of adolescent fathers. One program in the Southwest United States focused on the needs of the Latino community. In terms of minority populations, the majority of the limited research on adolescent fatherhood has focused on African American males when, in fact, the Hispanic population has the highest teenage birth rate of any minority group (Ventura & Hamilton, 2011). This particular program was initially designed for fathers in the juvenile justice system, but its tenets are universally applicable. The creators of the program described the goals as both "therapeutic and psychoeducational" with an emphasis on coping resources, an examination of their lives as sons themselves, and basic parent education (Parra-Cardona, Wampler, & Sharp, 2006). The program centered around group therapy sessions during which members discussed the following topics: family-of-origin issues, personal responsibility, the meaning of being a father, prevention of abuse and neglect, child development and child care, and fundamental parenting and discipline skills (Parra-Cardona et al., 2006). Working in groups helped to eliminate the potential for feelings of isolation among the young fathers. Group therapy is also conducive in forming a support system in a population that otherwise might not seek out one another (Anthony & Smith, 1994).

One especially noteworthy part of the therapy included a letter writing assignment. Participants wrote three letters: one to their own father expressing their emotions toward him, regardless of their relationship; one to themselves pretending to be their father highlighting what they wished their father had said to them when they were younger; and one to their child. The third was to include a pledge of commitment to active parenting to their child. Most notably, more than halfway through the program, all the participants had shared their writing with others (Parra-Cardona et al., 2006).

While there are limited programs in existence, counselors should consult the research to discover what adolescent fathers require in their treatment. One study found that the necessary components of a father-centric program included paternity establishment, employment and self-sufficiency training, effective parenting skills, and physical and mental health assistance (Weinman et al., 2002). Physical and mental health includes offering services to adolescents who may be engaging in high-risk behavior such as substance abuse or violence.

Becoming self-sufficient is extremely important for an adolescent father, as he will need to help support his child financially. For many adolescent fathers, a good father is one who can provide for his family. In one study, 47% of those surveyed believed that "being employed or finishing school would help them be better fathers." Career counseling involving interview skills, vocational training, or assistance in the job search is imperative to the success of an adolescent father. Counselors must "include strategies [in their treatment plan] that help young men succeed in overcoming these barriers [to employment]" (Lemay et al., 2010).

Programs should also highlight fatherhood as an ongoing part of a teen's life. Some experts believe that teens should develop a 10-year plan that includes their child in each step. Additionally, adolescent fathers must be trained to use contraceptives in the future to avoid unplanned pregnancies (Mazza, 2002).

Resources for Teenage Fathers

Federal initiatives that support the education of teen fathers continue to grow. In 1994, The National Fatherhood Initiative was established with the mission to "give our nation's children a brighter future by educating and engaging fathers" (National Fatherhood Initiative). Their website offers a variety of resources for new fathers of all ages. Much like other websites including Fatherhood.org, ResponsibleFatherhood.org, and MichiganFatherhood.org, there is very little information specifically targeted at teenage fathers on The National Fatherhood Initiative website. However, these websites are incredibly comprehensive, often with active discussion boards where new fathers can connect.

TeensHealth is a website directed at teens that have various medical questions. It can serve as a great resource for adolescent fathers who would like to learn more about prenatal and postnatal care for the mother of their child so that they can actively support her physically. For those fathers who may be unable to attend group therapy, counselors can direct them to the stories in the book *Teenage Fathers*, by Karen Gravelle and Leslie Peterson Caputo. The book follows 13 different stories of teenage fathers and the various ways in which the fathers handled their own situations. This may aid in helping an adolescent identify his own best practices as a parent during and after the pregnancy. Another book that may provide help to fathers is *Teen Fathers Today* by Ted Gottfried. Gottfried's book gives practical advice to teen fathers-to-be by debunking common myths in a language that is familiar to teens.

DATING VIOLENCE

The CDC (2010) has reported that 1 in 10 teens have been the victim of dating violence, and it is essential that adolescents are taught that violence does not belong in any relationship. Swahn, Simon, Arias, and Bossarte (2008) reported that in a survey of seventh graders in a high-risk school about a third of the boys reported being victimized within a romantic relationship and a quarter of the girls reported victimization. Dating violence comprises three types: physical, emotional, and sexual, and it typically begins in what many teens consider an innocuous way—by teasing or name-calling, but it can progress rapidly as a partner's defenses are gently eroded. Boys, as well as girls, are victims of forced sex: statistics show that fully 5% of males have been forced to engage in sexual intercourse (Howard & Wang, 2005). And the effects of intimate partner violence are long lasting for teens; a report from the CDC presented findings that victims of dating violence often have academic performance setbacks, increased substance use, and depression and anxiety that can lead to suicide attempts. And, not surprisingly, the perpetrators are more aggressive, more depressed, and show lower self-esteem than their peers. The CDC strongly believes that dating violence must be dealt with prior to its instigation, and it has developed a school-based program called "Safe Dates" that addresses social norms and enhances teens' problem-solving abilities.

Counselors must promote their offices as safe spaces in which victims of violence may reveal their experiences and appropriate assistance can be provided. Further, they must be aware of the laws and regulations in their state regarding the type of information that can be shared with students regarding sex education, birth control, and sexually transmitted infections. And they also must be aware that they are mandated reporters of any type of abuse involving minors.

It is important that counselors working in the schools or with adolescent clients in the community be aware of the strong pull that romantic relationships have on their clients. Davis and Benshoff (1999) stressed the importance of treating these relationships much as you would treat adult romantic relationships. The need for approval and acceptance can be strong during the teen years, and it is important that young couples are taught early how to respect and communicate with one another.

CASE STUDY: TEEN HEARTTHROB

Kyle is a 15-year-old, White male attending a suburban high school. He plays trumpet in the school band and plays lacrosse on the school team. Halfway through Kyle's sophomore year, his geometry teacher, Ms. Morrison, noticed Kyle repeatedly passing notes to Sarah, a female classmate. Ms. Morrison walked down the aisle of desks and picked up Kyle's notebook and the notes off Sarah's desk. She told Kyle he would have to retrieve his notebook at the end of class. While the class was wrestling with the next series of geometry theorems, she quickly looked over Kyle's note and the doodles in his notebook. The note contained requests for sexual favors, and the notebook had graphic pictures of sexual positions. Ms. Morrison considered marching Kyle directly to the principal, but instead decided to escort him to the school counselor, Ms. Rosewood.

Kyle swaggered into Ms. Rosewood's office behind Ms. Morrison. He appeared unconcerned, plopping himself in a chair, and began watching the phys ed class out the window. After quickly scanning Kyle's note to Sarah and the drawings, Ms. Rosewood asked Kyle how he felt about Sarah and how he would describe their relationship. Kyle shared that he and Sarah were in the early stages of their relationship and that Sarah and he were exclusive.

Interventions

Ms. Rosewood needs to quickly assess Kyle's behavior and psychological mindset in order to determine where his behavior stands on the continuum of adolescent sexual behavior. Though her initial questions assume Kyle's behavior is typical for an adolescent male with little to no knowledge of sexual mores, she is concerned he may be exhibiting a pattern of intentional sexual aggression and harassment of Sarah. Therefore, she first wants to determine whether or not Sarah is involved in the communications.

Kyle stated, "all the kids write those kinds of notes to each other. And Sarah and I have been kind of talkin' for a couple of weeks, she knows what I want the nex' step to be." Ms. Rosewood was a new counselor at this inner city school, but she knew that students in urban schools were typically much more sexually active than at her suburban internship placement site. She was also aware that about one-third of adolescents had been involved in "sexting," which is the sending of sexually explicit messages and photos via cell phone or e-mail (The National Campaign to Prevent Teen and Unplanned Pregnancy, 2008). She also remembered reading that about half of high school students have had sexual intercourse, so she wasn't as shocked at Kyle's comments as she would have been a year ago. However, she affirmed that school was not the place to communicate these types of messages and that sexually explicit drawings or messages were not to be brought into the classroom. Ms. Rosewood made a mental note that she would need to address these same issues with Sarah in a private meeting.

Ms. Rosewood then asked Kyle about his level of interest in fostering an emotional connection and relationship with Sarah. She also inquired about what he valued in her as a person. Kyle said that he wasn't ready to call her "his lady" yet, but that he wasn't "playin' Sarah," either. The counselor was exploring the overall relationship with Kyle, just as she would with adults, so that she could model the areas of a relationship that warranted attention: mutual respect, communication, negotiation, and so on. She also asked Kyle to talk about who his role models were when it came to creating romantic relationships as well as about any gender role expectations he felt placed on him by peers.

Luckily, they were in a school in which the counselors may address the importance of safe sex, and Ms. Rosewood shared this information with Kyle and referred him to a nearby center where he could pick up free condoms. She also encouraged him to engage Sarah in a conversation about safe sex and birth control. Kyle was surprised at the business-like tone that his counselor was able to take toward the topic, and he openly complimented her on her ability to be "kewl, like a jewel" and not treat him like a kid. Ms. Rosewood, herself, was also pleasantly surprised at how easily she'd been able to handle this initial discussion with Kyle.

Outcome

She asked that Kyle stop by for a follow-up chat in the next couple of weeks and reminded him that it was inappropriate to interrupt class lessons with the passing of notes and that if it persisted, it would become a matter of discipline that would be referred to the administration. She reiterated the importance of showing respect for Sarah, and all women, and again suggested that he might like to bring Sarah with him to a visit to her office. After Kyle left her office, Ms. Rosewood decided that she would develop some new groups and guidance lessons geared toward "couples communication" and "negotiating your relationship."

CASE STUDY: TEEN FATHER

Angel is a 16-year-old Hispanic male living in a low income inner city neighborhood. Angel's mother, Marisol, gave birth to Angel when she was 15 years old and, for the most part, raised Angel by herself.

Although Angel never had contact with his biological father, Marisol has dated different men over the course of his life. Over the course of several months, Marisol noticed that Angel's grades had slipped. She confronted him, and he responded defensively, which was uncharacteristic of him. In addition, Angel began arriving home from school much later than normal with an older crowd of boys who had a reputation for wild and erratic behavior. He seemed to be defying her every rule without any explanation.

Shortly after Marisol began to notice these changes in Angel's behavior, he was arrested on school property for his involvement in a minor drug deal with the older boys with whom he had been seen. Because he was a first time offender, the court ordered him to attend counseling so that the charge would eventually be expunged from his record. Over the course of the first few counseling sessions, Angel became more comfortable and began to speak about very personal subjects. During these conversations, Angel revealed that his 15-year-old girlfriend, Isabel, was pregnant. He also shared that he did not know how far along she was, nor did he know if she had even seen a doctor since she had taken a drugstore pregnancy test three months ago. He even asked his therapist, "I know it takes nine months to have a baby, but when do the nine months start?"

Angel described his emotions to his counselor in detail. Upon finding out that Isabel was pregnant, Angel's only thought was to make money so that he could pay for the baby. When Angel's counselor asked him if he had considered abortion or adoption, Angel seemed confused as though no one had made him aware of those options. Angel explained to his counselor that neither he nor Isabel had positive relationships with their fathers. Angel had actually never met his father, and he informed the therapist he "assumed he was dead." Angel acknowledged that because of the drug charge, he knew he would have difficulty getting a good job. No job meant no child support. In Angel's opinion, if he couldn't pay child support, then there was no real role for him as a dad. Whenever Angel became uncomfortable with the idea of being an inadequate financial supporter to his unborn child, his therapist noticed that he would insinuate that someone else might be the father of the baby. When the therapist suggested a paternity test, Angel refused the suggestion.

Interventions

In the next session, Angel's counselor suggested that they map out specific goals for him to accomplish over the remaining number of their court-mandated sessions. The first goal was to assist Angel in telling his mother about the pregnancy. The counselor offered to host both of them in her office in order to mediate the discussion between the two. She spoke with Angel about what the next steps on his road to being a father might be. She encouraged Angel to share this plan of action with Marisol in an effort to ask for her support.

Angel's counselor also felt strongly that in order to avoid becoming a repeat offender, Angel needs to receive vocational and job training. She reached out to several local organizations in order to gauge available programming. In doing so, she connected with a group sponsored by a local counseling center that offers group training for fathers-to-be. While the group is solely for teenage fathers, the program is designed for first-time fathers from low-income families. Angel's counselor was especially impressed by this program, as it focuses on designing a 5-year plan for each father. Angel is in a vulnerable demographic, and viewing this training as the first step toward being a lifelong father will be important to his success (Mazza, 2002). Angel's counselor was also pleased that successful hands-on fathers, in addition to responsible mothers, lead the program. Angel will be able to relate to the strong women, as he has a good relationship with his mother. The men will provide the much needed positive male role models for Angel to emulate.

Outcome

Because the counseling sessions were court-ordered, they were limited in number. Angel's counselor worked with Angel to pull together a network of resources that he can consult once termination has occurred. Over the course of the pregnancy, Angel and Isabel broke up, but Angel's pre- and postnatal training in his new father's group allowed him the opportunity to support Isabel physically and emotionally as he continued his education. Group therapy helped Angel develop a positive support system so that he no longer had to rely on the older boys at school who were with him at the time of his arrest.

Isabel was able to register in a school-supported teen mom program that allowed nontraditional class times to accommodate feeding schedules. Unfortunately, because nothing of the sort existed for Angel, he enrolled in vocational training in auto repair at the high school so that he could enter the job market immediately upon graduation.

In order to assist with childcare, Marisol has altered her work schedule so that she could keep the baby during the day. In Marisol's opinion, by increasing her involvement with his child, she would be able to monitor Angel's progress and his commitment to his 5-year plan.

Angel participated in eight court-mandated counseling sessions and then four additional sessions that the counselor provided pro bono. The group therapy program lasted 5 weeks, but Angel would be able to return at any time should he need to engage in discussion.

RESOURCES

Nonfiction Books

Corrina, H. (2007). *S.E.X.: The all-you-need-to-know progressive sexuality guide to get you through high school and college.* Cambridge, MA: Da Capo.

Daldry, J. (1999). *The teenage guy's survival guide: The real deal on girls, growing up and other guy stuff.* USA: Piccadilly.

Henderson, E. (2007). *100 Questions you'd never ask your parents.* Richmond, VA: Uppman.

Prescott, D., & Longo, R. (2010). *Current applications: Strategies for working with sexually aggressive youth and youth with sexual behavior problems.* Holyoke, MA: Neari.

Prescott, D. & Longo, R. (2005). *Current perspectives: Working with sexually aggressive youth and youth with sexual behavior problems.* Holyoke, MA: Neari.

Fiction Books

Chbosky, S. (1999). *The perks of being a wallflower.* New York: Pocket Books.

Flinn, A. (2001). *Breathing underwater.* New York: Harper Collins Children's Books.

Johnson, A. (2003). *The first part last.* New York: Simon & Schuster.

Online

www.scarleteen.com—This site is self-described as the best site for real-world sex education, and it offers information and education on almost any topic on sexuality that an adolescent might wonder about.

www.karenrayne.com—This site is authored by Dr. Karen Rayne, an expert on adolescent sex education. She offers frank advice to adolescents, and she is a strong supporter of parents taking an active role in the sharing of sex education information with their children. Her site has sections for adolescents as well as their parents.

www.teenwire.com—This site offers information for teens related to relationships as well as sex education for heterosexual and gay-questioning adolescents.

www.iwannaknow.com—This site is sponsored by the American Social Health Association and offers information for adolescents, parents, and educators. It has a strong focus on prevention of sexually transmitted diseases.

Dating Violence Resources

Choose Respect Initiative—www.chooserespect.org
National Domestic Violence Hotline—1–800-799-SAFE (7233)
National Sexual Assault Hotline—1–800-656-HOPE (4673)
National Sexual Violence Resource Center—www.nsvrc.org
National Youth Violence Prevention Resource Center—www.safeyouth.org

REFERENCES

Abma, J., Martinez, G. M., Mosher, W. D., & Dawson, B. S. (2004). Teenagers in the United States: Sexual activity, contraceptive use, and childbearing. *Vital and Health Statistics, 23* No. 24, 1–87.

Anderson, E. (1990). *Streetwise: Race, class, and change in an urban community.* Chicago: Chicago University Press.

Anthony, I. & Smith, D. (1994) Adolescent fathers: A positive acknowledgement in the school setting. *Social Work in Education, 16*, 179–186.

Armstrong, E. G. (2001). Gangsta misogyny: A content analysis of the portrayals of violence against women in rap music, 1987–1993. *Journal of Criminal Justice and Popular Culture, 8*, 96–126.

Barber, B. & Eccles, J. (2003). The joy of romance: Healthy adolescent relationships as an educational agenda. In P. Florsheim (Ed.), *Adolescent romantic relations and sexual behavior: theory, research, and practical implications* (pp. 355–387). Mahwah, NJ: Lawrence Erlbaum Associates.

Brown, J. D., L'Engle, K. L., Pardun, C. J., Guo, G., Kenneavy, K., & Jackson, C. (2006). Sexy media matter: Exposure to sexual content in music, movies, television, and magazines predicts black and white adolescents' sexual behavior. *Pediatrics, 117*, 1018–1028.

Carver, K., Joyner, K., & Udry, J. R. (2003). National estimates of adolescent romantic relationships. In P. Florsheim (ed.), *Adolescent romantic relations and sexual behavior: Theory, research, and practical implications* (pp. 23–56). Mahwah, NJ: Lawrence Erlbaum.

Cavanagh, S. E. (2004). The sexual debut of girls in early adolescence: The intersection of race, pubertal timing, and friendship group characteristics. *Journal of Research on Adolescence, 14*, 285–312.

CDC. (2010). Youth Risk Behavior Surveillance System: US, 2009. *MMWR, 57*(SS-4).

Coleman, E. (1981). Counseling adolescent males. *Personnel & Guidance Journal, 60*(4), 215–218.

Davis, K. M., & Benshoff, J. M. (1999). A proactive approach to couples counseling with adolescents. *Professional School Counseling, 2*, 391–394.

Degges-White, S., & Borzumato-Gainey, C. (2011). *Friends forever: How girls and women forge lasting relationships.* Lanham, MD: Rowman & Littlefield.

Dietrich, L. C. (1998). *Bitches, 'ho's, and schoolgirls.* Westport, CT: Praeger.

Erikson, E. (1980). *Identity and the life cycle.* New York: W. W. Norton & Co.

Forrest, S. (2000). 'Big and tough': Boys learning about sexuality and manhood. *Sexual and Relationship Therapy, 15,* 247–261.

Foshee, V. A., Linder, G. F., Bauman, K. E., et al. (1996). The Safe Dates project: Theoretical basis, evaluation design, and selected baseline findings. *American Journal of Preventive Medicine, 12*(Suppl 2), 39–47.

Giordano, P. C., Longmore, M. A., & Manning, W D. (2006). Gender and the meanings of adolescent romantic relationships: A focus on boys. *American Sociological Review, 71,* 260–287.

Howard, D. E., & Wang, M. Q. (2005). Psychosocial correlates of U.S. adolescents who report a history of forced sexual intercourse. *Journal of Adolescent Health, 36,* 372–379.

Kiselica, M., Gorczynski, J., & Capps, S. (1998). Teen mothers and fathers: School counselor perceptions of service needs. *Professional School Counseling, 2*(2), 146–153.

Kohler, P., Manhart, L., & Lafferty, W. (2007). Abstinence-only and comprehensive sex education and the initiation of sexual activity and teen pregnancy. *Journal of Adolescent Health, 42,* 344–351.

Lemay, C., Cashman, S., Elfenbein, D., & Felice, M. (2010). A qualitative study of the meaning of fatherhood among young urban fathers. *Public Health Nursing, 27*(3), 221–231. doi:10.1111/j.1525–1446.2010.00847.x.

Mazza, C. (2002) Young dads: The effects of a parenting program on urban African American adolescent fathers. *Adolescence, 37*(148), 681–693.

Milbrath, C., Ohlson, B., & Eyre, S. L. (2009), Analyzing cultural models in adolescent accounts of romantic relationships. *Journal of Research on Adolescence, 19,* 313–351.

Miller, D. (1997). Adolescent fathers: What we know and what we need to know. *Child and Adolescent Social Work Journal, 14,* 55–69.

National Fatherhood Initiative (2006). *How to create a reentry plan.* Gaithersburg, MD: Author.

National Vital Statistics. (August 9, 2010). Birth rates, by age and race of father: United States, 1980–2007. *National Vital Statistics Reports, 58*(24), 51–52.

Okazaki, S. (2002). Influences of culture on Asian Americans' sexuality. *Journal of Sex Research, 39*(1), 34–41.

O'Sullivan, L. F., Cheng, M. M., Harris, K. M., & Broks-Gunn, J. (2007). I wanna hold your hand: The progression of social, romantic and sexual events in adolescent relationships. *Perspectives on Sexual and Reproductive Health, 39*(2), 100–107.

O'Sullivan, L. F., Meyer-Bahlburg, H. F. L., & Watkins, B. X. (2001). Mother-daughter communication about sex among urban African American and Latino families. *Journal of Adolescent research, 16,* 269–291.

Ott, M. A., Millstein, S. G., Ofner, S., & Halpern-Felsher, B. L. (2006). Greater expectations: Adolescents' positive motivations for sex. *Perspectives on Sexual and Reproductive Health, 38*(2), 84–89.

Parra-Cardona, J., Wampler, R., & Sharp, E. (2006). Wanting to be a good father: Experiences of adolescent fathers of Mexican descent in a teen fathers program. *Journal of Marital and Family Therapy, 32,* 215–231.

Rosenthal, D. A. & Feldman, S. S. (1999). The importance of importance: Adolescents' perceptions of parental communication about sexuality. *Journal of Adolescence, 22,* 835–851.

Royer, H. R., Keller, M. L., & Heidrich, S. M. (2009). Young adolescents' perceptions of romantic relationships and sexual activity. *Sex Education, 4,* 395–408.

Shafii, T. (2007). Association between condom use at sexual debut and subsequent sexual trajectories: A longitudinal study using biomarkers. *American Journal of Public Health, 97,* 1090–1095.

Smith, L. H., & Guthrie, B. J. (2005). Testing a model: A developmental perspective of adolescent male sexuality. *Journal for Specialists in Pediatric Nursing, 10*(3), 124–138.

Smith, P., Buzi, R., & Weinman, M. (2002). Programs for young fathers: Essential components and evaluation issues. *North American Journal of Psychology, 4*(1), 81–92.

Swahn, M. H., Simon, T. R., Arias, I., & Bossarte, R. M. (2008). Measuring sex differences in violence victimization and perpetration within date and same-sex peer relationships. *Journal of Interpersonal Violence. 23,* 1120–1138.

Tabares, A., & Gottman, J. M. (2003). A marital process perspective of adolescent romantic relationships. In P. Florsheim (Ed.), *Adolescent romantic relations and sexual behavior: Theory, research, and practical implications* (pp. 337–354). Mahwah, NJ: Erlbaum.

The National Campaign to Prevent Teen and Unplanned Pregnancy. (2008). *Sex and tech: Results from a survey of teens and young adults.* Washington, DC: The National Campaign to Prevent Teen and Unplanned Pregnancy. Retrieved from http://www.thenationalcampaign.org/sextech/pdf/sextech_summary.pdf

Thornberry, T., Wei, E., Stouthamer-Loeber, M., & Van Dyke, J. (2000). Office of Juvenile Justice and Delinquency Prevention Bulletin.

Tuffin, K., Rouch, G., & Frewin, K. (2010). Constructing adolescent fatherhood: Responsibilities and intergenerational repair. *Culture, Health & Sexuality, 12*(5), 485–498.

Ventura, S. J., & Hamilton, B. E. (2011). *U.S. teenage birth rate resumes decline.* NCHS data brief, no 58. Hyattsville, MD: National Center for Health Statistics.

Weinman, M., Smith, P., & Buzi, R. (2002). Young fathers: An analysis of risk behaviors and service needs. *Child and Adolescent Social Work Journal, 19,* 437–453.

9

Counseling Gay and Questioning Boys and Young Men

EDWARD P. CANNON AND JOHN F. MARSZALEK

Although gay people, as a group, are more open than ever before—with almost 60% of U.S. residents reporting that they have a friend, coworker, or relative who is gay (Gallup, 2009)—gay and questioning boys and young men still receive mixed messages from society on whether or not it is acceptable to be gay. For example, in a recent poll, almost 60% of U.S. residents expressed the belief that homosexuality should be supported by society, but 46% opposed same-sex marriage (Pew Research Center, 2011). While homosexuality has not been considered a mental illness by the American Psychiatric Association (APA) since 1973, over half of the states do not prohibit employment discrimination based on sexual orientation (National Gay and Lesbian Task Force, 2011). Gay youth are coming out at earlier ages (Denizet-Lewis, 2009), but the Gay, Lesbian, and Straight Education Network (GLSEN, 2009) reported that of 7,261 gay and questioning middle and high school students surveyed, 85% reported experiencing verbal harassment based on their sexual orientation, 40% reported physical harassment, and 19% reported physical assault. It is not surprising, then, that gay and questioning youth report more symptoms of depression and higher rates of suicidal ideation (Almeida, Johnson, Corliss, Molnar, & Azrael, 2009). In fact, suicide prevention programs such as *The Trevor Project* and the *It Gets Better Project* were specifically created to reach out to gay and questioning youth.

This chapter presents important information for counselors and other helping professionals who work with gay and questioning boys and young men, including specific issues likely to be addressed in counseling. Following a description of the terms *sexual orientation, sexual behavior,* and *sexual identity*, we will discuss gay identity models and the importance of counselors and other helping professionals understanding the developmental process for gay and questioning boys and young men in coming out to themselves and others. Next, we will discuss implications for counseling, including specific challenges for gay and questioning boys and young men and present a case example. Finally, we will provide resources for counselors and other helping professionals who work with gay and questioning boys and young men.

SEXUAL ORIENTATION, SEXUAL BEHAVIOR, AND SEXUAL IDENTITY

To work effectively with gay and questioning male youth, helping professionals need to understand the difference between sexual orientation, sexual behavior, and sexual identity. According to the APA (2008), *sexual orientation* refers to an enduring pattern of emotional, romantic, and/or sexual attractions to men, to women, or to both men and women. Sexual orientation is likely to be established by birth or early childhood and is mostly stable, resistant to conscious control, and internally consonant. Research over several decades has demonstrated that sexual orientation ranges along a continuum, from exclusive attraction to the other sex to exclusive attraction to the same sex. Sexual orientation is usually described in terms of three categories: heterosexual, gay/lesbian, and bisexual. More recently, nonheterosexual individuals have begun describing themselves as "queer" to illustrate that they do not fit into any category. The term "queer" also has political connotations, since it has been historically used to oppress nonheterosexual individuals, but is now being used by this community as a source of pride.

Sexual behavior refers to sexual activities in which individuals engage. Depending on cultural and individual factors (e.g., religiosity, values of the family, race, ethnicity, gender, and age), sexual partners may be consistent or inconsistent with one's sexual orientation. For example, the "down low" phenomenon (Denizet-Lewis, 2003) represents individuals who engage in sex with partners of the same sex, but who overtly identify as heterosexual or straight. These individuals present an image of hypermasculinity, while rejecting a gay identity, and are very secretive. Unfortunately, due to this secrecy, individuals whose sexual identity does not match their sexual behavior are often unreceptive to safer sex messages directed at gay and bisexual men.

Sexual identity is a socially recognized label that names sexual feelings, attractions, and behaviors and is symbolized by statements such as, "I am gay" and "I am straight." According to the APA (2008), the core attractions that form the basis for adult sexual identity typically emerge between middle childhood and early adolescence. These patterns of emotional, romantic, and sexual attractions may arise without any prior sexual experience. In other words, people can be celibate and still know their sexual identity, whether gay, bisexual, or heterosexual. This is an important issue for helping professionals, since individuals are recognizing and naming their sexual identities at younger and younger ages.

Although most adolescents who come out do so in high school, researchers are finding that middle school students are increasingly coming out to friends or family, or to an adult at school (Savin-Williams, 2005). For many gay and questioning youth, middle schools and high schools are hostile territory. Recent statistics and news reports about antigay bullying are alarming. Even the perception by others that one has a gay identity can lead to social ostracism and bullying, thus complicating the issue. The majority of school personnel and administrators report feeling unprepared to work with a middle or high school student who comes out as gay (GLSEN, 2009).

Coming Out

Coming out, or disclosing one's same-sex attractions, is a complex sexual identity recognition process that begins when an individual has a sense of being different from other boys and culminates with disclosure to others. It is a lifelong process, but begins with the self-recognition of feeling same-sex attractions. Typically, a boy or young man will come out to himself first, followed by disclosure to a trusted friend, and then, eventually, he may come out to his family and wider social circle. It is also true that many people with same-sex attractions will never disclose to anyone or will selectively disclose to trusted friends. Because the importance of *fitting in* during adolescence is paramount, coming out can be fraught with anxiety and danger, both physical and emotional. Thus, staying in the closet, or not revealing one's true feelings, is quite common for many adolescent boys and young men.

Historically, coming out has been viewed as a developmental task that primarily involves establishing an identity as a gay person by specifically incorporating sexual orientation into one's identity (Cass, 1984; Troiden, 1989). In these models, nonheterosexual individuals move through a series of stages from *awareness* to *acceptance* of one's sexual orientation. For example, the Cass model includes the following stages: identity confusion, identity comparison, identity tolerance, identity acceptance, identity pride, and identity synthesis. Failure to navigate the stages in a timely and linear manner was once thought to result in negative outcomes, from minor delays in coming to terms with one's sexuality to stunted psychological growth.

More recently, researchers have conceptualized the coming out process in different ways. All adolescents, regardless of attractions, have a basic, stable sexual orientation and may engage in sexual behavior. In general, only same-sex attracted adolescents and young adults question the meaning of their sexual orientation and behavior and construct a sexual identity. Savin-Williams (2005) argued that same-sex development does not proceed in an orderly, universal manner, but rather constitutes a complex blending of typical adolescent development with specific commonly experienced milestones. These milestones include feeling different from other children of their biological sex, the onset of same-sex attractions (average age is 8 or 9), a first same-sex encounter, romance (e.g., merging emotional and sexual intimacy), and finally, disclosure of their same-sex attraction to friends, followed by disclosure to parents.

Rosario et al. (2001) asserted that coming out consists of five dimensions: (a) involvement in gay-themed activities; (b) the development of attitudes (from negative to positive) toward a gay identity; (c) comfort with a gay identity; (d) the number of disclosures of sexual identity to others; and (e) the type of sexual identity (e.g., how one self-identifies). Rosario and colleagues developed a model that links these five dimensions to psychological functioning (i.e., levels of distress and self-esteem) and sexual behaviors (i.e., number of sexual encounters). Initial negative attitudes toward homosexuality change over time for the adolescent as he begins to participate in activities such as the school's Gay–Straight Alliance (GSA) or perhaps a teen drop-in center for non-heterosexual youth. Exploring the associations between the coming out process for male adolescents, psychological functioning, and sexual behaviors, Rosario and colleagues found that positive attitudes and comfort with homosexuality correlated with high self-esteem, lower anxiety, and lower rates of depression.

Minority Stress Model

The minority stress model (Meyer, 2003) is a conceptual framework for understanding elevated rates of mental and physical illness among non-heterosexual boys and young men. According to the model, sexual minorities, similar to other culturally marginalized groups, suffer negative life events perpetrated by the majority culture that generate stress reactions. These reactions can lead to mental illness (e.g., depression and anxiety) as well as problematic behavior (e.g., promiscuity and delinquency. In this model, it is suggested that the stress is initially generated from feelings of unacceptability and inferiority. There are few experiences as alienating as growing up believing that a "natural" aspect of one's self is deemed morally and socially deplorable and knowing that one may become an outcast upon its disclosure.

According to the model, boys learn that a gay identity is unacceptable, and this leads to internalized homophobia, a perceived need to conceal important aspects of oneself, and a fear of rejection. Some learn that being gay would hurt or disappoint parents; others are directly warned by parents that they will be abused or thrown out of their homes if they reveal a gay identity. Although other stigmatized youth who are teased because of physical traits, ethnicity, or religion are almost certain to receive support and guidance from family and community, nonheterosexual boys and young men can feel isolated and alone. Because any nonheterosexual identity is often stigmatized and punishable by socially sanctioned violence and discrimination, the minority stress model observes that these young people endure states of chronic arousal and hypervigilance.

Some nonheterosexual boys and young men externalize stress by becoming overtly heterosexual, which can include vitriolic displays of aggression directed at those perceived to be gay, behavioral "proofs" of masculinity through promiscuous heterosexual sex, or antisocial or criminal acts. Others seek relief from stress by becoming asexual, by associating with other perceived social misfits such as "druggies," or by overcompensating in other areas, including academics. Numbing the pain through alcohol and drugs can be interpreted as an attempt to flee from unacceptable circumstances and to contain sadness and anxiety. Turning inward and becoming depressed or suicidal is another mechanism of coping.

RECOMMENDATIONS FOR COUNSELORS AND OTHER HELPING PROFESSIONALS

Having access to school staff members who are supportive of their needs and issues offers an important resource for gay and questioning youth. School counselors are often ideally situated to advocate for and provide services to nonheterosexual students (Whitman, Horn, & Boyd, 2007). However, school counselors may have an inadequate level of knowledge related to gay issues and a lack of understanding of how to help nonheterosexual youth in their schools. This creates a situation where the school counselors may have the desire to assist these students in their school but may not know how to be effective. The section that follows provides specific recommendations that counselors and other helping professionals can implement to ensure that the school experience is positive for gay and questioning students.

Challenge Homoprejudiced and Biased Remarks

Researchers have found that school personnel are *three times* less likely to challenge homoprejudiced comments than racist comments (Kosciw, Diaz, & Greytek, 2008). Sporadic intervention by school personnel to homoprejudiced language may send the message that this type of discrimination and bias are not only tolerated, but also accepted. By demonstrating that antigay verbal harassment is unacceptable, school counselors and other helping professionals can send a strong message to the student body and create an atmosphere of tolerance and acceptance for all students. Additionally, nonheterosexual students who have supportive school personnel also have higher grade point averages and are more likely to pursue postsecondary education than nonheterosexual students who do not have the support of school staff (GLSEN, 2009). The *Think Before You Speak Campaign,* created by the Ad Council, is a valuable resource for school counselors and can be found at http://www.thinkb4youspeak.com

Biblioguidance

Biblioguidance, frequently referred to as bibliotherapy, is the use of books to help the reader deal with social, emotional, or personal problems. The underlying premise is for clients to identify with literary characters similar to themselves, an association that helps the clients release emotions, gain new directions in life, and explore new ways of interacting (Gladding & Gladding, 1991). School counselors and other helping professionals working with gay and questioning adolescents have a duty to address the needs of their students; using biblioguidance is one way in which this may be accomplished.

Currently, gay and questioning teens rarely, if ever, see their history or stories reflected in the literary selections or textbooks used in their classes. This failure to acknowledge the existence and contribution of lesbian, gay, bisexual, and queer (LGBQ) people can be destructive to the students' development (Vare & Norton, 2004). The lack of visibility and the inability for students to "see" themselves in the curriculum sends an alienating message of denial and despair. School counselors and other helping professionals can combat these messages by building a professional library of LGBQ titles to break through this barrier of silence and to create a more hospitable environment. Although a large number of suitable fiction and nonfiction books written for LGBQ youth exist, school counselors need only a small selection of well-chosen books available to recommend to students. At the end of this chapter, you will find a cross section of literary titles available for students, as well as a brief selection of recommended books for counselors and other helping professionals.

Safe Spaces

GLSEN developed the *Safe Space* concept to visibly identify people and places that are "safe" for nonheterosexual students. Typically, the ally places a sticker, banner, or sign with a pink triangle, rainbow flag, or other recognizable gay symbol on their office door, bulletin board, filing cabinet, or desk as an affirmation of LGBQ people. It clearly lets others know that they are a safe person to approach for support and guidance. The *Safe Spaces* program helps to encourage an inclusive environment that is accessible and friendly to all students. This program increases the visible presence of allies who can help shape a school environment that is welcoming to all people regardless of sexual orientation, gender identity/expression, race, ethnicity, culture, nationality, religion, or other differences.

In an ideal world, the school administration would formally organize and publicize the program, provide the allies with basic training, and educate the greater school community about the meaning of the stickers and the importance of making the school safe for all students. However, this does not need to be formally organized or officially backed to be successfully implemented. Any individuals committed to equality and safety for all students can turn their office or classroom into a safe space. In these situations, it is very likely that word of mouth will spread the news that there is an ally and a safe place for gay and questioning youth. On their website, GLSEN offers a free how-to kit for developing the *Safe Space* program (http://www.glsen.org).

Gay–Straight Alliances

Gay–Straight Alliances (GSAs) are student-led, school-based clubs that address LGBQ issues. One of the unique qualities of these clubs is that membership is open to all students, regardless of sexual orientation or sexual identity (Hansen, 2007). GSAs typically provide support and foster a sense of belonging for nonheterosexual students and their allies. GSAs also help educate the school community about LGBQ issues and advocate for an improved school environment for all students (GLSEN, 2009). Research has shown that the presence of a Gay–Straight Alliance is the strongest indicator of a supportive environment for nonheterosexual students (Hansen, 2007).

Positive Role Models

Gay and questioning youth are in need of role models who can help counter negative messages and can help to create a more positive and supportive environment. School counselors must be willing to be this role model (Pope, 2003). Nonheterosexual counselors, teachers, and others who are "out" in the school can serve as role models for the gay and questioning youth in their school. By being visible as a LGBQ individual, the counselor can help dispel many of the myths and stereotypes about nonheterosexual people. If the counselor is either heterosexual or unable to come out of the closet because of the climate, he or she can still be a role model by actively combating heterosexism and homoprejudice.

School counselors and other personnel are the natural choice for students looking for someone to talk to about their concerns and feelings. Research has shown that if gay and questioning students are going to see the school counselor, they will take the initiative themselves (Fontaine, 1998). Counselors and other helping professionals who are seen as welcoming and understanding will find that the nonheterosexual students will seek them out.

CASE STUDY: MARTIN, AGE 16

Martin is a Hispanic, Catholic, 16-year-old boy who has come to counseling through a referral from his high school English teacher, Ms. Patterson. She had noticed that Martin seemed to be depressed; he rarely spoke in class and seemed to keep to himself. She had spoken to one of his teachers from the previous year, and he noted that that Martin had been one of his most talkative and engaged students. One day during lunch, Ms. Patterson walked by a picnic table on the school grounds and noticed Martin sitting alone. She approached him and asked if everything was okay. He paused for a moment, looked down at the ground, then raised his head, and nodded "yes." She noticed, however, that he seemed to be fighting back tears. She shared that she was concerned about him and that he could talk to her anytime; she would not judge him.

During class, Martin had noticed that Ms. Patterson had books on a variety of topics on the bookshelf behind her desk, including one on the history of gay and lesbian literature. He had also heard her mention that Tennessee Williams was gay in a matter-of-fact way as she talked about his life. The next day, he stopped by her office after school. He told her that he was gay and that he was afraid of anyone finding out. He did not know to whom he could talk and was afraid how his parents would react if he told them.

Families, and Friends of Lesbians and Gays (PFLAG) to provide to his parents should he decide to come out, as well as a copy of "A Resource Guide to Coming Out" (Human Rights Campaign Fund, 2011) for them to discuss as he considered whether or not he should come out to others. Finally, she explained to him that he did not have to make a decision right away and that she would be happy to conduct a family counseling session if he decided he would rather talk to his parents with her present.

Ms. Barnett also wanted to provide resources for Martin to connect with other gay students in the area so that he would feel less isolated. She told him about a youth group for LGBQ youth at the local community center. She had referred other students to this group, and she knew that they had benefitted from it. The youth group provided both a support and social outlet for gay and questioning youth. Martin did not know how he would be able to attend this group without his parents' knowledge, but he was excited that there was a way he could meet other gay and questioning youth in his area.

Martin met regularly with Ms. Barnett throughout the term as he worked through the coming out process. Counseling helped him to feel less isolated, and he was eventually able to come out to a few of his female friends but lived "two lives" throughout high school, being out only with these friends and his *Facebook* friends. He did eventually come out to his parents later that year, who were concerned that "this was a phase he was going through." Ms. Barnett met with his parents and provided them with information on PFLAG meetings and other resources. However, they eventually became increasingly supportive and provided their permission for him to attend the youth group, especially when they learned that in addition to being a social group, the group counselors provided education to participants on topics ranging from safe sex to how to choose a LGBQ-friendly college.

Discussion

This case example paints somewhat of an ideal picture of a gay youth's experience in coming out. First, he attended a school in which the school counselor and teacher felt free to display items such as relevant books and safe zone stickers to let gay and questioning students know that they were allies. This is not always the case in conservative areas and at religion-based schools. Second, Ms. Barnett worked in a school district that had the resources to hire school counselors who could meet with students individually. In addition, she could guarantee Martin's confidentiality based on his age and their state's law regarding confidentiality. In many schools, the school counselors would be required to refer a student out to a community counselor and/or obtain parental consent for treatment. Third, Martin lived in a large metropolitan area with a gay and lesbian community center. Gay youth living in rural areas do not have access to gay youth groups and community centers unless a high school has a gay–straight alliance; rural youth are thus likely to feel more isolated. Fourth, Martin's parents were supportive of him, which is too frequently not the case. According to Ray (2006), between 20% and 40% of homeless youth were LGBT youth who had experienced family conflict regarding their sexual or gender identities, including physical assault and being kicked out of the home.

The authors of this chapter have worked with adult clients who described their experiences as adolescents and being pulled from schools that had gay student groups; other clients described being sent to so-called reparative therapy clinics that purported to be able to change one's sexual orientation. Every national mental health organization recognizes that efforts to change a person's sexual orientation are, at a minimum, pointless (because sexual orientation is seen as innate and immutable), and at a maximum, harmful and damaging to people, because they are based on the false premise that there is something wrong with a gay sexual orientation (APA, 2008). For more information, please refer to the following resources.

HELPFUL INTERNET RESOURCES

Gay, Lesbian, and Straight Education Network http://www.glsen.org GLSEN is the leading national education organization focused on ensuring safe schools for all students.

Gay–Straight Alliance (GSA) Network http://www.gsanetwork.org Gay–Straight Alliance Network is a youth leadership organization that connects school-based GSAs to each other.

It Gets Better Project http://www.itgetsbetter.org The It Gets Better Project was created to show young LGBTQ people the levels of happiness, potential, and positivity their lives will reach if they can just get through their teen years.

National Gay and Lesbian Task Force http://www.ngltf.org National grass-roots organization.

Teaching Tolerance http://www.tolerance.org Teaching Tolerance is a place to find news, conversation, and support for those who care about diversity and respect in schools.

The Trevor Project http:// www.thetrevorproject.com The Trevor Project is the leading national organization providing crisis intervention and suicide prevention services to lesbian, gay, bisexual, transgender, and questioning youth.

RECOMMENDED BOOKS FOR YOUTH

Middle School

And Tango Makes Three by Peter Parnell, Justin Richardson, and Henry Cole (2006). Based on a true story, this story follows two male penguins that fall in love and adopt an orphaned penguin named Tango.

The Sissy Duckling by Harvey Fierstein and Henry Cole (2005). Elmer the duck is taunted for his non-gender-conforming behavior and is rejected by his family. However, his differences are accepted when he becomes a hero by saving his father.

Totally Joe by James Howe (2005). Joe is a seventh grader who has the assignment of writing an alphabiography (presenting his life from A to Z), which helps him to come to terms with his sexuality and the discrimination of others.

High School

Breathe by Blair Poole (2005). An African American teenager living in urban hip-hop culture must keep his sexuality a secret in the face of his homophobic friends and extremely religious family.

Eight Seconds by Jean Ferris (2003). A story about two teenage rodeo competitors coming to terms with, and coming out as, being gay.

Hero by Perry Moore and TK (2007). High school basketball star Thom Creed isn't just coping with being gay, he's also coping with being an undercover superhero in a heterocentric world.

Not the Only One: Lesbian and Gay Fiction for Teens by Jane Summer (2004). A collection of coming of age stories dealing with coming out, love, independence, and homophobia by many of today's most popular authors.

On Being Gay by Brian McNaught (1989). Thoughts on family, faith, and love.

Out Law: What LGB Youth Should Know About Their Legal Rights by Lisa Keen (2007). An analysis of the legal issues affecting LGBTQ teenagers in the USA.

The Gay and Lesbian Guide to College Life (College Admissions Guides) by The Princeton Review (2007). A resource for LGBTQ teens and their parents and counselors, this guide covers LGBTQ-friendly schools as well as tips on making the most out of college.

When You Don't See Me by Timothy James Beck (2007). A gay Midwestern boy tries to make a new life in New York as he navigates self-acceptance, economic troubles, and love.

Who's Who in Gay and Lesbian History by Robert Adrich (2003). Over 500 entries of some of the most famous (and not so famous) LGB persons throughout history, spanning from the pre-Roman era to more recent times.

RECOMMENDED BOOKS FOR COUNSELORS AND HELPING PROFESSIONALS

Gay–Straight Alliances: A Handbook for Students, Educators, and Parents by Ian K. MacGillivary (2007). This guide explains exactly how to begin a gay–straight alliance. There are chapters for students, counselors and teachers, principals, superintendents, and parents.

Lesbian and Gay Voices: An Annotated Bibliography and Guide to Literature for Children and Young Adults by Frances Ann Day (2000). A resource for counselors, librarians, and others who will be providing services to LGBQ youth, this book provides information on positive books for LGBQ youth and their families.

The Heart Has Its Reasons: Young Adult Literature With Gay/Lesbian/Queer Content, 1996-2004 by Michael Cart & Christina A. Jenkins (2006). It is a comprehensive overview and detailed discussion of 35 years of young adult books with lesbian, gay, bisexual, transgender, and queer/questioning (LGBTQ) content.

Understanding Gay and Lesbian Youth: Lessons for Straight School Teachers, Counselors, and Administrators by David Campos (2005). This book discusses the current state of affairs for LGB students in schools, lessons for working with LGB students, and strategies for creating a safe and accepting school atmosphere.

REFERENCES

Almeida, J., Johnson, R. M., Corliss, H. L., Molnar, B. E., & Azrael, D. (2009). Emotional distress among LGBT youth: The influence of perceived discrimination based on sexual orientation. *Journal of Youth and Adolescence.* doi:10:1007/10964-009-9408-x.

American Psychological Association. (2008). *Answers to your questions: For a better understanding of sexual orientation and homosexuality.* Washington, DC: Author. Retrieved from http://www.apa.org/topics/sorientation.pdf.

Cass, V.C. (1984). Homosexual identity formation: Testing a theoretical model. *The Journal of Sex Research, 20,* 143–167.

Denizet-Lewis, B. (2003). Double lives on the down low. *New York Times Magazine,* 28–33. August 3, 2003.

Denizet-Lewis, B. (2009). Coming out in middle school. New York Times Magazine, 34–43. September 23, 2009.

Fontaine, J. H. (1998). Evidencing a need: School counselors' experiences with gay and lesbian students. *Professional School Counseling, 1*(3), 8–15.

Gallup (2009). *Knowing someone gay/lesbian affects views of gay issues.* Retrieved from http://www.gallup.com/poll/118931/Knowing-Someone-Gay-Lesbian-Affects-Views-Gay-Issues.aspx

Gay, Lesbian, and Straight Education Network. (2009). *National School Climate Survey.* Author. Retrieved from http://www.glsen.org

Gladding, S. T., & Gladding, C. (1991). The ABCs of bibliotherapy for school counselors. *School Counselor, 39*(1), 7–13.

Hansen, A. L. (2007). School-based support for GLBT students: A review of three levels of research. *Psychology in the Schools, 44*(8), 839–848.

Human Rights Campaign Fund. (2011). *Resource guide to coming out.* Author. Retrieved from http://www.hrc.org/resources/entry/resource-guide-to-coming-out

Kosciw, J. G., Diaz, E. M., & Greytak, E. A. (2008). *2007 National School Climate Survey: The experiences of lesbian, gay, bisexual and transgender youth in our nation's schools.* New York: GLSEN.

McNaught, B. (1986). *On being gay: Thoughts on family, faith, and love.* New York, NY: St. Martin's Press.

Meyer, I. (2003). Prejudice, social stress, and mental health in lesbian, gay, and bisexual populations: Conceptual issues and research evidence. *Psychological Bulletin, 129*(5), 674–697.

National Gay and Lesbian Task Force. (2011). *Reports and research: Nondiscrimination laws map.* Washington, DC: Author. Retrieved from www.ngltf.org/reports_and_research/nondiscrimination_laws

Pew Research Center. (2011). Fewer are angry at government, but discontent remains high. Washington, DC: Author. Retrieved from www.people-press.org/files/legacy-pdf/3-3-11%20Political%20Release.pdf

Pope, M. (2003). *Sexual minority youth in schools: Issues and desirable counselor responses.* Washington DC: Education Resources Information Center. ERIC Document Reproduction Service No. ED480481.

Ray, N. (2006). *Lesbian, gay, bisexual, and transgender youth: An epidemic of homelessness.* New York, NY: National Gay and Lesbian Task Force Policy Institute and the National Coalition for the Homeless.

Rosario, M., Hunter, J., Maguen, S., & Smith, R. (2001). The coming-out process and its adaptational and health-related associations among gay, lesbian, and bisexual youths: Stipulation and exploration of a model. *American Journal of Community Psychology, 29*(1), 133–160.

Savin-Williams, R. (2005). *The new gay teenager.* Cambridge, MA: Harvard University Press.

Troiden, R. (1989). The formation of homosexual identities. In G. Herdt (Ed.). *Gay and lesbian youth* (pp. 43–73). New York: Harrington Park.

Vare, J. W., & Norton, T. L. (2004). Bibliotherapy for Gay and Lesbian Youth: Overcoming the Structure of Silence. *The Clearing House, 77*(5), 190–194.

Whitman, J. S., Horn, S. S., & Boyd, C. J. (2007). Activism in the Schools: Providing LGBQ Affirmative Training to School Counselors. *Journal of Gay & Lesbian Psychotherapy. 11*(3/4), 143–154.

Part III: Emotional and Mental Health Concerns

10

Attention Deficit/Hyperactivity Disorder in Young Males

IMELDA BRATTON

PREVALENCE AND DIAGNOSIS OF ATTENTION DEFICIT/HYPERACTIVITY DISORDER

One of the most common childhood neurobehavioral disorders is attention deficit/hyperactivity disorder (ADHD). As children enter a formal school setting, their ability to focus on tasks can be difficult to maintain. This can be especially difficult during the primary years when reading, writing, and mathematical concepts are first introduced. Taking this into consideration, it is comprehensible that the average age of diagnosis of ADHD is 7 years (NIMH, 2011), or around first or second grade. For those diagnosed with ADHD, 9% will have a lifetime prevalence of the disorder; with the majority of those diagnosed being male rather than female (NIMH, 2011). In fact, males are diagnosed up to three times as frequently as females in the United States (CDC, 2010; NIMH, 2011).

The Diagnostic and Statistical Manual of Mental Disorders IV-TR (DSM-IV-TR) (APA, 2000) describes ADHD as manifesting patterns of inattention, hyperactivity, and/or impulsivity. These patterns must be persistent and present for a minimum of 6 months before diagnosis can be made, and the impairments can negatively impact children in a variety of settings. The presence of this disorder makes completion of tasks that require focus and mental concentration a challenge. Shifting between tasks, avoidance, forgetfulness, and distraction are all characteristics of ADHD.

The majority of lay people have heard of ADHD and, generally, assume that it specifically refers to a person who is hyperactive; however, there are actually three subtypes of the disorder that vary from one extreme to the other: inattentive, hyperactive–impulsive, and combined type.

171

Focusing and maintaining attention can be a daily challenge for children and adults with inattentive type ADHD. The ability to carry out instructions (especially if they involve more than three steps) is difficult because many times they are unable to recall all of the information. These individuals may not appear to be listening when instructions are given, which can lead to frustration from those working with them. Unfortunately, these symptoms occur in various activities and situations, making it difficult to complete tasks effectively or promptly. Individuals may begin to feel incompetent and develop feelings of low self-worth as they become discouraged in their friendships, school, and work situations.

Being able to stay still and settle down is a challenge faced by children and adults with hyperactive–impulsive type ADHD. Impulsivity may cause individuals to speak more often or say inappropriate comments without thinking about them. Friends, teachers, and colleagues may be offended by the individual's inability to wait his turn or avoid interrupting during conversations. Additionally, they may be "wound up" physically and move around quickly without thinking, which can lead to clumsiness.

The third type is combined type ADHD. Individuals that meet the criteria of inattentive and hyperactive–impulsive ADHD are classified in the combined-type diagnosis. As described, social situations, such as group work, can exacerbate peer rejection. Individuals with this diagnosis are primarily male (Al-Karagully, 2006).

SUGGESTED INTERVENTIONS FOR TREATING ADHD

There are many effective interventions for those diagnosed with ADHD. Conventional treatment strategies consist of medications with or without cognitive–behavioral therapy (CBT). For many children, this is an effective treatment regimen; however, expressive art therapies have recently been found to be effective.

Psychopharmacological Treatments

A leading treatment is the use of pharmacology, either by itself, or in conjunction with counseling. Stimulant medications such as methylphenidate (Ritalin and Ritalin SR), methylphenidate extended-release tablets (Concerta), dextroamphetamine (Dexedine), and the combination of dextroamphetamine with amphetamine (Adderall) are commonly prescribed by physicians to assist with ADHD symptoms. Several studies explore the effects of methylphenidate. A study by Hood, Baird, Rankin, and Isaacs (2005) found that the use of methylphenidate improved cognitive attention of children (7–11 years old) diagnosed with ADHD. In addition, a study by

Mehta, Goodyer, and Sahakian (2004) stated that working memory was improved in adolescent male participants diagnosed with ADHD. In the past decade, nonstimulant drugs such as atomoxetine (Strattera) and guanfacine (Intuniv) have been an option for parents concerned about negative side effects produced from stimulant medications. Although guanfacine is primarily used to treat high blood pressure, it has also been used to treat children diagnosed with ADHD who experience aggression, tics, and sleep issues. A licensed professional counselor, psychologist, psychiatrist, school psychologist, or physician can diagnose ADHD. Even though various professionals can make a diagnosis, only physicians or psychiatrists can prescribe medication for treatment. Physicians begin with the lowest dosage of medication until they reach an effective level. This process can take a few months, as feedback is often requested from parents, teachers, and counselors who are in contact with the child on a regular basis. The process of obtaining feedback from various sources helps determine a baseline of behavior and identify an improvement or regression of behavior over the period of treatment.

COUNSELING, ACTIVITY-BASED, AND EXPRESSIVE INTERVENTIONS

Historically, CBT has been an approach used to work with children and adults with ADHD (Prince, Wilens, Spencer, & Biederman, 2006). In CBT, psychoeducational techniques are employed to assist children in reframing their thoughts and behaviors. Strategies such as teaching individuals to stop and think before they act and talking about various responses to stimuli are used in this approach. In addition, organization, planning, and reducing distractibility are also emphasized. This talk therapy encompasses these strategies in an active approach that teaches new skills to individuals.

For many children and adults with ADHD, the ability to perform daily tasks and socialization can be a challenge (Gol & Jarus, 2005). Being able to pay attention to, follow instructions, and complete tasks can be difficult for a child or adult with ADHD as many times the ability to follow organized actions is overwhelming. Furthermore, children, especially, may have a lack of fine motor skill development and coordination, which can interfere with writing skills and motor coordination (Barkley, 1997; Kadesjo & Gillberg, 1998; Raggio, 1999). Social skill training can improve this concern. Activities can be used in a group setting through the use of games, arts and crafts, and cooking. Meaningful activities such as these can develop organizational and problem-solving skills, as well as improve social skills in children (Gol & Jarus, 2005) and adults with ADHD. The counselor can provide an activity while assisting in any emotional, cognitive, sensory, or physical functions needed by group members. Having a counselor available during the activity can encourage and facilitate a positive development of the basic skills needed to function in the real world. For example, while a game is played, the counselor can be mindful of turn taking, rule following, and peer relationship development by the participants.

Over the past decade, use of the expressive arts has increased. Expressive arts can emphasize a client's artistic talents through a metaphoric activity. Adventure-based counseling (ABC, see Chapter 11) is based on behavioral and cognitive theory while integrating experiential learning and affective viewpoints. ABC can provide a positive physical outlet considered necessary for those with ADHD. Counselors employing ABC strategies select an appropriate metaphoric activity based on the client's issue. During the activity, the counselor will often refer to the metaphor, connecting the activity to their real-world situation. When the ABC activity is complete, the counselor facilitates a discussion to integrate change (Fletcher & Hinkle, 2002; Hinkle, 1999) and build awareness (Portrie-Bethke, Hill, & Bethke, 2009). Activities can vary from having the group build a structure out of Legos to an outdoor ropes course. The purpose is to create a team-building experience that incorporates some form of therapeutic risk. The client has the option of deciding how to work through the risk with the support of the counselor and group members. New coping skills can be taught during the activity to increase a client's growth. As children and adults with ADHD may be impulsive and energetic, this type of intervention could be valuable in the therapeutic process.

Another expressive art technique is the use of sand in a sandtray. Similar to ABC, sandtrays provide a tactile experience. Figurines are placed in the sandtray to represent thoughts, feelings, desires, or wishes. The sandtray is a protected space where the role of the counselor is to witness the creation of a final product (Allan, 1988), also known as a sand world. Like ABC, sandtray is metaphoric; however, interpretation is seldom a part of the process. This experiential activity is discussed further in the case study that follows.

As children and families do not live in isolation, the effects of ADHD can impact an entire family unit. Parents of children with ADHD or families of an adult with ADHD are also encouraged to seek counseling. Parents of children with ADHD can receive guidance on behavior management and parenting techniques and strategies that can enhance the child's counseling experience. Discipline is a main concern of parents, which can also be addressed. Parents and families of adults with ADHD can benefit from the support of an individual counselor or a group-counseling experience with others in similar situations. Being able to relate with others can reduce feelings of isolation and promote feelings of connectedness.

Issues such as guilt, disappointment, questioning, failure, and despair can be discussed, which can alleviate stress of day-to-day living with someone who has ADHD.

Children spend the majority of their day in school settings during school years. To encourage continuity of counseling, it is best to involve school personnel. Classroom teachers can work with parents and outside counselors to assist children with ADHD. Interventions employed by the counselor can be modified for use in the classroom. Children with ADHD need structure, which can be optimized if parents, counselors, and teachers all work together.

CASE STUDY: A JOURNEY THROUGH TYLER'S WORLD

Client Description

When Tyler was 6.5 years old, I began using sandtray therapy with him in an elementary school setting. Tyler was a slender, average-sized student of Anglo descent in the first grade. He lived with his birth mother, stepfather, and three siblings. Tyler was the second oldest of the siblings. Unlike his siblings, he was the only child who had a different birth father. During his mother's marriage, there was a brief time of separation and she became pregnant with Tyler by a different man. A few months after becoming pregnant, she reconciled with her husband. Tyler was aware that he had a different father than his siblings as he visited his biological father once a week. During these visits, he would often receive gifts of clothes or toys, which he highly prized.

Tyler lived in a small, conservative, Midwestern town where his family had lived for many generations. Living in a conservative community can be difficult when marital issues occur as this type of negative information can be quickly spread. His mother was embarrassed of the pregnancy and immediately believed that Tyler caused much of the marital issues she experienced with her husband after he was born. Although Tyler had a united family, he did not experience a warm and loving relationship with either his mother or his stepfather.

Presenting Issues

Tyler had been in first grade for approximately one month before his teacher approached me, the school counselor, with her concerns. She described Tyler as having difficulty concentrating and maintaining focus throughout the day. In addition, she was concerned about his impulsivity and lack of positive social skills. His teacher stated that he wanted his desk to be separated from his classmates. She noticed that during recess and free class time, he would play by himself and would rarely join others in play. During group time, when students would sit around the teacher on the floor, Tyler preferred to sit at his desk and observe from across the room. Although he wanted to be away from the group discussions, he would throw pencils or crayons while he was at his desk, or make noises to draw attention to himself. I noticed that after he would throw something, he would make sure that someone noticed what he was doing. It appeared that his behavior was motivated to gain attention.

As part of the school counseling consultation process, I arranged to go into the classroom to observe Tyler. I wanted to view him in his natural setting during a time that the entire class was participating in an activity. As a school counselor, it is common for me to go into classrooms and work with teachers and students. Tyler was unaware that I was observing him as I sat away from him with some of his classmates. The students were assigned to work on their journal writing. While the majority of students were working on their writing, Tyler was busy tearing off the paper wrappings of his crayons. He would throw them on the floor or at classmates near him and laugh. When the teacher would step over to redirect him, he would make grunting noises, stop momentarily, and then continue his behavior when she was not paying attention. This behavior continued throughout my observation.

My recommendation to the teacher was that both of us conduct a parent conference with Tyler's mother. Our goal was to explore any issues or concerns that they may also be experiencing at home. During the conference, in the initial parental session, Tyler's mother described him as her "devil child." She was very clear in her impatience with her son, and she related that he often got into trouble at home. It appeared that she was frustrated with what was going on at home and school and wanted Tyler to begin weekly counseling sessions to help improve his behavior.

Intervention

I chose to focus the following interventions on Tyler, the school, and the family. It was evident that Tyler did not have a genuine warm relationship with significant adults or peers. Due to this, I wanted to create an environment that fostered a relationship with unconditional positive regard for Tyler. In addition, I wanted to focus on helping

Tyler develop skills to self-regulate his behavior, improve social skills, and increase his attention span.

To create a safe and secure environment for Tyler, I used sandtray during our weekly counseling sessions. In my school counseling office, I have a complete play therapy room. Included in my play therapy room is a standard sandtray with approximately 900 figurines. This allows students to select figurines and to create sand worlds that represent their thoughts and images.

As school counselors are not able to diagnose in the school system, I encouraged his mother to take him to their pediatrician to make sure that there were not any medical issues that had not been identified up to this point. His teacher provided a brief written statement that described her observations and concerns in the classroom so that the pediatrician would have various viewpoints to consider.

I believed it was important to consult with the classroom teacher to develop consistent positive behavior interventions. We came up with a positive behavior plan that addressed several of his common behaviors such as improving time on task and classroom compliance. The positive behavior plan encompassed interventions such as offering choices, encouragement, and working toward goals. Tyler created the daily and weekly goal rewards such as extra time working on the computer, playing educational games, or being a classroom helper.

For family interventions, I referred Tyler's mother and stepfather to a local counseling agency that provided parenting skill classes. The classes were available at no charge and were conducted on a weekly basis. Furthermore, I shared the positive behavior plan with the family so that they would be aware of the plan we had at school. After obtaining signed parental permission to speak with the counseling agency, I was able to share intervention information with their counselor so that we would be able to work toward the same goals. Additionally, I shared the positive behavior plan with the counselor so that she could modify it for the parents to use at home. This provided a consistent structure and language to reinforce what Tyler was hearing at school.

Treatment Outcome

During Tyler's first counseling session in the play therapy room, he was unsure of what to do. He stood in the middle of the room staring at the figurines on the shelves. I was attentive to the reality that Tyler had experienced rejection and social isolation from family and peers, and I assumed that he expected the same type of reaction from me.

I encouraged him to create a sand world in the sandtray that showed
how he felt. In the beginning, he simply stood there and just stared
at the figurines. At first, it appeared that he was unsure of what to
do; however, I soon realized that he was searching for just the "right"
figurines. He carefully selected approximately 20 figurines, which he
arranged in an attack mode. Four Star Wars figurines were placed on
one side of the sandtray, facing toward a crowd of one large bug-like
figurine, and some smaller soldiers and action figures. I witnessed
Tyler vigilantly placing the figurines in their positions and he
proceeded to act out violently against them. He was very quiet while
he was creating his sand world; however, when he began to act out the
war he softly made war sounds. When I asked him what he wanted
to share about his sand world, he said he felt like the figurines that
were obliterated. It seemed that he believed that he could not protect
himself, no matter how many he had on his side. It was as if he had
no defense system against the attackers. This was an unmistakable
metaphor of how he felt throughout his life (Figure 10.1).

The annihilation theme in Tyler's sand world continued for
the next several months. He would consistently set up one group of
figurines against the other. Time after time, he identified himself with
the side that lost the war. I gradually began to reflect his feelings
of hopelessness, his perceived inability to protect himself, and his
loneliness and rejection. Tyler began to shake his head as he heard
my reflections, a sign that I validated his experiences and feelings. As

FIGURE 10.1 Annihilation scene.

we developed our relationship, Tyler began to open up and show me his thoughts and fears through his sand worlds. At first, I honored his personal space and sat off to the side witnessing the creation of his sand worlds. As we developed our counseling relationship, he wanted me to sit closer to him. In an attempt to increase his feelings of worth, I continued to reflect his feelings, accept his choices, and accept his acting out of his sand world creations.

A benefit to being a school counselor is the fact that I generally see the students on a daily basis in the hallway, playground, or classroom environments. Throughout the time I saw Tyler, I also went into the classroom to spend time with him each week. His teacher mentioned that Tyler had difficulty completing individual assignments such as math and writing. Reading and math assignments typically require concentration, which is a common challenge for children who have ADHD. In the beginning, it appeared that he did not like it when I spoke to his classmates. Intentionally, I made sure to make the interactions with them brief and quickly refocused my attention back to Tyler so that he knew my main objective was to be with him. As the year progressed, he understood and trusted that I was there for him and did not object to me working with others in the class. To assist Tyler with his attention, I provided a few sensory items at his desk so that he could self-soothe when he began to lose focus. I placed a few strips of hook and loop tape under his desk so that he could quietly rub them. A round rubber air-filled seat cushion was provided for him to sit on during the day. One side of the seat cushion was smooth, while the other side had small bumps on it. He was able to wiggle around on the cushion with minimal disruption to nearby classmates.

His teacher implemented the positive behavior plan soon after we created it. It was difficult in the beginning to use with fidelity, as it was a different way of interacting with students than she was accustomed to. After a few weeks, she was more comfortable in her daily interactions with Tyler and using the plan. The plan was shared with all the teachers, including his music, art, and physical education teachers. It took Tyler a few weeks to "test" his teachers to see if they would be consistent in implementing the plan. He gradually began to realize that all of his teachers consistently used the plan.

To support the positive behavior plans used at home and school, Tyler and I developed a list of goal rewards toward which he would work. The list included activities such as extra time at the end of the day playing with Legos, educational computer games, and drawing. One item that I suggested was to be a classroom helper in a kindergarten class. I believed that this would provide an opportunity for Tyler to take a leadership role with younger children. He liked the idea and we added it to his list of choices. As a visual reminder of what daily and weekly goal rewards he was working toward, I had Tyler make a "menu" of his choices on paper. I laminated it so that it could be placed on his desk and reused on a daily basis. Each day he would select his choice and circle it with a dry erase marker. This could be easily wiped off at the end of the day for a fresh start the following school day.

Two months after I began working with Tyler, I had another conference with his mother. She had recently taken Tyler to his pediatrician, and he was diagnosed with ADHD. The pediatrician prescribed Ritalin, a common medication provided to children with ADHD. His mother stated that she would begin to give Tyler the medication the following weekend and wanted the school to be aware in case there were any issues. The following Monday I met Tyler at the beginning of the school day and immediately began to notice some differences. He seemed to have a sense of calmness that I had not seen before.

Especially, I noticed a difference in Tyler's sand worlds that he created over the next few sessions. He spent quite a bit of time setting up extravagant scenes with great detail. I reflected this observation to him and he commented he was able to "think better." I believed that he was ready to develop his social skill set. We began to work on how to make and keep friends. As he created his sand worlds each week, I would search for opportunities to open up a discussion about how to treat others and choose appropriate responses to various social situations. I began to focus on basics such as how to ask someone if they wanted to play a game and how to say "no" without hurting someone's feelings. We began to act out responses in the sandtray as well as expand that to role-playing with various figurines. He began to gain insight into how his actions impacted the way others responded to him. After a few weeks, I was comfortable in how Tyler was responding to our role-playing scenarios, and I suggested that Tyler invite a classmate to come to the playroom so that he could have an opportunity to "try out" some of his new skills in a safe environment. He asked a male classmate with whom he had started to play with at recess. I was able to observe their interactions and facilitate any negotiations between the two when needed.

Toward the end of the school year and our individual counseling relationship, I began to notice how Tyler's sand worlds were evolving. His first sand worlds were full of despair and despondency. As he began to develop social skills, acquire friends, and improve his attention span in the classroom with medication, his sand worlds took on a dissimilar mood. He continued to use some of the same figurines; however, they were in a different role. Tyler no longer had fighting scenes in his sand worlds. He also began to show himself as being strong and self-reliant on his new social skills. In Figure 10.2, it is evident Tyler created a sand world which confirms these thoughts. He included only one set of figurines with a barrier to protect himself. Having only one group of figurines indicates that he no longer felt under attack. He placed himself behind the barrier, instead of being exposed in the sandtray, and even identified a few of his classmates in his sand world. As opposed to his initial sand world, he described a feeling of adequacy instead of vulnerability. This different take on his world could be attributed to the consistency between his home and school settings, medication, and his newly acquired set of internal resources and self-regulation skills.

Positive behavioral differences were observed in Tyler's classroom. By the end of the second semester, Tyler was complying almost 80% of the time. This was a significant increase to how he began the school year. Additionally, Tyler appeared happier as he was commonly seen with a smile on his face. Oftentimes, he preferred to play with a friend during recess; however, there were still occasions where he wanted to play by himself. His parents described similar behaviors at home as well.

FIGURE 10.2 Protective scene.

SUGGESTED RESOURCES

Barkley, R. (2010). Taking *charge of adult ADHD*. New York, NY: The Guilford Press.

Buitelaar, J., Kan, C., & Asherson, P. (2011). *ADHD in adults: Characterization, diagnosis, and treatment*. New York, NY: Cambridge University Press.

Corman, C., Trevino, E., & Dimatteo, R. (1995). *Eukee the jumpy jumpy elephant*. North Branch, MN: Specialty Press, Inc.

Gordon, M. (1991). *I would if I could: A teenagers guide to ADHD/Hyperactivity*. DeWitt, New York, NY: GSI Publisher.

Galvin, M. (2001). *Otto learns about his medicine: A story about medication for children with ADHD*. Washington, DC: Magination Press.

Hallowell, E., & Jensen, P. (2010). *Superparenting for ADD: An innovative approach to raising your distracted child*. New York, NY: Ballantine Books.

http://school.familyeducation.com/learning-disabilities/add-and-adhd/34474.html

Kapalka, G. (2009). *Counseling boys and men with ADHD (The Routledge series on counseling and psychotherapy with boys and men)*. New York, NY: Routledge.

Monastra, V. (2005). *Parenting children with ADHD: 10 lessons that medicine cannot teach*. Washington, DC: American Psychological Association.

Moss, S. (1989). *Shelley, the hyperactive turtle*. Kensington, MD: Woodbine House.

Nadeau, K., Dixon, E., & Beyl, C. (2004). *Learning to slow down and pay attention: A book for kids about ADHD*. Washington, DC: Magination Press.

Pera, G., & Barkley, R. (2008). *Is it you, me, or adult A.D.D.? Stopping the roller-coaster when someone you love has Attention Deficit Disorder*. San Francisco, CA: 1201 Alarm Press.

Ratey, N. (2008). *The disorganized mind: Coaching your ADHD brain to take control of your time, tasks, and talents*. New York, NY: St. Martin's Press.

Sleeper-Triplett, J. (2010). *Empowering youth with ADHD: Your guide to coaching adolescents and young adults for coaches, parents, and professionals*. Plantation, FL: Specialty Press, Inc.

Stein, K. (2010). *The gift of ADHD: How to transform your child's problems into strengths*. Oakland, CA: New Harbinger Publications, Inc.

Taylor, J. (2006). *The survival guide for kids with ADD or ADHD*. Free Spirit Publishing.

www.aap.org/healthtopics/adhd.cfm
www.add.org
www.addresources.org
www.adhd.com/index.html#
www.adhdsupport.com/adhd-resources.aspx
www.chadd.org/
www.help4adhd.org
www.nimh.nih.gov/health/publications/attention-deficit-hyperactivity-disorder/complete-index.shtml

REFERENCES

Al-Karagully, T. (2006). Attention deficit hyperactivity disorder: An overlooked problem in children. *Iraqi Journal of Medical Science, 5*(1), 48–54.

Allan, J. (1988). *Inscapes of the child's world: Jungian counseling in schools and clinics.* Dallas, TX: Spring Publications, Inc.

American Psychiatric Association (APA). (2000). *Diagnostic and statistical manual of mental disorders (4th ed.),* Text Revision. Washington, DC: Author.

Barkley, R. (1997). *ADHD and the nature of self-control.* New York, NY: Guilford Press.

Center for Disease Control. (2010). *Increasing prevalence of parent-reported attention-deficit/hyperactivity disorder among children.* Retrieved June 27, 2011, from www.cdc.gov/mmwr/preview/mmwrhtml/mm5944a3.htm?s_cid=mm5944a3_w

Fletcher, T., & Hinkle, J. (2002). Adventure based counseling: An innovation in counseling. *Journal of Counseling and Development, 80,* 277–285.

Gol, D., & Jarus, T. (2005). Effect of a social skills training group on everyday activities of children with attention-deficit-hyperactivity disorder. *Developmental Medicine & Child Neurology. 47,* 539–545.

Hinkle, J. (1999). Utilizing outdoor pursuits in mental health counseling. In J. S. Hinkle (Ed.), *Promoting optimal mental health through counseling: An overview* (pp. 179–186). Greensboro, NC: E.R.I.C.

Hood, J., Baird, G., Rankin, P., & Isaacs, E. (2005). Immediate effects of methylphenidate on cognitive attention skills of children with attention-deficit-hyperactivity disorder. *Developmental Medicine & Child Neurology, 47,* 408–414.

Kadesjo, B., & Gillberg, C. (1998). Attention deficits and clumsiness in Swedish 7-year-old children. *Developmental Medicine & Child Neurology, 40,* 796–804.

Mehta, M., Goodyer, I., & Sahakian, B. (2004). Methylphenidate improves working memory and set-shifting in AD/HD: relationships to baseline memory capacity. *Journal of Child Psychology and Psychiatry, 45,* 293–305.

National Institute of Mental Health. (2011). *Attention deficit hyperactivity disorder.* Retrieved June 27, 2011, from www.nimh.nih.gov/health/Topics/attention-deficit-hyperactivity-disorder-adhd/index.shtml

Portrie-Bethke, T., Hill, N., & Bethke, J. (2009). Strength-based mental health counseling for children with ADHD: An integrative model of adventure-based counseling and Adlerian play therapy. *Journal of Mental Health Counseling, 31*(4), 323–339.

Prince, J. B., Wilens, T. E., Spencer, T. J., & Biederman, J. (2006). Pharmacology of ADHD in adults. In R. A. Barkley (Ed.), *Attention-deficit hyperactivity disorder: A handbook for diagnosis and treatment* (3rd ed., pp. 704–736). New York, NY: Guilford.

Raggio, D. (1999). Visuomotor perception in children with attention deficit hyperactivity disorder-combined type. *Perceptual and Motor Skills, 88,* 448–450.

11

Navigating the Challenges of Connecting With Male Youth: Empowering Real-Time Interventions Through Adventure-Based Counseling

TOREY L. PORTRIE-BETHKE, DAVID CHRISTIAN,
WILLIAM BROWN, AND NICOLE R. HILL

ADVENTURE-BASED COUNSELING WITH YOUNG MALES

Working with adolescent males can be difficult, as evidenced by many mental health professionals describing them as the most challenging population with whom to work (Church, 1994; Gil, 1996; Hanna, Hanna, & Keys, 1999). One of the main reasons is that adolescent males are often difficult to engage in traditional talk therapy. Furthermore, some characteristics of males' verbal and nonverbal communication patterns often result in deficits in interpersonal relationships that make it more likely for males to be referred to treatment because of behavior problems (Cox, 2006; Polluck, 1999). Due to the high rate of comorbidity between behavior problems and deficient language development, males often struggle in traditional talk therapy (Hill, 2007). In order to respond to the needs of this population, a growing number of mental health professionals are turning to adventure-based counseling (ABC; Fletcher & Hinkle, 2002).

ABC is an action-based counseling approach that utilizes cognitive, behavioral, experiential, and Adlerian counseling theories to foster the improved mental and emotional health of individuals, families, and groups. Fletcher and Hinkle (2002) differentiated ABC from traditional talk therapy in that ABC utilizes a variety of settings, risks (real and perceived), supplementary skills, additional ethical considerations, added emphasis on metaphor, and the transfer of learning from an experiential activity to multiple life realms (e.g., psychological, educational, sociological, physical, and spiritual). Considering the action-based involvement needed to participate in ABC activities, the modality encourages engagement in the therapeutic process.

Gass (1995) proposed a seven-point reference for implementing ABC, which can be applied to understanding how this approach is beneficial for working with adolescent males. Given that males are charged with a level of energy that may push the limits of a chair-bound therapeutic interaction, an *action-oriented counseling approach* fosters learning of intra- and interpersonal development in the moment (Gass). While participating in various ABC activities, clients are engaging with their emotional responses to the elements experienced. Gass asserted that the most important aspect to ABC is that it utilizes *unfamiliar situations* by providing clients with new emotional awareness of self for potential application of problem solving and solutions to real-life experiences. Adolescent male clients in talk therapy might interact based on preconceived notions of how counseling works. For example, versions of counseling depicted in popular culture may shape behaviors during talk sessions. Clients may begin the counseling process by saying "so do you want me to tell you my dreams," "do you want me to lie down," or "my mother said you need to fix me, so tell me what is wrong with me so this can be over." When clients generate preconceived notions about counseling like those described, they have begun to develop a script of their future counseling experiences. Given that ABC provides clients with unfamiliar experiences, clients are unable to plan how they will respond. This leads clients to experience a perceived risk, which induces disequilibrium from homeostatic patterns of emotional responses and reactions resulting in *cathartic transformation* (Gass).

Adaption through healthy behaviors and choices leads to equilibrium (trust, effective communication, cooperation) with regained sense of self. Fostering an environment that challenges clients' mental and emotional balance is best implemented through a sequence of ABC activities that generates an *informal assessment* of clients' mental health needs (Gass, 1992). The counselor conceptualizes the individual's and group's potential needs and works toward *balancing group needs*. The counselor's professional opinion is applied to selecting ABC experiences to challenge participants. Through these challenges, counselors select what participants' experience and which dynamics to process for therapeutic gain (Gass).

Implementing ABC requires thoughtful decisions as the counselor selects activities that benefit clients' needs and is intentional when processing the experience. Gass (1992) describes the sixth reference point of ABC as being either *solution* or *problem focused*. Counselors oriented toward a strength-based approach will explore areas where the activity and interactions were most effective and build on this awareness for future growth. Humanistic counseling approaches believe the counseling relationship fosters mental health changes in clients. Therefore, ABC may enhance the clients' perceived beliefs about the counselor's involvement in the process. Clients may view *counselors integrated into the ABC* experience as fun and approachable (Gass). This also may make it easier for clients to perceive the games and interventions as fun and inviting. The invitational and approachable factor of ABC functions as therapeutic leverage for adolescent male clients in that they more willingly engage in this active counseling approach, as compared to traditional talk counseling. ABC has a long history of providing therapeutic benefits to clients who benefit from an experiential and engaged treatment modality (Gass, 1992).

A HISTORY OF ABC

Numerous theories exist describing the origins of ABC as a treatment modality (Gass, 1995). Just as the term ABC encompasses many different approaches to counseling and evades easy definition, the history of the field is equally ambiguous. There is little consensus in the literature regarding the origins of ABC. Valid arguments can be made tracing ABC's history to numerous different original sources. Many histories trace ABC's foundational programs to Outward Bound and Project Adventure in that they served as early models and catalysts for future ABC programming (Gass, 1995). The history of ABC described in this chapter looks to identify the philosophical, theoretical, and programmatic origins that helped found and shape contemporary approaches. This section will also explore how ABC evolved from these origins to take shape and earn its place in the empirically supported approaches to mental health counseling as a viable treatment modality for adolescent males.

Philosophical Origins

Inherent in ABC is the belief that natural settings are beneficial environments that have positive effects on people. Nature is more than simply the place in which ABC occurs. It is a "cofacilitator during therapeutic transformations" (Taylor, Segal, & Harper, 2010, p. 81). Activity in natural environments is an essential component in the process of change (Taylor et al., 2010). ABC is the contemporary expression of a healing motif present in human culture throughout history. The essential premise of ABC—that activity in the outdoors can serve as an effective setting and vehicle for change—long predates any recent clinical or theoretical approach.

Wilderness, nature, and the outdoors appear throughout history as the location for human introspection and growth.

Nearly every cultural tradition employs the motif of the natural world to signify the setting or vehicle for personal change. The natural world serves as a metaphor for the despair and disorientation that accompanies the process of change. The structure and purpose of wilderness spaces in change narratives are remarkably similar across human cultures. The most explicit expression of this theme appears in the spiritual traditions of numerous cultures. That the connection is established between spirituality and change is not surprising as, until the modern era, personal change was the domain of the spiritual, overseen by religious figures and designated through ritual practice. Here are a few examples to illustrate the use of nature as a motif designating change and growth.

In the Western tradition, Judaism, Christianity, and Islam each employ wilderness motifs to designate change narratives. When Moses is wandering and seeking guidance, he climbs a mountain to speak to god, receiving a new direction for himself and his people (Coogan, Brettler, Newsom, & Perkins, 2001, p. 110). Jesus, seeking to validate his ministry by testing his resolve, disappears into the desert to confront the devil and emerges "filled with the power of the spirit" (Coogan et al., 2001, pp. 102–103). And Mohammed, exhausted by a merchant's life in Mecca, retreats to a cave in which to meditate and find spiritual awakening and receive the word of god from the Angel Gabriel (Emerick, 2002, p. 57).

Similarly, the motif is present in the two primary Eastern religions: Hinduism and Buddhism. In his quest for enlightenment, Siddhartha Guatama abandons his princely upbringing, and then later his ascetic searching, for a solitary spot before the Bodhi tree (Smith & Novak, 2004, p. 9). In doing so, he realized the Four Noble Truths and became the Buddha. Similar themes appear in Hindu narratives as well, some of which are the oldest extant texts of any religious tradition. Among them is the Aranyaka, a book in the Hindu Vedas, which translates as belonging to the wilderness, also called the "forest manuals" (Easwaran & Easwaran, 2007a, p. 298). The text describes rituals that allow Hindus the release from rebirth, the most sacred of spiritual endeavors (Easwaran & Easwaran, 2007b, p. 24).

Two more examples illustrate how thoroughly saturated human cultures are with the use of wilderness spaces for places of change. Indigenous peoples in Australia and the Americas both employ ritualistic wilderness journeys to mark the beginning of adulthood. The walkabout and vision quest separates adolescent boys from the social support network, imposes an unmitigated experience of the natural world, and challenges the individual to redefine himself in light of the learning undergone in nature (Heart, 1998, p. 230).

Given the strong connection between the natural world and human growth and realization, it is not surprising that counseling has sought to employ outdoor settings as a vehicle in which, and through which, personal change might be motivated. Education and, then later, ABC, represents an evolution away from the religious institutions as the foundation of healing and change. In their place, secular organizations employ similar environments toward similar ends with a focus on mental and emotional—rather than spiritual—health.

Forerunners to ABC

During the 19th and early 20th century, a shift in practice and perspective occurred in Western culture. Behavioral and relational problems, which were previously conceived of as moral and character flaws, became understood as mental health concerns underlain by developmental, emotional, and cognitive pathology. At the same time, the institutions designed to address these concerns were shifting. When psychopathology was thought of as a matter of moral degeneracy, it was the religious institutions that were expected to address and facilitate the path toward personal and social righteousness. As these concerns became redefined as mental health diagnoses, secular institutions became responsible for treating such disorders.

In the intermediary, a number of social organizations intervened. These groups identified physical, mental, and moral wellness as essential to the full functioning of the individual. As a setting and focus for their programs, many chose the outdoors and physical activity to aid in the education and treatment of their participants. Three different threads converged to help form the basis for ABC, namely physical health, moral wellness, and outdoor education.

Physical Health
During the Industrial Revolution in Europe, urban spaces were becoming increasingly toxic environments. Soot filled air, polluted water, and contaminated food supplies were thought to blame for a number of illnesses endemic in the population (Weber, 1988, p. 21). Physicians recommended extended stays at health spas, known as curist retreats, away from the city. Those with financial means would escape the cities' filth for the rural surrounds. There, they were prescribed to take in the water and air. A regimen of exercise, relaxation, and a simple diet were often included as well. The retreats were intended to treat physical illness, but it was learned that "what salt water and sea air cured, above all, were the ills occasioning the characteristic urban light from strain, stress, and pollution, which ranged from depression, chlorotic languor, and hypochondria to neurosis, delirium, and assorted nervous strains" (Weber, 1988, p. 180). As people began

to seek out natural places as a source of wellness, it was learned that the curative effects extended to clients' mental conditions as well.

Moral Wellness and Character Building

Soon after the rise of curist retreats in Europe, other social organizations began utilizing the outdoors as a vehicle to encourage health. In these instances, health was perceived of as the moral and character wellness of boys. The YMCA and the Boy Scouts developed a notion of "character building [that] rested upon a popular psychology which conceived the mind of being composed of several major faculties: intellect, emotion, will, and sometimes conscience" (Macleod, 2004, p. 30). These organizations were applying nascent psychological understanding to shape behaviors in boys. Through carefully constructed activities, these organizations hoped to "suppress undesirable drives and channel the others to good ends" (Macleod, 2004, p. 97). Group leaders hoped to redirect the energy, sexuality, aggressiveness, and disrespect for rule toward more socially accepted outcomes.

The most powerful venue for such work was camping. Local chapters and summer camp destinations brought youth from the cities to the countryside. Here, camping served as a "world apart where [leaders] could recreate an ideal boyhood...[where] outdoorsmanship was not an end in itself" (Macleod, 2004, p. 233). This blank slate provided by the outdoors offered a setting to teach boys about how they might best understand themselves and relate to others according to the ideals set out by the organizations. Soon, advocates "touted camping as a cure for enervation, nervousness" as well as exhaustion, poor appetite, and pampering (Macleod, 2004, p. 234). The benefits extended beyond the original intentions, providing unexpected mental health benefits through group interaction in the outdoors.

Outdoor Education

It was from this early joining of outdoor activity and personal development that outdoor education evolved into a deliberate curriculum aimed at employing personal challenge as an opportunity for growth. Kurt Hahn, a physical education teacher from Germany, developed an outdoor education program for his school that, during the Second World War, took shape as a survival-training program for sailors (Nassar-McMillan & Cashwell, 1997). Shortly after, Kurt Hahn and Laurence Holt applied the knowledge gained from this program to the development of a "wilderness program incorporating helping interventions that later became known as Outward Bound" (Glass & Myers, 2001, p. 105).

Outward Bound began as a month-long course aimed at building "independence, initiative, physical fitness, self-reliance, and resourcefulness" (Hattie, Marsh, Neill, & Richards, 1997, p. 44). Personal and relational insights were not an unintended by-product of Outward Bound's programming. The explicit aim was to employ physical activity in the out-doors as an "effective medium for participants to recognize and understand their own weaknesses, strengths, and resources and thus find the wherewithal to master the difficult and unfamiliar in other environments" (Hattie et al., 1997, p. 45). Outward Bound recognized the metaphorical value of the outdoors. Personal and relational insights gained during activities became an integral part of the follow-up discussion, or processing, of each activity. These insights were then related to other activities and relationships in the participants' lives. The goal was to help individuals be more adaptive, responsive, and productive and to better manage challenging situations.

From Education to Counseling

In 1971, at the Hamilton-Wenham High School in Beverly, Massachusetts, another evolution occurred in the development of ABC. Jerry Pieh developed a program applying the methods of Outward Bound to the classroom setting. The program, called Project Adventure, was originally constructed to aid in the teaching of traditional academic subjects but later developed a focus on counseling for students with special needs.

Project Adventure developed the notion of "Challenge by Choice" (Warner, 2009, p. 72). In this model, participants choose the ways and levels in which they were involved in a given activity. This development marked a theoretical shift in adventure programming from educational to therapeutic underpinnings. The goal now was to provide opportunities that generated emotional experiences and to use the metaphorical experience to resolve broader emotional challenges. Attention was placed on the participants' subjective experiences and participants were encouraged to reflect on their experiences and abstract their insights.

The union between Outdoor Education and traditional counseling, now known as ABC, helped participants explore the thoughts and emotions they experienced during adventure activities (Haras, Bunting, & Witt, 2006). The goal was to examine how these experiences impacted self-perception, relationships, and functioning and to help clients develop healthy emotional experiences. The result was a new approach to counseling that offered healing opportunities for clients who might otherwise resist traditional approaches, especially adolescent male clients.

CURRENT APPLICATIONS OF ABC

In the preceding decades, various new expressions of ABC have taken shape. Along with ABC, "wilderness therapy...adventure therapy, wilderness adventure therapy, and outdoor behavioral healthcare (OBH)…are often used interchangeably" (Becker, 2010, p. 49). Each of these approaches combines the beneficial effects of outdoor activity, group interaction, and therapeutic theory to affect positive change in participants.

Despite the challenges that exist in empirically validating ABC, there is ample evidence linking ABC to successful therapeutic outcomes when working with various populations. Fletcher and Hinkle identify youth at risk, families, women, college students, corporations, athletes, and victims of abuse and trauma as common populations in ABC settings (Fletcher & Hinkle, 2002). Additionally, ABC approaches are used with clients experiencing depression, anxiety, addiction, posttraumatic stress disorder, and behavioral problems. Many studies have been conducted supporting the use of ABC approaches for these populations (Gillis, Gass, & Russell, 2008; Jones, Lowe, & Risler, 2004; Wilson & Lipsey, 2000). Although many of these studies call for additional research to continue exploring the connection between ABC and treatment outcomes, these studies suggest that ABC is as effective and, in some instances, more effective than other practices commonly used to treat clients.

Given the theoretical foundations and empirical support, ABC has expanded as a treatment approach and is currently being used in a wide range of settings. Outpatient counselors are integrating ABC techniques in office visits with clients using activities as a means of exploring clinical issues (Huber, 1997). Similarly, other outpatient counselors are offering ABC programs for clients outside of the office. Individuals, groups, and families can schedule sessions ranging from 2-hour weekly visits to longer retreats in which counselors use ABC techniques. ABC techniques are also being used with adjudicated populations (Jones et al., 2004; Wilson & Lipsey, 2000), in hospitals (Gillen & Balkin, 2006), and in ABC programs working with nonvoluntary youth and young adults, such as the wilderness therapy program Second Nature. Other programs, such as the REAL curriculum developed by Empowering Education, are applying ABC principles to school classrooms. These programs all seek to access clients in need of services who may benefit from ABC approaches.

ABC: A Unique Mode of Therapy

In most cases, ABC is used as an adjunct to traditional forms of talk therapy in order to enhance the therapeutic process (Gass, 1993). Activities, group interactions, outdoor experiences, and risk add elements to the therapeutic process not found in talk sessions. These elements can work in conjunction with other approaches, but they can also be used independently to engage clients differently.

The key difference between ABC and traditional talk therapy is setting. Although ABC can be facilitated indoors, it is preferable to be outside (Fletcher & Hinkle, 2002). One activity that illustrates the value of breaking free of the therapist's office invites the use of counselor-selected imagery. Find two photos of a wild animal. Choose one that shows the animal in a cage or in an enclosure such as a zoo setting. For the second image, choose a photo that shows the animal free in the wilderness of its typical habitat. Begin by asking clients to look at the first picture and write a list of words that describe the animal. Then have them repeat this exercise while looking at the second picture. Lastly, ask the clients to choose which of the animals that they would like most to become and to consider the reasons for their choice.

It is likely that for the first image, the list of words includes descriptors such as encaged, trapped, discouraged, sad, depressed, miserable, locked up, broken, or imprisoned.

For the second, the list might include proud, brave, courageous, free, happy, content, or strong. This connection to freedom and outdoor spaces is visceral and leads many to choose the second lion as the one they would rather become.

This activity illustrates the difference between doing ABC indoors versus outdoors. Being outside is liberating and empowering. It connects young males to something larger than themselves. Further, when you bring adolescents outdoors, they are immediately introduced to an unfamiliar setting (Gass, 1993) that aides in the change process. In addition, nature provides consequences that are both consistent and balanced (Hill, 2007). This allows the ABC practitioner to form a stronger connection with the participants. Being outside also allows for catharsis in the form of releasing frustration and anxiety through movement and verbal articulations that might not be feasible in an indoor setting (Miles, 1987). Kaplan and Talbot (1983) reported that being outside can increase awareness of one's environment, self-confidence, feelings of calm, and intrapersonal reflection, resulting in deeper insight and awareness. Similarly, Hanna et al. (1999) encouraged mental health practitioners working with adolescents to get out of the office as much as possible.

ABC relies heavily on experiential learning to produce change and growth in participants. Proponents of ABC believe that in order to change, participants need to be placed as close to the learning experience as possible (Gass, 1993). Thus, instead of being a spectator, ABC participants actively participate in the therapeutic process.

Another way that ABC differs from traditional talk therapy is that participant behavior is less inhibited. In traditional talk therapy, it is easier to disguise one's true behavior. This is much more difficult in ABC. As the unfamiliar situations bring out the participants true selves, they are forced to confront their behavior without excuses. At this point, the counselor is able to help the participant become aware of maladaptive behavior and choose new beneficial behaviors.

A very important distinction between ABC and traditional talk therapy is how ABC practitioners conceptualize participants (Gass, 1993). ABC practitioners strive to help participants focus on their strengths and encourage them to become empowered. As Erikson (1968) pointed out, the central task of adolescence is establishing a positive identity, without which, positive social interaction is unlikely to occur. ABC is an optimistic mode of counseling that does not view youth as deficient and necessitating categorical labels, but instead views participants as having yet to develop a positive self-identity (Gass, 1993).

One way that ABC helps adolescents develop a positive self-identity is through the use of activities (Gass, 1993). As adolescents engage in these tasks, they discover strengths and assets previously unknown. Hill (2007) reported that as adolescents successfully engage in ABC, they often experience gains in self-concept, increased internal locus of control, and elevated self-confidence.

Creating Meaning Through Experience

ABC experiences become metaphors for difficulties the participants face in their everyday lives (Fletcher & Hinkle, 2002; Gass, 1993; Hill, 2007; Kimball & Bacon, 1996). Thoughts, feelings, and actions exhibited during ABC are usually identical to problematic patterns that got them placed in counseling. One of the goals of ABC is to address these behaviors as they pertain to the tasks at hand.

Yalom and Leszcz (2005) refer to this process as the here-and-now. As the ABC activity triggers problematic behavior, the group becomes a social microcosm. The difference between what Yalom and Leszcz (2005) describe and what is experienced in ABC is a matter of manifestation. In ABC, the participant communicates the problematic pattern not only through verbal communication, but also through actions observed during the completing of the activity. Thus, the participant as well as the ABC practitioner creates meaning regarding the behavior through the actual experience.

During this process, the participant and practitioner are also heavily reliant on metaphor. It is through metaphor that participants are able to transfer their insights into their everyday lives (Fletcher & Hinkle, 2002; Kimball & Bacon, 1996). ABC practitioners help participants frame the activity as a metaphor for problems experienced outside the group. The way that they engaged in the activity serves as a metaphor for how they might behave in everyday life.

Risk Taking in ABC

According to Gass (1993), change is most likely to occur when people are placed outside their comfort zone. This discomfort is facilitated by introducing risk. The use of risk is a fundamental part of ABC (Fletcher & Hinkle, 2002) and is believed to be one of the prime mechanisms for change. Essentially, when participants experience an unfamiliar situation, they must choose a way to cope. This choice requires them to take a risk. ABC practitioners help participants take risks and engage in unfamiliar situations regardless of the expected outcome (Fletcher & Hinkle, 2002; Gall, 1987).

Risk can be real or perceived; both are necessary attributes of ABC (Fletcher & Hinkle, 2002). The experience of risk is a positive outcome of ABC participation (Fletcher & Hinkle, 2002). It was reported that participants who engaged in ABC were more likely to take risks in social situations. For adolescent males, this might include being more willing to meet new people, speak out in groups, or stand up for what they believe to be right. Further, as Walton (1980) posed, risk taking is a natural part of adolescent development. ABC not only acts as a socially appropriate outlet for risk taking (e.g., zip lines and high ropes course participation), it also facilitates the development of decision-making skills.

Creative Approaches to Problem Solving

As will be mentioned in the following sections, young males often struggle with thinking out of the box. They typically rely heavily on the left side of their brain, which is responsible for logical thinking (Cox, 2006). Therefore, they may approach problem solving in a straightforward manner. This reliance can be problematic in certain circumstances. Males often struggle in social situations, and instead of attempting to discover new and creative ways to navigate social relationships, young males often withdraw (Cox, 2006). Because of this, males may struggle to make safe or healthy decisions, particularly when peers pressure each other to participate in harmful activities.

ABC provides a setting where adolescent males can practice thinking out of the box. Most ABC activities can be completed using more than one solution. The group generates solutions to a problem. Often, participants' opinions on how to complete the tasks vary, and negotiating an agreed upon solution is a great opportunity for adolescents to practice creative thinking. Following the ABC intervention, participants discuss the decision-making process. They disclose their thoughts and emotions and any challenges they experienced during the problem solving. They may also explore the roles they play in the group dynamic. This process allows adolescent males to practice exploring creative approaches to problem solving as well as express their thoughts and feelings in a safe and supportive group environment.

MALE DEVELOPMENTAL CONSIDERATIONS

Gender differences between male and female adolescent populations impact treatment planning in ABC. Significant differences exist in brain functioning, language use and verbal expression, and behavioral issues. Understanding these developmental considerations allows counselors to construct interventions and activities that are appropriate for the population participating in the group.

Brain Development/Language

According to Cox (2006), males' language is distinctly different from females'. This difference is directly related to brain development and functioning. The right hemisphere of the brain is affiliated with creativity, insight, and comprehension of nonverbal communication. The left hemisphere is associated with the processing of spoken and written language as well as problem solving, reasoning ability, and skills related to math and science. Typically, due to a larger corpus callosum, females are better at combining the use of the left and right hemispheres of the brain. This combination allows them to communicate more effectively and exhibit greater perception in social situations.

In contrast, males are often at a disadvantage concerning social communication and interaction due to their restricted use of the right hemisphere. This increased dependence on the left hemisphere helps to explain why a majority of male adolescents tend to be goal oriented and prefer a straightforward approach to solving problems (Cox, 2006).

Language in Relation to Emotional and Behavioral Problems

According to Cox (2006), males also use language differently than females. In general, males typically use language in a more functional manner. For example, on average, males use language to make requests, such as asking permission to do something. They also use language to retrieve specific information, like asking why they have to clean their room or why they cannot do something. Cox (2006) noted that males typically experience a deficit in regards to using language for self-expression. Adolescent males will typically struggle to explain how they feel, what defines them, what they hope for, or what they believe in. Unfortunately, this deficit is directly related to the type of language required in most forms of traditional talk therapy.

Expressing oneself can be risky, especially for males. Polluck (1999) pointed out that males often avoid situations where they feel vulnerable or might experience shame. As boys struggle to understand and express what they are feeling, they will become more frustrated and are more likely to withdraw from social interactions in order to avoid potential embarrassment. This isolation and frustration likely contribute to increased feelings of anger as well as problematic behaviors (Polluck, 1999). Once this withdrawal process has begun, it becomes increasingly difficult for parents and mental health professionals to connect with the individual.

Developing the ability to express oneself through language is vital to human development. Deficits in expressive language often result in a lack of meaningful personal relationships (Cox, 2006). This lack of relationships is not only related to many mental health diagnoses, but it can also lead to a sense of isolation, frustration, and discouragement (Cox, 2006; Polluck, 1999) as well as limit the effects of talk therapy.

ABC's Applicability to Adolescent Male Developmental Needs

The applicability of ABC to counseling adolescent males can be showcased through experiential learning, as articulated in Kurt Hahn's and John Dewey's philosophy (Gass, 1993). Gass (1993) reported that, from the beginning, learning by doing was meant to build character in young men. As a result, ABC is often an appropriate and enhanced treatment modality for adolescent males because it engages clients through experiential learning, risk taking (real and perceived), metaphorical framing, and transfer of learning to multiple life realms (Fletcher & Hinkle, 2002).

When adolescent male clients experience ABC, natural consequences are encountered throughout the process, thereby enabling intrapersonal insight and change with minimal focus on language and maximum focus on metaphor. Adventure-based activities are selected to fit the participants, and they are framed in a logical manner that creates a linear pattern that is followed throughout the therapeutic process (Gass, 1993). Participants start at a clear beginning and finish the activity when they have reached its clearly marked ending (Gass, 1993). At the end of each activity, the participants discuss what occurred during the activity. During this processing discussion, adolescent males are utilizing both the right and left hemispheres of the brain, enhancing their ability to communicate the emotional connection with the activity. Although they will likely depend on the logic heavy left side (Cox, 2006), the discussion encourages emotional, interpersonal awareness, and intrapersonal insights.

According to self-efficacy theory (Bandura, 1977), the perceived consequence of insights made directly impacts the likelihood they will be generalized to other situations. Thus, when adolescent males participate in ABC, they are more likely to translate their new self-understanding and behaviors into their everyday life than if the same information was gained during a traditional talk therapy session. Creating a connection between the activity and life provides the participant a linear path with which to transfer their learning to everyday experiences.

Although ABC relies heavily on the experiential process to create change within the participants, some verbal and nonverbal language exchange is required. However, relying on the metaphoric understanding of the experience empowers male participants to take responsibility for change. All participants are encouraged to share during the processing time, but expecting all participants to fully process everything they have experienced or learned is unrealistic. To expect any or all change to occur through verbal processing would void the power of the experience and equate ABC to talk therapy. Instead, it is expected that true change and growth has occurred intrapersonally throughout the ABC experience. It is likely that this dependence on the intrapersonal therapeutic process makes it difficult to establish empirically based evidence of the efficacy of ABC.

Roles for Adventure-Based Counselors

Counseling in ABC programs requires a range of skills unique among therapeutic treatment approaches. Typically, ABC counselors divide their skill sets into two broad categories: soft skills and hard skills. In addition to counseling skills, ABC counselors require knowledge and understanding of the social dynamics of the population with whom they work. They need to be skillful in the specific activities the group is working through, and they must have appropriate medical training to respond to emergent concerns, particularly if the activity occurs in the backcountry. The counselors need to be knowledgeable of and feel comfortable within the natural environments to work constructively with therapeutic intentionality. Lastly, the counselor will benefit from employing methods specifically designed to help facilitate counseling in ABC programs.

Activities, settings, and discussions must be developmentally appropriate for the clients in a given ABC program. Finding ways to connect with clients that draw on their cultural experiences helps add a sense of familiarity in an environment that is otherwise unfamiliar. Counselors will be able to build rapport more effectively if they respond to clients in ways that are consistent with their social norms. Consideration is also given to the physical capabilities of participants. Recognizing their skill levels and physical abilities will help counselors construct activities that are challenging but possible for participants.

ABC approaches can be used at residential therapeutic schools, inpatient settings, and with clients on an outpatient basis. In any instance, ABC counselors will spend time with clients both within the structure of a given activity and during times when explicit therapeutic work is not being conducted. Because of this, it is important for counselors to recognize the different social spaces groups occupy. Although all of what happens within the program is "grist for the mill," distinguishing between "therapy" activities and downtime allows participants to engage in ways that are more free. If there are significant learning or therapeutic experiences that occur outside the activities, counselors should use judgment when deciding whether this is best addressed in the moment or at a later time.

Counselors should be trained in specific skills required for any activities employed. This knowledge may be necessary logistically to run the course, but it also becomes a basis for rapport. The skill and safety awareness of leaders help create an atmosphere of physical safety. This can be used to communicate empathy and positive regard and can be a foundation for mutual respect. Understanding the natural environment is also important as it constantly presents opportunities for learning. Having facts and narratives at quick recall allows the counselor to draw on information about the natural environment that may be pertinent to a client's work.

ABC inherently involves some element of physical risk. Although this risk is well managed and is often more a perceived element than an actual hazard, clients still have the potential to be physically injured. Counselors should have appropriate training to address whatever likely medical and safety concerns may arise during the activities. This may be as simple as basic first aid and CPR certification. It may also require additional certification including Wilderness First Responder or high angle/swift water rescue. Activity-specific training also increases the safety of the program.

Lastly, adventure-based counselors will benefit from using models created specifically for use in ABC settings. One such model is the Psychological Depth Model (Ringer & Gillis, 1995). This model provides an approach to ABC that helps counselors work from basic group building and social skills to significant personal exploration. According to the goals outlined through Informed Consent, counselors can direct the activity and conversation to meet appropriate levels of processing. The model moves through various levels of depth, each of which encourages the client to connect with and explore increasingly vulnerable and affecting aspects of himself (Ringer & Gillis, 1995).

Metaskills

In order for ABC practitioners to competently facilitate ABC groups, it is important to combine soft and hard skills into what Priest and Gass (1997) referred to as metaskills. They define six metaskills vital to ABC: leadership style, communication, judgment, problem solving, decision making, and professional ethics. A case example is described as follows, and Table 11.1 provides an overview of an integrated model of ABC sequenced activities that incorporate the metaskills as outlined.

(Text continues on p. 209)

TABLE 11.1

Integrated Model of ABC Activities and Counselor's Focus

ABC Sequence of Activities	ABC Activities	Counselor's Focus and Metaskills	Potential ABC Processing Statements
Full Value Contract (FVC)	*Building the Community*	*Building the Community*	*Counseling Process*
Facilitators generate a counseling environment that supports the cocreation of a group culture that is authentic and respectful of the individuals. In the FVC process, the counselors' process with the group how each member will attentively and mindfully respond to personal needs and the perceived and communicated needs of others.	Create a constructive conversation of building norms and values of respect and responsibility to self and others. Give participants a stuffed animal that squeaks to be caught by members standing in a circle facing into the middle of the circle. Once the stuffed animal is caught, the participant yells out a value such as trust, honesty, support, or friendship. Write down the values, and then process with the group if a value appears to be missing.	The counselors' democratic leadership role involves sharing the decision making and problem solving with the group members (Priest & Gass, 1997). Building the community is constructively designed by participants and counselors to create a working community built on an agreement to be open to communicating and listening to needs, paying attention, accepting responsibility for behaviors, exploring assumptions with others, and transferring learning of activities to further emotional and mental development.	Counselors process with the group the reasons for creating a working environment built on the list the group created. Have the members describe how the values will help the group community work together. Explore with the group how they will know if they are a group built on the values desired. Identify other needs of the group to help the members to feel safe and supported by others in the group.
Challenge by Choice (CbC)	*Community Construction*	*Involvement*	*Counseling Process*
The CbC principle is explained by the counselors as part of the FVC to help members understand their role and level of participation in	Create an environment to process the benefits of full emotional engagement and explore options for selecting the	Prior to engagement of ABC activities, counselors explore with participants their level of involvement in the ABC activities.	Describe the ABC experience to involve personal choice in participating in the activities. Although participants may not be

TABLE 11.1

Integrated Model of ABC Activities and Counselor's Focus (*continued*)

ABC Sequence of Activities	ABC Activities	Counselor's Focus and Metaskills	Potential ABC Processing Statements
the group. The principle communicated to members is that they are invited to participate in the ABC activities and select their level of participation. As a result of this open involvement principle, a participant may choose to sit out of an ABC activity, and this decision is respected by the counselors and supported by the members of the group.	degree of physical involvement.	CbC encourages members to take personal responsibility when choosing behaviors and actions. Counselors are encouraged to conceptualize and recognize when members decide not to physically engage in the activity so that these members potentially learn and grow more by refusing to participate on occasions than feeling resentful for participating.	physically engaged in the activities, they are encouraged to be supportive to the ABC community.\n\nWhen a participant decides to not be physically engaged in the ABC activity, they are encouraged to be emotionally supportive and communicative to the group members.
Opening Joining Initiative	*Group Juggle (Name Game)*	*Counseling task*	*Counseling Process and Metaskills*
Fun, inviting, and motivating activity to welcome full engagement of participants into a nonthreatening environment.	To facilitate this activity, counselors will request each participant to stand in a circle shoulder to shoulder facing the center. Once everyone is in place, explain the rules of the game. Tell the participants that the purpose of the game is to get to know each other in a fun and interactive way. Located in a bag (that is not transparent) have five stuffed	Counselors engage participants in a pattern of throwing the stuffed animals in a sequenced pattern. After the first round and once the pattern has been created, the counselors will add more stuffed animals for the group members to toss. This activity will become fast paced and fun!	Counselors are encouraged to begin the processing of the members experiences with a broad, open-ended question.\n\nDescribe your experiences with Group Juggle.\n\nWhat surprised you while you played Group Juggle?\n\nDescribe when you noticed a change in your interactions with others in the group.

(continued)

ABC Sequence of Activities	ABC Activities	Counselor's Focus and Metaskills	Potential ABC Processing Statements
	animals and one rubber chicken. Begin the game by stating your name and a value you will work to create in the group (e.g., trust) and passing one stuffed animal to a person across the circle. Have the participants remember whom they threw the stuffed animal to and received it from. Once the person receives the stuffed animal, he will say thank you "name" to the person throwing the stuffed animal and "here you go name" to another person intended to receive the stuffed animal. Each person will receive the stuffed animal once in the first round.		In what ways did you feel supported by others in the group?

Communicating using metaskills involves the counselors' role in developing processing norms with the group members. A few important processing norms include:

(a) helping members clearly state messages by speaking for themselves by using "I" statements; (b) processing the members' experiences, counselors need to connect key points communicated by the members through linking experiences and similarities; (c) fostering an environment where all thoughts are heard and acknowledged by demonstrating listening and interest among group members in an effort to encourage members to finish one message and thought before connecting or beginning new ideas. |

TABLE 11.1

Integrated Model of ABC Activities and Counselor's Focus (*continued*)

ABC Sequence of Activities	ABC Activities	Counselor's Focus and Metaskills	Potential ABC Processing Statements
Team Building—Ice Breaker Activity	*"Have You Ever" (Rohnke & Butler, 1995, p. 224)*	*Counselor's Task "Have You Ever"!*	*Counseling Process and Metaskills*
An ice breaker activity is a great first activity to engage adolescents in having fun. The activity involves short durations of attention, movement, and laughter. This activity begins the process of moving around, listening, and focusing energy in the activity.	To facilitate this activity, counselors will need to place chairs in a large circle with the number of chairs being one less than the number of participants engaging in this activity. The counselor of the activity will provide the instructions for the game, while the participants sit in the chairs waiting to begin. While providing the instructions, the facilitator will stand in the center of the circle and state: "Have You Ever is a game to explore our exciting adventures. Each of you will remain sitting in the chair until the person in the center of the circle states something he or she has participated in. For instance, if the center person asks 'Have you ever been scuba diving?' all of those who have been scuba diving will move out of their chair and run to	The counselor's role includes observing the interactions and reactions of the participants while playing the game. If the counselor notices challenges or inappropriate interactions between the participants, the counselors will then need to set limits to create a safe environment for the group.	Describe your experience while playing "Have You Ever?" When did you notice others were having fun too? What was it like for you when you were in the middle asking "Have You Ever?" Describe what it was like to feel stuck while in the middle? Explore what others in the group were thinking and/or feeling when they noticed someone stuck in the middle. Counseling process and metaskills involve focusing the discussion on creating communication norms. These norms involve generating communication or ideas and experiences, encoding how others understand the communication sent, checking impressions of the sent message, linking ideas and feelings with other members, and

(*continued*)

TABLE 11.1

Integrated Model of ABC Activities and Counselor's Focus (*continued*)

ABC Sequence of Activities	ABC Activities	Counselor's Focus and Metaskills	Potential ABC Processing Statements
	another empty chair. The center person will also quickly find a chair. The participant not seated will become the next person in the middle to ask "Have you ever..."		acknowledging the information gained by the communication (Priest & Gass, 1997).
Working Stage Activity	*Crossing the Great Divide*	*Counselor Statement*	*Counseling Process and Metaskills*
Crossing the Great Divide is utilized to develop cohesion in a group. Discussing group member's physical abilities, strengths, openness to share ideas, and willingness to ask for help is also an opportunity when dialoguing about the experience.	Set up two boundaries at either end of the room or designated area—one as a starting point and the other as the finishing point. It is essential that both the starting and finish line be in sight. Have the group line up shoulder to shoulder along the starting line. Group members need to line up by placing their right foot next to the person's left foot that is next to them, and so on down the line. As a group, they need to figure out when to move forward together in order to reach the other side at the same time. If anybody's feet become separated, the whole group needs to start over.	Welcome to the Great Divide. I'd like to point out a few rules that the group must follow to get to the other side of the divide. Note the two pieces of rope at either end of the divide—they indicate the starting and finish line for crossing the divide. One facilitator is needed to lay out the boundaries for the start and finish lines of the activity. This activity may be experienced inside or outside. One important consideration is to have enough space to accommodate the size of your group. A time limit for this experience may be provided if desired. If the group discovers	Counselors are encouraged to design the space between the starting line and finish line to represent the common issues, themes, or experiences of the participants engaging in the activity. For example, high school students engaged in the activity may conceptualize the distance to cross the Great Divide as the challenges and experiences within their high school experience. When processing the activity, facilitators make direct and intentional connections between what was working well during the activity (group process, communication, teamwork, asking for help, etc.) with what is needed

TABLE 11.1

Integrated Model of ABC Activities and Counselor's Focus (*continued*)

ABC Sequence of Activities	ABC Activities	Counselor's Focus and Metaskills	Potential ABC Processing Statements
		that they are unsuccessful in arriving at the finish line or at the metaphor created (e.g., graduation), have the group create a dialogue reflecting on the metaskill of judgment. A good rule of thumb is that learning will occur from all mistakes and challenges. Assist the group to reflect on the communication and experiences that are effective in reaching their goals. Connect these skills with the metaphor of graduation or finishing the school year. Assist the members to embrace the challenge, evaluate, and reflect on the process, and explore their predictions to achieve their goals as a way to improve their future judgments (Priest & Gass, 1997).	of them to complete the present school year or to arrive at graduation. *Processing statements and Metaskills* - How did you feel counting on everyone to cross the Great Divide? - What went well? What did not go so well? - How did you utilize others for support? - What might you do differently if you crossed the Great Divide again? - What communication method worked when crossing the Great Divide? - What did you learn about communicating with others in order to reach a goal?
Problem-Solving Activity	*Traffic Jam Activity*	*Counselor Statement*	*Counseling Process and Metaskills*
Creating a problem-solving activity promotes group members to embrace the ambiguity of not	Place seven stepping stones side by side in a straight line. Six group members will engage in this activity.	This activity presents a challenge of exchanging places. Everyone standing on the stones must move	In facilitating this activity, counselors may want to begin by front-loading the activity with the

(continued)

TABLE 11.1

Integrated Model of ABC Activities and Counselor's Focus (*continued*)

ABC Sequence of Activities	ABC Activities	Counselor's Focus and Metaskills	Potential ABC Processing Statements
knowing and discovering alternative methods for working together to overcome obstacles and challenges.	Have one person stand on each of the three left-hand stones, facing the center. Have one person stand on each of the three right-hand stones, facing the center stone. The center stone is not occupied to begin the problem-solving activity.	so that the members originally standing on the left-hand stepping stones move to the right-hand stones. Those members standing on the right-hand stones move to the left-hand stones. The center stone will remain unoccupied. Ask the group to transition to the other side by finding the least number of moves. Rules of the problem-solving activity: (a) After each move, one person must be standing on a stepping stone; (b) if you start on the right, you must only move to the left, and if you start on the left you must only move to the right; (c) you may jump another person if there is an empty stone on the other side; (d) you may not jump more than one person; (e) only one person will move at a time.	instructions and immediately identifying a metaphor for the activity to translate to real life. Given the members need for developing aptitude toward practicing life skills, motivation for completing high school, and for maintaining relationships, it may be possible for the counselors and members to cocreate a metaphor that defines the problems both in the activity and in real life. For example, as the members stand on the stones, ask them to identify (define) the presenting problem. Based on their responses, link the common themes and feelings to a problem in life. Next, the counselor will construct with the group possible solutions and pathways that may result in the anticipated results. Once the group physically moves through the identified plan, process with the members the communication

TABLE 11.1

Integrated Model of ABC Activities and Counselor's Focus (*continued*)

ABC Sequence of Activities	ABC Activities	Counselor's Focus and Metaskills	Potential ABC Processing Statements
			process that was effective, steps the members took to work together, and identify how others offered support and recognized when support was provided.
			Help the members to organize their responses to identify their process for decision making and how this model of working together benefited their overall goals.
			To connect the members with the activity and real-life challenges, directly explore how their communication, decision making, and the cocreated metaphor relates to presenting challenges that may be overcome by the skills gained through this activity.
Closing Activity	*Balloon Frenzy*	*Counselor Statement Balloon Frenzy*	*Counseling Process Balloon Frenzy*
Providing properly sequenced activities designed to connect participants learning of self and others as a final activity is important for transference of learning to	Ask the participants to stand in a circle facing in toward each other. Provide the members a choice of one balloon. Ask the members to blow up their balloons. While	Ask each member to identify a concern in their lives that impacts their ability to participate in the group. Announce to the group that during this activity, their balloon	Counselors are charged with directly connecting the group members' concerns with the group dynamics and interactions.

(*continued*)

TABLE 11.1

Integrated Model of ABC Activities and Counselor's Focus (*continued*)

ABC Sequence of Activities	ABC Activities	Counselor's Focus and Metaskills	Potential ABC Processing Statements
everyday life challenges. Two ABC activities are presented to integrate intra- and interpersonal learning as a means for connecting ABC experiences to real-life events.	observing the process of blowing up the balloons make a mental note of the difficulty of the task. Once the balloons are blown up ask the members to share with the group a concern or difficulty in life that impacts their ability to participate in the group. *Postcard Send-Off* Have the members stand in a circle facing inward toward an arrangement of postcards laying face up. Have more postcards available than members. Counselors will ask the members to select a postcard that represents their feelings and thoughts throughout the ABC activities. After the members have selected a postcard, begin processing how the postcard represents a metaphor for their experience. To conclude the activity, have each member write on the postcard something they have gained from	represents that concern. Set a goal for the group to work together to keep all the balloons in the air without letting any of them touch the ground. As balloons begin to touch the ground, stop the group, and process what is working and what presents as a challenge toward achieving the goal to work together. What can they do to better manage the balloons? Have them engage in the activity again and then process: what was working and what in the activity was similar to how they manage the concerns in everyday life. *Postcard Send Off* It is designed to create an integrated understanding of the participants' experiences through the ABC activities with their personal goals. Counselors begin the activity by announcing that this last activity will draw upon your experiences	Remember the goal was to work together to keep the balloons in the air. Help the group members to explore how their concerns impact their relationships in the group. Directly connect the metaphor of keeping the balloons in the air and needing supports in relationships to the members' experiences of the group. Develop a metaphor to connect the balloons to all the members' responsibilities toward achieving their identified goal of graduating, completing the year of school.... *Postcard Send-Off* Counselors will process with the group members how the picture represents their experiences with the activities and other group members. Explore with the group what they have gained from the activities and interactions with others. Connect this learning to relationships and

TABLE 11.1

Integrated Model of ABC Activities and Counselor's Focus (*continued*)

ABC Sequence of Activities	ABC Activities	Counselor's Focus and Metaskills	Potential ABC Processing Statements
	the experience or a goal they hope to achieve. Mail the postcards to the members after an agreed upon timeframe has passed! The postcards may need to be mailed in an envelope for confidentiality proposes.	today and your future goals. To begin, place numerous postcards (more postcards than participants) facing picture side up across a large space. Members are asked to stand in a circle around the postcards. As a group, ask the members to select a postcard that represents their thoughts and feelings of their experiences in the ABC activities. Counselors facilitate a group process of members' experiences through the metaphor of the postcard.	challenges outside the group experience to support the process of transferring intra- and interpersonal learning to lived experiences. Process with the group members how it may be to receive this self sent message in the mail. How may having this reminder of your experience promote continued transformation of your learning? If you were to experience ABC activities again, what may you do the same or differently?

Group Case Example

The group members are characterized as 15- to 17-year-old males who define themselves as lazy and lacking motivation in all areas of life. The members have been previously involved in either individual counseling and/or family counseling with little to no reported success and motivation to continue in the counseling process. As a result of their minimal desire to engage in the counseling work, their counselors made referrals for group counseling. The group members voluntarily agreed to participate in ABC as a way to appease parental complaints. Several members stated this will give them time to get their moms off their backs from wanting them to participate in family interactions and for the dads to stop pressuring them to finish homework and develop some level of motivation. Several members agreed that they preferred to spend their time in isolation playing online video games rather than engaging in any social interactions. As a result of their current behaviors, the members are at risk of failing their present year of high school and are struggling to have family relationships.

Leadership Style

Priest and Gass (1997) defined leadership style as the methods employed to influence a group. Three categories of leaders are presented in the article: autocratic, democratic, and abdicratic. Autocratic leaders make the majority of decisions, are often controlling, and allow little flexibility in how the group functions. Democratic leaders share decision making with the group and allow the members to influence how the group functions. Abdicratic leadership involves facilitating the group so that it creates its own decisions and faces consequences that result. Although ABC counselors will often rely heavily on democratic approaches to leadership, each style may be appropriate when working with clients.

Communication

Communication skills are pivotal to the facilitation of ABC. Without effective communication skills, all other skills are void. Because all human interaction relies on the use of some form of communication, it could be argued that healthy social functioning cannot be attained without effective communication skills. Communication consists of verbal and nonverbal messages sent between individuals (Priest & Gass, 1997).

Communication in ABC involves a sender and receiver. From a practitioner perspective, communication is used to establish one's role as leader, convey information such as norms and expectations, and facilitate interpersonal and intrapersonal relationships (Priest & Gass, 1997). Communication aides in the practitioner's ability to keep the participants safe and without effective communication, other parts of the process disintegrate. From a participant perspective, communication is the modus operandi by which insight, learning, growth, and change occur (Priest & Gass, 1997).

In order to be effective communicators, it is imperative that ABC practitioners are aware of how they are communicating their messages. Priest and Gass (1997) submitted a model of communication that entails a message being generated and encoded by the sender. The sender then connects with the recipient and sends the message by transmitting it via verbal and nonverbal pathways. After the recipient receives the message, it is decoded and interpreted. At this point, the recipient must decide how to respond to the information received in the message (e.g., change or not change).

When working with males, it is imperative that the sender encodes the message in a way that is decodable by the recipient. As mentioned previously, males process language differently than females and may also have a communication deficit. Therefore, the ABC practitioner must phrase messages in a way that the participants can understand and respond to appropriately.

Judgment

According to Priest and Gass (1997), "judgment is an experienced-based application of the human brain's ability to reason in a cycle of three reflections" (p. 261). They identify these three reflections as inductive, deductive, and evaluative. The term "reflections" is used because ABC practitioners believe that experience alone is insufficient to foster growth. Rather, it is through reflecting upon experiences that one is able to develop the ability to make appropriate evidence-based judgments.

Inductive reflections create concepts that are generalizable to future experiences. Deductive reflection is the process of using the general concepts to make specific statements or form particular predictions. The final reflection, evaluative, is possibly the most important reflection in the judgment cycle. It is during this process that you evaluate the accuracy of the judgment.

Developing experience-based judgment emerges based on the following, as detailed by Priest and Gass (1997): (a) listen to rules carefully and imagine possible exceptions, (b) gather as much information from others' experiences, (c) watch how other leaders make decisions, and ask questions about how they come to certain conclusions, (d) confront other ABC practitioners about judgments you disagree with, and (e) ask peers to participate in ABC with you as the leader, and get their responses to your performance. Priest and Gass also recommend that counselors gain as much supervised experience as possible so that there is a high level of processing of the experience. Developing a relationship with a mentor can also provide feedback and support as a counselor cultivates evidence-based judgment.

Problem Solving

"Problem solving is the process of finding answers to questions by determining a strategy applied to a situation to make it turn out the way you desire" (Priest & Gass, 1997). Priest and Gass (1997) present a multiphase problem-solving model that can be used in ABC. The phases include assessment, analytic, and creative.

The initial phase, assessment, is used to identify whether there is a problem that needs to be solved. If there is a problem, then the ABC practitioner moves to the analytic phase. This phase consists of five sequenced steps: definition, anticipation, identification, selection, and execution. First, the ABC practitioner defines the problem and anticipates characteristics of a satisfactory solution. Next, the practitioner identifies possible

solutions—pathways that will result in the anticipated result. After identifying multiple solutions, the practitioner selects and executes the solution
that appears to be the best fit for the problem. Although this process can
happen intrapersonally, it is often a process the ABC practitioner assists
the participants through as a group.

During the creative phase, six identified techniques (Priest & Gass,
1997) can be implemented if the practitioner or group comes to an
impasse. These techniques include brainstorming, extended effort, attribute listing, forced relationships, deferred prejudice, and judgment. For
a detailed description of these six techniques, refer to Priest and Gass
(1997). If there is still no agreed upon solution, the ABC practitioner must
be prepared to introduce creative means to foster communication and
compromise in order to arrive at a solution.

Decision Making

Decision making is the direct consequence of the previous two metaskills:
judgment and problem solving. Priest and Gass (1997) defined decision
making as "the process of choosing the most probable option from a
collection of possible ones" (p. 275). During this process, the ABC practitioner builds a list of potential actions and then works to narrow the
choices down to the best one. This process mandates the use of judgment,
problem-solving skills, as well as convergent techniques such as organizing and weighing the options, weeding out the less desirable ones, and
then selecting the preferred choice. Like problem solving, this process can
occur intrapersonally or with the group. How practitioners choose to make
decisions depends on their leadership style as well as the situation.

ABC Research for Adolescents

Although ABC addresses the developmental needs of adolescent males,
it is important to explore the counseling research to evaluate ABC's
treatment efficacy with such a population. ABC generally involves the
integration of different professional disciplines, counseling theories,
and treatment planning methods. This multifaceted approach seems to
maintain over time consistent struggles with purporting outcome-based
research findings that match the anecdotal reports of the ABC facilitators' perceptions of the participants' experiences and the participants'
self-reports. A few concerns outlined by Cason and Gillis (1994) highlight
the problems within the research, where several similar outcome-based
research findings purport different results for a similar study (Cason &
Gillis, 1994). Given that different professions are investigating the outcomes of ABC, it is possible that the adventure educational programs
have been designing different research studies to examine factors of

self-perception and self-esteem without the facilitators intentionally processing the emotional connections within the ABC experiences (Cason & Gillis, 1994). The challenge facing the counseling profession, related to ABC best practice methods, involves having counselors with training in research design and knowledge of implementation of the study to be facilitating the research. Attending to these methodology concerns will allow for studies to be duplicated by other professionals so that the research will continue to make the outcome-based results more effective and applicable in counseling training and ABC activity design (Cason & Gillis, 1994).

In response to the inconsistent research outcomes as a result of the ineffective measurement effectiveness (lack of a control group, randomization of participant involvement, and clearly defined methods for conducting ABC programs), Cason and Gillis (1994) conducted a meta-analysis within the field of adventure programming with adolescents. The meta-analysis was utilized to statistically integrate outcomes from numerous studies exploring the outcomes of ABC. The outcomes of each separate study were converted into an effect size (ES) to measure the amount of change experienced following an ABC experience. The researchers collected 99 potential studies within a 25-year period (1969–1994) of adventure programming with adolescents (ages 11–college freshman). The ESs were based on 11,238 adolescents who experienced adventure programming that was not specifically designed to evaluate therapeutic gains (Cason & Gillis, 1994).

Overall, the meta-analysis ES for adventure programming with adolescents was 0.31. This ES indicates a positive improvement and denotes a measurable difference since it is greater than zero. These findings are small to moderate with an average of a 12.2% improvement (Cason & Gillis, 1994, Cohen, 1977). The study specifically assessed if adventure programming experience was more beneficial for adolescents based on duration of experience, for contrasting populations (nonadjudicated/adjudicated youth), and for developments' (age) impact on the outcome. The outcomes of the study determined that the measurements and evaluation methods used to explore program effectiveness were diverse. Research discovered that although changes were noted to be positive based on adventure programming experience, the results compiled were not consistent for similar studies.

The researchers proposed several concerns and variables for future ABC researchers to attend to when conducting sound ABC methodology. Cason and Gillis (1994) recommended that studies need to better identify the group size and determine if the study is exploring the benefits of ABC experience on the group or separate individuals within the group (Cason & Gillis, 1994). The group leaders' qualification and experience for the specific ABC tasks, training for attending to group members' needs, and mental health diagnosis need to be documented and addressed (Cason

& Gillis, 1994). Researchers Cason and Gillis (1994) and Gass (1992) also suggested collecting regression data to help predict what client needs and characteristics are more successful in ABC.

Attending to several of the program design concerns noted previously, a study was conducted by Haras et al. (2006) to examine ropes course program outcomes through program design and delivery. The study explored participants' perceived involvement, based on two alternative ropes courses, through an experience sampling method (ESM) to study participants' immediate conscious experiences in a real-time and on-site context (Csikszentmihalyi & Larson, 1987; Haras et al., 2006). Of the 360 adolescent participants, 172 males and 188 females, ages 10 to 15 (average age 12.7), there was no random assignment to either the Challenge by Choice (CbC program) or the Inviting Optimum Participation (I-Opt program).

The CbC program invited participants to decide how involved they chose to be when engaging in an experience. The I-Opt program provided the participants information of the various levels of difficulty and challenges. It also involved participants in a discussion of their responsibility to select their own level of involvement and challenging roles (Haras et al., 2006). The I-Opt approach provided participants with three elements to achieve vertical elevation with multiple climbing sources to succeed in meeting vertical goals.

A multivariate analysis of variance (MANOVA) was conducted to determine if meaningful involvement differed between the CbC and I-Opt participants during high (belayed) and low (spotted) ropes course activities. The MANOVA results indicated that there was no significant main effect for sex on either the high elements or ropes course programs. A significant main effect was indicated on the I-Opt program, as participants reported that the option for multiple selections in ABC activities decreased apprehension about the experience and allowed for more desirable options to reach goals. High ropes courses in general have greater focus on individual achievement and success as the other participants are able to witness how the climber is performing. Given that the I-Opt program offers numerous participants multiple options for accessing the high elements, many climbers may be experiencing different aspects of the belayed experience at one time. With many options for climbing and accessing the high ropes course, the focus is less on one individual, allowing for participants to find an activity that they perceive themselves to be more successful at. Increasing the belief they may be successful and decreasing the number of other participants observing from below, participants have reported less anxiety that others will observe their shortcomings and compare performances.

Overall, this study documented the benefits of providing participants with choices when selecting desired routes for vertical climbing. A few concerns continue to exist within this research. The researchers noted that the facilitators were trained, but no specific training methods were indicated. The ABC programming activities were not documented, and no specific information was given for group size. Given that ABC is facilitated for emotional and relational development, it seems important to examine participants' psychological gain, emotional connections, inter- and intrapersonal growth, perceived self-efficacy and self-worth, and transference to real-life experiences (Haras et al., 2006). Future research studies are needed to demonstrate how specific activities promote emotional connection and transference of learning. Facilitator training experience, group member demographics, and size remain as important considerations within future research studies.

ABC Ethical Considerations

Many cautions exist for both professional training programs (Gillis & Gass, 1993). The American Counseling Association (ACA) and the accreditation bodies the Council for Accreditation of Counseling-Related Educational Programs (CACREP) and the Association for Experiential Education (AEE) offer guidelines and standards for training professionals in similar ways. These similarities include treatment planning, assessment and diagnosis, action-based counseling approaches, metaphor applicability, relationship building techniques, and safety measures (ethical standards; Gillis & Gass, 1993). Each training program assisting professionals in developing ABC skills needs to attend to three areas: train professionals to conduct ABC techniques, develop sound counseling skills and adhere to professional knowledge of mental health diagnoses and treatment planning, and complete courses in CPR and child/adult First Aid along with applying knowledge of CPR and First Aid in the field when required (Gillis & Gass, 1993).

When integrating two professional fields (ACA and AEE), it is important to be knowledgeable of the similarities and differences of the ethical standards. A few similar ethical guidelines for the ACA and AEE (Gass, 1993a) exist. These ABC concerns for ethical considerations (Fletcher & Hinkle, 2002) are Client Welfare and elements of risk: emotional/physical risk and physical/mental welfare are considered and explored through challenge by choice. An additional concern for both professionals is that counselors need to be prepared to counsel DSM diagnosis within the setting of the activity. Most importantly, it is difficult to train counselors for the unexpected challenges of the variable types of relationships that may develop during the long duration of activities. Therefore, it is important to conceptualize the potential challenges of the counseling relationship based on the length of time to experience ABC activities. The many hours or months in the field may inherently present benefits and challenges to the counseling relationship dynamics, which may pose additional challenges to professional boundaries, and the proper training to facilitate ABC techniques. Attending to training professionals to meet these challenges will be an ongoing mission of counseling professionals.

There are also specific ethical considerations related to the use of interactive virtual adventures (e.g., video games) to deliver counseling services to adolescent males. This trend is detrimental not only to the mental health of the participant, but also to the family and ABC as a field. Boys' tendencies to prefer an organized and goal-oriented approach to problem solving makes them good candidates for ABC as well as easy targets for video game distributors. Both are organized and highly goal oriented. However, video games lack the benefits of being outside in nature where consistent, balanced, and effective consequences are nonexistent. Furthermore, video games lack the ability to create a sense of real or perceived risk. Risk is a vital part in facilitating change within ABC participants; without risk, it is less likely that change will occur, and if it does, less likely it will be lasting.

Lastly, video games provide a form of social interaction that reduces the challenges presented by communicating and working directly with another person. The lack of personal connection reinforces social isolation and as Cox (2006) stated, "communicating with boys who have withdrawn into isolation...makes a parent's job much harder" (p. 17). Video game use may ultimately exacerbate symptoms particularly, as many are specifically designed to elicit addictive responses and repetitive play. Counselors must be cognizant of ethical considerations that globally apply to ABC as well as those that emerge more specifically in the realm of virtual interactive adventures.

THE FUTURE OF ABC

As ABC continues to expand, counselors and programs increasingly seek out opportunities to help individuals and families. Programs explore new recreational activities, drawing upon clients' interests to use the activity as the starting point for interventions, metaphor, and therapy. Researchers explore new aspects of ABC, testing the validity and reliability of approaches and adding to the body of research. Integrating this knowledge assists academic programs to continue developing courses of study devoted to ABC.

Two primary challenges face ABC in the future. The first is the ongoing problem of reaching clients in need of services. As with other therapeutic interventions, one goal of ABC is to work with clients currently suffering from mental health distress and disorders. Many individuals and families are unfamiliar with ABC as a treatment modality. Of those who are, some see it as a diluted version of more "serious" approaches. Others are concerned of the "boot camp" therapies in which clients are "whipped into shape" through physical trial and shaming techniques. Presenting an accurate view of ABC to clients will inform public perception as to the efficacy and safety of the approach.

The second challenge is to procure resources that will allow more clients with access to ABC. ABC programs are often expensive therapeutic interventions. Frequently, programs are time intensive. For instance, many programs are constructed around "retreats" in which clients go to a location where they will spend a period of time engaged in activities and therapy. Locations are often removed or remote and require travel. With the time and travel requirements, ABC can be an expensive intervention. Moreover, since insurance companies have policies that often only cover limited aspects of ABC programming, clients may be left to pay for large portions of treatment "out of pocket." In many instances, access is limited to clients who can afford these services or to those who have been adjudicated and are supported in the process by public funds. As such, a large portion of the population who might benefit from ABC is not being reached.

Lastly, ABC offers another opportunity to help clients by "treating" those who are not currently suffering. For instance, ABC can also be "effectively used as a preventive strategy" (Nassar-McMillan & Cashwell, 1997). ABC may be used as a proactive approach to helping clients build the skills needed to manage the inherent stressors of life rather than only as a reactive measure once clients have developed symptoms. This lends itself to working in schools and work environments. Because the activities and environments of ABC are often enjoyable, clients may choose to participate in order to build or strengthen healthy personal attributes. Generating resources that inform potential participants of the positive emotional gains and interpersonal benefits of ABC may bring clients to ABC programs who may not otherwise seek counseling services.

REFERENCES

Bandura, A. (1977). Self-efficacy: Toward a unifying theory of behavioral change. *Psychological Review, 84*(2), 191–215.

Becker, S. P. (2010). Wilderness therapy: Ethical considerations for mental health professionals. *Child & Youth Care Forum, 39*(1), 47–61. doi:10.1007/s10566-009-9085-7.

Cason, D., & Gillis, H. L. (1994). A meta-analysis of outdoor adventure programming with adolescents. *The Journal of Experiential Education 17*(1), 40–47.

Church, E. (1984). The role of autonomy in adolescent psychotherapy. *Psychotherapy, 31,* 101–108.

Cohen, J. (1977). *Statistical power analysis for behavioral sciences* (rev. ed.). New York, NY: Academic Press.

Coogan, M. D., Brettler, M. Z., Newsom, C. A., & Perkins, P. (2001). *The New Oxford Annotated Bible with Apocrypha: New Revised Standard Version, College Edition* (3rd ed.). New York, NY: Oxford University Press.

Cox, A. J. (2006). *Boys of few words: Raising our sons to communicate and connect.* New York, NY: The Guildford Press.

Csikszentmihalyi, M., & Larson, R. W. (1987). Validity and reliability of the experience sampling method. *Journal of Nervous and Mental Disease, 175,* 526–536.

Easwaran, E., & Easwaran, E. (2007a). *The Bhagavad Gita* (2nd ed.). Tomales, CA: Nilgiri Press.

Easwaran, E., & Easwaran, E. (2007b). *The Upanishads* (2nd ed.). Tomales, CA: Nilgiri Press.

Emerick, Y. (2002). *Critical lives: Muhammad: Muhammad.* Indianapolis, IN: Alpha.

Erikson, E. H. (1968). *Identity: Youth and crisis.* New York, NY: W. W. Norton.

Fletcher, T. B., & Hinkle, J. S. (2002). Adventure based counseling: An innovation in counseling. *Journal of Counseling and Development, 80,* 277–285.

Gall, A. L. (1987). You can take the manager out of the woods, but... *Training and Development Journal, 41,* 54–58.

Gass, M. A., (1995). Adventure family therapy: An innovative approach answering the questions of lasting change with adjudicated youth? *Monograph on Youth in the 1990s. 4,* 103–117.

Gass, M. A. (1993). The theoretical foundations for adventure family therapy. In M. Gass (Ed.), *Adventure therapy: Therapeutic applications of adventure programming* (pp. 123–137). Dubuque, IA: Kendall Hunt.

Gil, E. (1996). *Treating abused adolescents.* New York, NY: The Guildford Press.

Gillen, M. C., & Balkin, R. S. (2006). Adventure Counseling as an Adjunct to Group Counseling in Hospital and Clinical Settings. *Journal for Specialists in Group Work, 31*(2), 153–164. doi:10.1080/01933920500493746.

Gillis, H. L., & Gass, M. A. (1993). Brining adventure into marriage and family therapy: An innovative experiential approach. *Journal of Marital and Family Therapy 19*(3), 273–286.

Gillis, H. L., Gass, M. A., & Russell, K. C. (2008). The effectiveness of project adventure's behavior management programs for male offenders in residential treatment. *Residential Treatment for Children & Youth, 25*(3), 227–247. doi:10.1080/08865710802429689.

Glass, J. S., & Myers, J. E. (2001). Combining the old and the new to help adolescents: Individual psychology and adventure-based counseling. *Journal of Mental Health Counseling, 23*(2), 104–114.

Hanna, F. J., Hanna, C. A., & Keys, S. G. (1999). Fifty strategies for counseling defiant, aggressive adolescents: Reaching, accepting, and relating. *Journal of Counseling and Development, 77,* 395–404.

Haras, K., Bunting, C. J., & Witt, P. A. (2006). Meaningful involvement opportunities in ropes course programs. *Journal of Leisure Research, 38*(3), 339–362.

Hattie, J., Marsh, H. W., Neill, J. T., & Richards, G. E. (1997). Adventure education and outward bound: Out-of-class experiences that make a lasting difference. *Review of Educational Research, 67*(1), 43–87. doi:10.2307/1170619.

Heart, B. (1998). *The wind is my mother: The life and teachings of a Native American Shaman.* New York, NY: Berkley Trade.

Hill, N. R. (2007). Wilderness therapy as a treatment modality for at-risk youth: A primer for mental health counselors. *Journal of Mental Health Counseling. 29*(4), 338–349.

Huber, C. H. (1997). Outward Bound together (Indoors): Adventure family counseling. *The Family Journal, 5*(1), 49–52. doi:10.1177/1066480797051006.

Jones, C. D., Lowe, L. A., & Risler, E. A. (2004). The effectiveness of wilderness adventure therapy programs for young people involved in the juvenile justice system. *Residential Treatment for Children & Youth, 22*(2), 53–62. doi:10.1300/J007v22n02_04.

Kaplan, S., & Talbot, J. F. (1983). Psychological benefits of a wilderness experience. *Human Behavior & Environment: Advances in Theory & Research, 6,* 163–203.

Kimball, R. O., & Bacon, S. B. (1993). The wilderness challenge model. In M. Gass (Ed.), *Adventure therapy: Applications of adventure programming* (pp. 11–41). Dubuque, IA: Kendall/Hunt.

Macleod, D. (2004). *Building character in the American boy: The Boy Scouts, YMCA, and their forerunners, 1870–1920* (1st ed.). University of Wisconsin Press.

Miles, J. C. (1987). Wilderness as a healing place. *Journal of Experiential Education, 10,* 4–10.

Nassar-McMillan, S. C., & Cashwell, C. S. (1997). Building self-esteem of children and adolescents through adventure-based counseling. *Journal of Humanistic Education & Development, 36*(2), 59.

Polluck, W. (1999). *Real boys: Rescuing our sons from the myths of boyhood.* New York, NY: Owl Books.

Priest, S. & Gass, M. A. (1997). *Effective leadership in adventure programming.* Champaign, IL: Human Kinetics.

Ringer, M., & Gillis, H. L. "Lee." (1995). Managing psychological depth in adventure programming. *The Journal of Experiential Education, 18*(1), 41–51.

Rohnke, K., & Butler, S. (1995). *Quicksilver: Adventure games, initiative problems, trust activities and a guide to effective leadership.* Dubuque, Iowa: Kendall/Hunt Publishing Company.

Smith, H., & Novak, P. (2004). *Buddhism: A Concise Introduction.* San Francisco: HarperOne.

Taylor, D. M., Segal, D., & Harper, N. J. (2010). The ecology of adventure therapy: An integral systems approach to therapeutic change. *Ecopsychology, 2*(2), 77–83. doi:10.1089/eco.2010.0002.

Walton, F. X. (1980). *Winning teenagers over in home and school: A manual for parents, teachers, counselors, and principals.* Columbia, SC: Adlerian Child Care Books.

Warner, L. (2009). A place for healthy risk-taking. *Educational Leadership, 67*(4), 70–74.

Weber, E. (1988). *France, Fin de Siècle.* Cambridge: Belknap Press of Harvard University Press.

Wilson, S. J. & Lipsey, M. W. (2000). Wilderness challenge programs for delinquent youth: A meta-analysis of outcome evaluations. *Evaluation and Program Planning, 23*, 1–12. doi:10.1016/S0149-7189(99)00040-3

Yalom, I. D., & Leszcz, M. (2005). *The theory and practice of group psychotherapy.* New York, NY: Basic Books.

12

Autism Spectrum Disorders: Helping Young Males Connect

RITA BRUSCA-VEGA AND SUZANNE BEIKE

As diagnoses, autism and autism spectrum disorders (ASDs) have received an enormous amount of media attention in recent years. Highly publicized increases in the prevalence of autism; controversial claims about childhood vaccines as the cause of autism; books by celebrity parents of individuals with autism; and the influence of well-organized parent advocacy organizations, among other factors, are some of the circumstances that have contributed to this attention. The outcome of this increased publicity has been both positive and negative. Federal, state, and private resources are increasingly devoted to biological and educational research and professional development on autism. Many school districts now offer special programs and services. Physicians are more likely to recognize symptoms of autism than in the past. Yet many parents, educators, and counselors are feeling overwhelmed by the rapid pace of dissemination and increasing wealth of information focused on autism. This leads to the need to find answers to the following questions: How accurate are the findings being released? Why are diagnostic criteria for milder forms of autism changing? Which treatment option is the best fit for the individual? The purposes of this chapter are to provide background information on ASDs, to describe treatment options, and to help elucidate issues and services in treatment using case study examples of male children and adolescents whose conditions fall on the spectrum.

UNDERSTANDING AUTISM SPECTRUM DISORDERS

History

Leo Kanner and Hans Asperger are the names most frequently associated with providing detailed descriptions of the characteristics of children who are now recognized as exhibiting ASDs. Both of these men were physicians who specialized in child psychology and independently published their work around the time of World War II during the 1940s. Kanner (1943) described 11 children, noting that the majority were male, with symptoms that included atypical speech patterns (e.g., echolalia, pronoun reversal); difficulties in using language to communicate; a quality of "aloneness;" and repetitive behaviors. He named this set of symptoms "autistic disturbances of affective contact." Asperger (1944) described four cases, all males, whose sets of similar symptoms he termed "autistic psychopathology of childhood." While these children had symptoms similar to those described by Kanner, but with far milder features, they also exhibited a tendency to have highly developed skills in certain areas such as math. Asperger's work was not widely read, having been published in German, until British psychiatrist Lorna Wing (1981) used the term Asperger's syndrome in the 1980s and suggested that characteristics of autism were best conceptualized along a spectrum. Over the years, professionals, parents, and the public have become accustomed to thinking about autism existing on a continuum that ranges from significant autistic symptoms with accompanying intellectual disability to mild autistic symptoms with average to above-average intelligence.

Definition

There are two widely known definitions of ASDs. The legal definition appears in federal legislation, The Individuals with Disabilities Education Act (IDEA) 2004. This definition establishes eligibility for special education services in the schools:

> a developmental disability significantly affecting verbal and nonverbal communication and social interaction, usually evident before age 3 that adversely affects a child's educational performance. Other characteristics often associated with ASD are engagement in repetitive activities and stereotyped movements, resistance to environmental change or change in daily routines, and unusual responses to sensory experiences. The term does not apply if a child's educational performance is adversely affected because the child has an emotional disturbance [34 C.F.R. 300.8(c)(1)]

The second definition is an authoritative description that appears in the *Diagnostic and Statistical Manual of Mental Disorders* (*DSM-IV-TR*) of the American Psychiatric Association (APA, 2000). Physicians and psychologists use this description to make clinical diagnoses of ASDs that are often used by school staff to help determine eligibility for services under IDEA. In the *DSM-IV-TR*, ASDs appear in the category of Pervasive Developmental Disorders (PDDs) (APA, 2000). PDD includes autistic disorder, Asperger's disorder, PDD not otherwise specified (PDD NOS), and two additional disorders that are not common (Rett's disorder and childhood disintegrative disorder). For a clinical diagnosis of autistic disorder, there must be significant impairments in social interaction (e.g., lack of eye contact, social reciprocity) and communication (e.g., lack of spoken language, repetitive language use), as well as a restricted pattern of behavior or interests. Difficulties should be apparent prior to the age of 3. For a clinical diagnosis of Asperger's disorder, there must be significant impairments in social interaction and a restricted pattern of behavior or interests. However, the similarity to autistic disorder ends there, as there is no significant language delay or impairment of cognitive development evident for individuals with Asperger's disorder. As distinct as these two disorders may sound on paper, making differential diagnoses in practice has proven to be problematic as clinicians wrestle with questions such as these: Can social interaction skills be reliably separated from communication skills? Should cognitive delays always rule out a diagnosis of Asperger's disorder? What happens to the diagnosis when individuals display different skills under different circumstances?

In keeping with the continuum concept of ASDs, experts now propose that autism is best represented as a single diagnostic category in which symptoms range from mild to severe (APA, 2010). The next edition of the *DSM*, the *DSM-V*, is expected to replace PDD with ASD (http://www.dsm5.org/proposedrevision/pages/proposedrevision.aspx?rid=94). This revised category will include criteria for (a) social communication and social interaction; (b) restrictive, repetitive patterns of behavior or interests; (c) presence of symptoms in early childhood; and (d) limits in everyday functioning. The intent of this change is not to eliminate references to Kanner's classic "early infantile autism" or to Asperger's syndrome, as these descriptions help us to better understand the child with autism, but to emphasize the similarities in behavior that exist along a complicated and dynamic continuum. Another feature of the proposed definition is the designation of severity levels to indicate the type of support that individuals diagnosed with autism will need to be successful across life areas: (a) Level 1—requires support; (b) Level 2—requires substantial support; and (c) Level 3—requires very substantial support. These levels were developed to facilitate the conceptualization of symptoms as well as assist service providers and families as they make decisions about treatment plans.

Diagnosis

A complete diagnostic evaluation for ASDs includes extensive behavioral observation, interviews with significant caretakers, and the administration of formal instruments and informal strategies by trained professionals to assess intelligence, adaptive behavior, language and communication skills, social skills, and academic and developmental progress. While there is no medical test for autism, complete physical and neurological examinations are recommended, as they may identify issues apart from ASD. Over the years, a number of behavioral rating scales have been developed to aid the diagnostic process. These include the Modified Checklist of Autism in Toddlers (M-CHAT; Robins, Fein, Barton, & Green, 2001), the Childhood Autism Rating Scale (CARS; Schopler, Reichler, & Renner, 1988), the Autism Diagnostic Interview-Revised (ADI-R; LeCouteur, Lord, & Rutter, 2003), and the Gilliam Asperger's Rating Scale (GARS; Gilliam, 2001). Most clinicians agree that ASDs can be reliably diagnosed by around the age of 3, but children with more obvious symptoms may be identified as early as 12 months.

Prevalence

The current prevalence of ASDs is estimated to be 1 in 88 children (Autism and Developmental Disabilities Monitoring Network, 2008), representing a dramatic increase from earlier decades when autism was thought to be a rare condition. This increase is hypothesized to be the result of increased public and professional awareness as well as changes in the definition that have broadened the scope of symptoms. A review of epidemiological studies of ASDs indicated that approximately 70% of affected individuals have an intellectual disability, at least twice as many boys are affected than girls, and the male-to-female ratio increases among children with mild symptoms (Fombonne, 2003).

Causes of Autism Spectrum Disorders

A combination of genetic predisposition and environmental factors comprises the prevailing theory of causation for the majority of ASDs. The genetic link is based on evidence that a higher than expected rate of autism is seen in siblings of affected children, especially among identical twins (Chakrabarti & Fombonne, 2001; Folstein & Rutter, 1977). Teratogens (substances that are harmful to the developing fetus), vaccinations, and infections are environmental factors that have been examined as potential causes of autism. In a review of the causation literature, Hyman and Towbin (2007) concluded that teratogens and infections may indeed affect neurological development, although specific factors have not been solidly identified. However, the authors found no basis for the claim that the measles, mumps, and rubella (MMR) vaccine is associated with autism. In the past, autism was hypothesized to be caused by aloof and poor mothering practices (Bettelheim, 1967). This theory has been thoroughly discredited but not before having caused considerable angst among families seeking treatment. Additional research on biological and environmental causation can be expected in the future due to the commitment of the federal government to address and treat this disorder. Their efforts have also included the establishment of the Interagency Autism Coordinating Council (http://iacc.hhs.gov) and the passage of the Combating Autism Act of 2006.

TREATING AUTISM SPECTRUM DISORDERS

Treatment approaches for ASDs may be broadly categorized as behavioral approaches (i.e., interventions focused on increasing or decreasing specific behaviors through the use of consequences and/or environmental changes); social/developmental approaches (i.e., interventions with roots in developmental psychology and social cognitive learning); cultural approaches (i.e., interventions that reflect culturally responsive practices); and supplemental approaches (i.e., a highly diverse group of physiological therapies that purport to alleviate various symptoms of autism). Educational programs, whether school- or home-based, typically employ a combination of behavioral and social/developmental approaches. The interventions selected for inclusion in this chapter provide a representative sample of the treatment options for autism, some traditional and some novel. None of the interventions provides a cure for autism. They are intended to improve critical aspects of learning and behavior.

Behavioral Approaches

Behavioral approaches form the bedrock of instruction in special education and have been used successfully across a diverse range of learning and behavior problems. Based on the work of early behaviorists including Watson (1914), Pavlov (1927), and Skinner (1938), these approaches focus on well-defined, specific, and observable behaviors and the antecedent and/or consequent events that influence them. The overarching goal of the various behavioral approaches is to increase behaviors that are associated with positive life outcomes and decrease behaviors that interfere with optimal performance in education, home, vocational, and other settings. Target behaviors can range from relatively simple actions such as the individual making eye contact or offering yes/no responses to more complex actions such as completing class assignments or buying groceries. Behavior changes are brought about by manipulating antecedents of the target behaviors or by applying consistent consequences designed to increase or decrease behavior. Giving a picture schedule to a child who has difficulty in making transitions in the classroom is an example of changing antecedent events in order to decrease anxiety associated with change. Providing a favorite toy to a child who rarely speaks after he has made a verbal or signed request for it is an example of a consequence that increases the likelihood of desired behavior. In addition to these primary aspects of behavioral intervention, there are many other behavioral techniques and principles from which to choose when developing intervention plans, including shaping, chaining, differential reinforcement, levels of prompting, and schedules of reinforcement (Alberto & Troutman, 2009). This section includes a description of four behaviorally based treatment options that show the application of behavioral principles in systematic to more specific ways.

Applied Behavioral Analysis

Applied behavioral analysis (ABA) is the most comprehensive of the behavioral approaches. Hundreds of studies using ABA to treat autism have been reported in journals such as the *Journal of Applied Behavior Analysis, Focus on Autism and Other Developmental Disabilities,* and *Education and Training in Autism and Developmental Disabilities.* Positive findings exist in areas including language and communication, inter- and intrapersonal behavior, and academic skills. Intensive ABA programs are reported to be especially successful with young children who have been diagnosed with ASDs (Cohen, Amerine-Dickens, & Smith, 2006; McEachin, Smith, & Lovaas, 1993). An ABA approach requires that the behavior and related environment are carefully studied and documented, a well-designed intervention is implemented, and behavior change is carefully monitored so as to verify the functional relationship between the behavior and the intervention and to inform continued intervention procedures (Alberto & Troutman, 2009). A critical feature of ABA is to identify the cause or function of a behavior in order to help the individual make positive change. Once behavior and the environment have been studied extensively, an intervention is designed that (a) teaches new or replacement behaviors; (b) improves the environment; and/or (c) adjusts behavioral contingencies (Umbreit, Ferro, Liaupsin, & Lane, 2007). Teachers use ABA to perform functional behavior assessments (FBAs) and formulate behavior intervention plans (BIPs) for use in the school and other settings. In all cases, the intent of ABA is to address a socially significant problem.

Identifying the behavior in need of change for students with ASDs is often straightforward. Many behaviors are clearly displayed, such as a client's hand flapping that interferes with completing written school work; scratching which results in self-injury; or difficulty in making conversation that impedes social relationships. Identifying the function of the behavior can be more difficult and requires data collection that includes not only the target behavior but antecedent events and consequences. Antecedents and consequences help to define variables that might be reinforcing the behavior. There are six functions of behavior, and each must be understood in context in order to develop a successful intervention (Alberto & Troutman, 2009). Three functions are associated with positive reinforcement and involve actions to gain (a) attention from adults or peers; (b) a tangible such as an object, activity, or event; or (c) sensory stimulation that involves motor movements, touch, vision, smell, or taste. The remaining functions are associated with negative reinforcement and involve actions to escape (a) attention from adults or peers; (b) tasks that are boring or demanding; or (c) sensory stimulation that is discomforting or painful. Consider a student with ASD who begins yelling loudly whenever presented with a written task. If the consequence of the behavior is that the student is consistently allowed to take a "cool down" time and not complete the task, the function of the behavior is avoidance or escape. Depending on the characteristics of the student and other aspects of the environment, intervention options might include offering the student a choice of written tasks or choice of novel writing utensils or providing a tangible reward for spending an increasing number of minutes on the tasks. Opportunities for escape or avoidance would be greatly reduced by replacing the "reward" of escape with the reward of an appealing alternative reward. Because behaviors serve different functions and because personal and setting variables are so diverse, interventions are highly individual with regard to complexity of implementation, duration, and intensity of treatment. ABA allows for this individualization within the context of behavioral teaching principles and requires data collection that informs future actions.

With the use of ABA, there is an ethical implication that any behavior identified for change must have positive significance to the life of an individual with autism. This means that behaviors that are merely annoying or nonessential to day-to-day functioning should not be subject to this process. Some behaviors are merely a product of personality or developmental stage and, as such, must be accepted by the people around them. Professionals should be aware of treatment ethics and act as advocates in the ABA process. ABA is taught in many programs that train special education teachers and other individuals who provide services to individuals with autism, but having a credential as an ABA therapist is becoming more popular. The organization, Autism Speaks, offers suggestions for parents and others seeking individuals and organizations that claim to "do ABA" (www.autismspeaks.org).

Positive Behavioral Support

Positive behavioral support (PBS) is a philosophical approach to treatment as much as it is a system of behavioral intervention. The approach was conceptualized largely in response to interventions that involved punishment procedures (e.g., time out, physical restraints, electric shock), were not effective in improving quality of life, and did not respect the dignity of individuals with disabilities. The elements of PBS emerged from three sources: the field of ABA, the normalization/inclusion movement, and person-centered values (Carr et al., 2002). A life span perspective, ecological validity, systems change, and an emphasis on prevention are among the features of PBS (Carr et al., 2002). A cornerstone of the approach is person-centered planning, which includes a long-term plan that reflects the perspective of the individual being supported and significant others in that person's life. Three well-known person-centered planning approaches are Circle of Friends (Perske, 1998), Making Action Plans (MAPS; Forest & Lusthaus, 1990), and Group Action Planning (GAP; Turnbull & Turnbull, 1992). The approach also includes a comprehensive functional behavioral assessment, proactive interventions designed to reduce problem behaviors by teaching new skills, providing opportunities for reinforcement of positive behaviors, and/or making environmental changes. Like ABA, PBS provides a structure for change with interventions uniquely designed to match individual characteristics and situations. Options for positive support vary widely. Among the many examples are teaching self-monitoring strategies, providing choices, selecting appropriate assistive technologies, designing visual schedules, and developing the capacity of significant others to implement and maintain the selected interventions. The Association for Positive Behavior Support (www.apbs.org) is a good starting point for parents, educators, and other service providers to learn more about the approach.

Cognitive Behavioral Therapy

Cognitive behavioral therapy (CBT) refers to a variety of treatment techniques in which behavior change is facilitated by helping individuals to better understand and control their thoughts and emotions. Aaron Beck, who developed a cognitive treatment for depression (Beck, Rush, Shaw, & Emery, 1979), and Albert Ellis, who developed rational emotive therapy (RET; Ellis, 1962), are considered the founders of this movement. This approach, unlike a strict behavioral approach, considers the relationship of an individual's perceptions and his or her actions. In general, thoughts associated with anxiety or other unpleasant emotions are identified and gradually replaced with more adaptive and reasonable thoughts by teaching self-regulatory skills. Over the years, CBT has been used increasingly with children and adolescents to address issues including impulsivity, anger, aggression, depression, and anxiety (Graham, 2005; Kendall & Choudhury, 2003). Recently, CBT has been explored as a promising option for children and youth with mild autism, especially for issues related to social anxiety (Rotheram-Fuller & MacMullen, 2011; Wood et al., 2009). A young man with Asperger's syndrome, for example, might find it difficult to make friends because he believes that he will always be rejected by his peer group, and he then becomes anxious in social settings. Therapy sessions would include challenging that belief, replacing that belief with the more reasonable view that some peers may reject him while others will not, and having him test these new ideas by approaching others in various situations. Implementing CBT in school settings, as opposed to more typical clinic settings, offers the advantage of practice and feedback in real-life environments (Rotheram-Fuller & MacMullen, 2011) provided that staff members are trained and the educational program is designed to integrate treatment aspects. Many therapists practice CBT but may not have experience working with individuals with autism. State or local chapters of the Autism Society (www. autism-society.org) may provide referral information.

Picture Exchange Communication System

The Picture Exchange Communication System (PECS) is an increasingly popular augmentative communication strategy that utilizes the principles of ABA for improving initial functional language and communication skills in individuals with ASDs and other disabilities that cause significant impairments in these areas (Bondy & Frost, 1994, 2001). There are typically six phases of instruction that are taught sequentially as the individual gains skills. In the first phase, the goal is to establish spontaneous requests for items or activities. This is done by teaching the individual to pick up a picture or photo of what is wanted and to hand it to the facilitator in exchange for the desired item or activity. Two facilitators may be involved in this first phase; one person acts as the primary communicator, while the other person assists with physical prompts. In the second and third phases, the goal is to increase the repertoire of requests and to generalize requests across people and settings. The individual is taught to discriminate and make choices among an increasing number of items or activities in various circumstances. In the third phase, the focus is on sentence structure and making more complicated requests. The individual is taught to combine pictures into sentence strips, starting with the picture for "I want" and adding the requested item or activity. The remaining phases focus on expanding vocabulary, for example, "I want two blue balloons," and commenting on the environment using pictures that represent phrases such as "I feel" or "I see."

PECS is widely used in school and other settings because of factors including simplicity, practicality, flexibility, and low cost. Pictures can be easily carried from place to place by users and facilitators in forms such as small books or picture rings, like key rings, which can be attached to belts or used on necklaces. Since many people trained to be PECS facilitators (e.g., speech/language pathologists, special education teachers) are familiar with ABA procedures through their degree preparation, mastering the instruction and data collection strategies is a relatively straightforward process. PECS originators, Andy Bondy, Ph.D., and Lori Frost, CCC/SLP, offer professional development and materials, including the recent additions of PECS apps for the iPhone and iPad, through their company, Pyramid Educational Consultants (www.pecsusa.com). Over the years, research support for PECS has grown. A recent review of over 30 studies concluded that PECS successfully enabled the majority of participants who lacked functional communication skills to acquire extensive functional vocabularies and to use their skills with teachers, parents, and others (Sulzer-Azaroff, Hoffman, Horton, Bondy, & Frost, 2009).

Other Behavioral Interventions

Because the behavioral approach can be applied across a myriad of situations, there are many behavioral intervention options and variations from which to choose for individuals with autism and other related disabilities. Incidental Teaching (Hart & Risley, 1975; McGee, Morrier, & Daly, 1999) and Pivotal Response Training (Koegel & Koegel, 2006) capitalize on the child's interests and motivations to increase adaptive responding within a behavioral teaching paradigm that occurs in natural environments, including the child's home and inclusive school program. Discrete Trial Training (Lovaas, 1987) is especially helpful in establishing and shaping new behaviors and is a significant part of the broader Lovaas Method. The Lovaas Institute promotes this method and offers services to families and schools nationally (http://lovaas.com). Functional Communication Training (Carr & Durand, 1985), which has well-documented applications in school and other settings (Mancil & Bowan, 2010), is a strategy to determine the function of challenging behaviors and then replace them with appropriate communicative responses. Finally, the augmentative and alternative communication devices that may be prescribed for individuals with autism are typically introduced using behavioral teaching practices (Kaiser & Grimm, 2006).

Social-Relational/Developmental Approaches

Social and developmental approaches to the treatment of autism are based on the premise that typical developmental processes in the areas of language, cognition, social-emotional, and motor development are delayed or disrupted in individuals with autism due to neurological differences (Scheuermann & Webber, 2002). These differences lead to problems in learning and behavior that are obvious from very early ages, including difficulties in attending and imitating, limited responsiveness to social reinforcement, hyper- or hyposensitivity to sensory input, and restricted emotionality. Developmental educators address these issues by working on the developmental skills that the child lacks and then moving to age-appropriate, functional skills (Boutot & Myles, 2011, p. 75). Unlike behavioral approaches, where learning is considered primarily a function of reinforcement or environmental change, social and developmental approaches consider cognition and social-emotional development to be significant, dynamic, and mediating factors in learning (Bandura, 1977; Piaget, 1950; Stern, 1985; Vygotsky, 1978).

Denver Model

The Denver Model is a developmental treatment approach for toddlers and preschoolers with autism that began in the early 1980s as a federally funded project (Rogers, Hall, Osaki, Reaven, & Herbison, 2001; Rogers & Lewis, 1989). The model began as a center-based program focused on play as the means for improving social and communicative behaviors. Today, it is an inclusive service delivery model in preschool settings that follows a comprehensive curriculum and incorporates the use of ABA principles. In the preschool setting, the child typically spends about half the day in an integrated group and half the day in intensive teaching. The adults working with the child undergo training in the model, and team members regularly assess their actions and the child's progress. The Denver Model has expanded to include children as young as 12 months and is referred to as the Early Start Denver Model (ESDM; Rogers & Dawson, 2009). The models are similar and emphasize an interdisciplinary perspective, partnership with parents that includes home-based training and implementation, a developmental curriculum that includes the major domain areas, the development of reciprocal and spontaneous imitation, verbal and non-verbal communication, and cognitive aspects of dyadic play (Rogers & Dawson, 2009). ESDM includes a strong emphasis on Pivotal Response Training (PRT), an ABA-rich and evidence-based strategy that strategically uses the child's interests and motivations in naturalistic settings to encourage and build typical developmental responses (Koegel & Koegel, 2006).

Research on the Denver Model indicates gains in language, cognition, social-emotional, and motor domains (Rogers & DiLalla, 1991; Rogers & Lewis, 1989). A recent study of ESDM, using a randomized controlled design, showed that 18- to 30-month-old children with autism who received the ESDM intervention made significant gains in IQ, communication, and social interaction over children who received other community-based services over a 2-year period (Dawson et al., 2010). Children received 2 hours of treatment with trained therapists 5 days a week for 2 years in addition to receiving parent support at home. The findings of this study have been widely publicized as a means of showing how early intervention in children with autism under 2 years of age can be highly effective, and it is expected that interest in ESDM will grow. Individuals who are interested in becoming ESDM trainers or learning more about the program should visit the ESDM page at the website of the MIND Institute at the University of California, Davis (www.ucdmc.ucdavis.edu/mindinstitute).

Modeling Strategies

Social stories and video modeling are two increasingly popular strategies for improving social skills that have roots in social-cognitive learning theory. Social-cognitive theory deals with the capacity of individuals to develop knowledge and skills by observing the actions of others and the consequences of those actions (Bandura, 1986). More than simple imitation or mimicry, modeled activities also convey rules for behavior that can generate new behaviors and is a powerful tool for learning in children as well as adults. Observers perform modeled behaviors with or without reinforcement in different settings and in different ways. Attention and motivation are required for observational learning, and children will most likely attend to a model whom they admire or who shares characteristics similar to their own (Bandura, 1977).

Social stories are a means of influencing behavior by presenting a written and/or visual model of behavior in the form of a simple story. The idea of social stories was postulated in the early 1990s by Jean Gray (Gray & Garand, 1993) for students with mild disabilities such as Asperger's syndrome. Gray has since trademarked her story development (Social Stories™) and established The Gray Center for Social Learning and Understanding (http://graycenter.org), which provides information about training and materials. According to her format (Gray, 2000), a story is written with specific types of sentences (e.g., descriptive sentences, directive statements, perspective-taking sentences, and partial sentences) with attention paid to their ratio in the story. The story deals with a social issue in the student's life and may be written by anyone with training who is close to the student. The story is presented prior to the troublesome situation and may be read by the adult or student. A sample story from her website deals with having to pretend in order to complete story problems. Since many students with autism are highly literal, they have difficulties connecting with story problems, and the social story provides a model and insight about what might be done to solve the problems and get the work done. In contrast to many testimonials of their value, the results of two meta-analyses reported low/questionable overall effectiveness for social stories (Kokina & Kern, 2010; Reynhout & Carter, 2006). Kokina and Kern (2010) hypothesized that while social stories may promote social understanding, improvements in behavior may require more direct social skill instruction. Because Social Stories™ and its variations are simple to construct, inexpensive, and easy to implement, it is likely that the strategy will continue to be used and offer more opportunities for research and development.

Video modeling is a strategy that captures the target or desired behavior on camera (e.g., introducing oneself, controlling one's temper, and making a food request) and uses the video to illustrate the behavior to learners. The model can be an adult, a peer, or a self-model. The primary components of video modeling are to identify the target skill, produce the video, and implement the intervention (Ganz, Earles-Vollrath, & Cook, 2011). Recommendations include (a) conducting an ecological assessment before collecting baseline data on the skills to be improved; (b) shooting several short videos for the same targeted skill using different models, settings, and scripts to promote generalization; and (c) having a structured plan for intervention including when, where, and how often the videos will be viewed and providing opportunities for the skill to be practiced (Ganz et al., 2011). Video modeling has a well-developed history in the treatment of students with special needs and has been used to teach various functional, social, and communication skills (Dowrick, 1999; Hitchcock, Dowrick, & Prater, 2003). With regard to children and youth with autism, a meta-analysis of video modeling and video self-modeling interventions showed that both strategies were effective in the acquisition of social communication and functional and adaptive behavioral skills, in addition to promoting maintenance and generalization (Bellini & Akullian, 2007). These authors concluded that video modeling is an evidence-based practice that educators and clinicians should consider in treatment plans.

Other Social and Developmental Approaches

There are a number of social-relational and developmental programs gaining attention in the autism field that are focused on different age groups and emphasize different aspects of developmental theory relative to autism. Developmental, Individual-Difference, Relationship Based (DIR®/Floor Time™) is based on the theory that young children with autism will improve if supported through six developmental stages, depending on individual needs, using intensive relationship-based interaction (Greenspan & Weider, 1998, 2006). Responsive Teaching (RT) is a program designed for children from birth to 6 years with autism and other disabilities that uses a structured curriculum focused on teaching pivotal behaviors that the child is weak in (e.g., exploring, cooperating, and joint attention) (Mahoney & MacDonald, 2005; Mahoney & Perales, 2005). SCERTS®, which stands for *s*ocial *c*ommunication, *e*motional *r*egulation, and *t*ransactional *s*upport, is a program for children and adults with autism that features building social communication, preventing problem behaviors, and a coordinated team effort within a dynamic life span approach (Prizant, Wetherby, Rubin, Laurent, & Rydell, 2006a, 2006b). Each of these programs offers specialized training and support described in the websites of the developers: www.icd.com (DIR/Floor Time); www.responsiveteaching.org (RT); and http://scerts.com (SCERTS). As relatively new programs, comprehensive critical analyses are forthcoming.

Cultural Approach: TEACCH

The program highlighted in this section has elements of behavioral and developmental interventions but has been identified as a cultural approach for the treatment of autism (Hall, 2009, p. 133). A cultural approach recognizes and respects the culture, in this case the culture of disability and autism, and promotes culturally responsive teaching and support.

TEACCH (*T*reatment and *E*ducation of *A*utistic and *C*ommunication related handicapped *Ch*ildren) is a comprehensive program of instruction for students with autism that emphasizes understanding of the culture of autism (i.e., behavioral, cognitive, developmental, and social aspects of autism) and implementing responsive intervention practices. Educators are seen as cross-cultural interpreters, viewing the world through the eyes of individuals with ASD and then using this information to help them function in this outer world (Mesibov, Shea, & Scholper, 2004). TEACCH was established in the early 1970s at the University of North Carolina by Eric Schopler and colleagues, based on research that structured environments and visual supports would help to address the learning difficulties associated with autism (Mesibov et al., 2004; Schopler, Brehm, Kinsbourne, & Reichler, 1971). In addition to understanding cognition, perception, and the need for routine and structure to benefit individuals with ASD, parents are viewed as reliable reporters of their children's behaviors and history who can serve as cotherapists and collaborators (Mesibov et al., 2004). Today, the TEACCH program operates many centers in the state, provides diagnostic and many clinical services to children and adults with ASD and their families, and conducts national and international training and consultation about TEACCH practices and research. The TEACCH website, www.TEACCH.com, offers information to interested parents and educators.

The TEACCH methodology is referred to as structured teaching. Prior to implementing a structured teaching approach, educators must be aware of the culture or characteristics of autism and engage in individual assessment. Critical aspects of the autism culture are a focus on details rather than connections, distractibility, concrete versus abstract thinking, impaired organizational and sequencing skills, difficulty with generalizations, atypical sense of time, differences in learning, and differences in neurobehavioral patterns (Hall, 2009). Structured teaching strategies include careful physical organization of the teaching environment; the use of schedules, primarily visual schedules; independent work systems that emphasize a routine of work first, then play; and organization of tasks using visual supports (Hall, 2009). TEACCH is a popular approach in schools across the country, but it appears that districts and schools do not adopt or implement all aspects of the program. Instead, teachers and administrators who receive TEACCH training implement elements of structured teaching (e.g., work stations, visual supports) throughout programs or classrooms. Research on the TEACCH program and on aspects of structured teaching is expanding and recent studies are positive (e.g., Hume & Odom, 2007; Panerai et al., 2009).

Supplemental Approaches

In addition to the approaches typically used in education settings to fulfill individualized education program (IEP) goals, children and youth with ASDs may also participate in drug therapy to improve learning and behavior and receive occupational or physical therapy to improve sensory and motor functioning. Drug treatment for autism varies widely based on the knowledge and experience of the physician and individual symptoms. A recent report indicates that approximately 35% of children diagnosed with autism take at least one psychotropic medication, typically from the drug classes of stimulants, antipsychotics, or antidepressants (Rosenberg et al., 2010). Drug treatment for autism should be directed at specific behaviors and used as part of a comprehensive therapeutic program that includes a functional behavioral analysis (Hyman & Towbin, 2007, p. 337). Occupational or physical therapists may use sensory integrative (SI) strategies designed to provide a calming environment and/or increase the child's tolerance for sensory stimulation. Sensory integration rooms or spaces are relatively common in programs for students with autism and SI is considered a promising but not fully validated practice (Simpson et al., 2005). There is a growing and dynamic list of supplemental therapies that have been proposed for the treatment of autism (see Table 12.1). Often, these therapies are too quickly adopted or endorsed by some parents and professionals and too easily dismissed by others. A balanced approach to selecting complementary or alternative treatments combines open-mindedness with caution and practicality.

The Role of Counselors

The intensity of symptoms strongly influences the role that counselors play in the treatment of children and youth with ASDs. In the case of children such as Brian, who is described in the following case study, traditional counseling methods are not viable because of limited language and social communication skills. The counselor, who may mange the case or participate as a member of the school team, can contribute to treatment efforts by acting as a resource and consultant: keeping current with intervention options; advising team members about treatment in relation to the social-emotional needs of the child; and establishing

TABLE 12.1

Examples of Supplemental, Novel Treatments for Autism

Antifungal Therapy

Auditory Integration Training

Acupuncture

Biofeedback

Chelation

Craniosacral Manipulation

Gluten-Free/Casein-Free Diet

Homeopathy

Hyperbaric Oxygen Therapy

Intravenous Immunoglobulins (IVIG)

Reiki

Secretin Therapy

Sources:
Levy, S. E., & Hyman, S. L. (2005). Novel treatments for autistic spectrum disorders. *Mental Retardation and Developmental Disability Research Reviews, 11,* 131–142.
Autism Research Institute: http://www.autism.com
Healing Arts: http://www.healing-arts.org/children/autism-treatments.htm
About.com: http://autism.about.com/od/treatmentoptions/u/treatmentsuserpath.htm

communication with local autism networks and groups. Supportive inclusive environments are critical for students with autism. A school counselor who acts as an inclusion advocate can strongly influence how service delivery takes place in the school and how mindful teachers are of instructional and curricular adjustments. Counselors can also work with typical peers to establish friend and peer supports in and outside of the classroom and provide support to siblings of students with autism. In the case of young adults with mild autism, such as Eugene, who is described in the second case study, individual and group counseling can have a positive effect on some of the presenting concerns and behaviors (Shopler & Mesibov, 1992). Individual counseling can be helpful in terms of offering supportive specific explanations and feedback about the relationship between the events the client's experiences, his behavior, and the resulting outcomes. These individuals benefit from sessions that focus on how to avoid unwanted behaviors, provide coping strategies, and, in some cases, teach relaxation techniques (Schopler & Mesibov, 1992). Group counseling sessions can provide a safe environment in which to practice appropriate social skills, develop an interest in social interactions, and have multiple social experiences. Knowledge of the support services offered to students with disabilities at local colleges and awareness of the increasing number of web-based and other self-help groups and social networking sites for individuals with Asperger's syndrome are important for school and community counselors.

CASE STUDY: BRIAN—A THIRD GRADER WITH ASD

Brian is a 7-year-old child who is about to begin the second grade at a new school. He lives with his father, Dave, and three older brothers, ages 12 to 18 years, in a rural community close to extended family members. The oldest brother will be away at college in the fall, and the two middle brothers will be enrolled in middle and high school. Brian's mother died of complications related to breast cancer when he was six. Dave, a software designer who is able to work from home much of the time, moved the family from a nearby state to the hometown where he and his wife were raised. Dave is looking forward to the support of family and friends.

Like his brothers, Brian's birth was unremarkable. His mother was concerned early on about his language and communication skills, especially when she compared his development to that of his brothers. However, the pediatrician encouraged her not to worry about it, as some children "just need time to catch up." At the age of 18 months, however, Brian's behaviors were markedly different from those of his brothers at that age and his peers. He had difficulty playing with other children and cried often over the itchiness of the tags on his clothing. On most days, Brian would have breakfast after watching his favorite cartoon. But on days when this routine was changed in any way, he would engage in long-lasting temper tantrums. Gradually, Brian began to withdraw from any physical contact and spent much of the time "playing" with just one toy. Actually, Brian would hit the toy on his pillow repetitively and scream whenever the toy or pillow was removed. When Brian was about 2 years old, his parents took him for an evaluation at a university hospital that housed a special clinic for children with developmental problems. The multidisciplinary evaluation supported their concerns, and Brian was diagnosed with moderate autism.

Dave's insurance provided good coverage, and the family was able to consider several options for treatment in addition to a half-day public school program for preschool children with developmental disabilities that would become available upon Brian's third birthday. Brian's mother made the choice to begin an in-home ABA program, working with a trained therapist, which continued when Brian began the more developmentally oriented preschool program in the school district. Dave was never pleased with the in-home program, finding it too restrictive and time consuming. Around this time, Dave's wife became ill, and they employed a nanny to help with Brian and the other boys. The ABA program was discontinued, but Brian continued to attend the preschool program. His temper tantrums decreased, and he slowly began to seek out new toys and to look for social attention.

His teacher and parents were happy to see him also make progress in toilet training, self-feeding, and dressing skills. Gains in language were minimal. Shortly after Brian transitioned to the inclusive developmental kindergarten program, his mother passed away. Brian had a difficult time dealing with all the changes in the household after his mother's death, and his behavior deteriorated that year. The following year, Brian showed improvements once again and increased his receptive and expressive language.

Because of Brian's educational needs, Dave contacted the special education director in his hometown prior to the move. Penny Reynolds, the elementary education school counselor and special education case manager, was assigned to work with Dave and Brian. Penny brought Brian's case to the special education assessment team. Team members reviewed the file from Brian's previous school and decided that a reevaluation would be a good idea so they could get to know Brian better. Dave agreed and brought Brian in during the summer before school started. The team assessed Brian's cognitive, social, language, and motor skills using formal and informal measures. Following the assessment, Penny asked Dave to invite the important people in Brian's life to a series of planning meetings based on the Making Action Plans (MAPs; Forest & Lusthaus, 1990) approach. MAPs is a planning process that brings family members, service providers, and significant others together to help identify a shared vision for the client or student and to make that vision a reality. Penny's district has been using MAPs for about 5 years and she feels comfortable leading the group of educators and Brian's circle of family and friends in the collaborative process. At the sessions, group members answer and discuss the following basic questions:

What is Brian's story?
What are your dreams for Brian?
What are your nightmares?
What are Brian's strengths?
What are Brian's needs?
What would an ideal school day look like for Brian?

The first meeting is attended by Dave, Brian, Brian's brothers, Dave's sister who cares for Brian at her home several times a week, the district's speech/language therapist, the special education teacher, and Penny. Penny begins by explaining the process, and the members begin to write and/or draw their ideas on large easels. At this meeting, the first three questions are addressed and the following themes are evident: The family wants Brian to enjoy family life, including playing games and sports with his brothers, and become independent enough to eventually live in a community with other young people who have learning problems. Family members are most afraid that Brian will become ill or injured and not be able to communicate. Brian's brothers are afraid that Brian will not ever really know that they love him, and he is their brother.

Penny feels that the process has gotten off to a good start, and there will likely be one more meeting before the team begins to develop Brian's IEP. At this point, Penny thinks that she will ask the brothers to attend a group for siblings of students with special needs that she began last year in the district and will put Dave in touch with a parent support group whose members include families with young adults who have autism and intellectual disabilities.

CASE STUDY: EUGENE—A YOUNG ADULT WITH ASD

Eugene H. is a 19-year-old Caucasian American male with a history of multiple psychiatric diagnoses including PDD NOS, AD/HD, Major Depressive Disorder, Schizoaffective Disorder, and Asperger's Disorder. He came to the clinic with his parents for a psychological evaluation because he has completed his GED and now wishes to enroll in college. He will require evidence of a disability in order to request reasonable accommodations. He and his parents are also interested in counseling and other supports. He is a tall, thin young man who appeared at the intake session with satisfactory dress and hygiene. He was able to make consistent eye contact and to interact with his examiner consistently well. He was cooperative, fairly motivated, displayed good social skills and etiquette, and there was no semblance of elusiveness or evasiveness in his responses to a wide range of inquiries. However, his psychomotor activity was elevated, and he asked if he could stand up and stretch a couple of times during the session.

Eugene lives with his parents. His mother, age 56, continues to work, while his father, age 67, is retired. Eugene helps them around the house as they continue to support him. He also has two paternal half-sisters who are older. He occasionally talks to them, but they are not close. There is no reported family history of diagnosed psychiatric illness with the exception of alcohol dependency on his maternal side of the family (his grandfather). Eugene reports being closer to his mother than his father because she is more supportive, although overprotective, while his father is more demanding.

Mrs. H. reported an uneventful pre- and postnatal history. Developmental milestones (sitting, crawling, standing, walking, etc.) were within normal limits, or even early. For example, Eugene avoided baby talk altogether; started talking at 9 months; and behaved "like

a little adult." At about 3 years of age, however, he started looking/
gazing at his hands and, shortly after, began talking to his hands. This
continued until he began first grade. During second grade, his parents
took him to a counseling center because of anxiety about attending
school and socialization problems. He was seen at the center through
his middle school years, a time when he experienced an exacerbation
of psychosocial issues and felt increasingly isolated from his peers in
school. A psychological report indicated that Eugene had a repressed
"level of rage toward the other students," which preoccupied his
thoughts. He expressed these feelings indirectly, as in "markings on
walls at the school or in drawings or stories." He reportedly developed
a "vivid fantasy life," but he was also able to identify and observe
appropriate behavioral limits and boundaries and to differentiate
between thought/fantasy and action. There were no reported visual,
auditory, or other sensory hallucinations at the time.

Eugene was referred to a psychiatrist by the counseling center
at age 14, when symptoms were said to include a lack of energy and
inability to pay attention in school. He was believed to have AD/HD
and to be experiencing suicidal ideation; he was diagnosed with
schizoaffective disorder and prescribed two psychotropic medications.
Although he initially related that he never really had a suicide plan,
per se, suicidal ideation was said to increase to the extent that by age
16, he was giving thought to a plan. He was hospitalized for a week,
during which time he tried to escape twice. He was also diagnosed
with depression. Over time, his medication history has included
varying combinations of psychotropic prescriptions, but he was said
to have stopped taking all medications when he turned 18 and has not
been on medication since that time. He related that the medication(s)
made him feel "doped up" and that his mind became clearer once
medication was stopped.

Eugene's academic performance throughout his school career was
adequate overall, but he experienced periods in which anxiety, anger,
and a preoccupation with American history appeared to interfere with
the completion of his work. He dropped out of high school at age 17
and occasionally attended an alternative academic center, where he
received instruction for his GED. He and his parents report that it didn't
take a lot of effort from him to pass the GED exam. Eugene reports
that he "calmed down a lot" after leaving school and worked nearly full
time at a fast food restaurant for about a year. He had quit his job a few
months prior, hoping to find a part-time office job while taking college
courses, but he is currently home most of the time. He says he doesn't
have friends except for a cousin with whom he goes to the movies
occasionally. He would like to have a girlfriend and reports that he
has been visiting a couple of Internet sites where single young people

"who have problems like him" chat online. He has been accepted at two colleges within commuting distance from home. He wants to make sure that he can have extra time to finish assignments and take exams "if he feels nervous." He is also worried about controlling his hand movements in class and having other students stare at him. Since he has been out of school, he has read about Asperger's syndrome and reports seeing some TV characters who remind him of himself.

Jason Rush is the counselor assigned to Eugene. Jason recently received his degree and licensure and worked for a year as a counselor at the local community college before starting at the clinic. He has experience with college students who need accommodations, including a couple of young men who self-identified as having Asperger's syndrome. Eugene is one of Jason's first clients at the clinic. Jason was able to attend Eugene's intake session with the clinic psychologist, and he has read the psychologist's brief evaluation. This confirmed a diagnosis on the autism spectrum, an IQ score in the average range, and social anxiety. The report noted Eugene's previous problems with anger and thoughts of suicide. These have not been issues for about a year according to Eugene and his parents. Jason has seen Eugene for two counseling sessions and has decided that he will take a cognitive behavioral approach to treatment and develop an action plan with Eugene that emphasizes self-awareness and self-regulation. At the session this evening, Jason will present a plan to Eugene that consists of ideas they have discussed.

Eugene will attend weekly counseling sessions for the next 8 weeks, during which time he will complete the following activities and report on his progress during counseling sessions:

- Make a decision about which college he will attend and prepare to enroll on a part-time basis for the next semester. This includes making appointments with academic advisers and visiting the offices for students with disabilities to discuss his needs.
- Keep a journal in which he rates his overall anxiety each day on a scale from 1 (very low) to 10 (very high) with a rationale for his selection. Each week, he will also make a journal entry about his most positive social interaction and the most negative social interaction.
- Read at least two autobiographical books written by adult authors with ASD (e.g., *Beyond the Wall: Personal Experiences With Autism and Asperger's Syndrome* by Stephen Shore; *The Way I See It: A Personal Look at Autism and Asperger's* by Temple Grandin).
- At the end of the 8 weeks, Jason and Eugene will review Eugene's progress. Future ideas include joining a group for individuals with ASD, applying for part-time employment, and starting a regular exercise program.

CONCLUDING REMARKS

The field of autism and its treatment is ever growing and dynamic as we continue to explore biological and environmental factors in the development and treatment of the disorder. This chapter provided an overview of autism for counselors and other service providers that is hopefully a starting point for continued reading, research, and reflection. The reader is encouraged to seek out impartial sources that provide critical analyses of interventions for autism. Traditional print sources include the text by Simpson et al. (2005), which provides reviews of nearly 40 treatment options that consider possible negative or harmful outcomes and rates each option as scientifically based, promising, limited supporting information, or not recommended, and journals such as *Focus on Autism and Other Developmental Disabilities* and *The Journal of Autism and Developmental Disorders*. Web-based information can be easily accessed through the websites of government-sponsored institutions including the National Institutes of Health (www.ninds.nih/gov) and the National Dissemination Center for Children with Disabilities (www.nichcy.org), and other major organizations including the Autism Society of America (www.autism-society.org) and Autism Speaks, Inc. (www.autismspeaks.org).

REFERENCES

Alberto, P. A., & Troutman, A. C. (2009). *Applied behavior analysis for teachers* (8th ed.). Upper Saddle River, NJ: Pearson.

American Psychiatric Association. (2000). *Diagnostic and statistical manual of mental disorders* (4th ed., text rev.). Washington, DC: Author.

American Psychiatric Association. (2010). *A 09 Autism Spectrum Disorder.* Retrieved from http://www.dsm5.org/proposedrevision/pages/proposedrevision.aspx?rid=94

Asperger, H. (1944). Die 'Austistischen Psychopathen" im Kindesalter. *Archiv fur Psychiatrie und Nervenkrankheiten, 117*, 76–136.

Autism and Developmental Disabilities Monitoring Network. (2008). *Prevalence of autism spectrum disorders* (CDC/MMR Surveillance Summaries). Retrieved from www.cdc.gov/mmwr/preview/mmwrhtml/ss6103a1.htm?s_cid=ss6103a1_w

Bandura, A. (1977). *Social learning theory.* Englewood Cliffs, NJ: Prentice Hall.

Bandura, A. (1986). *Social foundations of thought and action: A social-cognitive theory.* Englewood Cliffs, NJ: Prentice Hall.

Beck, A. T., Rush, A. J., Shaw, B. F., & Emery, G. (1979). *Cognitive therapy of depression.* New York: Guilford.

Bellini, S., & Akullian, J. (2007). A meta-analysis of video modeling and video self-modeling interventions for children and adolescents with autism spectrum disorders. *Exceptional Children, 73*, 264–287.

Bettelheim, B. (1967). *The empty fortress.* Toronto, CA: Collier-Macmillan.

Bondy, A. S., & Frost, L. A. (1994). The picture communication system. *Focus on Autistic Behavior, 9*(3), 1–19.

Bondy, A. S., & Frost, L. A. (2001). *A picture's worth: PECS and other visual communication strategies in autism*. Bethesda, MD: Woodbine House.

Boutot, E. A., & Myles, B. S. (2011). *Autism spectrum disorders: Foundations, characteristics, and effective strategies*. Upper Saddle River, NJ: Pearson.

Carr, E. G., Dunlap, G., Horner, R. H., Koegel, R. L., Turnbull, A. P., & Sailor, W. (2002). Positive behavior support: Evolution of an applied science. *Journal of Positive Behavior Interventions, 4*, 4–16.

Carr, E. G., & Durand, V. M. (1985). Reducing behavior problems through functional communication training. *Journal of Applied Behavior Analysis, 18*, 111–126.

Chakrabarti, S., & Fombonne, E. (2001). Pervasive developmental disorders in preschool children. *Journal of the American Medical Association, 285*, 3093–3099.

Cohen, H., Amerine-Dickens, M., & Smith, T. (2006). Early intensive behavioral treatment: Replication of the UCLA Model in a community setting. *Developmental and Behavioral Pediatrics, 27*, 145–155.

Dawson, G., Rogers, S., Munson, J., Smith, M., Winter, J., Greenson, J. Donaldson, A., & Varley, J. (2010). Randomized, controlled trial of an intervention for toddlers with autism: The Early Start Denver Model. *Pediatrics, 125*, 17–23.

Dowrick, P. (1999). A review of self-modeling and related interventions. *Applied and Preventative Psychology, 8*, 23–39.

Ellis, A. (1962). *Reason and emotion in psychotherapy*. New York: Stuart.

Folstein, S., & Rutter, M. (1977). Infantile autism: A genetic study of 21 twin pairs. *Journal of Child Psychology, Psychiatry, and Allied Disciplines, 18*, 297–321.

Fombonne, E. (2003). Epidemiological surveys of autism and other pervasive developmental disorders: An update. *Journal of Autism and Developmental Disorders, 33*, 365–382.

Forest, M., & Lusthaus, E. (1990). Everyone belongs with MAPS action planning system. *Teaching Exceptional Children, 22*(2), 32–35.

Ganz, J. B., Earles-Vollrath, T. L., & Cook, K. E. (2011). Video modeling: A visually based intervention for children with autism spectrum disorder. *Teaching Exceptional Children, 43*, 8–19.

Gilliam, J. E. (2001). *Gilliam-Asperger's Disorder Scale (GADS)*. Austin, TX: Pro-Ed.

Graham, P. J. (Ed.) (2005). *Cognitive behaviour therapy for children and families* (2nd ed.). Cambridge, MA: Cambridge University Press.

Gray, C. A. (2000). *Writing social stories with Carol Gray*. Arlington, TX: Future Horizons.

Gray, C. A., & Garand, J. D. (1993). Social stories: Improving responses of students with autism with accurate social information. *Focus on Autistic Behavior, 8*, 1–10.

Greenspan, S. I., & Weider, S. (1998). *The child with special needs: Encouraging intellectual and emotional growth*. Reading, MA: Perseus Books.

Greenspan, S. I., & Weider, S. (2006). *Engaging autism: Using the floortime approach to help students relate, communicate, and think*. Cambridge, MA: De Capo Lifelong Books.

Hall, L. (2009). *Autism spectrum disorders: From theory to practice.* Upper Saddle River, NJ: Pearson.

Hart, B., & Risley, T. R. (1975). Incidental teaching of language in the preschool. *Journal of Applied Behavior Analysis, 8,* 411–420.

Hitchcock, C. H., Dowrick, P. W., & Prater, M. A. (2003). Video self-modeling in school based settings. *Remedial and Special Education, 56,* 36–35.

Hume, K., & Odom, S. (2007). Effects of an individual works system on the independent functioning of students with autism. *Journal of Autism and Developmental Disorders, 37,* 1166–1180.

Hyman, S. L., & Towbin, K. E. (2007). Autism spectrum disorders. In M. L. Batshaw, L. Pelligrino, & N. J. Roizen (Eds.), *Children with disabilities* (6th ed., pp. 325–343). Baltimore, MD: Brookes.

Kaiser, A. P., & Grim, J. C. (2006). Teaching functional communication skills. In M. E. Snell & F. Brown (Eds.), *Instruction of students with severe disabilities* (6th ed., pp, 447–488). Upper Saddle River, NJ: Pearson.

Kanner, L. (1943). Autistic disturbances of affective content. *Nervous Child, 2,* 217–250.

Kendall, P. C., & Choudhury, M. S. (2003). Children and adolescents in cognitive-behavior therapy: Some past efforts, current advances, and the challenge in our future. *Cognitive Therapy and Research, 27,* 89–104.

Koegel, R. L., & Koegel, L. K. (2006). *Pivotal response treatments for autism: Communication, social, and academic development.* Baltimore, MD: Brookes.

Kokina, A., & Kern, L. (2010). Social Story™ Interventions for students with autism spectrum disorders: A meta-analysis. *Journal of Autism and Developmental Disorders, 40,* 812–826. doi:10:1007/s10803–009-0931–0.

LeCouteur, A., Lord, C., & Rutter, M. (2003). *The Autism Diagnostic Interview: Revised (ADI-R).* Los Angeles, CA: Western Psychological Services.

Lovaas, I. O. (1987). Behavioral treatment and normal educational and intellectual functioning in young autistic children. *Journal of Consulting and Clinical Psychology, 55,* 3–9.

Mahoney, G., & Macdonald, J. (2005). *Responsive teaching: Parent-mediated developmental intervention.* Cleveland, OH: Case Western Reserve University.

Mahoney, G., & Persales, F. (2005). Relationship-focused early intervention with children with pervasive developmental disorders and other disabilities: A comparative study. *Journal of Developmental and Behavioral Pediatrics, 26,* 77–85.

Mancil, G. R., & Boman, M. (2010). Functional communication training in the classroom: A guide for success. *Preventing School Failure, 54,* 238–246.

McEachin, J. J., Smith, T., & Lovaas, O. I. (1993). Long-term outcome for children with autism who received early intensive behavioral treatment. *American Journal on Mental Retardation, 97,* 359–372.

McGee, G. G., Morrier, M. J., & Daly, T. (1999). An incidental teaching approach to early intervention for toddlers with autism. *The Journal of the Association for Persons with Severe Handicaps, 24,* 133–146.

Mesibov, G. B., Shea, V., & Shopler, E. (2004). *The TEACCH approach to autism spectrum disorders.* New York: Springer.

Panerai, S., Zingale, M., Trubia, G., Finocchiaro, M., Zuccarello, R., Ferri, R., & Elia, M. (2009). Special education versus inclusive education: The role of the TEACCH program. *Journal of Autism and Developmental Disorders, 39,* 874–882.

Pavlov, I. P. (1927). *Conditioned reflexes: An investigation of the physiological activity of the cerebral cortex* (G. V. Anrep, Trans. and Ed.). London: Oxford University Press/Humphrey Milford.

Perske, R. (1988). *Circle of friends: People with disabilities and their friends enrich the lives of one another.* Nashville, TN: Abingdon Press.

Piaget, J. (1950). *The psychology of intelligence.* London: Broadway House.

Prizant, B. M., Wetherby, A. M., Rubin, E., Laurent, A. C., & Rydell, P. J. (2006a). *The SCERTS model: A comprehensive educational approach for children with autism spectrum disorders: Volume I, Assessment.* Baltimore, MD: Brookes.

Prizant, B. M., Wetherby, A. M., Rubin, E., Laurent, A. C., & Rydell, P. J. (2006b). *The SCERTS model: A comprehensive educational approach for children with autism spectrum disorders: Volume II, Program planning and intervention.* Baltimore, MD: Brookes.

Reynhout, G., & Carter, M. (2006). Social stories for children with disabilities. *Journal of Autism and Developmental Disorders, 36,* 445–469.

Robins, D. L., Fein, D., Barton, M. L., & Green, J. A. (2001). The Modified Checklist for Autism in Toddlers: An initial study investigating the early detection of autism and pervasive developmental disorders. *Journal of Autism and Developmental Disorders, 31,* 131–144.

Rogers, S. J., & Dawson, G. (2009). *Early Start Denver Model for young children with autism.* New York: Guilford.

Rogers, S. J., & DiLalla, D. L. (1991). A comparative study of the effects of a developmentally based instructional model on young children with autism and young children with other disorders of behavior and development. *Topics in Early Childhood Special Education, 11,* 29–47.

Rogers, S. J., Hall, T., Osaki, D., Reaven, J., & Herbison, J. (2001). The Denver Model: A comprehensive integrated approach to young children with autism and their families. In J. S. Handleman & S. L. Harris (Eds.), *Preschool education programs for children with autism* (pp. 95–133). Austin, TX: Pro-Ed.

Rogers, S. J., & Lewis, H. (1989). An effective day treatment model for young children with pervasive developmental disorders. *Journal of the American Academy of Child and Adolescent Psychiatry, 28,* 207–214.

Rosenberg, R. E., Mandell, D. S., Farmer, J. E., Law, J. K., Marvin, A. R., & Law, P. A. (2010). Psychotropic medication use among children with autism spectrum disorders enrolled in a national registry, 2007–2008. *Journal of Autism and Developmental Disorders, 40,* 342–351.

Rotheram-Fuller, E., & MacMullen, L. (2011). Cognitive-behavioral therapy for children with autism spectrum disorders. *Psychology in the Schools, 48,* 263–271.

Scheuermann, B., & Webber, J. (2002). *Autism: Teaching does make a difference.* Belmont, CA: Wadsworth.

Schopler, E., Brehm, S. S., Kinsbourne, M., & Reichler, R. J. (1971). Effect of treatment structure on development in autistic children. *Archives in General Psychiatry, 24,* 415–421.

Schopler, E., & Mesibov, G. B. (1992). *High functioning individuals with autism.* Current Issues in Autism Series. NY: Plenum Press.

Schopler, E., Reichler, R., & Renner, B. R. (1988). *The Childhood Autism Rating Scale (CARS).* Los Angeles, CA: Western Psychological Services.

Skinner, B. F. (1938). *The behavior of organisms: An experimental analysis.* New York: Appleton-Century Crofts.

Simpson, R. L., de Boer-Ott, S. R., Griswold, D. E., Myles, B. S., Byrd, S. E., Ganz, J. B., Cook, K. T., Otten, K. L., Ben-Arieh, J., Kline, S. A., & Adams, L. G. (2005). *Autism spectrum disorders: Interventions and treatments for children and youth.* Thousand Oaks, CA: Corwin Press.

Stern, D. N. (1985). *The interpersonal world of the infant: A view from psychoanalysis and developmental psychology.* New York: Basic Books.

Sulzer-Azaroff, A. O., Hoffman, C. B., Bondy, A., & Frost, L. (2009). The Picture Communication Exchange System (PECS): What do the data say? *Focus on Autism and Other Developmental Disabilities, 24,* 89–103.

Turnbull, A., & Turnbull, R. (1992, Fall & Winter). Group action planning (GAP). *Family and Disability Newsletter, 1*–13.

Umbreit, J., Ferro, J., Liaupsin, C. J., & Lane, K. L. (2007). *Functional behavioral assessment and function-based intervention: An effective, practical approach.* Upper Saddle River, NJ: Prentice Hall.

Vygotsky, S. L. (1978). *Mind in society: The development of higher psychological processes.* Cambridge, MA: Harvard University Press.

Watson, J. B. (1914). *Behavior: An introduction to comparative psychology.* New York: Holt.

Wing, L. (1981). Asperger's syndrome: A clinical account. *Psychological Medicine, 11,* 115–129.

Wood, J., Drahota, A., Sze, K., Har, K., Chui, A., & Langer, D. (2009). Cognitive behavioral therapy for anxiety in children with autism spectrum disorders: A randomized, controlled trial. *Journal of Child Psychology & Psychiatry, 50,* 224–234.

13

Understanding and Treating Victimization and Abuse

NANCY E. SHERMAN AND BILL M. BLUNDELL

PREVALENCE OF THE PROBLEM

Although the number of reported cases of child abuse has been decreasing in the past 10 years, the maltreatment of children remains a major source of mental health issues in boys and youth. *Child Maltreatment, 2009* provided the latest statistics compiled by the Children's Bureau of the U.S. Department of Health and Human Services (2010). The total number of child victims of maltreatment in 2007 was 702,000, with children aged birth to 1 year having the highest rate of victimization at 20.6 per 1,000. Of the victims, 48.2% were boys, while 44% were White, 22.3% African American, and 20.7% Hispanic. In terms of type of maltreatment, the report identifies the following: more than 75% (78.3%) suffered neglect; more than 15% (17.8%) suffered physical abuse; less than 10% (9.5%) suffered sexual abuse; and less than 10% (7.6%) suffered from emotional or psychological abuse. Child maltreatment fatalities increased by 15% from the 2006 reported total.

Finkelhor, Ormrod, Turner, and Hamby (2005) conducted a national survey addressing childhood victimization with the goal of improving on studies that failed to show a comprehensive picture of childhood maltreatment. Their Developmental Victimization Survey covered a range of types of victimization of children from birth to 18 over the course of 1 year. The study divided maltreatment into five categories: physical abuse, sexual abuse, emotional abuse, neglect, and family abduction. Among the findings were that more than half (530 per 1,000) of youth were victims of a physical assault, with the highest rate occurring between the ages of

6 and 12. The rate for sexual victimization was 1 in 12, which included sexual assault and attempted or completed rape. Overall, the rate of child maltreatment was one in seven children, with emotional abuse occurring most frequently (Finkelhor et al., 2005).

Many children suffer more than one type of abuse, and this is an area that has not been well researched. *Polyvictimization* is the term used by Finkelhor to describe exposure to multiple types of victimization. Finkelhor, Ormrod, and Turner (2007), using a comprehensive measure of childhood victimization, found that half of a national sample of youth aged 2 to 17 had experienced two or more different types of victimization. The median number of types of victimization for this sample was three. Through this study, the authors demonstrated that "multiple contemporaneous victimization is the norm for victimized children" (p. 149). A previous study of the effects of victimization found that when multiple victimizations are controlled for, the effect of a single victimization virtually disappeared. These results suggest that youth suffering multiple victimizations are the ones manifesting trauma responses, while youth experiencing a single type of victimization display far less and sometimes no trauma response (Finkelhor et al., 2005). Although statistics continue to indicate that child maltreatment is a tremendous problem for society, estimates are that only one out of three cases of child abuse is ever discovered or reported.

SIGNS AND SYMPTOMS OF MALTREATMENT

Physical Abuse

The signs and symptoms of maltreatment of children vary according to the type of abuse as well as the age of the child among other factors. As noted previously, many children are victims of more than one type of abuse, and polyvictimization can result in more severe signs and symptoms. The Child Welfare Information Gateway (2001) lists signs and symptoms displayed by children and the abuser for each type of child maltreatment. Physically abused children may display unexplained injuries such as burns, bites, bruises, broken bones, or black eyes; fading bruises or other marks noticeable after an absence from school; fear of parents and protesting or crying when it is time to go home; and reports of injury by a parent or another. Signs of physical abuse shown by the abusing parent or caregiver may include conflicting, unconvincing, or no explanation for the child's injury, describing the child as "evil," or in some other very negative way; the use of harsh physical discipline with the child; and a history of abuse as a child.

The possibility of neglect exists when the child is frequently absent from school; begs or steals food or money; lacks needed medical or dental care, immunizations, or glasses; is consistently dirty and has severe body odor; lacks sufficient clothing for the weather; abuses alcohol or other drugs; and states that there is no one at home to provide care. The Child Welfare Gateway (2001) suggested considering neglect when the parent or other adult caregiver appears to be indifferent to the child; seems apathetic or depressed; behaves irrationally or in a bizarre manner; and is abusing alcohol or other drugs.

Sexual Abuse

Signs of sexual abuse in children vary according to age as well. According to the American Humane Association (2005), children up to age 3 may exhibit the following signs of sexual abuse: fear or excessive crying, vomiting, feeding problems, bowel problems, sleep disturbances, and failure to thrive. For children in the age range of 2 to 9 years, signs include fear of particular people, places, or activities, regressive behaviors such as bed wetting or stranger anxiety, victimization of others, excessive masturbation, feelings of shame or guilt, nightmares or sleep disturbances, withdrawal from family or friends, and eating disturbances. Older children and adolescents may display depression, nightmares or sleep disturbances, poor school performance, promiscuity, substance abuse, aggression and bullying, running away from home, eating disturbances, early pregnancy or marriage, suicidal gestures, and pseudo-mature behaviors.

An online resource for boys and men who have been sexually abused exists that is named, "1 in 6." This figure is also the estimate of the number of males who have experienced unwanted or abusive sexual experiences before age 16. A 2005 study conducted by researchers from the U.S. Centers for Disease Control and Prevention on San Diego Kaiser Permanente HMO members, reported that 16% of males were sexually abused by the age of 18 (Dube et al., 2005).

Boys from across the sociodemographic spectrum can be victimized by sexual abusers. Those at higher risk of victimization include boys younger than 13, who are non-White, are of low socioeconomic status, and who are living in a single-parent home. Family factors that contribute to higher risk include living with only one or neither parent; parental divorce, separation, or remarriage; parental alcohol abuse; and parental criminal behavior. Sexually abused boys are more likely to have other family members who are victims of sexual or physical abuse (Prevent Child Abuse America, n.d.).

Many people would like to believe the myth that most perpetrators of sexual abuse are strangers; however, children typically know and trust their perpetrator. Perpetrators of child sexual abuse come from different age groups, races, genders, and socioeconomic backgrounds. The majority of perpetrators are male (80%–95%), although female sex offenders victimize both boys and girls. In addition, juvenile perpetrators comprise as many as a third of all offenders (Finkelhor, 1994). Boys are more likely to be sexually victimized by someone outside of the family, such as a coach, teacher, neighbor, or babysitter, while girls are more likely to be victimized by close and/or extended family members. The Internet is the newest medium that sexual offenders use to reach their victims. Cruise (2004) reports that a study surveying youths 10 to 17 years old found 20% of participants who used the Internet at least once a month had received unwanted sexual solicitations and approaches in the last year. For some youths in the study, the solicitor attempted to gain further access by phone, mail, or in person.

Many believe that sexual abuse of males is underreported and that boys are less likely than girls to disclose abuse due to the stigma of homosexuality, fear of reprisal by the perpetrator against self or family members, and loss of self-esteem (Holmes & Slap, 1998). Valente (2005) states that although sexual abuse of boys and men is a serious problem, those who have been abused rarely report the abuse unless they are specifically asked during a "therapeutic encounter" (p. 11). Mental health professionals in all settings need to ask both boys and men about sexual abuse in order to provide appropriate and effective assistance.

The long-term effect of sexual abuse on males is an area of research that has, until recently, been neglected. Most studies have focused on children in general or only females (Dube et al., 2005). One study of 17,337 adults that investigated the effects of child sexual abuse on both men and women found that the male victims were twice as likely to attempt suicide as those who had not been abused. In addition, men who had been abused were 40% to 50% more likely to experience marital relationship problems and to marry an alcoholic (Dube et al., 2005). Wolfe, Francis, and Straatman (2005) studied the long-term impact of physical and sexual abuse of boys by an adult in a trusting, nonfamilial relationship at a religiously affiliated institution. Participants in the study were men who had substantiated claims for multiple and severe incidents of sexual, physical, and/or emotional abuse during childhood. Of the 76 men, the authors found that 42% met *DSM-IV* criteria for posttraumatic stress disorder (PTSD), 21% for alcohol abuse and/or dependence, and one-quarter met criteria for a mood disorder. In addition, more than one-third of the men suffered from chronic sexual problems, and over half had a history of criminal behavior. These long-term consequences of PTSD and depression, alcoholism and drug abuse, suicidal thoughts and attempts, problems in intimate relationships, and underachievement at school and work underline the necessity of early identification and intervention of sexual abuse of boys and youth.

SIBLING ABUSE

Research involving the subject of sibling abuse is lacking at best. The limited amount of research available does not show who is more likely to abuse if the sibling group involves both male and female. Sibling abuse, within the family unit, is often overlooked or minimized. Parents are often not willing to face the reality of abuse between siblings. Comments such as "boys will be boys" and "that's just what siblings do" are used by parents when faced with the knowledge of sibling abuse. Sibling abuse includes physical, sexual, emotional, and psychological abuse. Of these types, psychological abuse is often difficult to discern as "real" abuse. A brother calling his sisters "fat and ugly" may seem harmless to a parent, but over time, those words can have lasting psychological effects.

The parents' role and response to sibling abuse is vital to the development of their children. In many households where sibling abuse occurs, other types of violence such as child abuse or domestic violence between parents are also present. Hardy (2001) explains why parents may not intervene: "parents of children who physically abuse their siblings often experience significant stress and because they cope ineffectively with the stress, they are often unaware or fail to intervene adequately in abusive sibling relationships" (p. 258). Without parental intervention, sibling abuse can become a generational issue.

Sibling sexual abuse is more easily identified than psychological abuse, but tends to be underreported for different reasons. Parents may believe that their children are simply curious and are engaging in exploration. Most underreporting occurs as a result of not wanting child protective services involved with their family. Kiselica and Morrill-Richards (2007) found that "sibling incest might be the most common form of sexual abuse perpetrated by immediate family members" (p. 150). When sibling sexual abuse is disclosed within the family unit, the response by parents often dictates how effective counseling services will be, as well as eventual outcome for the victim.

ABUSE OF PARENTS

Similar to sibling abuse, the abuse of parents by their sons is not well researched. Boxer, Gullan, and Mahoney (2009) found that boys were more likely than girls to be physically aggressive toward both parents, at almost a 2:1 rate. Boys who are raised in homes with domestic violence tend to acquire the learned behavior of physical aggression. In addition, in homes where a youth is the victim of aggression, he can also be or become a perpetrator of violence. Pagani, Tremblay, Zoccolillo, Vitaro, and McDuff (2008) state that "regardless of gender, a childhood life-course of violence is likely to build up over time, especially if unmanaged by firm, yet kind and consistent parenting that teaches appropriate conflict resolution and mutual respect" (p. 181). Counseling professionals working with children who abuse their parents should integrate parents into the counseling process. In this way, psychoeducational work can be completed on how their children's needs might be met without the use of aggression. Parents can learn how conflict differs from aggression and how to deal with conflict without the use of aggression. Constructive communication can be a result of conflict between a boy and his mother/father, and this approach to resolving conflict should be normalized within the family unit. If done appropriately, the child in the conflict will not feel backed into a corner and justify the need to fight back, whether verbally or physically. Family counseling can be a place for families to come together in a neutral setting where expectations are set by the counselor and not by the parent or child. This creates an environment for all family members to learn how to express thoughts and feelings and learn to approach conflict constructively.

IMPACT OF MALTREATMENT

The impact of maltreatment and trauma on child development can occur in all areas, including health and physical, intellectual and cognitive, emotional and psychological, and social and behavioral development (Hagele, 2005). Examples of negative impact in these developmental areas include failure to thrive, attachment difficulties, learning disabilities, and failure of the brain to develop normally. Hagele (2005) describes maltreatment as "an extreme traumatic insult to the developing child" (p. 366). She cites recent neuroimaging studies that show significant changes in the neuroanatomy of children exposed to the trauma of maltreatment, as well as in adults with a history of abuse. The neuronal loss associated with maltreatment leads to significant deficits across developmental and cognitive domains. These deficits are manifested as deficits in attention, abstract reasoning, impulse control, long-term memory for verbal information, and lower IQ scores.

Although the impact of maltreatment may not be visible at an early stage except in the most severe cases, the effects of maltreatment are harmful and may be long lasting. Neglected and abused children often experience multiple consequences, and determining whether the impact is related specifically to the neglect, is caused by another factor, or arises from a combination of factors is difficult (DePanfilis, 2006). Research shows that the impact of victimization varies based on factors such as the child's age, the presence and strength of protective factors, the frequency, duration, and severity of the neglect, and the relationship between the child and the caregiver (English et al., 2005).

One way the societal impact of childhood abuse and neglect is measured is in economic terms (Child Welfare Information Gateway, 2008). Economically, there are both direct and indirect costs. Direct costs include funds necessary to run the child welfare system for investigating and responding to allegations of abuse and neglect. Direct costs also include judicial, law enforcement, health, and mental health system expenses incurred in adjudication and treatment. Indirect costs are associated with the long-term economic consequences of child abuse and neglect. These costs include expenses related to juvenile and adult criminal activity, mental illness, substance abuse, and domestic violence. Additional cost considerations may be loss of productivity due to unemployment and underemployment, the cost of special education services, and increased use of the health care system. According to Wang and Holton (2007), who researched the economic impact of child abuse and neglect for Prevent Child Abuse America, the estimated annual cost of child abuse and neglect is $103.8 billion in 2007 dollar value. This estimate was labeled a conservative figure.

Long-Term Effects of Childhood Maltreatment

The Child Information Gateway's (2008) Factsheet offers compiled findings from a variety of recent studies regarding the long-term effects of child maltreatment. Potential outcomes of maltreatment are listed in the categories of physical health, mental health, behavioral, and societal consequences. Physical health consequences include shaken baby syndrome, poor physical health, and impaired brain development. Psychological consequences are poor mental and emotional health, cognitive difficulties such as cognitive capacity, language development, and academic difficulties, and social and relationship difficulties.

Behavioral consequences are twice as likely to occur among maltreated children. In adolescence, problems such as delinquency, teen pregnancy, low academic achievement, alcohol/drug use, and mental health problems are at least 25% more likely among abused children (Child Welfare Information Gateway, 2008). Adult criminal behavior, domestic violence, and sexual abuse of others are more likely to occur and approximately one-third of child abuse victims will themselves become abusers (Prevent Child Abuse New York, 2003).

In researching the physical abuse of boys and outcomes later in life, Holmes and Sammel (2005) found that 51% of their sample of 197 adult men had been physically abused as children. Of those abused, 73% were abused by a parent. The investigators found that a history of childhood physical abuse was associated with depressive symptoms, PTSD symptoms, number of lifetime sexual partners, legal difficulties, and incarceration in adulthood.

O'Leary (2009) investigated the relationship between coping strategies used by men who had been sexually abused as children and clinical diagnoses. He found that the men who had been abused were 10 times more likely to have a clinical diagnosis than men in the general population. In addition, the coping strategy of seeking active assistance had a moderating effect on clinical diagnoses. Implications from these findings show the need for awareness among clinicians that "psychiatric symptoms" in men could be caused by past sexual abuse and are worthy of further exploration.

TREATMENT

Many treatment protocols and methods have been developed to respond to the emotional and behavioral concerns and problems of maltreated children and their families. Empirically based treatments are usually cognitive behavioral theoretical approaches and use behavioral and cognitive intervention procedures and techniques. These empirically supported treatments also typically involve both the individual child and family members. Many share specific treatment procedures and techniques, for example, cognitive restructuring, exposure procedures, and behavioral management skills that are applied to different problems (Saunders, Berliner, & Hanson, 2004). Empirically supported treatments generally have the following principles and components in common: they are goal-directed and structured; they teach skills to manage emotional distress and behavioral disturbances to children and adults; and they involve repetitive practice of skills both in session and in the larger environment. Key skills for children that are common among treatments are skills for identifying, processing, and regulating emotions, anxiety management skills, skills for identifying and changing maladaptive cognitions, and problem-solving skills. These general skills are employed in treating a variety of emotional and behavioral disorders and are considered basic and fundamental treatment components (Saunders et al., 2004).

Trauma-Focused Cognitive Behavioral Therapy

Trauma-Focused Cognitive Behavioral Therapy (TF-CBT) has been nationally recognized as an exemplary evidence-based, empirically supported treatment program. TF-CBT received an "Exemplary Program Award" in 2001 and recognition as a Model Program since 2003 by the U.S. Department of Health and Human Services Substance Abuse and Mental Health Services Administration (SAMHSA). In 2004, TF-CBT was named a Best Practice by the Kauffman Best Practices Task Force of the National Child Traumatic

Stress Network (NCTSN) and was given the highest classification for an evidence-based practice by the U.S. Department of Justice-sponsored report, *Child Physical and Sexual Abuse: Guidelines for Treatment* (2004).

TF-CBT, based on learning and cognitive theories, is designed to reduce children's negative emotional and behavioral responses to maltreatment and to correct maladaptive beliefs and attributions related to the abuse. It also provides support and skill-building to help nonoffending parents cope effectively with their own emotions and learn how to respond to their victimized children in appropriate and healing ways (Chadwick Center on Children and Families, 2004). Cohen, Mannarino, and Deblinger (2006) are leaders in research on and development of a treatment framework for TF-CBT. They describe TF-CBT as a components-based psychosocial treatment model that incorporates elements of cognitive-behavioral, attachment, humanistic, empowerment, and family therapy models.

Cohen, Mannarino, & Deblinger (2006) describe a number of well-designed studies that provide evidence that TF-CBT works in treating trauma symptoms in children, adolescents, and their parents. TF-CBT was originally developed to address trauma associated with child sexual abuse and has more recently been adapted for use with children who have experienced a wide array of traumatic experiences (National Child Traumatic Stress Network, 2004).

TF-CBT includes several core treatment components designed to be used flexibly in addressing the unique needs of each child and family. Treatment components of TF-CBT include the following:

- Psychoeducation about child abuse, typical reactions of victims, normalization of reactions, safety skills, and healthy sexuality
- Stress management techniques such as focused breathing, progressive muscle relaxation, emotional expression skills, thought stopping, thought replacement, and cognitive therapy interventions
- Constructing the Trauma Narrative—Gradual exposure techniques including verbal, written and/or symbolic recounting (i.e., utilizing dolls, puppets) of abusive event(s)
- Cognitive processing or cognitive reframing consisting of exploration and correction of inaccurate attributions about the cause of, responsibility for, and results of the abusive experience(s)
- Parental participation in parallel or conjoint treatment including psychoeducation, gradual exposure, anxiety management, and correction of cognitive distortions
- Parental instruction in child behavior management strategies
- Family work to enhance communication and create opportunities for therapeutic discussion regarding the abuse (Kauffman Best Practices Project, 2004)

TF-CBT is an effective treatment program for children (4–18) who have experienced any trauma, including multiple traumas. It works with children from diverse backgrounds in as few as 12 treatment sessions. TF-CBT has been used successfully in clinics, schools, homes, residential treatment facilities, inpatient settings, and with children in foster care (Cohen, Mannarino, & Deblinger, 2006). A free training course on TF-CBT developed by Cohen, Deblinger, and Mannarino (http://tfcbt.musc.edu/) is available online. This web-based learning program covers psychoeducation, stress management, affect expression and modulation, cognitive coping, creating the trauma narrative, cognitive processing, behavior management, and parent–child sessions.

CASE STUDY: BART, AGE 14

Bart is a 14-year-old Caucasian male, originally from a southern county in a Midwestern state. Bart is 20 pounds overweight, of normal height, and has no notable health issues. Bart functions at an average cognitive level according to intelligence testing and currently resides in a residential treatment facility roughly 1.5 hours from his home. Bart is the middle child in a sibling group of three. He has one sister who is older, age 16, and one who is younger, age 12. Bart lived with his mother, father, and two sisters for the first 5 years of his life. Bart's father was present in the home until the age of 5; after that, Bart had sporadic contact with his father. At the age of 12, Bart was removed from his mother's home by the Department of Children and Family Services due to his mother's chronic drug abuse that resulted in neglect. While in his mother's care, Bart was victimized physically, emotionally, and sexually. He was placed in foster care for 9 months before being placed in the residential treatment facility. Bart has family visits with his mother once a month and one sister twice a month. He does not have contact with his younger sister because she resides in a foster home and does not want contact with other family members. When Bart was 8 years old, his father was killed in an alcohol-related automobile crash.

Bart performed well in school during his early years; as time progressed, however, he began missing school on a frequent basis. His school absenteeism was based, in part, on his need to care for his mother and her increasing drug problem. Bart is currently in the 8th grade, attends the on-site school at the residential facility, and does well academically. He struggles at times with peer interactions but overall does well in the classroom. Bart is willing to partake in new activities and has a creative mind. He works well in group activities as well as independently, though at times he lacks motivation. Bart is willing to help others who need his help.

Presenting Issues

The presenting issue in Bart's case is sexual abuse and the claim that he sexually abused a foster brother. Bart was placed in the residential facility to focus on the issue of being a sexual perpetrator. Bart is a victim of abuse, physical, sexual, and emotional, and had multiple traumatic experiences in his life. Bart also displayed some problems with self-abuse, such as pulling his hair and punching himself. This issue was more historical than present, but was linked to Bart's low self-esteem. As mentioned, Bart is overweight, and this leads to self-esteem issues.

Bart also appears to be an adolescent who is questioning his sexuality. He has been called "gay" based on his perceived effeminate nature. He is soft spoken, caring, and meticulous, and some peers equate these features with homosexuality and make negative comments to him. This bullying was present prior to and while in residential treatment. Bart is defensive regarding his sexuality in reaction to the verbal abuse from his peers.

Bart has several issues that need to be addressed in the counseling setting. The most pressing issue or presenting problem is the trauma that Bart experienced in his 14 years of life. The presenting issue that brought Bart into a residential treatment facility was sexually inappropriate behavior, so while residing in residential treatment, he has 24-hour supervision and is not allowed to be alone with other residents. Placing the focus on the traumatic experiences in Bart's life is integral to his success in treatment.

Interventions

With the focus on the trauma Bart experienced, the treatment approach used is an integrative one. The main component of this integrative model is the use of TF-CBT. TF-CBT is a treatment modality used for children and adolescents who have experienced simple and complex trauma. TF-CBT consists of relaxation training, affect regulation, and creating a life or trauma story. Bart exhibits characteristics of a youth affected by complex trauma including self-esteem issues, anger, trust issues, generalized anxiety, and compound stress. Bart experienced multiple traumas during his youth including the death of his father, abuse, neglect, a drug-addicted mother, and removal from his family.

Bart benefited from the relaxation component of this modality, as he was able to learn coping skills to alleviate some of the stress of recurring thoughts of traumatic experiences in his life. These coping skills help Bart manage his anger, as his levels of anger fluctuated during the few months of placement in the residential facility. Bart needed some work in the area of affect expression and regulation. Bart has the ability to communicate his thoughts and feelings; however, at times, this leads to anger as he appears to be flooded with emotion. He is now able to use the coping skills learned in treatment. Even with this ability, Bart is still asked to do feelings exercises to help with affect regulation.

Part of affect regulation is the use of a thought-stopping technique. Bart has permission to wear a rubber band around his wrist and when he has negative thoughts about his family or himself he snaps the rubber band to remind himself to stop these thoughts. Bart is also encouraged to use daily positive self talk to help boost his self-esteem and to improve his overall mood. The Socratic method of questioning was employed early in treatment to identify the root of Bart's issues, which turned out to be his being removed from his mother's care.

An important component of TF-CBT was Bart's creation of his life story or trauma narrative. He was instructed on what the life story should include and was given creative freedom to create his life story in any format he chose. Bart chose to construct a scrapbook of his life. The life story covers from birth to his current age and could include his thoughts about the future if desired. The central theme for his life story was the one traumatic experience Bart feels affected him the most. This was discovered during the use of the Socratic method of questioning, which aims to help clients answer their own questions by making them think and drawing out the answer from them. Bart identified his removal from his mother's home as his most traumatic. An important aspect of TF-CBT is allowing the client to tell the therapist what was most traumatic. In working through Bart's trauma, it is therapeutic to focus on Bart's trauma "experiences" and not assume that he "suffered" trauma. When hearing Bart discuss finding his mother unconscious with a heroin needle in her neck, I assumed this was a traumatic event. I encouraged Bart to talk through how this experience affected him, rather than assuming that he was suffering as a result. I discovered that Bart felt pride in his ability to get help and save his mother. If, however, his reaction had been one of pain and suffering, it would have been appropriate to validate those feelings.

In conjunction with TF-CBT, Reality Therapy (Glasser, 2000) is useful in working with the client to address behavioral issues. Bart needs to understand the importance of taking responsibility for his own actions and focus on change. This is necessary to help work through the current problem of sexually inappropriate behavior and to discuss past instances of sexual abuse. Bart maintained his innocence in allegedly sexually abusing his foster brother.

Although aware that he cannot make excuses for his actions, he is reluctant to focus on his behaviors and will use his past as a reason for current behaviors. His feelings were validated for the traumatic experiences in his life, and he discussed how those experiences have had an impact on some of his life. Along with Reality Therapy, a strengths-based approach is being used to help confront the issues head on and to decrease tendencies to make excuses for past and present negative behaviors. Bart worked hard on creating a list of his positive attributes upon which he could build self-esteem. Low self-esteem was an issue Bart became aware of early in treatment. He continues to have self-image issues, mainly concerning body image, and is working hard on diet and exercise to help alleviate some of the stress of being overweight.

Outcome

Bart continues to make strides in the therapeutic setting and is dealing with many of the abuse issues he brought to the forefront through the therapeutic relationship. Bart is willing and able to continue in his treatment and make progress. Bart, even with multiple trauma experiences, is laid back and calm for a child his age. Bart attempts to be more mature than his age would suggest, but after reminders of his age and the lack of need to act older, he functions as a 14 year old. Part of Bart's tendency to act older is because he is a parentified child. He was asked to do things as a child a majority of children his age would not be asked to do.

Bart is willing to meet the demands of rigorous feelings exercises and is able to regulate his feelings in appropriate ways. Bart is willing to talk more about the sexual abuse that he experienced as a child, but remains steadfast that he is being falsely accused of being a perpetrator of sexual abuse. With commitment to his story, Bart was informed he would be referred for a more specific assessment of his history of sexual abuse. Bart agreed to take part in that assessment, and results are unknown at this time.

Bart is slowly increasing his self-esteem and continues to utilize methods to help bolster his self-esteem. Bart is willing to discuss difficult issues and situations, understanding the benefit to him and his feelings about self. Bart utilizes the coping strategies he learned, and this increases his self-esteem as well. Bart is able to hear negative comments about his weight and self-image and deals with them appropriately.

Bart was able to come to terms with the myriad of abuses he experienced as a child and continues work on dealing with how it affects him. Bart describes the abuse he suffered as painful, both physically and emotionally, and that he will not allow past experiences to dictate who he is going to be in the future. Bart comments he will never treat his children the way he was treated. Bart discusses the traumatic events in his life more openly and freely as time progresses.

Bart finished his life story and was willing to share it with the therapist in a counseling session. He worked hard on his life story, and it appeared to be the most important component in his treatment. It allowed him to express himself in his own way, without judgment or questioning. Bart will be able to add more to his life story and be able to present it to the important people in his life. Bart continues to reside in the residential treatment facility, while an appropriate foster home or possible family member is located for placement. Before leaving residential treatment, he will be required to present his life story again to his therapist and two other residential staff members. Bart is able to live in the community but does need supervision. He is not presently considered a threat to the community, but due to past allegations, supervision is needed in his reintegration to the community. Bart is aware of the effects of trauma he experienced and will continue to use his learning from treatment when necessary through the course of his life. Bart is now able to express how he feels when he experiences emotions. He does this in appropriate ways and has developed into a more emotionally and behaviorally healthy adolescent.

RESOURCES FOR PROFESSIONALS

1. Crimes Against Children Research Center website: http://www.unh.edu/ccrc/links/links.html
2. U.S. Department of Health and Human Services, Administration for Children and Families, Children's Bureau website: http://www.acf.hhs.gov/programs/cb/index.htm
3. Child Welfare Information Gateway website: http://www.childwelfare.gov/
4. Goodyear-Brown, P. (2010). *Play Therapy with Traumatized Children. A Prescriptive Approach*. Hoboken, NJ: John H. Wiley and Sons.
5. Cohen, J. A., Mannarino, A. P., & Deblinger, E. (2006). *Treating Trauma and Traumatic Grief in Children and Adolescents*. New York: Guilford Press.
6. Trauma-Focused Cognitive Behavioral Therapy website: http://tfcbt.musc.edu
7. National Child Traumatic Stress Network website: http://nctsnet.org/

RESOURCES FOR SEXUAL ABUSE

1. http://1in6.org/: The mission of 1 in 6 is to help men who have had unwanted or abusive sexual experiences in childhood live healthier, happier lives and includes serving family members, friends, and partners by providing information and support resources on the web and in the community.
2. Lew, M. (2004). *Victims No Longer: The Classic Guide for Men Recovering from Sexual Child Abuse*. New York: HarperCollins.
3. Levy-Peck, J. (2009). *Healing the Harm Done: A Parent's Guide to Helping Your Child Overcome the Effects of Sexual Abuse*. Bloomington, IN: Xlibris Corp.

4. Davis, L (1991). *Allies in Healing: When the Person You Love Was Sexually Abused As a Child*. New York: HarperCollins.
5. http://www.bigvoicepictures.com/boys-and-men-healing/: *Boys and Men Healing* is a documentary about the impact the sexual abuse of boys has on both the individual and society, and the importance of healing and speaking out for male survivors to end the devastating effects. The film portrays stories of three courageous nonoffending men whose arduous healing helped them reclaim their lives—while giving them a powerful voice to speak out and take bold action toward prevention for other boys. The film includes a support group of men and is testimony to the importance of men finding safe places to support one another and share their stories together. The film was produced in association with the International Documentary Association.
6. http://www.malesurvivor.org/default.html provides resources and support for men who were sexually victimized as children, adolescents, or adults.

REFERENCES

American Humane Association. (2005). *Child neglect* [Fact sheet]. Retrieved from http://www.americanhumane.org/children/stop-child-abuse/fact-sheets/child-neglect.html

Boxer, P., Gullan, R., & Mahoney, A. (2009). Adolescents' physical aggression toward parents in a clinic-referred sample. *Journal of Clinical & Adolescent Psychology, 38*(1), 106–116.

Chadwick Center on Children and Families. (2004). Kauffman best practices project final report. Retrieved from http://www.chadwickcenter.org/Documents/Kaufman Report/ChildHosp-NCTABrochure.pdf

Child Sexual Abuse Task Force and Research & Practice Core, National Child Traumatic Stress Network. (2004). *How to implement Trauma-Focused Cognitive Behavioral Therapy*. Durham, NC and Los Angeles, CA: National Center for Child Traumatic Stress.

Child Welfare Information Gateway. (2001). *In focus: Understanding the effects of maltreatment on early brain development* [Online]. Retrieved from http://www.childwelfare.gov/edtoolkit/pdfs/earlybrain.pdf

Child Welfare Information Gateway. (2008). *Long-term consequences of childhood abuse and neglect*. Retrieved from http://www.childwelfare.gov/pubs/factsheets/long_term_consequences.cfm#physical

Cohen, J. A., Mannarino, A. P., & Deblinger, E. (2006). Treating Trauma and Traumatic Grief in Children and Adolescents. New York: Guilford Press.

Cruise, T. K. (2004). *Sexual abuse of children and adolescents*. Retrieved from http://www.nasponline.org/educators/sexualabuse.pdf

DePanfilis, D. (2006). *Child neglect: A guide for prevention, assessment and intervention*. Children's Bureau, Office on Child Abuse and Neglect, Child Welfare Information Gateway. Retrieved from http://www.childwelfare.gov/pubs/usermanuals/neglect/index.cfm

Dube, S. R., Anda, R. F, Whitfield, C. L., Brown, D. W., Felliti, V. J., Dong, M., & Giles, W. H. (2005). Long-term consequences of childhood sexual abuse by gender of victim. *American Journal of Preventive Medicine, 28*(5), 430–438. doi:10.1016/j.amepre.2005.01.015.

English, D. J., Upadhyaya, M. P., Litrownik, A. J., Marshall, J. M., Runyan, D. K., Graham, J. C., & Dubowitz, H. (2005). Maltreatment's wake: The relationship of maltreatment dimensions to child outcomes. *Child Abuse and Neglect, 29,* 597–619.

Finkelhor, D. (1994). Current information on the scope and nature of child sexual abuse. *The Future of Children, 4*(2), 31,46–48.

Finkelhor, D., Ormrod, R. K., & Turner, H. A. (2007). Poly-victimization and trauma in a national longitudinal cohort. *Development and Psychopathology, 19*(1), 149–166.

Finkelhor, D., Turner, H. A., & Ormrod, R. K., & Hamby, S. L. (2005). The victimization of children and youth: A comprehensive, national survey. *Child Maltreatment, 10*(1), 5–25.

Glasser, W. (2000). *Reality therapy in action.* New York: HarperCollins.

Hagele, D. (2005). The impact of maltreatment on the developing child. *North Carolina Medical Journal, 66*(5), 356–359.

Hardy, M. S. (2001). Physical aggression and sexual behavior among siblings: A retrospective study. *Journal of Family Violence, 16*(3), 255–268.

Holmes, W. C., & Sammel, M. D. (2005). Brief communication: Physical abuse of boys and possible associations with poor adult outcomes. *Annals of Internal Medicine, 143*(8), 581–586.

Holmes, W. C., & Slap, G. B. (1998). Sexual abuse of boys. *Journal of the American Medical Association, 280*(21), 1855–1862.

Kiselica, M. S., & Morril-Richards, M. (2007). Sibling maltreatment: The forgotten abuse. *Journal of Counseling and Development, 85,* 148–160.

O'Leary, P. (2009). Men who were sexually abused in childhood: Coping strategies and comparisons in psychological functioning. *Child Abuse & Neglect, 33*(7), 471–479. doi:10.1016/j.chiabu.2009.02.004.

Pagani, L., Tremblay, R., Zoccolillo, M., Vitaro, F., & McDuff, P. (2009). Risk factor models for adolescent verbal and physical aggression towards fathers. *Journal of Family Violence, 24*(3), 173–182.

Prevent Child Abuse New York. (2003). *The costs of child abuse and the urgent need for prevention.* Retrieved from http://www.preventchildabuseny.org/files/6213/0392/2130/costs.pdf

Prevent Child Abuse America. (n.d.). *Sexual abuse of boys* [Fact sheet]. Retrieved from http://member.preventchildabuse.org/site/DocServer/sexual_abuse_of_boys.pdf?docID=127

Saunders, B. E., Berliner, L., & Hanson, R. F. (Eds.). (2004). *Child Physical and Sexual Abuse: Guidelines for Treatment* (Revised Report: April 26, 2004). Charleston, SC: National Crime Victims Research and Treatment Center.

Valente, S. M. (2005). Sexual abuse of boys. *Journal of Child and Adolescent Psychiatric Nursing, 18*(1), 10–16.

Wang, C., & Holton, J. (2007). *Total estimated cost of child abuse and neglect in the United States.* Chicago, IL: Prevent Child Abuse America.

Wolfe, D. A., Francis, K. A., & Straatman, A. (2006). Child abuse in religiously-affiliated institutions: Long-term impact on men's mental health. *Child Abuse and Neglect, 30*(2), 205–212. doi:10.1016/j.chiabu.2005.08.015.

14

Understanding the Child's World of Grief

CORIE SCHOENEBERG AND GEORGE R. SESSER

THE IMPACT OF LOSS

The loss of a loved one constitutes one of the most significant and life-altering experiences an individual can have. The death of an especially close loved one affects the physical, emotional, and spiritual self and can threaten to overwhelm even high-functioning adults. Children, who are often left with few resources, face a particularly difficult challenge of dealing with their grief when confronting a substantial loss (Muller & Thompson, 2003). A child's life after suffering a loss involves bereavement, which can be considered the act of adjusting to daily life without the loved one. Grief and mourning is the process through which a child makes this adjustment of learning to live in a world in which everything is the same, but the vacancy of the loved one endures as very profound (Worden, 1996).

This process of grief is not a specific or identified emotion, like anger or sadness, and often manifests in children through cognitions, physical sensations in the body, and disrupted behavior (Green & Connolly, 2009). Because children do not grieve in many of the same ways as adults, there is a misperception that children do not grieve at all (Worden, 1996). Children are often unable to verbalize the complicated feelings surrounding their grief, and they may appear to be unaffected, but these feelings more commonly emerge and are expressed in the child's behavior and play (Kirwin & Hamrin, 2005). Males in particular may present with fewer obvious expressions of grief because of stereotypical pressures to maintain the mantra that "boys don't cry" and remain unemotional and seemingly disconnected.

This chapter is a result of a specific child's grief work in individual counseling from within a public school setting in a Midwestern state. The play therapist implemented a Child-Centered Play Therapy (CCPT) approach from the initial session to termination. In the following sections, grief is examined from within an individual and developmental framework, the importance of grief work in children is explored, the tenets and philosophy of CCPT are reviewed, and the presentation of the child in the case study is visited. The format following these sections takes on a child-centered organization, through which highlights of the child's experiences in play therapy are presented session by session and connected with corresponding research, concluding with implications for counselors and play therapists.

Individual and Developmental Components of Grief

The grief experience in children is affected by both individual and developmental factors. Children respond to a loss in ways that reflect their individual temperament, preexisting coping strategies, access to external resources, cognitive-processing capabilities, and previous experiences with death (Green & Connolly, 2009). From a developmental perspective, abstract concepts linked with death, such as causality and irreversibility, are not fully comprehended until the child reaches Piaget's Concrete Operational stage around the age of 7 or 8 (Worden, 1996). A child who has not yet reached this cognitive developmental milestone will experience the loss in ways that adults often have a difficult time understanding. The child's grief may also be influenced by the circumstances surrounding the death. The loss becomes complex and especially difficult if the death was sudden or unexpected, violent, involved mutilation, occurred after a prolonged illness, or if the deceased was a child (Kirwin & Hamrin, 2005).

IMPORTANCE OF FACILITATING THE GRIEF PROCESS

The needs of this population of grieving children are profound. One out of seven children will experience a loss of a loved one or caretaker before the age of 10 (Green & Connolly, 2009). Research suggests that children are able to process their grief most effectively when they do so in the presence of a consistent adult, who can help them identify and express their feelings about the loss (Worden, 1996). Unfortunately, for many of these children, parents are so overcome by their own feelings that they are unable to parent effectively or be emotionally available to their grieving children, especially in cases of children who have lost a sibling

(Worden, 1996). Children who are learning to live with their loss may display extreme ranges of mood and behavior, such as appearing to cope positively then suddenly erupting with emotional distress and significant behavioral outbursts. Even when parents are able to help their child process grief, these parents may feel overwhelmed, confused, and powerless by the radical shifts in the child's mood and behavior (Schoen, Burgoyne & Schoen, 2004). Parents also believe that the task of helping a grieving child is so troubling and disturbing that the child's feelings are ignored or overlooked. In cases such as these, children may also experience post-traumatic stress disorder, or symptoms closely related, and complicated grief.

The facilitation of the grief process is imperative. Studies show that children who have not processed their grief and feelings about their loss have a significant risk for developing depression and anxiety as adults (Kirwin & Hamrin, 2005). In fact, up to one-third of individuals who have experienced grief and bereavement develop depressive symptoms or disorders, and children are also at risk for other psychiatric disorders (Kirwin & Hamrin, 2005).

Besides the mental health issues that may emerge as a result of suppressed grief, the child's developmental growth also may be negatively affected by the stress of bereavement if not effectively addressed (Kirwin & Hamrin, 2005). Mental health professionals must be aware of these risks and assist children in the grieving process in order to help ensure healthy coping skills and developmental growth. Research indicates that bereavement functions as a significant life event that has potential for positive and negative effects on the life span (Muller & Thompson, 2003).

CHILD-CENTERED PLAY THERAPY

CCPT emerged out of the counseling practices and works of Carl Rogers and Virginia Axline. CCPT leans fully on the child for the guiding of the counseling sessions through play, and the play therapist serves as a facilitator rather than a director in the child's growth. In order to do this, the play therapist must fully trust the inner resources of the child and embrace the belief that the child intuitively knows what to explore about him or herself and how to go about processing these ideas and feelings while in the playroom (Guerney, 2001). The child, rather than the problem, is the focus of the play therapist, and CCPT "is a way of being rather than a way of doing" (Landreth, 2002, p. 70). Critical to the effectiveness of CCPT is the play therapist's genuine approach, unconditional positive regard, empathy, and shared relationship with the child (Landreth, 2002). Rather than using words, children are allowed to express themselves and communicate through the language of play wherein toys serve as their vocabulary. In this kind of counseling environment, the play therapist gives voice to the child's patterns of behavior, thoughts, feelings, beliefs, and soulful evolution in the process of discovering self and mastery over troubling situations.

Child-Centered Play Therapy and Grieving Children

CCPT serves as an exceptional modality when working with grieving children because it allows them the lead in gaining a personal understanding of their loss (Green & Connolly, 2009). As is the case for adults, the intense and powerful feelings of grief in children can challenge and threaten to overwhelm their existing coping strategies. Through CCPT, children are able to explore some of these penetrating feelings from a safe distance and in an indirect fashion through the toys (Crenshaw, 2005; Worden, 1996). In male children, this safe emotional distance can be especially helpful if the child comes into the playroom believing he might be considered weak if he expresses his feelings. The toys and open nature of the counseling session provides him with powerful avenues to engage in his own unique grieving process, without violating his sense of masculinity.

Children between the ages of 5 and 7 have acquired pieces of the cognitive abilities needed to understand some of the permanency of death. However, a partial cognitive understanding of finality also makes them especially vulnerable because they still lack the ego strength and social skills to deal with the intensity of feelings surrounding their loss (Worden, 1996). CCPT allows them the opportunity to address their anxiety and conflict without overwhelming their coping capacity (Worden, 1996). CCPT provides ample room for children to go at their own pace, explore feelings as they are able, and lead the way in their own healing and growth.

Child-Centered Play Therapy in the School Setting

Historically, play therapy was viewed as a counseling intervention used only among private practitioners and community mental health professionals. In the 1960s, the presence of school counselors in elementary schools began a shift toward integrating play therapy into the school setting as part of preventive counseling strategies for students (Landreth, 2002). CCPT works in conjunction with one of the child's primary educational goals, which is ultimately to learn. If a child comes into school overloaded with raw, emotional tensions, it is unlikely that such a child will be able to focus energies into classwork and learning. CCPT allows the children to safely address difficult emotions so that their mind is freer to focus on academics. In this way, CCPT is in partnership with administrative goals as well as the child's primary educational interest, which is to learn and grow as a student. CCPT provides a powerful and effective avenue for children to increase their opportunities to learn (Landreth, 2002).

Efficacy of Child-Centered Play Therapy

In addition to the emotional safety provided for grieving children, CCPT has been shown to be an effective counseling intervention for children across all populations who are experiencing emotional and/or behavioral disturbances from any diagnostic category, except in cases of children with autistic and schizophrenic disorders (Guerney, 2001; Landreth, 2002). Research indicates that children who participate in play therapy increase positive coping behaviors while decreasing symptomatic behavior (Bratton & Ray, 2000). Empirical and clinical evidence has shown that client-led practice leads to improvement with adults as well as children for problems both mild and severe (Guerney, 2001). Research has demonstrated CCPT to be a reliable and efficacious modality when working with children, including those experiencing grief.

CASE STUDY: CCPT WITH TOM, A 7-YEAR-OLD BOY

Case History and Background

Tom is a 7-year-old, White, male from a low SES home in a rural Midwestern state. Tom's mother requested that her son begin seeing the school counselor regularly after the recent death of Tom's younger brother, Josh. In addition to Josh, Tom also has two other younger brothers. The mother explained that Josh had been violently killed in a child abuse-related incident at the hands of a trusted caregiver. Since the news of his brother's death, Tom had been acting out aggressively at home, including behaviors of biting, yelling, kicking, and general defiance toward his mother. However, Tom's teacher reported that she had no concerns for the child's behavior or mood at school; his anger and aggression appeared only at home. At the start of counseling, Tom was receiving special reading intervention services at school.

The school counselor began seeing the child for CCPT sessions less than 6 weeks after Tom's loss. Sessions occurred once a week or biweekly for 30 minutes in a playroom located in the child's school. Counseling consisted of 19 sessions that occurred over the course of most of the school year.

Tom's case presents a number of risk factors. Tom's loss is complicated by the nature of the death (unexpected, violent death of a child, betrayal of caregiver) and by the accompanying grief of his mother. Tom's externalizing behaviors at home warranted the need for counseling services, and play therapy served a preventive function for the child's educational interests.

Tom had few external protective factors at the time he began counseling. His family was low SES and not receiving any community support, such as a religious partnership. Additionally, Tom's mother was not attending a parenting group to which she had been referred, and she experienced problems with substance abuse. Live-in boyfriends changed frequently within the family, and the child had little to no contact with his biological father.

While Tom did not have much support from the outside world, he maintained tremendous inner resources and strengths. Tom displayed a vivid imagination, a major goal in the play therapy process, and had awareness of fantasy figures in which he strongly identified with, such as "Sam" and "Bumblebee" from the film "Transformers." Much like "Sam," Tom faced an overwhelming task that was truly alien in nature to him, and like "Bumblebee," he displayed moving loyalty and bravery.

Despite Tom's sadness, he maintained a joyful sense of humor and a childhood enjoyment of the toys in the playroom. Throughout the counseling process, he showed the depth of his character through tremendous courage, resiliency, and a passion to live fully despite a broken, grieving heart. The following are highlights from Tom's experiences in the playroom.

Play Therapy Intervention

Sessions 1–5

Session 1: Tom engaged in exploratory play (general play led by the child's curiosity of the contents of the playroom and the flow of the counseling session), and he quickly built a relationship with the play therapist. The child put on a police badge and stated that he "wants to destroy the whole world with it and not get in trouble."

Discussion: This statement within the context of play represents the child's view of those he sees as having a position of authority as well as the depth of a generalized anger at the world, which provides the play therapist with a powerful image of the child's current place in the grief process.

Session 2: Tom verbalized to the play therapist that his brother "died" and that he had "cried a lot." While telling the play therapist this, the child put the Hulk figure and a dinosaur in the sand tray, explaining that the dinosaur was the Hulk's "pet" and that they must "fight the bad guys." Tom's play intensified when the bad guys killed the pet dinosaur, and the Hulk became angry and tried to get back at them. At the end of the play, the Hulk was also killed by the bad guys.

Discussion: The impact of grief may sometimes create a worldview shift or change in the child's overall perception (Green & Connolly, 2009). Tom communicated a powerful message through the death of the pet, perhaps representing his brother, and later the death of the Hulk, which could represent a variety of important individuals in his life, like his mother or even himself. After a loss, a child may begin to experience the world as unstable and unpredictable, perhaps most especially when another child dies, and may respond with anger and confusion, which can be externalized and expressed through play (Green & Connolly, 2009). Children ages 6 to 9 can begin to reconcile that death is permanent, but they may experience it as spontaneous and contagious: one catches death like one catches a cold (Kirwin & Hamrin, 2005).

Session 3: Tom changed the role of the Hulk from the protector in the previous session to the villain. The Hulk killed a number of dinosaurs, and the Hulk was able "to trick them" several times into thinking that he was dead when he wasn't.

Discussion: The transformation of the Hulk may suggest a change in self-perception, which sometimes occurs in children who have lost a family member (Schoen et al., 2004). The play theme of a central figure who is "tricking" the others into thinking that he is dead becomes a reoccurring play sequence for Tom. In order to cope with feelings surrounding the finality of death, school-aged children may regress to former magical thinking patterns of those more similar to preschool children (Green & Connolly, 2009; Kirwin & Hamrin, 2005). The finality of death is far too frightening, and, therefore, a child creates a world in which it was all just a "trick" or joke in good fun to ease the intensity of the loss.

Session 4: The child reported, which the teacher also verified, that he no longer needs additional reading services at school. Tom spent most of the time talking with the play therapist rather than engaging in a play sequence. He stated that he "misses his little brother" and alluded to feeling guilty for "being mean to him."

Discussion: Guilt is a common reaction and theme among 5- to 9-year-olds experiencing bereavement (Green & Connolly, 2009). Children are naturally ego-central during this age range, and they may believe that as a direct result of some behavior that they did or did not do or because of an interaction they had with the deceased, they are somehow responsible and to blame for the loss of their loved one (Davenport, 1981; Schoen et al., 2004). Regarding Tom's graduation from Title 1 reading services, play therapy has been shown in studies to help children improve their reading performance (Landreth, 2002).

Session 5: Tom revisited a play theme from the initial session. Tom showed the play therapist the police badge and says that police "can do whatever they want," but "the judge can get them in trouble." The child went on to say that "a judge must have a thousand badges."

Discussion: Children will very often return to a previous play sequence or theme throughout the counseling process. This may stem from a child's need to return to more stable waters and go over an important area of need once again. Another reason children will sometimes return to an old play is that while the play is the same, the child has changed, and the focus is now on how the child is feeling and thinking differently about what is occurring in the play. In either one of these scenarios, the play therapist uses clinical judgment to reflect this phenomenon to the child and to allow him to process it. In Tom's case, he is reevaluating his thoughts about those who seem to have power and how they have attained it.

Sessions 6–10

Session 6: Tom again spent most of the session talking with the play therapist rather than engaging in a play sequence. Tom said that he "hates his mom" because it seems like "she just doesn't care." The child acknowledged that he feels mad at her most of the time and "talks back to her." The child mentioned wanting to "feel tough." Following this, the child said again that he "misses his little brother," and he referred to several other family members who have "died." The child agreed that he thinks about death a lot and worries that his mother may die too.

Discussion: Children may experience resentment and anger toward their parents for not being able to protect their sibling from death, especially in cases in which the death was violent or accidental as opposed to a natural death (Worden, 1996). In Tom's case, his anger seemed to emerge from the fear of losing other family members, especially his mother, as well as the fear of possibly not being protected himself. Tom also identified his struggle to feel tough while also feeling pain, and he is beginning to explore the paradox of how these two dichotomies can coexist.

It is also important to note that the child-centered mantra is to allow the child to lead, and the counselor must remain true to this by being flexible during the session, even if that means that the child chooses to move out of play therapy and into more traditional talk therapy as Tom demonstrated in this session. Skilled practitioners must be prepared to smoothly transition between different modes of counseling and through a variety of interventions. Truly, the most child-centered method of therapy is for the counselor to adjust the session to meet the needs of each unique individual, which may include a nondirective approach, guided activities, or alternative theoretical approaches. In many ways, the play therapist can view sessions like this one as a sign of growth and positive change. Movement from play therapy into talk therapy may indicate that the child is more able to overtly and directly address his concerns.

Session 7: Tom continued to revisit significant verbalizations and play themes in this session. He stated again that he is "always mad at his mom" and "likes to talk back to her." Tom engaged in play sequences very similar to those seen in Session 3. This time the good guy "tricked" the bad guys repeatedly by pretending to be dead and then coming back to life.

Discussion: Schoen et al. (2004) explains:

> At approximately 7 to 11 years of age, children are functioning in the concrete logical operational period, according to Piaget. As the child moves through this stage, the reasoning processes become more logical. Yet, the child will still struggle with complex, abstract situations. In addition, the child's egocentrism will cause continued need to validate his or her own thoughts. The impact of this thinking upon how a child of this age views death is an awareness of the finality of death and the fear of how the death personally affects her own life. (p. 145)

Session 8: The child continued the fight between the army men, who were the "good guys," and the Hulk, who was the "bad guy." By the end of the session, the Hulk had killed all except for one army man, and Tom explained that all those who were killed "were brothers." At the end of the session, the Hulk was eventually defeated and killed through a series of detailed events.

Discussion: Pieces of the play are becoming more literal, the death of the "brothers," which indicates the child's growing tolerance for directly confronting his loss and his increasing coping skills.

Session 9: Tom continued the good guy/bad guy play with the army men and the Hulk, this time, with the inclusion of "a boss" for each side. The child pointed to the army men and said, "If their boss is dead, then they fail." At the conclusion of this session, the Hulk was defeated and killed, but two army men survived as well as their boss. During this play, Tom again remarked how he misses his brother and was mean to him.

Discussion: The inclusion of the boss in this session may signify the child's recognition of his dependency on adults, namely his mother, for protection and survival. The child and his environment are inextricably linked to one another, so if a shift occurs within the surrounding environment, a shift also occurs within the child (Hayes, 1994). The two army men that remain alive under the care of the boss may also represent the child's two other surviving brothers.

Session 10: Again, this session presented with the theme of the "good boss" and "bad boss." Tom narrated his play by saying that "the bad boss killed one of the good guys," and the play continued with one of the other good guys attacking the bad guy, who had been the killer. Once the revenge had been exacted with the killer's death, the good guy was then able to bring the fallen good guy "back to life."

Discussion: This play sequence possibly represents the child's deepest wishes for his current situation, and being able to have revenge on the caretaker, or the "bad boss," who had killed his brother, and as well as being able to bring his brother "back to life" again. Many times children ages 2 to 7 believe that death is reversible due to their developmental stage (Schoen et al., 2004). For children who are cognitively able to begin understanding the permanence of death, magical thinking may still occur in order for the child to cope with this frightening reality of absolute finality (Green & Connolly, 2009; Kirwin & Hamrin, 2005). At age 7, Tom is in the process of emerging from one cognitive stage to the next, so his perspective on the permanency of death is more fluid and evolving.

Sessions 11–15

Session 11: The child continued on with play from previous sessions, which involved a fight between the good guys and bad guys. This time, Tom explained that "the good guys are stronger because they have more lives." Whenever a good guy was killed, he referred to the toy and said, "He has one more life," and continued on in the play. Midway through the session, the child had the main bad guy fall over and stated strongly, "He's dead." Immediately following this statement, the child said that he needed to use the bathroom, and he was gone from the session for approximately 10 minutes. Upon returning to the playroom, he did not go back to his play. Instead, he talked with the play therapist about the movie "Lord of the Rings" and how his favorite character, Frodo, "dies in the end."

Discussion: In this session, Tom began to experiment with the idea of death being final and permanent as opposed to previous sessions in which toys are able to "come back to life." He began this process at a safe distance for him by considering a bad guy to be dead, which was very anxiety provoking for him as demonstrated by urgently needing to go to the bathroom after stating, "he's dead." Even when children use symbols to represent their grief, this can create such intensity in emotion, such as anxiety or sadness, that there is a break off in the play (Crenshaw, 2005; Phillips,

1994). Even though Tom did not return to his play, he continued to go deeper into the significance of death of positive figures, like "Frodo." Fantasy can serve as a powerful vehicle through which the child begins to practice releasing control and experiencing intense emotions (Davenport, 1981).

Session 12: Tom stretched his work from the previous session further. Tom began by making a star out of play-doh, and he identified it as "a shooting star." Tom said that if he saw a shooting star, he would "wish to be with all his brothers." Tom went on to talk about how he had visited "the place where Josh is buried." Looking back at the star, Tom explained that he "can't wish for Josh to come back" because he "won't come back."

Discussion: Tom's very significant verbalizations in this session demonstrate how play can facilitate direct grief work. Through the play in the previous sessions, Tom experimented with his ideas and feelings about the finality of death so that he was then able to connect the process from the play directly with his own grief experience. Tom achieved this at his own pace and in his own way without prompting from the play therapist.

Session 13: Good guy/bad guy fighting play themes again emerged. Again, when toys were knocked over, representing that they had been "killed," the child requested to go to the bathroom. Once back in the playroom, the child said, "I miss Josh—he is dead." After this statement, the child went to the doctor's kit, removed the stethoscope, and held it to his chest. Listening to his chest, the child said, "I can hear my heart beating—thump, thump."

Discussion: Tom's play of listening to his heartbeat may symbolize his understanding that while his brother is dead, he is still alive. Research indicates that children who lose a sibling, as opposed to a parent, have a heightened sense of personal death awareness, which can result in phobia, separation anxiety, somatic complaints, and/or risk-taking behaviors (Worden, 1996).

Session 14: Tom's play was significantly less intense. The child continued with the good guy/bad guy "battle." During the play, Tom pointed to one of the toys and said "they thought he was a good guy but he tricked them and he is really a bad guy." After this, the child requested to go to the bathroom as he had done in previous sessions.

Discussion: Again, the link between play and reality is very clear: a trusted caregiver turned out to truly be a "bad guy." While the play appears less intense than previous sessions, Tom is still working hard to grapple with these frightening and troubling thoughts that arouse such powerful anxiety in him that it creates a physiological reaction.

Session 15: The play themes remained consistent with the exception of substituting different toys and figures to serve in the roles of the play sequence. Tom revisited the theme of characters "playing tricks" on the opposing side into thinking that they are dead when they were not.

Discussion: As mentioned previously, a return to old play themes does not necessarily indicate a regression in the counseling process. The play therapist continues to reflect the child's many thoughts and feelings about this significant play as well as the changes occurring in the sequence, even if these changes are very minimal.

Sessions 16–19
Session 16: The child engaged in a new play sequence. He got out the disc gun and began to shoot the foam discs around the room. Eventually, the child turned the gun so that it was facing his chest, and then he shot the foam discs at himself a couple of times. The child's affect seemed curious and focused while shooting himself.

Discussion: It is important for counselors and play therapists to remain aware that some children who have lost a loved one may express suicidal ideation and experience a desire to die; they believe that it is a way for them to be reunited with the deceased rather than wanting to die. This is different than suicidal ideations associated with depressive symptoms and/or guilt surrounding the loss (Kirwin & Hamrin, 2005; Worden, 1996). In Tom's case, his mood changed the context of this play to one of curiosity rather than morbidity. Children between the ages of 2 and 7 have an awareness and knowledge about their own bodies and may wonder about what it feels like to die (Schoen et al., 2004). Because this was the only time Tom engaged in this kind of play over the course of treatment and because he did not verbalize wanting to be with his brother in heaven or display any risk-taking behaviors, this shooting play was likely connected with the child's curiosity about the physical process of death and did not represent suicidal ideation.

Session 17: Tom continued the play theme of figures coming back to life. Toward the end of the session, the main good guy figure was "killed" and did not come back to life.

Discussion: Sometimes the timing of a very significant play or verbalization is just as important as the play itself. Tom almost always reserved a final death in a play sequence within the last 5 minutes of the session. Children will many times wait to do their most powerful and intense work at the end of a session because they know that the session will be coming to an end, and it gives them a sense of safety knowing that they don't have to sit with such intense feelings for very long. The timing becomes a consistent and secure container for them. This once again shows how important it is for the play therapist to move at the pace of the child since only the child is able to know how much he is capable of handling in any particular moment.

Session 18: Similar play sequences continued. During his play, Tom talked about his relationship with his mother by saying that they "don't fight anymore" and that now he's "being really good." The child had several play disruptions during the session. During one particular play disruption, Tom referred to a recent dream he had experienced. He explained, "I had a bad dream where I was a robot sent to destroy Tom." He went on to say that he "thought it was weird that it had my name" (referring to being sent to destroy himself). The child explained, "it was scary because I had no control over myself because I was a robot, but in the end, I became good and I saved Tom instead and I was really excited."

Discussion: The child's powerful and metaphorical dream may deeply symbolize Tom's internal struggle of not feeling in control of his life and possibly blaming himself for all the negative stressors that have occurred, for which, he believes he should be punished. The dream likely reflects the discovery and excitement of being able to regain his sense of a positive self-perception. In fact, around 30% of grieving children experience sleep disturbances during the first year of bereavement (Worden, 1996).

Session 19: Tom was aware that this would be the termination session, and his play changed significantly from previous sessions. The child arranged the Hulk figure facing four army men, with a mountain figurine behind the army men in the sand tray. On top of the mountain, Tom placed a gold stone, which he explained that army men "had to protect" because they "get power from it" (referring to the gold stone). Before the battle between the army men and the Hulk began, Tom pointed to the army men and stated that "they're not going to die" even though the Hulk "was very mad." The Hulk came very close to reaching the stone several times, but every time the army men were able to fight off the Hulk and keep the stone protected until, finally, the Hulk was "dead."

Discussion: Tom's play in the final session mirrored the rebuilding of his faith in being able to keep things that are most precious protected and safe. Through the work of his play, Tom discovered that he could indeed protect the source from which he draws his inner strength and power, even when faced with the monster of fear and grief. Following termination, Tom's mother reported that he no longer displayed any aggressive or acting out behaviors at home and their relationship had significantly improved.

IMPLICATIONS FOR COUNSELORS AND PLAY THERAPISTS

Tom's case and grief work through CCPT depicts both the power and importance of this therapeutic intervention with bereaved children. Play therapists, counselors, including school counselors, and all other mental health professionals must advocate for both preventative and intervention services to meet the needs of this population of children.

CCPT is an intervention that requires special training, education, and supervision. While counselors and other mental health professionals may practice play therapy, the Association for Play Therapy provides the national certification of a Registered Play Therapist and Registered Play Therapist Supervisor. Best and ethical practice calls for training in play therapy before implementing this intervention with clients. Some educational resources for beginning and experienced play therapists specifically regarding CCPT include, *Play Therapy: The Art of the Relationship* by Garry Landreth (2002), *Child-Centered Play Therapy* by Rise VanFleet, Andrea Sywulak, Cynthia Sniscak, and Louise Guerney (2010), and *Child-Centered Play Therapy: A Practical Guide to Developing Therapeutic Relationships with Children* by Nancy Cochran, William Nordling, and Jeff Cochran (2010).

There are several other issues to consider when working with parents of grieving children. Counselors should encourage families to allow children to take part in the grief process, which may involve attending funerals or discussing the child's feelings and memories about the lost loved one. Many parents believe that they are helping to protect their child by not exposing them to bereavement rituals when, in fact, ignoring the pain and grief that occurs within the child, and limiting these expressions of grief is counterproductive and isolating for the child (Schoen et al., 2004).

Counselors should also teach parents how children cope with death through their play. Many children have been observed playing only minutes after learning of the death of a close loved one, and such play may closely mirror the manner of death or appear completely removed, disconnected, and perhaps even insensitive to the current situation. While this sort of behavior may disturb some parents, counselors can take the opportunity to educate and normalize this coping strategy for adults involved in the child's life (Schoen et al., 2004).

Counselors must also remain aware of "red flags" and of serious emotional and behavioral disorders in some bereaved children. Grieving children who experience prolonged somatic symptoms, constantly talking about the deceased, marked aggressiveness, excessive anxiety, ongoing sleep problems, significant social withdrawal, major academic regression, persistent guilt and self-blame, self-destructive behaviors, and suicidal ideation may be experiencing more severe mental health issues (Worden,

1996). Counselors working with this population are advised to seek training and supervision so that they are able to identify these risk factors and take appropriate steps in intervention.

Play therapists and counselors should also remain aware of developmental and cognitive components that affect the grief process. Interventions that are appropriate for the child's developmental level, like play therapy, are more effective and well suited to facilitate the therapeutic process (Parr & Ostrovsky, 1991). When play therapists understand the current cognitive structure of the children and recognize their developmental experience of death, the counselor gains powerful insight into the play of the child, and facilitative responses acquire greater depth and significance (Fall, 1997).

Finally, it is essential that mental health professionals who work with this population allow the bereaved children to grieve at their own pace and in their own way. Processing grief requires great amounts of emotional energy and can very often be a stressful experience (Kirwin & Hamrin, 2005). Play allows the child to piece together the confusion of the situation as well as to process troubling feelings, which may accompany the situation from a safe distance (Landreth, 2002; Schoen et al., 2004).

Tom's story provides us with a touching look into the deep struggle children face when they are confronted with the frightening force of death. From within the playroom, Tom reminds us of the beauty found in regaining trust, faith, and hope in living. Through the powerful message translated by simple toys, play therapists have the extraordinary honor of witnessing and experiencing the child's world of grief.

REFERENCES

Bratton, S., & Ray, D. (2000). What research shows about play therapy. *International Journal of Play Therapy, 9*(1), 47–88.

Crenshaw, D. A. (2005). Clinical tools to facilitate treatment of childhood traumatic grief. *Omega: Journal of Death & Dying, 51*(3), 239–255.

Davenport, D. S. (1981). A closer look at the "healthy" grieving process. *Personnel and Guidance Journal, 59*(6), 332–336.

Fall, M. (1997). From stages to categories: A study of children's play in play therapy sessions. *International Journal of Play Therapy, 6*(1), 1–21.

Green, E. J., & Connolly, M. E. (2009). Jungian family sandplay with bereaved children: Implications for play therapists. *International Journal of Play Therapy, 18*(2), 84–98.

Guerney, L. (2001). Child-centered play therapy. *International Journal of Play Therapy, 10*(2), 13–31.

Hayes, R. L. (1994). The legacy of Lawrence Kohlberg: Implications for counseling and human development. *Journal of Counseling & Development, 72,* 261–267.

Kirwin, K. M., & Hamrin, V. (2005). Decreasing the risk of complicated bereavement and future psychiatric disorders in children. *Journal of Child and Adolescent Psychiatric Nursing, 18*(1), 62–78.

Landreth, G. L. (2002). *Play therapy: The art of the relationship* (2nd ed.). New York: Brunner-Routledge.

Muller, E. D, & Thompson, C. L. (2003). The experience of grief after bereavement: A phenomenological study with implications for mental health counseling. *Journal of Mental Health Counseling, 25*(3), 183–203.

Parr, G. D., & Ostrovsky, M. (1991). The role of moral development in deciding how to counsel children and adolescents. *School Counselor, 39*(1), 14–20.

Phillips, R. D. (1994). A developmental perspective on emotions in play therapy. *International Journal of Play Therapy, 3*(2), 1–19.

Schoen, A. A., Burgoyne, M., & Schoen, S. F. (2004). Are the developmental needs of children in America adequately addressed during the grief process? *Journal of Instructional Psychology, 31*(2), 143–148.

Worden, J. W. (1996). *Children and grief: When a parent dies.* New York: Guilford Press.

15

Emotional Concerns: When Life Doesn't Feel "Right"

RACHEL M. HOFFMAN

EMOTIONAL CONCERNS IN ADOLESCENTS AND YOUNG ADULTS

In this chapter, the author will discuss issues related to the treatment of emotional disorders in adolescent and young adult males. The conditions discussed in this chapter are anxiety disorders, mood disorders, body image and eating disorders, self-injurious behaviors, and suicide-related concerns. Historically, there has been a tendency for these disorders to be underdiagnosed in males. Contributing to the difficulty in identifying these disorders in males is a complex clinical presentation; often times, the various emotional disorders discussed in this chapter may present differently in males than in females.

There are a number of antecedents to emotional disorders in adolescents. Adolescents are routinely affected by their environment, and thus, it is not uncommon for adolescents to experience distress as a result of environmental stressors. Additional precipitants to emotional concerns include family, cultural, and biological predispositions. In the following sections, the author will review key contributors to emotional distress in adolescent and young adult males. A case example and discussion is provided to highlight presenting concerns and associated treatment.

ANXIETY DISORDERS

There are several anxiety-related disorders that are noteworthy in adolescents. These disorders include posttraumatic stress disorder (PTSD), obsessive-compulsive disorder (OCD), social phobia, specific phobia, and generalized anxiety disorder (GAD). In general, anxiety-related disorders are associated with difficulties in academic performance, impaired social relationships, and long-term impaired emotional health (Kendall, Furr, & Podell, 2010).

Anxiety-related disorders are the most prevalent mental health disorders among children and adolescents (Cartwright-Hatton, McNicol, & Doubleday, 2006). As is the case with most disorders, the development and clinical presentation of these disorders tend to differ across genders. Male adolescents and young adults may experience unique forms of anxiety-related problems. Anxiety problems in adolescent males tend to be associated with peer difficulties, family issues, and financial problems (Smith, Buzi, & Welnman, 2001). These interpersonal stressors can contribute to the development of disorders such as GAD or OCD.

Although traumatic reactions can develop from experiences such as abuse, neglect, witnessing violence, or being involved in a disaster, daily stressors may also contribute to posttraumatic symptoms. Penning, Bhagwanjee, and Govender (2010) found that repetitive stressful events (e.g., bullying) are related to PTSD and trauma-related symptomology in adolescent males. It is important that mental health professionals are cognizant of this associated risk so that proper interventions can be implemented to help mitigate potential traumatic situations.

Young adults diagnosed with anxiety disorders may also present with other comorbid conditions (e.g., ADHD, depression; Kendall et al., 2010). The most common comorbid pattern in adolescents is depression and anxiety (Essau, 2003). Once present, anxiety disorders in adolescents will rarely remit without treatment (Pahl & Barret, 2010). Effective intervention is necessary to treat anxiety-related concerns and avoid subsequent problems in later life, as research (e.g., Kendall et al., 2010) has found that anxiety disorders in adolescence increases the risk for comorbidity and psychopathology in adulthood.

MOOD DISORDERS

Depression in adolescents represents a complex disorder that causes serious impairment across several areas of functioning (i.e., academic, social, and physical; Jacobson & Mufson, 2010). The *Diagnostic and Statistical Manual of Mental Disorders, 4th edition* (*DSM-IV-TR*; American Psychiatric Association, 2000) identified that adolescent depression is most frequently characterized by depressed or irritable mood. Depression in adolescents also varies from depression in adults in that depressed adolescents may present with mood swings (i.e., intermittent periods of relative euthymia followed by periods of depressed mood; Jacobson & Mufson, 2010).

Research estimates are that depression affects approximately 2.5% of children and up to 8.3% of adolescents (Birmaher et al., 1996). Although the cause of depression is typically multifaceted, interpersonal conflict tends to play a significant role in the development of adolescent depressive symptoms (Jacobson & Mufson, 2010). Depressed adolescents may have experienced negative psychosocial events, such as family conflict, physical illness, and loss of friends (Lewinsohn, Allen, Seeley, & Gotlib, 1999).

Adolescent males may be less likely to report depression than females; however, there are serious risks associated with the depressive disorders in males (e.g., suicide, substance abuse, illegal activity; Pruitt, 2007). Untreated depression in adolescent males can have serious long-term consequences, such as impaired social interactions, poor academic performance, and suicide. Mental health professionals must be cognizant of the various ways in which depression might manifest in adolescent populations.

Male adolescents experiencing depression also tend to demonstrate aggressive conduct-related problems (Bardone, Moffitt, Caspi, Dickson, Stanton, & Silva, 1998). Oppositional defiant disorders have been shown to predict the later development of both anxiety and depressive disorders (Burke, Loeber, Lahey, & Rathouz, 2005). Male adolescents who are involved in interpersonal relationships marked by violence may also be at risk for the development of depressive disorders (Howard, Qi Wang, & Yang, 2008). It is noteworthy that, among male adolescents, there appears to be a thin line between externalizing behaviors (e.g., violent acting out) and internalizing behaviors (e.g., depression, sad mood). Male adolescents experiencing depression may be more likely to act out in physically aggressive ways, especially in situations where the depression is left untreated. Adolescent depression has been shown to be a risk factor for adult antisocial personality disorder in males (Loeber, Burke, & Lahey, 2002). Clearly, the risk of interpersonal violence toward self and others is related to symptoms of depression. Thus, it is important that mental health professionals have the ability to recognize signs of depression in male adolescents and refer these individuals for the appropriate counseling treatments.

Recent research (e.g., Uddin et al., 2010) has examined potential genetic differences in the development of depression in males and females. Although there is not one clear pathway for the development of depressive symptoms, it appears that depression can be caused by a complex interaction between biological and environmental factors. Effective assessment and timely intervention of depressive disorders are necessary to avoid later adult psychopathology.

BODY IMAGE AND EATING DISORDERS

Body image and eating disorders are generally considered to be issues that exclusively effect females. In the past, body image research has been related to women and thinness (Bergeron & Tylka, 2007). However, an emerging body of research (e.g., Furnham & Calman, 1998; McCabe, Ricciardelli, & Karantzas, 2010) has underscored that body image issues affect males. Prevalence estimates have suggested that males account for approximately 10% to 15% of eating-related disorders (Carlat & Camargo, 1991).

Researchers (e.g., Leit, Pope, & Gray, 2001; Pope, Olivardia, Gruber, & Borowiecki, 1999) have underscored that the cultural norm for the ideal male physique has become increasingly muscular. Because body image concerns tend to be related to muscularity (as opposed to thinness in females), it seems logical that body image issues in men might present differently than those in females. Body image issues in males tend to result in males viewing themselves as inadequately muscular (McCabe, Ricciardelli, Sitaram, & Mikhail, 2006).

Muscle dysmorphia (MD), a subtype of body dysmorphic disorder, is defined as a preoccupation with a lack of muscularity that results in clinically sufficient distress (Pope, Gruber, Choi, Olivardia, & Phillips, 1997). The core characteristic of MD is a preoccupation with becoming leaner and more muscular combined with a marked perceptual disturbance (i.e., seeing oneself as thin and weak despite evidence to the contrary; Hildebrandt, Schlundt, Langenbucher, & Chung, 2006). Preoccupation with a muscular physique may begin at a young age. In a study of the preadolescent and adolescent males, Baghurst, Carlston, Wood, and Wyatt (2007) found that preadolescent and adolescent males preferred physically larger action figures with a physically large physique.

Although eating disorders and body image concerns affect males, there is a clear distinction between these conditions among males and females. Boys tend to be more preoccupied with muscle development and, thus, may be more likely to endorse the use of anabolic steroids, excessive exercise, or other high-risk behaviors. Eating disorders in a clinical sample of adolescent males were related to anxiety and may be related to greater externalizing symptoms (e.g., drug abuse, violence, impulsivity; Zaitsoff & Grilo, 2010). Additionally, Carlat, Camargo, and Herzog (1997) found an association between homosexuality/bisexuality and eating-related concerns (especially bulimia nervosa).

Programs that promote healthy body image and self-esteem are likely good options to help prevent image-related concerns before they develop. However, healthy body image programs for males have been implemented with mixed results, and it appears that prevention programs for females do not work with males (McCabe et al., 2010). It is important that mental health professionals consider the unique characteristics of body image concerns and eating disorders in males when developing programs for promoting positive body image.

SELF-INJURIOUS BEHAVIORS

The phenomenon of deliberate, self-inflicted, self-injurious behavior has received considerable attention in scholarly literature, as well as the media, and popular press. Nonsuicidal self-injury (NSSI) is a type of self-injury that is not suicidal in intent, but does include purposely destroying body tissue. Yates (2004) described self-injury as a "self-inflicted, direct, socially unacceptable destruction or altercation of body tissue that occurs in the absence of conscious suicidal intent or pervasive developmental disorder" (p. 38).

Research estimates have suggested that 1% to 4% of the general population, and 21% to 66% of clinical samples engage in NSSI (Darche, 1990; DiClemente, Ponton, & Hartley, 1991). Among adolescents, research suggests that between 13% and 15% of adolescents have engaged in at least one act of deliberate self-injury (Ross & Heath, 2002; Laye-Gindhu & Schonert-Reichl, 2005). The secretive nature of NSSI may make it particularly difficult to identity deliberate self-injury in adolescent populations. For example, Evans et al. (2004) found that 20% of adolescents with a history of self-harm reported that no one knew about the behavior.

Early conceptualizations of NSSI identified the behavior as a female phenomenon (e.g., Favazza & Conterio, 1988). Although a limited amount of research has examined the male experience of NSSI, there are several noteworthy findings. Using a sample of undergraduate college students, Gratz and Chapman (2007) found that males and females engaged in self-injury at comparable rates.

Similar to the results of Gratz and Chapman (2007), in a sample of adolescents receiving treatment at an inpatient psychiatric facility, Nock and Prinstein (2004) found that approximately 82% of adolescents had engaged in at least one episode of NSSI, with no significant gender differences present between the rate of occurrence in males and females. Similarly, in a study of 428 homeless adolescents, 69% of the sample had engaged in NSSI on at least one occasion, with no significant differences between the rate of DSI between male and female participants (Tyler, Whitbeck, Hoyt, & Johnson, 2003).

Although previous research has identified gender differences in NSSI, a limited amount of research has examined the individual meaning of NSSI in the lives of women and men (Yates, 2004). In a study of 88 male psychiatric inpatients, White, Leggett, and Beech (1999) found that approximately 45% of participants reported a history of NSSI. Despite increases in the knowledge base of NSSI, the male experience remains a largely unexplored phenomenon. In men, NSSI may be less acknowledged, accepted, and understood than it is in women (Taylor, 2003).

It is worth noting that bias in research may prevent estimates of NSSI from being accurately represented in the male population. Basic methodological issues (e.g., defining NSSI as only self-cutting) may prevent NSSI from accurately being studied in male populations. Bowen and John (2001) described issues related to methodology biases in NSSI research, such as gender differences in willingness to seek treatment, ability to seek help, and reactions of others and society in general to the presence of the NSSI.

Understanding possible triggers to NSSI specific to males may be important for effective treatment of the behavior. Gratz and Chapman (2007) found that physical abuse and emotional dysregulation reliably distinguished men with NSSI behaviors from men without these behaviors. Similarly, in a study of male psychiatric inpatients, White et al. (1999) found that approximately 22% of self-injuring participants reported a history of sexual or physical abuse.

Compared to females, males may also display differences in the execution of NSSI. In a study of the differences between males and females who engaged in NSSI, males were found to injure themselves more frequently per day, they experienced more pain during acts of NSSI, and they took less care of their wounds and concealed them less than females (Claes, Vandereycken, & Vertommen, 2007). Men who engaged in self-injury were more likely to make suicide attempts rather than suicide gestures (Nock & Kessler, 2006). Males may also display high-risk comorbid self-endangering behavior, such as driving recklessly and abusing prescribed medication (Claes et al., 2007). These differences may suggest that males and females with NSSI may require different forms of treatment and interventions.

Although males may demonstrate unique NSSI behaviors, they may also share some commonalties with females who engage in NSSI. For example, Claes et al. (2007) found that both males and females endorsed engaging in NSSI for reasons related to tension relief as the most important function of NSSI.

SUICIDE: RISK ASSESSMENT AND PREVENTION

Suicide risk in adolescents is a nationwide public health concern. Of all the conditions that affect adolescents, suicide is perhaps the most concerning due to the life-or-death consequences of the action. Identification of risk factors for adolescent suicide can be difficult, and a thorough assessment is necessary to evaluate a client's risk. There are numerous factors that are implicated in the development of adolescent suicidal ideation. Although a detailed discussion of the numerous factors is beyond the scope of this chapter, the following paragraphs will highlight a few key contributors to suicidal ideation in adolescent males.

In a study of male adolescent suicide completers, Portzky, Audenaert, and van Heeringen (2005) found that in all of the cases, the individual had been diagnosed with one or more mental disorder(s) at the time of their death, and almost half of them were diagnosed with personality disorders. Other risk factors identified in this study included familial psychopathology, exposure to suicidal behavior, social problems, stressful life events, previous self-harm, childhood and/or adolescent difficulties, and lack of psychiatric care (Portzky et al., 2005). Other research (e.g., Wunderlich, Bronisch, Wittchen, & Carter, 2001) has found that alcohol use is a significant contributing factor to adolescent male suicidality.

Risk factors for suicide may differ among male and female adolescents. Becker and Grilo (2007) found an association between drug abuse and suicidality in male adolescents; this same association was not observed among female adolescents. Bearman and Moody (2004) found that having a friend who committed suicide increased the likelihood of suicidal ideation and attempts among male adolescents.

Concerns related to body image may predict suicidal behavior in male adolescents. Whetstone, Morrissey, and Cummings (2007) found that adolescent males who perceived their body as overweight or underweight were significantly more likely to have suicidal thoughts and behaviors compared to those without such body image issues. This is an important finding as it demonstrates that body image concerns can negatively influence male adolescents' well-being. Negative body image can contribute to feelings of suicidality among adolescent males.

Suicide is a complex situation, and there are number of contributing factors to this public health problem. It is worth noting, however, that concerns related to sexual identity are thought to have a disproportional contribution to suicide rates in adolescents. The process of questioning one's sexuality can result in significant distress for adolescents. In a nationally representative survey, Russell and Joyner (2001) found that adolescents with a same-sex orientation were more than twice as likely to attempt suicide. The increased suicide risk for gay adolescents can be attributed to the psychosocial distress associated with being gay (Kitts, 2005). How others react to a youth's sexuality may also contribute to the development of suicidal ideation and suicidal behaviors (Savin-Williams & Ream, 2003).

INTERVENTIONS

Adolescent clients' needs should be addressed in an understanding environment, exploring constructions of gender identity with attention paid to realistic societal and cultural demands (Bowen & John, 2001). In some cases, such as with NSSI, adolescents may be hesitant to disclose what they might consider a *female* behavior because they may fear being seen as feminine (Bowen & John, 2001). Men who self-injure may benefit from support groups, or other services designed to help them realize that males do engage in self-injury, and that they are not alone in their experiences (Taylor, 2003).

In situations where a gender bias for the disorder does exist, mental health professionals should take steps to determine the function of the behavior for the male client. Anorexia nervosa, where 90% of those diagnosed are women (APA, 2000), may offer a suitable example. Soban (2006) suggested that the successful treatment of anorexia nervosa in males is to regard it as its own disorder with treatment that addresses the gender bias that surrounds it. A similar approach with other conditions discussed in this chapter might be a helpful alternative to work with adolescent clients.

There are a number of different treatment approaches that have demonstrated effectiveness with the conditions discussed in this chapter. Cognitive behavioral therapy has demonstrated effectiveness in the treatment of anxiety-related concerns (Kendall et al., 2010; Pahl & Barrett, 2010) and the treatment of depression (Weersing & Brent, 2010). Dialectical behavior therapy has shown promise in the treatment of chronically suicidal adolescents (Miller, Rathus, & Linehan, 2007) and the treatment of eating-related concerns (Telch, Agras, & Linehan, 2001).

Motivational interviewing may be effective in the treatment of NSSI (Kress & Hoffman, 2008) and its demonstrated strong outcomes in the treatment of eating disorders (Tantillo, Nappa Bitter, & Adams, 2001; Treasure & Ward, 1997; Wilson & Schlam, 2004). Another externalizing approach to treatment, narrative therapy, may also be helpful in the treatment of NSSI (Hoffman & Kress, 2008).

Family treatment can be a helpful adjunct to individual counseling services. Family treatment has demonstrated promise in the treatment of depression in adolescent males (Pruitt, 2007), the treatment of anxiety disorders (Kendall et al., 2010), body image and eating disorders (Eisler, Dar, Hodes, Russel, Dodge, & Grange, 2000), and nonsuicidal self-injury (Trepal, Wester, & MacDonald, 2006).

CASE STUDY: HELPING JAKE MOVE OUT OF THE DARK

Client Demographics and Presenting Issues

Jake is a 17-year-old Caucasian male who presented for outpatient counseling services due to problems following rules at home and poor grades in school. Jake currently lives with his mother, stepfather, and 7-year-old sister, Mandy. Per his mother's report, Jake has recently been "temperamental" and "refuses to follow even the smallest direction." Mom reported that Jake is "out of control" and "spends all of his time in his room on that stupid computer." Mom also voiced her concern regarding Jake's recent "dark" behavior, stating that he has recently refused to wear anything but black clothes and only listens to "gothic" music. Mom stated that Jake and his stepfather, Simon, have had a "testy" relationship for the past 5 years. Mom stated that when she and Jake's stepfather married 9 years ago, "everything was fine for a while." Mom reported that Jake's biological dad lives in Atlanta, and Jake has very limited contact with him. Mom estimated that it has been several months since Jake last talked to his father on the telephone.

Despite the near 90-degree heat, Jake presented for the initial counseling session wearing a black hooded sweatshirt and long black pants. He presented as somewhat guarded and reported his reason for attending the session as "I'm trying to get my nosy mother off my back." Jake described his relationship with his mother as "a joke," stating that she clearly favors his sister Mandy because, "she's Simon's kid." Jake stated, "All Simon does is threaten me with 'juvie'; I wish he would just send me away and get it over with." When asked about his relationship with his biological father, Jake stated that he "doesn't care about him" and reported, "He's got a new family now, so he doesn't really care about his weirdo son." Jake reported that he feels like an "outsider," and stated that he does not feel love or supported by his family, stating, "no one gets me."

As the initial session progressed, Jake gradually became more forthcoming with information and confided that he and his girlfriend of 6 months had broken up within the last week because "I can't keep anything good in my life." Jake became tearful when discussing the breakup and admitted to frequent recurrent suicidal thoughts since the breakup. He stated, "I can't believe I messed it up. I really thought she was the one, ya know?" Jake reported that he has never attempted suicide in the past and reported that he did not have a plan to kill himself. Jake stated, "I just kinda wished I'd go to sleep and never wake up again." Jake did admit that he engages in intentional self-injury, stating that he first started cutting himself at about the age of 13 and has cut "off and on" since then. Jake reported that he typically cuts his upper thigh or stomach when he is angry. Jake also reported that he "likes to carve words" into his stomach and legs. Jake estimated that he currently cuts "a couple times a month, usually after fighting with my parents." Jake stated that his last episode of NSSI was 2 days ago when he carved his ex-girlfriend's name into his stomach. Jake stated that his mother had found out about the cuts a couple years ago, after a particularly deep cut on his leg required several stitches. Jake stated, "Mom totally freaked out and made me promise that I'd never do it again." Jake stated that his mother is not aware of his current self-injury and stated, "She'd kick me out of the house if she knew."

Intervention

During the initial session with Jake, the counselor obtained the following information as recommended by Kress (2003) and White, Trepal-Wollenzier, and Nolan (2002): a thorough biopsychosocial history and detailed mental status exam, information about the frequency and duration of the self-injury, additional information about past suicide attempts, cultural or religious factors, comorbid *DSM-IV-TR* diagnoses, and the history and level of medical attention required for wound care. Because of the client's expressed suicidal ideation, a more detailed risk assessment was conducted (see Hoffman & Kress, 2010, for a detailed discussion for risk assessment with NSSI).

After conducting a detailed assessment, the counselor then clarified with the client what he wanted to focus his attention on in treatment. The client reported that he felt "sad" since his breakup with his girlfriend, and he noted that he would like to "feel better." The client also indicated that he wanted to address his poor relationship with his mother and stepfather and, although he vacillated between wanting a good relationship with them and wanting to blame them for his problems, he did report that he was committed to accepting some responsibility for developing a good relationship with them.

It became apparent that relational problems within the family were contributing to the client's feelings of despair. It was also apparent that involving the client's mother and stepfather in treatment would help improve family communication patterns. In this case, the client was engaging in self-injury and had not disclosed that to his parents. In cases involving self-injury, counselors who work with adolescents must consider their adolescent client's confidentiality rights while simultaneously appreciating the parents' right to be apprised of their children's clinically related developments (Hoffman & Kress, 2010). Ultimately, it was beneficial to help the client feel empowered to disclose to his family, in session, that he had been using self-injury as a way to cope with his overwhelming feelings. Although the client initially did not want to disclose this information to his mother and stepfather, he reported being surprised at their understanding response. It was also helpful in this case to provide psychoeducation about self-injury to the family.

It may be helpful to approach clients with an element of curiosity, and a recognition that they may not be ready to, or want to, stop injuring, as this might prove helpful in facilitating open conversations related to self-injury (Kress & Hoffman, 2008). In this particular case, it was helpful for the client to not impose her viewpoints on the "whys" of the client behaviors, but rather, to approach the client as if he were the expert in his particular situation. The client reported feeling uncomfortable in his day-to-day interactions with his family, and he admitted to daily feelings of depression. In this case, the client was willing to work on his feelings of depression, and once these feelings had been identified, he was quite interested in engaging in the counseling process. As mentioned earlier, much of male adolescent dysfunction can be attributed to difficult interpersonal relations, and in Jake's case, it's clear that these issues had precipitated his current sad mood.

In my work with adolescents, I believe that it is important to work from a strength-based treatment approach. I generally incorporate elements of narrative therapy and motivational interviewing to help the client develop personal agency and empowerment as we collaboratively move toward the treatment process. In working with adolescents who self-injure, there is often an idea that the client must be taught by the counselor to apply cognitive and behavioral skills to stop engaging in the NSSI (Muehlenkamp, 2006). This approach may fail to consider the unique strengths and contributions of the client and may alienate the client by providing little opportunity for his preferences to be integrated into the counseling process (Hoffman & Kress, 2008).

Outcome

Jake began outpatient treatment at a frequency of once per week. Initially, the counselor met with Jake individually and, at Session 3, began involving his mother and stepfather in the counseling session. Both parents reported concerns about Jake's "dark" behavior, but they expressed a willingness to engage in counseling. Jake initially did not believe that his mother and stepfather would be receptive to hearing his thoughts and feelings, and, when he realized that they were committed to helping him, he began to demonstrate less acting out and irritable behaviors. Jake still struggled with allowing his stepfather into his life; however, he was willing to spend time with his mother and stepfather together, which represented a significant improvement compared to past interactions. Through the use of narrative therapy, Jake was able to externalize his feelings of depression, and throughout the duration of counseling, he experienced a decrease in self-injury. The NSSI behavior did not completely cease; however, the client reported feeling that he had more control over the behavior.

The client and his family participated in a total of 11 counseling sessions. At the completion of treatment, Jake was doing better in school and had experienced an increase in his social interactions with peers. Perhaps one of the most positive events happened when the client joined the school's art club. Interacting with his peers around a common shared interest (i.e., art) had a positive effect on Jake, and the use of art served as a healthy coping mechanism for dealing with periods of stress.

FURTHER READING

Unfortunately, the literature on emotional disorders in adolescent and young adult males remains scant. It is important for mental health professionals to appreciate the gender differences in clinical presentation. For additional reading, it is recommended that the reader consult the following references: Englar-Carlson and Stevens (2006) for a review of general counseling strategies in men; Weisz and Kazdin (2010) for evidenced-based practices in the treatment of child and adolescent concerns; Miller et al. (2007) for strategies for working with suicidal adolescents; and Muehlenkamp (2006) for information related to evidence-based practices in the treatment of NSSI.

REFERENCES

American Psychiatric Association. (2000). *Diagnostic and statistical manual of mental disorders* (4th ed. Text Revision). Washington, DC: Author.

Baghurst, T., Carlston, D., Wood, J., Wyatt, F. B. (2007). Preadolescent male perceptions of action figure physiques. *Journal of Adolescent Health, 41,* 613–615.

Bardone, M. A., Moffitt, T. E., Caspi, A., Dickson, N., Stanton, W. R., & Silva, P. A. (1998). Adult physical health outcomes of adolescent girls with conduct disorder, depression, and anxiety. *Journal of American Academy of Child Psychiatry, 37,* 594–601.

Bearman, P. S., & Moody, J. (2004). Suicide and friendships among American adolescents. *American Journal of Public Health, 94,* 89–95.

Becker, D. F., & Grilo, C. M. (2007). Prediction of suicidality and violence in hospitalized adolescents: Comparisons by sex. *Canadian Journal of Psychiatry, 52,* 572–580.

Bergeron, D., & Tylka, T. L. (2007). Support for the uniqueness of body dissatisfaction from drive for muscularity among men. *Body Image, 4,* 288–295.

Birmaher, B., Ryan, N. D., Williamson, D. E., Brent, D. A., Kaufman, J., Dahl, R., et al. (1996). Childhood and adolescent depression: A review of the past ten years: Part I. *Journal of the Academy of Child and Adolescent Psychiatry, 37,* 594–601.

Bowen, A. C. L, & John, A. M. H. (2001). Gender differences in presentation and conceptualization of adolescent self-injurious behavior: Implications for therapeutic practice. *Counseling Psychology Quarterly, 14,* 357–379.

Burke, J. D., Loeber, R., Lahey, B. B., & Rathouz, P. J. (2005). Developmental transitions among affective and behavioral disorders in adolescent boys. *Journal of Child Psychology and Psychiatry, 46,* 1200–1210.

Carlat, D. J., & Camargo, C. A., Jr. (1991). Review of bulimia nervosa in males. *American Journal of Psychiatry, 148,* 831–843.

Carlat, D. J., Camargo, C. A., Jr., & Herzog, D. B. (1997). Eating disorders in males: A report on 135 patients. *American Journal of Psychiatry, 154,* 1127–1132.

Cartwright-Hatton, S., McNicol, K., & Doubleday, E. (2006). Anxiety in a neglected population. Prevalence of anxiety disorders in pre-adolescent children. *Clinical Psychology Review, 24,* 817–833.

Claes, L., Vandereycken, W., & Vertommen, H. (2007). Self-injury in female versus male psychiatric patients: A comparison of characteristics, psychopathology and aggression regulation. *Personality and Individual Differences, 42,* 611–621.

Darche, M. A. (1990). Psychological factors differentiating self-mutilating and nonself-mutilating adolescent inpatient females. *The Psychiatric Hospital, 21,* 31–55.

DiClemente, R. J., Ponton, L. E., & Hartley, D. (1991). Prevalence and correlates of cutting behavior: Risk for HIV transmission. *Journal of the American Academy of Child and Adolescent Psychiatry, 30,* 733–739.

Eisler, I., Dare, C., Hodes, M., Russell, G., Dodge, E., & Grange, D. L. (2000). Family therapy for adolescent anorexia nervosa: The results of a controlled comparison of two family interventions. *Journal of Child Psychology and Psychiatry, 41,* 727–736.

Englar-Carlson, M., & Stevens, M. A. (2006). *In the room with men: A casebook of therapeutic change.* Washington, DC: American Psychological Association.

Essau, C. A. (2010). Comorbidity of anxiety disorders in adolescents. *Depression and anxiety, 18,* 1–6.

Evans, E., Hawton, K., & Rodham, K. (2004). Factors associated with suicidal phenomena in adolescents: A systematic review of population-based studies. *Clinical Psychology Review, 24,* 957–979.

Favazza, A. R., & Conterio, K. (1988). The plight of chronic self-mutilators. *Community Mental Health Journal, 24,* 22–30.

Furnham, A., & Calman, A. (1998). Eating disturbances, self-esteem, reasons for exercising and body weight dissatisfaction in adolescent males. *European Eating Disorders Review, 6,* 58–72.

Gratz, K., & Chapman, A. (2007). The role of emotional responding and childhood maltreatment in the development and maintenance of deliberate self-harm among male undergraduates. *Psychology of Men & Masculinity, 8*(1), 1–14.

Hildebrandt, T., Schlundt, D., Langenbucher, J., Chung, T. (2006). Presence of muscle dysmorphia symptomology among male weightlifters. *Comprehensive Psychiatry, 2006,* 127–135.

Hoffman, R. M., & Kress, V. E. (2008). Narrative therapy and non-suicidal self-injurious behavior: Externalizing the problem and internalizing personal agency. *Journal of Humanistic Counseling, Education, and Development, 47,* 157–171.

Hoffman, R. M., & Kress, V. E. (2010). Adolescent non-suicidal self-injury: Recommendations for minimizing client and counselor risk and enhancing client care. *Journal of Mental Health Counseling, 32,* 342–353.

Howard, D. E., Qi Wang, M., Yang, F. (2008). Psychosocial factors associated with reports of physical dating violence victimization among U.S. adolescent males. *Adolescence, 43,* 449–460.

Jacobson, C. M., & Mufson, L. (2010). Treating adolescent depression using interpersonal psychotherapy. In J. R. Weisz & A. E. Kazdin (Eds.) *Evidenced-based psychotherapies for children and adolescents* (2nd ed., pp. 140–158). New York: The Guilford Press.

Kendall, P. C., Furr, J. M., & Podell, J. L. (2010). Child-focused treatment of anxiety. In J. R. Weisz & A. E. Kazdin (Eds.). *Evidenced-based psychotherapies for children and adolescents* (2nd ed., pp. 45–60). New York: The Guilford Press.

Kitts, R. L. (2005). Gay adolescents and suicide: Understanding the association. *Adolescence, 40,* 622–628.

Kress, V. E. W. (2003). Self-injurious behavior: Assessment and diagnosis. *Journal of Counseling and Development, 81,* 490–496.

Kress, V. E., & Hoffman, R. M. (2008). Deliberate self-injury and motivational interviewing: Enhancing readiness for change. *Journal of Mental Health Counseling, 30,* 311–329.

Laye-Gindhu, A., & Schonert-Reichl, K. A. (2005). Nonsuicidal self-harm among community adolescents: Understanding the 'whats' and 'whys' of self-harm. *Journal of Youth and Adolescence, 34,* 447–457.

Leit, R. A., Pope, H. G., & Gray, J. J. (2001). Cultural expectations of muscularity in men: The evolution of the Playgirl centerfolds. *International Journal of Eating Disorders, 29,* 90–93.

Lewinsohn, P. M., Allen, N. B., Seeley, J. R., & Gotlib, I. H. (1999). First onset versus recurrent of depression: Differential process of psychosocial risk. *Journal of Abnormal Psychology, 108,* 483–489.

Loeber, R., Burke, J. D., Lahey, B. B. (2002). What are adolescent antecedents of antisocial personality disorder? *Criminal Behavior and Mental Health, 12,* 24–36.

McCabe, M. P., Ricciadelli, L. A., Karantzas, G. (2010). Impact of a healthy body image program among adolescent boys on body image, negative affect, and body change strategies. *Body Image, 7,* 117–123.

McCabe, M., Ricciardelli, L., Sitaram, G, & Mikhail, K. (2006). Accuracy of body size estimation: Role of biopsychosocial variables. *Body Image, 3,* 163–171.

Miller, A. L., Rathus, J. H., & Linehan, M. M. (2007). *Dialectical behavior therapy with suicidal adolescents.* New York: The Guilford Press.

Muehlenkamp, J. J. (2006). Empirically supported treatments and general therapy guidelines for non-suicidal self-injury. *Journal of Mental Health Counseling, 28,* 166–185.

Nock, M. K., & Kessler, R. C. (2006). Prevalence of and risk factors for suicide attempts versus suicide gestures: Analysis of the national comorbidity survey. *Journal of Abnormal Psychology, 115,* 616–623.

Nock, M. K., & Prinstein, M. J. (2004). A functional approach to the assessment of self-mutilative behavior. *Journal of Consulting and Clinical Psychology, 72,* 885–890.

Pahl, K., & Barrett, P. M. (2010). Interventions for anxiety disorders in children using group cognitive-behavioral therapy with family involvement. In J. R.

Weisz & A. E. Kazdin (Eds.) *Evidenced-based psychotherapies for children and adolescents* (2nd ed., pp. 61–79). New York: The Guilford Press.

Penning, S. L., Bhagwanjee, A., & Govender, K. (2010). Bullying boys: The traumatic effects of bullying in male adolescent learners. *Journal of Child and Adolescent Mental Health, 22*(2), 131–143.

Pope, H. G., Gruber, A. J., Choi, P., Olivardia, R., & Phillips, K. A. (1997). Muscle dysmorphia: An under-recognized form of body dysmorphic disorder. Psychosomatics, 38, 548–557.

Pope, H. G., Olivardia, R., Gruber, A., & Borowiecki, J. J.(1999). Evolving ideas of male body images as seen through action toys. *International Journal of Eating Disorders, 26,* 65–72.

Portzky, G., Audenaert, K., van Heeringen, K. (2005). Suicide among adolescents: A psychological autopsy study of psychiatric, psychosocial, and personality-related risk factors. *Social Psychiatry and Psychiatric Epidemiology, 40,* 922–930.

Pruitt, I. T. (2007). Family treatment approaches for depression in adolescent males. *The American Journal of Family Therapy, 35,* 69–81.

Ross, S., & Heath, N. (2002). A study of the frequency of self-mutilation in a community sample of adolescents. *Journal of Youth and Adolescence, 31,* 67–77.

Russell, S., & Joyner, K. (2001). Adolescent sexual orientation and suicide risk: Evidence from a national study. *American Journal of Public Health, 91,* 903–906.

Savin-Williams, R. C., & Ream, G. L. (2003). Suicide attempts among sexual-minority male youth. *Journal of Clinical Child and Adolescent Psychology, 32,* 509–522.

Soban, C. (2006). What about the boys? Addressing issues of masculinity within male anorexia nervosa in a feminist therapeutic environment. *International Journal of Men's Health, 5,* 251–267.

Smith, P. B., Buzi, R. S., Welnman, M. L. (2001). Mental health problems and symptoms among male adolescents attending a teen health clinic. *Adolescence, 36,* 323–332.

Tantillo, M., Nappa Bitter, C., & Adams, B. (2001). Enhancing readiness for eating disorder treatment: A relational/motivational group model for change. *Eating Disorders: The Journal of Treatment & Prevention, 9*(3), 203–216.

Taylor, B. (2003). Exploring the perspectives of men who self-harm. *Learning in Health and Social Care, 2,* 83–91.

Telch, C. F., Agras, W. S., & Linehan, M. M. (2001). Dialectical behavior therapy for binge eating disorder. *Journal of Consulting and Clinical Psychology, 69,* 1061–1065.

Treasure, J., & Ward, A. (1997). A practical guide to the use of motivational interviewing in anorexia nervosa. *European Eating Disorders Review, 5,* 102–114.

Trepal, H., Wester, K., & MacDonald, C. (2006). Self-injury and postvention: Responding to the family in crisis. *The Family Journal, 14,* 342–348.

Tyler, K. Whitbeck, L., Hoyt, D., & Johnson, K. (2003). Self-mutilation and homeless youth: The role of family abuse, street experiences and mental disorders. *Journal of Research on Adolescence, 13*(4), 457–474.

Uddin, M., Koenen, K. C., Santos, R., Bakshis, E., Aiello, A. E., Galea, S. (2010). Gender differences in the genetic and environmental determinants of adolescent depression. *Depression & Anxiety, 27,* 658–666.

Weersing, V. R., & Brent, D. A. (2010). Treating depression in adolescents: Using individual cognitive-behavioral therapy. In J. R. Weisz & A. E. Kazdin (Eds.) *Evidenced-based psychotherapies for children and adolescents* (2nd ed., pp. 126–139). New York: The Guilford Press.

Weisz, J. R., & Kazdin, A. E. (2010). *Evidenced-based psychotherapies for children and adolescents* (2nd ed.). New York: The Guilford Press.

Whetstone, L. M., Morrisey, S. L., & Cummings, D. M. (2007). Children at risk: The association between perceived weight status and suicidal thoughts and attempts in middle school youth. *Journal of School Health, 77,* 59–66.

White, J., Leggett, J., & Beech, A. (1999). The incidence of self-harming behaviour of a medium-secure psychiatric hospital. *Journal of Forensic Psychiatry, 10,* 59–68.

White, V. E., Trepal-Wollenzier, H., & Nolan, J. (2002). College students and self-injury: Intervention strategies for counselors. *Journal of College Counseling, 5,* 105–113.

Wilson, G. T., & Schlam, T. R. (2004). The transtheoretical model and motivational interviewing in the treatment of eating and weight disorders. *Clinical Psychology Review, 24,* 361–378.

Wunderlich, U., Bronisch, T., Wittchen, H.-U., & Carter, R. (2001). Gender differences in adolescents and young adults with suicidal behavior. *Acta Psychiatrica Scandinavica, 104,* 332–339.

Yates, T. M. (2004). The developmental psychopathology of self-injurious behavior: Compensatory regulation in posttraumatic adaptation. *Clinical Psychology Review, 24,* 35–74.

Zaitsoff, S. L., & Grilo, C. M. (2010). Eating disorder psychopathology as a marker of psychosocial distress and suicide risk in female and male adolescent psychiatric inpatients. *Comprehensive Psychiatry, 51,* 142–150.

Part IV: Behavior Disorders and Concerns

16

Identifying the Cycle: Assessing Addictions in Young Men

W. BRYCE HAGEDORN, JESSE FOX, AND TABITHA L. YOUNG

ADDICTIONS IN ADOLESCENT MALES

In working with boys and young men, perhaps one of the more challenging clinical issues counselors face lies in the realm of addictive disorders. Be it the debilitating effects that these disorders have on clients and those who care about them, clinicians' perceived lack of self-efficacy in addressing addiction and its complications (e.g., co-occurring disorders), or the high relapse/recidivism rates, many counselors may find themselves wanting to refer their addicted clients to those who specialize in addressing addictive disorders. To complicate matters further, addicted clients tend to resist clinician-led change efforts, and counselors themselves can become quickly frustrated with clients' ambivalence about change (e.g., "I really want to stop ruining my life with oxycodone, but I really like how it helps numb me out").

Although we note the importance of a high level of competence in order to effectively work with adolescents struggling with addiction-related concerns, we also believe that every counselor should be, at the very least, minimally equipped to assess, diagnose, and treat addictive disorders. This assertion has been legitimized by the newest version of the accreditation standards set forth by the Council for Accreditation of Counseling and Related Educational Programs (CACREP, 2008). In the CACREP Standards, the importance of this need is noted in core curricular Standard II.G.3.g., which states that all counselor education students are required to know, "[the] theories and etiology of addictions and addictive behaviors, including strategies for prevention, intervention, and treatment." Therefore, every counselor, regardless of their place of employment or scope of practice, should be able to accurately address their clients' concerns and note when the need arises to refer to an addiction specialist.

In following the lead set forth by CACREP and other authors noting the need for counselor preparation in this area (Merta, 2001; Schulte, Meier, Sterling, & Berry, 2010; Whittinghill, Carroll, & Morgan, 2004), we have designed this chapter to provide the necessary addiction-related information for the general practitioner. As there are entire books dedicated to this study, we will focus on those areas that will enable every counselor to at least minimally address their clients' concerns. As such, we begin with a set of definitions and criteria to aid in the identification process, which will be followed by two structured interviews to assist in the assessment of addictive disorders. Following this, we will highlight those chemicals and behaviors which most often plague adolescents, with a special emphasis on their impacts on boys and young men.

DEFINITIONS AND CRITERIA OF ADDICTION

The place to begin in defining addiction is broader than one might expect. Although most are familiar with addictions to such things as alcohol, marijuana, and nicotine (known as the "gateway drugs"), the concept of addictions to such behaviors as the Internet, sex, and gaming is gaining recognition. Some behavioral or "process addictions" have been formally legitimized by the American Psychiatric Disorder due to their inclusion in the *Diagnostic and Statistical Manual of Mental Disorders* (*DSM* [APA, 2000]) (e.g., eating disorders and compulsive gambling), whereas other processes are not currently considered (e.g., sexuality, spending, exercise, Internet use, and gaming). Since we do not have the space here to provide the rationale for seeing these behaviors as addictive, the interested reader is encouraged to read the article by Hagedorn (2009). We *do* want to note that alcohol and other drugs (AODs) and behaviors impact the brain similarly, with the neurotransmitters of epinephrine, dopamine, and serotonin all being affected (Bostwick & Bucci, 2008; Guay, 2009; Westphal, Jackson, Thomas, & Blaszczynski, 2008).

While it is our desire to broaden the traditional definition of addiction, we also caution readers from wearing their "addiction glasses" at all times. For if one misconstrues an adolescent's recreational use of Internet gaming as an addiction, or is quick to overreact to an adolescent's experimentation with alcohol with a diagnosis of chemical dependency, this may quickly distance the youth from accepting your clinical assistance. As a matter of fact, given our slant toward motivational interviewing (Miller & Rollnick, 2002), which will be explored in the following chapter, we caution counselors from *ever* naming a client's behaviors as addictive to them, but rather providing information to clients and their families and allowing them to wrestle with a definition.

By allowing clients to self-identify their concerns, ownership is bolstered and resistance is lowered. Nevertheless, we also recognize the need to work with other treatment providers, third-party payment sources, and parents desperate to understand, and thus advocate for, the proper definitions and diagnoses of client concerns using the criteria for abuse and dependence identified in the *DSM-V-TR* (APA, 2000). For those behaviors not identified in the *DSM* (e.g., process addictions), we use the set of criteria noted by Goodman (2001) and highlighted by others (Hagedorn, 2009; Hagedorn & Juhnke, 2005):

> A maladaptive pattern of behavior, leading to clinically significant impairment or distress, as manifested by three (or more) of the following, occurring at any time in the same 12-month period:
>
> *1.* Tolerance, as defined by either of the following:
>   *a.* A need for markedly increased amount or intensity of the behavior to achieve the desired effect
>   *b.* Markedly diminished effect with continued involvement in the behavior at the same level or intensity
>
> *2.* Withdrawal, as manifested by either of the following:
>   *a.* Characteristic psychophysiological withdrawal syndrome of physiologically described changes and/or psychologically described changes upon discontinuation of the behavior
>   *b.* The same (or a closely related) behavior is engaged in to relieve or avoid withdrawal symptoms
>
> *3.* The behavior is often engaged in over a longer period, in greater quantity, or at a higher intensity than was intended.
> *4.* There is a persistent desire or unsuccessful efforts to cut down or control the behavior.
> *5.* A great deal of time is spent in activities necessary to prepare for the behavior, to engage in the behavior, or to recover from its effects.
> *6.* Important social, occupational, or recreational activities are given up or reduced because of the behavior.
> *7.* The behavior continues despite knowledge of having a persistent or recurrent physical or psychological problem that is likely to have been caused or exacerbated by the behavior. (Goodman, 2001, pp. 195–196)

Although the criteria and definitions outlined in the *DSM* and by Goodman (2001) help those external to the counseling session understand the clinical significance of our clients' distress (e.g., other service providers, insurance companies), we find that there are several lay definitions that tend to have greater utility to the work we do with the youth sitting across from us and for their families. For example, Hagedorn and Young (2011) noted:

> One way to distinguish between "normal" and addictive behaviors is to use the definition developed by Goodman (2001), who suggested that a behavior moves from normal to addictive when it (a) both produces pleasure and reduces negative moods and (b) includes two key features: (1) the individual is unable to control, cut back, or stop the behavior, and (2) the individual continues to use the behavior despite substantial negative consequences. (p. 251)

Another definition that helps clients understand is that adapted from Nakken (1996): *Addiction is an abnormal love and trust relationship with an object or event in an attempt to control that which cannot be controlled.* We have found that our adolescent clients can relate to addiction as a relationship fairly easily, and by developing certain metaphoric language around the relationship process, they are better able to articulate how their behaviors progress through recognizable relationship "stages." A final definition that has proven useful was noted by Juhnke and Hagedorn (2006): *addiction is an increasing desire for something with an accompanying decreasing ability to satisfy that desire* (p. 3). The utility of any of these definitions is in the conversations they generate, in the meaning-making that occurs, and in the lowering of client resistance.

Having settled on some definitions that we have found that best help our young clients understand, we now turn briefly to two assessment strategies that counselors can use regardless of their setting or modality.

ASSESSMENT STRATEGIES

The field of addiction counseling is ripe with screening and assessment methods that can greatly aid in understanding the extent of our clients' presenting concerns. Put simply, *screening instruments* generally ask, "Are AODs and/or behaviors a problem?" with an outcome that points fairly clearly to answers of either "yes" or "no." That is, when an adolescent presents with depression, isolation from others, and a sudden drop in school performance, the competent clinician would employ a screening instrument as a part of any thorough intake process in order to determine if the client is using any form of depressant. If such a screening produces a "yes" result, a follow-up with a more detailed *assessment instrument* would be warranted. Such an intervention would answer the general question of "how *much* of a problem is it?" with a number or a range that would indicate a more precise explanation of the extent of the problem that can be attributed to AODs and/or behaviors.

Given that the focus of this chapter is on general practitioners and that entire books are written on the subject of addiction-related screening and assessment instruments, we would like to offer two structured interviews that we have found to be particularly useful and that can be employed by any counselor in any setting. The added benefit of a structured interview is that it can often answer *both* questions ("Is it a problem?" and "How much of a problem is it?") because it is incorporated into the session itself and lends itself to probing for additional information. In fact, answering affirmatively to *any* one of the yes/no questions found in these instruments would indicate that AODs/behaviors are of concern, whereas the more affirmative answers there are, the larger the concern becomes. The two interviews we use are the CAGE (Ewing, 1984) and the WASTE-Time (Hagedorn & Juhnke, 2005).

CAGE

The CAGE (Ewing, 1984) was originally developed to screen and assess for alcohol-related concerns, but it has found utility for all mind-altering substances in a variety of clinical settings over many years. The four questions proposed by the CAGE are:

1. Have you ever felt as though you should Cut down on your substance use?
2. Have you ever felt Annoyed by someone who was criticizing your substance use?
3. Do you ever feel Guilty about your substance use?
4. Do you ever use the substance in the morning to steady your nerves or to get rid of a hangover? (Eye-opener)

Given that each affirmative response is scored as a 1, one affirmative answer would indicate that the adolescent is experiencing "problem" use (all the way up to a diagnosis of *substance abuse*) and that further assessment would be warranted (Ewing, 1984). Two or more affirmative answers, on the other hand, would be indicative of meeting criteria for *substance dependence* (King, 1986; Mayfield, McLeod, & Hall, 1974). As such, given that the adolescent is meeting with a counselor in the first place, a referral to a specialist and/or inpatient treatment may be warranted given the severity of the problems that are indicated. For example, in receiving a "yes" to the fourth question and probing further, the counselor may find that the client reveals that she starts getting high first thing in the morning and does not stop until late in the evening. Ceasing such use without being medically monitored could pose a serious health risk, thus the need for a higher level of care. The various levels of care are noted later in this chapter.

WASTE-Time

The WASTE-Time structured interview (Hagedorn & Juhnke, 2005) evolved from the lack of any such instrument to determine the impact of a process addiction on clients' presenting concerns. The following seven questions align with Goodman's (2001) criteria for a process addiction and were noted in Hagedorn and Young (2011):

> *W: Withdrawal*: "How do you feel/what happens to you when you are unable to engage in ____ (fill in blank with the behavior that is being assessed)?"

> Responses may include irritability, anxiety, depression, anger, and/or other negative mood states. Clients may also reveal using other behaviors or chemicals to supplement their addictive behaviors as a means to avoid withdrawal symptoms.

> *A: Adverse Consequences*: "Have you experienced any negative (or adverse) consequences as a result of your behaviors?"

> Responses may include broken relationships, being grounded at home, lowered grades, lack of sleep, financial difficulties, physical injury, being kicked off a sports team, and/or psychological trauma (e.g., suicidal ideations). This can lead to further discussions about the cost of continuing the addictive behaviors.

> *S: Inability to Stop*: "Have you attempted to cut back, control, or stop your behaviors without success, even when you know that continuing will cause you harm?"

> Responses may include multiple attempts at stopping or controlling the addictive behaviors without success, even when faced with the knowledge that continuing poses a physical or psychological problem.

> *T: Tolerance or Intensity*: "Have you found it necessary to increase the amount or intensity of your behaviors to achieve the same high (or whatever reaction occurs whenever the behavior is used)?"

> Responses may mirror the tolerance that one would feel towards alcohol: whereas one alcoholic beverage used to provide an alteration in mood, tolerance would be evidenced by it taking six drinks to produce a similar effect.

E: Escape: "Do you find yourself engaging in the activity whenever you feel such things as stress, anxiety, depression, sadness, loneliness, or anger?"

Responses here may include any negative mood state and discussion can easily move into comorbid emotional concerns (e.g., depression, anxiety, etc.).

Time: Time Spent and Time Wasted

Time Spent: "Have you found yourself spending a lot of time preparing for, engaging in, or recovering from your activity?"

Responses often include time-consuming ritualistic behavior patterns that accompany addictive behavior, which can be followed by large amounts of time needed to recover from a binge episode.

Time Wasted: "Have you been spending more time and/or more resources on your activities than you planned to?"

Responses may include unintended hours spent on the Internet, a loss of sleep due to an entire weekend spent on voyeuristic activities, or a lost paycheck spent on gambling activities. (p. 260)

In scoring the WASTE-Time, Hagedorn and Juhnke (2005) affirmed that one to two affirmative answers (i.e. "yes") would indicate a strong possibility for an addictive behavior, which would be similar to a diagnosis of "abuse" for chemicals. This being the case, further assessment would be warranted and the adolescent should be referred to a trained counselor. An affirmative answer to three or more questions would likely indicate that the client has a process addiction. As such, the immediate referral to a specialist would be warranted, inpatient hospitalization may be considered (based on the severity of the behaviors), and at the minimum, outpatient counseling coupled with self-help support group attendance would be necessitated.

Armed with a definition with which clients can self-identify their concerns, and after obtaining a more precise answer to the extent of their concern, it is important next to understand how AODs and behaviors manifest themselves. We will begin the discussion with those *chemicals* to which adolescents most often gravitate and finish with the *behaviors* that can become addictive.

CHEMICAL ADDICTIONS

Adolescent substance abuse is a rapidly changing phenomenon that requires frequent monitoring and reassessment (Johnston, O'Malley,

Bachman, & Schulenberg, 2010). Monitoring the Future, an annual national survey comprising 46,000 adolescents, found that from 2005 to present adolescent consumption of illicit substances has moderately declined. In addition, they found that adolescent boys tend to have higher rates than adolescent females of illicit drug use; in particular, males report higher rates of heavy use. Despite this steady decline, it is estimated that approximately 10% of adolescents from the ages of 12 to 17 are currently abusing illicit substances (Stagman, Schwarz, & Powers, 2011). Using a national data set from 113 grantee treatment programs comprising 14,776 adolescents interviewed from 1998 to 2007, Dennis, White, and Ives (2009) found that the chemical substances most commonly abused by adolescents were marijuana (44%), alcohol (15%), cocaine (3%), heroin (2%), and other drugs (6%). In addition, they found that 52% reported using tobacco at least once a week. Dennis et al. warned, however, that these numbers are likely suppressed because 38% of the participants had completed 90 days of residential treatment or incarceration prior to being interviewed. The majority of the discussion will focus on marijuana and alcohol, since counselors are most likely to encounter these two substances in their work with adolescent addicts.

Marijuana

Background

By far the most prevalent illicit substance consumed by adolescents is marijuana (Johnston, O'Malley, Bachman, & Schulenberg, 2010) and is therefore given the most attention in this chapter. Doweiko's (2006) review found that marijuana use has a mean onset of 18 years of age, peaks in the early 20s, and generally ceases in the late 20s to early 30s. The drug, marijuana, comes from the *Cannabis sativa* plant. The exact mechanisms in the brain that marijuana acts upon to produce its effects are not entirely understood, but the primary acting agent is called Δ-9-tetrahydrocannabinol (THC) and is most concentrated in the plant's flowers (Kuhn, Swartzwelder, Wilson, Wilson, & Foster, 2008). One of the more significant findings concerning this substance is that it connects to cannabinoid receptors in the brain where natural compounds the body produces normally bind. One such compound is called anandamide (Sanskrit for bliss), which is thought to regulate mood and reduce pain. Kuhn et al. also noted that cannabinoid receptors are found primarily in the hippocampus, which plays a vital role in the formation of new memories and would help explain marijuana's effect on memory impairment.

Intoxication

Marijuana is notoriously difficult to categorize because it shares many psychoactive characteristics with other classes of drugs (Kuhn et al.,

2008). The subjective effects of marijuana are largely influenced by the expectations of the user. Doweiko's (2006) review found that marijuana users tend to believe that it will lead to cognitive impairment, relieve their stress, enhance their social, creative, and sexual experience, and increase their appetite. In addition, a user's experience generally follows two phases. The first involves a general sense of anxiety to be followed by an overall sense of well-being or euphoria. Marijuana use is generally accompanied by red eyes, dry mouth and throat, a decrease in body temperature, and an increase in heart rate (Craig, 2004). Lastly, some have speculated that marijuana inhibits the formation of new memories by acting on the area of the brain responsible for storing information, the hippocampus (Becker, Wagner, Gouzoulis-Mayfrank, Spuentrup, & Daumann, 2010).

Withdrawal
Historically speaking, controversy surrounds the legitimacy of a withdrawal syndrome from marijuana consumption. As a result, the *DSM-IV* did not include cannabis withdrawal in its diagnostic terminology (Milin, Manion, Dare, & Walker, 2008). However, Milin et al. found that withdrawal symptoms are present in adolescents for up to one month after the cessation of use and are most acute in the first 2 weeks. Furthermore, there is very little difference in the experience of withdrawal symptoms in respect to age, gender, and racial background (Copersino et al., 2010). Marijuana withdrawal is characterized by the following symptoms: insomnia, restlessness, loss of appetite, craving for marijuana, muscle pain, and chills, as well as irritability and heightened aggression in heavy users (Haney et al., 2004; Stevens & Smith, 2005).

Negative Consequences
The negative consequences of marijuana are fraught with controversy, and the debate over its influence on the lives of users is widespread. For example, Earleywine (2005) argued that "Despite consistent propaganda to the opposite, cannabis does not lead to aggression, reckless driving, infertility, amotivation, low grades, poor employment, mental illness, unwanted pregnancy, firearm accidents, or the use of harder drugs" (p. 240). However, this statement stands in direct contradiction to Kuhn et al. (2008) who warned that marijuana does impair judgment as well as coordination and that motor vehicle accidents or other dangerous circumstances are the greatest risk to marijuana users. For instance, Lenné et al. (2010) found that marijuana intoxication while driving is associated with increased variability in speed and lateral positioning on the road, impaired ability to judge the relative velocity of other vehicles on the road, and delayed reaction time. Furthermore, marijuana can impair verbal learning and memory, with more severe levels of impairment being associated with

earlier use, suggesting that marijuana can negatively affect brain development (Solowij, 2011). In Doweiko's (2006) review, there is evidence to suggest that marijuana impairs reaction time for up to 24 hours after use. Furthermore, heavy use can produce psychotic episodes called toxic or drug-induced psychosis, altogether doubling the risk of developing a psychotic disorder in adulthood (Arseneault, Cannon, Witton, & Murray, 2004).

On the other hand, some have acknowledged that thus far the research shows that the average intake of marijuana does not "kill" brain cells (Kuhn et al., 2008), while others have found that chronic users can develop a tolerance to marijuana that somewhat insulates them from acute impairment (Ramaekers, Kauert, Theunissen, Toennes, & Moeller, 2009). This was consistent with Doweiko's (2006) review, which concluded that it is not clear what permanent effects chronic marijuana use has on the brain. However, evidence is mounting that implicates marijuana in the development of other physiological complications. For example, researchers estimate that one marijuana joint (cannabis rolled in cigarette paper) may have about the same amount of tar as approximately three tobacco cigarettes (Wu, Tashkin, Djahed, & Rose, 1988). Furthermore, there is evidence to indicate a positive association between marijuana use and the development of cancer (Hashibe et al., 2005; Mehra, Moore, Crothers, Tetrault, & Fiellin, 2006). Lastly, marijuana may also adversely affect the reproductive systems of both males (Kolodny, Masters, Kolodner, & Toro, 1974) and females (Hubbard, Franco, & Onaivi, 1999).

Depressants

Alcohol

BACKGROUND. Behind tobacco and marijuana, alcohol is the third most abused substance by adolescents (Dennis et al., 2009). There are many different kinds of alcohol, but the one that is most often used for recreational consumption is called ethanol or ethyl alcohol (Doweiko, 2006; Kuhn et al., 2008). Alcoholic beverages vary in their relative concentration of ethanol; however, Kuhn et al. noted that the standard drink is classified as 12 ounces of beer, 4 ounces of wine, or 1 ounce of hard liquor. It is important to note that the body metabolizes roughly one alcoholic drink every 60 to 90 minutes (the exact time of which depends on such things as body composition [percentage of body fat, overall weight, etc.], age, and gender).

INTOXICATION. The effects of alcohol vary depending upon the concentration of ethanol in the blood stream, known as the blood alcohol level

(BAL). A person's BAL is measured by milligrams of alcohol per 100 milliliters of blood and serves as a rough approximation of a person's subjective level of intoxication. The effects of alcohol can vary from impaired judgment, fine motor coordination, and reaction time, which are symptoms that are seen with low BALs (up to 100 mg/100 ml, or 0 to 0.10) to respiratory and heart failure at the highest BAL (600–900 mg/100 ml, or 0.60 to 0.90).

Doweiko noted that BAL is influenced by a number of factors, most notably tolerance (e.g., past prevalence of use), gender, and body mass. This means that two people with different levels of past use, gender, or body mass will have different BAL's even if they drink the exact same amount of alcohol in the exact same time period. Kuhn et al. noted that outward appearance is not a reliable indicator of impairment. In other words, just because someone looks or acts sober does not mean that their BAL is below the legal limit.

WITHDRAWAL. One of the more important changes in the body from sustained alcohol use is called "metabolic tolerance" where the liver becomes more efficient at eliminating alcohol from the blood stream so that the drinker must ingest more alcohol to reach the same desired effect. Withdrawal from alcohol dependence can range from mild headaches, nausea, involuntary shaking, and vomiting to more severe withdrawal symptoms such as *delirium tremens,* which can involve hallucinations and confusion (Craig, 2004). Unlike many substances that only produce subjective discomfort during withdrawal, alcohol withdrawal can be potentially life threatening. Given that severe cases of alcohol withdrawal can result in death, Doweiko (2006) recommended that whenever there is evidence of alcohol withdrawal, an assessment by a physician be completed.

NEGATIVE CONSEQUENCES. The negative consequences of adolescent alcohol abuse are far reaching. It is important to note that alcohol affects adolescents differently than adults. Specifically, alcohol appears to have increased deleterious effects on adolescent's memory function, while concurrently producing decreased feelings of drowsiness (Kuhn et al., 2008). In particular, verbal learning and memory seem especially susceptible to impairment by adolescent alcohol use (Mahmood, Jacobus, Bava, Scarlett, Tapert, & Kelly, 2010), which is consistent with prior research that has found that alcohol reduces the size of the hippocampus (De Bellis et al., 2000). Kelly, Kazura, Lommel, Babalonis, and Martin (2009) reported that alcohol is responsible for 5,000 motor vehicle-related deaths among adolescents every year. In addition, alcohol use is also associated with the development of chronic diseases, negative social and cultural consequences, and elevated risks for liver disease as well as aversive effects to the endocrine and metabolic systems. They also found research to suggest that alcohol reduces the integrity of the neuronal cell membrane of the developing adolescent brain. Further, prolonged alcohol use in adolescence can result in structural changes in the brain including reduced volume of the prefrontal cortex and hippocampus, which is thought to be responsible for memory impairment. Doweiko (2006) found evidence to suggest that 20% of individuals will experience irrecoverable cognitive damage due to their chronic alcohol abuse, while only 20% showed evidence of complete recovery.

Benzodiazepines

The benzodiazepines are the closest we have to a panacea for anxiety and are the most prescribed medication for anxiety and insomnia (Kuhn et al., 2008; Stevens & Smith, 2005). In addition to providing immediate relief for anxiety, they also show little potential for risk of overdose if they are not combined with other drugs because they do not inhibit respiratory function. However, benzodiazepines have their drawbacks. They can cause drowsiness and impair coordination in their first few days of prescribed use, which makes them a hazard for operating a vehicle or heavy machinery.

Like all sedatives, when benzodiazepines are taken for long periods of time they inhibit neuroplasticity, the brain's physiological process for learning. However, neuroplasticity does return to normal when use ceases. In addition, like many other drugs of abuse, there is a clear pattern of withdrawal that includes sadness, inability to feel, fluctuating emotions, concentration difficulties, and reduced sleep (Vikander, Koechling, Borg, Tönne, & Hiltunen, 2010). Furthermore, they can be powerful enough to produce retrograde amnesia when combined with alcohol. This is particularly dangerous in incidents of date rape where flunitrazepam (Rohypnal, nicknamed "roofies") is covertly combined with a woman's alcoholic beverage, who is later sexually assaulted when she succumbs to the combined sedative effect of the benzodiazepine and alcohol.

GHB

Gamma-hydroxybutyrate (GHB) is an odorless and colorless liquid that is a popular depressant among adolescent males between 18 and 25 years of age, at raves and nightclubs (Kuhn et al., 2008; Stevens & Smith, 2005). It is a metabolite of GABA and activates the dopaminergic system, the brain's reward pathway. Like roofies, GHB can produce retrograde amnesia and is used in date rape scenarios. What makes GHB dangerous is that it is particularly unpredictable. At lower doses, it produces relaxation and alleviates stress. However, as the dosage increases, it can cause a loss of consciousness 15 minutes after consumption and a coma within 30 to 40 minutes. This is especially dangerous because a side effect of GHB is nausea and vomiting, making death by asphyxiation a plausible hazard.

Stimulants

Background

There are a number of chemicals that can be classified as stimulants, including cocaine, the amphetamines, and ephedrine (Dowieko, 2006), and they are the third most abused class of drugs by adolescents (Dennis et al., 2009). Given that most stimulants have a similar psychoactive effect, an exhaustive discussion of each stimulant is not needed, and instead they will be discussed in unison. However, it does benefit counselors to have some working knowledge of the stimulants most commonly abused by adolescents.

Intoxication

The subjective experience of stimulant intoxication is similar because each one activates many of the same areas and neurotransmitters in the brain (Dowieko, 2006; Stevens & Smith, 2005). However, cocaine and amphetamine intoxication can be differentiated by the following: (a) the high from cocaine is brief (one hour at the most), while the effect of amphetamines can be felt for hours, (b) cocaine is not effective when administered orally, and (c) cocaine can be used as a local anesthetic. Depending upon the level of intoxication, when a stimulant is consumed, it elicits a feeling of euphoria and intense agitation of the body's central nervous system (CNS) that at high levels can result in death (Freye & Levy, 2009). People generally die within the first 2 to 3 minutes of advanced CNS stimulation, making it unlikely for them to survive an overdose if medical personnel are not present when they first begin to experience signs of advanced toxicity (e.g., seizures, irregular pulse, rapid heartbeat, and irregular breathing).

Withdrawal

Amphetamine withdrawal is characterized by depressive symptoms, comorbid symptoms of psychosis, and a steady craving for the drug that can last well into the fifth week of abstinence (Zorick et al., 2010). Based on their systematic review, Pennay and Lee (2011) defined amphetamine withdrawal as "the presence of symptoms including depression, agitation, fatigue and cognitive impairment that are likely to last for at least a number of weeks" (p. 220). However, they also found that it is less likely to involve physical pain that is common in alcohol or opiate withdrawal. Similarly, cocaine withdrawal is also characterized by a disruption of mood, sleep, and appetite that is most prevalent immediately after use (24 hours) and is often described as a "crash" (Walsh, Stoops, Moody, Lin, & Bigelow, 2009). Furthermore, the severity of these withdrawal symptoms is an accurate predictor of relapse (Kampman et al., 2002). In other words, the more severe these symptoms are, the more likely a person is to return to active use.

Negative Consequences

Beyond the obvious potential for fatal overdose on stimulants, Degenhardt, Coffey, Moran, Carlin, and Patton (2007) found that adolescent onset of amphetamine use is associated with regular use of alcohol, tobacco, and marijuana. In addition, they found that adolescent amphetamine use is later associated with increased rates of drug dependence and mental health disorders in early adulthood. This was consistent with Marshall and Werb's (2010) review in which the authors found clear evidence that adolescent methamphetamine use is associated with depression, psychosis, behavioral problems, polysubstance use, suicidality, and overdose.

Opiates

Heroin

BACKGROUND. Heroin is the most commonly abused opiate among adolescents (Dennis et al., 2009). The opiates, notably opium, are a nitrogen waste product of the poppy plant (Nahas & Burks, 1997). In turn, heroin is derived from the chemical opium that also produces a number of opiate-like compounds (i.e., opioids) such as codeine and morphine (Landry, 1994). One of the most significant findings in neurology came in the 1970s when researchers discovered the presence of endogenous opioids and specific opioid receptors in the human brain, explaining why opiates had such a powerful binding ability in the CNS. As Nahas and Burk explained, the opiates mimic the nervous system's naturally occurring compounds and their effect on neurotransmitters. Technically, heroin is a CNS depressant and alleviates pain through general anesthesia.

INTOXICATION. When administered intravenously, heroin intoxication is characterized by a rush in the lower abdomen that is likened to an orgasm, followed by a pervasive sense of warmth throughout the body (Schuckit, 2000). This rush is linked to this drug's effects on the CNS by releasing a large volume of dopamine into the *nucleus accumbens*, which is subjectively experienced as "pleasure" (Doweiko, 2006, p. 186). In addition to the painkilling and pleasure-producing euphoria from intoxication, heroin is also a CNS depressant. Unfortunately, heroin can cause a fatal overdose by suppressing the respiratory system and can be identified by the "*narcotic triad*: coma, depressed respiration, and pinpoint pupils" (Stevens & Smith, 2005, p. 61).

WITHDRAWAL. Heroin withdrawal can typically be experienced within hours of abstinence. Opiate withdrawal symptoms are nearly identical to the flu, including nausea, vomiting, dysphoric mood, diarrhea, sweating, muscle aches, fever, running nose, watery eyes, and insomnia (Landry, 1994). Furthermore, withdrawal is characterized by a craving for heroin some have called a "drug hunger" (Stevens & Smith, 2005, p. 61) accompanied by "emotional irritability" (Schuckit, 2000, p. 161). These acute symptoms generally last between 7 and 10 days (Giannini & Slaby, 1989), giving way to a protracted withdrawal phase that can last for several months after abstinence and can include increased blood pressure, body temperature, respiration, and pupil dilation (Schuckit, 2000).

NEGATIVE CONSEQUENCES. Overdose is a constant danger of acute intoxication from heroin that can be compounded further if it is combined with another CNS depressant such as alcohol (Stevens & Smith, 2005). Petry, Bickel, and Arnett (1998) found that people who abuse heroin tend to lack the ability to envision the future consequences to their life choices. This "truncated" (p. 735) perspective of future events in heroin users may be one of the causes for both maladaptive behaviors as well as continued use despite negative consequences. Furthermore, Reimer et al.'s (2011) review found that since heroin is often administered intravenously, users are at a higher risk for contracting hepatitis B, hepatitis C, and HIV, as well as contribute to electrocardiogram disturbances, cardiac dysfunction, tuberculosis, and poor nutrition.

PRESCRIPTION PAINKILLERS. Prescription painkiller abuse is particularly popular with club-going youth (Kelly & Parsons, 2007) and is abused more often by female adolescents than male adolescents (Wu, Pilowsky, & Patkar, 2008). Wu et al. noted that prescription painkillers are often obtained from different sources as well as used for different reasons as compared to illicit substances. Kalb (2001) explained that oxycodone (Oxycontin or Oxy), the most powerful of the prescription painkillers, became popular among addicts soon after its release in 1996 because it offered a longer effect with fewer doses compared to other prescribed opioids. In addition, unlike other painkillers, oxycodone did not include acetaminophen in its chemical structure, allowing it to be abused without fear of causing liver damage. Although it is delivered in a time release capsule, abusers often crush the pill and inject it directly into the blood stream or take more than the prescribed dose to mimic the euphoric effect of heroin (Doweiko, 2006). Hydrocodone (Vicodon) is also a widely abused prescribed painkiller and is comparable to oxycodone in its power to counteract pain (Kuhn et al., 2008).

Hallucinogens

Ecstasy

BACKGROUND. Methylenedioxymethamphetamine (MDMA) is commonly referred to as "ecstasy." Ecstasy is categorized as a hallucinogen in this chapter; however, the drug seems to have effects consistent with both hallucinogens as well as stimulants (Kuhn et al., 2008). Originally, ecstasy was used in psychotherapy because it was thought to open clients up to self-disclosure and insight. However, the medicinal purposes of the drug were not realized, and its popularity grew recreationally during the 1980s. Since then, adolescent use of ecstasy has steadily increased in recent years, with females consuming more than males (Wu et al., 2010), and it is often used in clubs or parties, though recent trends suggest that it is becoming increasingly common in other settings (McCrystal & Percy, 2010).

INTOXICATION. When ecstasy is consumed, its effects peak within 90 minutes (Schwartz & Miller, 1997) and elicit a sense of elevated mood, euphoria, and closeness to others (Stevens & Smith, 2005). Hallucinogenic effects include sensory enhancement, distortion, and illusions. Physical effects of ecstasy include increased heart rate and blood pressure, as well as uncontrollable teeth clenching. However, there can also be a number of unwanted side effects to intoxication including depression, confusion, anxiety, insomnia, and paranoia (Craig, 2004). Furthermore, people who are particularly sensitive to the effects of ecstasy can experience numbness in their hands and feet, vomiting, as well as blurred vision and hallucinations (Doweiko, 2006).

WITHDRAWAL. Research seems to suggest that physical withdrawal from ecstasy plays a relatively minor role as compared to the psychological withdrawal in both animal and human studies (Degenhardt, Bruno, & Topp, 2010). However, the "down" users' report can resemble major depression, while others experience extreme irritability and aggression. Furthermore, some have experienced panic attacks after the high has dissipated. Although these symptoms eventually disappear, depending upon the level of use, they can last for months after ceasing use (Kuhn et al., 2008).

NEGATIVE CONSEQUENCES. There is some debate over ecstasy being a neurotoxin, though some research (Kuhn et al., 2008) suggests that heavy ecstasy use can have long-term effects on memory. However, the most dangerous adverse effects of using ecstasy are the potential for hyperthermia (elevated body temperature) and hyponatremia (low sodium), both of which can cause death (Gowing, Henry-Edwards, Irvine & Ali, 2002). In addition, ecstasy negatively affects cardiac function through arrhythmias and inflammation of the heart (Doweiko, 2006).

Inhalants and Volatile Hydrocarbons

Kuhn et al. (2008) explained that the chemicals that fall into the inhalant and volatile hydrocarbon category have little in common with each other except for the fact that they are all inhaled. In short, there are three types of chemicals that are often inhaled for their psychoactive effect: (a) nitrates, (b) gas anesthetic such as nitrous oxide, and (c) solvents. The nitrates relax smooth muscle in the body, lower blood pressure, increase heart rate and produce a calm sense of euphoria. Nitrous oxide, commonly used as a general anesthetic, relieves pain, elicits euphoria, reduces inhibitions, and induces sleep at higher doses. Solvents have similar effects to those of alcohol, though they can produce mild visual and sensory hallucinations. The adverse consequences of sustained inhalant use during adolescence are well documented (Doweiko, 2006; Garland & Howard, 2011). Potential health risks include harm to the heart, kidneys, liver, and lungs, as well as irreversible damage to the brain and death through hypoxia.

PROCESS ADDICTIONS

Having done a thorough exploration of problematic chemical use, the authors now move to those behaviors that can become problematic for children and adolescents: eating, gambling, sex, spending, exercise, the Internet, and video games. We offer a brief description of each behavior with a special emphasis on how they can impact adolescent males. For those interested in additional information related to these behaviors, resources are offered at the end of this chapter.

Addictive Eating

Addictive eating, which includes the eating disorders known as anorexia, bulimia, and compulsive overeating, affect more than 14 million Americans (APA, 2000). Addictive eating has been defined as a disease characterized by an excessive relationship with food, weight, and calories, as well as the loss of control over the amount eaten (National Institute of Mental Health, 2008). Further, addictive eating is created by a physiological, biochemical condition of the body that creates cravings for complex carbohydrates (Bate, 2003). This physical response has also been linked directly to psychological processes, such as depression and anxiety (Allen, Byrne, La Puma, McLean, & Davis, 2008). Individuals often experience difficulties distinguishing between emotions and physical hunger, difficulties describing and labeling their feelings, and issues of control. For example, an adolescent who struggles with addictive eating may interpret his feelings of loneliness and emptiness as hunger and use food to feel fulfilled. The relationship with food, weight, and calories represses such things as anxiety, depression, low self-esteem, social anxiety, and passivity (Allen et al., 2008).

Adolescents are perhaps the largest age group to suffer from addictive relationships with eating, which includes detrimental methods of weight control, chronic dieting, excessive exercise, self-induced vomiting, and the abuse of laxatives, diet medications, and water pills. Although such concerns have traditionally been associated with females, boys and adolescent males also struggle in this area, with between 5% and 10% of males reporting some form of addictive eating (Farley, 1997; Yager et al., 1993).

Addictive Gambling

Addictive gambling is characterized by a repetitive and consistent pattern of gambling behavior despite unfavorable outcomes (Dickson & Derevensky, 2006). This disorder is typically male-dominated and can be chronic, progressive, and consume the affected individual's life (Iancu, Lowengrub, Dembinsky, Kotler, & Dannon, 2008). Although individuals often gamble to escape their problems and relieve stress, this behavior typically further complicates their lives. Some of the specific consequences experienced by those addicted to gambling include the loss of family, decreased self-esteem, incarceration, loss of jobs, expulsion from school, and depression. Consequently, this addictive disorder has the highest rate of suicidal ideations and completions (Potenza, Fiellin, Heninger, Rounsaville, & Mazure, 2002). Slutske (2006) suggested that approximately one-third of individuals with a history of compulsive gambling recover from this disorder.

According to a study conducted by Harvard University, adolescents are twice as likely as adults to be addicted to gambling (Hardoon & Derevensky, 2002). Among the adolescent population, 4% to 7% are addicted, and an additional 10% to 14% are considered problem gamblers, which is exhibited by a loss of control and the beginning of negative consequences (Howard, Horard, George, & Cummings, 1995). In total, this would indicate that between 14% and 21% of adolescents struggle with gambling, with the vast majority being males. Some additional figures help demonstrate the magnitude of this problem: 75% of children 12 and under have placed bets (Proimos, DuRant, Dwyer Pierce, & Goodman, 1998), 76% to 91% of all seniors have gambled (Buchta, 1995), and 90%

of adult compulsive gamblers started in adolescence (Fong, 2006). Clearly there is a problem among adolescents.

According to Buchta (1995) common bets for adolescents include dares, video games, sports, Internet activities, personal possessions (for example Pokémon cards), other card games, games of skill (for example basketball or pool), and other betting venues. The two biggest venues for betting among adolescents are March Madness (the NCAA college basketball play-offs in the month of March) and the purchase of lottery and scratch off tickets.

Sexual Addiction

The prevalence and impacts of sexual addiction are very difficult to assess among children and adolescents, likely due to the sensitivity of parents and caregivers related to having their children assessed/surveyed in topics related to sexuality. Overall, between 6% and 13% of Americans are addicted to sexuality, which equates to between 17 and 37 million people (Carnes, 2001; Cooper, Delmonico, & Burg, 2000; Wolfe, 2000). Carnes (2001) identified three levels of sexually addictive behaviors: (a) Level 1 behaviors include compulsive masturbation, compulsive use of pornography, and multiple sexual partners; (b) Level 2 behaviors include those behaviors for which we have societal titles (e.g., exhibitionism, voyeurism, and frotteurism); (c) Level 3 behaviors, which include compulsive molestation, incest, and rape, have severe consequences for both victims and perpetrators alike.

Carnes (1994) offers a few noteworthy caveats in helping us to better understand those who struggle with sexual addiction. First, although there is progression in sexual addiction as in the other addictions (i.e., gone untreated, the addicted individual will move into more intense, frequent, and/or risky behaviors), not every sexual addict moves beyond Level 1 behaviors. Second, those who engage in the range of sexual behaviors such as prostitution, voyeurism, or rape are not necessarily sexual addicts: these behaviors have a variety of etiologies. Finally, these levels were created for the purpose of helping us better understand the behavior clusters that exist in sexual addiction: the term addiction should be clearly designated with the definition offered earlier by Goodman (2001) and not confused with a strong sexual appetite or curiosity that may be a part of many nonaddicted individuals' lifestyles.

As noted, there is a paucity of studies that have investigated the impact of sexual addiction on adolescent males. The studies that *have* examined sexuality among adolescents look more at "high-risk sexuality" and demonstrate a co-occurrence of such behaviors with the use of alcohol, drugs, cigarettes, and other risk-taking behaviors (Abrantes et al., 2009; Black, Kehrberg, Flumerfelt, & Schlosser, 1997; Delmonico & Griffin,

1997). Nonetheless, for those who are addicted to sex (as noted in the adult population), common feelings include a deep sense of shame, isolation, despair, and a fear of being discovered (Weiss, 2004; Young, 2008). As such, suicidal ideations can be very high among this population of adolescent males.

Addictive Spending

Addictive spending (also known as compulsive buying) has been defined as persistent and cyclical purchasing that occurs in relation to negative feelings or events (Kellett & Bolton, 2009; O'Guinn & Farber, 1989); prevalence rates in the United States range between 1% and 10% (Benson, 2000). The consumer or "purchase on credit" mentality in this country has perpetuated this disorder (Rose, 2007) among adolescents who often view their parents spending beyond their means, particularly in response to some form of need fulfillment. In terms of addictions that co-occur with addictive spending, television, and Internet addictions are quite common given that these are two sources where spending can occur from home. Furthermore, smoking, drug use, alcohol consumption, and addictive eating are common among adolescents with addictions to spending (Faber, Christenson, de Zwaan, & Mitchell, 1995). Feelings common to those that use spending to self-medicate include depression, anxiety, intense frustration, and low self-esteem (Miller, 2007; Rindfleisch, Burroughs, & Denton, 1997). In addition to negative feelings, other etiological foundations of spending addiction include familial patterns of spending and inconsistent communication styles (Edwards, 1993). In terms of possible consequences for the addictive spender, financial destruction of the individual or the family, and legal-related issues (bad check writing, extortion, shoplifting, and forgery) can have devastating effects (Clark & Calleja, 2008; Lee & Mysyk, 2004).

In terms of how spending affects adolescents, some have alluded to its impact by reporting that 6% of adolescents struggle with addictions to spending (the majority of whom are female), with most compulsive buyers starting in their late teens or early 20s (Black, 2007; Lee & Mysyk, 2004; Miller, 2007). Given that the possession of credit cards and addictive spending are highly correlative, the societal trend to decrease the age that individuals can possess credit cards has yielded predictable results. Specifically, a recent study conducted by Baylor University indicated that 40% of those born between the years of 1977 and 1997 reported that they received their first credit cards in high school (Pirog & Roberts, 2007). What is more, the study also concluded that there has been a significant rise in addictive spending among adolescents in recent years. Although more research is needed in this area, addictive spending is impacting more adolescents today than in any other time in history.

Addictive Exercise

Given the emphasis for physical health and exercise in the United States, it can be challenging to determine the difference between healthy and unhealthy patterns of exercise. Perhaps the best way to separate healthy exercisers from those who abuse exercise is their attitude. Unlike those who view exercise as a part of their wellness routine (i.e., missing a workout has no detrimental consequences), for those addicted to exercise, the ability to workout/perform encompasses their daily thoughts and emotions and dictates how they organize their time (Aidman & Woollard, 2003).

Exercise abusers will often lie about their exercise patterns, tend to disregard sickness and injury, and experience withdrawal symptoms such as anxiety, irritation, and even severe depression when unable to exercise (Adams & Kirby, 2002; Allegre, Souville, Therme, & Griffiths, 2006; Zmijewski & Howard, 2003). They may also experience sleeping problems, muscle soreness, changes in appetite, and mood swings. Compulsive exercisers (a) tend to be dissatisfied with their body and/or themselves; (b) may exercise to gain control of something in their lives, but find themselves becoming controlled by the activity; (c) suffer from a lack of free time; (d) can become dependent on the euphoric and calming benefits of exercise; (e) are avid goal-setters and can struggle with perfectionism, and; (f) can become socially withdrawn when the exercise becomes more important than any other person or activity in their lives (Aidman & Woollard, 2003; Bamber, Cockerill, & Carroll, 2000; Draeger, 2005; Zmijewski & Howard, 2003).

Little has been written about how addictive exercise directly affects adolescents. This may be due in part to the difficulty in separating these behaviors from those seen as a part of disordered/addictive eating (i.e., those who struggle with an addictive relationship with food often struggle with maladaptive weight loss methods such as exercise) (Davis, 2000). Another possible complicating factor involves the developmental and physical changes that occur in adolescence and how these impact body image, weight distribution, and the use of exercise. Nonetheless, the research that has been done in this area has identified some typical factors that predispose adolescent males to exercise addiction, including low self-esteem, body dissatisfaction, and eating disorders (Bamber, Cockerill, & Carroll, 2000; Davis, 2000). Adolescents are particularly vulnerable to becoming obsessed with working out, either to excel at a sport or to become "fit" as defined by cultural norms, media images, and peer influences (McCabe & Ricciardelli, 2004). These same authors noted in their study that males tend to use compulsive exercise as a means to a stronger and more fit body (in response to cultural expectations of having a "manly" physique). Although concerns about body image have traditionally been thought to be a preoccupation among females, with some studies noting that adolescent females struggle with addictive exercise more so than males (e.g., McCabe & Ricciardelli, 2004), other research suggests that body image concerns have been affecting young males in increasing numbers (e.g., O'Dea & Abraham, 2002).

Internet Addiction

Like the other behaviors we have mentioned, when done in moderation, few negative consequences occur with the use of the Internet. However, when adolescents become addicted, consequences such as negatively impacted relationships with family and friends, poor school performance (procrastination, poor time management, and decreased productivity), exacerbated comorbid conditions (loneliness, depression, impulse control problems, low self-esteem), financial difficulties, physical complaints (e.g., dry eyes, back aches, wrist and finger cramping), and illegal activities (e.g., child pornography, sexual harassment, cyberbullying) can occur (Davis, Flett, & Besser, 2002; Griffiths, 2003; Hagedorn & Young, 2011; Hall & Parsons, 2001; Young, 1999). Addictions to spending, gambling, gaming, and pornography are exacerbated by the Internet, with between 17 and 41 million Americans reportedly being addicted (National Center on Addiction and Substance Abuse at Columbia University, 2003).

Of those reportedly addicted to the Internet, some studies have identified that between 6% and 10% are adolescents (Chou & Hsiao, 2000; Park, Kim, & Cho, 2008). Adolescents in today's world have always had instant access to such things as information, e-mail, instant messaging, online games (discussed in the following section), online gambling, online pornography, and social media (Facebook, MySpace, etc.). Not surprisingly, youth have often been exposed to inappropriate content at a very young age, to include pornography, violence, and information about illicit drug use (Stanley, 2003). Although the results of such early access have not been conclusively determined, addicted adolescents often experience the full gamut of consequences that were noted earlier (Nalwa & Anand, 2003).

Gaming Addiction

Hagedorn and Young (2011) wrote much on the impact of gaming addiction on adolescents. Upward of 90% of American youth play video and/or online games, with approximately 10% to 15% meeting criteria for addiction (the majority of which are male) (Chak & Leung, 2004; Griffiths & Hunt, 1995; Grusser et al., 2007). The consequences of

Internet-based gaming has garnered recent attention and includes such things as withdrawal from primary relationships, poor hygiene and nutritional deficiencies, drops in school performance, and even suicidal and homicidal behaviors (Hart et al., 2009; Smahel, Blinka, & Ledabyl, 2008; Tanner, 2007). Those who struggle in this area experience cravings, mood swings (particularly when unable to engage in gaming: anxiety, anger, irritation, and depression), poor impulse control, continued use despite negative consequences, and significant losses at work, school, recreation, interpersonal relationships, and spirituality (Grusser et al., 2007).

Adolescents can experience significant negative consequences should they get hooked on the biggest culprit: massive multiplayer online role-playing games (MMORPGs), also known as MMOs (Chappell, Eatough, Davies, & Griffiths, 2006). These competitive games are played simultaneously with millions of people around the world, with the action occurring in real time. MMO games never end, as they are built upon mission completion, the attainment of escalating skills, powers, and weapons, and the need to work together as a unit. Team members may live anywhere in the world. Therefore, if an American teenager living in California wishes to participate in a mission that is being led by a German youth beginning at 9 o'clock in the morning German time, the mission would start at 12 a.m. California time. One can imagine how this time table would impact sleep patterns and the resulting consequences on such things as school performance. More and more youth are being swept up in the online gaming community, with Smahel et al. (2008) reporting that many average upward of 23 hours per week playing these games, with almost 9% reporting having spent 40 hours per week.

CONCLUSION

Given the complexity and prevalence of addictive disorders with young men and adolescents, it is important that clinicians be equipped with the necessary tools to identify, assess, and refer clients with primary or comorbid disorders that fall within this classification. In an attempt to further inform practitioners, this chapter explored methods for assessing addictive disorders. In addition, both broad and specific definitions of the chemical and behavioral addictions that commonly plague boys and young men were introduced. Being that we assert it is equally important for general practitioners to possess the skills and knowledge necessary for effective treatment and intervention with addicted populations, the subsequent chapter, *Stopping the Cycle: Treating Addictions in Young Men*, turns its focus to strategies for intervening with addicted young men and boys.

REFERENCES

Abrantes, A., Lee, C., MacPherson, L., Strong, D., Borrelli, B., & Brown, R. (2009). Health risk behaviors in relation to making a smoking quit attempt among adolescents. *Journal of Behavioral Medicine, 32*(2), 142–149.

Adams, J., & Kirkby, R. (2002). Excessive exercise as an addiction: A review. *Addiction Research & Theory, 10*(5), 415–437.

Aidman, E., & Woollard, S. (2003). The influence of self-reported exercise addiction on acute emotional and physiological responses to brief exercise deprivation. *Psychology of Sport and Exercise, 4*, 225–236.

Allegre, B., Souville, M., Therme, P., & Griffiths, M. (2006). Definitions and measures of exercise dependence. *Addiction Research and Theory, 14*(6), 631–646.

Allen, K., Byrne, S., La Puma, M., McLean, N., & Davis, E. (2008). The onset and course of binge eating in 8- to 13-year-old healthy weight, overweight and obese children. *Eating Behaviors, 9*(4), 438–446.

American Psychiatric Association. (2000). *Diagnostic and statistical manual of mental disorders* (4th ed., Text Revision). Washington, DC: Author.

Arseneault, L., Cannon, M., Witton, J., & Murray, R. (2004). Causal association between cannabis and psychosis: examination of the evidence. *The British Journal of Psychiatry: The Journal of Mental Science, 184*, 110–117.

Bamber, D., Cockerill, I., & Carroll, D. (2000). The pathological status of exercise dependence. *British Journal of Sports Medicine, 34*(2), 125–132.

Bate, R. (2003). Addiction inflation. *American Enterprise Institute for Public Policy* Research. Retrieved June 23, 2008, from http://www.aei.org/publications/pubID.19586,filter.social/ pub_detail.asp

Becker, B., Wagner, D., Gouzoulis-Mayfrank, E., Spuentrup, E., & Daumann, J. (2010). Altered parahippocampal functioning in cannabis users is related to the frequency of use. *Psychopharmacology, 209*(4), 361–374.

Benson, A. (2000). *I shop, therefore, I am*. Northvale, NJ: Jason Aronson, Inc.

Black, D. (2007). Compulsive buying disorder: A review of the evidence. *CNS Spectrums, 2*(2), 124–132.

Black, D. W., Kehrberg, L. L. D., Flumerfelt, D. L., & Schlosser, S. S. (1997). Characteristics of 36 subjects reporting compulsive sexual behavior. *American Journal of Psychiatry, 154*, 243–249.

Bostwick, J., & Bucci, J. (2008). Internet sex addiction treated with naltrexone. *Mayo ClinicProceedings, 83*(2), 226–230.

Buchta, R. (1995). Gambling among adolescents. *Clinical Pediatrics, 34*(7), 346–349.

Carnes, P. (2001). *Out of the shadows: Understanding sexual addiction* (3rd ed.). Center City, MN: Hazelden.

Carnes, P. (1994). *Contrary to love: Helping the sexual addict*. Center City, MN: Hazelden.

Chak, K., & Leung, L. (2004). Shyness and locus of control as predictors of Internet addiction and Internet use. *CyberPsychology & Behavior, 7*, 559–570.

Chappell, D., Eatough, V., Davies, M., & Griffiths, M. (2006). EverQuest—It's just a computer game right? An interpretative phenomenological analysis of online gaming addiction. *International Journal of Mental Health and Addiction,* *4*(3), 205–216.

Chou, C., & Hsiao, M. C. (2000). Internet addiction, usage, gratification, and pleasure experience: The Taiwan college students' case. *Computers and Education, 35,* 65–80.

Clark, M., & Calleja, K. (2008). Shopping addiction: A preliminary investigation among Maltese university students. *Addiction Research & Theory, 16*(6), 633–649.

Cooper, A., Delmonico, D. L., & Burg, R. (2000). Cybersex users, abusers, and compulsives: New findings and implications. *Sexual Addiction & Compulsivity, 7,* 5–29.

Copersino, M. L., Boyd, S. J., Tashkin, D. P., Huestis, M. A., Heishman, S. J., Dermand, J. C., Simmons, M. S., & Gorelick, D. A. (2010). Sociodemographic characteristics of cannabis smokers and the experience of cannabis withdrawal. *American Journal of Drug & Alcohol Abuse, 36*(6), 311–319.

Council for Accreditation of Counseling and Related Educational Programs (2008). *CACREP 2009 standards.* Retrieved on August 29, 2008, from: http://www.cacrep.org/ 2009standards.html

Craig, R. J. (2004). *Counseling the alcohol and drug dependent client: A practical approach.* Boston: Pearson/Allyn and Bacon.

Davis, C. (2000). Exercise abuse. *International Journal of Sport Psychology, 31,* 278–289.

Davis, R. A., Flett, G. L., & Besser, A. (2002). Validation of a new scale for measuring problematic internet use: Implications for pre-employment screening. *Cyberpsychology and Behavior, 5,* 331–345.

De Bellis, M., Clark, D., Beers, S., Soloff, P., Boring, A., Hall, J., Kersh, A., & Keshavan, M. (2000). Hippocampal volume in adolescent-onset alcohol use disorders. *The American Journal of Psychiatry, 157*(5), 737–744.

Degenhardt, L., Bruno, R., & Topp, L. (2010). Is ecstasy a drug of dependence? *Drug & Alcohol Dependence, 107*(1), 1–10. doi:10.1016/j.drugalcdep.2009.09.009

Degenhardt, L., Coffey, C., Moran, P., Carlin, J. B., & Patton, G. C. (2007). The predictors and consequences of adolescent amphetamine use: findings from the Victoria Adolescent Health Cohort Study. *Addiction, 102*(7), 1076–1084.

Delmonico, D. L., & Griffin, E. (1997). Classifying problematic sexual behavior: A working model. *Sexual Addiction & Compulsivity, 4,* 91–104.

Dennis, M. L., White, M. K., & Ives, M. L. (2009). Individual characteristics and needs associated with substance misuse of adolescents and young adults in addiction treatment. In C. G. Leukefeld, T. P. Gullotta & M. Staton-Tindall (Eds.), *Adolescent substance abuse: Evidence-based approaches to prevention and treatment* (45–72). New York: Springer.

Dickson, L., & Derevensky, J. (2006). Equipping school psychologists to address another risky behavior: The case for understanding youth problem gambling. *Canadian Journal of School Psychology, 21*(1), 59–72.

Doweiko, H. E. (2006). *Concepts of chemical dependency.* Australia: Thomson/Brooks/Cole.

Draeger, J. (2005). The obligatory exerciser. *Physician and Sports Medicine Journal, 33*(6), 13–23.

Earleywine, M. (2005). Cannabis. In M. Earleywine (Ed.), *Mind altering drugs: The science of subjective experience* (240–257). New York: Oxford University.

Edwards, E. A. (1993). Development of a new scale for measuring compulsive buying behavior. *Financial Counseling and Planning, 4*, 67–85.

Ewing, J. A. (1984). Detecting alcoholism: The CAGE Questionnaire. *JAMA, 252*, 1905–1907.

Faber, R., Christenson, G., de Zwaan, M., & Mitchell, J. (1995). Two forms of compulsive consumption: Comorbidity of compulsive buying and binge eating. *Journal of Consumer Research, 22*(3), 296–304.

Farley, D. (1997). *On the teen scene: Eating disorders require medical attention.* U.S. Food and Drug Administration FDA Consumer. Retrieved March 12, 2009, from http://www.cfsan.fda.gov/~dms/fdeatdis.html

Fong, T. (2006). Pathological gambling in adolescents: No longer child's play. *Adolescent Psychiatry, 29*, 119–147.

Freye, E., & Levy, J. V. (2009). *Pharmacology and abuse of cocaine, amphetamines, ecstasy and related designer drugs: A comprehensive review on their mode of action, treatment of abuse and intoxication.* Dordrecht, NY: Springer.

Garland, E. L., & Howard, M. O. (2011). Adverse consequences of acute inhalant intoxication. *Experimental and Clinical Psychopharmacology, 19*(2), 134–144. doi:10.1037/a0022859.

Giannini, A. J., & Slaby, A. E. (1989). *Drugs of abuse.* Oradell, NJ: Medical Economics Books.

Goodman, A. (2001). What's in a name? Terminology for designating a syndrome of driven sexual behavior. *Sexual Addiction & Compulsivity, 8*, 191–213.

Gowing, L. R., Henry-Edwards, S. M., Irvine, R. J., & Ali, R. L. (2002). The health effects of ecstasy: A literature review. *Drug & Alcohol Review, 21*(1), 53–63.

Griffiths, M. (2003). Internet abuse in the workplace: Issues and concerns for employers and employment counselors. *Journal of Employment Counseling, 40*(2), 87–96.

Griffiths, M., & Hunt, N. (1995). Computer game playing in adolescence: Prevalence and demographic indicators. *Journal of Community & Applied Social Psychology, 5*(3), 189–193.

Grusser, S. M., Thalemann, R., & Griffiths, M. D. (2007). Excessive computer game playing: Evidence for addiction and aggression? *Cyberpsychology & Behavior, 10*(2), 290–292.

Guay, D. (2009). Drug treatment of paraphilic and nonparaphilic sexual disorders. *Clinical Therapeutics, 31*(1), 1–31.

Hagedorn, W. B. (2009). The call for a new Diagnostic and Statistical Manual of Mental Disorders diagnosis: Addictive disorders. *Journal of Addictions & Offender Counseling, 29*, 110–127.

Hagedorn, W. B., & Juhnke, G. A. (2005). Treating the sexually addicted client: Establishing a need for increased counselor awareness. *Journal of Addictions & Offender Counseling, 25*(2), 66–86.

Hagedorn, W. B., & Young, T. (2011). Identifying and intervening with students exhibiting signs of gaming addiction and other addictive behaviors: Implications for professional school counselors. *Professional School Counseling, 14*(4), 250–260.

Hall, A. S., & Parsons, J. (2001). Internet addiction: College student case study using best practices in Cognitive Behavior Therapy. *Journal of Mental Health Counseling, 23*, 312–327.

Haney, M., Hart, C. L., Vosburg, S. K., Nasser, J., Bennett, A., Zubaran, C., & Foltin, R. W. (2004). Marijuana withdrawal in humans: Effects of oral THC or divalproex. *Neuropsychopharmacology, 29*(1), 158–170. doi:10.1038/sj.npp.1300310.

Hart, G., Johnson, B., Stamm, B., Angers, N., Robinson, A., Lally, T., et al. (2009). Effects of video games on adolescents and adults. *CyberPsychology & Behavior, 12*(1), 63–65.

Hardoon, K. K., & Derevensky, J. L. (2002). Child and adolescent gambling behavior: Current knowledge. *Clinical Child Psychology and Psychiatry, 7*(2), |263–281. doi:10.1177/1359104502007002012.

Hashibe, M., Straif, K., Tashkin, D. P., Morgenstern, H., Greenland, S., & Zhang, Z. (2005). Epidemiologic review of marijuana use and cancer risk. *Alcohol, 35*(3), 265–275. doi:10.1016/j.alcohol.2005.04.008.

Howard, G., Horard, S., George, E., & Cummings, T. (1995). *North American think tank on youth gambling issues: A blueprint for responsible public policy in the management of compulsive gambling.* Harvard University, MA: Council on Compulsive Gambling and MCCG/NATI.

Hubbard, J., Franco, S., & Onaivi, E. (1999). Marijuana: medical implications. *American Family Physician, 60*(9), 2583.

Iancu, I., Lowengrub, K., Dembinsky, Y., Kotler, M., & Dannon, P. N. (2008). Pathological gambling: An update on neuropathophysiology and pharmacotherapy. *CNS Drugs, 22*(2), 123–138.

Johnston, L. D., O'Malley, P. M., Bachman, J. G., & Schulenberg, J. E. (2010). *Monitoring the Future: National Results on Adolescent Drug Use. Overview of Key Findings, 2009.* NIH Publication No. 10–7583. National Institutes of Health, Retrieved from EBSCOhost.

Juhnke, G. A., & Hagedorn, W. B. (2006). *Counseling addicted families: A sequential assessment & treatment model.* New York, NY: Brunner-Routledge.

Kalb, C. (2001). Painkiller crackdown. *Newsweek, 137*(20), 38.

Kampman, K. M., Volpicelli, J. R., Mulvaney, F., Rukstalis, M., Alterman, A. I., Pettinati, H., Weinrieb, R. M., & O'Brien, C. P. (2002). Cocaine withdrawal severity and urine toxicology results from treatment entry predict outcome in medication trials for cocaine dependence. *Addictive Behaviors, 27*(2), 251–260. doi:10.1016/S0306–4603(01)00171-X.

Kellett, S., & Bolton, J. (2009). Compulsive buying: A cognitive–behavioural model. *Clinical Psychology & Psychotherapy, 16*(2), 83–99.

Kelly, B. C., & Parsons, J. T. (2007). Prescription drug misuse among club drug-using young adults. *American Journal of Drug & Alcohol Abuse, 33*(6), 875–884. doi:10.1080/00952990701667347

Kelly, T. M., Kazura, A. N., Lommel, K. M., Babalonis S., & Martin, C. A. (2009). A biological/genetic perspective: The addicted brain. In C. G. Leukefeld, T. P. Gullotta & M. Staton-Tindall (Eds.), *Adolescent substance abuse: Evidence-based approaches to prevention and treatment* (pp. 15–45). New York, NY: Springer.

King, M. (1986). At risk among general practice attenders: Validation of the CAGE Questionnaire. *Psychological Medicine, 16*, 213–217.

Kolodny, R. C., Masters, W. H., Kolodner, R. M., & Toro, G. (1974). Depression of plasma testosterone levels after chronic intensive marihuana use. *The New England Journal of Medicine, 290*(16), 872–874.

Kuhn, C., Swartzwelder, S., Wilson, W., Wilson, L. H., & Foster, J. (2008). *Buzzed: The straight facts about the most used and abused drugs from alcohol to ecstasy.* New York, NY: W.W. Norton.

Landry, M. J. (1994). *Understanding drugs of abuse: The processes of addiction, treatment, and recovery.* Washington, DC: American Psychiatric Press.

Lee, S., & Mysyk, A. (2004). The medicalization of compulsive buying. *Social Science & Medicine, 58*, 1709–1718.

Lenné, M. G., Dietze, P. M., Triggs, T. J., Walmsley, S., Murphy, B., & Redman, J. R. (2010). The effects of cannabis and alcohol on simulated arterial driving: Influences of driving experience and task demand. *Accident Analysis & Prevention, 42*(3), 859–866. doi:10.1016/j.aap.2009.04.021.

Mahmood, O. M., Jacobus, J., Bava, S., Scarlett, A., & Tapert, S. F. (2010). Learning and memory performance in adolescent users of alcohol and marijuana: Interactive effects. *Journal of Studies on Alcohol and Drugs, 71*(6), 885–894.

Marshall, B., & Werb, D. (2010). Health outcomes associated with methamphetamine use among young people: a systematic review. *Addiction, 105*(6), 991–1002.

Mayfield, D., McLeod, G., & Hall, P. (1974). The CAGE Questionnaire: Validation of a new alcoholism screening instrument. *American Journal of Psychiatry, 131*, 1121–1123.

McCabe, M., & Ricciardelli, L. (2004). A longitudinal study of pubertal timing and extreme body change behaviors among adolescent boys and girls. *Adolescence, 39*(153), 145–166.

McCrystal, P., & Percy, A. (2010). Factors associated with teenage ecstasy use. *Drugs: Education, Prevention & Policy, 17*(5), 507–527. doi:10.3109/09687630902810691

Mehra, R., Moore, B., Crothers, K., Tetrault, J., & Fiellin, D. (2006). The association between marijuana smoking and lung cancer: A systematic review. *Archives of Internal Medicine, 166*(13), 1359–1367.

Merta, R. J. (2001). Addictions counseling. *Counseling and Human Development, 33*(5), 1–15.

Milin, R., Manion, I., Dare, G., & Walker, S. (2008). Prospective assessment of cannabis withdrawal in adolescents with cannabis dependence: A pilot study. *Journal of the American Academy of Child & Adolescent Psychiatry, 47*(2), 174.

Miller, M. (2007, January). Compulsive buying. *Harvard Mental Health Letter.* Harvard Health Publications. Retrieved on May 12, 2008 from: https://www.health.harvard.edu/newsletters/harvard_mental_health_letter/2007/January

Miller, W. R., & Rollnick, S. (2002). *Motivational interviewing: Preparing people for change* (2nd ed.). New York, NY: The Guilford Press.

Nahas, G. G., & Burks, T. F. (1997). *Drug abuse in the decade of the brain.* Amsterdam, Netherlands: IOS Press.

Nakken, C. (1996). *The addictive personality: Understanding the addictive process and compulsive behavior* (2nd ed.). Center City, MN: Hazelden.

Nalwa, K., & Anand, A. P. (2003). Internet addiction in students: A cause of concern. *CyberPsychology & Behavior, 6*(6), 653–656.

National Center on Addiction and Substance Abuse at Columbia University. (2003). CASA conference food for thought: *Substance abuse and eating disorders*. Retrieved April 18, 2004, from http://www.casacolumbia.org/pdshopprov/files/fod_far._ihou^_12_C6.pdft5eaidi='fixd%20fa-%20thoughn%20Substance%2C6buse%20Mid%

National Institute of Mental Health (2008). *Eating disorders*. Retrieved March 12, 2009, from http://www.nimh.nih.gov/health/publications/eating-disorders/index.shtml

O'Dea, J. A., & Abraham, S. (2002). Eating and exercise disorders in young college men. *Journal of American College Health, 50*, 273–278.

O'Guinn, T., & Faber, R. (1989). Compulsive buying: A phenomenological exploration. *Journal of Consumer Research, 16*, 147–157.

Park, S., Kim, J., & Cho, C. (2008). Prevalence of Internet addiction and correlations with family factors among South Korean adolescents. *Adolescence (San Diego): An international quarterly devoted to the physiological, psychological, psychiatric, sociological, and educational aspects of the second decade of human life, 43*(172), 895–910.

Pennay, A. E., & Lee, N. K. (2011). Putting the call out for more research: The poor evidence base for treating methamphetamine withdrawal. *Drug & Alcohol Review, 30*(2), 216–222.

Petry, N. M., Bickel, W. K., & Arnett, M. (1998). Shortened time horizons and insensitivity to future consequences in heroin addicts. *Addiction, 93*(5), 729–738. doi:10.1080/09652149835576.

Pirog, S. F., & Roberts, J. A. (2007). Personality and credit card misuse among college students: The mediating role of impulsiveness. *The Journal of Marketing Theory and Practice, 15*(1), 65–77.

Potenza, M., Fiellin, D., Heninger, G., Rounsaville, B., & Mazure, C. (2002). Gambling. *Journal of General Internal Medicine, 17*, 721–732.

Proimos, J., DuRant, R., Dwyer P. J., & Goodman, E. (1998).Gambling and other risk behaviors among 8th- to 12th-grade students. *Pediatrics, 102*(2), 1–6.

Ramaekers, J., Kauert, G., Theunissen, E., Toennes, S., & Moeller, M. (2009). Neurocognitive performance during acute THC intoxication in heavy and occasional cannabis users. *Journal of Psychopharmacology, 23*(3), 266–277.

Reimer, J., Verthein, U., Karow, A., Schaefer, I., Naber, D., & Haasen, C. (2011). Physical and mental health in severe opioid-dependent patients within a randomized controlled maintenance treatment trial. *Addiction, 106*(9), 1647–1655.

Rindfleisch, A., Burroughs, J., & Denton, F. (1997). Family structure, materialism, and compulsive consumption. *Journal of Consumer Research, 23*, 312–325.

Rose, P. (2007). Mediators of the association between narcissism and compulsive buying: Theories of materialism and impulse control. *Psychology of Addictive Behaviors, 21*(4), 76–581.

Schuckit, M. A. (2000). *Drug and alcohol abuse: A clinical guide to diagnosis and treatment*. New York: Kluwer Academic/Plenum Publishers.

Schulte, S. J., Meier, P. S., Sterling, J., & Berry, M (2010). Unrecognized dual diagnosis—A risk factor for dropout of addiction treatment. *Mental health and Substance Use: Dual Diagnosis, 3*(2), 94–109.

Schwartz, R. H., & Miller, N. S. (1997). MDMA (ecstasy) and the rave: A review. *Pediatrics, 100*(4), 705.

Slutske, W. S. (2006). Natural recovery and treatment-seeking in pathological gambling: Results of two U.S. national surveys. *The American Journal of Psychiatry, 163*, 297–302.

Smahel, D., Blinka, L., & Ledabyl, O. (2008). Playing MMORPGs: Connections between addiction and identifying with a character. *Cyberpsychology & Behavior, 11*(6), 715–718.

Solowij, N., Jones, K., Rozman, M., Davis, S., Ciarrochi, J., Heaven, P., Lubman, D. I., & Yücel, M. (2011). Verbal learning and memory in adolescent cannabis users, alcohol users and non-users. *Psychopharmacology, 216*(1), 131–144.

Stagman, S., Schwarz, S., & Powers, D. (2011). *Adolescent substance use in the U.S.: Facts for policymakers.* Fact sheet. National Center for Children in Poverty.

Stanley, J. (2003). "Downtime" for children on the Internet: Recognizing a new form of child abuse. *Family Matters, 65*, 22–27.

Stevens, P., & Smith, R. L. (2005). *Substance abuse counseling: Theory and practice.* Upper Saddle River, NJ: Pearson.

Tanner, L. (June 21, 2007). AMA considers classifying video game addiction as a mental illness. *Associated Press.* Retrieved on June 22, 2007 from http://news.yahoo.com/s/ap/20070621 /ap_on_hi_te/video_game_addiction

Vikander, B., Koechling, U. M., Borg, S., Tönne, U., & Hiltunen, A. J. (2010). Benzodiazepine tapering: A prospective study. *Nordic Journal of Psychiatry, 64*(4), 273–282. doi:10.3109/08039481003624173.

Walsh, S. L., Stoops, W. W., Moody, D. E., Lin, S., & Bigelow, G. E. (2009). Repeated dosing with oral cocaine in humans: Assessment of direct effects, withdrawal, and pharmacokinetics. *Experimental and Clinical Psychopharmacology, 17*(4), 205–216. doi:10.1037/a0016469.

Weiss, D. (2004). The prevalence of depression in male sex addicts residing in the United States. *Sexual Addiction & Compulsivity, 11*(1), 57–69.

Westphal, J., Jackson, A., Thomas, S., & Blaszczynski, A. (2008). A review of pharmacological approaches to intervention in pathological gambling. *Journal of Social Work Practice in the Addictions, 8*(2), 192–207.

Whittinghill, D., Carroll, J., & Morgan, O. (2004). Curriculum standards for the education of professional substance abuse counselors. *Journal of Teaching in the Addictions, 3*(2), 63–76.

Wolfe, J. L. (2000). Assessment and treatment of compulsive sex/love behavior. *Journal of Rational-Emotive & Cognitive-Behavior Therapy, 18*(4), 235–246.

Wu, P., Liu, X., Pham, T., Jin, J., Fan, B. & Jin, Z. (2010). Ecstasy use among US adolescents from 1999 to 2008, *Drug and Alcohol Dependence, 112*(1–2), 33–38.

Wu, L., Pilowsky, D., & Patkar, A. (2008). Non-prescribed use of pain relievers among adolescents in the United States. *Drug & Alcohol Dependence, 94*(1–3), 1–11.

Wu, T., Tashkin, D., Djahed, B., & Rose, J. (1988). Pulmonary hazards of smoking marijuana as compared with tobacco. *The New England Journal of Medicine, 318*(6), 347–351.

Yager, J., Andersen, A., Devin, M., Mitchell, J., Powers, P., & Yates, A. (1993). American Psychiatric Association practice guidelines for eating disorders. *American Journal of Psychiatry, 150*, 207–228.

Young, K. (1999). Internet addiction: Symptoms, evaluation, and treatment. In L. VandeCreek & T. Jackson (Eds.), *Innovations in clinical practice: A sourcebook* (pp. 19–31). Sarasota, FL: Professional Resource.

Young, K. (2008). Internet sex addiction: Risk factors, stages of development, and treatment. *American Behavioral Scientist, 52*(1), 21–37.

Zmijewski, C., & Howard, M. (2003). Exercise dependence and attitudes toward eating among young adults. *Eating Behaviors, 4*(2), 181–195.

Zorick, T., Nestor, L., Miotto, K., Sugar, C., Hellemann, G., Scanlon, G., Rawson, R., & London, E. D. (2010). Withdrawal symptoms in abstinent methamphetamine-dependent subjects. *Addiction, 105*(10), 1809–1818.

17

Stopping the Cycle: Treating Addictions in Young Men

W. BRYCE HAGEDORN, JESSE FOX, AND TABITHA L. YOUNG

STRATEGIES FOR TREATING YOUNG MEN WITH ADDICTIVE DISORDERS

In the previous chapter, we spent considerable time exploring the details of the problem. In this chapter, we address the solution: competent care for the addicted adolescent. We will explore the various treatment settings that are available for working with addicted youth, discuss ways in which the family can be involved, and then make a recommendation for a therapeutic approach based upon our years of clinical experience. To conclude this chapter, we will take a brief look at some specific interventions and unique treatment strategies that have proven successful with adolescents.

Inpatient Detox

Inpatient detox is often used to provide a safe environment for users to cope with the debilitating physical effects of alcohol, barbiturate, hallucinogen, and heroin withdrawal. Typically, inpatient detox takes place in a hospital where medical staff are available in the event of complications arising from the withdrawal process, though others do exist (Stevens & Smith, 2005). During detox, medical staff will often administer small doses of an agonist or partial agonist (e.g., methadone in the case of heroin withdrawal) to reduce the severity of withdrawal symptoms. Generally speaking, the length of stay in a detox facility is less than 2 weeks. It is important to realize that detox will only rid the user of acute withdrawal symptoms and is really just the beginning of the process of recovery and by no means the end.

Inpatient Residential

Many residential programs embrace the Minnesota Model of residential treatment that incorporates medical, psychological, and self help strategies for treating chemical dependence (Stevens & Smith, 2005). A key assumption of residential programs is that in order to recover, users must be separated for a time from the environment that is sustaining their addiction. While in residence, patients are expected to be respectful of other patients and staff as well as attend lectures on the 12 steps and participate in a mix of individual and group therapy (Doweiko, 2006). Depending upon their progress, patients can be discharged as early as 30 days and as late as 90 days.

Intensive Outpatient

Intensive outpatient (IOP) or intensive long-term outpatient treatment (ILTOT) is designed for patients who are experiencing moderate to severe levels of substance use (Doweiko, 2006). These programs typically are tailored to the individual needs of the patient, yet they can last from 3 to 6 months in the short term to 12 to 18 months in the long term. During treatment, patients usually attend group therapy 3 to 4 days a week, 3 hours at a time, with at least one of those groups being multifamily (Stevens & Smith, 2005). The goals of an IOP or ILTOT is to (a) convince the patient that drugs have had a negative influence on his life, (b) secure a commitment to sobriety as a lifestyle, (c) develop and sustain a supportive environment that is conducive to recovery, and (d) find appropriate referrals for long-term care.

Outpatient

Outpatient programs are the most utilized treatment format for chemical dependence (Doweiko, 2006). These programs employ a number of modalities including individual, group, marital, and family therapy as well as often requiring involvement in a 12-step program. Abstaining from use is a requirement to continue in the program, and drug testing is common practice. The goal of outpatient programs is to offer support and structure as the addict learns to cope with the problems of daily living without using substances while they live at home.

Therapeutic Community

There is still some controversy regarding the effectiveness and some of the intervention strategies, including ego stripping and unquestioned compliance to community rules, that take place within therapeutic communities (Doweiko, 2006). Although therapeutic communities vary in their format (including some outpatient modalities), they have a common philosophy in which the community is seen as the primary agent of change. Therefore, they tend to include a structured living environment that exists somewhat in isolation, with the residents and staff seen as family. The length of stay can vary from several months to 3 years in some communities.

THE FAMILY'S INVOLVEMENT

It has been said, and we ascribe to the belief, that addiction is a family-based concern. When one person (i.e., the adolescent) in a system is struggling with an addictive relationship with alcohol, food, cocaine, or gaming, the *entire* family struggles. Therefore, when possible, it only seems prudent to treat the entire system rather than solely focusing on the individual addict. We have all seen (admittedly with some significant frustration) the consequence of discharging a newly recovering client back to his family system, only to see him back in treatment soon thereafter. Without going into *too* much detail, families are systems with their own set of roles, rules, and boundaries. When an addiction is present in the system, the family will initially resist the change but eventually will adjust to the roles, rules, and boundaries that best maintain homeostatic balance for the system, even when these bring extreme discomfort. Similarly, when the addicted individual exits treatment as a *changed* person, the very same system will resist this change because it is unknown and unpredictable and thus a threat to homeostasis. Even when on a cognitive level the family members can see how much better their recovering adolescent is acting, they have become accustomed to their maladaptive behavior and are left with being unsure as to how to proceed. Without addressing the entire family system, it is unlikely that change for the adolescent will last.

The Sequential Family Addiction Model

Although there is likely no one best way to work with addicted adolescents and their families, some treatment approaches have garnered more empirical support than others. In deciding which approach to take, the Transtheoretical Model of Change (TTM; Prochaska, DiClemente, &

Norcross, 1992) has demonstrated strong efficacy and offers a roadmap that can help guide helping efforts. This model helps to conceptualize where clients are in their readiness to make changes, which fits quite well for those considering changing an addictive lifestyle. The model includes the following stages: *Precontemplation* (characterized by an inability to recognize the existence of a problem and/or need for change), *Contemplation* (noted as a recognition of a problem/need to change but no intention to change at the present time), *Determination/Planning* (recognized when the client begins to formulate a plan to change), *Action* (seen when the client is making overt changes), *Maintenance* (conceptualized as the consolidation phase where the forward momentum is maintained and the source of problems can be rooted out), and *Termination* (when the change process is complete and no additional effort is required). Within each stage, relapse (or recycling to an earlier stage) is quite possible and is an expected part of the change process.

Being able to conceptualize change according to the TTM can be *extremely* valuable for client and counselor alike. For clients, it normalizes the difficulty with making changes, particularly the obtaining and maintaining of recovery from an addiction. Similarly, it releases them from the guilt and shame that can ensue from relapse. It also offers counselors an explanatory construct in which to view the change process. Therefore, when the counselor has helped an adolescent client to see the need for change (i.e. helped him move from *Precontemplation* to *Contemplation*), that is success. It is not necessary (dare we say impossible) to move a client from *Precontemplation* to *Action* in one sitting (let alone several).

As noted earlier, the TTM helps to guide helping efforts as it offers suggestions as to what therapies and techniques can be most efficacious for each stage of change. Juhnke and Hagedorn (2006) took advantage of this guide when they proposed the Sequential Family Addiction Model (S-FAM) as a part of their text, *Counseling Addicted Families*. This model employs seven distinct treatment theories that match clients wherever they happen to be in the change process; that is, one does not need to begin in the first theory if the client is already in the *Action* stage. In the following section we follow Juhnke and Hagedorn's work by offering a *brief* exploration of each theory (given that entire texts have been written on each one), with an emphasis on those techniques from each theory that can best aid clients along their journey to change. Readers are encouraged to investigate the original works cited as references in each section for a more thorough review of the theory and its applications for working with addicted clients.

Readers will note that the first several theories of the S-FAM can be conceptualized as "here-and-now" approaches that focus on present-day concerns, goals, behaviors, and thoughts. These theories are necessary for those newly entering recovery as they help address resistance, ambivalence, uncertain directions for recovery, and maladaptive thought/ behavior patterns. Given additional time, or for clients who have already accomplished the early work of recovery and who now require deeper therapeutic work, the model shifts focus to more insight-oriented theories with a focus on "there-and-then." These theories investigate the impact of the client's family system (the reason for which was noted earlier) and incorporate a wrap-around approach to sustaining the recovery process.

"Here and Now" Theories

Motivational Interviewing
One of the newest postmodern treatment approaches, Motivational Interviewing (MI; Miller & Rollnick, 2002) can best be described as a directive form of client centered therapy. Miller and Rollnick stated that MI provides counselors with a *way of being* with clients, rather than prescribing a set of techniques or exercises. The theory is best used to address *resistance* and *ambivalence*, two things common to those in the *Precontemplation* stage of change and for those traversing from any one stage in the TTM to any other stage (as each stage shift will involve various amounts of resistance and ambivalence). According to the S-FAM (Juhnke & Hagedorn, 2006), MI is quite useful for the first several initial sessions. We will spend a bit more time on this approach than the other theories as we believe that a strong foundation in MI will set the overall tone for working with addicted adolescents.

MI conceptualizes resistance as a product of a relationship (i.e., the only reason clients will resist change efforts is because counselors give them something to resist *against*) and sees such resistance as a natural by-product of the change process. This approach is quite unique in that other therapeutic approaches describe resistance as an element of the addictive disorder or as an inherent characteristic of addicted clients themselves. MI, on the other hand, cautions counselors from being an advocate for change in their clients' lives as this lean *toward* change on the counselor's part is exactly what clients will *push back* against.

MI offers prescribed ways to avoid evoking resistance (Miller & Rollnick, 2002). These include *demonstrating empathy* (done through reflecting warmth, acceptance, and a nonjudgmental attitude), *avoiding arguments* (e.g., overt confrontation, quarreling, clinical labels, and defending oneself all must be avoided), *rolling with resistance* (which involves avoiding common communication traps), *supporting self-efficacy* (i.e., bolstering clients' beliefs in their ability to change, reminding them that they are responsible for their own decisions about change, and offering a spectrum of therapeutic alternatives from which they may choose), and *developing discrepancies* (done by emphasizing any distance between clients' current behaviors and choices and their identified values or goals).

The task of developing discrepancies is also useful to address the second aspect that MI is designed for: addressing ambivalence. Miller and Rollnick (2002) normalized ambivalence as a part of every change process. In fact, they noted that without ambivalence (e.g., if the client has no desire to change whatsoever), change will never be realized. As a result, for some clients, the task of MI is to *create* ambivalence, which can be accomplished through six sets of questions. These series of questions include the *positive questions* (designed to elicit information related to the positive aspects of the current behaviors, e.g., "What are some of the good things about smoking marijuana?"), the *not-so-positive questions* (used to explore some of the negative aspects of the current behaviors, e.g., "What won't you miss about smoking marijuana?"), the *life goal questions* (focused on trying to determine what the client would like to be doing in the future, e.g., "If things work out the way you want, what would you like to do after high school?"), the *comparison questions* (centered on helping the client see some distance between current behaviors and future goals, e.g., "How does your future 'airline pilot' fit with your current marijuana smoking?"), the *asking for a decision questions* (done after the comparison questions have created ambivalence, e.g., "Now that we've looked at these things, what do you think might be a way to proceed to getting your goals met?"), and the *setting a short-term goal questions* (used to help the client to choose a direction, e.g., "What do you think should be the first step at this point?").

Throughout their work with clients, counselors must (a) do their best to suspend their judgment, (b) resist their natural tendencies to guide clients toward making "better decisions," and (c) support clients' self-efficacy. Done correctly, we believe that MI has earned its title as the *jujitsu of counseling*.

Solution-Focused Counseling

Once clients have accepted that a problem exists and that some ownership in the problem is theirs to assume (i.e., they have moved from *Precontemplation* to *Contemplation*), it is time to help them consider how their lives will be once their goals are realized. Solution-Focused Counseling (SFC) is a strength-based way to meet clients in this stage of change and to help them to begin this forward-thinking process (O'Hanlon & Weiner-Davis, 1989). Rather than spending exorbitant amounts of time disserting the problem or status quo (though it is important to cocreate a shared definition of the problem), SFC directs clients' focus to what the solution will be and how the future will look once they have successfully navigated their change process. SFC begins by probing the client for *exceptions* (times when the problem does not exist, is not as bad or intense, or when it is not as noticeable) and then helping them discover what is different about them, their circumstances, and/or their choices during those times. Once these exceptions are identified and patterns are recognized, clients are directed to continue doing those things that align with their goals for change. In solidifying gains, counselors help their clients to visualize the future and to set goals that will help them to realize future aspirations. Juhnke and Hagedorn (2006) suggested that SFC best serves clients for three to seven sessions before moving on to the next theory.

Several techniques are offered by SFC to aid in the goal-setting and goal-attaining processes including *Miracle Questions* and *Scaling Questions* (O'Hanlon & Weiner-Davis, 1989). The *Miracle Questions* and its derivatives (the Crystal Ball, the Movie Director, the Mapping Technique, etc.) are useful in helping clients to conceptualize how their lives will be once they are living the life they want to live. For example, the first author (Hagedorn) typically asks something akin to the following: "Say we jumped 90 days into the future and videotaped our session. In that session, you are describing to me how well things are going in your life: how your parents are off your back about smoking, how you've been able to earn that money toward the car you wanted, and how you're excited about the application you've submitted to start your flying lessons. We decide to grab that video and bring it back to the present day and watch it right now in session. How would you be talking about those events? How would you be acting in that session? How would you describe how you were able to make all those things happen?" Once the client articulates answers to all these questions (obviously such questions would be asked throughout the session and not all at once), then the counselor can start helping the client to set treatment goals around obtaining these future goals.

The second technique, *Scaling Questions*, is useful for several purposes. First, these can be used to check clients' readiness: "On a scale from 1 to 10, with 1 meaning "not at all ready right now" and 10 meaning "completely ready to move forward," where would you place yourself right now in relation to taking the next step?" Second, Scaling can be used to check clients' and family members' levels of commitment: "Family, on a scale from 1 to 10, with 1 indicating a 'very low level of investment' and 10 meaning 'you're completely on board,' how would you rate your commitment to helping your son to maintain his sobriety this week?" Finally, counselors can help their clients to scale the severity of their symptoms by asking, "On a scale from 1 to 10, with 1 being a complete absence of cravings and 10 meaning that you're feeling overwhelmed by the desire to use, how would you rate your cravings today?"

Whenever you use Scaling Questions, be cautious in how you respond to clients' low rankings (or high for that matter). That is, avoid asking, "Why would you rate yourself so low in your readiness to move forward? I thought you created some really good plans!" Instead, see the client's ranking as "data," process the data, and see what will help the client to move forward or backward along the scale, be it resources, more time, or something else: "So you'd give yourself a three in your readiness to move forward, which indicates to me that you have some pretty good motivation. What do you think it would take for you to feel like you were ready enough to give yourself a four?" Be it *Scaling* or *Miracle Questions*, SFC offers the counselor a way of connecting with clients strengths, solidifying gains made during the MI phase, and transitioning to the cognitive behavioral phase.

Cognitive Behavioral Theory

Cognitive Behavioral Theory (CBT) is more of an umbrella term for a variety of theories, be it Choice/Reality Theory (Glasser, 1965), Rational Emotive Behavior Theory (REBT; Ellis, 1973), Cognitive Theory (Beck, 1997), or a variety of others. For the sake of the S-FAM, Juhnke and Hagedorn (2006) highlighted CBT techniques that are common to most of these theories and suggested that counselors work within this realm after resistance and ambivalence have been addressed (*Precontemplation*) and after goals have been visualized (*Contemplation*). During the *Determination/Planning* and *Action* stages of change, counselors will use CBT techniques for three to 11 sessions to aid clients in setting realistic goals for change and then taking actual steps toward this change. Juhnke and Hagedorn identified techniques such as (a) examining thoughts, feelings, and behaviors, (b) evaluating negative and positive consequences, (c) identifying high risk situations, and (d) creating contingency contracts, as these are all effective ways of aiding clients during these stages of change.

When clients are challenged to *Examine Thoughts, Feelings, and Behaviors*, they are asked to critically analyze the motivations behind decisions that they make. Counselors use a variety of methods to help clients to identify (a) what they say to themselves ("If I smoke pot, people will think I'm cool"), (b) how they feel ("I'm feeling left out right now"), (c) what they do ("I'll just call to see if the guys are hanging out but won't actually go over there right now") and (d) what they say to others ("Why can't you just get off my back Mom, I'm just going to hang out with the guys for a while!") before they engaged with their addiction. By peeling these processes apart, clients can begin to recognize a broader range of available thoughts, feelings, and behaviors that can be used to break the cycle. Similarly, in *Evaluating Negative and Positive Consequences*, clients are aided in recognizing how their maladaptive behaviors are connected to negative consequences ("I'm never going to get a girlfriend; staying high helps me to deal with my loneliness") and positive consequences ("I'm not so lonely when I hang out and party with the guys"). Part of the CBT approach would then be to help the addicted adolescent to develop healthier ways of getting his relational needs met.

In the third CBT approach, *Identifying High Risk Situations*, counselors help their clients to create two lists as it relates to gaining and maintaining their sobriety. The first is a list of *risky people, places, and things* that may trigger an addictive episode. From this *Trigger List* of people (e.g., "my friends who smoke pot, my mother who irritates me, my boss who thinks that I'm a lousy worker"), places ("concerts, parties, my friends' houses"), and things ("the sounds of a lighter, certain songs, playing video games, junk food"), the counselor helps the client to rank order his triggers, from those that will most likely lead to an immediate addictive episode to those that are not as risky. From here, the counselor aids the client in creating a *Nonuse List* of people ("my friend Jacob, my art teacher Mrs. Erin, my dad on his weekends"), places ("sporting events at school, walking in the woods, youth group at church"), and things ("shooting hoops, playing guitar, painting"). This too would be rank ordered from those that will definitely keep him from using marijuana to those with least appeal. The task is then to pair the highest risk situation (e.g., "hanging out with my friends playing video games") with the highest deterrent ("shooting hoops at Jacob's) and planning how the client can best make the decision to go to Jacob's house whenever he is feeling the need to spend time with friends. This would be solidified by the client choosing positive consequences for making consistent healthy decisions (e.g., "After 60 days of clean urinalyses, I'd like to earn the right to go hiking in the woods on my own") and identifying negative consequences for less healthy choices (e.g., "If I do smoke pot, I'll follow through on that 90 meetings in 90 days suggestion that I've heard at the Narcotics Anonymous meetings that I've been to"). Helping the client to articulate these plans into a more formal *Contingency Contract*, with input from his family members and other healthy people in his life, would then clarify for all involved the intentions for movement into and through the *Determination/Planning* and *Action* Stages.

Moving Into Insight Theories

As we noted earlier, the first several theories in the S-FAM are focused on the here-and-now and are best utilized within the first 6 months of treatment. In fact, if you add the suggested number of sessions attached to each individual theory, you will find that MI, SFC, and CBT should focus your work for approximately 20 to 24 sessions, which, if done weekly, would take approximately 6 months. In fact, the first author (Hagedorn) uniformly suggests a "6-month rule" be applied to therapeutic work with addicted clients. By this, it is suggested that counselors remain with here-and-now–oriented treatments that aid clients in developing healthy coping mechanisms and creating sobriety-sustaining communities for the first 6 months of treatment. This also aligns well with the *Maintenance* stage of the TTM (Prochaska et al., 1992), for it is in this stage that counselors can help clients recognize the sources of their maladaptive and addictive behaviors.

Moving clients too quickly into the insight-oriented theories listed next can result in unintentional relapses, because in so doing, the counselor uses psychotherapy as a scalpel, digging around at the tumor of pain and family dysfunction that has often lead to addictive behaviors in the first place. Without a way to cope with the resulting pain and a community from which to garner strength during this phase of treatment, the client is left to resort to the only way he knows how to cope with pain in the first place: drinking, drugging, or misbehaving. We will spend less time than we did previously on the following theories as they would likely be employed by a counselor trained to work with addicted family systems. In these next phases of treatment, the client is moved from individual treatment to family and/or couples counseling, for at this point in the care cycle, the family system is addressed (a) because the client has enough time in sobriety to address some of the underlying sources of pain or (b) because earlier forms of treatment outlined by the S-FAM have not resulted in continued sobriety, and therefore, a deeper look into the addicted family system is warranted. As before, we gleam the following information from a review of Juhnke and Hagedorn's (2006) text, *Counseling Addicted Families*.

The fourth phase of the S-FAM involves the counselor moving into 5 to 10 sessions of *Structured Family Therapy*. Structured Family Therapy (Minuchin, 1974; Minuchin & Fishman, 1981) focuses on organizing the family into various subsystems (*Marital Subsystem*, *Parental Subsystem*, and *Sibling Subsystem*). In so doing, the counselor helps to highlight the various *boundaries*, *tasks*, and *rules* inherent to each subsystem. In identifying the structural patterns of each subsystem, the counselor works with the family to strengthen and/or loosen those subsystems that are contributing to the clients' distress. For example, in an attempt to bond with his son (the marijuana smoker), the father in the family system has been acting like a best friend, defending his actions in front of the mother, who is left to being the sole disciplinarian. As such, during this phase of treatment, the counselor would use various techniques to strengthen the parental subsystem so that both adults act in accord with one another and share equal parenting responsibilities.

Moving into the fifth phase of the S-FAM, the counselor shifts into 5 to 10 sessions of *Extended Family Systems Therapy* (Bowen, 1975). This theory investigates the cascading effects of family pathology handed down from generation to generation. This, and subsequent levels of care, would be warranted when the identification and evaluation of the families subsystems (as noted) were insufficient to break the maladaptive familiar patterns that contribute to the addictive disorders being treated. Those requiring this level of treatment often find it difficult to think logically without being encumbered by emotions that hinder most of their relationships (this is known as a lack of *Differentiation of Self*). In Extended Family Systems Therapy, the counselor attempts to address *triangulations*, which is when two people pull in a third person (or an addictive disorder) to help escape the high levels of tension in the relationship. Similarly, the counselor would address each member's family of origin issues with an extended *Family Genogram*. Once a couple can recognize the impact of their family of origin on their current relationships and make appropriate adjustments, this form of therapy would be successful.

If Extended Family System Therapy is unsuccessful at helping to maintain the family's sobriety, the counselor would move to the final stage of treatment, *Psychodynamic Object Relations Therapy*. Prior to this stage, there is an optional intervention called the *Modified Intergenerational Family of Origin Experience* (Framo, 1992). This involves bringing the *entire* extended family together for a family session (hence its optional nature as this would not be feasible for some families for a variety of reasons—history of family violence, members living out of state/country, etc.). This intervention can be helpful for the adults in the parental subsystem in that it highlights each other's family of origin experiences, role, and rules within the context of their adult vision (i.e., they are no longer children). Should the couple want to head in this direction, the counselor would help them to identify an agenda that addresses three points: (a) What will a successful session look like? (b) What will the couple do if the session goes unexpectedly? (c) How will the data that emanates from such a session aid them in removing the addiction from their current family system? Put simply (and believe us when we say this is not a simple intervention!), the counselor begins the family of origin experience by asking the individual members of the couple two questions (and then facilitates the data that results): "What was it like to grow up as a child in this family?" and "What things come to mind as you recall life as a child in this family?" As noted, a bevy of data results from this session that can intentionally be used to help the couple break their maladaptive relational styles.

The final phase of treatment is *Psychodynamic Object Relations Therapy*, which can involve 15 or more sessions for the addicted family system. The goal here is to increase clients' understanding of their internalized perceptions of self and others, which tend to be held in the unconscious realms of the mind. The counselor provides a *corrective emotional experience* for each member of the family by exploring their *initial attachments to primary caregivers*, working through *transference and countertransference issues*, and directly *confronting resistances* that are experienced in the context of the session (*very* different from MI). The counselor creates a *holding environment* where each adult is basically *re-parented* and supported to address their resulting insights and feelings. As noted, this level of care would only be reached when other forms of care have proven ineffective. When the family has been with the counselor for this amount of time, the level of trust and acceptance has grown to the point where the counselor does serious digging into the client and the system in which he lives.

The S-FAM has proven to be a very effective way of addressing adolescent addictive disorders. Beginning with those treatments that have been found to be empirically supported to address clients' here-and-now therapeutic needs, the model follows the TTM from start to end. To finalize this chapter, the authors now turn to an extended case study where the concepts found earlier can be seen to play out with a fictitious client. We suggest the use of the mnemonic device called "DO A CLIENT MAP" (Seligman, 1990), which includes the following elements as it pertains to creating an extensive and creative treatment plan: Diagnosis, Objectives, Assessment, Clinician, Location, Interventions, Emphasis, Number, Timing, Medication, Adjunct services, and Prognosis. Readers should note that the various aspects of the treatment planning format do not necessarily have to be followed in order, but each element is important and therefore included (and will be noted in italics).

CASE STUDY: DON'T BET ON IT

Presenting Problem

Chen is a 17-year-old Asian American male who is preparing for his senior year of high school. Recently, Chen and his parents have been fighting more often than normal and have been seeking family counseling where Chen's addictive behaviors became known to the family. Chen's parents are fortunate enough to be well off financially and have tried to always instill in Chen and his two younger siblings the importance of hard work and fiscal responsibility. As such, they opened a credit card for Chen when he was 16 years old and gave him the responsibility of paying it on time using the money he earns at an afterschool job. Unfortunately, since he has gotten the card, he has maxed out the credit limit primarily because of gambling with his friends and securing cash for crystal meth.

Every Friday night, Chen goes to a house with a group of friends, and he plays video games with them. For the past year, he and his friends have been betting on the games they play together and occasionally sneaking into a riverboat casino to play slots and blackjack. In addition, Chen often goes to the gas station near school during his lunches and buys scratch-off lottery tickets. About the same time, Chen and his fiends started experimenting with drugs including alcohol, marijuana, and crystal meth. Though he has tried a number of substances, Chen would consider crystal meth his drug of choice and has been using it weekly for the past year. He likes using crystal meth because he is able to stay up well into the night gambling or playing video games. Furthermore, since more and more of his time has been taken up gambling and getting high, when he needs to catch up on a school assignment, he uses the crystal meth to pull all nighters. In total, Chen was able to amass $10,000 in credit card debt.

To keep his parents from becoming aware of what he is doing, Chen has a number of hiding places for amphetamines all over their house. In addition, when he goes out to the casinos, he tells his parents that he is staying the night at a friend's house. When his parents confronted him about the credit debt, Chen lied and said that he had been spending the cash withdrawals on food, movie tickets, gas for the car his parents bought him to go to school and work, and other "stuff" he does with friends. In the past year, Chen's grades went from being in the high A's to low C's, and his parents are worried about Chen being accepted into a good college that can set him off on the right path into his future career. In addition, his teachers at school have noticed that Chen goes from looking exhausted and irritable one day to hyperactive, impulsive, and defiant the next. He has had a slew of detentions in the last month partly due to his oppositional behavior in class and partly due to being truant from class periods.

During the initial interview, Chen's parents drifted back and forth between being tearful and being irate at Chen for his recent behavior. Though his parents were aware that Chen has been using drugs, they are unaware of the extent of his use. During most of the interview Chen looked out the window trying his best to look like he did not "care" about what his parents were saying, only to engage in the conversation when he believed his parents were "lying" about his behavior. Chen's parents were scared and were looking for any answers that could help their son get his life back together.

Response

In order to obtain an accurate diagnosis of what is happening with Chen, we must begin with the *Assessment* process. Employing the WASTE-Time structured interview (Hagedorn & Juhnke, 2005) and the CAGE (Ewing, 1984) would help us to gain the necessary information to determine an accurate *Diagnosis* for Chen. Overall, Chen presents with two viable options for diagnoses: Amphetamine Dependence (Methamphetamine) and Gambling Addiction. Chen often spends late nights combining gambling and his crystal meth use, both on the weekends and on school nights, which is affecting his performance at school. He often ditches classes and spends his lunches gambling. Chen's behavior is also affecting his relationships at home through the many lies he has told his parents to continue his use, as well as the financial toll he has cost his parents.

Based upon the severity of Chen's use, the most appropriate *Location* to begin his treatment would be an IOP followed by a step-down approach (outpatient and then support group attendance). Using the S-FAM as the *Intervention*, we would begin helping Chen by using MI to bypass some of the resistance he is experiencing based upon his initial presentation as being "coerced" into the office by his parents. As Chen would most likely fit into a Precontemplative stage of change, the *Emphasis* of treatment should be direct and structured, striking a balance between providing support and gentle confrontation, with a low level of exploration of Chen's past history (employing the 6-month rule). The most appropriate *Clinician* for Chen would be someone who specializes in chemical and process addictions, works well with adolescents, and who is well-versed in multicultural counseling.

To combat the severity of Chen's addictive disorders, a series of attainable short-term, mid-term, and long-term *Objectives* is prudent. In the short term (those objectives that can be reached within days or weeks), Chen should be encouraged to sign a no-harm contract (given the high rates of self-harm associated with these addictive disorders) that would include an agreement to avoid all high-risk situations that include casinos, ditching classes, and contacting his dealers. In addition, he should abstain from all forms of gambling and mind-altering substances for the next two weeks while attending Narcotics Anonymous (NA) and Gambling Anonymous (GA) meetings (some *Adjunct services*). While at those meetings, he must secure a temporary or permanent sponsor (someone on whom he can call for support). Given his level of use, Chen will also be admitted to IOP-based counseling for three to four times per week (*Timing*), the majority of which will be group counseling with one individual session per week (*Number*), and complete a formal assessment by a physician to rule out any complicating medical concerns (*Medication*).

For mid-term objectives (which can take weeks or months), Chen must complete the IOP program and complete the first step of the 12-steps for both NA and GA (*Adjunct services*). In addition, to move toward changing his social network, we would help him to reinitiate or create a list of at least three nonusing/nongambling friends. To keep his investment in the 12-step groups consistent, a good mid-term objective would be to attend 90 meetings in 90 days. After completing the IOP program, the step-down approach would involve his continuing with an individual counselor and a family counselor (*Location*) once a week (*Timing*) to address his reasons for use and repair his relationship with his family. Finally, in order to provide relapse prevention strategies (*Intervention*), Chen should be assisted in identifying his triggers, identifying four stress management strategies, and creating a relapse prevention plan that outlines what he should do when he experiences triggers and how to respond if he falls back into active use.

In the long term (which occurs over months and into years), Chen could complete the first six of the 12-steps in NA and/or GA and continue to develop a relationship with his higher power that could include a variety of spiritual or religious exercises and experiences (*Adjunct services*). In addition, during the course of his individual and family therapy, he needs to identify any possible maladaptive relational patterns that inhibit his recovery (*Emphasis*). To remediate his credit card debt, Chen should complete a financial plan (*Adjunct services*) that outlines steps to paying his parents back. Finally, to continue his growth as a person and maintain his sense of wellness, he could be encouraged to maintain a healthy diet and exercise plan.

While we like to be hopeful about our clients' successful recovery, we also need to be fair and accurate about their *Prognosis* so that we can help them to plan for setbacks and assist their family members to set up reasonable expectations. Prognosis, which is the counselor's belief about the successful resolution of all client concerns within the given treatment setting and timing, is based on the course of the disorder (i.e., if it was addressed at the start or after the addiction has had time to cause severe consequences), the number of client concerns (the more addictive disorders, the more challenging the treatment will be), the stage of change (those in Precontemplation or Contemplation have much work to do, which takes time and experience), and the number of times treatment has been sought (someone who has been through treatment more than once begins to recognize the amount of effort it takes to maintain recovery). Given that Chen's addictive disorders have caused significant consequences, that he has two significant addictive disorders, that he is in Precontemplation, and that this is his first time in treatment, a fair prognosis would be "fair," "poor," or "guarded." As such, we would want to prepare him and his family for the work ahead, noting that people *do* recover with concerted efforts and a family-based approach, and that as his counselors we will stand beside them as they move forward into recovery.

CONCLUSION

This chapter expanded upon information presented within the previous chapter to include empirically supported methods for treating young men and boys afflicted with addictive disorders. Furthermore, readers were furnished with a practical, applied case study from which to conceptualize the material presented within this and the previous chapter. As previously mentioned, these chapters are merely introductions to identifying, assessing, and treating addictive disorders with young men and boys. Thus, readers are encouraged to seek continued education in order to better serve their addicted clientele.

REFERENCES

Beck, A. T. (1997). The past and future of cognitive therapy. *Journal of Psychotherapy Practice and Research, 6*, 276–284.

Bowen, M. (1975). Family therapy and family group therapy. In H. Kaplan & B. Sadock (Eds.), *Comprehensive group psychotherapy*. Baltimore, MD: Williams and Wilkins.

Doweiko, H. E. (2006). *Concepts of chemical dependency*. Australia: Thomson/Brooks/Cole.

Ellis, A. (1973). My philosophy of psychotherapy. *Journal of Contemporary Psychotherapy, 6*, 13–18.

Ewing, J. A. (1984). Detecting alcoholism: The CAGE Questionnaire. *JAMA, 252*, 1905–1907.

Framo, J. L. (1992). *Family-of-Origin therapy: An intergenerational approach*. New York: Brunner/Mazel.

Glasser, W. (1965). *Reality Therapy*. New York: Harper & Row.

Hagedorn, W. B., & Juhnke, G. A. (2005). Treating the sexually addicted client: Establishing a need for increased counselor awareness. *Journal of Addictions & Offender Counseling, 25*(2), 66–86.

Juhnke, G. A., & Hagedorn, W. B. (2006). *Counseling addicted families: A sequential assessment & treatment model*. New York: Brunner-Routledge.

Miller, W. R., & Rollnick, S. (2002). *Motivational interviewing: Preparing people for change* (2nd ed.). New York: The Guilford Press.

Minuchin, S. (1974). *Families and family therapy*. Cambridge, MA: Harvard University Press.

Minuchin, S., & Fishman, H. C. (1981). *Family therapy techniques*. Cambridge, MA: Harvard University Press.

O'Hanlon, W. H., & Weiner-Davis, M. (1989). *In search of solutions: A new direction in psychotherapy*. New York: Norton.

Prochaska, J. O., DiClemente, C. C., & Norcross, J. C. (1992). In search of how people change: Applications to addictive behaviors. *American Psychologist, 47*(9), 1102–1114.

Seligman, L. (1990). *Selecting effective treatments: A comprehensive, systematic guide to treating adult mental disorders*. Hoboken, NJ: Jossey-Bass.

Stevens, P., & Smith, R. L. (2005). *Substance abuse counseling: Theory and practice*. Upper Saddle River, NJ: Pearson.

18

Out of Bounds: Oppositional Defiant Disorder and Conduct Disorder

MARGERY J. SHUPE

OVERVIEW

Our youth now love luxury. They have bad manners, contempt for authority, and disrespect for their elders. Children nowadays are tyrants. — (Socrates, 470–399 BC)

Children with severe acting-out problems have long been a concern to parents, teachers, and society. Such behaviors are often considered the path by which some youngsters will develop a life of juvenile delinquency and adult criminality. Although the most severe forms of youth violence (e.g., homicide) in the United States have been decreasing since the mid 1990s, other forms of severe acting out have not declined (Brenner, Simon, Krug, & Lowry, 1999; Snyder & Sickmund, 1999). During adolescence, there is clearly an increase in behavior that can be considered "problematic" or "at risk," such as the use of drugs, truancy, school suspensions, vandalism, stealing, and precocious and unprotected sex (DiClemente, Hansen, & Ponton, 1996; Ketterlinus & Lamb, 1994; U.S. Congress, Office of Technology Assessment, 1991). In fact, approximately 70% of adolescents engage in some form of delinquent behavior. Fortunately, fewer are involved in more-serious offenses (such as robbery and aggravated assault), but many more are involved in problematic but less-serious behaviors (such as underage drinking, running away from home, truancy from school, traffic violations) (Elliott, Huizinga, & Ageton, 1985, Farrington, 1995).

Conduct disorder (CD) and oppositional defiant disorder (ODD) are two of the most common reasons for referral of juveniles for mental health treatment (Robins, 1991; Selzer & Hluchy, 1991). It has been estimated that between one-half and two-thirds of youth seen in child guidance clinics have been diagnosed with CD or ODD (Comer, 1995; Webster-Stratton & Dahl, 1995). This high rate of referral is attributed to the fact that the symptoms of CD are external, and are therefore frequently observed by others, and are likely to bring the youth into contact with the law or authorities. In addition, these behaviors are frequently more distressing to those who are around the youngsters than to the youngsters who exhibit them. Although estimates of the prevalence of conduct problems vary greatly, in the general population of approximately 70 million children and adolescents in the United States, it is estimated that from 6% to 16% of boys and 2% to 9% of girls have acting-out behavioral problems (Mash & Wolfe, 2005); this translates to between 5.6 to 17.5 million youths. There are also longer-term consequences for youth diagnosed with these disorders, as about 80% of youths who demonstrate severe acting-out behavioral problems are likely to meet criteria for some type of psychiatric disorder in the future (Kazdin, 2004). There are also numerous long-term consequences for others who have to deal with such youths—parents, siblings, teachers, peers, as well as strangers who are the target of aggressive or antisocial acts. CD and ODD are financially costly to society, in part, because of the large percentage of diagnosed children who remain involved with mental health agencies and criminal justice systems over the course of their lives. Even before they reach adulthood, the economic impact borne by our society is great, with the average cost of incarceration for a juvenile exceeding $60,000/year (Webster-Stratton & Dahl, 1995).

Conduct Disorder and Oppositional Defiant Disorder

In general, childhood behavior problems can be viewed along the broad dimension of externalized versus internalized conflict. Disruptive acting-out behaviors are "externalized" in the sense that the conflict that occurs is typically in the youngster's relationship with societal norms and other rules of conduct. This stands in contrast to "internalized" disorders, such as anxiety and depression, in which the symptoms lie primarily within the youngster.

Although externalized behavior problems have long been identified in children and adolescents, it was not until 1980 that a formal distinction was made between CD and ODD, which are closely linked and can involve defiance of rules, problems managing anger, and failure to assume responsibility for one's behavior. The current *Diagnostic and Statistical Manual of Mental Disorders-IV-TR* (American Psychiatric Association, 2000) describes ODD as "a recurrent pattern of negativistic, defiant, disobedient, and hostile behavior towards authority figures" (p. 100). Such oppositional defiant behaviors are usually apparent by the preschool years and have been linked to problematic temperaments in infancy and child-hood (e.g., high reactivity, difficulty being soothed, and/or high motor activity). On the other hand, CD reflects a "persistent pattern of behavior in which the basic rights of others or major age-appropriate societal norms or rules are violated" (p. 93). The problem behaviors associated with CD include aggressive behavior that causes or threatens physical harm to another or an animal, property damage or loss, theft or deceitfulness, and/or serious violations of rules. Three or more of these behaviors must have been present during the last year, and one of them must have been present in the last 6 months. Furthermore, the behaviors must have reached a level as to have significantly impacted the individual's social, academic, or occupational functioning. Such acting-out behaviors occur under various conditions and vary in terms of chronicity, severity, and frequency.

With both ODD and CD, it is important to distinguish between persistent aggressive antisocial acts such as setting fires, cruelty to people and animals, and destruction of property and theft; and the less-serious pranks often carried out by "normal" children and adolescents. It should also be noted that both ODD and CD involve behavior that may or may not be considered illegal. *Juvenile delinquency* is a legal term that refers to violations of the law committed by minors, but a juvenile who has been found to have violated a law may not meet diagnostic criteria for CD or ODD. That is, a youth may be adjudicated for vandalism or theft, but if these behaviors do not reflect a persistent pattern of rule/law violations, he is not correctly identified as having CD or ODD. Further, the behavior seen in ODD, and especially in CD, can reflect the early stage in the development of an antisocial personality disorder (Axis II Diagnosis, APA 2000). An antisocial personality disorder involves a "pervasive pattern of disregard for and violation of the rights of others that begins in childhood or early adolescence and continues into adulthood" (APA 2000, p. 701).

It is often difficult to distinguish between ODD and CD. It is even more difficult to distinguish between CD delinquent patterns of behavior and the early stages and development of an antisocial personality disorder. Behaviorally, the patterns are similar. Indeed, there is considerable evidence that some children's disruptive behavior problems (especially the early-onset type) develop gradually from childhood onward (Loeber, Green, Keenan, & Lahey, 1995). Thus, it appears that, for some children, there is a developmental sequence from ODD to CD to antisocial personality disorder, and there are common risk factors for these disorders (Hinshaw, 1994). More specifically, virtually all cases of CD (especially in the early-onset subtype) were preceded developmentally by ODD; although only about 25% of children with ODD go on to develop CD within a 3-year period (Lahey, Loeber, Quay, Frick & Grimm, 1992). Children who develop CD at an earlier age are more likely to develop an antisocial personality disorder as adults than youths who develop adolescent onset

CD (Hinshaw, 1994; Moffitt, 1993). Approximately 35% to 40% of youths diagnosed with early-onset CD go on to develop adult antisocial personality disorder. Over 80% of boys who develop early-onset CD, however, continue to have multiple problems of social dysfunction characterized by disrupted friendships, problems in intimate relationships, and vocational problems, even though they do not meet full criteria for an antisocial personality disorder (Hinshaw, 1994; Zoccolillo et al., 1996). By contrast, youths who develop adolescent-onset CD typically do not go on to develop adult antisocial personality disorders. Instead, their behavior problems are limited to their adolescent years. These "late-onset" youngsters do not share the same cluster of risk factors that "early-childhood onset" cases have, such as low verbal intelligence, neuropsychological deficits, impulsivity, and attention problems (Hinshaw, 1994; Moffit & Lynan, 1994).

Age of onset of CD has been found to be an important factor not only in the outcome, but also in terms of the severity of the problem presented (Sanford et al., 1999). Individuals who are found to have the child-onset form of the disorder tend to be more aggressive, are more likely to drop out of school, tend to have a higher probability of persisting in their antisocial behaviors as adults, and have a higher probability of developing substance abuse problems. In short, they are likely to have more chronic, intense acting-out problems. Thus, it appears that the primary developmental pathway to continued serious conduct problems into adulthood is established during the preschool period (Campbell & Ewing, 1990). This suggests perhaps a strategic point for primary interventions in a CD or ODD-diagnosed individual's development, which may be in the preschool and early elementary school years (i.e., ages 4–7). Unfortunately, not all CD children can be identified early on, and practitioners are often required to intervene with such youths over the course of their lives.

The Oregon Research Institute has been the site of one of the most comprehensive, programmatic, and longest-running research programs regarding CD and ODD. Since the 1960s, research has been carried out by Gerald Patterson and his colleagues to explicate the pathways by which a child develops a CD or ODD. Two major paths have been identified: early starters and late starters.

The "early starter" pathway (Patterson, Capaldi, & Bank, 1991) is also referred to as "life-course persistent" (Moffitt, 1993) and "childhood onset" (Hinshaw & Anderson, 1996). This pathway consistently leads from early conduct problems and oppositional behaviors to more-serious overt conduct problems and precocious arrests. Later, CD/ODD behavior expands the children's behavioral repertoire rather than replacing earlier problem behaviors (Frick & Jackson, 1993). The settings where the behaviors emerge broaden to include places beyond the youth's home or school (Lahey & Loeber, 1994). Often, antisocial personality disorder and other serious diagnoses follow in adulthood (Robins, 1966, 1978).

The "late-starter" pathway has been proposed, but there is less evidence to support it. Patterson et al. (1991) described families of late starters as "marginally effective," as they exhibit somewhat stronger parenting skills than early-starter families. With the onset of a significant family stressor or change (e.g., divorce) or even the typical growing strains of teenage rebellion, these families are no longer able to parent as effectively. Supervision tends to drop off, and the adolescents affiliate with groups of peers who are engaging in conduct-related and behavioral problems. However, because the "late starters" have experienced a longer period of social skill development and possess greater personal and family resources than "early starters," they are seen as less likely to persist in conduct problems over time.

In summary, it is clear that (a) several million children and adolescents engage in problematic acting out and are in need of some type of treatment; (b) these children and adolescents experience many and varied types of problems; (c) they frequently experience several problems concurrently (e.g., have comorbid disorders, experience learning problems in school); and (d) these problems can appear at different points in a youngster's life (Kazdin, 2004).

SUGGESTED INTERVENTIONS/TREATMENT STRATEGIES

Effective treatment planning relies on accurate clinical assessment prior to treatment selection. The pretreatment assessment is essential for gathering information needed for disposition or treatment planning including developmental, medical, academic, social, and family history; parameters of the target problems and current contingencies; comorbid disorders; strengths within the child, family, school, and larger community; and potential barriers to treatment. It is also important to understand the family's expectations for treatment and to clarify any misperceptions and treatment demands. The initial assessment not only lays the groundwork for implementing an appropriate evidence-based treatment (EBT), but also identifies collateral treatments that may be indicated, such as medication or academic remediation (Table 18.1).

Once an EBT is selected, it is important to maintain treatment integrity by following treatment manual guidelines. It is also important to understand the function of ongoing assessment in tailoring the EBTs to the needs of the individual child, family, and setting. In parent training, for example, therapists need to assess both parental learning and child response and to pace the steps of treatment accordingly. Treatment applications should be matched to family cultural preferences, parent personality styles, child developmental levels, and other individual differences.

TABLE 18.1

**Recommendations for the Assessment and
Diagnosis of ODD and Conduct Disorder**

- Employ multiple informants in the assessment process
- Multimodal/multidimensional—Full Battery Assessment—To include the following:
  - Behavioral assessment (Achenbach Scales; Achenbach, 1991)
  - Personality/Projective: Younger children (TAT, FAT, CAT) Teens: RISB
  - Intelligence Scales (WPPSI; WISC-IV)
- Psychopathology (MMPI-A)—Employ multiple informants/assessors: PhD, psychologists/ counselors, social workers, case managers, teachers, parents, and psychiatrists
- Diagnosis of CD/ODD is not always clear cut and often there are co-occurring, comorbid mental health disorders
- Use diagnosis with caution: always start with the least restrictive and work your way up, as per the DSM guidelines
- It can be an overused diagnosis; be mindful of this, with certain cultural groups/settings/areas
- Work for early identification and implement early treatment interventions for the best possible outcomes
- The earlier the acting out behavior become a problem and the more severe the behavior, the more likely such patterns of behavior will persist
- The earlier the intervention the more likely it will be effective

Suggested Interventions and Best Practices

Despite extensive treatment research on disruptive behavior over several years, no single intervention emerges as "best." In a review of 16 Evidence-Based Treatment Programs (EBTs) by Eyberg, Newlson, & Boggs (2008), for use with children and adolescents with severe disruptive behavior disorders, the researchers found strong support for both parent-training and child-training EBTs for youth with CD/ODD. It is recommended that clinicians consider parent training as the first-line approach for young children and reserve direct child-training approaches for older youth. Please see Table 18.2 for a list of suggested interventions.

For older children and adolescents, there are two evidence-based multicomponent treatment approaches (MST and MTFC), which are for adolescents with severely delinquent behavior. These include both parent- and child-training components, involve multiple agents of change (e.g., parents, foster parents, teachers, behavior specialists, physicians), and incorporate a greater number of adjunctive treatments beyond psychosocial interventions. A therapist working on a case with a child or adolescent with disruptive behavior disorder should actively engage in research and ongoing case evaluation and ask themselves the following questions: *Does treatment work? How does this treatment work? When is*

TABLE 18.2

Evidence-Based Treatment Interventions

- CBT/BT Programs
- Parent Training/S.T.E.P. (Strategic Teaching of Effective Parenting)
- Multisystemic Therapy (MST)
- Family Therapy
- Multicomponent Treatment Approaches (MTFC)
- Inpatient/Residential Treatment Programs
- Play Therapy—for Assessment
- Adventure Therapy/Boot Camp
- Recreational Therapy/Equine Therapy
- Expressive Arts/Movement Therapy (Dance/Exercise/Yoga/Meditation/Karate)
- Psychopharmacological Interventions

this treatment not enough? and *Is this treatment cost effective?* These contemplative questions serve as an ongoing guide for the therapist to ensure that they are employing the most efficacious treatment strategies to harvest the best possible case outcome. In the following section, a case study will be presented that highlights the difficulty in effectively eliminating the behavioral problems and the intractability of the disorder.

CASE STUDY: ALEX, AGE 7

Alex was a 7-year-old, Caucasian male, and somewhat small in stature and weight for his age. Alex's mother, Terri, was 25 and had given birth to Alex at 18. Alex's father, Martin, had been 19. Although Alex was socially engaging, his mother reported that the behaviors that he had been exhibiting were noxious, severe, developmentally inappropriate, and acute enough that Alex had already been involved with the juvenile justice system at age 7. Despite being born prematurely, Alex appeared to proceed through early infancy with no major development delays or problems. Terri did report that he was difficult to soothe, and seemed to have a "demanding" temperament as an infant and toddler.

His early development was normal, though his speech was slightly delayed. Alex was described by Terri as a highly active baby with little need for sleep, which caused stress and pressure for her and Martin as young parents. Terri also noted that Alex was destructive early on with toys, possessions, and property. He got into things he shouldn't and climbed on furniture and countertops, seemingly fearless even as a small child. When Alex was 4, his mother discussed her concerns about his challenging behavior and his hyperactivity with his pediatrician. The doctor mentioned that these might be symptoms of AD/HD, but advised her to wait until he was in kindergarten and have him evaluated then, and if Alex met the criteria, the doctor would consider medication for him. During the early years of his life, Alex was expelled from numerous daycares and preschool programs. Reasons included severe behavioral disruption, physical aggression, violence toward other children, throwing things, destroying property, yelling/screaming/inappropriate laughing/ swearing, disrespecting staff and teachers, an inability to follow the rules, and urinating openly in the hallway (post toilet training at age 4½). By the time Alex was age 5, with no formal assessment, Alex's pediatrician placed him on Ritalin to see if this would remediate some of the extreme behaviors that Alex was displaying. These behaviors were not just contained to the school or public setting. Alex's behavior was often even more pernicious, manipulative, and, at times, violent at home. Terri revealed that just recently, Alex had been involved in property damage that had brought him to the attention of the law. Alex had walked through the trailer park where his family resided, and using a rock, he had "made designs" on over 35 cars in the neighborhood. When confronted by a neighbor who caught him "in the act," Alex professed innocence and denied wrongdoing. The police were called, and Alex was arrested and charged as a juvenile for vandalism and malicious destruction of property. The arraigning judge chose to hold Alex overnight at the local juvenile justice center due to the severity of the crime, and his parents were charged with failure to control and supervise their minor child. One of the recommendations of the probation of his case was for Alex to receive counseling services and behavior management and for his parents to receive parent training to help them to learn to manage their child's behavior.

After taking on Alex as a client, the therapist would work with him and his family on and off over the course of 7 years. Alex showed inconsistent and only minor improvement in his ability to control his behavioral impulses. His out-of-bounds behavior in school would result in suspensions and expulsions. He was eventually placed in a special alternative school that offered a behavioral modification/ token economy system for children with severe behavioral difficulties. Alex seemed to function much better in this educational setting where he received immediate feedback from the environment about his behavior and where he could earn tokens for his good behavior, and he would lose tokens for negative/unacceptable behavior. He did very well when there were very specifically outlined behavioral expectations of him and where he was actively monitored, which helped him to learn to control his highly impulsive behavior. Over the years at home, however, his behavior still challenged his parents. He was cruel to animals as well as aggressive and violent with family as well as others.

Unfortunately, but not unexpectedly, Alex's parents eventually divorced when he was a preteen and, while at his father's home, he began to display further inappropriate behaviors (e.g., drinking beer, viewing pornography) that were not controlled by his father. Left largely unsupervised, Alex found a group of youths who were similar to him in their predilection for impulsive, destructive, and illegal behaviors. This led to him being charged, again, with vandalism and placed on probation for his uncontrolled behavior. A summary of his behavior over the years in which he was in treatment with this therapist is found in Table 18.3.

TABLE 18.3
Case Study Highlights

- Early display and symptoms of oppositional and defiant behavior
- Alex had always been a highly active young boy, even as an infant and toddler. He was the first child born to the young parents, then 18 and 19 years old, from a semirural community just outside of Cincinnati
- Initially identified diagnosis was AD/HD at age 6, though symptoms were evident as early as age 2
- Inability to relate to others' emotions and no display of empathy
- Limited/lack of ability to modulate emotional responses (i.e., vacillating between blunted/flattened affect and overly reactive)
- Destruction of property and increasingly severe acts of vandalism
- Early involvement in Juvenile Justice System
- Multiple expulsions due to violent behavior at school (pencil incident), encopresis/urination incidents
- Behavior "ratcheted up" as time progressed
- Mother spoke of how heartbroken, ashamed, and embarrassed she had become over Alex's behavior
- Trend toward permissive/neglectful parenting (parents didn't know how to parent/what to do with this child; nor did they agree on how to handle discipline)
- Child ran the household practically since he first learned to walk and talk
- Harmed animal: kicked dog so hard, collapsed his lung, mom had to take the dog to the pound
- Mother was 8 months pregnant; Alex kicked her in the stomach; she fell down the stairs and miscarried
- Alex showed little affect/emotion for his actions; virtually no remorse
- Unable to comply with even the simplest of rules
- Father took no responsibility for parenting him; saying "boys will be boys"

Therapeutic Goals

Based on the history, testing, and interview material, the therapist's primary goals in the short term were to improve the relationship between Alex and his mother and reduce both their conflicts and Alex's conduct problems. In the longer term, improving Alex's prosocial behaviors and skills to promote responsible behaviors, altering his peer affiliation, eliminating aggressive/hostile behavior, improving affect identification in self and others (development of empathy), and improving his ability to behave according to the code of conduct at his school as well as work toward improving his academic achievement were the goals.

Family-Based Behavioral Interventions

Given the evidence that parenting skills deficits are at least in part responsible for the development and maintenance of CD/ODD, the behavioral approach includes family members of the identified patient. Kazdin (1996) pointed out that parent training is the best researched of all the interventions for CD/ODD, and its effectiveness has been supported by empirical evidence (Christophersen & Mortweet, 2002; Kazdin, 1995). Kazdin outlined core elements of parent training. First, treatment is conducted primarily with the parents, with relatively less emphasis on therapist–child interaction. Second, treatment emphasizes prosocial goals and removes some of the focus from the undesirable conduct. Third, the treatment reflects the underlying learning theory. This means that defining, monitoring, and tracking the child's behavior are the foci. Parents are taught methods of reinforcement that involve positive parent attention and extinction/punishment methods such as ignoring, response cost, and time out. They also learn ways to give clear commands and problem-solving techniques. The methods of teaching are behavioral in nature with frequent use of modeling, role playing, and structured homework. The goal is to replace unproductive parenting with a less coercive method. Please see Table 18.4 for the treatment interventions chosen.

In a unique program *Helping the Noncompliant Child* (Forehand & McMahon, 1981), parents were taught to change their patterns of interaction in the "here-and-now" of the clinic by the use of the "bug in the ear" mechanism. Skills were taught didactically, rehearsed, then coached during practice with the child. This program teaches tracking of the problem behaviors or concerns and institutes a simple token economy based on points with back-up reinforcers. Research has indicated (Patterson & Forgatch, 1995) the need for punishment to change the behaviors of children with CD/ODD. Thus, this program

TABLE 18.4

Cognitive Behavioral-Based Treatment for Alex

- Individual CBT
- Token Economy/Level Behavioral Program based at the school
- Parent Training: structural parent/family model that uses natural environmental consequences with positive (+) and negative (–) reinforcers for the child's self-regulation and inhibition and impulse control
- Teach child empathy, affect identification in self and others
- Delivery of Therapy with a Humanistic Approach—developed a relationship with Alex hoping that the relationship would be healing
- Developmental Therapy—consider where he was in the continuum, and also consider that he may not be developmentally capable of mastering the goals of treatment

introduces response costs and chores for use with older children. Sells (2001) wrote a detailed book for parents wanting to change the way their teenagers behave when the teen is "out-of-control." It focused on the need for parents to enforce accountability in their children through "ironclad" behavior contracts. Sells encourages involvement of the wider community of adults, and sometimes peers, in the interventions. He also appeals to parents to develop stronger positive relationships with their adolescent children, even when they are exasperated and angry at the youth for his unacceptable behavior.

In-School Behavioral Treatment Program

Since the 1960s, behavioral management in the classroom has been the topic of considerable research. Despite teachers' beliefs that they frequently praise their students for positive behaviors, classroom observations have shown low rates of positive attention for prosocial behaviors (Martens & Hiralall, 1997). Strategies that help the teacher create classroom contingencies that favor prosocial behaviors and reduce classroom disruption are especially helpful with children with mild-to-moderate conduct problems (Walker, Hops, & Fiegenbaum, 1976). Token reinforcement systems have been used with success for classroom management of disruptive behaviors, especially to increase the prosocial behaviors that are compatible with conduct problem behavior. Abramowitz and O'Leary (1991) reviewed the use of token systems in schools and report consistent decreases in aggressive and disruptive behaviors along with an increase in more desirable classroom behavior. Fading the token system needs to be carried out carefully and strategically so that more naturally occurring environmental contingencies can maintain the newly developed behaviors.

Treatment Outcome

Alex's therapist worked with him and his parents for a number of years, yet his father was seldom available and had limited investment in managing his son's behavior. His mother felt overwhelmed and frightened by her son, and this limited her ability to enforce behavior limits. Unfortunately, Alex was one of the cases in which a therapist's assistance can only do so much. His refusal to stay in school or to abide by the law resulted in his incarceration. Please see Table 18.5 for the summary description of his treatment outcome.

TABLE 18.5
Outcome Description

- Best Practices & Evidence-Based Treatment models—unexpected outcomes despite researched methods
- Incarceration due to limited ability to self-modulate and lack of consistent external environmental controls
- Poor prognosis for Alex due to the extremely early onset of a lack of demonstrated ability to develop empathy, and an inability to understand the consequences
- Challenges (a therapist and treatment team needs to be prepared for ...)
- Consistency/lack of compliance with treatment plan and interventions
- Inconsistency between parental figures
- Inconsistency between environments (school and home)
- Maintaining hope and encouragement in the face of chronic case difficulty
- Inpatient long term—deciding when, and if, residential therapy is the best possible modality for this child
- Brain/biology/genetic factor—unsurpassable?

CONCLUSION

This chapter focused on boys and adolescents who exhibit CD and ODD. It is difficult, if not impossible, to distinguish between ODD, CD, predelinquent behavior, and early stages in the development of an antisocial personality disorder. Behaviorally, the patterns are alike and may simply represent four ways of describing or accounting for the same problematic acting-out behavior. Although a number of factors are related to CD/ODD, no single factor can be identified as producing the disorder. Instead, it likely arises from genetic/constitutional factors, shaped by problematic interactions with parents, teachers, and peers, and influenced by sociocultural factors. It seems most likely that the disorder develops as a result of an interaction of a complex set of factors that result in a spiraling sequence that exacerbates the tendency toward conduct problems and even later antisocial behavior. The earlier the acting-out behavior becomes problematic and the more severe the behavior, the more likely such patterns of behavior will persist. In general, the earlier the assessment and identification of the presence of the disorder and the earlier the intervention, the more likely it will be effective.

ADDITIONAL RESOURCES

For Clinicians

Treating Explosive Kids: The Collaborative Problem-Solving Approach by Ross W. Greene and J. Stuart Ablon, The Guilford Press; 2005.

Clinical Handbook of Assessing and Treating Conduct Problems in Youth by Rachael C. Murrihy, Antony D. Kidman, and Thomas H. Ollendick; Springer; 2010.

Helping Children With Aggression and Conduct Problems: Best Practices for Intervention by Michael L. Bloomquist, PhD and Steven V. Schnell, PhD; New York: Guilford Press, 2002.

Helping the Noncompliant Child: Family Based Treatment for Oppositional Behavior by Robert J. McMahon and Rex L. Forehand; New York: The Guilford Press, 2nd Edition, 2003.

Defiant Teens: A Clinician's Manual for Assessment and Family Intervention by Russell A. Barkley, Gwenyth H. Edwards, and Arthur L. Robin; Guilford Press; 1999.

Conduct and Oppositional Defiant Disorders: Epidemiology, Risk Factors, and Treatment by Cecilia Essau; Lawrence Erlbaum; 2003.

Conduct Disorders: A Practitioner's Guide to Comparative Treatments by W.M. Nelson III, A.J. Finch, Jr., and K.J. Hart; Springer; 2006.

Working with Challenging Youth: Lessons Learned Along the Way by Brent Richardson; Routledge; 2001.

Conduct Disorder and Behavioral Parent Training: Research and Practice by Dermot O'Reilly; Jessica Kingsley; 2005.

Handbook of Disruptive Behavior Disorders by Herbert C. Quay and Anne E. Hogan; New York: Kluwer Academic/Plenum Publishers; 1999.

For Parents

American Academy of Child and Adolescent Psychiatry (AACAP)—Oppositional Defiant Disorder Resource Center. Retrieved from http://www.aacap.org/cs/ODD.ResourceCenter

The Explosive Child: A New Approach for Understanding and Parenting Easily Frustrated, Chronically Inflexible Children by Ross W Greene; Harper Paperbacks; Rev Updated Edition, 2010.

Your Adolescent: Emotional, Behavioral, and Cognitive Development from Early Adolescence Through the Teen Years by David Pruitt, M.D., AACAP; Harper Paperbacks; 2000.

Your Child: Emotional, Behavioral, and Cognitive Development From Birth Through Preadolescence by David Pruitt, M.D., AACAP; Harper Paperbacks; 2000.

Your Defiant Teen: 10 Steps to Resolve Conflict and Rebuild Your Relationship by Russell A. Barkley; Guilford Press, 2008.

The Whipped Parent: Hope for Parents Raising an Out-Of-Control Teen by Kimberly Abraham, Marney Studaker-Cordner, and Kathryn O'Dea; Rainbow Books; 2003.

Parenting Your Out-of-Control Teenager: 7 Steps to Reestablish Authority and Reclaim Love by Scott P. Sells; St. Martin's Griffin; 2002.

Skills Training for Children with Behavior Problems, Revised Edition: A Parent and Practitioner Guidebook by Michael L. Bloomquist, PhD; Guilford Press; Revised Edition, 2005.

REFERENCES

Abramowitz, A. J., & O'Leary, S. G. (1991). Behavior interventions for the classroom: Implications for students with ADHD. *School Psychology Review, 20*, 220–234.

Achenbach, T. M. (1991). *Manual for the Child Behavior Checklist and 1991 profile.* Burlington, VT: University of Vermont, Department of Psychiatry.

American Psychiatric Association. (2000). *The DSM-IV-TR.* Washington, DC: Author.

Brenner, N. D., Simon, T. R., Krug, E. G., & Lowry, R. (1999). Recent trends in violence-related behaviors among high school students in the United States. *Journal of the American Medical Association, 282,* 440–446.

Campbell, S. B., & Ewing, L. J. (1990). Follow-up of hard-to-manage preschoolers: Adjustment at age 9 and predictors of continuing symptoms. *Journal of Child Psychology and Psychiatry, 31,* 871–889.

Christophersen, E. W., & Mortweet, S. L. (2002). *Treatments that work with children: empirically supported strategies for managing childhood problems.* Washington, DC: American Psychological Association.

Comer, R. J. (1995). *Abnormal psychology* (2nd ed.). New York: W. H. Freman.

DiClemente, R. J., Hansen, W. B., & Ponton, L. E. (Eds.). (1996). *Handbook of adolescent health risk behavior.* New York: Plenum.

Elliott, D. S., Huizinga, D., & Ageton, S. S. (1985). *Explaining delinquency and drug use.* Beverly Hills, CA: Sage.

Eyberg, S. M., Nelson, M. M., & Boggs, S. R. (2008). Evidenced-Based Psychosocial Treatments for Children and Adolescents with Disruptive Behavior. *Journal of Clinical Child & Adolescent Psychology, 37*(1), 215–237.

Farrington, D. P. (1995). The development of offending and anti-social behavior from childhood: Key findings from the Cambridge study in the delinquent development. *Journal of Child Psychology and Psychiatry, 36,* 929–964.

Forehand, R., & McMahon, R. J. (1981). *Helping the noncompliant child: A clinicians guide to parent trainings.* New York: Guilford Press.

Frick, P. J., & Jackson, Y. K. (1993). Family functioning and childhood antisocial behavior: Yet another reinterpretation. *Journal of Clinical Child Psychology, 22*, 410–419.

Hinshaw, S. P. (1994). Conduct Disorder in childhood: Conceptualization, diagnosis, comorbidity, and risk status for antisocial functioning in adulthood. In D. D., Fowles, P. Sutker, & S. H. Goodman (Eds.), *Progress in experimental personality and psychopathology research.* New York: Springer Publishing Co.

Hinshaw, S. P., & Anderson, C. A. (1996). Conduct and oppositional defiant disorders. In E. J. Mash & R. A. Barkley (Eds.), *Child psychopathology* (pp. 113–149). New York, NY: Guilford.

Kazdin, W. E. (1995). Child, parent, and family dysfunction as predictors of outcome in cognitive-behavioral treatment of antisocial children. *Behavior Research and Therapy, 33*, 371–381.

Kazdin, A. E. (1996). *Conduct disorders in childhood and adolescents* (2nd ed.). Thousands Oakes, CA: Sage.

Kazdin, W. E. (2004). Psychotherapy with children. In M. J. Lambert (Ed.), *Bergin and Garfield's handbook of psychotherapy and behavior change* (5th Ed.). New York: Wiley.

Ketterlinus, Z. R., & Lamb, M. E. (Eds.). (1994) *Adolescent problem behaviors: Issues and research.* Hillsdale, NJ: Erlbaum.

Lahey, B. B., & Loeber, R. (1994). Framework for a developmental model of oppositional defiant disorder and conduct disorder. In D. K. Routh (Ed.). *Disruptive behavior disorders in childhood.* New York: Plenum.

Lahey, B. B., Loeber, R., Quay, H. C., Frick, P. J., & Grimm, J. (1992). Oppositional defiant and conduct disorders: Issues to be resolved for DSM-IV. *Journal of the American Academy of Child and Adolescent Psychiatry, 31*, 539–546.

Loeber, R., Green, S., Keenan, K., & Lahey, B. (1995). Which boys will fare worse? Early prediction of the onset of Conduct Disorder in six year longitudinal study. *Journal of the American Academy of Child Adolescent Psychiatry, 34*, 499–600.

Martens, B. K., & Hiralall, A. S. (1997). Scripted sequences of teacher interaction. *Behavior Modification, 21*, 308–323.

Mash, E. J., & Wolfe, D. A. (2005). *Abnormal child psychology* (3rd Ed.) Belmont, CA: Wadsworth.

Moffitt, T. E. (1993). "Adolescence-limited" and "life course persistent: anti-social behavior: A developmental taxonomy. *Psychological Review, 100*, 674–701.

Moffitt, T., & Lynan, D. (1994). The neuropsychology of Conduct Disorder and delinquency: Implications for understanding antisocial behavior. In D. Fowlers, P. Sutker, & S. Goodman (Eds.), *Progress in experimental personality and psychopathology research* (pp. 233–262). New York: Springer Publishing Co.

Patterson, G. R., & Capaldi, D., Bank, L. (1991). An early starter model for predicting delinquency. In D. J. Pepler & K. H. Rubin (Eds.), *The development and treatment of childhood aggression* (pp. 139–168). Hillsdale, NJ: Lawrence Erlbaum Associates.

Patterson, G. R., & Forgatch, M. S. (1995). Predicting future clinical adjustment from treatment outcome and process variables. *Psychological Assessment, 7*, 275–285.

Robins, L. N. (1966). *Deviant children grown up.* Baltimore, MD: Williams & Wilkins.

Robins, L. N. (1978). Sturdy childhood predictors of adult antisocial behavior: replications from longitudinal studies. *Psychological Medicine, 8,* 611–622.

Robins, L. (1991). Conduct disorder. *Journal of Child Psychology & Psychiatry, 32,* 193–212.

Sanford, M., Boyles, M. H., Szatmari, P., Offord, D. R., Jamieson, E., & Spinner, M. (1999). Age-of-onset classification of Conduct Disorder: Reliability and validity in a prospective cohort study. *Journal of the American Academy of Child and Adolescent Psychiatry, 36,* 405–414.

Sells, J. N. (2001). Purpose, process and product: A case study in marital intervention. *Family Journal: Counseling & Therapy for Couples, 9(2),* 186–190.

Seltzer, J. D., & Hluchy, C. (1991). Youth with conduct disorder: A challenge to be met. *Canadian Journal of Psychiatry, 36,* 405–414.

U.S. Congress, Office of Technology Assessment. (1991). Adolescent health. (OTA-H-468). Washington, DC: U.S. Government Printing Office.

Snyder, H. N., & Sickmund, M. (1999). *Juvenile offenders and victims 1999 national report.* Pittsburg, PA: National Center for Juvenile Justice, US Department of Justice.

U.S. Congress, Office of Technology Assessment. (1991). *Adolescent health.* (OTA-H-468). Washington, DC: U.S. Government Printing Office.

Walker, H. M., Hops, H., & Fiegenbaum, E. (1976). Deviant classroom behavior as a function of combinations of social and token reinforcement and cost contingency. *Behavior Therapy, 7,* 76–88.

Webster-Stratton, C. & Dahl, R. W. (1995). Conduct Disorder. *Advanced abnormal child psychology.* Hillsdale, NJ: Erlbaum Associates.

Zoccolillo, M., Tremblay, R., & Vitaro, F. (1996). DSM-III-R and DSM-III criteria for conduct disorder in preadolescent girls: Specific but insensitive. *Journal of the American Academy of Child and Adolescent Psychiatry, 35,* 461–470.

19

Bullying and Its Opposite: Harnessing the Power of the Heroes in the School Room, Therapy Room, and on the Playground

JAMES R. PORTER AND BRIAN J. MISTLER

OVERVIEW

This chapter will address the roles of bully, bullied, and bystander and ways to help these young males at the elementary, middle, and high school levels. This chapter is written with two primary audiences in mind—the individual clinician who may be working with an individual victim or perpetrator of bullying, and the therapist, school counselor, teacher, or administrator who is looking for a place to begin to understand available tools to reduce bullying in schools. In the former case of individual or group therapeutic intervention, each clinician will come to the situation with a particular theoretical orientation. The authors presenting the case are heavily influenced by, in one case, a combination of Solution-Focused, Positive Norming, and Narrative Therapy, and in another, Gestalt Therapy. If we are true to our identities we expect, and hope, this influence will shine through. At the same time, we have each worked with colleagues and supervisors from cognitive behavioral therapy, family systems, interpersonal, and other models and have seen the same factors present, and the same information useful. Thus, our hope is that the case is presented in such a way as to be useful to clinicians across orientations.

In the latter case, the number of roles from which an individual may be called upon to offer a "big picture" intervention are numerous, and so too the variety of interventions. Yet, many or most of them have powerful features in common—trying to reduce misperceptions, increase support for successful "peer pressure" in the direction of the desirable behaviors, and ultimately to reduce the acceptance of bullying to begin with. While punishment can be a deterrent, we know that many events go unreported, and many students become repeat offenders. We would especially like to draw your attention to two models—the social norming model and empowerment intervention model. Both approaches are well documented. The social norms marketing approach in particular is presented much more thoroughly elsewhere than we could do herein (e.g., Perkins, Craig, & Perkins, 2011; Perkins, 2003). The empowerment intervention approach, which is being used ever more widely with great success (Porter, 2009), is the one on which we will primarily focus herein in our school-wide case study. However, we feel these two ideas are not contradictory—indeed, they can and should be seen as complimentary. The empowerment intervention model suggests a "what" to target (and in a social context, even a "who" as bystanders are a core group for intervention). The social norms marketing approach suggests another possible, and very powerful, "how" that we recommend you explore further, beginning with the references given earlier in this paragraph. First, let us examine how awareness of social norms and empowerment can be understood and supported in a clinical context.

INTERVENTIONS AND BEST PRACTICES FOR INDIVIDUAL AND GROUP THERAPY

Typically, children are brought into therapy by adult referral. For example, a parent or school personnel may be dissatisfied with a child's behavior or performance. These adults may also be concerned for a child's welfare. The child may appear emotionally vulnerable, or the child is experiencing mistreatment from others at school. Thus, a child is often "subjected" to therapy not of his own initiative and not based on a positive goal but a negative one (i.e., the removal of a problem). In this context, the therapist must begin by establishing rapport with both the family and the child and by making clear to himself or herself and to all involved who is being helped with what. Without such a foundation and an initial demonstration to the child that the therapist can be trusted by both the family and the child, the therapist may be viewed antagonistically by either of them, and one or both may consciously or unconsciously sabotage the relationship and the work.

The Critical Role of Empowerment

When the clinician's task is empowering a child, then the therapist must seek to build trust and rapport in a situation that is often especially difficult. The situation is that the child was introduced by one adult to the counselor (another adult) to do what no other adult has done for the child—namely, empower the child. However, it may be especially in the contexts where a child feels disempowered in multiple contexts that this approach is paramount. Bullying is a power cycle, in which one child seeks empowerment by aggression and another is disempowered through aggression. The primary goal of the therapist is empowerment of the client. In this case, the client is the child and the referring person. If it is within the counselor's means to do so, he or she should try to reach both.

Simultaneously, a therapist can assume that the referring adult is also in a perceived state of disempowerment because they are seeking help. The adult can be counted on to point out various behaviors on the part of the child that frustrate the adult. The adult will probably describe being mystified by many of the behaviors and hard pressed to know what to do about it. Therefore, the counselor can seek to empower the adult.

The core of the approach described herein is present in models such as solution-focused, positive norming, and narrative therapy. In order to revive in the client an internal sense of empowerment, instances of that internal power in each client must be rediscovered and highlighted. These instances are different in children than in adults. For example, most children cannot look back on a life of creating income for themselves in the midst of fear of failure. This is a powerful remembrance for an adult, even one who has occasionally failed to provide for himself or herself. However, many children can remember having stood up and spoken their minds on one occasion at least, even if they were not always effective according to their own ideal. Regardless of age group, all hopelessness is dependent on selective memory. Remembering, in therapy or via the "educational" efforts of program developers, the numerous losses we have suffered or the many horrible things that can happen on the playground creates a compact story of negative events, ignoring the rest. Selectively creating a new story of remembered triumphs creates an assessment that is simultaneously honest and empowering. Not only does it make a person *feel* empowered, it also stimulates solutions that can create powerful responses to problems.

In addition, truer direction is probably best achieved by an almost Skinnerian focus on positive reinforcement. Skinner argued that while positive reinforcement creates clear directions toward the behavioral achievements, punishment carries the potential for paradoxical side effects (Skinner, 1998). First, punishment teaches punishment strategies, a lesson we do not want to be teaching children who are in trouble for punishing others already. Second, punishment works by coupling a punishing stimulus with an undesired behavior in order to decrease it.

Unfortunately, humans associate a punishment they receive not only with the behavior they themselves committed, but also with the human who is doing the punishment. Third is reactance, in which a punishee attempts to extinguish the punitive behavior of the punisher by committing behaviors intended to prove to the punisher that the punishment is not working. This well-reasoned response should reasonably be countered by intensified punishment, but reactance supersedes reason when anger, confusion, hopelessness, and especially lack of direction are present. Therefore, the introduction of exemplary behaviors appropriate to bullying situations and the systematic and meaningful reward thereof seem indispensable in a culture where males are typically rewarded for bully-like attitudes and behaviors.

In aggressive and victimized children, stories of hopelessness incorporate their views of themselves, other people (children and adults), and the world. They will sometimes point out that "this is just the way I am" whether it is aggressive, unpopular, or shy. They will also point out that all of the "cool" or popular students in a particular school look down on all of the shy or uncool children in the school. In the case of the aggressive child, he or she perceives no way out of bullying that does not lead to being victimized. In the case of the victimized child, he or she simply sees no way out of being bullied. Because of the chronic nature of bullying and because examples of disempowered adults seem to abound in some schools, many children will create a worldview in which power is a linear top-to-bottom structure consisting of the powerful, the middle, and the powerless.

In such situations, symptoms of depression and anxiety may appear, which if untreated may increase a person's risk of suicide (Klomek et al., 2008, 2009). This makes sense if you imagine an aggressive child looking ahead to a lifetime of struggle to maintain dominance. Think about a victimized child seeing no end to his or her victimization. This hierarchical fight need not be true of the world. The happiest children are not involved in this struggle, but are the ones who seek to help others out of this struggle.

Highlighting the Positive Reality

In narrative therapy, positive social norming, and solution-focused approaches, the positive reality is highlighted. In narrative therapy, this is done to restructure the story by which a client views the world. In positive norming, it is done to show that healthy behavior is typical behavior. In solution-focused therapy, these positive examples are highlighted to get the client aware of past successes and present opportunities.

Awareness of defending presents opportunities for aggressive and victimized children alike. Defending becomes an "out" or a "third way." The presence of a third way unhinges a dichotomous thought structure consisting of the powerful "top dog" and the powerless "underdog." In the case of defending, power is inherent in empowering others. This is evident in the highly desirable personal and social attributes of children who defend. In therapy, examples can be brought out of the child client's life and from research literature. Examples of "top dog/underdog" (dominant/submissive) interactions may also be found in parts of the individual, as a child or any client struggles with the internal dialog between "I want" and "I should."

Therapy presents a situation in which an adult is offering to struggle side-by-side with a child to find such examples, brainstorm action plans, and reap the benefits of a new worldview. Children trapped in the bullying cycle need to understand that there are defenders in their schools and that they themselves can become defenders. In the case of adults, empowerment can be achieved in very much the same way. Adults who refer children to therapy for bullying others or due to being victimized need concrete reasons to believe that they and their children are powerful. Educating adults of the statistical likelihood that there are healthy, proactive, prosocial children in schools allows them to come up with solutions or opens them to suggestions from the therapist. Parents can expose their children to the most altruistic friends. Adults can assess, approve of, and disapprove of friends for their children. Adults can reshape the relationship with their kids based on their knowledge of what has not worked and what has worked, as well as on ideas of what "might" work that has not been tried. Adults can change their discipline styles. Both suggestions from the therapist and ideas from the client are valuable here. As an example of adult empowerment, a clinician has the immediate fact of the adult deciding and following through on therapy for his or her child.

Group Therapy Considerations

These same dynamics play out in similar but slightly different ways in a group context. In groups, individuals will often reenact familiar patterns, either falling into known roles or identifying group as an opportunity to explore new roles within familiar dynamics. The skillful group therapist will help label these processes and support/challenge appropriately to allow members to experiment with new patterns that transcend these choices rather than continuing to feel stuck selecting among them. Group can also play an important role in helping participants to experience a sense of empowerment as they witness their power to effect change in themselves.

For open groups especially, older members also see how far they have come and are given an opportunity to be altruistic as they offer their wisdom by example to newer members. As participants try on new behaviors in group, and later outside the group, the group can also play an important role in providing support for persisting with the new, more desirable behaviors. This is especially critical as participants return to school or family systems where their new role has a destabilizing effect—one which the system can often unconsciously push back on with great force, making it difficult for the person to maintain new patterns of behavior. Talking explicitly about strategies for enlisting support from important adults in the child's life outside the group can help prepare the person for a better chance of success.

Beyond the Therapy Room

Indeed, adults often have more power than they realize. When they enter complaining about their children's behavior and emotional needs, they enter with a problem-laden story and will probably resist the clinician who is not willing to hear that story. However, once the clinician honors that reality, he or she can begin helping the client tell a more nuanced version of the story by finding positive exceptions in the story of their lives with the child. As the adult comes to see him or herself as empowered, he or she becomes both an advocate and a model for the child. As the counselor works to empower the child and the parent, he or she must remember to also empower the parent to empower the child. Just the way the therapist has taught the child to see the positive potential in him or herself, the parent can function to do the same.

Empowerment has some hard realities, however. Some problems cannot be solved without changing a child's environment. Some schools have predominantly harsh environments. Rare perhaps is the school with catastrophic problems. Empowerment of children does not suggest a mandate that a child go down with a ship that is sinking. Sometimes a change of schools is indicated. However, this is difficult to assess case by case. A negative worldview in a client may cause him or her to run from school to school finding insurmountable problems in each. This can add to the pervasiveness of the view of the world as hostile. On the other hand, an acknowledgement that a particular school has a better environment than the child's current school can result in a hopeful search for a better life. The therapist's job is to present this duality in all its difficulty and uphold the capability of the adult and child client to make the decision and live with the consequences. Support, during and after such decisions, helps bolster coping. Let us turn to examine a clinical case—one in which norms and empowerment also play a key role.

CLINICAL WORK WITH A VICTIM OF BULLYING

This case study was chosen to describe a situation in which both the child perpetrating and the child receiving the bullying were males. In addition, two flavors of bullying are sampled here: social bullying and physical aggression. Traditionally, literature found that girls were more likely to be involved in social bullying, while males were involved in physical bullying (e.g., Crick, Casas, & Ku, 1999). This case shows that boys can summon up the social know-how to create a sophisticated and damaging form of social exclusion. It shows also how verbal, social, and physical bullying can easily go hand in hand.

CASE STUDY: RICHARD, AGE 12

"Richard" was a 12-year-old, African American, male, sixth-grade student. Both of his parents had private businesses. His father owned a bookstore, and his mother ran a law practice. Richard had no known learning disabilities and appeared average in size and build for his age. According to his mother, his grades in elementary school were average or above, until about the fifth grade. Richard was often shy, he and his mother stated, but he was very interested in girls since fourth grade. In addition, Richard said he was very outgoing when he played soccer. Richard apparently had occasional friends, but he said it was always because they approached him or because his parents organized "play-dates" when he was young. He stated that most kids were nice to him until the past year. His relationship with his best friend "Charles" was strong and had lasted from the beginning of first grade until recently.

Presenting Issue

Richard said that the trouble began the summer before fifth grade. Richard had made some new friends at soccer camp. Most of the boys at camp did not go to Richard's elementary school, but almost all of them would be attending his middle school the following year. One night, after the camp had ended and just before the school year was to begin, Richard confided to one of his soccer camp friends "Colt," via a private message on a social networking website, that he had a crush on a girl named "Shania." Richard went on to describe some romantic, and even sexual, fantasies he had had about her. Reportedly, Colt called Richard a "wuss" for not being able to approach Shania.

The following day, Richard discovered that Colt had published his private message about Shania on his own and Richard's public pages that were available for access by registered friends and by anyone on the Internet. In addition, several other people had added comments to the posting, including one of Shania's friends who said that she was crying because of what Richard and the others who commented had said. Richard noted that he did not know many of the people who made comments, but a few were soccer friends and some were school acquaintances. Richard responded angrily to Colt with a new public posting. After that, Richard and Colt began trading insults on the website. When asked why he insisted on arguing publicly, Richard said that he "knew" that Colt would make all of his private postings public anyway. By the time the school year came around, Colt had gone from insulting Richard to inventing stories about him and convincing others who saw the posts that Richard was a "psycho" and not to hang around him. Others had long since joined in on insulting Richard via the Web.

When Richard got to sixth grade, children avoided him and some even went on to insult him to his face. At one point, a child kicked Richard's crutches, used for a minor sports-related injury, out from under him. The most bizarre turn of the story was relayed by Richard and his mother both. The kids had printed t-shirts with coded insults about Richard using a language devised by one of the children who had taken Colt's side. Some children wore them to school. Richard stated he did not pay the shirts any mind because he did not know what they meant. Throughout most of this, his friend Charles had stood by Richard, but when the insult language was created, Charles joined in talking about Richard behind his back though never obtaining a t-shirt. Richard communicated that he was alone in the world, that he wanted to change schools, and that no one would help him.

Interventions

Many things happened in therapy with Richard after the initial intake session was completed. His mother was a willing advocate, but Richard believed her past attempts at helping had failed. Instead of helping, teachers embarrassed him by telling the entire class not to pick on him. The teasing increased and Richard said it proved that nothing would help. After some encouragement, his mother was determined to continue communicating to the school until she and Richard started to see positive change. Even before big changes occurred at school, Richard reported improved feelings of self-worth due to his mother's show of advocacy.

In addition, he began to verbalize that his mother's example of persistence reminded him of how persistence once paid off for him. He had been failing in math one year, but was determined to at least pass by the end of that term. His insistence on better study habits earned him a "D" (passing) that term and transformed him into a "math genius," as he put it, by the end of the following year. With encouragement, he began to approach his fellow students and his teachers until he found a way to communicate, which, along with his mother's alliance with one of his teachers, created better treatment from many of the students. An important "re-storying" of Richard's complaints came when he remembered that his best friend Charles had been the one who had informed him of the insult language. Feeling a rekindling of his fondness for Charles, he approached him in school to ask him why he eventually joined in the bullying. Charles stated that he had been told by one of the ringleaders that Richard had been insulting him behind his back. By the time Richard had made it to his next counseling appointment, he had already begun playing with Charles again after school.

Outcome and Reflections

Richard and his classmates made many strides during his course of therapy. In other cases, the therapist had intervened by attending meetings with the school faculty to help create a plan. However, in Richard's case, his mother's persistent advocacy had created change in the school. Richard felt safer, loved, and more powerful and began initiating changes in his social behavior that resolved conflict—or at least made it clear that he would do whatever it took to stop the bullying. He and his mother felt safe enough to end therapy. Although he reported that one day he would like to deal with some long-standing feelings of poor self-image and a tendency to sacrifice himself for the approval of others, he said he would like to show himself that he could handle school without further therapy. His mother, too, was determined that he would become more independent without therapy now that his environment had become friendly.

   This situation is a good description of how therapy can create change in a boy's thinking, his behavior, and his environment. In addition, it shows the value of solving acute problems and allowing the client to judge when he is ready to cope without professional intervention.

SCHOOL INTERVENTIONS AND STRATEGIES

In the previous section, adults and children have been seen as in need of empowerment when therapists are introduced to a child client involved in bullying situations. However, adults as we have discussed heretofore have been primarily the parents or family of the child. School staff, faculty, and administration have not been discussed. For school personnel and leadership, finding new ways of addressing bullying can involve some risk. The positive social attitudes that children need to learn to avoid bullying or being victimized are not usually prioritized in school curricula. Often school personnel have crowded agendas, and intervening to prevent and alleviate bullying represents dropping the ball in another arena. In a state of disempowerment, risk aversion supersedes opportunity seeking. However, empowering adults who work for schools is crucial in creating examples for children in the adult world that defending-type behavior works in the real world—that adults are not expecting better from their kids than they are from themselves.

Empowerment of Actors in a Whole School Approach

The therapist and parent must also be empowered to deal with the school environment. In many cases, this will be done on a step-by-step basis and will vary with each case. For example, sometimes a therapist advocates for the child and family by proxy, by empowering the parent to advocate for the child at school. In the case of one of the authors this has been a frequent and rewarding method of creating change at a school. In addition, therapists can make themselves available as consultants to schools, for free or for fee. Therapists may also offer to accompany students and parents to meetings with school faculty. Therapists simultaneously build clientele and help educators educate when they send informational letters to school guidance counselors about the nature and presence of defending in their schools and how to encourage it.

Indeed, somewhere between 16% and 28% of children in schools, on their own initiative, attempt to interfere with bullying when they see it (Porter, 2009). Over half of the time, they succeed within 10 seconds (Hawkins, Pepler, & Craig, 2001). Children who act to intervene in bullying or to help those victimized by bullying in some other way are termed "defenders." These children are defined by their actions rather than their attitudes, for many a bystander wishes to intervene and does not.

Life is good for defenders of those victimized by bullying. They have high "genuine self-esteem" as opposed to the well-faked self-esteem of bullies (Salmivalli, Kaukiainen, Kaistaniemi, and Lagerspetz, 1999). Defenders feel that they are effective in their behaviors, emotions, and family and social lives (Salmivalli, 1998). Defenders are popular among other children (Goossens, Olthof, & Dekker, 2006; Monks, Ruiz, & Val, 2002; Salmivalli, Huttunen, & Lagerspetz, 1997; Salmivalli, Lagerspetz, Björkqvist, Österman, Kaukiainen, 1996).

Defenders are "good kids," the kind you might want your children getting closer to. They are altruistic and agreeable (Tani, Greenman, Schneider, & Fregoso, 2003). Defenders are highly concerned with the morality of people's actions (Gini, 2006). Defenders are against bullying (Salmivalli & Voeten, 2004). They are more empathically aware than other children, particularly aggressive children (Gini, Albiero, Benelli, & Altoè, 2007; Maeda, 2003). They are not aggressive like bullies and their "henchpersons" (Maeda, 2003).

Defenders have powerful abilities. Defenders can infer other people's motives better than many of us (Gini, 2006; Maeda, 2003). Defenders have self-control (Monks, Smith, & Swettenham, 2003). They are also good at regulating their own emotions (Maeda, 2003). More than anything being a defender probably does not rely on an inborn trait, but rather on environmental context. It seems that just hanging around defenders (Salmivalli, Lappalainen, & Lagerspetz, 1998) or friends who expect you to be a defender (Porter, 2009), increases your likelihood of being one. So too is a general perception of the norms of a peer group critical, and a social norms marketing approach can play a key role (Perkins, Craig, & Perkins, 2011).

In short, defenders are happier and healthier than other kids are, and kids who are not defenders can become happy, healthy defenders. At a time when the media, schools, parents, and policymakers are finally starting to take bullying seriously, and in a book about aggression in young people, you may be surprised to read in this chapter that focusing on bullying and aggression is lamentably iatrogenic and that we do not plan to fall into that path.

A core premise of this chapter is that the solution is bigger than the problem. This is not to say, however, that "everything's fine" and that we should starve bullying of attention with the aim that it will die on its own. No, the solution to bullying is bigger than the problem, but it needs to be bigger. This chapter describes the problem of bullying only inasmuch as to help discuss the solution. The reason the solution is highlighted is that, even without the problem of bullying, the solution to bullying involves attitudes and behaviors that are generally applicable to success in life. Augmenting the solution to bullying in schools involves nurturing, teaching, and training students, faculty, and administration in skills that can be applied generally to life. These skills do not derive their importance from the damage done by bullying. Rather, the consequences of bullying derive from the absence of benefits associated with training in prosocial behavior. Furthermore, we will assert that these skills are equally crucial to our children living effective lives as are the most highly prioritized subjects covered in our schools today.

For bullying to end, the art of standing up for others should be taught formally. In addition, the skills, attitudes, and characteristics of children who defend are abilities, mind-sets, and qualities that can be taught in schools. Furthermore, without learning these, boys are handicapped by schools rather than bolstered by them in their attempts to succeed in career, family, and society. It is important to apply a number of ways of intervening to prevent, reduce, and address bullying. We suggest a range of treatment strategies, including social norms marketing approaches, psychoeducational interventions, and creative approaches including drumming and the use of costumes and role-play for those working to address systemic issues and help prevent bullying.

Whom Should Community Interventions Target?

In general, three important and often complimentary targets for interventions are school administrators, teachers, and students. It is also possible in some cases to intervene with parents, siblings, and even community members as well as any other stakeholder who has interest in preventing bullying and/or influence of students' behaviors. Forty percent of surveyed teachers admit to bullying students at least once, and 33% admit to bullying them more than once and even frequently (Twemlow, Fonagy, Sacco, & Brethour Jr., 2006). It is likely that the bullying problem in our nations' schools does not start with students and will not end with students.

A strongly supported perspective of intervention for various mental health concerns is the cognitive-behavioral part. It holds that beliefs held by persons form their interpretations of life circumstances, and that these interpretations can inform behavior in predictable ways. A person whose beliefs about the world, other people, and themselves promote positive coping is likely to be highly resilient and perhaps prosocial in his or her behavior. Evidence suggesting that the expectation for males to behave as defenders is smaller than that for females also suggests that these expectations are linked to less self-reported defending behavior by males as compared to females (Porter, 2009). The implications of this are large for males, particularly if further research supports the concept that gender expectations in bullying-scenario behaviors lead to behavior based on those expectations.

During a consultation with an elementary school principal about a social-exclusion pattern that was occurring in one of her grade levels, the principal asked the consultant whether "friendly guy-style jabs" that she had taken on as a form of humor with the kids made her a bad person. The response that this researcher would now give to that question is that children are sent to school to be educated in thinking skills that will serve them for their lifetimes. Faculty and staff are charged with teaching math, science, and reading because they are thought to promote success later in life. Now, research suggests that attitudes about the world, other people, and themselves predict such things as relationship success, longevity, and career performance. This being the case, it becomes perhaps of equal importance to inculcate children systematically in optimism, altruism, self-efficacy, and positive self-concepts. Thus, a teacher or other school personnel who engages in jocular mini-insult upon children may be committing an action that is parallel to actions that would sabotage the learning of math, science, and reading. Just as schools have been charged to teach those subjects to children because their parents were not capable of teaching them, it stands to reason that schools are the only place for some children in our society to learn positive responsible attitudes in a structured and consistent way.

Bullies, Victims, or Bystanders?

Direct interventions with students can be understood broadly as aiming to directly reduce acts of bullying and/or educating and empowering bystanders to speak up against and report incidents of bullying they witness. Much research has pointed to the importance of peer-influence in both cases. Indeed, students and adults alike frequently look to those around them to make decisions about their behaviors (Perkins, 2003).

Victims are perhaps the most invested in seeing an end to bullying, but they perhaps feel themselves to be the most powerless. Bullies are not thought to be "happily mean" people, and so may also have some motivation to change. Bystanders can be divided roughly into two types: those who intervene and those who do not. Salmivalli (1999) recommends employing the children who intervene as agents of change in bullying programs perhaps making them the theoretical primary target of intervention among children. We present now an example of a prevention program at a public school designed to measurably increase defending behavior and decrease the number of bullying instances for an entire school. Noncritical details of the target school have been obscured.

CASE STUDY: SYSTEMATIC PREVENTION PROGRAM

Initial Meetings and Requests for Programming

A small urban charter school had asked to have an antibullying program implemented at the school. It was a middle school with about 15 children at each grade level. However, incidents of violence between children had increased. After administrators had done some investigation, it became apparent that (a) only a few children were typically targeted for aggression, (b) those targeted children had begun retaliating and were becoming difficult in class, and that (c) most of the aggression was rooted in making fun of children for their weight, skin color, or other physical attributes. The assistant principal asked if the program developers could make presentations to the school about the causes and effects of bullying, teasing, and other aggression. She added that some of the children were from homes in which drug use, parental absence, and even gang membership existed. The program developers convinced the assistant principal that, though violence in the children's lives can affect their behavior at school, the chronic, power-imbalanced, and targeted nature they described at their school had turned general anger and aggression into laser-like diminution of a select group of kids.

Programming Selected

After some discussion, the assistant principal was able to find some "exceptions to the rule." At the request of the program developers, she was able to name a few kids whom she had observed standing up for others verbally, reporting instances of actual child-on-child abuse, and befriending children who would otherwise have no friends. She gave program-developers permission to do a paper and pencil survey to determine by self-, peer-, and teacher-report who the school's "defenders" were. These defenders were then trained via "encounter experiences," lectures, role-play, and ordinary group games. The goal was to show them that they each were not alone in their desire to help kids who are victimized, to keep them safe, to encourage them to continue trying to help, and to create the best possible solutions for their particular school environment. In addition, awareness lectures on the topic of defending were provided to all students at the school, grade by grade.

Follow-up sessions with those children revealed that they were feeling more empowered on the playground and in the classroom. They reported some successes. However, the number of children in the original group diminished as the time went, as administrators had insisted on having the trainings scheduled after school. A high-stakes academic test season had begun during the program implementation, and communication with administrators became more difficult for the intervention specialists as well as for the children. Children reported being ignored by faculty members when they reported instances of bullying.

The group itself seemed to increase in enthusiasm—even while reporting more frustration. Children who remained in the group asserted that they got much from the discussions. They reported some successes. One child invited a former victim into the group. Some students identified a pattern in which they confronted a bully on his actions, the bully threatened retaliation, but that the retaliation rarely came. However, the program implementers found that, without adequate school support, it would not be fair to continue encouraging the children in the group to intervene more. Some of them had taken risks beyond what the interventionists had suggested.

Informal conversations with faculty members suggested that the actual violence and name-calling had decreased. Many reported that, it being a small school, the "bullies" and "victims" had largely become friends again in cases where they had been friendly before. They stated that, while arguments and misunderstandings were common, physical violence was rare and resolutions came naturally among the children.

Outcome and Reflections

Implementation Outcomes

Implementation as originally conceived was difficult due to priorities of the specific school that reflect priorities at the state and national level. Measurement of outcomes did not occur due to the difficulties inherent in an already full school schedule. Nor did a sufficient portion of the school, or even the grade-level selected, participate in the training due to the decision by the school leadership to hold the training after school hours were over. Teacher training occurred as planned, although the selection of and communication with a "defender-liaison" among the faculty did not occur.

Behavioral and Attitude Outcomes

Scheduling constraints, and perhaps ennui as detected in the school staff during teacher training and from reports by student participants, limited the program's promotion of altruistic behaviors, as well as altruistic and confident attitudes. It was observed that the training encouraged children to "stick their necks out" without sufficient peer support due to low participation rates. Children reported backlash from their efforts. However, reconstructing the training based on student feedback did appear to have a strengthening effect on the trainees and the potential to create lasting change in those affected by the training. Children who followed up with faculty or peers on their efforts to intervene in bullying and support children targeted by bullying thought they eventually conveyed the belief that backlash was merely initial resistance to change, which gave way under persistence.

It appears that this somewhat large-scale, complex program created more benefit from adapting to specific needs of students and others in the school. In addition, limits in the workability of the program were not wholly due to constraints within the school system. Future implementations of the program may involve more direct talks with administrators to create a customized plan for intervention. In addition, implementing such a strategy at a "full-size" public school will probably involve more of the same type of time and investment conflicts. However, the concept of selecting defenders in some reliable and valid way appears to create a training group that is highly motivated.

School investment is a primary factor in the success of such a program as that described here. In order to implement the complex data gathering and systematic access to students that such a program requires, schools in many areas would have to change operating procedures and priorities for the time the program is being implemented.

CONCLUSIONS AND SUMMARY

If we can simultaneously hold in our minds two somewhat opposing thoughts about bullying, we can perhaps find motivation to address it more seriously, enthusiastically, and hopefully. What is called abuse in homes is called bullying in schools, playgrounds, and online. Verbal, physical, and sexual abuse committed between children outside the home often earns the term bullying. In point of fact, verbal abuse committed by adults upon children in schools will often be termed bullying. The line blurs even more when teens land themselves on a sex offender list by "sexting" nude photos of other teens (e.g., Feyerick & Steffen, 2009). However, it appears that children who face adversity and overcome it may have higher resiliency than children who face no adversity at all (Seligman, 1998). Furthermore, as was discussed earlier in this chapter, at least one role children assume in the bullying process—the role of children who intervene in bullying—is associated with enviable mental health qualities.

As described, a large portion of children in our schools could be termed successful antibullies. Their contributions, however, are underrecognized in antibullying efforts and bullying-related literature. Concepts such as "the boomerang effect," "positive norming," social-learning theory, and Skinner's "differential reinforcement of an incompatible behavior" suggest that presenting these young "defenders" as examples gives heretofore illusive direction to bullying reduction approaches. Examples of recommended strategies include using defending behavior as the primary selection criterion for recruiting peer mentors in antibullying programs, normalizing defending behavior by "marketing" the high prevalence of that behavior in schools, teaching defending strategies, and highlighting the positive social status and personal attributes associated with becoming a defender.

Let us also be clear that these recommendations are not only for children. Becoming an example can be a breakthrough experience for staff, faculty, and parents. Strategies for adults involve refusing to be bullied in the workplace, at home, and in school. In addition, adults can learn not to bully coworkers, students, offspring, other family members, and other members of their social network. Crucially, however, the replacement behavior of defending and befriending victims must be exemplified somewhat blatantly to children by educators, administrators, and parents—but most importantly by their peers.

The gender gap in aggression, and bullying in particular, is not thought to be subject to trait differences in males and females, but in socialization differences. By and large, children spend at least 6 to 7 hours of their weekdays in the school environment, and that does not include the potential for an additional 3 hours a weekday in school-site aftercare. Yet, it does not seem that schools commonly target appropriate socialization for children in their curriculum. Furthermore, school personnel are apparently not socialized into their profession in a way that encourages appropriate example and treatment of children. It may seem that large institutional changes would be required to adequately train school personnel in the effective socialization of their student population—and that such a focus would detract from the traditional academic priorities. However, such efforts may incur a high reward for all involved, and the difficulty may be less than perceived. It appears that a nation of children, particularly boys, may be suffering from the current level of intervention. Conversely, the higher than normal resiliency that comes from facing adversity with the appropriate attitudes and behavioral responses seems to be commensurate with the benefit schools are expected to garner: success into adult life.

Concepts of perseverance, self-efficacy, and altruism can be part of the academic stratagem because highly demanding academic exercises tackled from a correct attitude mimic the kind of adaptive coping that helps in careers and that seem to be associated with the altruistic behavior of defending. Views of boys as highly academic, nurturing, and indefatigable can be inserted into the traditional subject instruction, whereas currently attitudes and behaviors come forward merely by chance if at all. There does appear to be a different socialization for boys than for girls as a force of cultural habit, and this seems to affect boys negatively in terms of bullying and academics.

More than family, schools have the structural foundation to systematically counter this and other cultural habits to create a relief from bullying and broader benefits for boys and girls alike. We have tried to outline ways that understanding the roles of bully, bullied, and bystander can help young males especially at the elementary, middle, and high school levels. We have also presented two cases in the hope that they will be useful to clinicians across orientations, administrators and educators across venues, and other stakeholders invested in helping overcome bullying. What is clear, above all, is that each individual reading this book and each individual he or she comes in contact with will have an opportunity to act in a way that makes the world a safer place; we hope you have found something in the last few pages that will better equip you for that opportunity the next time you are aware of it.

REFERENCES

Crick, N. R., Casas, J. F., & Ku, H. (1999). Relational and physical forms of peer victimization in preschool. *Developmental Psychology, 35*(2), 376–385.

Feyerick, D., & Steffen, S. (2009, April) 'Sexting' lands teen on sex offender list. *CNN's American Morning.* Retrieved May 17, 2011 from http://articles. cnn.com/2009–04-07/justice/sexting.busts_1_phillip-alpert-offender-list-offender-registry?_s=PM:CRIME

Gini, G. (2006). Social cognition and moral cognition in bullying: What's wrong? *Aggressive Behavior, 32*(6), 528–539.

Gini, G., Albiero, P., Benelli, B., & Altoè, G. (2007). Does empathy predict adolescents' bullying and defending behavior? *Aggressive Behavior, 33*(5), 467–476.

Goossens, F. A., Olthof, T., & Dekker, P. H. (2006). New participant role scales: Comparison between various criteria for assigning roles and indications for their validity. *Aggressive Behavior, 32*(4), 343–357.

Hawkins, D. L., Pepler, D. J., & Craig, W. M. (2001). Naturalistic observations of peer interventions in bullying. *Social Development, 10*(4), 512–527.

Klomek, A. B., Sourander, A., Kumpulainen, K., Piha, J., Tamminen, T., Moilanen, I., Almqvist, F., & Gould, M.S. (2008). Childhood bullying as a risk for later depression and suicidal ideation among Finnish males. *Journal of Affective Disorders, 109*(1–2), 47–55.

Klomek, A. B., Sourander, A., Niemela, S., Kumpulainen, K., Piha, J., Tamminen, T., Almqvist, F., & Gould, M. S. (2009). Childhood bullying behaviors as a risk for suicide attempts and completed suicides: A population-based birth cohort study. *Journal of American Academic Child and Adolescent Psychiatry, 48*(3), 254–261.

Maeda, R. (2003). Empathy, emotion regulation, and perspective taking as predictors of children's participation in bullying (Doctoral Dissertation, ProQuest Information & Learning). *Dissertation Abstracts International Section A: Humanities and Social Sciences, 64* (11), 3957–3957. (UMI 3111101) Retrieved from http://search.ebscohost.com.lp.hscl.ufl.edu/login.aspx?direct=true&db=psyh&AN=2004-99009-050&site=ehost-live

Monks, C., Ruiz, R., & Val, E. (2002). Unjustified aggression in preschool. *Aggressive Behavior, 28*(6), 458–476.

Monks, C. P., Smith, P. K., & Swettenham, J. (2003). Aggressors, victims, and defenders in preschool: Peer, self-, and teacher reports. *Merrill-Palmer Quarterly, 49*(4), 453–469.

Perkins, H. W. (2003). The emergence and evolution of the social norms approach to substance abuse prevention. In H. W. Perkins (Ed.), *The social norms approach to preventing school and college age substance abuse: A handbook for educators, counselors, and clinicians* (pp. 3–18). San Francisco, CA: Jossey-Bass.

Perkins, H. W, Craig, D., & Perkins, J. (2011). Using social norms to reduce bullying: A research intervention among adolescents in five middle schools. *Group Processes Intergroup Relations.* doi:10.1177/1368430210398004.

Porter, J. (2009). Children's tendency to defend victims of school bullying: Gender social identity, and normative pressure. (Doctoral Dissertation, Proquest Information & Learning). Retrieved from http://proquest.umi.com/pqdlink?d id=1845742601&Fmt=7&clientI d=79356&RQT=309&VName=PQD

Salmivalli, C. (1998). Intelligent, attractive, well-behaving, unhappy: The structure of adolescents' self-concept and its relations to their social behavior. *Journal of Research on Adolescence (Lawrence Erlbaum), 8*(3), 333–354.

Salmivalli, C. (1999). Participant role approach to school bullying: Implications for interventions. *Journal of Adolescence, 22*(4), 453.

Salmivalli, C., Huttunen, A., & Lagerspetz, K. M. J. (1997). Peer networks and bullying in schools. *Scandinavian Journal of Psychology, 38*(4), 305–312.

Salmivalli, C., Kaukiainen, A., Kaistaniemi, L., & Lagerspetz, K. M. J. (1999). Self-evaluated self-esteem, peer-evaluated self-esteem, and defensive egotism as predictors of adolescents' participation in bullying situations. *Personality and Social Psychology Bulletin, 25*(10), 1268–1278.

Salmivalli, C., Lagerspetz, K., Björkqvist, K., Österman, K., & Kaukiainen, A. (1996). Bullying as a group process: Participant roles and their relations to social status within the group. *Aggressive Behavior, 22*(1), 1–15.

Salmivalli, C., Lappalainen, M., & Lagerspetz, K. M. J. (1998). Stability and change of behavior in connection with bullying in schools. *Aggressive Behavior, 24*(3), 205–218.

Salmivalli, C., & Voeten, M. (2004). Connections between attitudes, group norms, and behaviour in bullying situations. *International Journal of Behavioral Development, 28*(3), 246–258.

Seligman, M. E. P. (1998). *Learned optimism: How to change your mind and your life.* New York: Pocket Books.

Skinner, B.F. (1988, June). A statement on punishment. *APA Monitor,* 22.

Tani, F., Greenman, P. S., Schneider, B. H., & Fregoso, M. (2003). Bullying and the big five. *School Psychology International, 24*(2), 131.

Twemlow, S. W., Fonagy, P., Sacco, F. C., & Brethour Jr., J. R. (2006). Teachers who bully students: A hidden trauma. *International Journal of Social Psychiatry, 52*(3), 187–198.

20

Anger Management for Adolescents

KEVIN A. FALL AND STEPHANIE EBERTS

THE DYNAMICS OF ANGER

Anger is a multifaceted dynamic emotion that affects everyone regardless of age, gender, socioeconomic status, or any other demographic variable. As with any emotion available to humans, it is a part of the fabric of life. Despite its ubiquity, anger is expressed phenomenologically, and its characteristics differ across individuals. In an effort to understand the complexities of anger, many studies have explored the similarities and differences between the anger expressed across a wide variety of demographic characteristics (Ghazall, 1998; Matsumoto, 1990; Park, Kim, Cheung, & Kim, 2010; Scherer, 1997). These and other studies have noted that there are differences in the ways large groups internalize and externalize anger; in addition, they have managed to provide some guidance as to what constitutes healthy and unhealthy manifestations of anger. This chapter examines one population in particular, adolescent boys, and details the unique features of anger, apart from explaining how an Adlerian approach can help counselors understand anger and facilitate change.

What Is Anger?

There are many ways to define anger. Descriptions received from adolescent male clients include, "Anger is when I get all tense inside. I feel like I'm about to explode," "It's when I get pissed off and start yelling at people…usually my little brother," "I just get mad. I can feel my face getting red, and I want to go off on someone, but I don't. I just keep it inside," and "My anger is like a fire. It comes on fast and hot and then burns itself out, leaving me tired." If we define anger from these representative comments, we can infer that anger is an intense emotion that has both internal and external effects. Anger also seems to arise when a person is upset about something.

Deffenbacher (1999) defined anger across four major domains:

1. Emotional/experiential: This is the feeling domain, where people commonly report feeling irritated, mad, and furious, to name a few.
2. Physiological: Common examples include elevated heart rate, tightening of the major muscle groups, and stomach- or headaches.
3. Cognitive: Thought patterns that tend to create anger, such as thoughts of blame—"It's her fault I got in trouble," thoughts of intentionality—"He ignored me because he hates me," thoughts of retaliation—"That jerk deserves what he gets from me," and thoughts of demandingness—"This isn't fair! I should be treated better by him!"
4. Behavioral: Verbal and physical aggression, withdrawal, substance use, and defensiveness.

Although each emotion is apparently different across the domains, it is easy to get a holistic flavor of anger while simultaneously getting a clear sense of how it differs from other core emotions, such as happiness and sadness.

Anger can escalate to extreme aggression, violence, and other antisocial behavior. The *Diagnostic and Statistical Manual of Mental Disorders* (DSM-TR, American Psychiatric Association, 2000) includes two disorders, conduct disorder and oppositional defiant disorder, which include anger and anger-related issues. Apart from these two disorders, other diagnosable conditions, such as attention-deficit disorder, major depression disorder, substance-abuse disorders, and bipolar disorder, also include elements of anger among their diagnostic criteria. These disorders are, however, rare and extreme manifestations and are best treated through a multidisciplinary treatment approach (McMahon, Wells, & Kotler, 2006; Webster-Stratton, 1996; Wicks-Nelson & Israel, 2005).

Anger in Adolescent Boys

Anger can be differentiated from other emotions, and its expression in adolescent boys is unique. Across many cultures, anger is one of the few emotions that males feel comfortable about expressing openly (Campbell, 1993). As Shields (2002) commented, "Emotion is identified as feminine, but anger, a prototypical emotion, is identified as masculine" (p. 11). Backed by societal approval, males use anger to convey a wide variety of feelings (threat, intimidation, fear, shame, guilt, anxiety, sadness, embarrassment, and others), which makes the understanding of male anger confusing to some. In many cases, anger is the default emotion for many adolescent males.

Research paints an interesting picture of anger in adolescent males. Burney (2006) studied the differences in the expression of anger between adolescent males and females and concluded that adolescent males are more impulsive in their anger and that they also use their anger as a tool to achieve a goal, which is most often focused on revenge or power. Many studies link anger in adolescent males to overt aggression, violence, substance abuse, and bullying (Broidy & Agnew, 1997; Boveja & McFadden, 2001; Clarey, Hodoka, & Ulloa, 2010; Hubbard, McAuliffe, Rubin, & Morrow, 2007). Adolescent males who consistently struggle with anger issues and express the emotion in unhealthy ways are more likely to be diagnosed with a wide range of disorders that include anger-related criteria, such as attention-deficit disorder, conduct disorder, and oppositional defiant disorder.

The cultural acceptance of male anger coupled with the research outcomes that focus on how anger leads to psychological disorders and violence puts adolescent males in a bind. Despite literature that links anger to aggression, all adolescent males feel angry at some point, yet not all of them are violent. In the same vein, just because adolescent males express their anger, it does not mean they are more prone to being labeled with a psychological disorder. What is needed is a holistic method for understanding anger in adolescent males and, subsequently, translating that understanding into appropriate methods that help adolescents manage their anger in more constructive ways.

A THEORETICAL FRAMEWORK FOR UNDERSTANDING AND TREATING ANGER

The Adlerian theory provides a comprehensive theoretical structure for conceptualizing the wide variety of anger-based expressions, even in a specific population such as adolescent males. The Adlerian theory holds at its core the notion that all people are creative and unique. Within this philosophy are five key underpinnings: teleology, phenomenology, holism, social embeddedness, and responsibility.

The term teleology, derived from the Greek *teleos*, meaning "goal," highlights Adler's premise that all behavior is purposeful and directed toward a goal. To understand an individual fully, one must not only discern the goal of the individual, but also understand the movement of the person toward the chosen goal. The Adlerian theory maintains that all people have the same general life goal: striving for superiority. In this sense, superiority does not mean conquering other people or being "better than" others. Instead, superiority refers to the feeling of a sense of belonging, of fitting in, and being significant. Each person creates a unique set of strategies to move along the road to significance. Adlerians call the collection of these strategies a "style of life," and it represents a consistent way of being; it can be considered an individual's blueprint for belonging and connectedness. Some might refer to this aspect as one's "personality."

If all behavior is purposeful, then the emotions that coexist and underlie behavior are also goal oriented. Specifically, Adler (1956) characterized emotions as either conjunctive or disjunctive, as a way to illuminate the ways that people tend to use emotions to either move toward people (conjunctive) or to create a distance between one's self and others (disjunctive). Viewing emotions and the corresponding behavior as being directed toward a goal has interesting implications for working with anger issues. Instead of conceptualizing anger as being an out-of-control state, suddenly the focus is on the purpose behind the chosen emotion. Consider the following example:

> Billy's parents tell him he can't go out with his friends on Friday night. Billy responds by yelling at his mom and punching a hole in the wall. After the incident, Billy continues to storm and finally his parents tell him to go ahead and go out, because "we are tired of you making life miserable for us around here."

Can the purpose of the anger be identified? Billy is confronted by a situation that he does not like. From an Adlerian perspective, Billy chooses anger to motivate certain behaviors that will lead to a desired outcome, in this case, intimidating or wearing down his parents to get them to give in and create a distance between them and Billy (disjunctive purpose). Teleology also helps explain how anger differs in intensity across episodes. According to Adlerians, people modify the intensity of their emotions depending on what level is necessary to achieve the specified goal. The emotional and behavioral tools chosen by Billy are not only purposeful, they are specifically chosen by Billy to fit his family dynamics.

In teleology, the intensity of the cluster of symptoms is only important in the sense that it represents a clearer intensity of the purpose. In this context, diagnosable disorders are conceptualized in the same way as any other manifestation; the symptom profile represents a collection of symptoms directed toward the achievement of the client's goal. Creation of highly disruptive patterns of behavior, such as oppositional defiant disorder or conduct disorder, represent a rigid and stuck way of striving, but, in some ways, may be effective when the goal is considered. The unique way in which individuals choose their own expression of anger highlights the next concept, namely, phenomenology.

Phenomenology is a strand of philosophy that stresses that each individual has a unique and personal view of life and its events. Therefore, to understand an individual, one must investigate how that person perceives and comprehends the world. Working with anger provides a reminder that, to help, counselors must first understand how that anger fits into the life of the client. Paired with teleology, Adlerians focus on the goal of the behavior and understand that the choice of using anger is not a given fact, but instead a reflection of the client's unique world. In Billy's case, he chose anger to move his parents away and give in to his demands. That would not be the case in every household. Some children use sadness or guilt to create the same end, whereas in others, the parents may respond differently and render the strategy ineffective. The choice is both teleological and phenomenological.

Social embeddedness places the point of individual assessment of health within the social context and network of that individual. As mentioned, the process of striving toward superiority is best understood as a striving to connect and to feel a sense of belonging. Therefore, anger, although a phenomenon that begins internally, should be examined and understood through a social and interpersonal lens.

Adler valued the social nature of humans so much that he chose one concept, *social interest*, to be the gauge of mental health within his theory. Adlerians believe that unhealthy people develop strategies that move them away from goals of superiority that emphasize connection or develop goals that focus on gaining superiority over others. In either case, these maladjusted goals can be considered to lack social interest and to involve a diminished sense of community feeling and cooperation. The emphasis on social embeddedness is a natural fit for work with adolescent males. The social arena provides an avenue to include the family system in the counseling process, and topics about friendships and dating relationships are less defended in the case of adolescent boys.

The last philosophical underpinning is responsibility. Adlerians believe that people are responsible for their own thoughts, feelings, and behaviors. People choose their thoughts based on their style of life, which guides each person to an individually constructed sense of identity and belonging. According to the theory, every person must strive to meet the tasks of life: work, love, friendship, self, and spirituality. The chosen style of life provides the strategies and direction for the striving process within each task. People are free to choose to strive in socially interested ways, characterized by a sense of belonging and connection; or they can choose a path that is disconnected, selfish, and avoidant toward the tasks of life. Regardless of the usefulness of the path, it is chosen by the individual.

Some people criticize the emphasis on responsibility as an effort to blame the person for their struggles. However, Adlerians view acceptance of responsibility as an empowering force that provides an avenue for change. The acknowledgment of personal responsibility by the client is very important when working with anger. Anger is largely, but not always, a disjunctive emotion: it serves to move the individual away from others. As the person uses anger to disconnect, usually, an emerging facet of the anger dynamic is to blame another person for the conflict. The blame is a manifestation of a lack of responsibility and, therefore, a barrier to change. As the individual becomes aware of the personal role and choice involved in the expression of anger, avenues can open up for change. In a very real sense, a greater sense of control over the anger is achieved once the client understands the role of choice in selecting the emotion. Anger does not just randomly occur. One chooses it for a specific purpose. If I can choose it, I can also not choose it.

So, the big question is, can anger ever be a part of a healthy style of life? The answer according to this theory is, yes. Anger itself is neither healthy nor unhealthy. From an Adlerian perspective, anger can be used in healthy or unhealthy ways. In any situation, anger, when chosen, can be used in socially useful (usually characterized by honest expression, connection, and cooperation) or unhealthy (intense, violent, controlling, and disconnected) ways. The following case provides an in-depth exploration of one client's use of anger, along with the Adlerian conceptualization and treatment of the issues involved.

CASE STUDY: THE CASE OF JASON

Presenting Problem

Jason is a 16-year-old African American boy, who has been struggling with anger related to some bullying in school. Jason is overweight and larger than the other boys in his class. His teachers believe that he has some anger issues, yet he is typically a very quiet student. His parents and teachers say that they have a hard time knowing what he is thinking or feeling because he does not express himself until he is so angry that he goes into a rage. He has been physical with other students at times. He has hit walls and thrown items both at home and at school. Last week, Jason was confronted by a math teacher about some missing homework. Jason erupted into a rage that included yelling at the teacher and overturning his desk. The school recommended counseling.

Jason is the youngest of three children. His brother, Milton, is 4 years older than Jason. Milton is in college but reportedly struggles with anxiety. Two months ago, he told his parents, "I might be gay." This created a lot of emotional turmoil in the family, and Jason is confused about how he feels about his brother. His sister, Margie, is 19 years old, 3 years older than Jason, and she has also created chaos within the family and recently has been asked to move out of the family home.

Jason's mother and father report an up-and-down relationship. Mom states, "We are too busy with our kids to focus on ourselves." His mother is a stay-at-home mom. His father works as a mechanic. Jason is reportedly very close to his mother. When Jason turned 13, his father distanced from him because his father didn't want to "baby him."

Apart from the incidences at school, Jason also reports being distant and angry most of the time. He has stopped playing sports and now spends most of his time in his room playing video games. His mother worries that the games that he plays are very violent; but she says that taking the games away is not an option because he would become very angry. She also worries about the other kids making fun of his weight at school and that his obesity will lead to poor physical health in the future, even though he is currently not suffering from any physical illnesses.

Adlerian Treatment of Jason

The Adlerian approach is a comprehensive counseling process that includes overlapping phases: (1) building a therapeutic relationship, (2) exploring and understanding the client's style of life, and (3) reorientation. The case of Jason is used to demonstrate the use of these three phases.

Phase 1: Building a Therapeutic Relationship

The first phase of counseling is focused on developing an egalitarian relationship between the client and the counselor. Inherent in any emerging therapeutic relationship is the obvious power differential between the client and the counselor. Adlerians, with a firm belief that their clients are capable human beings, strive to create a team-based collaboration to explore the client's presenting problem, moving from the role of an expert to that of a consultant.

The building of an egalitarian relationship is especially important and attractive to male adolescents, many of whom enter counseling at the demand of parents or other figures of authority. In the case of clients with anger issues, one can expect that merely coming for counseling and being pressured to change would elicit feelings of anger. Not acknowledging this reality and treating the client as a broken person merely increases the use of maladaptive anger. Alternatively, creating a cooperative relationship provides a model for relating that will be used later in the process.

The opportunity to build the relationship begins from the moment of first contact. In the process of treating adolescents, most of the time, the first contact will be with the parents. Consider the following phone call from Jason's mother:

> Mrs. McMahon: *Hello, I was calling to get some counseling for my son.*
>
> Counselor: *Sure, what are some good times and days for you all to come in for an initial visit?*
>
> Mrs. McMahon: *Well, Tuesdays work, but do we all have to come in? I mean, I would be happy to come in before and let you know what's going on with him. There's a lot to discuss and I wouldn't necessarily want him to listen.*
>
> Counselor: *I would like to hear your perspective, but I would like a chance to meet with your son first. What is his name?*
>
> Mrs. McMahon: *Jason*
>
> Counselor: *For our initial meeting, I would like to talk with Jason and get a sense of him and what he would like to work on. He would need to decide if he thinks he and I could work together. I would then invite you to join us for the last bit of the session. Perhaps any other family members that are involved could come as well.*
>
> Mrs. McMahon: *Hmmm....Well, I know Jason doesn't want to come. He'll be angry when I tell him. He has a brother and sister, but they don't live with us, and his father is pretty busy with work. Can I talk to you about some of his problems?*
>
> Counselor: *I prefer to do that in person. Why don't we meet next Tuesday, and we'll go from there?*
>
> Mrs. McMahon: *Okay...*

This excerpt is typical of many first phone calls and may seem fairly superficial; but, underneath the details are several important process elements that are the beginning of a respectful, collaborative relationship. For example, the mother requests a meeting to discuss the problems of the client, but the counselor insists not only on dialoguing in person, but also states that the first contact will be with the client, not the parents. The Adlerian counselor understands that although Jason's family's perspective may be important, to better understand him, one must speak directly to Jason and give him a chance to define himself. By talking to the parents first, the counselor's view of Jason has been originally defined by them, thus increasing the distance between the counselor and the client. As one client stated, "Why should I tell you anything? You already know everything about me from them. If you want something, ask them." By the same token, the counselor invites all family members to participate. Not only will their information provide valuable information about the social system of Jason, but the counselor can also get a sense, merely by their willingness to attend, of the connection among the members.

Once the first session begins, counselor and client continue their work on the relationship. This work does not end at the transition into the next phase, but extends until the termination of counseling. The methods for building a relationship are fairly standard across theories. Techniques such as reflection of feeling and content, summarizing, and open-ended questions are all acceptable ways to validate and explore the client's world.

The challenge with Jason is creating an egalitarian relationship with a client who does not want to be in counseling and whose presenting problem is anger. From an Adlerian perspective, Jason may possibly respond to both his predicament and his sense of helplessness with reference to his decision to be in counseling by using anger to shut down the process. By understanding this possibility, the counselor can anticipate it and focus on the choices Jason does have in relation to his treatment, instead of focusing on what he has limited control over. The following interchange demonstrates how this might proceed:

Counselor: *Thanks for coming in. Let me share with you my expectations of today. I really don't know anything about you; so, today will be about you teaching me about what your life is like. I may ask questions, but I am mainly interested in what you would like to share. When we have about 20 minutes left, I would like to invite your family in. You are welcome to stay. I am most interested in hearing about what their concerns are and to learn a bit about them. That will be it for today.*

Jason: *That's fine. I mean, I think this is sort of stupid, but whatever.*

Counselor: *You are wondering if counseling is going to be beneficial to you. I don't know the answer to that. You will have to decide that as we go along.*

Jason: *Well, I don't have much say in it. No offense, but I didn't want to come.*

Counselor: *Yeah, it's difficult to be excited about something you don't have a choice in. Well, I told you about today, but let me go a bit further. I would like you to give our relationship 3 weeks, 3 hours of your time each. In those 3 hours, the only goal is for me to get a good understanding of what your world looks like to you. At the end of the 3 weeks, we'll decide whether we need to continue. A lot could happen in that time. You could decide you want counseling, but not with me. You could decide you don't want counseling. I could decide I didn't want to work with you. We could also decide that we should continue. We will then let your parents know of our decision. They may have brought you here, but you get to decide what you talk about and we'll work together to decide when to stop.*

Jason: *Hmmm. . . . That sounds good.*

Counselor: *Great. Well, it's now up to you to start teaching me about what it is like to be you.*

The important pieces to notice in the dialogue are how the counselor anticipates the area of resistance and uses the desire to create a cooperative relationship as a means to disarm the choice to use anger and, consequently, avoid connection. By framing the counseling process as an opportunity to talk about oneself, the counselor avoids the pitfall of focusing on the perceived problem, while simultaneously conveying a sense of interest in the holistic story of the client. In addition, the use of the word "teach" helps even out the power differential, for it is the client who has the expertise and teaches the counselor. The counselor also removes the forced aspect of counseling, by asserting the "new rule" of the client having a say in the continuation and termination of counseling. Although some might fear that the client will automatically leave after the third session, to fear this occurrence misinterprets the reason the client did not want to come in the first place. The resistance initially was not to counseling per se, but to the situation of feeling forced. Once the force is removed, there is no real reason to use the resistance. As the relationship deepens, the counselor begins work on the second phase involving exploration of the client's style of life.

Phase 2: Exploring and Understanding the Client's Style of Life

In the second phase of Adlerian counseling, the aim is to both explore the client's style of life and understand how it impacts the client's ability to meet the tasks of life (Mosak, 1995). To meet this goal, the counselor has many creative techniques designed to illuminate the client's style of life. However, counselors may not need to employ all the techniques but merely apply enough of them to discern (1) the client's style of life or strategy for belonging and being significant and (2) how the client's current movement is impeding growth. Some of the more common techniques include mapping the family constellation, the goals of misbehavior, early recollections, dream work, personality priorities, and sandtray work, among others (Carlson & Slavik, 1997; Carlson, Watts, Maniacci, & Ellis, 2005; Sweeney, 2009). Discussing all the techniques associated with the exploration of a client's style of life is beyond the scope of this chapter; but, a few are outlined below in relation to the case of Jason.

Mapping the family constellation is a form of exploration that often takes place as the counselor builds a relationship with the client through discussion about family members. With adolescents, it is a logical place to begin and most clients readily talk about their family members; the discussion gives the counselor good information about how the client fits into their home "society" and how the system functions. As the counselor explores the interconnectedness of the members, tentative hypotheses can begin to form about the client's unique way of fitting into the family. What makes him special? These hypotheses are the foundation for understanding the client's style of life.

When exploring the family constellation, Adlerians also consider the impact of birth order on the client's life. It is important to note that Adlerians do not consider ordinal positioning to be as important as the client's psychological birth order. Ordinal positioning is the actual birth order, whereas psychological order means that children can take on the characteristics of any ordinal position depending on the "space" left open and the child's choice of how they want to strive for superiority. Firstborn children, although getting the privilege of choosing what space they occupy, may choose roles more in line with the firstborn (responsible, bossy); or may instead choose roles associated more with the youngest (creative, helpless). The emphasis on psychological positioning honors the individual differences and helps explain why all firstborn children, or children of any other space, do not fit the characteristics of their ordinal position.

Jason is the youngest of three children. In looking over the known case material, it appears that all the children are experiencing some form of chaos. The counselor would explore each sibling, asking for the client to describe the individual and the relationship between the sibling and the client. The following is a typical chart of the sibling constellation:

Milton, + 4	Margie, + 3	Jason, 0
Smart, good at school	Crazy	Get along
Takes care of things	Always needs help	Don't make waves
Takes care of my sister	She gets all the attention	Nice person
Ignores me	Doesn't know I exist	Good at music

From an Adlerian perspective, Jason exhibits characteristics of a middle-born child, while his older sister apparently chose the role of the younger child. Jason sees himself as a "peacemaker" but often feels ignored due to the chaos created within the system, primarily emanating from his older sister. Jason seems to have found a place for himself in the chaos by flying under the radar and creating a sense of peace by staying apart from the chaos. One excerpt from his discussion about his sister exemplifies this strategy:

> About a month ago, I was really struggling with some friend issues. I wanted to talk to my parents about it, but when I went home, they were upset because my sister had stolen a bunch of money from them. I realized my stuff wasn't that big of a deal, so I just stayed out of their way. I even made supper for them that night so they could do what they needed to do. I just stayed out of their way. I didn't want to add to their burden.

Discussions with Jason's parents seem to validate the emerging hypothesis about Jason's attempt to stay out of the chaos. Both parents have trouble clarifying specific strengths of their son other than, "He doesn't cause as much trouble as his brother or sister. Well, except for his anger issues." His mother states that she does worry that he isn't getting the attention he needs due to the other familial distractions, but they both are not sure what else they could do to help.

Although the counselor has only completed one exploratory technique, the themes in the client's style of life are beginning to crystallize. Based on Jason's family-constellation exploration, the counselor hypothesizes that Jason has chosen the middle-child role to fit into his family system. His family is characterized by a large amount of chaos and he is choosing to try to not be a further distraction within the family, almost as if he is saying, "I cannot compete or be special by being chaotic; therefore, I will be unique by not creating waves." This strategy is consistent in his friendships, "People like me because I go with the flow;" and at his work (school), "My teachers generally like me but don't know me very well." The role of anger and its purpose is still murky; so, the counselor continues the exploration through the use of early recollections.

Adler believed there are no chance memories. One's recollections of past events represent summaries of the basic philosophy of life and, thus, provide insight into the client's style of life. The events we choose to remember validate the current perspective of life and reinforce the current style of life. In fact, research indicates that, as change occurs, the themes associated with the early memories gradually change to become congruent with the new view of self, others, and the world (Clark, 2002; Savill & Eckstein, 1987; Taylor, 1975).

A small collection of specific early memories will usually suffice to discern noticeable themes. It is important that the client provide a recollection, a specific memory, rather than a report, which is more general in nature. For example, "My father seems to not like me" is too general, whereas "One time I was playing with a truck, and I really wanted my father to see how I could make it roll in a straight line. I remember looking up at him and him just laughing and walking away" is a much more detailed and fertile memory. Jason's early recollections were recorded for review and analysis.

Early recollection #1 (4 years old): I am at my birthday party. Everyone is there, and I am feeling pretty good. My sister got into a fight with one of my friends. I think she pushed him down and he started crying. Everyone rushed over there to see what happened. They stayed there so long that I wandered outside and sat on the porch. It seems like it took them forever to come find me. When people finally came out, I remember my mom and dad freaking out. They were screaming, "We thought you ran away!" I was there all along.

Early recollection #2 (6 years old): My parents are helping my brother and sister do "real homework" while I was to sit in my room for "quiet time." On this particular night, I remember them screaming at each other, which was usual. What was different is that on this night, I went to my door and opened it, like I wanted to be in there with them, but then closed it again. I think I must have opened and closed the door a million times. Weird.

Early recollection #3 (6 years old): This was the first time I can remember getting angry. I was at the doctor's office and was getting a shot because I was sick. The shot hurt and I got sad. I think I was crying, but my sister knocked over a jar of cotton balls. Everyone was making sure she was okay, and I just started yelling at the nurse, "You are stupid!" I have no idea why I did that. My mom was so upset, she pulled me out of the office, and we sat in the car alone while she gave me this long lecture.

Processing and interpreting early recollections is a collaborative venture between counselor and client. For example:

Counselor: *Thanks Jason. Nice job on coming up with these memories. As you read over them, do you see any common themes?* (Here, the counselor wants to give the client a chance to gain awareness of themes. The counselor is also ready to provide insight as well.)

Jason: *Um . . . it's just so weird. Why did I do stuff like that? That's pretty messed up* (laughs).

Counselor: *What are you most aware of when you look over them?*

Client: *Well, my sister is in there a lot. I guess she has been sucking the energy out of the room forever* (laughs).

Counselor: *That's an interesting observation. What do you notice about your response to the distraction?*

Jason: *Hmmm . . . well it seems like I either disappear, like a ghost, or I explode.*

Counselor: *So, when you experience those situations, it's like you have two options: either disappear, go "ghost," or you make your presence known by getting angry?*

Jason: *Hmmm . . . . I guess so.*

As the discussion progresses, the aim of any technique in this phase is to gain some awareness of the client's strategy for striving for significance in life. In processing the early recollections of Jason, both the client and the counselor were able to see that Jason operates under two modes of functioning. Because he sees life as chaotic, his preferred mode of relating is to exist outside of the fray where he can neither be too impacted by the conflict, nor add to the burden of those engaged in the chaos. He gets a feeling of significance, which is reinforced by those around him for this approach. However, there are times when Jason feels this strategy is not effective. Often, he feels ignored, and his needs are marginalized. In those times, he chooses anger as a mechanism for making his needs known. While he temporarily gets the attention he needs, he is left feeling internally conflicted because it violates his preferred method of connecting. This dynamic process is validated by Jason's perspective, "I always feel guilty after I explode. I feel like I have added to my parents' issues, and I don't like that; but sometimes, it's like it is the only way I can get people to listen."

To further explore Jason's style of life, the goals of his misbehavior must be examined (Dreikurs, 1957). Because Adler viewed all behavior as purposeful, the goals of Jason's behavior are particularly important. The four goals can be summarized as a progression, starting with attention-seeking and then moving on to power, revenge, and finally, withdrawal. If the goals of the behavior are not met at any given stage, a child might progress on to the next stage. Jason's early recollections demonstrate his progression through these goals. In his earliest memory, his sister is receiving attention during his birthday celebration. Leaving the party is often a great way to get attention; however, his family did not know that he was on the porch. His attention-seeking behavior had failed. In his second recollection, Jason remembers opening the door to his room while his parents were arguing. Jason attempted to insert himself into the power struggle between his parents; but again, he failed. His third recollection demonstrates his move toward revenge-seeking behavior. When a child is seeking revenge, it is as though that child is saying, "I have been hurt, so I want you to hurt, too." What can often be confusing about this goal of behavior is that children may not lash out at the person who has hurt them; they may do so with someone who is safer. For example, Jason called the nurse stupid, rather than yelling at a member of his own family. Jason's "explosions" can be seen as a revenge-seeking behavior; but if the goals are not met, Jason may progress to withdrawal. Children and adolescents who withdraw often inspire a sense of hopelessness in the adults around them. When children use withdrawal as a goal of behavior, it is much harder to engage them in the counseling process. It is as though they are saying, "I have tried everything; nothing has worked, so why bother?" Jason is still striving to belong, but he is discouraged.

The exploration of the client's style of life through techniques such as family constellation, early recollections, and the goals of misbehavior is designed to illuminate the client's style of life and begin to discern the purpose of the client's current behavior. Although anger can be used for a wide variety of reasons, Jason seems to use it as a secondary strategy for being heard. He tends to use anger when his primary method, fading into the background, is not working for him. As with most clients, this holistic exploration of the client allows for an understanding beyond the presenting symptom of anger and puts it into a context where the client can now explore and choose different ways of relating at many different levels. For example, as he moves forward, Jason can now choose to change the way he makes himself heard and/or he can make changes to his primary mode of relating, that is, does being a "ghost" really work for you across all the tasks of life?

The general purpose of this phase is for the counselor and the client to gain deeper awareness of the adaptive and maladaptive aspects of the client's style of life. More specifically, the client begins to understand both the importance of the style of life and how each thought, feeling, and behavior reflects this strategy, even maladaptive or painful thoughts, feelings, and behavior. For example, Jason gained an understanding of how his low-drama mediator role is both useful and, at times, not useful in his life. He also can recognize how he chooses anger as a way to compensate for the occasional shortcomings of his primary strategy and, in turn, is able to see the consequences and benefits of choosing anger in those scenarios.

As Jason is both aware and accountable for his choices, he is better situated to make choices about if and how he would like to create change.

Phase 3: Reorientation
For Adlerians, insight alone is not enough to produce change. Once the clients are aware of their style of life, they are then responsible for any changes in the blueprint. However, it is possible that no change is desired by the client. In many cases, the client understands the purpose of the behavior and feels that changing would be more burdensome or painful than the consequences of the current behavior.

For Jason, as he gains some understanding of how he uses his anger, he can make choices on whether that tool is the best one to reach his goal or whether he would like to develop another. The goal of this process is not to eradicate anger from his life. That is unrealistic. Jason will need to understand that although anger can be healthy, some of its manifestations are not. One possibility will be for him to experiment with low-intensity forms of anger or behaviors associated with the emotion. For example, he may choose to hit walls when he is angry, but that is not the only possible choice. Jason can make different choices with his anger while honoring its purpose in his life: "I use it as a tool to get noticed and get my needs met." The task for Jason is to find a different way of achieving that purpose. Consider the following exploration of this issue:

> Counselor: *Well, Jason, I think we understand that you choose anger because you feel that is the language your family, friends, and teachers understand. It's your way of saying, "I am here and I want you to listen to me."*
>
> Jason: *Yeah, I mean, especially at home. It's like they just want me to be the good kid. I'm sick of being ignored, but I don't want to be broken and needy like my sister, or even my brother.*
>
> Counselor: *That makes sense. I guess what you have to decide is twofold. First, is there something else you could do to make your needs known; and second, are you interested in doing those things instead of being angry in that way.*

The deeper change will involve changing the path toward the goal of superiority. The real maladjustment in Jason's anger is that it disconnects him from his family and leaves him with the belief that he is "broken."

From an Adlerian perspective, counseling is terminated once the clients have a greater understanding of their style of life and the choices made to achieve a sense of belonging and significance. As mentioned, insight without action is not useful or curative; but it is the client's responsibility to use the insight to make a change. It is possible that the client could decide that no change is needed; that it would be more difficult to change than it would be to stay the same. As unfortunate as that decision may be, it is, in the end, the client's decision. Jason, through counseling, was able to see that he seemed caught between two ways of being. Toward the end of counseling, he summed up his stance this way:

Jason: *Basically, what I know now is I am special because I am a good mediator and I am not a drama generator. My family is freaking crazy (laughs). I mean, people in my family have chosen to create chaos in order to feel unique and fit in. It seems like my brother and sister have been engaging in a crazy arms race to be the best screw up in the family. It seems weird, but it is working for them, I guess. They get a lot of resources and attention from people for that. I have always been the "ghost." I like that metaphor. I understand that I fit in because my parents, teachers, and friends don't have to worry about me. I take care of myself. I think I do that too much, and when I need something, I don't ask and people don't notice. Then, I become an angry ghost and start throwing shit (laughs).*

Counselor: *That's a great summary of the work you have done. I'm wondering if you can't find a middle ground. You know, keep the good parts of being a ghost, but let people know sooner about your needs.*

Jason: *Yeah, I guess I am afraid I am going to burden them with something stupid.*

Counselor: *Here's the deal, your needs are not stupid, they are just your needs. It seems that bottling them up and then erupting creates more chaos than getting to them when they are smaller.*

Jason: *Hmmm, that's a good point. It seems dumb that I create tons of burden when I am trying to avoid it. Damn.... Yeah, I could change that.*

SUMMARY

Anger is an emotion that is a recurring part of everyday life. Adolescents struggle with anger as they straddle the world between adulthood and childhood, and male adolescents also carry the weight of societal expectations of being "tough." As adolescent males deal with this emotion, the Adlerian theory provides a comprehensive approach to understanding and managing the emotional, cognitive, and behavioral aspects of anger. From an Adlerian perspective, each person develops a blueprint for living, a style of life, which guides the person's behavior, thoughts, and feelings in everyday life. Within this consistent way of being, emotions are used as tools to achieve the client's individual goals of significance and belonging. Anger, like other emotions, can be used in both healthy and unhealthy ways. Through the process of counseling, Adlerians help their clients understand the chosen uses of anger and help each client make changes that allows for a greater expression and understanding of self and the world around them.

SUGGESTED RESOURCES

Adlerian Theory

Online Resources
Adler School of Professional Psychology, Chicago: http://www.adler.edu
North American Society for Adlerian Psychology: http://alfredadler.org

Books
Adler, A. (1956). *The individual psychology of Alfred Adler* (H. L. Ansbacher & R. R. Ansbacher, Eds.). New York, NY: Basic Books.
Carlson, J., Watts, R. E., & Maniacci, M. (2006). *Adlerian therapy: Theory and practice.* Washington, DC: American Psychological Association.
Dreikurs, R., & Soltz, V. (1964). *Children: The challenge.* New York, NY: Hawthorne Books.
Sweeney, T. J. (2009). *Adlerian counseling and psychotherapy: A practitioner's approach.* New York, NY: Routledge.

Adolescents

Carlson, J., & Lewis, J. (2007). *Counseling the adolescent: Individual, family, and school interventions* (5th ed.). Denver, CO: Love Publishing Co.
Hitchner, K., & Tifft-Hitchner, A. (1996). *Counseling today's secondary students: Practical strategies, techniques, & materials for the school counselor.* San Franciso, CA: Jossey-Bass.
Geldard, K., & Geldard, D. (2010). *Counseling adolescents: The proactive approach for young people* (3rd ed.). New Delhi, India: Sage Publications.
McWhirter, J. J., McWhirter, B. T., McWhirter, E. H., & McWhirter, R. J. (2007). *At-risk youth: a comprehensive response for counselors, teachers, psychologists, and human service professionals* (4th ed.). Belmont, CA: Brooks/Cole~Thompson Learning.

Straus, M. B. (1999). *No-talk therapy for children and adolescents.* New York, NY: W.W. Norton.

Anger

Books

Golden, B. (2006). *Healthy anger: How to help children and teens manage their anger.* New York, NY: Oxford University Press.
McKay, M., Rogers, P. D., & McKay. (1989). *When anger hurts: Quieting the storm within.* Oakland, CA: New Harbinger.

Group Work

Online Resources

The Association for Specialists in Group Work at: http://www.asgw.org
Booklist provided by the American Group Psychotherapy Association: http://www.agpa.org/pubs/Booklist.htm

Books

Ashby, J. S., Kottman, T., & DeGraaf, D. (2008). *Active interventions for kids and teens: Adding adventure.* Washington, DC: American Counseling Association.
Berg, R. C., Landreth, G., & Fall, K. A. (2006). *Group counseling: Concepts and procedures* (4th ed.). New York, NY: Routledge.
DeLucia-Waack, J. L., Bridbord, K. H., Kleiner, J. S., & Nitza, A. (Eds.). (2006). *Group work experts share their favorite activities: A guide to choosing, planning, conducting, and processing* (Rev.). Alexandria, VA: Association for Specialists in Group Work.
Foss, L. L., Green, J., Wolfe-Stiltner, K., & DeLucia-Waack, J. L. (Eds.). (2008). *School counselors share their favorite activities: A guide to choosing, planning, conducting, and processing.* Alexandria, VA: Association for Specialists in Group Work.

REFERENCES

Adler, A. (1956). *The individual psychology of Alfred Adler* (H. L. Ansbacher & R. R. Ansbacher, Eds.). New York, NY: Basic Books.
American Psychiatric Assocation. (2000). *Diagnostic and statistical manual of mental disorders* (4th ed., text revision). Washington, DC: Author.
Boveja, M. E., & McFadden, J. (2001). Urban adolescents and violencia. In D. Sandhu (Ed.), *Faces of violence,* (pp. 143–154). Huntington, NY: Nova Science.
Burney, D. M. (2006). An investigation of anger styles in adolescent students. *The Negro Educational Review, 57,* 35–47.
Broidy, L., & Agnew, R. (1997). Gender and crime: A general strain theory perspective. *Journal of Research in Crime and Delinquency, 34,* 275–306.

398 Counseling Boys and Young Men

Campbell, A. (1993). *Men, women, and aggression*. New York, NY: Basic Books.

Carlson, J., Watts, R., Maniacci, M., & Ellis, A. (2005). *Adlerian therapy: Theory and practice*. Washington, DC: American Psychological Association.

Carlson, J., & Slavik, S. (1997) *Techniques in Adlerian psychology*. Washington, DC: Accelerated Development.

Clark, A. J. (2002). *Early recollections: Theory and practice in counseling and psychotherapy*. New York, NY: Routledge.

Clarey, A., Hodoka, A., & Ulloa, E. C. (2010). Anger control and acceptance of violence as mediators in the relationship between exposure and interparental conflict and dating violence perpetration in Mexican adolescents. *Journal of Family Violence, 25*, 619–625.

Deffenbacher, J. L. (1999). Cognitive-behavioral conceptualization and treatment of anger. *Journal of Clinical Psychology, 55*, 295–309.

Dreikurs, R. (1957). *Psychology in the classroom*. New York, NY: Harper & Row.

Ghazall, Z. (1998). From anger on behalf of God to forebearance in Islamic medieval literature. In B. Rosenwien (Ed.), *Anger's past: The social uses of an emotion in the middle ages* (pp. 203–230). Ithaca, NY: Cornell University Press.

Hubbard, J. A., McAuliffe, M. D., Rubin, R. M., & Morrow, M. T. (2007). The anger-aggression relation in violent children and adolescents. In T. A. Cavell & K. T Malcolm (Eds.), *Anger, aggression, and interventions for interpersonal violence (*pp. 267–280). Mahwah, NJ: Lawrence Erlbaum.

Matsumoto, D. (1990). Cultural similarities and differences in display rules. *Motivation and Emotion, 14*, 195–214.

McMahon, R. J., Wells, K. C., & Kotler, J. S. (2006). Conduct problems. In E. J. Marsh & R. A. Barkely (Eds.), *Treatment of childhood disorders* (pp. 137–268). New York, NY: Guilford.

Mosak, H. (1995). Adlerian psychotherapy. In R. J. Corsini and D. Wedding (Eds.), *Current psychotherapies* (5th ed.). Itasca, IL: Peacock.

Park, I. J., Kim, P. Y., Cheung, R. Y., & Kim, M. (2010). The role of culture, family processes and anger regulation in Korean American adolescents' adjustment problems. *American Journal of Orthopsychiatry, 80*, 258–266.

Savill, G. E., & Eckstein, D. G. (1987). Changes in early recollections as a function of mental status. *Journal of Individual Psychology, 43*, 3–17.

Scherer, K. R. (1997). The role of culture in emotion-antecedent appraisal. *Journal of Personality and Social Psychology, 14*, 902–922.

Shields, S. A. (2002). *Speaking from the heart: Gender and the social meaning of emotion*. Cambridge, UK: Cambridge Press.

Sweeney, T. (2009). *Adlerian counseling: A practitioner's approach* (5th ed.). New York, NY: Routledge.

Taylor, J. A. (1975). Early recollections as a projective technique: A review of some recent validation studies. *Journal of Individual Psychology, 31*, 21–36.

Webster-Stratton, C. (1996). Early onset conduct problems: Does gender make a difference? *Journal of Consulting and Clinical Psychology, 64*, 540–551.

Wicks-Nelson, R., & Israel, A. C. (2005). *Behavior disorders of childhood* (6th ed.). Upper Saddle River, NJ: Prentice Hall.

21

Gang Membership and Interventions

LORI A. WOLFF AND EDWARD HUDSPETH

BACKGROUND OF GANGS IN THE UNITED STATES

Although gang membership in the United States declined during the late 1990s and early 2000s, recent estimates are that more than 750,000 members actively participate in over 25,000 different gangs (Egley & O'Donnell, 2008). Some sources estimate the number of gang members as more than 1 million (Paterson, 2010). Larger metropolitan areas remain the most affected by gangs, but some of the largest increases during that past 10 years in both gang membership and number of gangs were within smaller cities and rural areas (Egley & O'Donnell, 2008). Gangs are prevalent in schools as well, and nearly 40% of K–12 students note such a presence in their schools (Pesce & Wilczynski, 2005), and schools at all levels within K–12 report an increased level of gang activity since 2005 (Paterson, 2010). Gangs are enticing to a diverse array of adolescents of many ethnicities. According to data collected by law enforcement agencies reporting gang problems, the demographic make-up of gangs in larger cities included 48% Hispanic or Latino membership; 35% Black or African American membership; 9% White membership; and 7% other ethnicities (National Gang Center, 2011).

Gangs are not an American phenomenon. In the United States, a widely used definition is that "a gang is a group of three or more individuals who engage in criminal activity and identify themselves with a common name or sign" (National Criminal Justice Reference Service, 2011). In Europe, which has seen a more recent emergence of gang activity (Alleyne & Wood, 2010), a similar definition is used where "a street gang (or troublesome youth corresponding to a street gang elsewhere) is any durable, street-oriented youth group whose involvement in illegal activity is part of its group identity" (Weerman et al., 2009, p. 20). That illegal activity and membership in gangs, regardless of country in which it occurs, spans across race, ethnic, and even gender lines, as female involvement in such activity is increasing steadily and includes physical violence as well (Alleyne & Wood, 2010; Cobbina, Like-Haislip, & Miller, 2010). It is still true, however, that males predominate gang membership, and, for that reason, most research on gangs includes only males or a large gender imbalance toward males (Alleyne & Wood, 2010). As this book is focused on males, that is the stated focus of this chapter as well, but the increase of females in gangs begs the need for additional research centered on females, even though such is outside the scope of this book.

Youth who are not members of gangs also participate in illegal activity. Yet, unlike those in the nongang group, not only are the gang members disproportionately responsible for adolescent crime but also membership in a gang itself is related to an increased level of participation in criminal and delinquent activity, as well as level of seriousness and violence of crimes committed (Melde & Esbensen, 2011). Such levels are lower both before and after gang life (Craig, Vitaro, Gagnon, & Tremblay, 2002). Gang members themselves attribute this escalation in criminal activity to "easy access to cars, guns, lots of money which ma[k]e it easy for them to have girls, and lack of any legitimate means to accomplish all that" (Sirpal, 1997, p. 18). There is a certain "glamour and power" (Sirpal, 1997, p. 18) in being a member of a gang that affords a lifestyle different from that to which many are accustomed, as gang members are often pulled from disadvantaged, low socioeconomic backgrounds (Ryan, Miller-Loessi, & Nieri, 2007).

Three theories provide explanations for this distinctive increase in criminal and delinquent activity that occurs just by virtue of gang membership. Under the first theory, selection, gangs are purposeful in the members; they seek and tend to select or attract those for whom criminality and delinquency is already the norm in their lives (Thornberry, Krohn, Lizotte, & Chard-Wierschem, 1993). The second model, social facilitation, relates to the norms of the group itself and, within this model, gang members follow the social norms of the group by participating in criminal and delinquent activity (Thornberry et al., 1993). The last theory, enhancement, combines attributes of the other models, and indicates that gangs not only seek or attract those who already have a tendency to commit criminal and delinquent acts, but also provide a conducive and necessary environment, as well as social structure, to allow for the enhancement of participation and level of such activity (Craig et al., 2002).

Why Do Juvenile Males Join Gangs?

The primary objective of this chapter is to present information regarding "best practices" in prevention and intervention strategies/programs centered on juvenile males and gang membership. Some researchers suggest that such programs lack efficacy (Sirpal, 1997). In certain cases, programs go beyond lacking effectiveness as, in addition to showing no positive outcomes, participation in the programs appeared to solidify group cohesion and increase the level of illegal and delinquent pursuits of the members who were a part of the programs (Boerman, 2001). Shortage of research, particularly up until the mid-1990s, on why someone joins a gang, is cited as one of the reasons for low efficacy, and thus, it provides an argument that the effectiveness of prevention and intervention programs would increase if more research were available on the factors that cause or lead one to participate in a gang, as then programs could be focused on addressing those predictors (Lahey, Gordon, Loeber, Stouthamer-Loeber, & Farrington, 1999; Sirpal, 1997).

Sirpal and others have since conducted studies related specifically to identifying factors related to gang membership. Juvenile males, as we all do, seek what is missing or broken in their lives. These sought items include "power, popularity, recognition, and acceptance" (Sirpal, 1997, p. 14) as "gangs reflect universal needs among young people for status, identity, and companionship" (Alleyne & Wood, 2010, p. 425). Gang members may feel lonely and lack friends and social activities in which to participate, making gangs initially attractive to meet those purposes (Sirpal, 1997). Also, as noted previously, a juvenile male's economic disadvantage may make the lure of money overwhelming, regardless of whether the money is gained illegally (Sirpal, 1997).

In addition to potential and current gang members often coming from families who are considered poor and as having a low socioeconomic status, other familial-related factors are found when considering the reasons why someone joins a gang. Families, unfortunately, may not always provide positive role models, and parents may not have appropriate parenting, discipline, and supervision skills (Alleyne & Wood, 2010; Lahey et al., 1999). Communication with parents, whether initiated by a parent or the child, is vital to the child having and achieving healthy goals (Ryan et al., 2007). A child discussing his life with his parents is particularly important and "self-disclosure to parents [is] inversely associated with norm-breaking" (Ryan et al., 2007, p. 1055). In terms of other familial factors, a young male also may have family members involved in criminal activity or who have current or former gang affiliation themselves (Alleyne & Wood, 2010; Chu, Daffern, Thomas, & Lim, 2011). Although perhaps not providing any better role models, gangs may offer a juvenile male a replacement for his family (Krohn, Schmidt, Lizotte, & Baldwin, 2011).

Relationships with those outside the family are important as well in the discussion of why someone joins a gang as, in addition to seeking a replacement for a dysfunctional family, juvenile males attracted to gang membership may be searching for a peer group (Craig et al., 2002). A gang member may have had positive peers and good relationships with other adults, such as school personnel, at one time, and thus, had typical or "prosocial" relationships, but having peers and friends who are involved in antisocial or delinquent activity is one of the major predictors of gang membership (Lahey et al., 1999; Melde & Esbensen, 2011). "[N]egative peers disrupt...positive social relationships and prosocial activities" (Egan & Beadman, 2011, p. 749). Teachers and other school personnel can affect whether a life path goes positively or negatively, particularly for someone already at-risk due to economic or social situations (Ryan et al., 2007). Having a positive attachment to teachers can counteract antisocial or delinquent peers and friends (Ryan et al., 2007). Overall, however, membership in gangs tends to close off other relationships either because the member was not particularly skilled or successful in that area anyway or because the gang demands such relationships be severed (Craig et al., 2002; Melde & Esbensen, 2011).

GANG PREVENTION AND INTERVENTION PROGRAM STRATEGIES

There are various strategies for gang membership intervention, and among the most commonly used are the five identified and developed by Spergel and Curry in 1993 (as cited in Decker & Curry, 2000; Scherer, Dorsey, & Catzva, 2009). The five strategies include "(1) suppression, (2) social intervention, (3) social opportunities, (4) community mobilization, and (5) organizational change" (Decker & Curry, 2000, p. 130). Although many programs incorporate aspects of more than one from the list, when considering city-based programs, just short of half use suppression as their primary strategy, one-third use social intervention, 5% percent use social opportunities, 9% use community mobilization, and 11% use organizational change (Decker & Curry, 2000). The strategies are discussed in the following sections individually based on the frequency of use of strategy.

Suppression

Suppression involves a prosecutorial focus on ending the illegal activity by arresting, prosecuting, and incarcerating gang members associated with the activity (Decker & Curry, 2000). Although contact with law enforcement and judicial personnel can be positive, often gang members have a negative view of those in positions of authority, a negative view that can be reinforced through the type of constant interaction with law enforcement often found within intervention programs focused on suppression (Alleyne & Wood, 2010). Suppression efforts, by putting the spotlight on the problem, also put the spotlight on the gangs, which may lead to an increase in the status of the members, which may work against positive outcomes of the program (Decker & Curry, 2000). Under suppression programs, juvenile male gang members are seen as threats, rather than as people with at least the potential to be positive members of society (Sirpal, 1997), and removing the threat by suppression may only serve to remove the young men from the possibility of leading successful, positive lives.

Social Intervention

Social intervention strategies tend to focus on crisis situations, which often require some sort of immediate action (Decker & Curry, 2000). Taking programs that use social intervention as their focus beyond the initial action or reaction to the crisis is vital to their success, as then there is more opportunity for involvement of several agencies, which may include law enforcement, social services, and health care, as well as inclusion of gang members' families and the provision of more long-term assistance (Decker & Curry, 2000). Interventions with this focus may include mentoring programs to introduce positive role models and relationships into a gang member's life (Decker & Curry, 2000).

Organizational Change

The typical manner in which intervention programs include organizational change is the development of a task force, which may be initiated following some major crisis event, but is meant to create an avenue for more long-term response and agency and community involvement (Decker & Curry, 2000). Of course, facilitating the work of a task force can by unwieldy in terms of scheduling meetings and helping members feel engaged in the process and maintain confidence that the process is moving in a positive direction (Grekul, LaBoucane-Benson, & Erickson, 2009).

Community Mobilization

Just as any single prevention or intervention program may include several of the strategies noted here, the use of one strategy may lead to another strategy. This is especially true in terms of organizational change and community mobilization. A task force may outline the needs and approaches a community plans to undertake, and then community mobilization is used or required to implement the plan (Grekul, 2011). "Effective community mobilization must include both immediate social institutions such as the family, and schools, community agencies and groups, churches, public health agencies; and criminal and juvenile justice systems" (Decker & Curry, 2000, p. 131). Ideally, a community mobilization program confronts the root causes of why someone joins a gang and then "coordinates and targets services so that the needs of gang members may be met more effectively" (Decker & Curry, 2000, p. 131).

Social Opportunities

Prevention and intervention programs that may be categorized under the social opportunities strategy are those focused on provision of information and programming related to employment and education (Decker & Curry, 2000). More than any other strategy, centering a program on jobs and educational opportunities addresses the factors associated with why someone joins a gang, and thus, such programs carry the highest likelihood for success (Decker & Curry, 2000). Recall, however, that the strategies are presented here in the order of frequency of use, and programs incorporating social opportunities rank last on that list, with only 5% of city-based programs containing that feature (Decker & Curry, 2000).

SPECIFIC GANG PREVENTION AND INTERVENTION PROGRAM COMPONENTS AND EVALUATION

Within this section, information on specific programs is presented, along with research-based advice regarding "best practices" involving prevention and intervention programs targeting juvenile males and gang membership. Two common themes emerge from successful programs: community collaboration in the development and implementation of such programs and an individualized treatment focus within the programs for potential or current gang members.

Scherer et al. (2009), in addition to outlining the five strategies presented earlier in this chapter, delineates the components essential to an effective intervention program: "1) family; 2) employment; 3) criminal; 4) social; and 5) education" (p. 31). Scherer et al. (2009) discussed an evaluation of a national program created under the auspices of the Office of Juvenile Justice and Delinquency Protection of the U.S. Department of Justice called the Gang-Free Schools and Community (GFS) initiative.

In addition to highlighting the significance of "community capacity" (Scherer et al., 2009, p. 41), the evaluation noted the importance of the project coordinator role and that, although partnership between schools and law enforcement was vital, it was best to have the school be the recipient of the grant rather than a law enforcement agency based on the school's access to personal information regarding the children and their home and school situations (Scherer et al., 2009). Given that delinquent acts occur earlier and earlier in a child's life, the evaluators suggested starting the program in elementary school (Scherer et al., 2009). An intervention program should be "holistic" and address "education, employment, mentoring, mental health counseling, and parenting classes for the young person and his or her family" (Scherer et al., 2009, p. 37). While being holistic, the program should also be individualized to "target their unique needs" (Scherer et al., 2009, p. 37).

GFS is a school-based program, as many prevention and intervention programs are, but it is of note that, although many researchers advocate for school-based programs (Paterson, 2010; Pesce & Wiczynski, 2005), others point to the high dropout rate for gang members, which may decrease the success of such programs as the target group is not present where the program is given (Craig et al., 2002). Gang members also may be detached from school and its personnel due to real or perceived negative treatment from both school officials and law enforcement (Rios, 2010). Starting intervention programs early, as noted by Scherer et al. (2009), may alleviate this problem as could involving school counselors in the process, focusing on positive rather than negative behaviors of students so as not to inappropriately place a spotlight on gangs and their members (Paterson, 2010), and, where possible, creating alternatives to suspension and expulsion to keep the current or potential gang members as part of the school system (Pesce & Wilczynski, 2005).

Building connections with law enforcement to help show young males that meaningful and positive relationships are possible between students, school personnel, and law enforcement can aid in success of a program as well (Paterson, 2010; Rios, 2010). "[P]ositive interaction with police officers in recreational, educational, and athletic activities in conjunction with schools and community creates an avenue for adolescents to become involved in their neighborhood in a constructive manner [and] [g]iven the right opportunities and interactions, adolescents will build a healthy, positive attitude toward the police, school, themselves, and society" (Koffman et al., 2009, p. 245).

The program from which that quote is based was a collaboration between the Los Angeles Police Department, California State University, and the Los Angeles Unified School District and was conducted at a high school in a poor neighborhood highly infiltrated by gangs and taught by trained resource officers (Koffman et al., 2009). The program focused on elements of resistance, empowerment, leadership, and parenting, and since the implementation of the program, the school has experienced a decrease in incidents warranting full-day suspensions. There is some preliminary evidence that the "whole child" approach was "an effective tool to promote mental health and reduce depression among youth with multiple risk factors, most of whom might otherwise be reluctant to take advantage of mental health services" (Koffman et al., 2009, p. 244). One interesting aspect is that "graduates" of the program often return as volunteers to help with the next set of students and also become involved in a program designed "to recruit qualified young men and women and prepare them for future careers in law enforcement" (Koffman et al., 2009, p. 243).

Another example of a school-based program that shows the collaboration between a school and law enforcement is the Gang Resistance Education and Training (GREAT) program, which is delivered in middle schools by law enforcement officials (Esbensen et al., 2011). The program began in Phoenix, but has since become a national program, which originally was based on the widely known Drug Abuse Resistance Education (DARE) programs. This was initially a problem for the GREAT program, as DARE lacked a strong research base for its curriculum, but both programs changed in that regard and, that the GREAT program is now theoretically based, is considered one of its strengths (Esbensen et al., 2011). The two main goals of GREAT are to assist youth with avoiding gang membership and associated activity and developing positive relationships with law enforcement personnel (Esbensen et al., 2011). In the first iteration of the program, no short-term differences were found between students who participated in the program and those who did not, although there were some positive outcomes 3 and 4 years down the road, but those were focused primarily on the second goal of positive relationships with law enforcement (Esbensen et al., 2011). Once the program was changed, however, and became more evidence based, there were positive short-term effects in both gang membership and relationships with law enforcement (Esbensen et al., 2011).

The GFS program referred to community capacity and other programs focused on community involvement as well. The Community Solution to Gang Violence (CSGV) is based in Canada, but its structure and evaluation results are applicable to other countries as well, including the United States (Grekul et al., 2009). The two primary goals of CSGV, which was a task force comprising representatives of 30 agencies created by a joint effort between law enforcement and the Native Counseling Services of Alberta in the early 2000s, are "preventing youth gang involvement and community collaboration" (Grekul et al., 2009, p. 54). The first evaluation of the program, conducted 5 years after its initiation, focused largely on how well CSGV gained and disseminated knowledge to the community on gangs and gang membership (Grekul et al., 2009). The evaluation determined that the group had done well in this area and that the group and the community recognized the importance of agencies working collaboratively, and that the group, primarily through its website and outreach, was seen as the experts to whom to turn when an incident occurred (Grekul et al., 2009).

A later evaluation of CSGV conducted 2 years later verified many of the positives found in the first evaluation (Grekul, 2011). The group had further focused its goals and articulated four pillars of its existence and work: knowledge translation/transfer, community awareness, engaged network, and community leader/funder awareness (Grekul, 2011, p. 30). Even more organizations are involved, which was both positive and negative, as the frustrations associated with scheduling meetings and keeping everyone engaged in the process had grown as well, but the commitment of those involved kept the difficulties manageable (Grekul, 2011). The group had learned to take small steps rather than trying to fix poverty levels and family structures of gang members, but also had recognized the importance of creating individualized plans for potential and current gang members in helping them address the individualized factors that lead to gang involvement (Grekul, 2011). One of the major downfalls noted was that, of all the groups and agencies represented, no youth were actually involved in the group (Grekul, 2011). As one CSGV member stated, "CSGV needs to get the kids that are involved in gangs involved themselves" (Grekul, 2011, p. 37).

In addition to having the youth involved in the program, according to several researchers, focusing on each individual youth is vital to the success of a program. According to Chu et al. (2011), a successful program will match the treatment to the client and is one where "treatment delivery is adjusted to accommodate the clients' idiosyncratic characteristics" (Chu et al., 2011, p. 131). Chu et al. (2011) also emphasizes the need for evidence-based programs. Boerman (2001) advocates for the consideration of each individual's treatment needs by assessing not only the behavior of the individual, but also the context of that behavior in terms of both biological and psychological characteristics (Boerman, 2001). Alleyne and Wood (2010) determined "that by identifying cognitive processes associated with gang membership there is potential for developing interventions to address youth interest in gangs *before* they develop into fully fledged members" (p. 434). A program based on individual needs and processes, as well as one that is a comprehensive model, tends to lead to success (Densley, 2011).

Use of the suppression strategy does not tend to lead to success, however, as was noted in an earlier section (Alleyne & Wood, 2010; Decker & Curry, 2000; Sirpal, 1997) and verified when looking at programs that focus on stricter or enhanced punishment for criminal offenders who are members of gangs. Such "gang injunction" programs are at odds with programs using other effective strategies and "in fact have great potential to exacerbate factors that contribute to gang involvement" (Caldwell, 2000, p. 243).

Another type of program that may not work well to address juvenile males and gang membership is a substance abuse program. Drug use and drug selling are two separate problems within gangs, although they are often treated as one (Decker & Curry, 2000). If a gang member is using drugs, then a substance abuse program, particularly one that is individualized to the gang member, is appropriate (Chu et al., 2011). Although drug selling is an activity in which many gang members are engaged, primarily because of the economic "benefits" associated with it, drug use is not (Craig et al., 2002; Sirpal, 1997).

An innovative approach, which builds on both the community collaboration and individual treatment needs themes, is to consider juvenile males who are members of gangs as a vulnerable population in terms of public health intervention by nurses (Sanders, Schneiderman, Loken, Lankenau, & Bloom, 2009). Nurses have a unique opportunity to collaborate with school officials, through school nurse positions, and also can partner with law enforcement officials through the health care system and other programs that may include law enforcement and social service agencies (Sanders et al., 2009). As noted by Sanders et al. (2009), "nurses are in the position to lead the important effort in providing primary, secondary, and tertiary health prevention to [youths involved in gangs], but must be encouraged to develop creative partnerships to gain access" (p. 351).

As gang membership continues to rise, prevention and intervention is vital for the health of our juvenile males who are disproportionately associated with gang membership. Community collaboration coupled with individualized attention is key to a successful program. Although desistance from gangs is important, that outcome is not enough, as a successful intervention program "should focus on the restoration of [positive] social bonds with conventional others" (Melde & Esbensen, 2011, p. 539). In addition, a successful intervention should "provide youth with avenues to build on sources of social capital, such as improved relationships with prosocial peer networks, school officials, and their families" (Melde & Esbensen, 2011, p. 539). Restoring identity, which is important in the development of adolescents, is vital as well (Melde & Esbensen, 2011). A successful program must focus on the factors that are known as predictors of gang membership and focus on the individual—all individuals—not just the "most salvageable" (Rios, 2010, p. 210).

More information on gang membership prevention and intervention programs may be found within the references listed at the end of the chapter. In particular, the National Criminal Justice Reference Service (www.ncjrs.gov) provides a wealth of information on gangs, gang membership, and intervention programs.

The following case is offered as support for interventions mentioned previously. The case describes a child engaged in pre-gang behavior. The specific intervention utilized highlights aspects recommended for individual treatment.

CASE STUDY: REGGIE, AGE 11

Reggie was an 11-year-old biracial youth (African American and Latino) who was referred to therapy by a counselor from the local youth court who felt he needed more intensive work than she was able to provide. He and two friends had appeared in youth court to address charges of vandalism, specifically gang-related graffiti. They had spray painted gang symbols on a school bus and were suspects in several other similar taggings.

Developmental and Family History

During the intake interview, Tina, Reggie's mother, described him as a *dream child*, prior to age 11. He had been a happy, easy to soothe baby and an energetic, yet easily satisfied, toddler. Tina noted that he met and exceeded all of the early childhood developmental milestones. By the time he was in kindergarten, he was reading at a second grade level. Reggie had never been hospitalized, had no chronic medical conditions; until youth court, he had never received counseling.

According to Tina, many maternal family members lived nearby; most of her family lived within a 50-mile radius of the small, southern town where Reggie was born. Reggie's father had been a migrant worker that Tina briefly dated. By the time she learned she was pregnant, he had left town. Reggie had never met his father, and she had never attempted to locate him. When Reggie was 4, he began to ask about his father, and Tina shared what little she knew of him. Tina had not dated in years because she felt life was complicated enough with work and caring for Reggie.

For many years, Reggie's primary male role model had been Tina's older brother, Carl, who was stable, hardworking, and available. Tina stated that this had changed when her older sister's son, Devon, 16, visited during the summer prior to Reggie entering the sixth grade. Devon was manipulative, sneaky, and unpredictable. Tina described that the purpose for Devon's visit was to get him out of the city where he lived and spend time with positive male role models such as her brother and father. Devon had been arrested several times and was currently on probation for his involvement in a petty theft and possession of marijuana with intent to distribute. He was a known gang member.

Tina noted, with recent changes, that she could describe Reggie's behavior in two ways: last 6 months and prior to age 11. She described his first 6 years in school as uneventful. He had excelled in reading, math, and science. Reggie seldom earned a B, and his teachers loved him. He was motivated and eager to please. Over his first 6 years in school, Tina revealed the few times Reggie was dissatisfied with school was when he had not been chosen, by a teacher, to do a task for the teacher or class. Reggie was more of a follower than a leader.

Starting in Grade 6, Reggie began to display problem behaviors consistent with attention-deficit hyperactivity disorder and disruptive behavior disorder. Specifically, he had become less attentive, easily distracted, and his grades had dropped. Also noted were oppositional and attention-seeking behaviors at home and in school. He frequently disrupted class and was now considered the class clown. Reggie had received in-school suspension several times this school year. One instance was for doodling gang symbols on a test and another was for using gang gestures in the lunchroom. Reggie had a select group of friends with whom he spent much of his time in and out of school, and his primary peers were the two boys with whom he had been arrested. These two friends were described as very similar to Reggie with similar family structures and rearing.

Assessment

The Child Behavior Checklist 6–18 parent and teacher form (CBCL; Achenbach & Rescorla, 2001) were completed for Reggie. The instrument was chosen because it includes eight syndrome scales, a scale for Internalizing Problems and Externalizing Problems, and an overall Total Problem score as well as Competence Scales for Activities, Social, and School. Specific assessment data for Reggie, from both the parent and teacher report form, included a normal range Total Competence, Internalizing Problems, and Total Problems score. Of the syndrome scales, the Social and Attention Problems, and Aggressive Behavior scales were borderline clinical range. Of particular interest were clinical range scores for Rule-Breaking Behaviors and Externalizing Problems. Reggie's mother and teacher both reported more problems than are typically reported by parents and teachers of boys aged 6 to 18.

Intervention

Play therapy was the intervention chosen, as it is expressive, developmentally versatile, nonconfrontational, and allows the client to direct his progress. Play therapy was selected also because a previous, purely directive intervention had been unsuccessful in effecting change. When Reggie came to his first play therapy session, he was 3 months away from his 12th birthday. Although some may consider him too old for play therapy, the therapist believed it was an appropriate choice, as it specifically addressed issues identified during the intake interview (viz., the desire to please others, problems with attention, and rule-breaking behaviors). The playroom was equipped and arranged as suggested by Landreth (2002) in his book, *Play Therapy: The Art of the Relationship*. The room had been modified to include games and a sand tray. During the initial stage of therapy, nondirective play therapy with limit setting was utilized. The working and termination stages included directive and nondirective measures. Listed as follows are the sessions, themes, and outcomes.

Sessions 1–4

The goal of the initial stage of play therapy is to build rapport, allow the child to explore, and be in control of his direction and ensure the child that he is safe (Nash & Schaefer, 2011). During this phase, the play therapist primarily attends to behaviors and continues to assess the child. When the child attends his first session, it is customary for the therapist to tell the child that he can decide what to do as long as no one is in danger.

During his initial session, Reggie seemed apprehensive as he attempted to explore the room. He asked what his therapist wanted him to do. When the therapist returned responsibility for the decision to the client, Reggie sighed, kicked over a chair, and sat in the floor. The therapist set a limit about kicking things in the playroom. After a few minutes, Reggie began to bounce a ball against the wall. When it landed near the therapist, he picked it up and tossed it back. This began a game of toss, and Reggie seemed to relax in the session. Ball toss led to a game of checkers and back to a game of toss. Near the end of the session, while tossing the ball, Reggie stated, "I use to toss the ball with Uncle Carl." When the session was over, the therapist asked Reggie if he would like to return and Reggie said, "Yes."

Sessions 2 through 4 were similar to the initial session by primarily involving cooperative play. However, at some point in each session, Reggie's rambunctious play would require that the therapist remind him of the playroom limits. As Reggie became more self-directed, he would talk more, yet kept the dialogue nonspecific. Near the end of Session 4, after having set several limits about how hard the ball could be thrown in the playroom, the therapist attempted to remove the ball from the room. Reggie became angry and attempted to stop the therapist. He came close to the therapist and said he wanted the ball back. The therapist explained that Reggie's disregard for the clearly set limits required that he remove the ball from the room. Reggie backed off and mumbled, "Devon would get it if he were here." This was the first mention of his cousin Devon. When asked about Devon, Reggie refused to respond and left the room.

After the fourth session, the therapist summarized the prior sessions and noted that Reggie had now displayed many of the behaviors that had brought him to therapy. He believed Reggie was moving toward a working stage. During this stage, client play involves the development of recurrent themes that represent the needs and unresolved conflicts the child is facing (Nash & Schaefer, 2011). With this in mind, the plan for the next few weeks was to talk about Devon and begin to talk about how Reggie had changed since Devon's visit.

Session 5

Prior to this session, Reggie's mother called and stated that Reggie was being resistant about coming to therapy; however, she had gotten him to agree to come. When Reggie entered the room, he sat on the floor and began to sift sand in the sand tray. Despite an invitation to talk about the last session, Reggie would not speak and continued quietly sifting sand for the remainder of the session. The therapist served as a silent witness to Reggie's quiet play.

Session 6

As he had done the previous week, Reggie entered the room and began to sift sand. After a few minutes, the therapist remarked that it seemed Reggie was trying to sort things out. Reggie responded, "Yes, a lot of things." In the dialogue that followed, Reggie and the therapist talked about Devon and the troubles Reggie was having at and away from school. As Reggie talked about Devon, it was evident how much he admired Devon. He described Devon as strong, powerful, well liked, and smart. The therapist asked, "How did Devon get so powerful?" Reggie responded, "Because he's not afraid to get in your face and take what he wants." The therapist responded, "Sounds like that could be good or bad." Reggie looked puzzled and began to talk about going to youth court. During the conversation, Reggie disclosed many of the problems he had at school and why he was referred to youth court. At the end of the discourse, Reggie stated, "Nobody messes with me now. I've been to jail." The session ended with Reggie initiating a game of toss.

Session 7

Reggie willingly came to this session. For the first time, he picked up the miniature soldiers and began to line them up as he talked about his friends. The therapist remarked that Reggie had set up a big group of soldiers facing a small group of soldiers. He then observed that the small group must be powerful because they had guns. Reggie agreed. He said, "This is us [Reggie and friends]. They don't mess with us now." When asked about who *they* were, Reggie mentioned some names and said, "They use to call us nerds, because we do good in school." The session ended with a discussion about being bullied in school.

Session 8

As the session started, the therapist summarized what Reggie and he had talked about over the last few weeks. The therapist said, "You seem powerful now, but do you like this kind of power?" Reggie said, "Yes and no. I don't get bullied, but I worry my mom and teachers." The therapists response was, "So how can you be powerful and not worry people?" During the remainder of the session, the therapist helped Reggie create a list of positive things that could help Reggie feel powerful. At the end of the session, the therapist asked Reggie to pick one activity or behavior and to practice it during the next week. Reggie chose *being responsible.*

Session 9

Prior to the session, Reggie's mother called. She seemed happy and stated that Reggie had been busy and had a lot to talk about. When Reggie came in, he blurted out, " I, I mean, *we* cleaned it up." He and the two other boys had cleaned up the graffiti. He talked about how he asked his Uncle Carl to take them to the seven different locations they'd tagged. Reggie also talked about doing his chores at home. When leaving, he chose another task to complete during the upcoming week.

Sessions 10–13

Each week, Reggie came to therapy full of energy, focus, and pride. He reported his successes as well as areas still unachieved. During these weeks, he and his therapist worked on coping skills (viz., assertiveness and anger management). The skills were practiced using role-plays and puppet shows. At first, Reggie dismissed the puppet shows as stupid and childish; however, after trying it, he found pleasure and benefit in the activity. At the end of Session 12, Reggie complained that although his grades were improving, they were not yet where he expected them to be. The therapist suggested they work on time management and study skills during the next session. In Session 13, time management charts and study tips were addressed.

Sessions 14–16

The final three sessions were utilized for termination. As this is the final stage of play therapy, much of the time is spent recapping progress and planning for ongoing work toward goals (Nash & Schaefer, 2011). In many ways, it is similar to relapse prevention.

As part of termination, Reggie and his therapist discussed the changes Reggie had made. They practiced skills and created a collage representing Reggie's life. The collage included four boards that Reggie named *Before*, *In the Middle*, *Play Therapy*, and *After*. Each was detailed and descriptive except for the last one. The *Before* collage was upbeat, the *In the Middle* collage was chaotic and dark, and the *Play Therapy* collage was part chaotic and part organized. He started the *After* collage, yet decided to leave it unfinished. Since Reggie's last session was near the end of the school year, he and his therapist talked about his plans for the summer. To support his progress, Reggie's mother had enrolled him in daily activities at the local Boys and Girls Club. This would provide socialization, mentoring, and routine supervision.

Summary

This case illustrates the versatility and therapeutic power of play. It shows the integration of nondirective and directive techniques to facilitate change in a child displaying pre-gang involvement and disruptive behaviors. Nondirective periods are necessary to allow the child to explore, choose, and self-direct. Once the therapeutic relationship has developed, the child feels safe and begins to display the deeper themes associated with his issues. At this point, noncoercive, directive measures may be introduced to address specific concerns. Finally, the case study in this chapter is descriptive and narrative in nature. It may serve as a guide, but not a blueprint. Each child is unique; therefore, each application of play therapy will be unique.

REFERENCES

Achenbach, T. M., & Rescorla, L. A. (2001). Manual for the ASEBA School-Age Forms & Profiles. Burlington, VT: University of Vermont, Research Center for Children, Youth, & Families.

Alleyne, E., & Wood, J. L. (2010). Gang involvement: psychological and behavioral characteristics of gang members, peripheral youth, and nongang youth. *Aggressive Behavior, 36*, 423–436.

Boerman, T. (2001). Ecological assessment: Establishing ecological validity in gang intervention strategies—a call for ecologically sensitive assessment of gang affected youth. *Journal of Gang Research, 8*(2), 35–48.

Caldwell, B. (2010). Criminalizing day-to-day life: A socio-legal critique of gang injunctions. *American Journal of Criminal Law, 37*(3), 241–290.

Chu, C. M., Daffern, M., Thomas, S. D. M., & Lim, J. Y. (2011). Elucidating the treatment needs of gang-affiliated youth offenders. *Journal of Aggression, Conflict and Peace Research, 3*(3), 129–140.

Cobbina, J. E., Like-Haislip, T. Z., & Miller, J. (2010). Gang fights versus cat fights: Urban young men's gendered narratives of violence. *Deviant Behavior, 31,* 596–624.

Craig, W. M., Vitaro, F., Gagnon, C., & Tremblay, R. E. (2002). The road to gang membership: Characteristics of male gang and nongang members from age 10 to 14. *Social Development, 11*(1), 53–68.

Decker, S. H., & Curry, G. D. (2000). Responding to gangs: Comparing gang member, police, and task force perspectives. *Journal of Criminal Justice, 28,* 129–137.

Densley, J. A. (2011). Ganging up on gangs: Why the gang intervention industry needs an intervention. *British Journal of Forensic Practice, 13*(1), 12–23.

Egan, V., & Beadman, M. (2011). *Personality and Individual Differences, 51,* 748–753.

Egley, A., Jr., & O'Donnell, C. E. (2008). *Highlights of the 2007 national youth gang survey.* Washington, DC: Office of Juvenile Justice and Delinquency Prevention. Retrieved from https://www.ncjrs.gov/pdffiles1/ojjdp/225185.pdf

Esbensen, F. A., Peterson, D., Taylor, T. J., Freng, A., Osgood, D. W., Carson, D. C., & Matsuda, K. N. (2011). Evaluation and evolution of the gang resistance education and training (G.R.E.A.T.) program. *Journal of School Violence, 10,* 53–70.

Grekul, J. (2011). Building collective efficacy and sustainability into a community collaborative: Community solution to gang violence. *Journal of Gang Research, 18*(2), 23–45.

Grekul, J., LaBoucane-Benson, P., & Erickson, K. (2009). "By working together we can support youth": Observations from a preliminary evaluation of the community solution to gang violence. *Journal of Gang Research, 17*(1), 45–67.

Koffman, S., Ray, A., Berg, S., Covington, L., Albarran, N. M., & Vasquez, M. (2009). Impact of a comprehensive whole child intervention and prevention program among youth at risk of gang involvement and other forms of delinquency. *Children & Schools, 31*(4), 239–245.

Krohn, M. D., Schmidt, N. M., Lizotte, A. J., & Baldwin, J. M. (2011). The impact of multiple marginality on gang membership and delinquent behavior for Hispanic, African American, and White male adolescents. *Journal of Contemporary Criminal Justice, 27*(1), 18–42.

Lahey, B. B., Gordon, R. A., Loeber, R., Stouthamer-Loeber, M., & Farrington, D. P. (1999). Boys who join gangs: A prospective study of predictors of first gang entry. *Journal of Abnormal Child Psychology, 27*(4), 261–276.

Landreth, G. (2002). *Play therapy: The art of the relationship* (2nd ed.). New York, NY: Brunner-Routledge.

Melde, C., & Esbensen, A. (2011). Gang membership as a turning point in the life course. *Criminology, 49,* 513–552.

Nash, J. B., & Schaefer, C. E. (2011). Play therapy: Basic concepts and practices. In C. E. Schaefer (Ed.), *Foundations of play therapy* (2nd ed., p. 9). Hoboken, NJ: John Wiley & Sons, Inc.

National Criminal Justice Reference Service. (2011). *In the spotlight.* Retrieved from https://www.ncjrs.gov/spotlight/gangs/summary.html

National Gang Center. *National Youth Gang Survey Analysis.* Retrieved November 18, 2011, from http://www.nationalgangcenter.gov/Survey-Analysis.

Paterson, J. (2010, May). Getting inside the gang mentality. *Counseling Today.* Retrieved from http://ct.counseling.org/2010/05/getting-inside-the-gang-mentality/

Pesce, R. C., & Wilczynski, J. D. (2005, November). Gang Prevention. *Student Counseling.* Retrieved from http://www.nasponline.org/resources/principals/nassp_gang.pdf

Rios, V. M. (2010). Navigating the thin line between education and incarceration: An action research case study on gang-associated Latino youth. *Journal of Education for Students Placed at Risk, 15*, 200–212.

Ryan, L. G., Miller-Loessi, K., & Nieri, K. (2007). Relationships with adults as predictors of substance abuse, gang involvement, and threats to safety among disadvantaged urban high-school adolescents. *Journal of Community Psychology, 35*(8), 1053–1071.

Sanders, B., Schneiderman, J. U., Loken, A., Lankenau, S. E., & Bloom, J. J. (2009). Gang youth as a vulnerable population for nursing intervention. *Public Health Nursing, 26*(4), 346–352.

Scherer, J., Dorsey, D. T., & Catzva, D. (2009). Lessons learned from the national evaluation of the gang-free schools and community program. *Journal of Gang Research, 17*(1), 29–44.

Sirpal, S. K. (1997). Causes of gang participation and strategies for prevention in gang members' own words. *Journal of Gang Research, 4*(2), 13–22.

Thornberry, T. P., Krohn, M. D., Lizotte, A. J., & Chard-Wierschem, D. (2003). The role of juvenile gangs in facilitating behavior. *Journal of Research in Crime and Delinquency, 30*(1), 55–87.

Weerman, F. M., Maxson, C. L., Esbensen, F., Aldridge, J., Medina, J., & van Gemert, F. (2009). *Eurogang program manual.* Retrieved from http://www.umsl.edu/~ccj/eurogang/EurogangManual.pdf

Conclusion

It is better to build boys than mend men. — Author: Unknown

Boys and young men comprise one of the most "at risk" groups in our society today. The explosion of technology, changes in family structure, influence of the media, unstable economy, and shifting demographics have all created greater pressures on a vulnerable group, which is already overwhelmed with stress and insecurity. This has led to an increase in emotional instability; addictive, aggressive, and violent behavior; inadequate academic performance; relationship difficulties; and confusion about life roles and careers for boys and young men. Young males are not well educated in how to handle their negative emotions and often seek unproductive—and even dangerous—ways to express their feelings or attempt to gain a sense of power over their environment. Parents and educators, who most often interact with this group, are looking for assistance as they try to help this group navigate more easily through the tumultuous stages of childhood and adolescence. In their quest, they often turn to therapists and school counselors for their expertise and guidance.

This book was conceived and developed in the hope that it would provide helping professionals with current research findings and best practices to enhance their ability to work successfully with this population. The professionals who have contributed chapters to this book offer the expertise and experience that they have gleaned through their own work, and we hope that their insights and wisdom will help readers feel better prepared to meet the developmental and emotional needs of boys and young men. We appreciate the contributors who so graciously shared their experience working with young clients who have faced a variety of challenges as well as their strategies for helping these young males over-come obstacles. Young men need guidance, support, and our belief in their ability to change—we hope this book gives you reason to offer these to the young males with whom you work.

Index

Action-oriented counseling approach,
186
Addiction
  in adolescents, 295–296
  assessment strategies, 298–299
  CAGE, for screening alcohol-related
    concerns, 299–300
  chemical, 301–311
  definitions and criteria of, 296–298
  process, 311–317
  WASTE-Time structured interview,
    for screening alcohol-related
    concerns, 300–301
Addictive disorders, therapeutic
    approach to
  Chen's story, 338–341
  cognitive behavioral theory (CBT),
    334–335
  family's involvement, 329–338
  inpatient detox, 327–328
  intensive long-term outpatient
    treatment (ILTOT), 328
  Motivational Interviewing (MI),
    331–332
  outpatient programs, 328
  residential programs, 328
  Sequential Family Addiction Model
    (S-FAM), 329–331
  solution-focused counseling,
    332–334
  within therapeutic communities, 329

  Transtheoretical Model of Change
    (TTM), 329–330
Addictive eating, 311–312
Addictive exercise, 315
Addictive gambling, 312–313
Adolescent male clients
  African Americans, 44–45
  Asian Americans, 44–45
  assessment for counseling, 46
  biopsychosocial–spiritual under-
    standing of, 46
  boundary testing, 53
  cognitive skills, development
    processes, 52–53
  conceptualization of, 47
  creativity-based interventions, 49–51
  cultural identity, 44–45
  ethnic identity, 43–45
  gender roles, 42
  Hispanic and European Americans,
    44–45
  insight-oriented talk-focused
    techniques, 49
  intervention selection, 48–51
  involvement in risky or illegal
    behaviors, 45
  Latinos, 44–45
  monitoring of countertransference,
    52
  multicultural counseling competen-
    cies and framework, 46–48

Adolescent male clients (cont.)
physical activity-based
interventions, 51
process of collecting information, 46
sexual orientation, 42–43
talk-based intervention, 49
13-step cultural auditing process, 52
tips for counsellors, 51–53
Adolescents. *See also* Bullying; Gang
membership
African Americans' sexual activity,
139–140, 143
anger in, 380–381
boy's sexual identity and sexual self,
138
Erikson's stages of development,
135
family networks, 101–102
grandparent relationships, 102
influence of family communications
and family expectations, 139
Kyle's behavior and psychological
mindset, 145–147
peer relationships, 101, 105–107
perception about self-concept and
self-esteem, 136
sexual activity, 139
sexual development, 137–138
sibling relationships, 102
social world of male, 135
suicide risk in, 284–285
"therapeutic and psychoeducational"
education for, 143
Adventure-based counseling
of adolescent males, 197–199
as an approach to problem solving
technique, 195, 211–212
application of, 191–192
approaches, 192
for attention-deficit hyperactivity
disorder (ADHD), 174
balancing group needs, 186
brain development/language, 196
communication skill development,
210–211
considerations in use of interactive
virtual adventures, 216

counseling relationship, 215
creative approaches to problem
solving, 195
decision making skill, development
of, 212
ethical considerations, 215–216
experience-based judgment development, 211
experiences, 186, 194
forerunners to, 189–191
functions, 187
future of, 216–217
group case example, 209–212
indoors *vs* outdoors, 193
informal assessment of clients'
mental health needs, 186
integrated model of activities and
counselor's focus, 200–209
language development in relation to
emotional and behavioral
problems, 196–197
leadership style development, 210
metaskill development, 199–209
moral wellness and character
building, 190
origins of, 187–189
Outdoor Education *vs* traditional
counseling, 190–191
philosophical origins, 187–189
physical health and, 189–190
research for adolescents, 212–215
risk taking, 195
as a treatment approach, 192
as a unique mode of therapy,
192–194
with young males, 185–187
Adventure-based counselors, 198–199
Adventure therapy, 131
Alcohol
background, 304
intoxication effects of, 304–305
negative consequences of, 305–306
withdrawal effects of, 305
American Counseling Association
(ACA), 215
American Psychiatric Association
(APA), 155

Anger
  Adlerian theory, 381–384
  in adolescent boys, 380–381
  definition, 379–380
  Jason's story, 384–395
Anorexia, 311
Anorexia nervosa, 286
Anxiety-related disorders, 279–280
  Jake's story, 286–289
  traumatic reactions, 280
Anxious-avoidant attachment, 10
Applied behavioral analysis (ABA),
    226
Art therapy, 127–129
Asperger's syndrome, 222–223
Association for Experiential Education
    (AEE), 215
"At risk" groups, 417
Attachment, 9–12
  as a developmental process, 9–12
  Stefan's story, 15–17
  theory, 17
Attention-deficit hyperactivity disorder
    (ADHD), 30
  adventure-based counseling for, 174
  atomoxetine, 173
  cognitive–behavioral therapy (CBT)
    for, 172–174
  dextroamphetamine, 172
  dextroamphetamine with amphet-
    amine drug, 172
  effects of, 174
  guanfacine, 173
  methylphenidate, 172
  methylphenidate extended-release
    tablets, 172
  pharmacological treatments for,
    172–173
  prevalence and diagnosis, 171–172
  team-building experience for
    patients, 174
  Tyler's story, 175–181
Autism and autism spectrum disorders
    (ASDs)
  behavioral approaches to, 225–230
  behavior intervention plans (BIPs)
    for, 226

Brian, case example of, 237–239
causes of, 224–225
cognitive behavioral therapy (CBT)
    for, 228–229
definition, 222–223
diagnostic evaluation, 224
Eugene, case example of, 239–241
functional behavior assessments
    (FBAs) for, 226
genetic predisposition and environ-
    mental factors, 224–225
history, 222
individualized education program
    (IEP), 235
modeling strategies, 232–233
positive behavioral support (PBS)
    for, 228
prevalence of, 224
role of counselors, 235–236
social and developmental
    approaches to, 230–233
social-relational and developmental
    programs, 233
teratogens, role of, 224–225
video modeling strategy, 233
Autism Diagnostic Interview-Revised
    (ADI-R), 224
Autistic psychopathology of
    childhood, 222

A Beautiful Mind, 90
Behavior intervention plans (BIPs),
    226
Benzodiazepines, 306
Bibliotherapy, 131, 160–161
Body image and eating disorders,
    281–282
Bonding, 12
*Boys of few words: Raising our sons to
    communicate and connect,* 108
Bulimia, 311
Bullying
  challenges in therapy, 364
  clinical work with a victim, case
    study, 365–367
  group therapy, 363–364
  misperceptions of, 360

Bullying (cont.)
role of empowerment, 360–362
school interventions, 367–371
Solution-Focused, Positive
Norming, and Narrative
Therapy, 362–363
systematic prevention program, case
example, 371–374

Career adaptability
application of, 75
as "developmental lines," 75
dimensions of, 75, 77–78
Career construction counseling, 75
children begin forming opinions
about life, 78
collaborating with children
regarding career issues, 78
Career Construction Theory (CCT),
74–76, 78, 82, 90
Career counseling with adolescent
males, 85–91
Career development in childhood,
76–78
Career identity development, 78–81
career story interview questions, 90
children's play, role of, 82–85
parental role, 79
preoccupation, 90
Super's causal model, 81–82
Career self-concept development, 79
Career Story Interview, 86
Cass model, 157
Cathartic transformation, 186
Challenge by Choice (CbC) program, 214
Child abuse
Bart's story, 256–260
behavioral consequences, 253
impact of maltreatment and trauma,
252–254
by parents, 251–252
physical abuse, 248–249
physical health consequences, 253
prevalence of, 247–248
resources for, 260–261
sexual abuse, 249–250
by sibling, 251

treatment protocols and methods,
254–256
Child-centered play therapy, 265–266
efficacy of, 267
and grieving children, 266
implications for counselors and play
therapists, 276–277
in the school setting, 266–267
Tom's story, 267–275
*Child-Centered Play Therapy: A
Practical Guide to Developing
Therapeutic Relationships with
Children* (Nancy Cochran
et al.), 276
Child-Centered Play Therapy (Rise
VanFleet et al.), 276
Childhood disintegrative disorder, 223
Childhood victimization, 247
Child Information Gateway's Fact-
sheet, 253
Child Maltreatment, 2009, 247
Choice/Reality Theory, 334
Christianity, 188
Cognitive behavioral theory (CBT)
addictive disorders, 334–335
for anxiety-related concerns, 286
autism and autism spectrum
disorders (ASDs), 228–229
Cognitive Theory, 334
Combating Autism Act of 2006, 225
Coming out/disclosing one's same-sex
attractions, 157–158
Compulsive overeating, 311
Conduct disorder (CD), 343–347
interventions/treatment strategies,
347–349
Contingent communication, 11
Council for the Accreditation of
Counseling and Related
Educational Program (CACREP),
49, 215
Counseling, boys and male adolescents, 30
attention-deficit hyperactivity
disorder (ADHD), 30
beginning and building rapport,
34–35

case study, 36–38
feelings ensemble, 35
interventions and best practices,
32–35
process of empathy, 35
traditional psychotherapy and
relational styles, 30–32
use of drumming groups, 32–34
Counseling Adolescent Males, 136
Counseling implications for
relationship, 107–109
empathic understanding in
relationships, 108
less-desired behavioral
dimensions, 108
Nathaniel's story, 109–112
*Counseling Theories: Essential
Concepts and Applications* (Sam
Gladding), 49
Cultural differences in sexual behaviors, 139–141

Dating violence, 145
Denver Model for developmental
treatment approach, 231
Depressants
alcohol, 304–306
benzodiazepines, 306
gamma-hydroxybutyrate
(GHB), 306
hallucinogens, 310–311
inhalants and volatile
hydrocarbons, 311
opiates, 308–309
stimulants, 307–308
Developmental, Individual-Difference,
Relationship Based (DIR®/Floor
Time™), 233
Developmental disability, 222
Developmental path, childhood to
adulthood
adhering to a societal code of
conduct, 12–15
cognitive development and
gender, 5–12
emotional and social
development, 3–5
gender difference, 1–3

*Diagnostic and Statistical Manual
of Mental Disorders,
4th edition (DSM-IV-TR),*
63, 223, 280
Dirty Harry, 87
Discrete Trial Training, 230
Disorder of written expression, 59,
63–65
academic achievement in, 63
bypass strategies, 64
impaired transcription skills
and neuropsychological
processes, 64
morphological or phonological
awareness training, 64
treatment and intervention
strategies, 64–65
"Do ABA," 227
Doing Anger Differently (DAD), 33
"Down low" phenomenon, 156
Dueling messages, 137
Dyslexia, 60

Early childhood experiences, 79
Early family relationships, 98
Early infantile autism, 223
Early Start Denver Model
(ESDM), 231
Education
gender implications, 6–9
Emotional and social
development, 3–5
Emotional disorders in
adolescents, 279
Enterprising occupations, 89
Ethnic identity, 43–45

Familial relationship, 101
Family networks
in adolescence age, 101–102
in childhood, 98–101
Father–son relationship, 100
"missing dad," 121–122
Four Noble Truths, 188
Functional behavior assessments
(FBAs), 226
Functional Communication
Training, 230

Gaming addiction, 316–317
Gamma-hydroxybutyrate (GHB), 306
Gang membership
    child engaged in pre-gang behavior,
        case example, 409–414
    Community Solution to Gang
        Violence (CSGV), 406–407
    Drug Abuse Resistance Education
        (DARE) programs, 406
    Gang-Free Schools and Community
        (GFS) initiative, 404–405
    "gang injunction" programs, 408
    Gang Resistance Education and
        Training (GREAT) program, 406
    juvenile males and, 401–402
    specific programs in, 404–409
    strategies for prevention and
        intervention, 402–404
    in the United States, 399–400
Gay, Lesbian, and Straight Education
    Network (GLSEN), 155
Gay–Straight Alliances (GSAs),
    158, 161
Gender-based differences between
    boys and girls, 6
Gender roles, 42
Generalized anxiety disorder (GAD), 280
Gestalt Therapy, 359
Giftedness, 66–67
Gilliam Asperger's Rating Scale
    (GARS), 224
Gilligan, Carol, 97
Gottfredson's Theory of
    Circumscription and
    Compromise, 79–80
Grandparent relationships in
    adolescence age, 102
Gray Center for Social Learning and
    Understanding, 232
Grief experience in children, 264
    facilitating grief process, 264–265

Heterosexual dating
    relationships, 106
High-conflict divorce cases and
    parent–child relationship, 120
Hinduism, 188
Homophobia, 159

Homosexual, bisexual, and
    questioning (HBQ) males, 106

Incidental Teaching method, 230
Individuals with Disabilities Education
    Act (IDEA), 61, 222
Individuation, 105
*Inner Harbour Therapeutic
    Drumming Program,* 33
Insight-oriented theories, 335–338
Instrumental exchange, 13
Interagency Autism Coordinating
    Council, 225
Internet addiction, 316
Interpersonal conformity, 13
Intimate relationships, 135
Inviting Optimum Participation (I-Opt
    program), 214
It Gets Better Project, 155

Judaism, 188
Judeo-Christian morality, 139

Kohlberg's moral development model,
    24–25

Learning disorders, 59–60
Learning environment, 6–9
Lesbian, gay, bisexual, and queer
    (LGBQ) people, 160
Loss of a loved one
    grief experience in children, 264
    impact of, 263–264
Lovaas Method, 230

Marijuana use
    background, 302
    intoxication effects of, 302–303
    negative consequences of, 303–304
    withdrawal effects of, 303
Masculine relationship style, 106
Mathematics learning disorder (MLD),
    59, 65–66
Mental representations, 11
    Bowlby's postulates, 11
Minority stress model, 158–159
Mixed-sex friendship networks, 106
Mood disorders, 280–281

Moral development theory, 17–19
Morality
  Stefan's story, 15–17
Motivational interviewing, 286
Movement therapy, 131
Music therapy, 129–130

National Campaign to Prevent Teen and
    Unplanned Pregnancy, 139
Nonsuicidal self-injury (NSSI), 282
Nonverbal cues, 11

Obedience, 13
Obsessive-compulsive disorder (OCD),
    280
Oppositional defiant disorder (ODD),
    343–347
  Alex's story, 349–354
  interventions/treatment strategies,
    347–349
Outdoor behavioral healthcare (OBH),
    192
Outward Bound intervention,
    190–191

Parental relationships
  in childhood, 98–99
  development of interpersonal
    conflict skills, 100
  father–son relationship, 100
  and gender atypical traits, 99
  and homosexual men, 99
Parental relationships (cont.)
  influence on emotional stability of
    males, 99
  maternal relationships with boys,
    100
  mother–son relationship, 100
  parent–child conflict, 101
  positive parent–son relationships,
    101
  on self-concept, 99
Parent–child conflict, 101
  during high-conflict divorce cases,
    120
Peer relationship
  adolescence, 105–107
  childhood, 102–104

peer networks and relational
    patterns of children, 102–104
Pervasive Developmental Disorders
    (PDDs), 223
Picture Exchange Communication
    System (PECS), 229–230
Pivotal Response Training (PRT),
    230, 231
Play, role in emotional and social
    development, 3–4
  sex differences in the type and
    style of, 4
Play therapy, 131
*Play Therapy: The Art of the Relation-
    ship* (Garry Landreth), 276
Polyvictimization, 248
Positive psychology/positive
    masculinity model of
    psychotherapy, 107
Positive role models, 162
Posttraumatic stress disorder (PTSD),
    250, 280
Prevent Child Abuse America,
    249, 253
Process addiction, 311–317
  addictive eating, 311–312
  exercise, 315
  gambling, 312–313
  spending, 314
  gaming, 316–317
  Internet addiction, 316
  sexual addiction, 313–314
Project Adventure, 191
Psychological Depth Model, 199
Punishment, 13

Queer, 156

Rational Emotive Behavior Theory
    (REBT), 334
Reading ability, evaluation of, 61
Reading disorder (RD), 59–63
Reciprocity of feelings, 13
Responsive Teaching (RT), 233
Rett's disorder, 223
Romantic relationships
  communication in, 136–137
  as normal development, 135–136

Safe Space concept, 161
Same-sex friendships, 105–106, 135
SCERTS®, 233
Secure attachment, 10
Self-efficacy theory, 197
Self-injurious behaviors, 283–284
Sexual abuse in children, 249–250
    long-term effect of, 250
    of males, 250
Sexual addiction, 313–314
Sexual behavior, 156
Sexual identity, 156–157
    coming out/disclosing one's
        same-sex attractions, 157–158
    counseling and recommendations,
        159–162
    helpful internet resources for, 166
    Martin's story, 162–166
    minority stress model, 158–159
    positive role models and, 162
    recommended book resources
        for counselors, 167–168
        for youth, 167
Sexual orientation, 42–43, 156
    stages from *awareness* to *accep-*
        tance of, 157–158
Sexual relationship development,
    138–141
Sibling abuse, 251
Sibling relationships, 100
Sibling sexual abuse, 251
Single-parent home
    Abrahim's story, 128–129
    adventure therapy, 131
    African American children, 121, 124
    art therapy, 127–129
    attachment-formation with primary
        caregiver, 124
    bibliotherapy, 131
    boys coping with an incarcerated
        parent, 123–126
    children of deployed parents, 122–123
    children of incarcerated parents,
        123–126
    child's difficulty in adapting to
        stress, 122
    difficulties for women, 121

    evidence-based interventions and
        innovative approaches, 126–132
    impact of being raised in, 119–120
    Jessie's story, 130–131
    maintaining healthy
        relationships, 125
    military families, 122–123
    "missing dad," 121–122
    movement therapy, 131
    music therapy, 129–130
    negative changes in children, 123
    play therapy, 131
    resources for interventions and
        innovative approaches, 132–133
    risk factors, 120
    school-based interventions, 126–127
    in the United States, 119
Social-cognitive theory, 232
Social contract, 14
Social order, 14
Social phobia, 280
Societal code of conduct
    conventional morality, 13–14
    postconventional morality, 14–15
    preconventional morality, 13
Solution-Focused, Positive Norming,
    and Narrative Therapy, 359
Specific phobia, 280
Spirituality, 188
Stefan's story, 15–25
    attachment theory, through the lens
        of, 17, 19, 21, 24
    family constellation and relationship
        development, 15–16
    moral development theory, through
        the lens of, 17–25
    physical challenges, 16
    school education, 16–17
Suicide risk in adolescents, 284–285

Talk therapy, 185
TEACCH (*T*reatment and *E*ducation of
    *A*utistic and *C*ommunication
    related handicapped *Ch*ildren),
    234–235
Team play, 4
Teen fatherhood, 141–144

Angel's story, 147–150
 resources for, 144
*Theories of Counseling and Psycho-
 therapy: Systems, Strategies,
 and Skills* (Linda Seligman and
 Lourie Reichenberg), 49
*Theory and Practice of Counseling
 and Psychotherapy* (Gerald
 Corey), 49

Think Before You Speak Campaign, 160
Trauma-Focused Cognitive Behavioral
 Therapy (TF-CBT), 254–256
The Trevor Project, 155

Universal ethical principles, 14–15

Victimization of children, 247–248
Vygotsky, Lev, 3